Chimpanzees, War, and History

Advance Praise for *Chimpanzees, War, and History*

"Are men born to kill? Some have been quick to assume evolved killer tendencies exist in both humans and chimpanzees. Drawing upon a truly impressive body of evidence, R. Brian Ferguson reopens the case. He casts substantial doubt on the assertion that chimpanzees and humans have been selected to kill. *Chimpanzees, War, and History* is meticulously researched, convincingly argued, and fascinating to read as Ferguson unveils a very different explanation for why chimpanzees kill."
　　—**Douglas P. Fry**, author of *Beyond War* and co-author of *Nurturing Our Humanity*

"Debates about the evolutionary 'nature' of war and the innateness of male violence are ubiquitous. And our close cousins, the chimpanzees, are often at center stage. In a book sure to enrage some, and please others, R. Brian Ferguson offers a truly comprehensive presentation and analysis of the available data on chimpanzee warfare and violence and opines on its relation to humanity. Agree or disagree with the conclusions, there is no denying the value of this in-depth, historical, socioecological, and sociocultural treatment of the chimpanzee wars. Ferguson furthers our understanding of war and violence in chimpanzees and beyond."
　　—**Agustín Fuentes**, author of *Why We Believe: Evolution and the Human Way of Being*

"This is a magnificent work by the greatest living scholar of human warfare. Ferguson applies his intellect to chimpanzee warfare, and makes, in my consideration, an air-tight case AGAINST speaking of 'our chimp ancestors' when it comes to war. He has turned the standard view (given, for example, in Wrangham and Peterson's *Demonic Males*) upside down. He is convincing, and, moreover, he is entertaining. This is an important work not just for scholars of war and chimpanzee researchers but for all people interested in human nature. A single word sums up my view: Magisterial!"
　　—**Jeffrey Moussaieff Masson**, author of *When Elephants Weep* and *The Assault on Truth*

"Are chimp intergroup killings the evolutionary precursors to human warfare? Has our evolution given us deadly proclivities? From R. Brian Ferguson, in this book, we get a firm and definitive 'no'. Human killing and warfare cannot, he argues, be attributed to our primate heritage. A fine contribution to an ongoing debate."
　　—**Vernon Reynolds**, Professor Emeritus, School of Anthropology, University of Oxford

"'Men are not born to kill, but they can be cultivated to kill. Don't blame evolution.' The last line of Ferguson's incredible survey of studies of the higher primates, showing definitively that all the analogy-based talk of humans as the killer apes—those ferocious monsters at the beginning of *2001: A Space Odyssey*—is just that: talk. In an age when it seems that war will never end,

understanding human nature and the distorting effects of culture is vital. There can be no better starting place than *Chimpanzees, War, and History*."
　　—**Michael Ruse**, author of *Why We Hate: Understanding the Roots of Human Conflict*

"Many scholars view warfare as inevitable, with deep and ancient roots. But this is a myth, arising from cherry-picking data, confusing mobile and sedentary hunter-gatherers, and ignoring Westernized causes of war among indigenous peoples. Ferguson has led the debunking of this myth. In this superb, important book, he demolishes two of its building blocks—the supposed inevitability of chimpanzee proto-warfare, and our link to a supposed chimpanzee-like past."
　　—**Robert M. Sapolsky**, John A. and Cynthia Fry Gunn Professor of Biology, Neurology, and Neurosurgery, Stanford University

Chimpanzees, War, and History

Are Men Born to Kill?

R. BRIAN FERGUSON

OXFORD
UNIVERSITY PRESS

Oxford University Press is a department of the University of Oxford. It furthers
the University's objective of excellence in research, scholarship, and education
by publishing worldwide. Oxford is a registered trade mark of Oxford University
Press in the UK and certain other countries.

Published in the United States of America by Oxford University Press
198 Madison Avenue, New York, NY 10016, United States of America.

© Oxford University Press 2023

All rights reserved. No part of this publication may be reproduced, stored in
a retrieval system, or transmitted, in any form or by any means, without the
prior permission in writing of Oxford University Press, or as expressly permitted
by law, by license, or under terms agreed with the appropriate reproduction
rights organization. Inquiries concerning reproduction outside the scope of the
above should be sent to the Rights Department, Oxford University Press, at the
address above.

You must not circulate this work in any other form
and you must impose this same condition on any acquirer.

CIP data is on file at the Library of Congress

ISBN 978-0-19-750675-2

DOI: 10.1093/oso/9780197506752.001.0001

Printed by Integrated Books International, United States of America

Contents

List of Illustrations — ix
Preface — xi
Acknowledgments — xv

PART I: CONTROVERSIES

1. From Nice to Brutal — 3
2. The Second Generation — 9
3. Theoretical Alternatives — 22

PART II: GOMBE

4. From Peace to "War" — 31
5. Contextualizing Violence — 44
6. Explaining the War and Its Aftermath — 59
7. Later Gombe — 69
8. Interpreting Gombe Violence — 87

PART III: MAHALE

9. Mahale: What Happened to K Group? — 105
10. Mahale History — 122

PART IV: KIBALE

11. Kibale — 145
12. Ngogo Territorial Conflict — 157
13. Scale and Geopolitics at Ngogo — 166
14. The Ngogo Expansion, RCH + HIH — 179
15. Kanyawara — 192

PART V: BUDONGO

16. Budongo, Early Research and Human Impact — 217
17. Sonso — 228

PART VI: ELEVEN SMALLER CASES

18. Eastern Chimpanzees, *Pan troglodytes schweinfurthii* — 251
19. Central Chimpanzees, *Pan troglodytes troglodytes* — 259
20. Western Chimpanzees, *Pan troglodytes verus* — 275

PART VII: TAI

21. Tai and Its Afflictions — 287
22. Sociality and Intergroup Relations — 294
23. Killings and Explanations — 304

PART VIII: BONOBOS

24. *Pan paniscus* — 315
25. Social Organization and Why Male Bonobos Are Less Violent — 335
26. Evolutionary Scenarios and Theoretical Developments — 353

PART IX: ADAPTIVE STRATEGIES, HUMAN IMPACT, AND DEADLY VIOLENCE: THEORY AND EVIDENCE

27. Killing Infants — 375
28. The Case for Evolved Adaptations, by the Evidence — 388
29. Human Impact, Critiqued and Documented — 406

PART X: HUMAN WAR

30. The Demonic Perspective Meets Human Warfare — 419
31. Species-Specific Foundations of Human War — 436
32. Applications: An Anthropology of War — 443

Tables — 457
References — 471
Index — 547

List of Illustrations

Part II

2.1 Gombe Map and Groupings	34
2.2 Three Researchers Photographing Chimpanzees	46
2.3 Gombe Feeding Bunker in System E	49
2.4 Gombe Chimpanzee Body Mass over Time	49
2.5 Gombe Number of Adult Males and Community Range Size	91

Part III

3.1 Mahale Territories and Feeding Stations	124
3.2 Chimpanzees Surrounded by Tourists at Mahale	131
3.3 Map of Baboon Invasion, Mahale	133

Part IV

4.1 Composite of Habitat Loss and Chimpanzee Groups	155
4.2 Ngogo Range with Infant Killings c. 1999	159
4.3 Ngogo Killings and Range Expansion	160
4.4 Chimpanzee Population Change at Ngogo 1975–2007, by Encounters along Observation Transects	168
4.5 Red Colobus Hunts around Ngogo, 1995–1998 and 1999–2002	184
4.6 Kanyawara Forest Disturbance	195
4.7 Kanyawara Territorial Encounters and Kills	200

Part V

5.1 Busingiro Ranges	222
5.2 Infant Killings and Attacks at Sonso	243

Part VI

6.1	Chimpanzee Subspecies and Bonobo Research Sites	253
6.2	Kalinzu Chimpanzee with Snare Injury	254
6.3	Goualougo Sociogram of Individual Associations	261
6.4	Lope Fruiting Levels 1987, 2017	273

Part VII

7.1	Tai Community Numbers	292

Part VIII

8.1	Average Taxonomic Differences between Species and Locations	337
8.2	GG Rubbing Positions among Bonobos and Chimpanzees	340

Part IX

9.1	Relation between Density and Kills Per Year	404

Preface

Between two World Wars, as a bloodied world grasped at a League of Nations, Albert Einstein asked Sigmund Freud why men can be roused to the carnage of war, a question publicly known as "Why War?" The physicist passingly noted the machinations of "the governing class" and arms makers, supported by organizing minions in schools, press, and church. That much was obvious. But the deeper question, he thought, was why do human beings readily join into such horrific violence? Einstein believed he already knew why. "Only one answer is possible. Because man has within him a lust for hatred and destruction." What he wanted from Freud was a scientific understanding of this lust. Freud obliged. Psychoanalysis had shown that humans have a biologically based "death instinct"—a fundamental urge of self-destruction that is better turned outward against others. "It may perhaps seem to you as though our theories are a kind of mythology and, in the present case not even an agreeable one. But does not every science come in the end to a kind of mythology like this?" (Einstein 2002 [1932]:189; Freud 2002 [1932]:198). Freud's death wish does not get much credence today, but other theories of innate depravity are alive and well.

Why do people make war? Why is war so common? Is it human nature for *men* to kill outsiders? Many say yes. In the 1960s legendary fossil hunter Raymond Dart (1959) traced our blood-drenched heritage in damage done to early hominid bones. Nobel Prize–winning ethologist Konrad Lorenz (1966) explained that we have an innate aggressive drive requiring discharge, and a triggerable program of "militant enthusiasm" to express it. Robert Ardrey (1961:322–323; 1968) crafted the verdict of science for popular consumption: we are "Cain's children," "bad-weather animals" born with a "territorial imperative," and "a natural instinct to kill with a weapon." We are "killer apes"—but that is a *good* thing. It made us "free of the forest prison" which still confined our primate cousins. That story went large. In *2001: A Space Odyssey*, when those obelisk-apes started killing each other—that was us. *Lord of the Flies* lies lurking within all men.

Is war an expression of human nature? Of course, no question. People *do* war. It's a human thing, mostly a men's thing. The question is what *kind* of nature paves our roads to war? On that, anthropologists split between "materialists," who see war deriving from practical interests in resources and power, and "symbolists," who see war as acting out scripts of cultural value systems. Both stances make assumptions about human nature, what makes us tick and why we do what we do, but neither suggests that people are *born* predisposed to war.

Another approach asserts exactly that. "Biological" or "evolutionary" theories claim that humans are not just capable of war, but that we naturally lean into it, we seek it out. Men are innately primed to kill outsiders. Specific wars are culturally molded expressions of a species tendency, which evolved because it promoted male reproductive success in our evolutionary past. That is the ultimate causation behind all proximate causes of war. Born-to-kill tendencies are proposed in countless variations (see

Milam 2019), but a touchstone for many is modern research on chimpanzees, *Pan troglodytes*.

Do chimpanzees make war? Until the 1970s nobody thought so. Then at Gombe National Park in Tanzania, over four years a group of chimpanzees stealthily patrolled their borders, entered a neighbor's rangeland, and sometimes attacked and killed single individuals. Eventually the targeted group was gone, and the attackers ranged in their territory. Since then, deciding whether chimpanzees make war depends on one's definition.

I always opted for a minimalist definition of war: collective and potentially lethal action by members of one group, directed against people outside that group (Ferguson 1984:5). By that minimal definition, chimpanzees can make war. But in that definition, I was thinking about people only, and so took much for granted, starting with complex and layered group social and political dynamics, and symbolic configuration of enemies that makes killing them acceptable and meaningful. My definition *assumed* the presence of *culture* (see Chapter 30). To anticipate my conclusions, chimpanzees are not cultural, which makes chimpanzee "war" essentially unlike human war. For clarity, their "war" is put in quotes.

I am not a primatologist. As an anthropologist of war I was drawn into the chimpanzee literature very reluctantly, because of prominent assertions that we cannot understand war without recognizing its evolved biopsychological substrate, supposedly shared by chimpanzees and people. Some version of "the first step in controlling war is understanding its biological roots" has been the refrain ever since Lorenz and Ardrey. We humans are born with predispositions to kill outsiders, irrespective of any immediate material needs or competition. This is the initial message from Jane Goodall's work at Gombe. It is the central point in Richard Wrangham and Dale Peterson's *Demonic Males*, and countless other publications.

The basic idea is that males of both species are naturally inclined to kill outsiders when there is little risk involved to themselves. Males are primed to *seek* opportunities to kill because in our evolutionary past that enhanced males' access to resources and females, and so enhanced reproductive success. Although advocates of this perspective invariably note qualifying, complicating, and modifying factors of culture, their main point is that ultimately, war is *man's* nature.

Wrangham (2005:18) puts this bluntly in *Harper's Magazine*, following a discussion of war by human hunter-gatherers:

> The principle that underlies the mayhem is simple: When the killing is cheap, kill. In any particular instance it may or may not lead to a bigger territory, but from the perspective of natural selection, killing need only lead to benefits sufficiently often. Just as the first male fig wasp that emerges from pupation will immediately attempt to kill any other males he finds in the same fig, so humans, chimpanzees, and wolves benefit by killing rivals when it's reasonably safe to do so. The killers may think of their action as revenge, as a rite of manhood, or as placating the gods– or they may not think about it at all. They may do it simply because it's exciting, as seems to be the case for chimpanzees. The rational doesn't matter to natural selection. What matters, it seems, is that in future battles the neighbors will have one less warrior.

Chimpanzees, War, and History: Are Men Born to Kill? challenges that perspective. It shows that *Pan* territorial behavior and intergroup relations vary greatly by circumstance, and sometimes include intergroup mixing and toleration. Intergroup killings of adults are few, and mostly limited to just two situations. Border patrolling is a pattern in only a minority of study sites. Adult males that disappear cannot be presumed dead, much less killed by outside chimpanzees. Chimpanzees have killed as many within their own groups as outsiders. Many other canonical "facts" are similarly contested.

My alternative explanation is that most killings are attributable to anthropogenic change. Killings are not a "normal" expression of evolved reproductive strategies, but situational reactions to *specific* human disturbance. That is my main argument. Along with human impact, another partly overlapping hypothesis is that killings of defenseless individuals can be related to "political" circumstances *within groups*. Supporting both those hypotheses with evidence is the task of this book.

The bottom line is that chimpanzee males are not innately predisposed to kill outsiders. To understand where, when, and why they kill, violence must be *historically* situated in the realities of its time and place. If that is done, the lesson of chimpanzees is that they, like people, are *not* inclined to war.

Many times a human disturbance explanation has been pronounced dead. The debate is called settled, closed. Killing it is said, is proven beyond reasonable doubt to be an evolved adaptive strategy, not seriously affected by human activities (Wilson et al. 2014a). That proclamation does not stand against the evidence presented here.

This is not an attack on evolutionary explanations but rather an argument for a different perspective on evolution. Humans are animals. Our minds and capacity for culture are ultimately the product of evolution. The question is, where has evolution brought us? To specific violent predispositions—what some still call instincts—or to open coping, with nature and nurture interacting? I argue that deadly violence is but one expression of behavioral plasticity. Many primatologists will say "of course!" Some—more than a few I hope—will agree with positions in this book. But as Part I and subsequent chapters show, that is not primatology's often proclaimed message to the public.

Who am I, an anthropologist, to contest theory about chimpanzees with researchers who spent years observing in the field? I do not know a single chimpanzee personally. Yet I have been immersed in this literature for over 20 years. Why do primatologists publish research findings if others cannot evaluate their findings independently? In science, theories and evidence must be subject to scrutiny and debate.

The book has ten multichapter Parts. Part I sets up everything to come. It shows how the idea of ape and human demonism—the Gombe paradigm—arose; and lays out major theoretical positions, both within primatology and my own. Parts II through VII go deep into all field observation sites: II Gombe, III Mahale, IV Kibale, V Budongo, VI eleven "smaller" cases across Africa, and VII Tai. Each considers *every* killing reported or suspected, and contextualizes every one within local history of human disruption and status politics. Part VIII about bonobos examines their territoriality and intergroup behavior; offers a *social* evolutionary explanation for pattern differences between them and chimpanzees, with the latter enabling violence and killing as political display; and considers nature–nurture interactions in hormonal and other biological characteristics in light of recent developments of evolutionary theory.

The final two Parts are synthetic. Part IX evaluates all that came before, first in two chapters that deconstruct demonic and broader adaptive explanations; beginning with sexually selected infanticide in Chapter 27, then moving to attacks on adults in Chapter 28. Chapter 29 rebuts critiques of human impact explanations and summarizes abundant supporting evidence. Throughout Part IX, special attention goes to refuting recent and widely cited claims that "Lethal aggression in *Pan* is better explained by adaptive strategies than human impacts" (Wilson et al. 2014a).

Part X wraps up with the biggest question of all, why do people make war? Chapter 29 evaluates all the proposed applications of chimpanzee analogies to human warfare, and finds them less than illuminating. Chapter 30 provides the foundation of my own unifying, species-specific anthropological theory of war, based on two fundamental differences between *Pan* and *Homo*. On that foundation, Chapter 31 outlines many ways I have employed that theory, to explain why war happens, the war patterns of particular societies, and actual decisions to go to war. That leads to a closing comment on my subtitle, "Are Men Born to Kill?"

Readers will approach this book from different angles. Researchers will want to scrutinize all the fine points; people just interested in chimpanzees or conservation may skim to get on with the main story; and those most concerned with innate tendencies to war will go for the theoretical discussions and evidentiary summaries (Part 1, Chapters 4, 8, and 26, Parts IX and X). Wherever possible, the narrative is simple and straightforward, with more technical but necessary points discussed in extensive footnotes. But often detail is required in the main text, to challenge existing positions or construct new ones. To avoid any appearance of cherry picking, the text presents a *complete* record of reports of even suspected killings, from published research on all major research sites, from initial observations to 2021. All this detail is necessary because *Chimpanzees, War, and History* aims to overturn a disciplinary consensus which concludes that killing is adaptive, and to substantiate a human impact explanation often declared disproven. That is why this book is so comprehensive and detailed, and why it took so long to research and write (and read).

Acknowledgments

Acknowledgments are difficult for a two-decade project. I have talked ideas through with many, many people, some whose names I never knew, and surely will not remember even all who were the most involved. Those I omit, I do apologize.

First are my loving and *patient* wife Leslie Farragher who put up with thousands of "I'm working," listened attentively every time I went on about something I'd just read, and always encouraged me; and my *inspiring* daughter Elise Ferguson who literally grew up with this book and inspires me with her smartness and moral commitment. Those two made this long journey possible, and Leslie checked my numbers and made the tables. My larger family also heard about it so many times, and believed in me (even though I've been saying "it's almost done" since 2004): sister Kate, her husband Bob Hirsh, son Ian Ferguson and his husband Ryan Brandau; sister Margaret, husband Mitch Kleinman and children Ben and Alex; brother Phil and his wife Linda; brother Bob, wife Diane, and anthropologist son Michael, with Kathy, not forgetting Charlie and Greer; and in-laws Carla Farragher and Mike McCrobie. To them all—the next book on the origin of gangsters in New York won't be so bad.

Friends and colleagues who listened and asked clarifying questions include Claudia Amos, Connie Anderson, Pat Antoniello, Gay Bradshaw, Antonio Campos, Charlotte Cerf, Aldo Civico, Ira Cohen, Steve Daley, Chris Duncan, Jeff English, Brian Felicetta, Frank Fischer, Steve Franklin, Douglas Fry, Agustin Fuentes, Rosa Gonzales, Brian Grant, Jonathan Haas, Clay Hartjen, Carol Henderson, Haram (Adam) Henriquez, Alex Hinton, John Horgan, Peter Kincl, Kate Korten, Chris Kyle, Jamie Lew, Jonathan Marks, Bill Mitchell, Sean Mitchell, Bryan Muldoon, Zoe Ngonyama, Hank Penza, The Phantom, Barbara Price, Steve Reyna, Nicole M. Rivera, Isaias Rojas-Perez, Dolores Shapiro, Kurt Schock, Genese Sodikoff, Leslie Sponsel, Allen Steinhauer, Bob Sussman, Joel Wallman, Alisse Waterston, and Maxine Weisgrau. Again, apologies to those left out. A special category is my high school friends, the Delmartians, who check in on progress when we get together every year, always interested and encouraging: Yael Harris, Tim Hewitt, Rob Longley, Janet Mattox, Richard Oldreik, Dick Phelan, Stephen Phelps, Molly Reynolds, Chris Rosaria, and Scott Vonnegut. Two graduate students did most of the bibliography, Alea Rouse and Michael Toomey—thank you! John Driscoll, Joy McDonald, and Dawn Wilson helped keep me going many times. I am grateful to the fabulous librarians at Rutgers—their interlibrary loan can find anything; and to the undergraduate and graduate students at Rutgers University-Newark, especially in the Master's Program on Peace and Conflict Studies, who heard many of these ideas and asked good questions. It would be remiss to leave out the crews and customers who respected my odd work habit of writing at local bars, and also asked good questions.

The Rutgers University Research Council twice stepped in with important funding when it was really needed.

A special debt is owed to Elizabeth Knoll, formerly at another press. We could not bring the book to publication together, but for years as my editor she encouraged me, asked pointed questions, and made my writing better. This book project might have gone nowhere without her encouragement and editorial advice.

PART I
CONTROVERSIES

1
From Nice to Brutal

How did chimpanzees get such a killer reputation? Where did the idea come from that people get their mean streak from apes? It wasn't always that way. Understanding the construction of our image of chimpanzee violence is the first step in evaluating scientific claims about humanity's supposedly lethal heritage.

An Image of Peace

Robert Ardrey, who called people "killer apes," had a much nicer opinion of chimpanzees. In being deadly dangerous, humans were *different* from forest apes, "nonaggressive vegetarians" condemned to "eternal munching." Although chimpanzees were hostile to neighbors, they "maintain each other's exclusive space by avoidance," not killing (Ardrey 1961:322–323; 1968: 245). In a public discussion with Louis Leakey, Goodall's mentor, Ardrey said that clashes between primate groups were mere "charades," just stimulating "fun." Leakey, referring to reports from Gombe, said that the *only* serious aggression there was between baboons and chimpanzees in the "contrived situation" of banana feeding (Leakey and Ardrey 1971:16–17). Ashley Montagu (1968:12) wrote that studies of wild primates, including Goodall's, "show these creatures to be anything but irascible. All the field observers agree that these creatures are amiable and quite unaggressive, and there is not the least reason to suppose that man's pre-human primate ancestors were in any way different."

Pioneering field studies of chimpanzees seemed to confirm this pacifistic orientation, or go even farther. From his own early observations in Budongo forest and other reports, Vernon Reynolds (1966:444; also Sugiyama 1968) concluded that chimpanzees lived in open groups, that they "recognize and tolerate other individuals in a network of acquaintances extending beyond any local community," and that old acquaintances reunite with "affectionate greeting." This he saw as the evolutionary template for hominid social organization.

Goodall (1986:503) recognized that her studied chimpanzees fell into "northern and southern 'subgroups'" where individuals spent most of their time, but thought there was no barrier between them or even beyond. Chimpanzees had open unbroken networks, with strangers being excitedly welcomed among them.

> Since chimpanzee groups in the reserve freely unite from time to time without signs of aggression, they cannot be divided into separate communities. It seems likely that only a geographic barrier would constitute a limiting factor on the size of a

community, although individuals living at opposite ends of the range might never come into contact. (Goodall 1965:456–457)

One of these "reunions" of separate groups is a central event in her first *National Geographic* (1967) special, "Miss Goodall and Her Wild Chimpanzees."

Another pioneer, Toshisada Nishida (1968:167) broke with this consensus by reporting that at Mahale in Tanzania, groups with overlapping territories were closed and antagonistic. Yet the "inter-unit-group interaction is peaceful; the subordinate unit-group avoids the dominant one" (Nishida 1980:21)—as Ardrey said.[1]

Goodall was the great communicator about chimpanzees. Her message was that chimpanzees are like humans, and humans like chimpanzees (Lehman Haupt 1971; Stade 1972; Scarf 1973). In regard to *war* however, at first there was *no* comparison.

> Two neighboring communities of chimpanzees may occasionally indulge in displays of power as individuals hurl rocks and wave branches or even briefly attack one another. But they show nothing even remotely comparable to the horror of human warfare. (van Lawick-Goodall 1973a:11)

"[C]himpanzees, though very much like us in behavior, were rather *nicer*" (Goodall with Berman 1999:111).

The Great Revision

That image shattered during what Goodall (1999:127) named "the Four Year War" at Gombe. First, the Kakombe community split into northern (Kasakela) and southern (Kahama) groups. Then, from 1974 to 1977, Kasakela males deliberately, brutally attacked members of the southern group, beating, biting, and sometimes killing those they caught, until none were left. Then Kasakela chimpanzees began to forage in their old range—they took Kahama's land! This was stunning news. Chimpanzees could brutally kill other chimpanzees. Like men. "Sadly, the 'noble ape' was as mythical as the 'noble savage'" (Goodall with Berman 1999:112).

These developments along with findings from Mahale, led to what I call the Great Revision, totally changing our picture of chimpanzee groups and interactions between them. Post-revision, it seemed that early observers were misled by the messy way daily parties of chimpanzees continually break up and reform in new combinations (Ghiglieri 1984:8, 173–174). That masked the existence of hostile, territorially exclusive communities that defined the limits of this "fission/fusion pattern" of association. With little further consideration, the earlier views of wide-ranging sociality were consigned to the dust bin, disappearing from the master narrative of belligerent chimpanzees.

---

[1] As developments unfolded over time at Gombe, Nishida's view gained credence there, and researchers reconceptualized northern and southern subgroups as parts of one community, called Kakombe (Teleki et al. 1976:581).

Human Influence

It took time to make any sense of these attacks, and interpretation went through two very different phases. The first is registered in a paper written by Goodall et al. (1979) and seven associates at Gombe. They start with an idea from David Bygott, a doctoral student who did much of the chimpanzee following away from the field station in the early 1970s. "Bygott (1974) has put forward a theory that increasing agriculture outside the boundaries of the park may have driven more chimpanzees into the area, thus increasing their density. This is plausible ... If the theory is true, it might account for an increased aggressiveness between males of different communities." However, "it does not seem to us that there is enough overcrowding to account for the severity of the three attacks perpetrated by the Kasakela community against Kahama males" (Goodall et al. 1979:42, 51).

Elsewhere Goodall (1977a:272–273) is even more clear about the impact of human encroachment. "We do not understand this violent behaviour." But she had good idea. Recent cultivation around the Park may have pushed a large group, later called Kalande, into Kahama's rangelands.

> It is possible that this large community may have moved into the Park from outside and that the density of the chimpanzees within the Park has, therefore, increased.... So far as we can tell, there is, as yet, no serious overcrowding of the chimpanzees at Gombe. Nevertheless, with the encroachment of another large community, there is increasing likelihood of encounters between males of one community and individuals of another.

Human interference was considered as a likely, though not complete, explanation of intergroup violence. Commentators said that "rigorous testing" of the effects of crowding on aggression would need to be done in the future (Trudeau et al. 1981:38). That never happened. The idea that external habitat loss led to crowding within the Park and so to intergroup aggression kept on in a few research publications (Goodall 1983:6; 1986:49–50; Williams et al. 2008:774). But in the theory and master narrative of Gombe, the point rarely surfaces.

Human impact was not limited to habitat impaction. Much fighting occurred over provisioned bananas. The feeding chaos was so intense that research almost ended. Teleki, at Gombe in the late 1960s, believed that the provisioning drew southern chimpanzees northward, to concentrate around the feeding station (Nishida 1979:117). Reynolds (1975) titled an article "How Wild Are the Gombe Chimpanzees?" Margaret Power (1991), the most important critic of the idea that *pan*icide was "natural," argued that changes in banana provisioning were responsible for the violence between Kasakela and Kahama. That is not the direction Goodall's thinking would take, nor researchers after her.

Although Goodall never credited banana competition as a cause of intergroup violence, she emphasized conflict over resource territories. With Kahama eliminated and the Kasakela chimpanzees occupying their range, recovering what had been lost became her immediate explanation of the fighting (Goodall 1977b). "The most likely cause of the Four-Year War at Gombe was the Kasakela males' frustration at being denied access to an area over which they had roamed until it was occupied by the breakaway community" (Goodall with Berman 1999:127–128). Yet resource competition alone was not seen as enough to explain the intensity of attacks.

Tilting toward the Dark Side

Goodall felt that the severity, the brutality of the attacks on chimpanzees that for years had lived together and socialized, had more disturbing implications. In *National Geographic* (Goodall 1979:594), she told the world that chimpanzees "had their own form of primitive warfare," and they used it to acquire territory. The caption for an illustration of "warmongering apes" ended with a hint of the perspective to come: "Whatever the reason, the events point up dramatically an aspect of chimpanzees behavior that she finds disturbingly similar to the darker side of human nature" (1979:611; and see Goodall with Berman 1999:117).

Dark Times

Goodall's view of human nature itself took a sharp turn for the worse at this moment. The mid-1970s was a time of human war near to Gombe. Across Lake Tanganyika in Zaire, Goodall sometimes saw villages in flames. Refugees came in from Burundi. In May 1975 rebels from Zaire crossed the Lake and kidnapped four student researchers, three of them from Stanford University, which had become the sponsor of the Gombe Stream Research Center (*New York Times* 1975). It took months of seriously strained relations between Stanford and the Ugandan government to get all the captives back. Goodall was enmeshed in nasty fights and recriminations (Peterson 2006:556–557, 567–568). Much of her energy and resources went to countering these criticisms. That was her personal low point. "I only mention it here because it was so devastating at the time, and because it taught me so much about human nature." "What a horrible commentary on human nature" (Goodall with Berman 1999:104–105).

Besides having a profound impact on Goodall personally, these events marked the "end of an era" in Gombe research (Goodall with Berman 1999:105). Her teaching position at Stanford ended, funding dried up, and the Tanzanian government greatly restricted her or any outsiders' access to Gombe. In 1976 wealthy friends helped establish the Jane Goodall Institute. Research revived, but for some time would rely primarily on trained Tanzanian observers rather than graduate students.

Goodall tells us that this sudden, dramatic reversal of fortune had a profound effect on her view of human nature. It happened at the same time she was trying to make sense of the Four Year War—and an array of other shocking violence among Gombe chimpanzees. Goodall refers to this period as "Paradise Lost," "my world turned upside-down" (Goodall with Berman 1999:97).

Meanwhile, events at Mahale, about 160 km to the south in Tanzania, added to the darkening picture. Antagonistic interactions but not serious violence had been observed between two chimpanzee communities: K-group, the initial focus of study, and the larger M-group to its south. Several K group males disappeared over the years with researchers making little of it. After word of the Gombe events spread, Nishida and colleagues thought again. Those and subsequent disappearances were *reinterpreted* as possibly being killings. Ultimately, with more male disappearances, K-group was gone (Nishida 1980; Nishida et al. 1985).

Many researchers concluded that at *two* research locations, one chimpanzee community "wiped out" another. Interpretive caution did not rule. For many, by 1985 the verdict was in: the Four Year War was no aberration. It is in the nature of chimpanzees to make war, to conquer territory—just like humans (Ghiglieri 1988:258–259; Goodall 1986:519–522).

Goodall's Theory

In her magnificent opus *The Chimpanzees of Gombe*—a true masterpiece of scholarship—Goodall (1986) mapped out the dark side. Chimpanzees had behavioral tendencies that they shared with human beings, which were "precursors" for human warfare. First, they are territorial.

> In the chimpanzee, territoriality functions not only to repel intruders from the home range, but sometimes to injure or eliminate them; not only to defend the existing home range and its resources, but to enlarge it opportunistically at the expense of weaker neighbors; not only to protect the female resources of a community, but to actively and aggressively recruit new sexual partners from neighboring social groups. (Goodall 1986:528)

Second, chimpanzees, especially young males, are "often strongly attracted to intergroup encounters, even to the extent of approaching a number of potentially dangerous neighbors." They are excited by it, they seek it out. "[I]if early hominid males were *inherently* disposed to find aggression attractive, particularly aggression directed against neighbors, this trait would have provided a biological basis for the cultural training of warriors" (1986:531).

Third, they have "an inherent fear of, or aversion to strangers, expressed by aggressive attack" (1986:531). Yet there is something more complicated here than simple xenophobia. They can draw a line cutting off *known* individuals, former companions, as Kasakela did to Kahama, in a deadly divide. When Kasakela males attacked, their behavior demonstrated an "intent to kill." "If they had firearms and had been taught to use them, I suspect they would have used them to kill" (1986:529, 530). Chimpanzees outside the group "may not only be violently attacked, but the patterns of attack may actually differ from those utilized in typical intracommunity aggression. The victims are treated more as though they were prey animals; they are 'dechimpized,'" just as humans dehumanize their enemies through a process of "pseudospeciation" (1986:532).

Years later, after the horrifying human wars of the 1990s, Goodall (with Berman 1999:131) brought the point home. "Our tendency to form select in-groups from which we exclude those who do not share our ethnic background, socioeconomic position, political persuasions, religious beliefs, and so on is one of the major causes of war, rioting, gang violence, and other kinds of conflict." All of that violence is largely due to the fact that humans share with chimpanzees a tendency to attack and kill members of other groups.

A new paradigm was being born. Not one developed from many researchers working over years on related problems, but from a few startling observations, rapidly reinforced by other events at Gombe and Mahale, and impressed on all the primatologists who would follow.

Jane Goodall is a hero. From humble beginnings, she dared to open up a new field of research. With courage and determination—with pure grit—she overcame self-doubt, physical hardship, malaria, a plane crash, professional scorn, a terrifying night raid, wrenching emotional turns, financial reverses, and personal tragedy. This young, former secretary made the most momentous discoveries in the history of chimpanzee research—that they make and use tools, that they hunt, and that in their emotional and behavioral range they closely resemble human beings. With these three discoveries, she changed forever our cherished notions of human uniqueness within the animal kingdom.

Goodall conducted superb research on many aspects of behavior, and organized a much larger project that resulted in one of the finest monographs of 20th-century science. Perhaps most extraordinary, in *The Chimpanzees of Gombe*, she faithfully presents information that does not seem to support her own ideas. When she turned from research to activism, she became the world's conscience about human abuse of chimpanzees. For decades she has worked tirelessly to promote natural conservation and peaceful cooperation among people, even busier during Covid with televisits. She built an organization, The Jane Goodall Institute, that has been a crucial moving force behind many chimpanzee protection programs, as seen repeatedly in this book.

In 1991, from her front porch in Tanzania, she began "Roots and Shoots," a youth empowerment network. It has operated around the world (Pusey et al. 2007:626), in all 50 US states and over 60 countries. "Since 1991, millions of students have taken on the challenge of making the world a better place for people, other animals and the environment we share. Roots & Shoots youth are not only the future—they are the present—and they are changing the world" (https://www.rootsandshoots.org/about-us/). Goodall is an incomparable role model for young people, especially but not limited to girls (Greene 2005). In 2002 Secretary-General Kofi Annan appointed her a United Nations Messenger of Peace (Hunt 2002:303). Her brilliant ideas in conversation with Douglas Abrams in *The Book of Hope* (Goodall and Abrams 2021) show not only great knowledge, from individual lives to planetary scale, but also wisdom. Wise hope is very scarce today. The world needs Jane Goodall.

But Dr. Goodall began her career as a scientist, and became one of incalculable influence. I treat her with great respect, as a scientist. It would be a disservice to do otherwise. Science progresses as new ideas are evaluated against new theory and evidence. There has been a lot of both since she gave up active chimpanzee research in the 1980s. All of that is included in this book.

2
The Second Generation

Sociobiology

There was another important development in the middle 1970s, not in chimpanzee behaviors, but in evolutionary theory to explain those behaviors. The year 1975, the middle of the Four Year War, saw the publication of E.O. Wilson's (1980) extremely influential and controversial *Sociobiology: The New Synthesis*.

Inclusive fitness theory explained many aspects of animal and human behavior as strategies designed by evolution to maximize an individual organism's genes in future generations. For males–which were the focus of most theorizing about primates and human origins (see Haraway 1989)—specific behaviors were selected for because they increased access to females, and/or increased food resources, which enabled reproductive success. Since close kin shared genes, nepotistically helping them helped to pass along those shared genes, selecting for behaviors favoring kin, or kin selection. Everything came down to the currency of maximizing genes in future generations.[1]

Goodall's findings were not inconsistent with the emerging field of sociobiology, but she was not a sociobiologist. She believes "it is pointless to deny that we humans harbor innate aggressive and violent tendencies," and scorns those who say those are all learned. Yet she pointedly distances herself from those who emphasize the calculus of reproductive success, singling out Richard Dawkins's *The Selfish Gene*. "Sociobiological theory, while helpful in understanding the basic mechanism of the evolutionary process, tends to be dangerously reductionist when used as the sole explanation of human—or chimpanzee—behavior" (Goodall with Berman 1999:141). Inclusive fitness approaches "provided an excuse for human selfishness and cruelty. We just couldn't help it . . . . [Referring to Nazi Germany, she asks, did] Dawkins's theory help to explain how, in a supposedly cultured, civilized country, mass killing and genocide on such a scale could have taken place?" (1999:119–122). Goodall's point is that tendencies to war are *innate*—not that humans or chimpanzees follow an inborn calculus for maximizing genetic success.

Settling In

Goodall was the beginning, not the end, of theory about chimpanzee war and its relevance to humans. Elaborating the evolutionary rationale behind "demonic males"

---

[1] Goodall herself does not dwell on theoretical issues in positing innate tendencies. She characterizes herself as a field researcher trying to understand chimpanzee behavior, while leaving high-level theoretical debates to others (Goodall with Berman 1999:122–123). Her basic approach is more in tune with the ethological observations of Konrad Lorenz, Niko Tinbergen, and Irenaeus Eibl-Eibesfeldt (Goodall 2000:311).

would be taken up by the next generation of chimpanzee researchers, some of them students of Goodall, and they would line up with Dawkins. Ghiglieri (1987) describes the spread of this perspective, explaining how it "plumbed the roots of social structure by seeking to explain it as a result of adaptations to maximize the reproductive success of the social individual." Despite arguments, "it is generally agreed that social systems have evolved to maximize the reproductive success of individuals in them" (Ghiglieri 1984:2–3). Wrangham's approach was close (1982a), with some differences.[2]

> Where does human violence come from, and why? Of course, there have been great advances in the way we think about these things. Most importantly, in the 1970s, the same decade as the Kahama killings, a new evolutionary theory emerged, the selfish-gene theory of natural selection, variously called inclusive fitness theory, sociobiology, or more broadly, behavioral ecology. Sweeping through the halls of academe, it revolutionized Darwinian thinking by its insistence that *the ultimate explanation of any individual's behavior considers only how the behavior tends to maximize genetic success*: to pass that individual's genes into subsequent generations. The new theory, elegantly popularized in Richard Dawkins's *The Selfish Gene*, is now the conventional wisdom in biological science because it explains animal behavior so well. It accounts for selfishness, even killing. And it has come to be applied with increasing confidence to human behavior, though the debate is still hot and unsettled. (Wrangham and Peterson 1996:22–23, my emphasis)

Throughout this book, I will occasionally refer to "sociobiology." I understand that few primatologists today would use that label for their own work. But the main theory of chimpanzee violence was built on that foundation, and for many explanations, the foundational theory has not changed.

Scientific Methods

Along with the new theories came a new methodology, focused on formulating and testing narrow hypotheses (McGrew 2017:240–242). Goodall exemplified an older, ethnographic, or natural history approach.

> Natural history data were the focus of primatology until the 1970s and 1980s, when there was a major shift toward hypothesis-driven research (the collection of a limited set of data used to test specific hypotheses) .... As a result of this shift, natural history data are currently undervalued, and it can be challenging in primatology (and other biological fields) to obtain funding specifically for the collection of broad behavioral and ecological data and to get natural history information published in leading primatological journals (Campbell et al. 2007:703; cf. McGrew 2017:240–242).

---

[2] And rather than sociobiology, he favored the label "comparative socioecology" (Rodseth et al. 1991:429–431; Rubenstein and Wrangham 1986:3–4).

That shift is very apparent in this book, for instance in the more restricted information we got about Gombe after Goodall withdrew from field research around 1981.

The New Mindset

By the end of the 1970s, the Four Year War was being reframed in terms of hypotheses about genetic relatedness and reproductive striving. Researchers who had done Gombe fieldwork before the kidnappings proposed that relations between males of different groups were fearful and hostile because males of one group shared common genetic interests, while they competed with less related males of other groups. It was a matter of inclusive fitness (Bauer 1980:117–118; Wrangham 1979a:358).

> If it is normally true that the larger party wins the encounter then the community which can most frequently form large parties will achieve territorial gain at the expense of its neighbours . . . the functional consequence of territorial expansion was the acquisition of females, since there is some evidence that they do not always follow a retreating male community. If so, we may view the formation of large parties as improving the reproductive success of a male community . . . (Wrangham 1977:536).

Bygott (1979:423) proposed that because of this reproductive advantage, "there would be strong selection for males to be rapidly aroused to attack strangers, particularly males on sight."

Wrangham, who would be the most thoughtful, prolific, influential, and provocative theorist on chimpanzee intergroup violence, made the most important contributions toward the adaptive explanation of male belligerence. Much of my disagreement in this book is with his theory. At Gombe he (1977; 1979b) concluded that females ranged alone or with offspring in the center or core of a territory; while males roamed in larger parties over a larger area.[3] The larger range of males surrounding the females, he deduced, enabled males to pursue their own internal political alliances, and simultaneously protect the females from stranger males. The alliances were for reproductive success (Wrangham and Smuts 1980:30).

Interference Mutualism

Deepening the evolutionary selfishness, Wrangham brought in a new principle, interference mutualism. Mutualism occurs when two organisms both benefit by participating in the same behavior at the same time (Clutton-Brock 2009). With chimpanzees, hunting will an example. Single hunters have less chance of catching a monkey than

---

[3] In traditional ecology, "territory" that is defended, is distinguished from a larger "home range," used but not defended (Burt 1943). This distinction does not work for primates (Grant et al. 1992). For instance, chimpanzee intergroup conflict often occurs at or beyond use peripheries. Chimpanzee studies often use "range" and "territory" interchangeably (Mitani and Rodman 1979), as I do in this book.

if several try at once. Many have written about mutualism across the animal kingdom as a powerful selective force—those who cooperate both directly benefit (Fry 2018; Sussman and Chapman 2004; Sussman and Cloninger 2011; Sussman and Garber 2004; Sussman et al. 2005; Zihlman and Bolter 2004; cf. Lawler 2011; Sussman et al. 2011).

But as the demonic perspective was being formed, in the salad days of sociobiology, mutualism itself was seen not just as a path to mutual benefit, but also as a way to *harm others*. "Non-interference mutualism" (NIM) confers benefits to all those participating in a behavior. "Interference mutualism" (IM) confers rewards on cooperators, but also imposes costs on others. IM is expected among genetically related individuals, against nonrelatives. Interferers would thus prosper at the expense of generally cooperative noninterferers. Relatively more of their genes would be passed along (Wrangham 1982b:272-273). This could be the origin of "us" vs. "them." This is the sort of "hard truth" on which sociobiology thrived.

If true, "individuals should associate with their closest possible relative at all times . . . stable groups of considerable size may develop. Relationships between these groups would normally be aggressive, unlike those between NIM groups" (1982b:274). Within-group conflicts should be limited in violence. "For example winners should refrain from killing defeated rivals . . . Aggression between males of different communities, however, can lead to serious injuries and deaths" (1982b:282).

Building a Theory

A related concept was already in wide use: coalitional aggression. "In ethology, a coalition is defined as cooperation in an aggressive or competitive context . . . the interests of the cooperating parties are served at the expense of the interests of a third party. It is this well-coordinated 'us' against 'them' character that sets coalition formation apart from other cooperative interactions among conspecifics" (de Waal and Harcourt 1992:2). Goodall (1986) uses the concept frequently in regard to mostly nonviolent conflicts within the group. It was easily applied to intergroup attacks and killings.

By the later 1980s, Wrangham acknowledged that "the value of biology for an understanding of warfare is still a matter of faith" (1988:79). But he was still building. He drew comparisons between intergroup violence among chimpanzees and human hunter-gatherers, arguing that both species shared a common ancestor with "closed social networks, hostile and male-dominated intergroup relationships with stalk-and-attack interactions" (1987:67-71). One statement from this time is crucial for the theory to follow: "The implication from these studies is that natural selection favors unprovoked aggression provided that the target is sufficiently vulnerable, even when the benefits are not particularly high" (1988:81).

Michael Ghiglieri was a graduate student closed out of Gombe in the aftermath of the 1975 rebel raid. He initiated chimpanzee observations in Kibale, Uganda. In 1987 and 1988 Ghiglieri, published a popular article and book supporting the sociobiological explanation of "War among the Chimpanzees," emphasizing its similarity to human warfare. "Primitive hunting and gathering societies the world over exhibit . . . territorial defense and warfare basically identical in form *and* function to that of chimpanzees" (1988:259; 1987).

The Imbalance of Power Hypothesis

In 1991, different ideas gelled into a major hypothesis (Manson and Wrangham 1991). The imbalance of power hypothesis (IoPH) grew out of the authors' long-standing interests in social organization across the primate order. It stressed the importance of two structuring conditions: male philopatry, and fission/fusion association within a group.

Key Concepts and Big Splashes

Male philopatry means that while most chimpanzee females migrate to another group after they reach sexual maturity,[4] males remain in their group of birth. (This generalization is substantially qualified in chapters to come.) A group's males, it was thought, were more genetically related than the group's adult females, mostly immigrants. Males thus are seen as likely to act in concert against the male mini-gene-pool of the next group. "If generations of males remain true to the territory of their natal community, then they will be more closely related to one another than to the immigrant females or to the average chimpanzee in their population. Solidarity between these males is predictable on the basis of increased inclusive fitness and kin selection" (Ghiglieri 1984:4). "The hypothesis [is] that the more closely related males form a kin group that cooperates to defend a territory, thereby increasing access to females and resources" (Morin et al. 1994:1195).

The *fission-fusion pattern* means that within a "unit-group" or larger community, daily foraging groups range from individuals to large parties, continually breaking up and coming together in new combinations.[5] *Combining* male philopatry and genetic relatedness was inferred to mean that sizable parties of gene-sharing males from one group occasionally encounter a solo genetic competitor from a neighboring group. In the developing adaptationist perspective, this combination set the evolutionary stage for lethal xenophobia and war.

> Examination of comparative data on nonhuman primates and cross-cultural study of foraging societies suggests that attacks are lethal because where there is sufficient imbalance of power their cost is trivial, that these attacks are a male and not a female

---

[4] Female migration at maturity has been attributed to incest avoidance (Pusey 1980), although Wrangham (1975:5.57–58) proposed that maturing females need to find their own core ranges, away from those occupied by their mothers and other adult females. The reason most leave remains an open question (Arcadi 2018:31; Walker and Pusey 2020).

[5] This was once thought to be extremely rare in other species. Further research and consideration has shown that "fission-fusion" is apparent across many species, varying by spatial cohesion, party size, and party composition (Aureli et al. 2008). Comparatively, chimpanzees and humans have a high degree of fission-fusion dynamics.

activity because males are the philopatric sex, and that it is resources of reproductive interest to males that determine the causes of intergroup aggression. (Manson and Wrangham 1991:369)

Male chimpanzees are said to be genetically predisposed to kill outside males whenever they can do so with impunity—and human males are too.

This perspective achieved much greater prominence in 1996, with Wrangham and Peterson's *Demonic Males: Apes and the Origins of Human Violence*. The "demonic" human male represents one point on a broader great ape spectrum, in the nasty things they do in pursuing genetic selfishness. "We think about this as being demonic male behaviour because, of course, females don't do it" (Wrangham quoted in O'Connell 2004). Then Ghiglieri (1999) published *The Dark Side of Man: Tracing the Origins of Male Violence*, with a similar explanation of men behaving despicably.[6]

Specifying an Urge to Kill

What, exactly, does the imbalance of power hypothesis claim about chimpanzees and humans?

We must start with a significant complication, the label "imbalance of power" itself. One ordinary understanding of that label is uncontroversial: whatever the issue, chimpanzees or humans are less likely to attack others when they lack a numerical advantage, and more likely to attack with one. I fully agree that both species normally abide by such elementary calculations. But the imbalance of power hypothesis as advocated by Wrangham and others goes much further than that.

The imbalance of power hypothesis attributes a murderous proclivity to male chimpanzees and humans. Both have "an appetite for lethal raiding," "a hunt-and-kill propensity" (Wrangham 1999:1, 5), both "are wont to kill adult neighbors" (Wrangham and Peterson 1996:165). "For humans, chimpanzees, and wolves it makes sense to kill deliberately and frequently" (Wrangham 2005:18). "Chimpanzees, our closest ape relatives, also have a tendency to organize into coalitions of related males to defend shared territory and to kill their enemies" (Wrangham 2005:15).

This inborn propensity makes male chimpanzees act "as a gang committed to the ethnic purity of their own set" (Wrangham and Peterson 1996:14). The suite of associated behaviors includes collective border patrols and at other times avoidance of border areas, deep incursions into enemy territory, and coalitionary attacks and kills (Wrangham 1999:6).[7] Intergroup violence as at Gombe is said to be confirmed

---

[6] Ghiglieri stopped publishing on chimpanzees at that point, while Wrangham has been a prolific researcher, theorist, writer, and mentor ever since.

[7] Patrols differ from "excursions." The latter is a collective move to a peripheral area of a range, including females and young. These may involve periods of silent watchfulness, but otherwise have normal amounts of noise and feeding. A patrol may include a female or two, but otherwise are adult and adolescent males only. Patrols are distinguished by silence, great attention to surroundings, and not feeding (Goodall 1986:489–491). Some movements are difficult to classify as one or the other. As we shall see, patrol-like behavior also appears when chimpanzees feed on human crops, or make a long passage through open savanna.

by research elsewhere as *normal* (Wrangham and Peterson 1996:12). "[I]ntergroup aggression, including lethal attacks, is a pervasive feature of chimpanzee societies" (Wilson and Wrangham 2003:364).

> Does this mean chimpanzees are naturally violent?... Alas, the evidence is mounting and it all points the same way.... In this cultural species, it may turn out that one of the least variable of all chimpanzee behaviors is the intense competition between males, the violent aggression they use against strangers, and their willingness to maim and kill those that frustrate their goals. (Wrangham 1995:7)

"It's in the nature of chimpanzees to kill" (Wrangham 2006:48).

Sufficient to Kill

A crucial part of this model is that intergroup violence and killing among chimpanzees is *not linked to any immediate resource scarcity or competition*. Action depends, instead, on the ability to kill without risk of serious injury (Wrangham 1999:14–16) "[U]nrestrained attacks on opponents are favored merely because their cost is low," "attacks will be restricted to occasions of overwhelming superiority" and "will occur whenever the opportunity arises" (Manson and Wrangham 1991:371, 385). "[A] necessary and sufficient condition for intercommunity aggression is a perception that an opponent is sufficiently vulnerable to warrant the aggressor(s) attacking at low risk to themselves" (Wrangham 1999:14). "[N]o resources need be in short supply at the time of the raid. Instead, unprovoked aggression is favored by the opportunity to attack 'economically,' that is at low personal risk" (Wrangham 1999:15; and see Wilson and Wrangham 2003:381). "In theory, killing might be a response to competition: but there's no indication that it happens more when resources are in short supply—more likely, it happens when food is abundant" (Wrangham 2006:51).

In the imbalance of power hypothesis, killing is not driven by current resource scarcity, intent to acquire more territory or mates.

> [T]he killers don't get immediate matings or even (normally) any immigrating females as a result. Nor is there any short-term benefit in the form of access to contested food supplies.... In the event of a successful attack there is not immediate pay-off other than the satisfaction the aggressors experience from the act itself. The implication is that natural selection has favoured in chimpanzees a tendency to relish the prospect and performance of such brutality. (Wrangham 2006:51, 53)

This disconnect from any current competition or need for resources is an essential point, with huge implications for chimpanzees and humans. Few would dispute that many human wars are over scarce resources. The imbalance of power hypothesis holds that even without immediate scarcity or competition, both species are inclined to war just because individuals are from different groups. It is the difference between a *capacity* and a *predisposition* for collective violence. This book turns on that distinction.

The Dominance Drive

So if it is not food or even females that pushes males forward—what does put a fire in their bellies? What motivates them to seek out, attack, and if possible kill males from other groups? It is the "dominance drive," the motor for males' struggles for status within the group, the quest to be alpha or close to it. This emotional system has been mobilized for employ in intergroup relations.

> The problem is that males are demonic at unconscious and irrational levels. The motivation of a male chimpanzee who challenges another's rank is not that he foresees more mating or better food or a longer life. Those rewards explain why sexual selection has favored the desire for power, but the immediate reason he vies for status is simpler, deeper, and less subject to the vagaries of context. It is simply to dominate his peers. Unconscious of the evolutionary rational that placed this prideful goal in his temperament, he devises strategies to achieve it that can be complex, original, and maybe conscious. In the same way, the motivation of male chimpanzees on a border patrol is not to gain land or win females. The temperamental goal is to intimidate the opposition, to beat them to a pulp, to erode their ability to challenge. Winning has become an end in itself.

It looks the same with men (Wrangham and Peterson 1996:199).

This is what the fighting is about. "From the raids of chimpanzees at Gombe to wars among human nations, the same emotion looks extraordinarily important, one that we take for granted and describe most simply but that nonetheless takes us deeply back to our animal origins: pride" (Wrangham and Peterson 1996:190).

> The immediate causes of wars are as varied as the interests and policies of those who launch them, but deeper analysis leads to a consistent conclusions: Wars tend to be rooted in the competition for status.... We could well substitute for Sparta and Athens the names of two male chimpanzees in the same community, one rising in power, the other anxious to keep his higher status. (Wrangham and Peterson 1996:192)

Comparing chimpanzees to human youth gangs, "the principal biological influence on collective violence is the male's concern for status. We assume that this status drive is an inherent tendency of both humans and chimpanzees" (Wrangham and Wilson 2004:234).

Gaining Advantage in Numbers

The imbalance of power hypothesis holds that a dominance driven tendency to kill when killing can be done with impunity was favored by natural selection because it reduced the adult males of neighboring groups, thus weakening their strength compared to the killers' group (Wilson et al. 2001; 2002:1107–1108; Wrangham 1999:15; Wrangham and Peterson 1996:190–193). That leads to "increased probability of winning intercommunity dominance contests (nonlethal battles);

this tends to lead to increased fitness of the killers through improved access to resources such as food, females, or safety" (Wrangham 1999:11–12; Wilson and Wrangham 2003:381).

"In any particular instance [killing] may or may not lead to a bigger territory, but from the perspective of natural selection, killing need only lead to benefits sufficiently often" (Wrangham 2005:18).

> A strong evolutionary rational for killing derives from the harsh logic of natural selection. Every homicide shifts the power balance in favor of the killers, giving them an increased chance of outnumbering their opponents and therefore of winning future territorial battles. Bigger territories mean more food, and therefore more babies. (Wrangham 2005:18)

Note carefully that the evolved goal is *not to kill off all the males* of another group, not to exterminate them, but to *reduce the relative number of males*, so the killers would win in future nonlethal contests when two communities clash. "[E]xterminating all of a rival group's males is an extreme outcome of a more general strategy: killing individual rivals whenever possible" (Wilson and Wrangham 2003:379–380).

Applied to Humans

Hunter-gatherers are said to share this generalized hostility to any male beyond their primary social group. In both species, "natural selection has favored specific type of motivational systems" that, "over evolutionary time . . . give individuals access to the resources needed for reproduction."

> The motivations that drive intergroup killing among chimpanzees and humans, by this logic, were selected in the context of territorial competition because reproduction is limited by resources, and resources are limited by territory size. Therefore, it pays for groups to achieve dominance over neighboring groups, so that they can enlarge their territories. To achieve dominance, it is necessary to have greater fighting power than the neighbors. This means that whenever the costs are sufficiently low it pays to kill or damage individuals from neighboring groups. Thus, intergroup killing is viewed as derived from a tendency to strive for status. (Wilson and Wrangham 2003:384)

That is, from the dominance drive.

Wrangham asks: "Did humans get their demons after leaving nature, or have we inherited them from our ancient forest lives?" His answer: "We are apes of nature, cursed over 6 million years or more with a rare inheritance" (1995:7). "[S]election has favored, in chimpanzees and humans, a brain that in appropriate circumstances, seeks out opportunities to impose violence on neighbors. In this sense, the hypothesis is that we have evolved a violent brain" (Wrangham 1999:6). "Chimpanzees and hunter gatherers . . . seek, or take advantage of, opportunities to use imbalances of power for males to kill members of neighboring groups" (Wilson and Wrangham 2003:384).

The position is unchanged in his new book, *The Goodness Paradox* (Wrangham 2019:257–258). After claiming functional similarities between "simple warfare" raiding and chimpanzee intergroup aggression, and noting how New Guinea villagers praised killers, he writes:

> Similar accounts, in which warriors perceive no benefits other than the thrill of making a kill, are rife. From an evolutionary perspective, we can explain their action as we can among animals. Why do they kill? The unnerving answer that makes biological sense is that they enjoy it. Evolution has made the killing of strangers pleasurable, because those that like to kill tended to received adaptive benefits....The rewards do not have to be anticipated consciously. All that is needed is enjoyment of the kill. Sexual reproduction works in a parallel way. A chimpanzee, or wolf, or any other animal, cannot be expected to know that an act of mating will lead to babies. Why do they mate? They enjoy it. (2019:257–258)

If the urge to kill seems alien to us, that is because we do not live in a Pleistocene world. A popular article hammers the message home.

> [S]election has favored a human tendency to identify enemies, draw moral divides, and exploit weaknesses pitilessly across boundaries. Among hunter-gatherer societies, inner-city gangs, and volunteer militias at the fringes of contested national territories, there are similar patterns of violence. The spontaneous aggressiveness of humans is a harsh product of natural selection, part of an evolutionary morality that revels in short-term victory for one's own community without regard for the greater good. (Wrangham 2005:19)

Ghiglieri's approach is consistent with Wrangham's, although not as theoretically nuanced. He (1987:74; 1988:260) concludes that the chimpanzee record shows that war does "run in our genes like addictive behavior, diabetes, and baldness." "[A]nyone insisting that men do not possess an instinct to kill other men in certain conditions is in factual error" (Ghiglieri 1999:178). His message for mankind is blunt.

> Unfortunately, every race, ethnic group, and tribe has its prejudices. Nearly all have led to atrocities, many lethal, often including full-scale war. The message here is that the human psyche has been equipped by kin selection to urge men to eliminate genetic competitors—males first, females second—when such killing can be safely accomplished. War itself, declared or otherwise, is often motivated by these instinctive genocidal goals. I believe this happens because men are born ethnocentric and xenophobic by nature. (Ghiglieri 1999:215)

Are men born to kill? They answer yes. Our DNA whispers from within, "kill thy neighbor." This was the big picture as the sociobiological generation theorized the trail blazed by Goodall. Although I will spend this book criticizing it, I must acknowledge that this is a very well-developed theory.

Since then, many *panologists*[8] have written on chimpanzees' (and humans') supposedly innate proclivity to attack and kill outside males. With some variations, the basic idea of implacable intergroup hostility, border patrols and avoidance unless in numbers, stealthy penetrations, and attacks with intent to kill as a reproductive strategy, has hardened into dogma as typical chimpanzee behavior. This is what I will refer to as the *Gombe paradigm*, or Gombe vision, or the demonic perspective. What does it mean for men, and "why war?"

The Moral of the Story

Goodall (with Berman 1999:141–144) is decidedly the most positive, in her *Reason for Hope*. She sees humans and chimpanzees sharing a tendency to care about others—not the selfish altruism of sociobiology, but true empathy that counters tendencies toward violence. Just as human brutality exceeds that of chimpanzees, so does our benevolence and self-sacrifice. "So here we are, the human ape, half sinner, half saint, with two opposing tendencies inherited from our ancient past pulling us now toward violence, now toward compassion and love." "[W]e really do have the ability to override our genetic heritage.... Our brains are sufficiently sophisticated; it's a question of whether or not we really *want* to control our instincts."

One does not get this sense of balance in Ghiglieri (1999:256–257). For him rising above our *Dark Side*

> will eventually require us to make a gigantic leap—on a level never before achieved—away from our instincts of individual and kin group selfishness, xenophobia, and distrust, all of which fuel war and the male violence we face in rape and murder. This leap must propel us to patriotic loyalty within our national community and carry us beyond it toward global cooperation between nations. That this latter goal is not a natural human tendency anyone can realistically expect (outside Earth being invaded by hostile aliens) almost goes without saying. But it is the only way to win against men's violence.

And in *Demonic Males*?

> So does this study of our warts help us at all? Does it help us take the step we would all like, to create a world where males are less violent than they are today? It would be nice to answer yes, of course, but nothing suggests that a long view of the problem can seriously reduce the violence projected outward from a human society: the Us versus Them problem of human aggression. (Wrangham and Peterson 1996:249)

Well that doesn't sound too good. Yet don't despair!

---

[8] "*Panologist*" is a neologism I use to denote primatologists who specialize in the study of chimpanzees *Pan troglodytes* or bonobos *Pan paniscus*, as distinct from the much broader discipline of primatology. Similarly, *panology* is comparative study of chimpanzees and bonobos, and *pan*icide any killing of one by another.

But with an evolutionary perspective we can firmly reject the pessimists who say it has to stay that way. Male demonism is not inevitable. [It has typically reflected the interests of men in power, and] the nature of power, its distribution and effects and ease of monopolization, all depend on circumstance. Add to the equation some of the more obvious unknowns, such as the democratization of the world, drastic changes in weaponry, and explosive revolutions in communication, and the possibilities quickly expand in all directions. We can have no idea how far the wave of history may sweep us from our rougher past. (Wrangham and Peterson 1996:251)

True. Earth might be invaded by hostile aliens.

In *The Goodness Paradox*, Wrangham (2019:251–255) disputes that this is a message of despair. Just because something is biological does not mean it cannot be successfully fought, like disease.[9] He notes leading scholars associated with research at Gombe—Jane Goodall, Robert Hinde, and David Hamburg—who saw the biology in collective violence yet worked for peace. That is true, but the issue as I see it is what message is conveyed to a larger public about the chances of reducing or even eliminating war.

"A key question is whether, if our ancestors were adapted for war in the Pleistocene, we are biologically driven to conduct war today. As I will explain, my answer is that while war is not inevitable, conscious effort is needed to prevent it" (Wrangham 2019:251). Specifically, "continuing intense efforts will be needed to regulate international relations.... There will bebumps along the road, but if international law is pursued with sufficient vigor and cunning it at least has the potential to avert catastrophe.... The idea that warfare has evolved, and that even today it is facilitated by adaptive features of our psychology, does not make it inevitable" (2019:271). The answer to the question of whether we are biologically driven to make war today is yes.[10]

---

[9] "I know of no factual basis to support the claim that a belief in ancient war induces fatalism" (2019:252). Nor can I produce supporting studies. But as I worked on completed final revisions in September 2019, I received an unsolicited email from a PhD student in the Max Planck Institute for the Physics of Complex Systems. He told me of discussions with his peers, which I repeat here with his permission, but as requested, without identification.

> One of the common points of view is that violence is part of our genetic endowment. Moreover, since violence is part of our genetic endowment being violent to others is a common trend in history. This then leads to the assumption of war being something inevitable. Then the dogmatic point of view is that since we are somehow violent beings, having wars is a natural consequence of our genetic endowment. Of course nobody would agree that war is a good thing, but they will accept it as a normal part of our societies. What I find dangerous about this dogmatic point of view, is that by developing a small theoretical framework that gives them an answer which they find reasonable enough, they might normalize war. I believe that when some things become normalized, we stop making efforts in order to stop or change them. (Anonymous 2019)

I call that evidence, and in my experience such thinking is very widespread.

[10] In this discussion, Wrangham criticizes "Rousseauian" scholars for suggesting "biology is destiny." I am singled out, and partially quoted (2019:251). Since he brought it up, the complete quote is (Ferguson 1984:12):

> But the image of humanity, warped by bloodlust, inevitably marching off to kill, is a powerful myth and an important prop of militarism is our society. Despite its lack of scientific credibility, there will remain those "hard-headed realists" who continue to believe in it, congratulating themselves for their "courage to face the truth," resolutely oblivious to the myth behind their "reality."

Every biologist proposing evolved tendencies toward war will stress that "biological" does not mean "unmodifiable." Expression of any trait is shaped by environment. There is no predestination, no biological determinism. Unlike chimpanzees, humans have the *ability to choose* a different way.

This is the standard disclaimer. Talking about an earlier generation of theories of innate hostility toward outsiders, early Budongo researcher Reynolds (1980:309) highlights the reflex cliche: "there is always an 'avowal of optimism' ... We can improve! But we need to be aware of the predispositions lurking in our evolved human nature in order to know what steps we must take in order to improve ourselves." Original sin meets free will. This formulation is the talisman that defends against charges of biological reductionism.

But human nature being what neo-Darwinists say it is, for many the message is simple and clear: it is human nature to war. If that message was not intended, perhaps *Demonic Males* was not the best title. *Chimpanzees, "War," and History* argues this message it totally wrong. We begin with theoretical alternatives to the Gombe perspective.

This was in my first discussion of innatist theory, surveying James, McDougall, Freud, Lorenz, Ardrey, E.O. Wilson, and others. Their positions have not fared well. I also note that: "Proponents of innate aggressive drives have become much more temperate in recent statements" (1984:10). I stand by that assessment.

3
Theoretical Alternatives

Chapter 3 presents theoretical alternatives to the Gombe paradigm, both from mainstream *pan*ology, and my own. From *pan*ology comes the resource competition hypothesis. I go along with that, but with human impact a necessary addition, contributing to scarcity and competition. Plus, I add something seemingly similar to the dominance drive but actually quite different: politically motivated violence.

Competition for Scarce Resources

Wilson, Wallauer, and Pusey (2004) is a theoretical compass point in *pan*ological theory about intergroup killing. It distinguishes and names the rival coalition reduction hypothesis (RCRH), from the resource competition hypothesis (RCH). The RCH argues that intergroup violence is to defend or enhance access to resources. The RCRH is close to the imbalance of power hypothesis (IoPH), but with a difference in emphasis.

For most of this book, IoPH and RCRH can be used interchangeably, referring to the two-part concept of numerical superiority and reducing rivals, but occasionally those must be distinguished. I will use RCRH if putting emphasis on the rival reduction aspect, and IoPH if focusing on significance of numerical advantage for attackers.

RCH vs. RCRH

Wilson et al. (2004) note two measurable differences between the RCRH and the RCH. One is the sex of the victims. The RCRH expects males not females to be targets, while the RCH makes no distinction by sex. The other is that the RCRH, but not the RCH, expects that male chimpanzees will try to *kill* stranger males whenever they can, rather than just drive them away. On those criteria, those authors argue from the total Gombe record, resource competition is a somewhat better explanation than rival coalition reduction.

There are two additional differences that Wilson and colleagues do not raise. The RCH is supported if unusually high resource competition precedes unusually intense intergroup clashes—which Wrangham specifically denies. Groups not driven to actively compete should have less intense interactions. Identifying high resource competition is one goal of this book. Such competition is best revealed, and usually *only* revealed, when the local impact of human activities is brought into focus.

Coming as I am from the anthropology of war, another big difference between the RCH and RCRH is the most important of all. The two approaches support radically different conceptions of the innate nature of chimpanzees, and by extension of humans, and the role of inborn xenophobic predispositions in generating warfare. Do chimpanzees and humans kill members of another group because of *circumstances that put those groups in conflict*; or rather do we both seek opportunities because of *an inherited impulse to kill outsiders*? The RCH is close to competition-for-scarce-resources (CSR) approaches, that have been common in the anthropology of war for decades (see Ferguson 1984b).[1]

The RCRH leads in an entirely different direction, to a long tradition of Social Darwinist/ethnocentrism theories, and "primordialist" explanations of recent group violence in former socialist states, Africa, and elsewhere. Primordialists see current civil wars as caused by inbred loyalties and hostility directed at those who are different. This is close to what is claimed for chimpanzees.[2] I side with the RCH, against the RCRH, and so side with one *pan*ological position vs. another. But the RCH is not sufficient in itself. It needs historical specificity. It must be informed by the effect of human activities.

Human Impact

*Pan*ologists hardly ignore human impact. Many write and labor mightily in the cause of conservation, and have accomplished much. But publications on human hazard and chimpanzee protection usually are separated from theoretical research. One doctoral student recognized this in her thesis.

> Although human influence and conservation issues are surfacing with increasing frequency in scientific publications, research and conservation have remained almost entirely exclusive of one another.... Indeed, the most disturbed settings may be extremely important in enabling us to observe the full range of primate behaviors, including those that may not be seen in less disturbed conditions... [R]eports from field sites that have experienced high degrees of human influences may misrepresent the normative behavior of chimpanzees. (Sanz 2004:21)

A decade later, the situation was much the same.

> [M]any great ape researchers are interested in understanding the adaptive significance of behavioural tendencies, which are assumed to have evolved in habitat undisturbed by human activity. Therefore, behaviour evinced by great apes in human-influenced habitats can be perceived as being less interesting.... In reality,

---

[1] Anthropological CSR hypotheses come in many varieties. Cultural ecology, popular in the 1960s and 1970s, explained war as a *cultural* adaptation to limited resources. Anthropologists moved on from there, putting more weight on structural, political, cultural, and historical considerations than on simple intersections with the environment. But practical gain remains a major orientation of many anthropological analyses of war, including my own.

[2] Few scholars who actually study such civil wars believe that story. "Ancient loyalties and animosities" are shown again and again to be recent cultural constructions, an expression, not the cause, of intergroup violence. But the superficial explanation lives on in public and policy discourses (Ferguson 2003). Primordialist interpretations make it seem that people readily take to mass killing because of their own instinctive tribalism. See Chapter 31.

few long-term great ape research sites are unaffected by human influences. The environment and behaviour recorded at most sites is influenced to varying extent by current or former human presence and activities. (Hockings et al. 2015:216, references omitted)

Ethnoprimatology

That topical separation is a choice forced by a paradigm oriented to demonstrating *evolved* adaptive tendencies. This is not the only way to go. Anthropologist Leslie Sponsel (1997) examined culturally patterned interactions of people and monkeys, in an article titled "The Human Niche in Amazonia: Explorations in Ethnoprimatology." His lead gave rise to an expanding field centering on human relations with other primates (Fuentes 2012; Fuentes and Wolfe 2002; Paterson and Wallis 2005; Riley 2006; Riley and Ellwanger 2013).

Ethnoprimatology topics range from long-term, sustainable relations of primates with indigenous peoples, to massive changes that developed in the late 20th century. Human beings have lived around and presumably affected chimpanzees for a very long time. But for African great apes, the past half century has been anything but long-term coexistence. Recent human activity radically transformed their lived experience and threatens their survival.

> It is vital to view these interconnections as more than just "interference" with, or perturbation of, a "natural" state. Rather these may be drivers for specific behavior patterns and or shifts that we observe in primates, and what we consider "normative" behaviors for primates are in fact stimulated by specific anthropogenic contexts. (Fuentes and Hockings 2010:841–842)

For instance, regarding deadly violence. The state-of-naturism implicit in theoretical research on chimpanzees and bonobos fogs understanding of why chimpanzees do what they do. But that is not a new idea.

Margaret Power

Gombe researchers initially identified human induced changes as the cause of intergroup violence, before everything went sociobiological in the Great Revision. After that, the outstanding exception—an ethnoprimatologist before ethnoprimatology—was Margaret Power (1991). In *The Egalitarians—Human and Chimpanzee*, Power shows that reported aggressiveness was less pronounced in earlier reports than in later ones. The now-standard explanation for these different portrayals is that the earlier ones were mistaken, misperceptions by inexperienced observers of elusive chimpanzees. Power, to the contrary, argued that the different observations were all accurate, but for their own times. She saw the difference representing *social change* in chimpanzee behavior, a result of human influence, primarily but not exclusively in practices of provisioning.

Power (1995:9) also emphasizes the importance of paradigms, the master narratives acquired by young researchers as they enter a discipline. Paradigms set the questions they ask, and shape their interpretation of findings. Power argues that chimpanzee studies in the 1970s—the formative years of *pan*ology—were shaped by observations of *provisioned* chimpanzees. This early training shaped perceptions thereafter. We will see the power of the Gombe paradigm in important ways: in the repeated inference that chimpanzees that disappeared were killed; in ignoring evidence that goes against theoretical expectations; and, above all, in the insistence that chimpanzee "wars" are "normal" and "natural."

Power's argument was roundly rejected by primatologists (e.g., Moore 1992). Her version of the human impact hypothesis is brushed off by citing intergroup clashes where there was no provisioning, as if provisioning is the only way humans impinge on chimpanzee environments. I say that Power was basically correct about intergroup violence and the shaping effect of the Gombe paradigm. *Chimpanzees, War, and History* follows in her footsteps as an extended exercise in ethnoprimatology. It challenges the artificial separation of conservation issues and theory, instead joining them for historically contextualized understanding of why chimpanzees sometimes kill.

The Human Impact Hypothesis

The human impact hypothesis holds that deadly violence by chimpanzees, especially but not limited to intergroup adult killings, usually is a response to anthropogenic changes in their environments. Human impact comes in several forms. Two forceful drivers are artificial provisioning and habitat disturbance or loss in areas outside but near to the focal group's home range. Both come in many variations, changing over sometimes short periods of time. Specific details must be foregrounded to understand effects, which may (or may not) include sharply increased competition over food resources. When that happens, resource competition and human impact combine. I call that RCH + HIH. Human impact leads to intensified resource competition and other disturbances which are conducive to deadly violence.

Another human impact is population loss from introduced disease, snaring, and deliberate killings or captures. Those may reduce pressure on resources, and so make intergroup violence unlikely. However, they can also upend existing intergroup balances, causing more conflict. I will connect provisioning, habitat disturbance, and population losses, always in detail and often in combination, to most intergroup killing and much within-group violence as well.

Those killing connections are clear. Others are more conjectural. What are the psychological consequences of human researchers appearing and following them everywhere? Or hordes of tourists, group after group, often close and with little restraint? In the very social world of chimpanzees, what happens downstream when multiple adults die or disappear in short order? In some places, wire snares mutilate a quarter or more of adults. They survive, but do they live with something like post-traumatic disorders? For all these questions, there are no answers. I cannot demonstrate that human induced psychological disturbance plays a role in killings, but we should still keep it in mind, especially when unusual sorts of violence appear as these unknowns add up.

Typically, several human-induced changes come together. Parts II through VII dive deep into all of this, case by case, killing by killing. Each context is unique, but always context is necessary for understanding. Comparing so many situations establishes the general parameters of human disturbance and deadly violence. Part XIII uses the same method to explain the *absence* of severe violence among bonobos. Comparison of bonobos to chimpanzees adds another dimension to explanation by offering a *social* organizational theory of cross-species similarities and differences. Chimpanzee males, but not bonobo males, are socialized into a male competitive status system, where violent aggression plays an important role. Which brings us to a second hypothesis, argued throughout the cases to come.

Status-Linked Violence

Power (1991:248) argued that the pronounced status hierarchies of Gombe and Mahale were not typical for chimpanzees, but responses to human disturbance. In contrast, Boehm (1999:131) can stand for the general consensus.

> [I]t is evident that wild chimpanzees—whether they are baited or not, whether they are habituated to humans or not—are given to status rivalry that leads to a high degree of political, social, and reproductive inequality. In no important sense are they politically egalitarian, for they always have alpha males.

Here I differ from Power. Sometimes male status competition may be aggravated by human disruption. But all known chimpanzee groups have a strictly male status hierarchy, with higher status commonly conferring deference, priority of access to preferred foods, and greater opportunity to copulate and reproduce.[3]

My display violence hypothesis is that within the chimpanzee form of social organization (as contrasted to bonobos), an adult male actively competing for high status with others for the highest status—a younger male rising, or an alpha with challengers, or one recently deposed—may *perform* severe violence against a helpless opponent to intimidate internal rivals. This occurs by leading in group assaults against single adults of a neighboring group, but also in attacks on infants, even inside their own group. Male chimpanzees commonly make aggressive displays to intimidate

---

[3] "A characteristic shared by most male chimpanzees is the preoccupation, from adolescence on, with maintaining and bettering their social rank, and many of their interactions are devoted to this end" (Goodall 1986:184). Different scholars from different situations portray this drive differently. For Mahale, Nishida (2012:217) waxes hyperbolic: "Male chimpanzees compete for social status. Winning the top rank in the dominance hierarchy appears to be the main lifetime goal of most, if not all, male chimpanzees. They breathe, eat, and live to dominate others." Later Mahale scholars are more temperate. "Although there can be dozens of biological benefits to being high-ranking, it seems to us that apart from such benefits, many male chimpanzees somehow have inclination to become high-ranking only in itself." Yet they add that in 1992 Mahale, "only two highest-ranking males and three lowest-ranking males were unequivocal in their ranks.... Furthermore, adult males rarely display overt dominance to each other" (Hosaka and Nakamura (2015b:390, references omitted).

others—piloerection, charging, flailing branches. I argue that this carries forward into what I call display violence, and display killing. If human disturbance is shaking up the status hierarchy, this may be more likely, but it could happen even without that. Much depends on individual personalities, the general belligerence of particular high-status individuals.

A second form of status-related violence is payback for past bullying. An overbearing alpha may build animosity among his male subordinates. The payback violence hypothesis predicts that when that alpha is past his prime or otherwise vulnerable, accumulated grudges can erupt in gang attacks within the group. The danger of severe attack makes many go into temporary or permanent exile. Once again, such attacks may come during intense human disturbance, but not necessarily.[4]

Superficially, status-related violence may seem like the dominance drive. The difference is that in this formulation, neither type of status-related violence is due to an inborn tendency of males. Instead, it depends on three different considerations: (1) species constructed social organization that channels males into direct and sometimes coalitional contest; (2) current circumstances within a status hierarchy that heighten status competition; and (3) individual male personalities that incline some toward unusual violence. The display violence and payback hypotheses are an important addition to the human impact hypothesis.[5]

---

[4] Payback violence against ex- or even current alphas was anticipated by the 1980 coalitional killing of Luit at Arnhem Zoo (de Waal 1986). There had been status turmoil, and the artificial conditions "created an *opportunity* [that made] the fatal attack possible." de Waal notes parallels in the wild, displaced alphas sometimes go into exile to avoid attacks. But Luit had just attained a very uncertain alpha status, and did not have a history of overbearing rule. As recognized by de Waal (1986:101), why deadly violence occurred here is not clear.

[5] When this manuscript was near completion, I found an important development about internal killings. Christopher Boehm, a cultural anthropologist who logged 18 months of observation at Gombe, in cross-site research discovered the same pattern I did, of within-group coalitional killing of ex-alphas and alphas (and some others). This finding is too important and too close to my position to leave unaddressed, but too late for thorough incorporation. And so this long note, which unavoidably gets far ahead of the book's story.

Boehm (2018a:691; 2018b) tallies nine within-group attacks which killed or drove into exile ex-alphas or alphas, plus five on non-alphas (including one suspected bonobo killing). Wrangham (2021:11–12) presents an almost identical list, with additional information about attacks and attackers. These lists are very close to my own findings.

Boehm is interested in the evolution of human morality. (That, and *all theories about hominin evolution*, are beyond the scope of this book). Boehm found no sign of moral behavior among Gombe chimpanzees. He did, however, find evidence suggesting *collective intent*—more than just individuals wanting the same thing—which he proposes as an evolutionary building block for later moral evolution. Boehm sees collective intent in patrolling, external violence, hunting, and in collective killing of adults within groups. I take no position on the collectivity or individuality of intent. But why kill one of their own?

"What we do know is that certain politically prominent males are singled out—but a confounding factor is that many others are not" (2018:692). So—why? Disliking the target's "dominance style" is one possibility . . . if his style of domination has been unusually aggressive, or if he isn't very proficient at maintaining allies, or if as a peacemaker he fails to be impartial and breaks up fights on a partisan basis, incurring enmities, he might be a likely target for a gang-attack (2018: 293).

The idea that chimpanzees do premeditated coalitional killing within their own groups goes against Wrangham's (2019) recent theory (see note 37, Part XIII—sorry about that), that deadly violence directed at out-groups is proactive, but internal violence is reactive, not planned. He argues for several distinctions between the two, mostly that they don't show the same premeditation as external killing. That is not an important distinction for me. Whether from collective premeditation or spontaneous actions of individuals doesn't matter—it is payback.

The idea of impartial peacemakers, breaking up fights is an issue for Boehm, not me; but being "unusually aggressive" and having few allies are like in my argument. Boehm does not include status turmoil at the

But there is a common problem in arguing the HIH or DVPH. Generally, the more detailed context available, the more firmly can particular acts of violence be tied to human impact or display violence. Instances with *the least description often seem most supportive* of the demonic perspective. For some research sites, detailed description of historical disturbance in research sites, and of reports of field behavioral observation, decrease to little or nothing by the mid-2000s. What can be gleaned from disparate source makes clear that disruption got considerably worse. Many were killed over these recent years, especially within groups. Understanding of those will remain limited until field researchers turn on the historical lights.

Now, on to where it all began, Gombe.

---

top. Wrangham (2021:13) does: "within-group attacks showed a strong tendency to be related to within-group tensions incurred by competition for alpha rank," which I emphasize as a condition for display violence. Yet mostly, ex-alphas are killed after their fall, more payback than contest. Nor does Boehm include social organizational differences that distinguish chimpanzees from bonobos in male coalitional violence (see Part XIII).

As will be shown in detailed case description of highly belligerent alphas, Boehm's observation of accumulated grievances against targets holds up well against Wrangham's (2021:14) counterclaim: "Current evidence does not support bullies being 'singled out for lethal attacks.'" Yes it does. Very belligerent alphas often incur later wrath.

PART II
GOMBE

4
From Peace to "War"

This begins seven Parts of detailed evaluation and comparison of the observational literature. Gombe is the longest Part, because more was observed and analyzed there than anywhere else. It is fairly said that "Gombe chimpanzees became the iconic wild chimpanzees, and to a large extent remain so for many" (Wilson et al. 2020:3). It is certain that they are iconic for chimpanzee "war."

Chapter 4 introduces the place, with Goodall and others' research from 1960 to the middle 1970s, including the "Four Year War." Chapter 5 contextualizes the War in terms of anthropogenic changes and the total array of chimpanzee violence. With this context, Chapter 6 offers a human impact explanation of the Four Year War, and the subsequent "Invasion from the South." Chapter 7 moves forward in time at Gombe, beginning with human-induced changes which got worse after the middle 1990s and then evaluating two periods: 1984–1997 with relatively little serious violence, then more intense violence from 1998 to 2013, when coverage ends. Chapter 8 evaluates all hypothetical expectations outlined in Part I against evidence in the key case of Gombe.

Gombe introduces the reader to the methods and rhythms of this book. Discussion of every research area follows its own logic. Chronology always provides orientation, but each narrative is shaped by what has been reported and argued for that particular case. Gombe also raises many topics that reappear in later chapters: nutrition and food preferences, hunting, infanticide, predation by leopards, cognitive capabilities, individual personalities, male status hierarchy and conflict, male and female ranging patterns, (nearby) habitat loss and crop raiding, tourism, disease, hunting by people, conservation efforts, chimpanzee attacks on people, departures of males, and exodus of females from a declining group.

Gombe National Park

Tanzania's Gombe National Park is on the east shore of Lake Tanganyika. Gombe Stream Game Reserve was created in 1943. Local human population was already growing, although habitat destruction was minimal as late as 1958. With creation of the Reserve, local residents within its boundaries were evicted. Gombe became a National Park in 1968, largely due to the international renown conferred by Jane Goodall's work. This was salvational for the chimpanzees of Gombe. Still, even during her early field work, habitat loss accelerated around the Park, especially to the north and northeast.

Gombe National Park is small compared to other protected habitats, just 35 square kilometers, although the steepness of terrain adds surface area. Eighty percent of the land is in slopes over 25%, most of that over 45%. Sharply rising hills lead up to the rift escarpment on the east, cut through by the steep valleys of a dozen named streams.

Five streams, Mitumba, Kasakela, Kakombe, Kahama, and Kalande, have lent their names to local communities of chimpanzees. Vegetation mixes dense forest, shrubs, and open grassland, varying by elevation. The north is more heavily forested, with more chimpanzee foods than the south (Goodall 1986:43–51; Pintea et al. 2011:228, 231, 233, 241; Pusey et al. 2007:624–625; Teleki 1973:28; Wilson 2012:358).

Gombe Found

Jane Goodall left England for Africa in 1957 to work as the secretary of the famed paleoanthropologist Louis Leakey. Leakey, at the time, was promoting field research on great apes (Itani 1996:305). Recognizing her love of animals during an excavation at Olduvai Gorge, he suggested she study wild chimpanzees. He arranged funding from tool manufacturer Leighton Wilkie for a six-month preliminary field project. Leakey also secured permissions, placed her in study in London, and set up a short exercise observing vervet monkeys before she went to Gombe in July 1960. There, the Game Ranger and local villagers helped her get established.

At first, Goodall worked out of a lakeside tent, accompanied by her mother, Vanne. Her observations were from chance encounters, sometimes informative but typically frustrating. "[N]one of the chimpanzees, in those days, would tolerate my following them." She would take her binoculars to high ground, "The Peak," and watch chimpanzees below in the fruit-filled valley of Kakombe. It was during the first year of observations that Goodall made her momentous discoveries of chimpanzees hunting and eating meat, and stripping twigs to fish for termites. But for some 15 months no chimpanzees allowed her to approach, bolting as she got near (Goodall 1963; Greene 2005:26–44; Kevles 1976:17–19; *National Geographic* 1967; van Lawick-Goodall and van Lawick 1967:14 ff.).

Goodall passed 45 months at Gombe from 1960 to March 1965 (van Lawick-Goodall 1968:165), gradually habituating chimpanzees to her presence. In the summer of 1963 she began providing bananas to chimpanzees that visited her camp. As more chimpanzees began to appear and stick around, her ability to observe them increased dramatically.

The Project Matures

As Gombe's fame spread, field operations went from lake shore to interior valley, from tents to buildings, from uncertain to secure funding, and from just Goodall with her mother or sister, to a growing number of student researchers. In January 1962 Goodall began to study for a PhD under Robert Hinde at Cambridge, which took her away from Gombe for months at a time (see Kelley and Sussman 2007). Beginning in March 1965, two or three trained assistants from different universities were in the field for much of the time Goodall was away. By 1967 she was off on lecture tours or other projects, and most research at Gombe was being done by others. The student population grew dramatically in the early 1970s, up to 22 by 1975. After a young researcher died of a fall in 1968, Goodall insisted that all students be accompanied by a local guide. (These guides took over as Goodall's observers after the kidnapping). With local staff and project managers, this placed about 50 humans in the center of Gombe. This time was the buildup and start of the Four Year War, which is why we have so much good information about those developments. For *The Chimpanzees of Gombe*, Goodall had some 80 years' worth of research observations to draw on (Goodall 1971; 1986:51–52; Greene 2005: 80–84, 98, 115; Kevles 1976:31, 49–56, 61–63; van Lawick-Goodall 1968:165).

Through the early years, the benign image of chimpanzee behavior prevailed. Then came the Four Year War. For the demonic males view, that is where the tale of Gombe begins. What came before is just as important, and very different from that to come.

Initial Views on Territorial Organization

The first report of Gombe chimpanzee territoriality is pre-Goodall (Thomas 1961:36), from H.F. Lamprey, Game Department Biologist for Gombe Stream Game Reserve. "Chimpanzees are very strongly territorial. (There are about six troops within the reserve) and seems to each have its own well defined areas." This is important. When Goodall arrived, chimpanzees already were seen as separate, territorially fixed groups. However, during her years of binocular observations from The Peak, Goodall saw these localized groups meet and mix.

Big Reunions

In the summer of 1960:

> Often I saw parties of chimpanzees traveling from Linda, in the north, down into Kakombe to feast on the figs. Frequently chimpanzees also arrived from the south. Several times I observed excited and noisy reunions as a large party from the south charged down the slope into the valley to join those who had arrived from the north, or vice versa. After a period of feeding, during which members of both parties mingled peacefully, the large gathering sometimes divided again, one group moving off to the north, the other to the south.... Sometimes virtually all the chimpanzees moved in a large party to the north to feed on the fruits in Linda Valley. At the time I was of the opinion that I was observing two separate social groups, which frequently encountered each other without undue hostility. (Goodall 1986:503; and see Goodall 1971:41–42)

One reunion, which began with great aggressive display and left at least one chimpanzee wounded, is seen in her first *National Geographic* film (1967). As many chimpanzees are shown arriving, the narrator explains: "With much excitement, the visitors head for the group of chimps, so peacefully grooming away in the quiet afternoon. There's to be a grand reunion. It will seem like a clash between enemies, but it's really a reunion of friends." Footage shows chasing, screaming, group charges, branch dragging, rock throwing, tumbling fights, and ends with a wounded chimpanzee hobbling away on two hands and a foot. The narrator explains, "For a chimpanzee, a hurt foot seems a small price to pay for the unbridled joy of meeting, by chance, friends and lovers again."

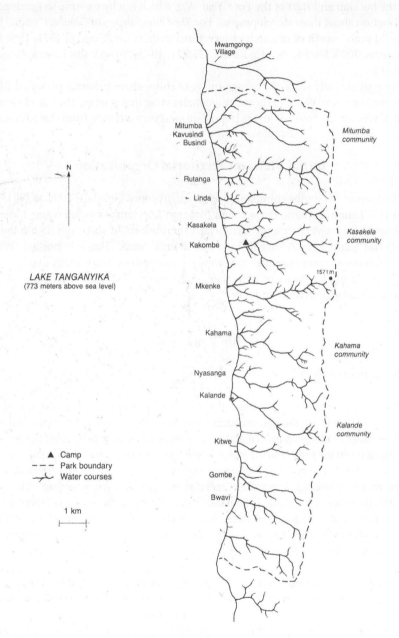

Illustration 2.1 Gombe Map and Groupings
Source: Goodall, J. (1986). *The chimpanzees of Gombe: Patterns of behavior*. Belknap Press of Harvard University.

The Great Revision reinterpreted these meetings as fission and fusion within one community, Kakombe, rather than two separate communities coming together. But Goodall's descriptions and the highly agitated film encounter do not seem like a within-group fusion. And if it *was* a single community, it was a community with two geographically centered and usually separate subgroups.

Even when they all came together over bananas, the distinctiveness of those later called Kasakela and Kahama remained. "By 1966 it was clear that the males could be divided into two groups: those who spent more time south of the Kakombe Valley (where camp is situated) and those who spent more time to the north. We referred to these as the northern and southern 'subgroups'" (Goodall 1986:503).

> Because of the peaceful interactions of all these chimpanzees from the beginning, it is likely that most or all of them had been associating together before provisioning began, and that they probably belonged to one community. From 1963 onward, there was always a subgroup of chimpanzees who arrived from the south and visited less frequently than the others. (Pusey 1979:467)

Ambiguous Observations, Defining Concepts

In the standard Gombe story, one community, Kakombe, divided and went to war. Yet other possibilities were recognized by contemporary field observers. Geza Teleki spent 26 months at Gombe from 1968 to 1971 (Teleki 1977:ii), and analyzed field data from 1963 to 1973. He and colleagues saw the Gombe behavioral record very differently.

> Indeed, several of these individuals never seemed to achieve full social membership in the resident community, and often traveled as a cluster in the main study zone. Coupled with these qualitative impressions, the demographic data suggest that many of the migrants observed at the start and the end of the decade may have belonged to another social community. (Teleki et al. 1976:581)

Teleki et al. describe how Japanese researchers' views on exclusive communities gradually took hold at Gombe, thus making the study population seem as one group, rather than part of a chain of chimpanzee populations. That is why, when banana provisioning was reduced and the southern chimpanzees went separate ways, this was seen as fissioning.

> The ethological evidence favoring this interpretation of a fissioned community may seem strong, especially when investigators are looking outward, so to speak, from the observation base of the study population; yet the demographic picture presented here suggests that the fissioning interpretation may have been premature. The segmentation of the study population was, in other words, perhaps no more that the

departure of a transient group whose members originally and also finally belong to a neighboring community. (Teleki et al. 1976:581)

Stubborn Facts

Substantial evidence indicates porous intergroup boundaries. Going against the standard image of a female core surrounded by protective males[1] are adult "peripheral females,"

> whose preferred core area is situated toward the outer limits of the community range, who associate with other community members when they are nearby but seldom (unless cycling) travel with them when they leave her area ... After giving birth, the female typically makes a commitment to one of the two communities. If her preferred area is very close to the boundary, however, there is the possibility that, at least for a while, she may maintain ties with members of both groups.

From 1965 until the early 1980s, three to six late adolescent or mature females and their offspring were peripheral (Goodall 1986:89–92). Around 1973 in the buildup to the war, peripherals outnumbered central, 10 to 6 (Wrangham 1975:5.56). Even some central adult females from within the protected range left to visit other groups while they were in estrus (Pusey 1979).

What about males?

> [K]nown males were encountered both at the northern boundary of the reserve and within 3 miles of the southern boundary. On five occasions small groups were seen leaving the reserve, crossing the eastern boundary; on only one of these occasions was I close enough to see that such a group consisted of known individuals. The small number of these observations is due to my having spent most of my time in the central area away from the boundaries of the reserve. (van Lawick-Goodall 1968:214)

That places recognized Kakombe males squarely within the ranges of the communities to their north (Mitumba) and south (Kalande), and probably in the range of the vaguely known Rift Community to their east. Given the number of sightings and the limited opportunities to observe them, it seems that such visits were pretty common in the early 1960s. Teleki (1977:56) also notes Kakombe chimpanzees far outside their usual home range, and strangers seen within it.

One could speculate that those were aggressive patrols and penetrations. That cannot explain direct observations of relaxed interactions. Kahama and Kasakela males peacefully associated with males that were not members of either group.

---

[1] An early issue in chimpanzee sociality is whether unit-group were "bisexual," with adult male and female members; or whether only, or primarily, males formed a group, with females scattered over the usable landscape, associating with males when they are around. Observations have supported both positions, and the group status of peripheral females were part of the debate (Wrangham 1975:5.53, 5.57).

In 1971, before the community split, unhabituated males were twice seen in association with the "southern" males (i.e., those who subsequently formed the Kahama community): once three prime males were seen traveling with habituated individuals, and a second time one adult male was feeding with them in a tree (Bygott 1974). Did the Kahama males once enjoy a peaceful relationship with males to the south, similar to that which existed until 1972 between the Kasakela and Kahama males? Were these unhabituated chimpanzees part of the same community, but ones who normally ranged even further to the south and who never traveled as far at the feeding station? If so, it suggests that communities at that time were much larger and less compact. Or were intercommunity interactions, in the past, less aggressive in nature.... More recently, a male chimpanzee who could not be identified by an experienced field assistant (H. Bitura) was seen to make his nest some 100 meters from Figan. When this male was approached, he threatened the observers but did not flee: early the next morning the two nests were empty. Although it is difficult to believe that a neighboring male could wander into the heart of the Kasakela core area and nest so close to its alpha male, we withhold final judgement. (Goodall et al. 1979:41–42)

During the Four Year War, after Goliath was brutally attacked, observers thought they saw him traveling with a small party including at least one unhabituated individual (Goodall et al. 1979:40).

Most intriguing is the Kasakela male Evered. Wrangham (1975:5.39) observed Evered heading north with three females, toward a calling group of northern chimpanzees. After he fell from being an alpha-contender, he would repeatedly disappear toward the north for up to 10 weeks at a time (Goodall et al. 1979:42).

He was observed during one such absence in Mitumba Valley, apparently in consort with a stranger female in estrus. From this incident we assume that during some, maybe all, of his visits to the north he was consorting with unhabituated females. After Faben's disappearance Evered spent less time wandering in the north and once again became a central community male. But he continued to make occasional mysterious visits outside the central part of the Kasakela range. (Goodall 1986:476)

Evered never became a secure alpha (though close), yet he was "thought to have sired more infants than any other Gombe male." Referring to his sojourns with females from the Mitumba community, Goodall (1986:64) quips, "Even in temporary exile it seemed that he was able to take advantage of the situation!"

This is more than an interesting curiosity. The Mitumba Valley is the center rangeland of the Mitumba group, Kasakela's northern neighbor. For a solo Kasakela male to go there once would be by demonic expectations suicidal—but to take local females on consortships, repeatedly over years, for weeks at a time? Evered should be dead. Yet he is never reported to have reappeared wounded. This record suggests that Mitumba males allowed Evered to be in their range, and to consort with local females. "Evered's behavior . . . seemed not to be consistent with a model of permanent aggression between males of different communities" (Wrangham 1975:5.40).

In the early 1970s, there is no indication that Mitumba was greatly impacted by people as their southern neighbors were—no provisioning or follows, and while much of their former habitat beyond the Park border had farms, it remained accessible for foraging until after 1979 (Chapter 7). These less disturbed males *let an outside male in*. Kasakela had connections to its northern neighbors, as Kahama had to its southern.

These early observations are ignored, but will not go away. They cannot be dismissed as fission/fusion confusion. The Gombe evidence remains consistent with a pre-Revision understanding of intergroup relations. Kasakela and Kahama were geographically centered but overlapping networks. They could meet with some antagonism or even violence, but settle down and feed together. With the artificial incentive of bananas, they joined together, but remained partly distinct in ranging patterns, and separately bound by "kinship, consort, coalition, and other special relationships" (Teleki et al. 1976:581). Before and even after bananas drew them together as Kakombe, both communities may have had similar sorts of contacts and associations with other communities around them, as Goodall originally surmised. But this was not to be the narrative of Gombe.

The Four Year War

In 1970, Kakombe numbered around 40 individuals, excluding 8 which only came for the bananas (Teleki et al. 1976:565). Although "the frequency of visits to camp by Southern males fell almost continuously... from 1968 to 1972" (Wrangham 1975:6.2), in 1970 they still spent most of their time near the station (Feldblum et al. 2018:737). From then on, Kakombe chimpanzees began to segregate into northern and southern bands, called Kasakela and Kahama. But the two groups sometimes met, and after agitation settled down. Separation increased over 1971. "Thus the situation in 1971 was strongly reminiscent of that which I had observed in the early sixties" (Goodall 1986:504). Beyond January 1972, of adult males, only old Hugo from the north, and old Goliath from the south, still associated across the divide. But three adult Kahama females kept coming to the feeding station. "Southern males occasionally came to camp during 1972, and associated briefly with Northern males after an aggressive encounter" (Wrangham 1975:5.39, 5.44). After year's end, most southern males never appeared at the research camp. Only Sleeping Valley remained an overlap zone, used by both groups (Goodall 1986:504).

In 1973, Kasakela had eight adult males, six prime and two old. Kahama had one late-adolescent male, four adults—one partially crippled by polio—and one old male. From May 1972 to September 1973, Kasakela males went to ridges between the groups 14 times, apparently looking for Kahama. Three times they chased a solo male they encountered. In June the males of both groups called and displayed across Mkenke stream, until Kasakela retreated. In 1974, separation turned to violence, as intrusive Kasakela males fiercely attacked solo chimpanzees they encountered, in what would later be called "raiding" (Goodall 1986:504–514; Wrangham 1975:5.37–5.39).

The first assault came in January. Seven adult or adolescent Kasakela males coalesced around sexually swollen Gigi. They traveled deliberately south, and hearing calls, went deep into the center of Kahama's range. They found Godi up a tree, grounded and chased him, held him down, severely beat on his shoulders and back, bit him "several" times, and after about 10 minutes, left. Godi slowly rose and walked off, never to be seen again.

In late February 1974, evenly matched parties (both three adult males and one female), ran into each other in the overlap zone. Kahama's De, weakened by prior illness, was separated from the others, and brutally attacked for 20 minutes by the Kasakela males and female, with pieces of skin torn off in strips—a singular image often invoked to highlight chimpanzee violence. Two months later he was seen foraging alone, emaciated, with visible damage from the assault, and trouble climbing trees. He was not seen thereafter, despite searching.

A year later, in February 1975, five Kasakela males went south. They climbed a tree and waited. They spotted old Goliath, and caught him. Three males beat and bit him for 18 minutes, stomped him, and drummed on him. The Kasakela male Faben "sat on the old male's back, took one of his legs and, with his one good arm, tried to twist it around and around." ("Tried"?) Finally abandoned by his attackers, Goliath, bleeding and shivering, had difficulty sitting up. He too was sought by researchers, and may have been spotted once but without positive confirmation (Goodall et al. 1979:40).

In May 1977 local fisherman heard the sounds of fierce fighting, and saw five habituated males pass by. Two days later, two local field assistants found the body of Charlie by Kahama stream, with a spread of wounds typical for extreme chimpanzee violence.

In late 1977 it seemed that late-adolescent Sniff was the only remaining Kahama male, since adult Willy Wally's pant-hoots were never heard. On November 11, six Kasakela males patrolled near Kahama stream and then continued further south. They caught Sniff and took turns assaulting him for some 35 minutes. He was so badly injured he could barely move. Goodall decided on euthanasia, but the field assistants were not able to locate him. Four days later, searchers thought they smelled his putrefying body. Both Charlie and Sniff—the two most conclusive outside male killings in the Four Year War—were killed while Goodall checked in by radio with local assistants, who by then were taking over observations (Goodall 1986:509–510).

A repeated victim was older female Madam Bee, sometimes with her daughters Little Bee and Honey Bee. All were attacked by Kasakela males in September 1974, a mild attack on Madam was seen in February 1975, and a another more serious one on Madam and Honey in May. Madam appeared with additional wounds over the next four months. Finally in September, four adult Kasakela males beat and beat on her. When they left, she could hardly move. Five days later she died.

Little Bee was of great interest to Kasakela males. Commentators on Gombe see her as an example of female acquisition through violence.

> Little Bee, in estrus, was traveling with De, the second of the victims; after the attack the Kasakela males forcibly led her back to the north. On three other occasions there is evidence that Little Bee, when in estrus was recruited by parties of invading Kasakela males who led her back to their range. Eventually, in 1974, she remained in the north even when anestrous and was thereafter classified as an immigrant. (Goodall 1986:87)

That was early in the War, before the death of Madame Bee. Little Bee was actually traveling with the males who killed her mother.[2] Honey Bee was sometimes seen with Kasakela males for the next few years, but never transferred. Kahama females Mandy and Wanda just disappeared, though Goodall wondered if they had been killed. She suspects killings also for the vanished Willy Wally, and Hugh, an older Kahama male who disappeared before the observed incursions began. By the end of 1977, after Sniff, Kahama was no more (Goodall 1986:61, 65, 94, 503–514, 528–530; 1988:11–12; Goodall et al. 1979:18–39, 45; Wrangham and Peterson 1996:17–18). That is the Four Year War.

How Many Killings?

It is not clear how many Kahama chimpanzees were *pani*cides. Three individuals counted as confirmed killings in Wilson and Wrangham (2003:373) and Wilson et al. (2014a:Extended Data Table 1—hereafter *EDT*) are questionable. De, as noted, was seen foraging alone two months after being attacked, although in very bad shape. He certainly was not killed in the attack, but the assault, along with his prior illness, may have contributed to his demise. There is no way to know. Regarding Godi, Wrangham and Peterson (1996:6) write, "He may have lived on for a few days, perhaps a week or two. But he surely died." Yet as Goodall (1986:506–507) describes it, Godi's visible wounds were a gash on the lower lip and chin, a swollen upper lip, bleeding from the nose and cuts on the side of his mouth, puncture marks on his right legs and ribs, and some cuts on his left forearm. Bad, but chimpanzees survive worse than that.[3]

Regarding Goliath, Goodall (1986:528) wrote, "Goliath and Sniff could in no way have survived." Circumstances (barely able to move, the stench of decay) support that conclusion in the case of Sniff, and the intensity of the assault on old Goliath assuredly *might* have caused his death. But an earlier report was very clear that his death was uncertain: "We do not know whether Goliath survived this brutal assault. Intensive searches were made in all likely places, and once he was thought to have been seen, but the small party was with an unhabituated individual and ran off before positive identification could be made" (Goodall et al. 1979:40).

The fact that De, Godi, and Goliath disappeared is why they are counted as confirmed killings. The "suspicious disappearances" of Willy Wally, Mandy, and Wanda, add to the number of supposed war casualties (Wilson and Wrangham 2003:373).

---

[2] Females mate promiscuously. "[E]stimates of the average number of times a female copulates per conception range from more than 400 to several thousand" (Arcadi 2018:58). Sexually interested males commonly "herd, harass and aggress against females" (Stumpf and Boesch 2006:761–762; Arcadi 2018:60–62; Muller et al. 2009; Muller et al. 2011; Novak and Hatch 2009; Smuts and Smuts 1993; Tuttle 1986:278–279). This is well studied at Gombe (Goodall 1986:453–487), where coercive males sire more offspring (Feldblum et al. 2014). Sexual coercion often involves displays and attacks directed at a swollen female, to compel her to accompany the male on a "consortship" away from other males. Such aggression may also happen any time during a female's cycle, possibly to make her more pliant during swellings. This coercion, however, is directed at females within the group, not at outside females (Smuts 1993:6–7, 20–23). Little Bee was in between.

[3] At Budongo, two grappling adult males fell 60 feet straight to the ground. One walked away unfazed, the other limped for a week before seeming fine (Reynolds 2005:53).

Goodall (1986:64) also suspects foul play in the disappearance of the healthy Kasakela male Faben sometime during 1975. But chimpanzees disappear often, 14 Gombe adults from before the War, 1966 to about 1973 (Wrangham 1974:92).

Also casting doubt on *pan*icides is an important observation from the time, not published until much later (McGrew/Pierce 2009). In November 1974, during the War, a leopard was observed close to Kahama stream. Six of the Kahama group saw it, lurking in the vegetation. Despite loud displays, the leopard lunged toward Sniff and Charlie, in what was interpreted as an attempted kill. A solo chimpanzee, especially if weakened, would be an easy target. There was a feline killer stalking the Kahama group just as disappearances began to mount.

Yet the assumption that came to rule Gombe and other research is that for adult males, disappearance equals death, and often suspected *pan*icide. "We assumed that all adult males, most juvenile males . . . died if they disappeared" (Williams et al. 2008:767). That assumption is very problematic.

Exit

In my research on warfare among shifting horticulturalists of the Amazon basin, a major factor working against the outbreak of actual war was the ability to move away from conflict situations. As serious tensions developed, one or both sides removed the threat by removing themselves. This pattern was so widespread that I coined a term for it: "almost wars" (Ferguson 1989a:197). The facts as reported regarding De, Goliath, Godi, and Willy Wally are consistent with a similar hypothesis: that males may abandon their territory for parts unknown, especially when under duress, either to roam alone or to join unhabituated neighbors.

What duress? In addition to being directly attacked by Kasakela chimpanzees, Kahama was increasingly squeezed between Kasakela and Kalande to their south. In 1974–1975 Kahama was down to four males in 1.8 km^2, "and even this was sometimes entered by parties of Kasakela individuals" (Goodall 1986:228, 505–506). Although total numbers for Kahama are not reported, 2.2 grown males per km^2 suggests a population density far above reports from other research sites. Yet compared to tropical forest, the mixed forests and grasslands of Gombe are somewhat marginal as a chimpanzee habitat, and more so in the south (Goodall 1986:44, 49).[4] With such a tiny range, the Kahama chimpanzees may have had trouble getting enough to eat.

The *possibility* of exit is clear. In the mid-1970s, Gombe was not the isolated island forest it would become, with large areas of forest and woodland adjacent to the Park (Pusey et al. 2007:629). Unknown chimpanzees called from the east, where the preserve's streams tumbled down from the rift escarpment. In February 1971 Kahama males traveled with three stranger males near the eastern edge of their usual range

---

[4] Although Goodall (1986:231) states that "healthy chimpanzees have no difficulty finding enough to eat during most dry seasons," nutritional stress is not uncommon. Gombe chimpanzees average 3–4 pounds lighter than those of Mahale or eastern Zaire, which some interpret as due to less food, especially in the dry season (Pusey et al. 2005:24; Stanford 1998a:45). Wrangham et al. (1996:47) note that "[d]uring fruit poor seasons in Gombe . . . fruit scarcity leads to relatively intense food stress (apparently responsible for weight loss, ill health, increased mortality and reduced reproductive effort.)"

(Bygott 1974:226–227). In November 1971, "[f]or four weeks, the southern males could not be found despite repeated searches" (Bygott 1974:232), even though with the openness of the land, "[a]n observer on a ridge crest could quite easily locate any chimpanzees who vocalized in the valleys to either side" (Bygott 1974:13).[5] A month of dedicated searching, in a small area, with no sight or sound? Kahama group went *somewhere*. They knew a place to go.

Is it possible that Godi, De, Goliath, Willy Wally, Mandy, and Wanda went off to roam alone, or with occasional contacts? Yes. Later discussions document many solo male exiles. For areas beyond the scope of observation—for instance, the rising rift lands to Gombe's east—we know practically zero about chimpanzee existence, other than nest spotting in some low-resolution surveys. If lonely chimpanzees are out there, their lives are unknown to us.

If the assumption that adult males that disappear are dead is unsustainable, the claim that Kasakela males "killed off all the Kahama males" (Williams et al. 2002:349) is also unsustainable. Up to four males and two females may have moved out.

Keeping Count

For Gombe, the toll of chimpanzee killings has been exaggerated. Numbers matter, and I will keep count of all certain to suspected killings throughout this book. Here I introduce the system of keeping track. The initial number indicates the relative certainty or probability of a killing.

1 = *a certain killing*, both a witnessed attack and a body.
2 = *a killing beyond reasonable doubt*, where either an assault is witnessed that leaves the victim incapacitated but no body is found, or where a body is found that seems almost certainly the result of assault by chimpanzees.
3 = *a very likely killing*, where a very severe assault is observed, and subsequently the chimpanzee disappears.
4 = *a possible killing*, where observations indicate a chimpanzee assault that could be lethal (like a 3), but where some factor raises doubt about that conclusion; and where a body is found that could be the result of a chimpanzee attack, but could also be the work of a leopard. Some infant deaths, such as when adults are seen eating a dead one but no attack is witnessed, will be classified as a 3 or a 4, depending on other circumstances.
5 = *a hypothetical killing*, where a chimpanzee disappears without any direct evidence of an assault, but a researcher publishes a suspicion that it was a result of death by violence. I call these "hypothetical" instead of "suspicious," because the suspicions rest on a hypothetical point: that living adult males never leave their group. That point is challenged.

---

[5] "Chimpanzees pant-hoot throughout the day . . . Pant-hoots can be heard over distances of 1–2 km" (Wilson et al. 2001:1204).

In concluding theoretical discussions, I will simplify this, so that all 1's, 2's, and 3's—very likelies to certains—will be lumped together as "killings," even though some of them may not be. I do not undercount *pan*icides. 4's, possible killings, will also be considered as indicators of potentially deadly violence, under possibles-to-certains. The 5's however, do not carry probative weight. Yet these, typically listed as "suspected" killings, amount to over a third of all claimed *pan*icides (Wilson et al. 2014a:EDTs).

I also keep track of what kind of chimpanzee is the victim. These codes indicate whether the victim is from outside or within the group; whether it is an adult, subadult/adolescent (about 9–15 years old), juvenile (about 5–8 years old), or infant (birth to around 4 years old); and whether it is female or male. The codes are:

O/W/? = outsider, within-group, unknown
I/J/As/A/? = infant, juvenile, adolescent, adult, unknown
F/M/? = female, male, unknown

These codes will be followed by the date, as far as can be determined. Thus a very likely killing of an adult male from a neighboring group in 1981 would be: 3-O-A-M 1981.

Here is the tally so far, in order of decreasing certainty of death:

Madam Bee, 1-O-A-F 1975
Sniff, 2-O-A-M 1977
Charlie, 2-O-A-M 1977
Goliath, 4-O-A-M 1975
De, 4-O-A-M, 1974
Godi, 4-O-A-M 1974
Willy Wally, 5-O-A-M 1977
Hugh, 5-O-A-M 1972
Wanda, 5-O-A-F 1977?
Mandy, 5-O-A-F 1977?
Faben, 5-O-A-M 1975

From this same set of events, Wilson and Wrangham (2003:373), and Wrangham et al. (2005) count all six of the witnessed assault victims of the 1970s—Madam Bee, Sniff, Charlie, Goliath, De, and Godi—as certain intercommunity killings. Wilson et al. (2014a:EDT 1) list them as observed, except for Charlie, as inferred. Going from the published evidence however, Goliath, De, and Godi are only possibles.

5
Contextualizing Violence

At Gombe an intermingling population went separate ways, and members of one group eliminated the other group. Why? Is that "normal" chimpanzee behavior, an expression of an evolved tendency? This book argues that deadly violence must be seen in historical context.

Chapter 5 establishes the context for the War, first describing human impact, then discussing other kinds of bloodletting at the same time—a "war" with baboons, a surge in hunting of red colobus monkeys, internal cannibalism of infants, and severe assaults on females. It was a disturbed time, an aggressive time. With this context given, Chapter 6 can move on to explaining the Four Year War itself.

Human Impact

During and after the Four Year War, Gombe researchers explained it as due largely, not entirely, to habitat loss around the Park. Human population in the surrounding Kigoma region went from 473,443 in 1967 to 648,441 in 1978, with substantial forest clearing (Pintea et al. 2011:241). Gombe is quite small compared to other chimpanzee sanctuaries. Researchers thought that habitat loss forced more chimpanzees to spend more time inside its border, especially the southernmost Kalande group. They surmised that this increased density increased food competition. Now we take up other forms of human impact, beginning with some of frustrating ambiguity.

Preliminary Unknowns

A human effect of the long term is introduction of the oil palm, *Elaeis guineensis*. Rich in calories and fats, fruiting all year long with regularity, this was the most significant plant food for Gombe chimpanzees (Goodall 1986:234–235). The oil palm is a domesticated plant from west Africa, introduced along Lake Tanganyika at an unknown time (Stanford 1998a:30–31).[1] Oil palms quite likely raised the carrying capacity of Gombe habitat.

The disappearance of big cats from the area would have reduced predation on chimpanzees, although one Gombe chimpanzee may have been killed by a leopard

---

[1] Chimpanzee consumption of different parts of the oil palm varies radically across Africa (see Hartley 1977:6–7; McGrew 1992:2–10; Sousa et al. 2011). This foreshadows issues that loom large in later discussions: the complexities of nutrition, dietary preferences, and local traditions. Not incidentally, primates around the world today are threatened by rapid expansion of industrial palm oil plantations (Linder and Palkovitz 2016; Wich et al. 2014).

(Stanford 1998a:27), and as noted, a leopard tried to kill Sniff and Charlie. Proliferating oil palms and diminishing predators may have increased population density within Gombe Park. On the other hand, diseases such as polio, which killed six and partially incapacitated others in 1966 (van Lawick-Goodall 1968:170; 1986:84–85), and a respiratory infection that killed four in 1968 (Williams et al. 2008:769), somewhat reduced population. This soup of demographic unknowns provides little guidance, but suggests a larger, more concentrated chimpanzee population as a result of human activities.

Observers

Another human impact-unknown is observation by researchers. In defense of the feeding program, Goodall (1986:57) poses a question: "We should also ask how disturbing it is for a chimpanzee to be followed through the forest by one or two humans, sometimes for days on end. Some chimpanzees show what appears to be a total lack of concern, of interest even, in the close proximity of one or more humans. Others are far more anxious."[2]

Although *captive* chimpanzees cannot be taken as representative of chimpanzees in the wild, research in captivity indicates that human observers markedly increase aggressive interactions.[3] Keep that in mind as we move forward through thousands of hours of field observers' reports.

In 1972 there was a major intensification of observation methods. Chimpanzees appeared less frequently at the feeding station after provisioning was reduced (below), while more students were on site through the program with Stanford University. Following habituated chimpanzees through the forest soon became standard procedure for gathering information (Boesch 1994a:114; Busse 1978:767). Figan, the Kasakela alpha during the Four Year War, was followed for 50 consecutive days in 1974 (Riss and Busse 1977). Goodall goes on to describe instructions to the research

---

[2] The possibility of significant, unanticipated effects of human observation on aggression by wild animals is illustrated by a study of elephant seals on California islands by Klopfer and Gilbert (1966:757–758). These huge creatures seemed oblivious to observers who approached to 10 m or closer. It seemed normal that females bit and sometimes flung others' pups, about four per hour. Females with pups aggressively challenged other females with pups, at about the same rate. Concerned in principle about the possible effects of their presence, the researchers retired to a hidden observation point. Although the female/female aggression continued unabated, the biting of pups stopped completely. "Thus, attacks directed upon young may in fact have been unwittingly instigated by the observers and can not be assumed to represent a normal state of affairs. Such attacks probably represent what has been called 'redirection.'"

[3] In one research colony, the presence of even one new student or scientist led to significantly higher aggression between chimpanzees (Maki et al. 1987). Records on eight research populations amounting to 416 observation years, compared weekdays when many people interacted with chimpanzees, to weekends. Woundings on weekdays averaged 70.6, compared to 19.5 for Saturday and Sunday (Lambeth et al. 1997:329–330). A zoo study found that the higher weekend crowds affected many behaviors, that the chimpanzees spent >9% of their time watching people, and that people reacted intensely to aggressive acts or dominance displays among chimpanzees (Wood 1998:227–228). Records at the Oakland Zoo "confirmed that human presence is the main factor that triggers aggressive behaviors" (Virgens 2013:1). Details of situations, reactions, and measurements are complex and not entirely consistent (Hosey et al. 2016; Williams et al. 2010:361), but together suggest that captive chimpanzees react to human presence with heightened belligerence.

Illustration 2.2 Three Researchers Photographing Chimpanzees
Source: Teleki, G. (1973). *The predatory behavior of wild chimpanzees*. Bucknell University Press.

followers for minimizing chimpanzee agitation, but some of these follows were quite intrusive.

Field research at Gombe and elsewhere contributed enormously to protection of chimpanzees and conservation of their habitat (see Chapter 7). The fame brought to Gombe by Goodall led to creation of the Park. Work by Goodall and those who followed raised international consciousness and concern about the fate of chimpanzees. Research provided a basis for tourism, which brought income to the government and local people, giving both a stake in chimpanzee protection. The knowledge of subsistence and social organization gained by field workers provides guidelines for conservation efforts, and researchers trained at Gombe spread these benefits to other chimpanzee locations (Collins and Goodall 2008; Pusey et al. 2007). "Virtually all of the major in situ ape conservation programs now operating started out as research projects and researchers still play a central role in ape conservation efforts" (Walsh 2008:719).

Benefits such as these are frequently noted in favor of expanding field research. However, field research also creates disturbance and hazards (Malone et al. 2010). Without doubt it represents a major change in chimpanzees lives. There is no way to evaluate the impact of these close research follows, just as Kahama and Kasakela transitioned from separation into violence.[4] Whether intensified observation of Gombe chimpanzees just before and during the Four Year War heightened aggression, as in captivity, is destined to remain unknown—as it will be for all other research sites across Africa. The impact of another form of human impact however, is very clear.

---

[4] See McLennan and Hill (2010) for some general issues of habituation and response.

Bananas

Provisioning began in a time of innocence (Goodall 2001). One day, David Greybeard snatched some bananas from a camp table. Goodall instructed local staff to set out bananas every day. The next step was described in a letter from "Chimpland" to Goodall's family dated August 17, 1962. "[T]oday is the happiest, the proudest, of my whole life to date. Something has occurred—an achievement which I value far higher than any prize, degree, praise—oh anything you like. David G—yes—he has TAKEN BANANAS FROM MY HAND." Others followed, and soon there was "the Banana Club." The next summer, a permanent feeding station was set up to draw in chimpanzees—which it did with great success (Greene 2005:67–68; Wrangham 1974:84).

I do not question the decision to initiate the feeding program. It was essential for facilitating the close observation that has done so much for our understanding of chimpanzees. There was no way to anticipate what would follow, or that it would encourage aggression. If I had been in Goodall's situation, I would have done the same. But the unintended effects were massive and negative. In a 2004 BBC documentary, Goodall commented: "If I had gone to Gombe and had access to information about the effect of feeding bananas on wild chimpanzees I wouldn't have done it" (BBC 2004).

Over 1963, more and more chimpanzees were drawn to the camp by large quantities of bananas. Chimpanzees sought these avidly, even invading tents to get them. When they could grab them, they would eat 40 or even 60 bananas at one sitting. As of mid-1967, chimpanzees were *averaging* about 30 bananas per day (Goodall 1971; 1968:166; Goodall 1986:51–57; Wrangham 1974). That is over 3,000 calories. At its peak, the bananas provided some 44,000 calories per day (Wrangham 1974:91)—a huge nutritional supplement.

In 1963, bananas caused increased aggression. As chimpanzees rushed to grab and hoard, they fought over bananas, throwing rocks at humans who got too close. Goodall's response was to construct a large steel cage in the feeding area, a refuge *for humans* in case chimpanzees got too violent (Greene 2005:77–78). By 1964, things were out of hand. Many chimpanzees hung around camp waiting to be fed. Some ransacked huts of fisherman on the lakeshore looking for food (Goodall 2000:281). Goodall was away from Gombe for about a year from 1965 to 1966, but provisioning continued. When she returned, she was shocked by "how much the chimps had changed in a year. Incidents of intimidation and fighting had increased among the chimps, driving many to seek permanent refuge in the camp" (Greene 2005:85).

Of observed chimpanzee-on-chimpanzee attacks, "66 per cent were undoubtedly due to competition for bananas" (van Lawick-Goodall 1968:278). "Attacks between chimpanzees were mostly by adult males and were either protracted interactions involving components such as charging, grappling, biting, slapping, and slamming, or brief physical contact together with a chase." There are even suspicions of fatalities.[5]

---

[5] Old Huxley sustained a major facial wound in within-group fighting in 1967, that did not heal before he vanished. In my view, he may have walked away, but Gombe researchers later counted him as a casualty of within group aggression (Goodall 1986:111; Williams et al. 2008:771) (Count 4-W-A-M 1967). In 1966, Sophie's baby disappeared, and she was not seen carrying the corpse—as often occurs—leading to suspicion it was cannibalized (see below) (Count 4-W-I-? 1966). A similar event happened in 1968, but it is not referred to as suspicious in a recent review of Gombe records, so is not included here (Goodall 1977a:275; Pusey et al. 2008:966). Wilson et al. (2014a:EDT 4) note an inferred internal infant killing of Jane, in 1965.

In any case, the violence, including with baboons (below), got so terrible "that observation was almost ended (Goodall, personal communication)" (Wrangham 1974:85).

But provisioning was the foundation of research, and of hopes for its future. Far from abandoning this tool, Goodall was ready to expand it. "Goodall, working in conjunction with the National Park officials, began collaborating on a number of projects including the building of a second feeding station in the southern area for tourists and other visitors" (Greene 2005:89–90).

New Systems

Goodall sought to diminish violence by modifying how bananas were provided (Goodall 1971:151–153; Wrangham 1974). Four feeding regimes were tried from March 1965 to June 1969. In one phase, physically aggressive acts were 25 times more frequent on days when bananas were available than on days when they were not (Wrangham 1974:89).

Efforts to restrict feeding were stymied by the chimpanzees' unceasing efforts to get at bananas, bashing open, or even pulling hinges from closed boxes (Goodall 2000:339). In June 1969 researchers settled on System E. In System E, 8 boxes of 15 bananas could be sprung on chimpanzees through trap doors in a concrete bunker, when other chimpanzees were not near. The initial goal was to feed the regular visitors every 10–14 days, but it settled into "about once a week" (Wrangham 1974:85). One ration of bananas supplied less than 20% of an adult's daily food requirements. Less than 10% of the northern community were fed per day, a mean of 2.2 individuals. Added up, System E feeding area contributed less than 2% of total food intake (Wrangham 1977:506).

The number of visitors per day dropped with more restricted feeding in 1968. "Individuals began to visit camp much less often ... Some individuals visit camp only three or four times a year despite the fact that they almost always receive bananas when they do come" (Goodall 1986:54). This will be a key point later—chimpanzees which remained around the camp were not fed most of the time; but if they went away for a while then came back to visit, they were fed. Changed provisioning greatly reduced aggressive interactions at the camp. For the chimpanzees, it also meant a massive nutritional and weight loss.

At Gombe at different times, chimpanzee body weight was measured by attaching bananas to a rope with a hanging scale. Climbing, the chimpanzee is weighed. In 1967, average body weight was the *highest* that has ever been recorded at Gombe. "The very high masses in 1967 were recorded after a prolonged period of heavy provisioning with bananas" (Pusey et al. 2005:17). In 1970, the next year of data, it was down to the *lowest* that has ever been recorded, a loss of approximately 20% in three years.[6]

Pusey et al. (2008:966) report only the disappearance of Sophie's baby around this time, leading me to believe that the two are the same.

[6] Average weight recovered by about a third of that loss by 1972—as hunting increased, below—and remained around that level through the next few years (with one unexplained spike in 1976) (Pusey et al. 2005:17).

Illustration 2.3 Gombe Feeding Bunker in System E
Source: Goodall, J. (1986). *The chimpanzees of Gombe: Patterns of behavior*. Belknap Press of Harvard University.

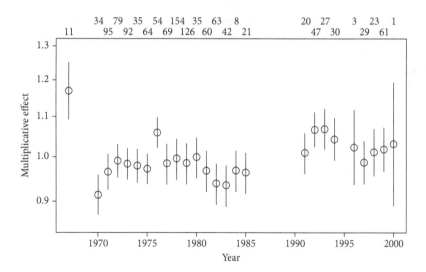

Illustration 2.4 Gombe Chimpanzee Body Mass over Time
Caption: Multiplicative effect of year on mass. For example, the effect for 1976 is 1.06, meaning that masses in 1976 were c. 6% higher than average. Numbers along the top give the counts of observations in each year.

Source: Pusey et al. (2005). Influence of ecological and social factors on body mass of wild chimpanzees. *International Journal of Primatology, 26,* 3–32.

This nutritional crash is a critical fact omitted in the standard Gombe story, but important for understanding development of the Four Year War. Before getting to that War, we must consider other contemporaneous violence at Gombe. Much blood was shed besides that of Kahama adults. That violent context helps in understanding the War.

Hunting

In the 1960s, chimpanzee hunting or meat eating was thought an oddity, maybe related to disturbance.[7] That question was resolved by studies across Africa. It is very common, not abnormal or due to provisioning.[8] In this book, hunting comes up in different ways in different contexts. I am not concerned with short-term variations in frequency. But a major point, starting now, is that a sharp *intensification* of hunting over time can be a response to changes in local resources and competition, itself due to human impact.

The Baboon "War"

By 1966 the provisioning was accompanied by violence not only among chimpanzees but between chimpanzees and baboons, which also came for bananas (Goodall 1971:149). In the late 1960s Gombe hunting took a highly unusual form: predation focused on baboons rather than the more typical prey of red colobus monkeys. Baboon hunting was not new—one killing and possibly a few unsuccessful attempts were witnessed 1961–1964 (Goodall 1986:278). But from March 1968 to August 1970, observers counted 12 kills and 22 attempted kills of infant or young baboons by chimpanzees, with a peak in 1968. There were only four kills of red colobus monkeys over those years (Teleki 1973:52–59, 69).[9]

Observers agreed that the focus on baboons was a result of banana feeding, at least in that feeding put the two species in frequent proximity (Goodall 1986:281; Teleki

---

[7] "[W]e must not start running away with the idea that chimpanzees are 'primitive hunters.' They are vegetarians. The eating incidents mentioned above are extremely rare in the apes studied by Jane Goodall, and her apes were unusual and atypical of the species in general, living as they do in un-chimplike surroundings" (Morris and Morris 1966:228).
"Predation by chimpanzees is thus not a common or frequent event" (Reynolds 1975:124). When Teleki (1973) published his book on intensive hunting at Gombe, debate ensued about whether this was normal, or related somehow to provisioning (de Pelham and Burton 1976; Gaulin et al. 1976; Teleki 1973:106–107; Teleki 1977).

[8] "Observation of chimpanzees hunting for a wide variety of mammalian species . . . in all ecological contexts in the ensuing decades, has silenced the argument" (Stanford 1998a:30). Yet other important questions are very open. Levels and targets of predation vary widely. Little hunting occurred for years at Budongo, but at Ngogo, chimpanzees nearly extirpated the red colobus within their range. Bonobos hunt much less than chimpanzees. Why?

[9] Only one other research site, Mahale, has recorded predation on baboons—see Chapter 10.

1974; Stanford 1998a:30–31). But it was not just proximity that increased attacks. It was direct, violent competition for bananas. In this, the attacks on baboons foreshadow the Four Year War to come.

There were two baboon troops in Gombe near the feeding area. In May of 1966, baboons were still too timid to enter the camp often. A year later, baboons were right in there, and fighting chimpanzees for bananas. "Attacks over common food items are rare outside the feeding area, but the provision of bananas provoked many attacks by the frustrated baboons, and the chimpanzees often retaliated" (Wrangham 1974:91).

> Sometimes the ensuing interspecific aggression resulted in absolute pandemonium with chimpanzees and baboons (often including females) screaming, roaring, barking, and lunging. During skirmishes of this sort the combatants sometimes engaged in physical conflict, standing up and hitting out at one another. On six occasions male baboons leaped onto chimpanzees and appeared to be slashing with their canines at the chimpanzees' backs. An adolescent male, Mustard, was only released when an adult male, Evered, displayed toward the scene so that the baboon ran off. (Goodall 1986:279)

The killing of the baboon infant Amber, offspring of Arwen, on March 19, 1968, is particularly well described, because four observers were there to record it. This was during System B, when bananas were put in 19 widely spaced boxes, released by underground wires (Wrangham 1974:84). I quote at length from Teleki, as this is the best description of direct violence around provisioning. Mike was the alpha male at the time.[10]

> Since boxes have been filled with bananas the previous evening, banana distribution begins at 7:11 A.M. as the first chimpanzees arrive. Only a few boxes are open by the time Camp Troop baboons appear at 7:15. Hugh (adult male), Mike (adult male), and a few others continue eating bananas. As the boxes cannot be closed, there is no alternative but to let the chimpanzees finish even as baboons of all ages stream into the feeding area. By 7:40 most of the troop (ca. 60) is here, so the remaining boxes are kept shut in the hope that at least a part of the troop will leave shortly.
> During the next half hour, while Mike eats nearly a whole box full of bananas (ca. 25), chimpanzees continue arriving from different directions until, by 8:15, 18 are in camp . . .
> Several chimpanzees, particularly the adult males, become increasingly agitated (or frustrated) as the minutes pass: knowing the boxes are full of bananas, all are

---

[10] Mike was a relatively small chimpanzee, which did not engage in direct attacks on others. He rose to the top by displaying and making noise with kerosene cans and other human objects (Goodall 1971:117–122; 1986:426).

expectant. In spite of this growing tension, feeding is delayed a bit longer in order to avoid the chaos that would result from having more than 60 individuals of both species present.

At approximately 8:20, tension suddenly erupts in action as Leakey (adult male) attacks Figan (adult male). Possibly taking advantage of the ensuing uproar and general distraction, Mike chooses this moment to quickly leave Charlie and Hugh on their branch and, with a flick of his right hand as he steps down from the tree trunk behind Arwen baboon, grabs infant Amber. Breaking into a bipedal run slightly up and then across the south slope, Mike flails Amber overhead, twice striking her against the grassy ground.

Mike's actions instantly elicit a burst of excited *screaming* from chimpanzees and *barking* from baboons which drop from trees all around camp. In a matter of seconds Mike covers about 15 yards while male chimpanzees and baboons converge from many directions. *Screeching* repeatedly, Arwen baboon darts about in the melee. Perhaps so that he can ward off mobbing baboons with both hands, Mike transfers Amber to his mouth while continuing his bipedal arms-flailing advance ...

Mike's speed slows considerably as a number of milling chimpanzees and baboons (ca. 12 by now) impede his movement across the open slope.... At least 3 male baboons harry him closely as the milling throng approaches a patch of taller grass ...

Suddenly one male baboon leaps onto Mike's back and, riding there by gripping hair with hands and feet, repeatedly rakes his open mouth across Mike's shoulder. Stopping abruptly, staggering, Mike takes Amber baboon into his left hand; while still bipedal, Mike rapidly rotates his body from side to side and violently waves both extended arms at shoulder level in an effort to dislodge his assailant. Mike smashes the back of his left hand against the trunk of a nearby sapling during one rotation, the impact breaks his grip, and Amber presumably flies into the tall grass.

It all took just two minutes. Then things calmed down, and individuals drifted away. "The mother baboon, Arwen, is the last to leave the site." As for Amber, the chimpanzee Humphrey, tangential to all the fighting, grabbed her from the grass. A few minutes after 9:00 he was seen up a tree, eating the limp infant (Teleki 1973:62–64). Mike here exhibits a trait to be seen in many *pan*icides: exceptional violence by an alpha. You will hear more about Humphrey.

This was not mere predation. It was battle, in direct and immediate competition over bananas. Otherwise, chimpanzees and baboons tolerated each other well, even playing together. The shift to violence could be sudden. "Once a juvenile baboon who had been playing with an infant chimpanzee was captured and eaten only hours afterwards by adult chimpanzees" (Teleki 1973: 42, 47).

System E greatly reduced cross-species violence. "The policy of feeding only in the absence of baboons led to a reduced attack frequency in May 1969 (system D) and during May 1970 (system E) no attacks were recorded at all. During 1968 chimpanzees were seen to prey on nine infant baboons in or near the feeding area; from 1969 to 1972 only one such case was seen each year" (Wrangham 1974:91). Baboon kills fell to zero from 1973 through 1978 (Goodall 1986:283). "It is noteworthy that chimpanzees still encounter baboons frequently in the forest and at camp in Gombe, but rarely hunt them.... The reason that baboons are today hunted only a few times a year is ambiguous" (Stanford 1998a:30). Lack of opportunity cannot explain this change in prey. Competition for provisioned food can.

In early debate on hunting at Gombe, Reynolds (1975:125) took issue with Teleki's downplaying provisioning. "I feel that Teleki has seriously under-rated the impact of the Gombe feeding technique, especially during the year 1967–1968, on chimpanzee–*baboon* relations and thus on chimpanzee–*baboon* predation." Antagonism was not confined to moments of feeding. Attacks happened far from the feeding site, and it took some three years after the direct competition was reduced for the attacks to end. As Reynolds perceived, a violently hostile *relationship* had been created. Something like that developed between Kasakela and Kahama chimpanzees.

Hunting, Nutrition, and Preferences

Hunting baboons was abnormal in the choice of prey and the intensity of violence. More consistent with later findings elsewhere is what followed in the early 1970s: increased predation on red colobus monkeys.

Red colobus hunting is intensively studied at Gombe and elsewhere (see Stanford 1998a; Watts 2020). Most work focuses on short-term variations in frequency. For that, key variables are number of males together, the presence of lead hunters, seasonality, and "binges" that can last more than a week (Stanford 1998a:182, 202–206; Stanford et al. 1994:225). My concern is not short-term variation, but major step increases of hunting over time. Do those indicate sharpened nutritional needs?

Nutrition is an extremely complex topic, involving very different models, approaches, and measures (Raubenheimer et al. 2009; Sommer et al. 2011; Thompson 2017; Wrangham 2006). Perhaps underappreciated is taste, which may or may not reflect nutritional value (Nishida 2012:48–52)—but sure does count in what people eat. Noninvasive testing of C-peptide levels measures energy balances for individuals, the net difference between intake and expenditure of calories (Sherry and Ellison 2007; Thompson et al. 2009). This is an important diagnostic, but does not address other questions of nutrition, or—obviously—tell us anything about past situations.

Much research pertains to plant foods. Animal food adds complications. Meat can be an important source of calories, but energy is not everything. Protein is an especially knotty problem, since quality depends on specific amino acids, and assessment of that is pursued through several noncomparable methods (Ortmann et al. 2006:401–402). Besides protein, meat contains micronutrients (vitamins A, K, and B_{12}, and calcium, sodium, and potassium) and fats that chimpanzees need, so even "meat scraps" may be nutritionally important (Tennie et al. 2009; Watts 2000:8–9).[11,12]

---

[11] "[C]arcass consumption indicated that Gombe chimpanzees seek fat from the brain and from limb-bone marrow over other body parts after a kill" (Stanford 1998a:195; and see Gilby and Wawrzyniak 2018).

[12] Although my focus is on hunting vertebrates, Gombe (and some other) chimpanzees spend more time going after insects. In 1979 and 1980, 45% of all one-day focal follows observed chimpanzees eating insects (Goodall 1986:284). That entails substantial opportunity costs—they could be looking for fruit. Data indicates low energy return from termite fishing, but important gains in amino acids and lipids (Hladik 1977:496, 500; and see O'Malley and Power 2012).

Stanford (1998a:194–195, 201–203) concludes that chimpanzees can get all the nutrients they need from plant foods, and that diverting effort into predation entails opportunity costs probably in excess of benefits. "It appears that chimpanzees are able to obtain both calories and nutrients from their consumption of plant foods without resorting to hunting for animal prey" (1998:196). He concludes that at Gombe, meat and its sharing is political. "Captured carcasses are not simply an end, but a means to an end. Meat is used as a currency in political and reproductive behavior as well" (Stanford 1998a:233).

> Males use meat to secure and maintain political alliances, to publicly snub rivals, and at times to attract estrous females . . . Once a kill is made, the carcass is likely to become the focus of intense political activity. We see cultural diversity from one wild chimpanzee population to the next in the pattern of sharing that follows. Gombe chimpanzee are utterly nepotistic and Machiavellian in their use of the carcass. (Stanford 2001:110)

Yet "if possession of a colobus carcass has political value, the value stems from its nutrients, without which it would have no currency in chimpanzee society" (Stanford 1998a:190; and see Pickering and Dominguez-Rodrigo 2010:109–110). And Gilby and Connor (2010:223–225) conclude for Ngogo that even if meat sharing is used socially, the nutritional benefit rather than possible political use better explains hunting.

Meat is nutritionally valuable, even if not nutritionally essential. Some chimpanzees and most bonobos get along with little meat (or insect) consumption. Yet even when plant nutrients are more than adequate, meat may be avidly sought. Nutritional value and preference may be overlapping but not identical. *Preferred* food is a big consideration going forward.

Whatever the reason, *some* chimpanzees put great effort into procuring animal flesh. The historical question is why, sometimes, intensity of hunting registers a sharp and persisting increase. To understand that one has to consider human impact. Unusual predation on baboons is one example. The hunting surge on red colobus and other species in the early 1970s is another.

The Gombe Hunting Surge

While predation on baboons fell off after banana competition ended, hunting of red colobus monkeys—the prey of choice across Africa—greatly increased over subsequent years. Hunting except of baboons—of bushpigs, bushbucks, etc.—increased during the 1970s War years. Total predation jumped fivefold, and on red colobus by 13 times. Over this time, red colobus developed a fearful, hostile response to chimpanzees that was not seen earlier. The rise in hunting began in 1972–1974, peaked in 1977, and fell back to level-off around the 1976 rate by 1980 (Boesch 1994:1144; Goodall 1986:269; Wrangham and Bergmann-Riis 1990:166). At its peak, red colobus take-off seemed abnormal. "It is doubtful that a predation rate of >40% of the population killed annually could be sustained" (Wrangham and Bergman-Riss 1990:168).

Total meat consumed is considerable. Teleki (1981:327) estimated it at about 10 kg per year per adult chimpanzee. But during the 1974–1975 hunting surge, males that hunted could average 50 kg of meat per year (Wrangham and Bergman-Riis 1990:167). That's about a burger a day. Leaving aside all the other nutrients in flesh, they reckon that this could amount to upward of 12% of annual caloric intake.

Wrangham and Bergman-Riis (1990:163) puzzle over the higher rate of predation in the early 1970s.

> The reasons for long-term changes in predation rate are obscure. There is no indication that artificial feeding has had any effect on the rate of predation except in increasing the number of baboon kills over the period of heavy banana provision in 1968 and 1969. Possible factors influencing predation rates include changes in individual composition (and predatory tendency) within the community, changes in size of parties (sub-groups), and changes in prey availability (1990:166).

All those could be factors in increasing hunts and kills. But why not consider the possibility that nutritional stress, in the aftermath of intensive banana feeding followed by its drastic reduction, could figure in this great leap in meat-seeking? With the banana feeding reduction, Gombe chimpanzees experienced a huge food loss. Shouldn't behavioral ecologists *expect* nutritional stress, and consequent reactions?[13]

There is a plausible connection between the massive nutritional loss accompanying System E provisioning and subsequent intensification of red colobus hunting. This, along with the fall in body mass, suggests that Gombe chimpanzees were experiencing substantial dietary stress as they headed into "war." And hunting was better in the southern rangelands, by then closed off to northern chimpanzees. From 1972–1975 Kahama chimpanzees had a monkey kill rate 2.3 times that of Kasakela (Wrangham and Begman-Riis 1990:160).

In coming chapters, hunting intensification is linked to dietary stress from human impact at Mahale, Kibale, and Budongo. That is a hypothesis. But it is a fact that predatory violence against other species increased up to and during the Four Year War. Hunting was not the only kind of bloodshed. Another sort was particularly shocking to the Gombe researchers: chimpanzees killing and eating chimpanzee infants.

---

[13] I do not suggest that this was a mechanistic unfolding of effect from cause, but a subsistence shift along the lines of human subsistence shifts, which are anything but simple. Changing relative costs and benefits of different subsistence efforts and options lead to differing individual choices. When this happens frequently enough with enough individuals, a new pattern is established. The process is complex, contingent, and sometimes idiosyncratic. The factors noted by Wrangham and Bergmann-Riis could be engaged in a gradually changing pattern of relationships and behaviors. If this is seen as a systemic social change, we should not expect an intensified hunting pattern to snap back to the status quo ante even if subsistence stress eased, once a new behavior pattern is learned and normalized.

Attacking Chimpanzees

Killing Infants

The first recorded instance of infant-eating was in September 1971, by Humphrey, then the alpha. He and four males raced toward chimpanzee calls in the distance. They found a stranger female with infant and violently attacked her. Humphrey snatched the infant, and with one other male, began to eat it while alive (Goodall 1977a:262; 1986:495) (Count 1-O-I-? 1971).

Humphrey is noteworthy. He was the eater of rumble-snatched Amber baboon in 1968. In general, he was violent, "a big bully" (Goodall 1971:12). He frequently attacked females. "It is extraordinary how often, if his victim was in estrus, he managed to rip open her swelling during his attacks; it almost seems that he must have done it intentionally" (Goodall 1986:70). Three years later, Humphrey would lead the first assault on a Kahama male, starting the Four Year War. He was an especially belligerent leader. Both this outside infant killing and later the first attack of the Four Year War illustrate status-related display violence.

In August 1975 came the horror that would haunt Goodall's dreams (Goodall with Berman 1999:118)—and it was not even by one of those demonic *males*. The Kasakela female Passion and her daughter Pom began attacking other Kasakela mothers within the community. Three times they were witnessed killing and/or consuming the victims (Otta, Orion, and Genie): (Count 1-W-I-F 1975, 1-W-I-M 1976, 1-W-I-F 1976). The body of another other most-likely victim was seen (Count 3-W-I-M 1976). Goodall suspected the pair to be responsible for several other infant disappearances (Goodall 1986:112, 354–355; Wilson et al. 2014a:EDT 4).[14]

It is a striking fact, that "[d]uring the four-year period 1974 to 1977," the exact years of the Four Year War and the peak of red colobus hunting, "only one mother, Fifi, was able to raise her infant," Frodo (Goodall 1986:284). (He would turn out bad.)[15] After a few years, Passion and Pom just stopped killing. The last dated, unsuccessful attack was in May 1978 (Goodall 1986:78, 354–355; with Berman 1999:113–115; 2001:193–196).

Why this unique serial infanticide, just as the Four Year War was raging? Two considerations were noted at the time. First, Passion exhibited aberrant behavioral

---

[14] The number of suspected infanticides has varied in different accounts (Goodall 1977a:261; 1986:78 351; Goodall with Berman 1999:115). Goodall's most specific discussion notes that two disappeared at about three weeks old, and five infants were brought to term but never seen by observers (1986:112). Williams et al. (2008:770) put it at three suspected. Wrangham et al. (2006:23) note four suspected internal infanticides, one female, one male, and two of unknown sex. Wilson et al.'s list (2014a: EDTs) for Gombe in the middle 1970s is Otta, female, in 1975; Genie, female, 1975; Orion, male, 1976—all observed; Melissa's infant, male, 1976, inferred. With minor adjustment in dates, these fit the four already counted. But in addition to those, Wilson et al. add only a single additional suspected internal infanticide, Banda, a female, in 1976 (Count 5-W-I-F 1976). Given Goodall's suspicions, and the violent character of this time, I add the three additional infants noted in Wrangham et al. (2005) as suspected (Count: Gandalf 5-W-I-M 1974, Patti's 5-W-I-? 1975, Little Bee's 5-W-I-? 1976).

[15] Goodall's (1986:62) data, however, show three more infants born in 1977 that survived. One was Passion's own son Pax. Another, Tubi, was barely saved from the cannibalistic duo in August, when Pax was a week old, by her mother Little Bee (Goodall 1986:355). Perhaps the discrepancy in number of survivors is from the way field seasons are counted.

qualities. In 1973, just before the infant killings began, seven resident researchers were asked to evaluate Gombe chimpanzees by 10 basic personality characteristics. Passion was exceptional among the females. "The overall impression of Passion was that of a disturbed, isolated, aggressive individual who would be considered in human terms to exhibit a paranoid spectrum of traits." She also displayed "unusually inefficient and indifferent maternal behavior.... Pom had to fight continually for her own survival," often ignored and left to catch up as her mother moved off (Buirksi and Plutchik 1991:208–209, numerical assessments omitted).

On their infanticidal motive, Goodall put it bluntly: they attacked "*only in order to acquire the infants* as meat" (1986:284, emphasis in original). Yet she (with Berman 1999:113) also claims, "[t]here was no shortage of food at Gombe at the time—Passion had not needed the infant's flesh for her survival."[16] Since in 1975, the Gombe chimpanzees were still well under their 1967 weight (Pusey et al. 2005:17), since males were simultaneously hunting more than they had ever done, and since cannibalistic attacks ended as hunting returned to lower levels and Kasakela acquired Kahama's range—how can dietary stress be so easily dismissed?

Assaults on Females

Other infants—outside infants—also died, but during attacks on their mothers. During the 1970s, Kasakela males (and occasionally females) repeatedly and severely attacked outside adult/females who came into their range. This is especially noteworthy because up to 1970, stranger females were seen on several occasions deep within Kakombe territory, without being attacked (Teleki 1977:51–55). As with red colobus hunting, the pattern that emerged after the cutback in provisioning was very different from early observations, a change consistent with the expectations of the resource competition + human impact hypothesis.

In 1973, Kahama males went to a body of an unknown female, possibly of the Kalande community which was to Kahama's south. The wounds were consistent with a chimpanzee attack, but also could be from leopard (Goodall 1986:493–500; 1990:102–103). Because Kahama chimpanzees led the observers to the body, I count this as a very likely *pani*cide (Count 3-O-A-F 1973).[17]

From 1971 through 1982, there were 16 serious attacks on stranger females, most with infants or children. The wounds were often serious, sometimes life-threatening. No actual killings were witnessed or bodies found, and all the female victims eventually escaped or were left. Yet as described, four attacks seem potentially lethal.[18] Surveying all field observations, Hashimoto et al. (2020:172) find peaceful intergroup interactions of females understudied, but the attacks at Gombe from 1975 to 1982 stand out for their violence.

---

[16] Gombe females hunt far less frequently than males (Stanford et al. 1994:220), but they spend considerably more time feeding on termites and ants (Goodall 1986:254–262).
[17] Goodall puts this as 1974, Wrangham et al. (2006:22) as 1972, but Wilson et al. provide an actual date, August 12, 1973.
[18] #3 November 1975, #6 March 1977, #8 October 1978, and #14 May 1979 (Count: 4-O-A-F 1975; 4-O-A-F 1977; 4-O-A-F 1978; 4-O-A-F 1979).

More definite are deaths of infants with the adult female victims, with two in 1975, and one in 1979 (Goodall 1977a:261–263; 1986:499) (Count 1-O-I-F 1975, 2-O-I-M 1975, 1-O-I-? 1979). In two, infants were eaten by males, and in three, male captors engaged in ostentatious acts of brutality that observers characterized as "bizarre" (Goodall 1977a:262–265). That is what I call display violence.

Other Violence

This still does not exhaust the varieties of violence of the middle 1970s, the War era. Nonlethal violence among Kasakela adults was frequent, and sometimes severe (Goodall 1986:68–78, 313–356). In 1968, 12-year-old Pooch sustained a severe groin wound. She survived, but disappeared six months later during a pneumonia epidemic, and Gombe researchers suspect her weakened condition contributed to death (Goodall 1986:89, 105, 111). Wilson et al. (2014a:EDT 3) record it as a suspected internal killing (Count 4-W-A-F 1968). From 1971 through 1978, 18 severe wounds—involving one or more deep, bleeding gashes—were recorded within Kasakela (Goodall 1983:34; 1986:317). Two especially severe internal attacks on females occurred in 1973 and 1977 (Goodall 1986:329–330).

The Four Year War's Context

Leading up to and during the Four Year War, human impact included: habitat and range loss around the park, a probable rise in density within the Park, massive increase in direct contact with human observers, and above all, artificial provisioning—first in abundance and then sharply curtailed. By 1966, intense aggression and violence among chimpanzees resulted from banana feeding. Provisioning led to killing and eating baboon competitors. Its reduction was followed by a surge in red colobus hunting, infanticide and cannibalism, severe attacks on outside females, and much nonlethal violence within Kasakela. Provisioning inadvertently *conditioned* Gombe chimpanzees to be violent. Violence became normal in a time of great disruption.

Most of these facts are left out of the simple tale of the Four Year War, of one group splitting in two, with one exterminating the other. They are not factored into theory about this, the type case, for the rival coalition reduction hypothesis. Putting this context in the foreground changes dramatically our understanding of what the War was all about.

6
Explaining the War and Its Aftermath

Why the War?

While Gombe researchers acknowledge that surrounding habitat loss increased density and food competition within the Park, they ignore or dismiss the possibility that banana provisioning fostered the War. Provisioning is the focus here.

Frustration and Favoritism

Power (1991:3, 28–35, 136–147) sees the Four Year War resulting from *frustration* after the restriction of the banana feeding. Intensely frustrated at being unable to get what once had been regular and abundant, aggression was redirected in a noninstrumental way. It had no tangible goal. The idea that frustration leads to aggression, or "the frustration-aggression response," has a venerable history in human psychology and anthropology.

Unquestionably, chimpanzees take it out on others when frustrated. See how Goodall (1990:148) imagines the 1980s alpha male Goblin after a setback: "seething as he stumped through the forest, spoiling to vent his frustrated fury, really directed against Satan and Evered, on anyone he met." Or go back to the tensions preceding the attack on the baboon infant when the banana boxes stayed closed. Goodall (1986:323) generalizes that attacks within the community are often a result of frustration and redirected aggression, often considerably displaced in time.

It cannot be doubted that System E of banana feeding frustrated the hell out of the Gombe chimpanzees. After years of all you could eat, suddenly it became—nothing, nothing, nothing, POP, SURPRISE!, nothing, nothing.... I do not disagree that frustration contributed to aggression of all sorts, among chimpanzees already conditioned to act violently. But in attacks on Kasakela, I believe there is something more deliberate involved. To see that, we need to add in other details usually left out of the Gombe story.

Competition for Food

As time passed after feeding reduction, the southerners were seen less and less at camp. Researchers wanted to entice them in, so starting in 1971 they fed them when they did appear. While Kasakela chimps that stayed around camp were reduced to a fraction of their former bananas, sprung unpredictably, *whenever* Kahama chimps showed up, they got bananas (Goodall 1986:503). "[A]lthough at that time, bananas were being handed out much less frequently, this did not affect the Kahama individuals since when they *did* visit camp (visits which became increasingly rare) they were *always* fed" (Goodall 1983:52, emphasis in original). Moreover, when the Kahama chimps came, they came *as a group*, intimidating and scattering the local Kasakela chimps.[1]

To add injury to insult, in this time of drastic caloric reduction, Kahama chased out Kasakela chimps visiting their old southern ranges. Bygott, who pioneered the research method of daily follows, and who chronicled developing tensions in 1971, wrote:

When a large party of southern males encountered northern males (in *any* part of their range) they tended to display charge in parallel and cause the northern males to scatter, although after the initial excitement both sides usually settled down to groom or feed peacefully. It was perhaps for reasons of security that northern males, when they traveled south, usually went in parties of at least five. Thus there developed a pattern of "expeditions." (1974:231–232)

At least nine such intimidations *by Kahama* were observed in 1970–71 (Goodall et al. 1979:45).

Kahama's last visit to the feeding station was around September 1972. Maybe they kept away because Hugh went missing. Formerly, Hugh would charge aggressively alongside Kahama alpha Charlie. It was not numbers that made Kahama so intimidating, but two fierce males charging in tandem (Goodall 1986:61). With Hugh gone, the effective balance of power had tipped. In January 1974 came the first possibly deadly attack, on Godi of Kahama.

Madam Bee and Goliath support the inference that intergroup violence was about provisioned food. Both had maintained contacts with Kasakela. They mostly ranged with Kahama, but hadn't severed ties. Both were attacked shortly after they paid their first visit in a long (unspecified) while to the feeding station (Goodall 1986:511–513). Goliath visited for the last time in 1975 "just a few months before he was brutally attacked and left to die by the Kasakela males" (1986:69).

For Madam Bee, the linkage was more immediate. She had frequently associated with Kasakela males, but in August 1974 came to the feeding station for the first time in two years. The first Kasakela attack on Madam Bee came the next month. The deadly line of division that Goodall saw drawn between Kasakela and Kahama was extended to these two only after they returned to be given bananas.

Goodall (1983:52–53) rejects suggestions that provisioning "may have caused the inter-community violence." Although it affected movements at first, "the feeding system was drastically revised once this was realized and the chimpanzees rapidly reverted to their former ranging patterns." Since the provisioned group raided the unprovisioned group, she concludes that "it is difficult to see" how banana feeding at any time had "anything to do with those events."

---

[1] "'We would hear these pant-hoot calls from the south and say to ourselves: the southern males are coming! All the northern ones would go up trees, and there'd be a lot of screaming and displaying" (Anne Pusey, quoted in O'Neill 2018).

Goodall once explained violence between Kasakela and Kahama as a result of the northerners being excluded from the southern range (Goodall 1977b; Goodall with Berman 1999:12, 127–128). No reason was ever offered to doubt that. On the contrary, long-term data confirms that Kasakela's regaining access to the southern area was associated with higher body weight and shorter interbirth intervals (Pusey et al. 2005:9; Williams et al. 2004:10; see Chapter 8). The southern exclusion developed after banana provisioning was drastically curtailed, removing thousands of calories from daily diets. Provisioning brought Kakombe together, and provisioning tore it apart.[2]

Psychology

Why the deadly brutality of attacks? Goodall thought their ferocity implicated something beyond food competition. Agreed. But do we need evolutionary selection to account for the fury, or will historical circumstances do? After years of severe individual and interspecific violence over bananas, intense hostility became group vs. group: as Kahama dispersed the hungry, frustrated Kasakela chimpanzees at the station and were then fed; and as Kahama chased away Kasakela males when they sought food in southern rangelands. Is it any wonder that Kasakela would develop a deep animosity toward their old companions?

Does that give chimpanzees too much cognitive credit? Primatologists give them more than sufficient brain power (Newton-Fisher 1997). They can "a) construct abstract categories of behavior, b) make predictions about future behaviors that follow

---

[2] When this book was in late editing, Feldblum et al. (2018) offered a new explanation of the Kasakela-Kahama fission, based on data from 1963 to 1973. They conclude Kakombe was one community that fissioned, rather than two groups that came together over bananas and later went separate ways. Their data suggest associations began to segregate in early 1971, increasing through 1972. In their view, this supports the one community hypothesis.

They do not address Goodall's observations of two distinct groups prior to 1963; or respond to observers' conclusions 1963–1966 of distinct northern and southern subgroups. They hypothesize that the cause of group separation was a status conflict between Humphrey on one side, and Charlie and Hugh on the other, intensifying from December 1970. But such conflicts are commonplace, without resulting in fission. Moreover, frightened Humphrey avoided Charlie and Hugh, yet it was Charlie and Hugh that drifted away. Feldblum et al. discount the shift to System E provisioning as causal for the split because it happened in mid-1969, "a year and a half before the onset of increased modularity" (2018:737); and because "beginning in 1971, researchers fed southern males every time they visited the feeding station in an ultimately fruitless attempt to reverse their declining attendance" (2018:735). Social change is a process. The provisioning context kept changing. After the boon years chimpanzees went through Systems A–D, starting May 1965. System D already reduced banana availability. "[T]he frequency of visits to camp by southern males fell almost continuously in successive six-month blocks from 1968 to 1972" (Wrangham 1975:6.2). With the severe reduction of System E, all chimpanzees were hungry and unpredictably fed—but waiting. Ranging data shows that *all* adult males spent most of their time near the feeding station until later 1970 (2018:737). In early 1971 they *all* drifted away, Kahama more distanced southward than Kasakela. Although "northern and southern males continued to interact peaceably elsewhere in the community range" in 1972 (2018:732), in early 1971 Kahama began chasing Kasakela away from southern ranges, initiating the overt food competition that Goodall and colleagues identified as the principle reason for the War. *Immediate* fission upon shift to System E is hardly expected. Changes like that take time.

from past behaviors, and c) adjust their own behavior accordingly" (Povinelli and Vonk 2003:157).[3] Kasakela's drawing a deadly line in the sand against Kahama, seeing them as enemies that took their food when they were hungry, seems elementary (and see Roscoe 2007).

Sex and Politics

Sex

Intergroup hostility was not simply a matter of resource competition. Along with food availability, the most significant determinant of chimpanzee party size is the reproductive status of females (Boesch 1996:109; Matsumoto-Oda et al. 1998; Reynolds 2005:91-93; Wittiger and Boesch 2013). When a female is in estrus, this is apparent by the pronounced swelling of her sex skin. Males, and even noncycling females, come together around them. One or more swollen females leads to larger parties. If no local females are in estrus, Gombe males seek them out in peripheral areas Gombe (Goodall 1986:158).

Those factors pertain during the Four Year War. Kahama expeditions that barged northward into Kasakela territory often coalesced around Kasakela female Mandy when she came into estrus (Goodall 1986:487). In 1974, the number of cycling females in Kasakela dropped to a low point. That year Gigi, infertile and so regularly cycling, "was the nucleus of eleven of the seventeen parties (about 65 percent) that were followed as they patrolled in the south of the Kasakela range" (Goodall 1986:486-487). With reduction of provisioning, peripheral females stopped coming to the feeding station, and southerly patrols may have been looking for them (Goodall 1983:19-20). "In 1974 there was a decrease in the number of available cycling females. This coincided with the first of the observed attacks, by Kasakela males on Kahama individuals" (1983:22). Kasakela males were drawn to Madam Bee's daughter, Little Bee, who "actually attracted the hostile Kasakela males into the area of conflict" (Goodall 1986:487).

Except possibly for Little Bee, Kasakela's moves were not about recruiting new females, as in sociobiological theory. Little Bee was a late adolescent, when a female would normally leave her natal group. She transferred to Kasakela very early in the War. Madame Bee was attacked and killed *after* that. One parous female, Joanne, might be a Kahama female that transferred; or maybe a peripheral female that moved into central Kaskala range in 1979 (Goodall 1986:88; Williams et al. 2004:529). Little Bee and Joanne are the only two female movements that *might* be considered a result of the Four Year War, and the connection is weak.

Groupings and some of the movements were in one sense about sex. Were it not for the drought of receptive females, the Four Year War might never have happened. But sex does not explain how or why things got so deadly bad. Such groupings and movements happen all the time, with little if any violence.

---

[3] Experimental situations suggest a "revenge system"—in coalitional maneuvering, chimpanzees intervene against those who previously intervened against them (de Waal and Luttrell 1988; Jensen et al. 2007).

Bringing Politics In

Another factor that may contribute to the intergroup clashes is male status competition. In the complicated world of chimpanzee politics, coalitionary behaviors acted out in patrols, incursions, and attacks on outsiders, all affect and are affected by maneuvers, alliances, and oppositions for status *within* the Kasakela community.

Christopher Boehm, a cultural anthropologist, brought a practiced political eye—and a videocamera—with him to Gombe. He concluded that chimpanzees were "particularly good at sizing up situations involving competition or agonism," and at "making decisions as groups, and some of these decisions are quite complex." He also found that conflict decisions were actively steered by dominant males (Boehm 1997:354–356). For example, in a *New York Times* story about videos from Gombe in 1986, involving then-alpha Goblin:

> Goblin was leading a troop on patrol when the animals caught sight of an enemy troop approaching. Would the encounter result in a screaming match, or a fight, or would one or both troops retreat? What the camera recorded, in Dr. Boehm's interpretation, was a group "decision" about how best to proceed. Dr. Boehm said one member of the troop began to vocalize softly, then choked off his sounds and turned to look at his leader, Goblin, who then rushed past him to get a better look at the enemy. Goblin looked at the chimp who served him as a sort of first mate and at the chimp who issued the initial scream. Within 54 seconds, after having visually "consulted" with his mates, Dr. Boehm said, Goblin made a decision and the entire troop began screaming and hooting and jumping about in a display of toughness. The approaching troop did the same, and after a while both troops withdrew and went home. (Brody 1996)

On patrol, Goblin had exercised leadership and dominance, and activated his alliances (see Boehm 2018a:685–687).

Was all of that compartmentalized and left behind after the screaming and hooting ended? What if a high-status male on patrol displays extreme violence? If, as Povinelli and Vonk conclude, chimpanzees construct abstract behavioral categories (e.g., he is extremely violent), make predictions about future from past behaviors (e.g., he could be really violent again), and adjust their own behavior accordingly (e.g., I don't want him to be really violent to me), then inflicting deadly violence on outsiders while on patrol, when there is little or no risk, would be a good stratagem for an ambitious, dominant, or challenged male. Given a context of greatly heightened competition and antagonism, this hypothesis helps explain the initiation of deadly intergroup attacks.

The Display Violence Hypothesis Applied

Up to and through the Four Year War, Kasakela males engaged in intensive status competition (Goodall 1986:64–70, 178–180, 418–428). Humphrey deposed old and slipping Mike in early 1971, probably in a single fight. He faced capable challengers and was never secure. In September 1971 came the first outside killing recorded at Gombe, as Humphrey killed and ate a stranger infant. Not only did he kill it, he displayed what observers called "bizarre" violence. He "smashed the infant's body time and again onto the ground" and moved off, "flailing the corpse so that the head smashed against the ground." He "pounded on the corpse with his fist, pressed down hard on the chest so that air was forced audibly through the lungs" and poked the body repeatedly. Then he shared the carcass with Mike and other males, reinforcing political support. He flailed the body some more, until leaving it for Figan to pick up and flail it for another hour (Goodall 1977a:263).

But Humphrey—the big bully—appeared frightened of the Kahama chimps, especially of co-charging Charlie and Hugh of Kahama. "When they made one of their periodic visits to the north in 1971, Humphrey always tried to avoid them" (Goodall 1986:70). He usually quit patrols that headed south, while others continued on without him, tensely listening for Kahama (Goodall 1986:209). Afraid, he left leadership to others, notably Figan. In May 1973, Figan, in tight alliance with Fagan, toppled Humphrey and his ally Evered. Things remained unsettled, with ever-shifting alliances and oppositions involving Figan and Humphrey.

These fraught males walked out in varying combinations to tensely enter their old rangeland. In January 1974, Humphrey did accompany one southward patrol. He made chimpanzee history by leading the first attack of the Four Year War, when Godi was encountered alone. Humphrey grabbed him, pinned him, and held him down while others beat him. Figan and others followed his lead and beat him (Goodall et al. 1979:33–36, 45; 1986:504–507).

My interpretation is that Humphrey, weakened by his fear of Kahama, took this opportunity to gain some cred. But over time, his rivals Figan and Fagan were more consistent. Figan went on more patrols than any other individual; and was tied for second behind Fagan for direct attacks on Kahama chimpanzees (Goodall et al. 1979:24). Their leading roles in the War coincided with their high though unstable position in the hierarchy. Figan, on top, had the most to lose.

In October and November 1975, more extreme violence was seen in outside infant killings. Several males participated, but Figan displayed the most severe, "bizarre" aggression. In October, he "seized the body and began to display with it, dashing it repeatedly against the ground and tree trunks. Next he sat down and pounded on its head with his fists, time and again. He pushed his hand into the thoracic cavity, withdrew and sniffed it, then wiped his hand on the ground. Then he abandoned the body." In November 1975, Figan got the corpse and "began to leap through the branches in a charging display, smashing the infant against the branches and trunks as he did so. He leapt to the ground and continued to flail his victim against the rocks as he ran" (Goodall 1977a:264–265).

Humphrey and Figan's demonstrations of violence against dead infants were truly extreme. Added to Mike's overhead flailing and bashing of the baboon infant, that makes three alphas in a row that engaged in this sort of extraordinary display.

Why Did It Happen?

That's the Four Year War. Driven by competition for food, encouraged by years of conditioning for violence, and with a good deal of sex and politics thrown in. How human! How *unlike* an inborn propensity to kill members of another group whenever possible. And how impossible to understand without a good grasp of the total context, the local history beginning with the impact of humans. The Four Year War did not happen in a vacuum. No war does.

Young Wrangham (1974:92), discussing the impact of banana provisioning, warned that if scholars ignore it regarding aggressive behavior, "a false impression may be gained of what is normal." However he restricted this point to actions directly connected to feeding competition at the camp. Nothing suggests chimpanzees compartmentalize their behavior so. Baboons were killed elsewhere.

Thirty years later on the BBC (2004), Wrangham would dismiss the whole issue: "people could say oh well Gombe is all special and peculiar, you know. They had, they gave bananas to them for a few years so that would have caused them to kill each other, which to some of us seems a little bit absurd."

Invasion from the South

The Four Year War set the mold for a demonic vision of chimpanzees. Further support seemed to follow almost instantly. Right after the disappearance of Kahama, came the "Invasion from the South" by the "powerful Kalande community" (Goodall 1986:514). Kalande, which previously roamed to the south of Kahama, foraged more and more to the north, pushing the smaller Kasakela group back.

In the post-War interpretive framework, this was seen as a repeat of Kasakela's violent capture of Kahama's range. Along with the supposed extermination of K-group by M-group at Mahale (Part III), the Invasion—*as it was interpreted*—confirmed that territorial conquest was *normal*. But unlike Kasakela and Mahale groups, Kalande— supposedly—was never provisioned, so this encroachment was taken to rule out human impact as causative of "war."

Kalande Prehistory

To understand Kalande's movements requires looking into its history. In the 1960s Kalande was Kahama's southern neighbor, probably pushed deeper into the Park by external habitat loss (Goodall 1977a:272–273). Kahama and Kalande chimpanzees were seen peacefully associating in 1971. But in 1974, three agonistic encounters occurred between Kalande and Kahama, without physical contact (Goodall 1986:488, 492). Kahama's post-provisioning southerly orientation may have increased competition with Kalande.

A map of the range of the Kakombe community united (Kasakela and Kahama together) c. 1971 has their core area end at Kahama stream, and Kalande's core begin at Nyasanga stream, with about 1½ km of overlapping peripheral range (Teleki 1977:42). A map of 1973 has Kahama core range right up to the Nyasanga stream (Goodall 1986:505). What makes this especially intriguing, is that something *human* was happening at Nyasanga.

In 1967 a small ranger station set up four kilometers south of Kakombe camp. Gombe researchers began at least occasional observation (McGrew/Pierce 2009).

For 11 months in 1968 and 1969, they operated a feeding station in the Nyasanga Valley, trying to habituate them (Greene 2005:89–90; Teleki 1977:44). It worked. More than 20 individuals were recognized (Wilson 2012:370). The fate of this project is unreported, but observers were there in 1970, when eight Kakombe males (including northerns and southerns) were reported at Nyasanga station for several days (Teleki 1977:53). The 1971 map (Teleki 1981:319) notes a National Park ranger station at Nyasanga, and marks a "Gombe Valley Research site, proposed tourist station" in the Gombe valley, three valleys *south* of Nyasanga, in the center of the Kalande range. It would be surprising if that project did not involve banana provisioning.

Kalande Intrudes

Kalande expansion is a bad fit with the imbalance of power hypothesis (IoPH). Estimated at over 40 individuals, they greatly outnumbered Kahama males in the early 1970s (Pintea et al. 2011:239), but "did not push their boundaries to the north until 1 year after the males had gone" (Williams et al. 2004:12). They did not exploit numerical superiority to expand into Kahama territory.

Once Kahama was gone, however, and Kasakela sometimes foraged in their former range, Kalande chimpanzees began moving north during the wet season to eat ripening fruit, returning to the south in April or May. Kasakela retreated northward in front of them, and returned south behind them. This territorial oscillation is quite different from the relatively fixed border between Kahama and Kasakela. It closely resembles however, the pattern between K-group and M-group at Mahale (Chapter 9). Goodall herself (1983:54–55; 1986:230) compares these two situations.

From 1978 onward, sightings and hearings of Kalande chimpanzees caused visible tension within Kasakela. They began frequent, alert patrolling along their southern frontier (Goodall 1986:515). By 1981 Kasakela had lost half its range. Kalande's advance pushed them against the Mitumba community to their north (Goodall 1986:516; Pusey et al. 2005:25). At one point, Kalande males called from the ridge south of camp, and Mitumba males from one valley north (Goodall 1990:110). In the wet season of 1981–82, Kalande moved into the next valley below the research site to feed on abundant fruit. Then they entered the valley of the research station itself (Goodall 1986:515–516). At this point, Kasakela was down to its smallest range ever on record, 5.3 km^2 (Pusey et al. 2005:25).

Casualties of War?

Kalande's push northward is portrayed as a repeat of Kasakela's attacks on Kahama, with several killings inferred. That inference is because events are seen through the lens of the Four Year War. There is no direct evidence of severe violence between Kalande and Kasakela.

Goodall's (1986:110, 112, 516) suspicion of female and infant victims during the Invasion is couched in general terms. Sorting through that and later commentary about wounds on mothers and infants and infant disappearances (Pusey et al.

2008:966–968; Williams et al. 2008:77), the firmest estimate is two outside female and one male infant suspected as killed[4] (Count 5-O-I-F 1981, 5-O-I-M 1981, 5-O-I-F 1982).

That is not evidence of a killing invasion. Infants frequently die from introduced disease. Females are wounded and their infants killed when they individually wander into a foreign community. Plus both mother-wounding and infant-killing happen in within-group violence, and this was a time of great contestation in the male status hierarchy[5] (Goodall 1986:425)—which in other situations led to display violence against infants, and payback against ex-alphas. There are alternative explanations besides Kalande expansionism for these signs or suggestions of violence, and no way to pick among them.

What about *adult males*? "Some of the Kalande raids may have been lethal. Humphrey died near the border in 1981, his body found but his death unseen" (Wrangham and Peterson 1996:19). That is a stretch. Goodall (1986:70) says his *skull* was found. "They *fail* to mention that Humphrey was approximately 35 years old, and wild chimps rarely live past 33 years" (Sussman 1999:127). Goodall (1986:70) clarifies: "We do not know how Humphrey died" (Count 5-O-A-M 1981).[6]

Three adult male chimpanzees disappeared from Kasakela during this time (Williams et al. 2002:514–516). Sherry was the first to go, his "disappearance in 1979 remains a mystery" (Goodall 1986:71). Humphrey makes two. Figan was third. He vanished in 1982, not long after being deposed as alpha. "[T]he reason for his disappearance and presumed death in 1982 is not known" (Goodall 1986:65). Wrangham et al. (2006:22) and Wilson et al. (2014a:EDT 1) count all three as suspicious. We will see that a toppled alpha male may become a special target of within-group payback violence, and/or may roam away solo. Figan may have lived. If he was killed, it could be an inside job—and Humphrey too (Count 5-O-A-M 1979, 5-?-A-M 1982).

In all this, there is no direct evidence at all of a *violent* invasion by Kalande. If these events had not followed upon the Four Year War, they would have been interpreted as a give and take based on numerical superiority, not violence.

---

[4] In 1980, Passion—the infanticidal mother during the Four Year War—returned to Kasakela with serious wounds. Her infant son Pax was severely wounded. He survived, effectively castrated (Wilson et al. 2004:531). Female Nope also returned, wounded, without her infant. Goodall notes that Hepziba, Barbet, and Dapples lost infants, which she suspects might have been killed by Kalande. Wrangham et al. (2006:23) do not include any of these in their list of intergroup infanticides. Only the last three are recorded as suspected killings in Wilson et al., though in Hepziba's case, the suspected aggressors were from Mitumba (Wilson et al. 2014a:EDT 2). Acknowledging uncertainty, I go with that.

[5] "Figan's status as alpha was challenged in mid-1979 when young Goblin made a determined bid to overthrow him. Another period ensued when, for five months, there was no obvious alpha. Once again Figan worked his way back to the top, but five months before his disappearance, Figan finally lost control. Once again there was no clear-cut alpha, this time for just over two years.... In 1984 Goblin finally qualified as alpha male." (Goodall 1986:425)

[6] Up to 1973, the projected maximum age was about 38 (Teleki et al. 1976:572). More recent demographic data gave them more years. About 18% of Gombe chimpanzees survived 33, with the oldest dying at 46 (Hill et al. 2001:444). Although chimpanzees are still considered "old" by their mid-30s, what was the oldest ever known in the wild, Sparrow, was about 52 and in good health (Wilson 2012:368–369). In captivity one female was estimated to be 78. A recent comparative study however, suggests ecological factors lead to higher or lower life expectancies by location, with the maximum age for Gombe at 55, Tai 46, Kanyawara 64, and Ngogo 66 (Wood et al. 2017:41–42).

Why "Invade?"

Wrangham and Peterson (1996:19) say that Kalande "had never been provisioned with bananas," and use this encroachment against Power's thesis. But banana provisioning and habituation efforts were carried out within the Kalande range in 1968 and 1969, and it is not clear when they ended. It is not surprising that the feeding station attracted Kalande during its northerly forays.

From its inception, the Gombe feeding station drew in chimpanzees that first observed it from outside (Goodall 1971:105).

> A chimpanzee does not necessarily have to visit the feeding area to learn that bananas are available, since it is visible from a distance and the exposure of bananas may elicit excited calls audible through much of the valley. During system E [from 1969 on] individuals were sometimes found looking towards the feeding area from several hundred yards for periods of several minutes. (Wrangham 1974:84)

The possibility that provisioning attracted Kalande chimpanzees makes sense of an otherwise inexplicable occurrence. "On a never-to-be forgotten day in 1982 four Kalande males actually appeared in camp." Unless attracted by the feeding and accustomed to humans, how is that possible? Visitor behavior was rather mild. Fifi and her offspring ran away. "Melissa rushed up a palm tree and was chased by a Kalande male and mildly attacked. Her four-year-old son, Gimble, encountered a second male—but was only sniffed. The four males left after this, moving back towards the others of their group, who were still calling" (Goodall 1986:516).

This tension soon ended. By late 1982, Kasakela was regaining land, and by 1984 was back to its old range, including the former Kahama area. The inferred reason was that maturation doubled adult and adolescents to join patrols. This increase spotlights a central idea of the rival coalition reduction hypothesis (RCRH): losing a single male marginally reduces ability to dominate intergroup clashes. Here, loss of three adult males was more than reversed in a couple of years. For the human impact hypothesis (HIH), there is a big question: were the Kalande chimpanzees fed during the 1982 visit to camp? If not, they may have gone away wondering what all the fuss was about.

The Invasion seemed to confirm chimpanzees' predilection toward intergroup killing only because the Four Year War suggested that inference. With the Invasion added in, the interpretive paradigm gained solidity. Adoption of the paradigm shaped the future of chimpanzee research. The demonic perspective on chimpanzee intergroup conflict rose upon the Four Year War and the Invasion from the South. Yet that Gombe model *never applies to Gombe again.*

7
Later Gombe

In writing this book, Chapter 7 was the toughest. Reading it may not be so easy either, because the factual material does not lend itself to coherent narrative. Having analyzed the "war" years, where the paradigm formed, this chapter takes the Gombe story up to the most recent (and very limited) reports, or from around 1984 to 2013. In the universal coverage of this book, complete history is important, and appraising all deadly violence necessary. But both are complicated, disjointed, and as time goes on, poorly described.

Chapter 7 begins with the many faces of impactful human disturbance. These only partly map on to each other over time. But over time, they accumulate and compound each other. This allows a very rough but necessary periodization: increasing but less critical disruption from the mid-1980s up to the late 1990s, say to 1997; then cascading disruption to a chaotic peak around 2004. Great disruption continues largely unimpeded after that, but with more patchy coverage or no context at all, up to 2017 when description of killing ends. This periodization then frames description of deadly violence among chimpanzees, which also gets much worse going into and through the 2000s. Chapter 7 is devoted to presenting the record. Theoretical discussion comes in Chapter 8.

A major fact: with a few exceptions, the killing happens within, not between, groups. Those killing allow, indeed require, elaboration in Chapter 8 of my hypothesis about status-related violence, which provides insight on the timing of killings in both periods. This extended discussion ends the main coverage of Gombe.

Finally before diving in, another factor impeding coherent narrative is that just after the "war years," Gombe loses its best scientific storyteller.

Jane Goodall Leaves Gombe

After the kidnapping, research efforts picked up again from 1981 (Greene 2005:114). But Goodall's systematic data for her book ends with 1981. The last anecdotal observations date to 1984, the closing date of the southern encroachment. Goodall officially ended field observation in 1986.[1]

---

[1] She was asked, "Why did you quit research?"
  I made that decision literally overnight at a conference in 1986. I was planning to go back to Gombe, but after I heard all the delegates speak about the extent of habitat destruction across Africa, I came out knowing that I would never go back. Since that day I haven't spent more than three weeks in any one place, but have spent my time traveling the world lecturing on conservation and cooperation. (Middleton and Else 2005)
She compares this moment to Saul's conversion on the road to Damascus (Greene 2005:120–122).

Her work since then for chimpanzees, nature, and humanity is deservedly legendary. Chimpanzees and the world are better for her decision. However, that does mean our knowledge of Gombe drops off dramatically. It is *The Chimpanzees of Gombe* that put everything together. In that anthropologically holistic book, you can see how one aspect of chimpanzee existence connects with another. Goodall was criticized for "personalizing" chimpanzees, giving them names and following their family histories. But it is that practice that enables me to consider how individual life histories, character, and ambition play a role in larger events. After Goodall left the field, behavioral observations, data series, and references to human activities must be cobbled together from narrow, hypothesis-driven research articles. Much knowledge of the sort found in *Chimpanzees of Gombe* is not available at all. Chimpanzee history kept on happening, but we can read much less about it, and put aspects together with much less clarity, once Jane Goodall left off field research.

The Changing Human Context, post 1983

Research and Tourism

There is nearly no information about changes in provisioning methods in the later literature, but change it did. Referring to the bunker system of feeding, Wallis and Lee (1999:805) note without elaboration: "when the equipment fell into disrepair and the subjects became more comfortable with humans, a trend developed for the habituator to hand food directly to the chimpanzees."

Research spread out and intensified over time. Effort was made to habituate Kalande in the 1970s and 1980s, but didn't continue. Research monitoring of unhabituated Kalande chimpanzees picked up in the later 1990s, and became systematic in 1999 (Pintea et al. 2011:230, 239). Habituation of Mitumba began in 1985 or 1986, and research became intensive through the 1990s, with a banana feeding station in 1992. All-day follows began in 2002 (Mjungu 2010; Nutter 1996; Pusey et al. 2007:627; Rudicell 2010:12; Williams et al. 2002:351; Wilson et al. 2004:528).

In 2000 with increased fear of disease transmission (below), *artificial provisioning ended*, though the impact is not assessed. In 2010 there were about 90 resident researchers, staff, local field assistants, and their families (Parsons et al. 2015:3, 8), compared to slightly over 100 chimpanzees (Wilson 2012:360).

Little is published about tourism. Attracting tourists already was a goal in 1971 (Teleki 1981:319). By 1992, it merited a 72-page guide to the Park (Bygott 1992). In the 1980s habituation aimed to establish Mitumba as the tourist center, but its rugged terrain and dwindling chimpanzee population squelched that, so tourism continued to focus on Kasakela (Mjungu 2010:10–11).

Tourism at Gombe was more limited than the out-of-control program at Mahale (Chapter 10). Accommodations have been limited, and in 2006 the high cost of a visitor permit kept numbers to about half of capacity, to 700–800 annually (Thaxton 2006a). Rarely did more than one group of tourists visit chimpanzees per day, and sometimes none at all (Lukasik-Braum and Spelman 2008:735, 736). Yet by 2006, on most days, Kasakela chimpanzees were treated to a tourist visit. A 2020 Internet search of tourism/Gombe/chimpanzee found many visitor plans, from day trips to five days in the Park, with no mention of quarantine. Did the increasing human presence inside the Park affect chimpanzees' behavior? Unknown, although captivity studies indicate that more and different human observers correlates with more aggressive acts between chimpanzees.

Habitat Destruction

Farming spread around Gombe in the 1980s and 1990s, with refugees from Burundi and then from Zaire (Collins and Goodall 2008:159; Goodall 2003:80). In 1984 and 1987 chimpanzees abducted and killed human infants somewhere in the Gombe area, circumstances unknown (Fallow 2003:2).[2]

Immigration accelerated over the 1990s. Population growth doubled, from 2.4% annually up to 1988, to 4.8% by 2001. The surrounding Kigoma region went from 648,441 people in 1976, to 854,817 in 1988, and 1,674,046 in 2002 (Pintea et al. 2011:241). On the Lake Shore, just north of the Park, the village of Mwamgongo by 2010 swelled to a town of 5,000 (Parsons et al. 2015:3).

Chimpanzee habitat loss proceeded apace. From 1979 to 1991, surrounding deforestation averaged 87.5 hectares per year. For 1991 to 2003 it went to 171 hectares/year. By 2003, only scattered patches remained of what had been forest connecting Gombe Park to chimpanzee areas further north (Pusey et al. 2007:627, 629, 631; Pintea et al. 2011:237).

In the middle 1990s Gombe became an island, cut off from chimpanzees elsewhere (Parsons et al. 2015:3). "New maps produced by Gombe researchers clearly show that it has become a 13.5-square-mile patch of forest surrounded by farms and denuded hillsides" (Goodall 2003:80). Mitumba lost much of its former rangeland, yet still used ridge-top forests to leave and re-enter the Park, foraging in remaining forest patches and on crops. To judge their original territory from those positional sightings, Mitumba's total range had been 19–25 km^2, of which only 12 km^2 was protected inside the Park. Chimpanzees to the south of the Park were eliminated even earlier between 1976 and the late 1980s (Goodall 1989:360). To the east, those of the Rift community were "displaced or killed . . . sometime after 1972" (though that same source has them on a map labeled 1975–1992) (Pintea et al. 2011:233; Williams 1999:3, 10).

Conservation

Alarmed by these trends, the Jane Goodall Institute in 1994 began an integrated conservation and development project, the Lake Tanganyika Catchment Reforestation and Education Project, TACARE. One goal was to foster local interest in long-term

---

[2] This was not the first chimpanzee attack on humans in the Gombe area. Three (two on infants) occurred before Goodall first arrived (Goodall 1986:282–283; Thomas 1961:37). That tells us humans were in places where chimpanzees lived, but also highlights that we know nothing about human disturbance prior to Goodall's work.

conservation, but population growth overwhelmed their efforts. Starting in 1997, the JGI working with the Nature Conservancy and funded by USAID, made strategic efforts to engage local people in habitat conservation and restoration (Pusey et al. 2007:631).[3] Still, the Park kept settlers out. LANDSAT imaging indicates *more* forest cover inside the Park in 1999 than in 1972, although not so much in southern ranges (Pintea et al. 2011:235; Pusey et al. 2007:629; Wilson 2012:361).

In 2005 the Jane Goodall Institute and Tanzania National Parks Authority began a new project with USAID to protect the greater Gombe ecosystem. This provided incentives to restore forest corridors to other chimpanzee areas, including a known community 12 km north of the Park. Results have been mixed. By 2009 13 villages had joined the effort and set aside 96.9 km^2 of forest for chimpanzee use, with village monitors, much of that within a North of Gombe Wildlife Corridor. Conservation and land use issues are addressed at multiple levels, from village to national. Yet tree cutting, land clearing, and new houses continue inside Village Land Forest Reserves, and illegal harvesting of some food trees remains a problem even inside Park borders. Hopeful signs are that chimpanzee nests are found even in highly impacted areas, and two unknown females appeared in the Park after 2011 (Pintea et al. 2011:236, 238, 243; Walker et al. 2018:3; Wilson et al. 2020:6).

Habitat suffered a severe setback in 2004. Fires are not rare at Gombe, often spreading in from people outside. The scrubby miombo woodlands found throughout the Park, especially in the south, are adapted to low-intensity burning (Pintea et al. 2011:235). But after local fires in June and July, a great blaze swept through in August 2004, charring half the Park, with the south most affected (Wilson et al. 2005:35). Whether or not people started it, chimpanzees not penned in by farming could forage elsewhere until regrowth. No longer.

Fire wasn't the only subsistence problem. Many of the once-cultivated oil palms, a Gombe staple, died off in the 2000s (Pintea et al. 2011:240–241). Post-provisioned chimpanzees experienced diminishing food availability, especially after 2004. Those would be especially violent years.

Human Assaults

Poaching is an enormous problem for primates across Africa. Often chimpanzees are caught and mutilated "accidentally" by wire snares set for other animals. Poaching hit Gombe in the late 1990s, after more Congolese settled nearby. Unlike local Tanzanians, they both ate and traded in wild game. Surveys of the Kalande range in later 1998 encountered "snares, hunters, hunting dogs, local villagers fleeing from

---

[3] TACARE Project staff quickly learned that community buy-in was essential for success in conservation activities. Therefore, TACARE added agriculture, health, social infrastructure and community development, and clean water components to the range of interventions under the project. Activities included microcredit schemes for community groups, education for girls, introduction of fuel-efficient stoves, environmental education in primary and secondary schools, family planning, water services, and HIV mitigation measures (Pintea et al. 2011:242–243).

inside the Park, and the case of a dead male chimpanzee found without his hands and genitals." Semiautomatic gunfire was sometimes heard at night (Greengrass 2000a; 2000b).

Locals attacked Mitumba and Kalande chimpanzees when they left the Park to forage. "Crop raiding" is another major issue across Africa, resulting in many dead apes (Hockings and McLennan 2012). Kalande chimpanzees frequently left the Park, using two gullies to reach villages up to 3 km south and 1 km east, where they munched on palm nuts, mangos, and bananas. This was former Kalande range cleared for firewood and charcoal, which was especially painful because "both food quality and quantity in the Kalande's range is much poorer than in either of the other two communities in the Park" (Greengrass 2000). Two chimpanzees were found dead in their nests near one village in 1998 or 1999. A decomposing female was found two valleys south of the Park, just when a chimpanzee infant was offered for sale from a village along the southern border. By the late 1990s, Kalande was a bad place to live, and some of their chimpanzees may have gone off outside the Park (Greengrass 2000). Mitumba had it bad too. Rumor had it that three males were deliberately killed (Mjungu 2010:23; Pusey et al. 2007:628).

Information about population and resources dries up by the mid-2000s. One brief note (Langat 2019) indicates continuing human population growth and forest loss for charcoal and small-holder palm oil production. The conservation corridors to other chimpanzee areas are in poor shape, with farms inside them. Gombe researchers and others developed a new chimpanzee conservation plan for Tanzania (TAWIRI 2018); and the Jane Goodall Institute encouraged nearby villages to set aside small forest patches for chimpanzees. With only that information, all that can be said about all the later deadly attacks is that they occurred during times of continuing human disruption.

All these disruptive trends combined—intensifying research, tourism, habitat destruction around the Park, mutilating snares, and deliberate killings characterize the post-"war" years—got worse over time. But population losses may have worked against actual resource scarcity, with most of that loss due to new diseases.

Disease

"[D]eath associated with observable signs of disease [is] the leading cause of mortality" at Gombe (Lonsdorf et al. 2016:1). From the 1966 Gombe polio epidemic it was suspected that human diseases had deadly effects among chimpanzees. Little was done about it for many years (Pusey et al. 2007:630). Janet Wallis, the director of Chimpanzee Research at Gombe from 1990 to 1994, coauthored a highly critical article (Wallis and Lee 1999:805, 808; and see Lonsdorf et al. 2006; 2011), saying that neither tourist programs nor researchers took necessary measures to prevent transmission of disease to chimpanzees. The farmers and fishermen around Gombe are another possible source of infection.

The general danger of anthropogenic disease was confirmed when deadly viruses at Tai were found to be of human origin (Kondgen et al. 2008). One author with 14 years of data calls for a new way of thinking about anthroponosis.

[D]isease dynamics are notoriously nonlinear. And in nonlinear dynamical systems, emergent population patterns are not simple additive sums of individual behaviors. Rather, relatively simple behavior by individuals results in complex, often nonintuitive patterns at the population or community level. (Walsh 2008:719)

His illustration: simultaneous death of multiple infants leads to reproductive synchronization of their mothers, which leads to high gregariousness when new offspring reach the peak of playfulness three years later, and that leads to higher potential of disease transmission. (Could that relate to the dearth of cycling females at Gombe in the early 1970s, which encouraged Kasakela males to roam further afield, and into violence?)

Emerging Infectious Diseases

Diseases of obviously human origin are not the only pathologies afflicting Gombe chimpanzees. They also carry SIVcpz, similar to human HIV. Usually, chimpanzees infected with SIV do not show AIDS-like symptoms (Wilson et al. 2005:5). However some Gombe chimpanzees do, and infection contributes to increased mortality (Keele et al. 2009). From 2002 and 2009, 12.7% of Mitumba chimpanzees and 12.1% of Kasakela were SIVcpz positive. Kalande was much higher with 46.1% incidence. Investigators surmise that early losses at Kalande were due to afflictions just described, but that some of the later mortality was contributed to by SIVcpz (Rudicell et al. 2010:10).

A different disease since 2002 is "skinny male syndrome," characterized by rapid deterioration, sudden weight loss, and weakness. It contributed to Goblin's death at 40 in 2004; and debilitated Beethoven before he disappeared in 2002. Frodo had it, falling from alpha, but he recovered, as did Kris and Apollo.

In response, the Gombe Stream Research Center began to actively monitor chimpanzee health, performing necropsies in collaboration with several universities (Lonsdorf et al. 2016; Wilson et al. 2005:6–7, 17). Necropsies revealed high infection by a parasitic nematode *Oesophagostomiasis*, associated with weight loss and other symptoms. Infection is "thought to occur via ingestion . . . within contaminated water, soil, or food" (Terio et al. 2018:2, 8).

SIVcpz and *Oesophagostomiasis* are not of human origin. Yet the question arises, how and why did they reach high levels of infection recently? Alternatively, high levels of infection may have been there all along, asymptomatic. (Testing from excreta samples began only in 2000 [Keele et al. 2009:3].) Could human disturbance contribute to either their spread or manifestation? Sure.

For example, another intestinal parasite, "*Cryptosporidium* is of special concern in this chimpanzee population, as SIVcpz illness may be complicated by *Cryptosporidium* co-infection" (Parsons et al. 2015:3). In humans, "cryptosporidiosis was one of the original AIDS-defining illnesses and as such was associated with an increased risk of death compared to other AIDS-defining illnesses" (O'Connor et al. 2011:549). The combined rate of infection among Gombe (nonhuman) primates was 16%. "[F]indings reinforce the notion that habitat overlap and anthropogenic disturbance increase the risk of interspecies transmission between wildlife, humans, and livestock and that transmission can occur both via direct physical contact with ingestion of contaminated feces, and by indirect exposure via a shared (potentially contaminated) watershed" (Parsons et al. 2015:8).

That is consistent with understandings of emerging infectious diseases (EIDs). Forest clearing is associated with host switching of parasites and pathogens (Hoberg and Brooks 2015; Weiss and McMichael 2004; Yale et al. 2013). Two-way transmissions between primates and humans are of central concern (Chapman et al. 2005; Nunn and Alitzer 2006). When a new illness and a newly debilitating illness appear simultaneously, in a place experiencing extensive anthropogenic changes, suspicion of connection is warranted.

How These Afflictions Dis-Balanced Gombe Groups

All of the above taken together had massive demographic impact. Each community suffered losses at different times. The respiratory infections fell like bombs. In 1987, Kasakela lost 14 chimpanzees in one, shrinking them—other things included—from 57 to 40. Kalande numbered 60–80 individuals at this time. Although this created a great imbalance in power, nothing suggests renewed territorial pressure from Kalande (Nutter 1996; Pusey et al. 2007:627; Williams et al. 2002:351; Wilson et al. 2004:528). By 1992, Kasakela recovered to 45, with 12 adult and subadult males, in a territory of 18 km^2 (= 2.5/km^2) (Stanford 1995:578).

In 1997 Kasakela endured a debilitating epidemic of scabies, or sarcoptic mange. Three infants died. It was first thought to be from surrounding people. Microscopic examination showed the mite was not a human parasite, although it could be from their cattle (Wallis and Lee 1999:807, 810–811; Williams et al. 2008:773).

In 2000 respiratory infection killed two of Kasakela. That led to terminating provisioning to reduce risk of disease transmission (Pusey et al. 2007:630; Williams et al. 2008:773). In 2003, the Jane Goodall Institute proposed a comprehensive list of guidelines to prevent researchers from introducing diseases, including a five- to seven-day quarantine before beginning to follow primates (Collins 2003). No requirement of tourist quarantine is indicated.

Neighbors

Mitumba fared even worse. When habituated in the later 1980s, they were estimated at no more than 31, far fewer than expected, suggesting that they already lost members (Wilson 2012:370). In 1996, a respiratory infection killed up to 11,[4] including a female, Rafiki, and her new twins. Also dead were "the alpha male and his primary lieutenants. With only one adult male surviving, it is unlikely the Mitumba community

---

[4] Elsewhere this drop is said to go from 25 to 20 (Wilson 2012:370).

will recover" (Wallis and Lee 1999:806, 823, and see Mjungu 2010:24). Wallis and Lee (1999:810) suspect that the infection came from researchers or Park personnel.

Yet Mitumba stabilized around 20 for a decade and a half (Pusey at al. 2007:627–628; Wilson 2012:361), numbering 25 in 2011 (Parsons et al. 2015:3). They were greatly outnumbered by Kasakela, and that affected intergroup relations. A very practiced observer makes the connection squarely: habitat loss and other human impacts reduced Mitumba numbers, and that encouraged Kasakela encroachments (Mjungu 2010:2, 29). But in a few years Mitumba grew "and subsequently recovered a substantial portion of their range from the Kasakela chimpanzees" (Mjungu et al. 2016).

Kalande's history was even more destructive. They were never fully habituated, and researchers looked for them or their signs. Sightings sharply decreased in the mid-1990s. A nest census—chimpanzees make a new tree nest to sleep in every night—indicated that the numbers dropped to 20–30 individuals by late 1999. One cause was poaching (Greengrass 2000). Closer observation put Kalande at 28–36 in 2002, falling to 14–18 in 2009. "In 2002 alone, six to ten individuals died, leaving the community with only a single adult male" (Rudicell et al. 2010:3–4).

Beginning in 1998, accelerating in 2002, and perhaps pushed by the fire that hit Kalande particularly hard, adult females disassociated from Kalande to join Kasakela. At least 15 Kalande individuals emigrated to Kasakela. "Many" were females. Three were mothers with offspring. Whether any older males went over is not clear. Seven additional chimpanzees seemed to be "moving between the two communities." This brought Kalande down to a low point of eight full-time members—with "a maximum of 1 adult male" (Murray et al. 2007:26)—against Kasakela's 62, (plus seven alternating) (Pusey et al. 2007:627–628).[5] Only two comparable "mass" female transfers have been noted elsewhere in Africa, at Mahale and Budongo.

Although various factors had negative effects, human impact in general was the main cause of drastic population losses among Kasakela's neighbors. An overview (Pintea et al. 2011:239) by leading researchers including Anne Pusey, Michael Wilson, and Jane Goodall concludes: "Habitat loss outside the park along with disease and killing by people were thought to be the major causes of the decline in numbers of the Mitumba and Kalande communities." Gombe Park had gone from 120–150 chimpanzees in the 1960s, to 96–100 in 2013. Data from 2005 to 2012 put Kasakela at 45–62, Mitumba at 19–29, and Kalande at 5–10 (Lonsdorf et al. 2016:3–5).

Kasakela's Big Expansion

Kalande's demographic collapse transformed its relations with Kasakela. As their numbers fell in the later 1990s, Kalande withdrew from northern ranges. Kasakela then moved in to this vacuum, "without meeting any resistance." By 1998, Kasakela added nearly two kilometers. By 2000 they were feeding in the Nyasanga valley, once Kalande's core. Kasakela's territory reached "its largest since records began in the early 1960s" (Greengrass 2000).

---

[5] A later study by Rudicell et al. (2010:4–5) estimated that 11 Kalande individuals relocated to Kasakela or Mitumba.

But note well for future discussions of adaptation: Kasakela moved into largely vacated land, rather than displacing prior residents by force. Acquisition of females derived from human disruption, not intergroup conflict.

This concludes the human impact overview, from the early 1980s until information peters out in the late 2000s. With the exception of the 1987 epidemic in Kasakela, the general picture is of human harm gradually increasing into the middle 1990s, but turning markedly worse from the late 1990s onward. The next task is to relate that to violence, first from 1984 to 1997, then from 1998 to 2013. With a few exceptions, 1984–1997 is a peaceable time. In 1998–2013, that changed.

(Relative) Peace Returns, 1984–1997

Post-Invasion Stability

After Kalande went back southward in 1983, Gombe's three unit groups mostly kept out of each others' way. Intergroup encounters plummeted. During 1980 tensions there were 13, but from 1984 to 1992, only zero to three per year (Williams et al. 2002:351). One of them is the videotaped calling led by Goblin. Goblin also led another patrol into Mitumba, which attacked a female and infant (Goodall 1990:98–99).

In 1984 and 1991 two Kasakela infants were suspected *internal* killings. In 1984 the Kasakela female Sprout's newborn disappeared, suspected as killed by others within Kasakela (Pusey et al. 2008:966) (Count 5-W-I-? 1984). In 1991 Kenitum's infant was thought injured during a within-group attack, and disappeared (Wrangham et al. 2006:23; Wilson et al. 2014a:EDT 4) (Count 4-W-I-M 1991). Nothing can be inferred from those two bare reports, other than they don't involve external conflict.

The dramatic exception to this generally peaceful time is violence against Goblin *within* Kasakela. My argument in Chapter 8 is that Goblin and another belligerent male, Frodo, were the main instigators of later Gombe violence. Understanding that requires the kind of biographical detail that only Goodall provided.

Goblin

Goblin began his political rise as junior ally to Figan, the mid-1970s alpha (Goodall 1986:418–425; 1990:138–149). At 13, barely out of adolescence, he displayed at senior males, temporarily toppling Figan. As Kalande encroached in 1979, in what became known as "the Great Attack," Figan and four others thrashed Goblin, leaving him "very badly wounded" (Goodall 1990:145). He backed off for a while, but in 1983–1984 rose to alpha.

Goblin was so aggressive that he frequently attacked human observers. Goodall was a particular target: "I went through a trying few years, never quite knowing when Goblin might charge out of the undergrowth, run up behind me, and slap me or even stamp on my back. There were times when I was quite black and blue" (Goodall 1990:140).

In September 1989 second-ranked Wilkie attacked Goblin (Goodall 1992:133). Both were visibly wounded, but Goblin got the worst of it, with severe bites all over and damage to his scrotum, which became infected. A television special shows Goodall sitting with feeble Goblin while he hid out, tenderly talking to him and feeding him bananas loaded with medicine (Home Box Office 1990). Finally he was anesthetized for treatment, and recovered. A few weeks later, most Kasakela males attacked him again. "[T]he gang attack led by Wilkie was by far the most savage intracommunity aggression that has been observed between males during our 30 years at Gombe" (Goodall 1992:139). Again, he was medically treated, and barely survived. For a while, Goblin became submissive. Wilkie became the alpha.

I count Goblin as one very likely killing, recuperated with medical attention (Count 3*-W-A-M, 1989). Contrary to the rival coalition reduction hypothesis (RCRH), these nearly deadly within-group attacks took out the fiercest "warrior" of Kasakela, right when it was greatly outnumbered by neighbors. The ferocity of attacks on Goblin suggests it was payback for his years of aggressive domination. This is the first illustration of internal gang violence directed at individuals with a history of bullying.

Goodall (1990:149–150) asks why Goblin was so unusually aggressive. Since she had seen him well-mothered, she leans toward a genetic explanation. That is possible of course. But learning does not stop with Mom. Goblin, as an adolescent, went along with the grown-ups on ten patrols from 1973 to 1975 (Goodall et al. 1979:24). If he were human, we would say he had a warrior upbringing.

Over three violent encounters, Goblin changed. In the attack on Godi, "Goblin kept out of the way." A year later, against Goliath, "Goblin repeatedly ran in, hit Goliath, and raced off again." Almost two years later, in the attack on Sniff, when the severely wounded victim vainly attempted to sit up, "Goblin at once approached and hit his nose several times" (Goodall 1986:506–510). There was much other violence during his tender years. Before he became a problem for his elders, they had shown him the way of violence. After Kalande's regression southward in 1984, most severe violence for the next nine years revolved around Goblin.

A Bad Patch, 1993–1994

In March 1993 Goblin led a large Kasakela excursion (10 adult males and four females) into Mitumba range. They encountered Rafiki with her female infant Rejea, and attacked. Prof killed Rejea with a bite to the stomach, then pulled her away from Rafiki. The adult males fed on the corpse. Rafiki seemed about to expire, but got up and ran away. Eleven days later she appeared to be healthy except for some cuts—illustrating why caution is warranted about inferring death from even very severe attacks. If Mitumba itself was not under study, Rafiki would be counted among the choir invisible. Goblin was the main eater of Rejea (Wilson et al. 2004:530–532). "The carcass was also used in a display" (Kirchoff et al. 2018:112) (Count 1-O-I-F 1993).

In 1993 Evered, at 41 years, died from an infected scrotal wound (Williams et al. 2008:772). Gombe researchers suspected the injury was inflicted by other Kasakela chimpanzees (Wilson et al. 2014a:EDT 3) (Count 4-W-A-M 1993).

The month before Kasakela chimpanzees killed Rafiki's infant, in February 1993, an enduring grudge match first played out within Kasakela. Three Kasakela females—Fifi, her daughter Fanni, and Gigi (who was drawn in by the others)—repeatedly attacked Kasakela female Gremlin, displaying, chasing, kicking, slapping, and punching. All the females involved except sterile Gigi had their own infants clinging to them throughout the action.[6] Some of Fifi's kicks seemed directed at Gremlin's infant. Yet two days later Gremlin was feeding in a tree with Fifi, Fanni, and others (Pusey et al. 2008:959–961).

Recall that Goodall believed Passion killed infants for meat. Fifi and Gigi were the two most accomplished female red colobus hunters, and Kasakela was at an unparalleled peak of hunting (Stanford et al. 1994:220–221; below). They too may have sought meat.

In the mid-1990s, Mitumba females hunted more than females of Kasakela (Gilby et al. 2015:5–8, 11; Gilby et al. 2017:90). In 1994, when some but not all of Mitumba were habituated, observers came upon a feeding group with both known and unhabituated individuals. Up a tree, an unknown female sat eating Rafiki's infant. Rafiki was wounded, limping with a dangling hand (Count 1-W-I-? 1994).[7] Whether or how much meat seeking may explain it, infant killings *by females* is a repeated occurrence at Gombe.

Lastly in this bad patch, in October 1994 the 10-year-old Kasakela orphan male Mel died. His "freshly killed body was observed with injuries consistent with intraspecific violence, but researchers were close by and had not heard the vocalizations such an attack would entail" (Williams et al. 2008:772). I count that as a possible (Count: 4-W-As-M 1994), and highlight their point about noise for later comparison.[8]

The key adjective for the few incidents of severe violence 1984–1997 is *internal*. This contradicts expectations of the Gombe vision. As human impact worsened in the late 1990s, so did violence. But even those incidents provide little support for the imbalance of power/rival coalition hypotheses (IoPH/RCRH). We start with the *best cases* for that perspective.

1998–2013, External Violence

In October 1998, some Kasakela silently entered the Kalande area. They found two Kalande mothers with infants and attacked. Goblin and Frodo both grabbed an infant. One pair got away, the other mother lost her daughter, which was eaten. Kasakela

---

[6] Sterile Gigi came into estrus every month. Never having a dependent child, her "behavior is very much like that of a male." She was seen to capture monkeys and other prey more often than any other female (Goodall 1986:66–67).

[7] Poor Rafiki gave birth to twins in March 1995, but all three died in the Mitumba respiratory epidemic of 1996 (Pusey et al. 2008:956–959).

[8] Williams et al. put this under death by "injury," and do not mention it in discussions of intraspecific attacks. Mel does not appear in Wrangham et al. (2006:22–23), but does in Wilson et al. (2014a:EDT 3) as inferred.

males ignored the mother once they had the infant (Wilson et al. 2004:533–535) (Count 1-O-I-F, 1998). Along with Rejea, that makes two external killings of *female* infants—not reducing rival males.

The Kalande Juvenile

In August 1998 four Kasakela males penetrated far south into the newly vacant Kalande northern range, visibly apprehensive about entering the space of their once formidable neighbor. Finally they descended into Nyasanga itself, where they encountered and caught a 10-year-old Kalande male (Wilson et al. 2004:536).

Frodo, then alpha, charged into the underbrush in attack, and inflicted severe and sustained violence. (Details of this attack are discussed in Chapter 8.) Two other adult males in the group mostly stayed out of it, then left. Only developmentally stunted Pax beat and bit the stunned juvenile. Then Pax left and the battered juvenile slowly got up and walked off.

At the peak of the frenzy, for minutes at a time Frodo had his mouth clamped on the juvenile's neck, pinning him to the ground. The young male could have been killed on the spot. He was not.

> Whether the wounds proved fatal remains unknown, though the observers agreed that the victim was unlikely to survive. The attack was comparable in duration and intensity to fatal attacks of the Kahama community during the 1970s. Nonetheless, some caution is warranted, as chimpanzees have shown remarkable resilience. (Wilson et al. 2004:538)

Such as Rafiki.

Wrangham et al. (2006:22) count this a "certain" intergroup killing; and Wilson et al. (2014a:EDT 1) record it as observed. In my tally, it is a "possible" (Count 4-O-J-M 1998). Since there are so few intergroup killings of grown males in the field record, the reader should mark the words of the original report. This young male may have lived. No other violent altercations between Kasakela and Kalande are reported after this point.

Territorial Jostling in the North

In the later 1990s Kasakela chimpanzees moved deeper into Mitumba range, following Mitumba's human-induced population drop (Mjungu 2010:2, 29). By early 2002 Kasakela males regularly entered the center of the Mitumba range (Wilson et al. 2004:542). Concern that accompanying researchers might embolden Kasakela chimpanzees led to a moratorium on follows beyond their usual range, 2000–2002. But Kasakela kept going in (2004:529–530).

Yet while Kasakela did that, in 2004 Mitumba traveled and fed into their south. "Despite repeated incursions from Kasakela, the Mitumba community also expanded their range, traveling into areas that they had not been observed visiting for many years" (Wilson et al. 2005:16). There is no suspicion of deadly violence between the two although they ran into each other frequently, and sometimes clashed.

From 1994 to 2007 when Kasakela had 11–13 grown males and Mitumba 2–5, there were 225 between-group encounters. 47 were observed by research followers on both sides. 210 were vocal, ten visual, and five physical. In most cases the groups avoided each other (Mjungu 2010:155–163), but on one occasion Kasakela attacked.

One physical clash is described. On December 18, 2004 (a few months after the great fire), about 27 Kasakela males and females, including Frodo, came upon 13 of Mitumba within their home ground. Mitumba mothers gathered their infants and juveniles and fled, but one female, delayed by getting her son, was caught and hit before running away. She had some small injuries to her lips. The two groups then exchanged calls (Wilson et al. 2005:17).

All together, this seems more like a pattern of conflicted coexistence, rather than a deadly struggle for territory.

Mitumba's Rusambo—A Classic Intergroup Killing?

There *might* be one deadly clash (Wilson et al. 2004:539–542). Since there are so very few instances of intergroup killing of grown males outside of the Four Year War and the Ngogo expansion, this incident merits careful scrutiny.

One interrupted follow of Kasakela involved Frodo and Goblin and five more adult males, entering the Mitumba range in June 2002. The next day Mitumba researchers found the body of the 12- to 14-year-old male Rusambo near the center of his range, about 140 m from trampled vegetation, with many visible wounds. They ask "What Killed Rusambo?" At the time, a leopard was known to be in the Park. "Researchers initially considered a leopard the most likely attacker" (Wilson et al. 2004:541). Then they changed their mind: Rusambo was most likely killed by the males of Kasakela. This revision supports the demonic perspective. So, what killed Rusambo?

The killing wound, a large hole in the neck, could come from either species. But the bruising, spread of small puncture wounds, "no obvious claw marks," the absence of wounds on the back, as if Rusambo were held down, are all consistent with chimpanzee violence. No leopard tracks were found, nor calls recorded (Wilson et al. 2004:542). But as detailed in Chapter 18's "crime scene investigation" at Loango, leopard claws usually are used to hold, rather than rake, leaving surface puncture wounds. Tracks and calls are hit or miss. Leopards prefer to pounce from behind, and so wounds usually are on the back. But if an animal turns, a leopard will go for the neck from the front. Inconclusive.

Another point counted for a chimpanzee attack is "dragging and final location of the carcass." Rusambo appears to have been dragged from an attack site, down a slope for about 140 meters, and left out in the open in a dry streambed by a trail. Being left exposed is the "opposite of what would be expected from a leopard attack. Leopards typically either take their prey up a tree or drag it ≤1600 meters to secluded place" (Wilson et al. 2004:542).

Yet while chimpanzees sometimes drag victims, never for such a distance. Wilson et al. (2004:542) reference dragging of the Kalande juvenile, but that was just pulling him around a small area. Since human observers were searching for or following chimpanzees that and the next day, it is quite possible that they scared a leopard away, mid drag. That fact that the victim was not eaten overnight is more supportive of chimpanzee attackers, but leopards do sometimes kill, leave, and come back some time later (Chapter 18).

Most of Rusambo's genitals were bitten or torn off—penis, testicles, and 70% of the scrotum. Loss of testicles was seen in two chimpanzee killings before Rusambo, and four after.[9] With that pattern, Rusambo's genital wounds are the strongest support for *pan*icide. Yet leopards often *begin* eating with the groin—so even this point is not definitive (see Chapter 18).

The main point *against* the chimpanzee-killer theory is lack of noise. Leopards are quiet, ambush predators, quickly breaking the neck or tearing the throat. The opposite is true when chimpanzees kill. "Observed intercommunity killings have included many loud vocalizations including screams, pant-hoot, roars and waa-barks," which go on for many minutes. In this case, neither research team reported any. That in itself would rule out a chimpanzee killing, except that:

> observers were ≥ 1 km from Rusambo's death site and the rugged terrain in the region limits transmission distance of calls. Moreover, a heavy rainfall lasted from 10:40 to 11:10 h; if the attack occurred during the rains, researchers would have had great difficulty hearing any distant chimpanzee call. No blood was near Rusambo's body, suggesting he was killed before or during the rain. (Wilson et al. 2004:542–543)

This may account for the lack of reported vocalizations, but only for half an hour. In 14 years of Mitumba research follows, the single deadly attack had to occur within a very small window. Plus, when it rains heavily, chimpanzees usually stop whatever they are doing. "Very heavy rain . . . tends to depress all activity; the chimpanzees sit huddled waiting for it to end" (Goodall 1986:335). It seems improbable that Kasakela killers would encounter Rusambo during heavy rain, much less gang attack him. In sum, Rusambo may have been killed by chimpanzees, and he may have been killed by a leopard.

If it was other chimpanzees, which chimpanzees? "The injuries inflicted on the Mitumba male together with circumstantial evidence suggests that Kasakela males killed him" (Wilson et al. 2004:523). But in subsequent years Mitumba killed several of their own males amid other internal violence (below); while there is no other instance of Kasakela severely attacking a grown Mitumba male.

Circumstantially, although the Kasakela chimpanzees were within a kilometer the day before the body was found, Rusambo was last seen in company of Mitumba, two days before, and 500 m from where his corpse was found (Wilson et al. 2004:539). The day of death is not known, so it could have happened then. If chimpanzees killed

---

[9] Luit, killed in Arnhem Zoo in 1978 (deWaal 1986:65), the Sebitole stranger killed in 1998 in Uganda's Kibale National Park (Muller 2002:118), two more in Kibale (Watts et al. 2006:167), and two in Tai (Boesch 2009:80–82).

Rusambo, it could be the home team. Given all the uncertainties, but to avoid appearance of undercounting, I mark this as a possible outside killing (Count 4-O-As-M, 2002).[10]

That ends Wilson et al.'s (2004:523) presentation of evidence in "support of the view that intergroup violence is a persistent feature of chimpanzee societies."[11] With the Kalande juvenile also downgraded to a possible, there is not a single very-likely-to-certain, intergroup, adult male killing at Gombe in the three-plus decades after the Four Year War. Not one.

Intergroup Attacks on Mothers and Infants

All the remaining noted (if not described) intergroup violence involves attacks on mothers and/or infants. In September 2005, "44 year old Patti was a Kasakela community member who was fatally attacked by Mitumba chimpanzees while on a consort in the Mitumba area" (Williams et al. 2008:771). The attack was observed (Wilson et al. 2014a:EDT 1) (Count 2-O-A-F 2005). Earlier, females had been killed in external attacks around the Four Year War. What is remarkable here is that old Patti was on a consort inside the Mitumba range. In that she was not unique.

As Kalande females transferred into Kasakela and Mitumba, some Kasakela females passed more time within the Mitumba range. In this intensely disrupted time, female group association seems in flux. One of those drifting more was Fifi, the only remaining pre-Goodall chimpanzee. "For most of the year she had been seen infrequently, having shifted her range to the remote northern valleys of Linda and Rutanga." Fifi and her 2-year-old were traveling with "northern mothers." She was seen once in August 2004, soon after the great fire, then not again (Wilson et al. 2005:11). Wilson et al. (2014:EDTs 1, 2) list her and child as suspected intergroup killings. Given her advanced age of 46, in a highly stressed environment, natural causes seem more likely (Count 5-O-A-F 2004; 5-O-I-F 2004).

In August 2006 a large, mixed Kasakela party traveling in the Mitumba range, heard Mitumba calls and went toward them in "stalking" way. They met and clashed. Although the action was not seen, female infant Andromeda was killed and recovered by Mitumba. She had multiple wounds, including punctures to the skull (Kirchoff et al. 2018:112–113; Mjumbu 2010:25–26, 45; Wilson 2013:368–269) (Count 1-O-I-F 2006) (reported as 2005 in Wilson et al. 2014a:EDT 2).

---

[10] Wilson and Wrangham (2003:373) count Rusambo as an "inferred" intracommunity killing; Wrangham et al. (2006:22) elevate it to "certain"; and Wilson et al. (2014:EDT 1) knock it back down to "inferred."

[11] However, Wilson et al.'s (2014a:EDT 1) indicates one other possibility. The 28-year-old Kasakela male Prof is tallied as a suspected killing by Kalande in 1998. Since this is not noted in any other publication, and since Kasakela was said to expand into Kalande territory without resistance, I suspect this notation expresses the standard assumption that a disappeared adult male has been killed (Count 5-O-A-M, 1998).

1998–2013, Internal Violence

Kasakela

Things were worse on the inside, starting with Fifi + Fanni again attacking Gremlin. In July 1998 Gremlin had 2-day-old twins. Mother Fifi—red colobus hunter—was heavily pregnant. Daughter Fanni had a clinging infant. They attacked, triggering chaos, including young sons and protective older males, and conciliatory gestures interspersed with displays and lunges. Fanni led the punching and grappling, and at one point grabbed for the twins. Gremlin protected them well. Eventually all walked off, and the three antagonists met without incident later that day (Pusey et al. 2008:962–964).

Act III came in January 2004. Gremlin appeared with another newborn. Fifi, with her own new infant, and Fanni approached hostilely. Then they all ran off. When observers caught up, "chimpanzees were screaming and charging and displaying in all directions." None seemed injured (Pusey et al. 2008:964). In April the Kasakela female Kipara appeared with injuries, her infant missing (Pusey et al. 2008:966). Wilson et al. (2014a:EDT 4) count this as an intracommunity killing (Count 3-W-I-M 2004).

Kasakela chimpanzees were under special stress by mid-2004, with skinny male syndrome, a particularly severe dry season (May–October), and smaller fires followed by the widespread blaze in August. Difficulty feeding during dry season contributed to the death of Goblin, suffering from skinny male syndrome (Wilson 2012:365). His death ended a particularly violent life path, but Frodo was still there to carry on violently.

In June 2004 an older infant died in a particularly strange way. Five Kasakela chimpanzees were feeding. Freud and female Tatiana engaged in a long mutual grooming bout, sometimes including her 3.5 yr son, Tofiki. Suddenly, Freud grabbed Tofiki from Tatiana's lap, ran away, and bit him in the head. Others recovered Tofiki, but over a few hours he lost function, and was never seen again. 3.5 years is older than any infanticide at Gombe. (Murray et al. 2007:28–30) (Count 1-W-I-M 2004)

It fits no profile, but does fit into a time of psychological disturbance and status-related killing (Chapter 8).

Mitumba

In December 2004 Mitumba chimpanzees killed one of their senior males, Vincent, formerly Mitumba's alpha. After being injured in a fall, he was deposed, then disappeared for some months. Excited by the calls of a hunt, he tried to rejoin the group, but was attacked and killed by the two other Mitumba adult males, Rudi and Edgar (Kirchoff 2019:76) (Count 1-W-A-M 2004).

Contrary to the idea that it requires several males to kill an adult male, here just two did the job. "The death of Vincent leaves Mitumba with only two adult males, and thus extremely vulnerable to intercommunity attack from the much larger Kasekela community" (Wilson et al. 2005:12). Vincent's death exemplified the internal killing of an ex-alpha, although how much of a bully he had been is not reported.

In 2005 juvenile Mitumba male Ebony was found dead with wounds indicating a chimpanzee attack. Researchers suspected Rudi did it (Mjumbu 2010:25–26) (Alone?) (Count 3-W-J-M 2005). Rudi became alpha (Massaro et al. n.d. 3).

Back to Kasakela

We come now to one of the densest listings of observed-to-suspected violence, as of this writing known mostly and merely by entries in EDTs 3 and 4 of Wilson et al. (2014a). In 2007 both Schweini and Imani lost an infant, suspected as internal infanticides (Count 5-W-I-M 2007, 5-W-I-? 2007). In 2010 alpha Ferdinand severely attacked 28-year-old Kris, who subsequently disappeared (Massaro et al. n.d. 3) (Count 4-W-A-M 2010).

The years 2012–2013 saw another surge in internal violence. In 2012 Eliza's infant, and in 2013 the infant Tarima, were seen killed (Count 1-W-I-F 2012, 1-W-I-F 2013). Also in 2012, what looked like a deadly internal attack on an infant by a female was interrupted by a male (Pusey and Schroepfer-Walker 2013:5) (Not counted). Ferdinand, who reigned by himself without allies, was the primary culprit (Mjiungu and Collins n.d.).

> [T]he alpha male of the Kasekela community (Ferdinand) killed an infant (Tarime), directed apparent infanticide attempts at three others (Tabora, Shwali, and Fifi), and led an attack on a mother (Eliza) during which the mother's newborn infant was snatched, killed and eaten by females (Sandi and Sparrow). These attacks are unusual in several respects. First, few other Gombe males have committed within-group infanticides, much less made multiple attempts within a single year. Second, genetic evidence indicates that Ferdinand is the father of at least one of the infants he targeted (Tabora). Third, Ferdinand has been alpha males for five years, during which he has frequently monopolized matings with fertile females (Mjungu et al. 2014).

In 2016 several males attacked Ferdinand, and might have killed him, but he got away and fled (Mjungu and Collins n.d.).

The final recorded Kasakela death, in November 2013, might seem like poetic justice—Frodo got his. Though the table only notes him as a suspected internal killing (Wilson et al. 2014a:EDT 3), a news account adds: "He was found dead in November 2013. A necropsy concluded that he had died from an apparent bite to his genitals that had become infected" (Morin 2014:3) (Count 4-W-A-M 2013).

Mitumba Again

Moving forward, internal violence within Mitumba also posed far more danger than external threat. In 2005–2012 health monitoring found they had more visible wounds than Kasakela. "This may relate to the fact that during the study period, there was more intense intracommunity aggression in Mitumba, as well as several intercommunity interactions during which Kasakela chimpanzees initiated aggressive interaction against Mitumba" (Lonsdorf et al. 2016:15). A later study, however, had the two about the same in total aggressive acts. However, Mitumba excelled in killings.

Edgar repeatedly challenge Rudi and became alpha in 2008. Rudi was positive for SIVcpz and disappeared in 2013, presumed dying of the illness.

> Edgar injured three other males in severe attack. Forest (2012), Apple (2015) and Fansi 2017. Forest and Apple disappeared soon after the attacks; we infer they died from injuries inflicted by Edgar. In 2017, observers found Edgar displaying near Fansi's freshly killed body; we infer Edgar was the killer. (Massaro et al. n.d. 3)

(All three are identified as weaned, but without ages. I count them as adults, but they may be younger) (Count 4-W-A-M 2012; 4-WA-M 2012; 2-W-A-M 2017). Thus four possible-to-certain killings (one shared with Rudi) are attributed to Edgar. Possible explanations are discussed in Chapter 8.

Summing up 1984–2017

Combining all the incidents discussed in this chapter, the 14 less disturbed years of 1984 to 1997 saw a total of six possible-to certain killings, .42/year. The 20 more disrupted years from 1998 to 2017 saw 16, or .8/year. More deadly violence 1984–2017 is within group (16) rather than between (6). For grown individuals—more the focus of demonic perspective—1984–2017 saw 13, and infants 9 (this includes the two recovered-with-care attacks on Goblin as one likely killing).

8
Interpreting Gombe Violence

Gombe is the type case for chimpanzee "war," and has the greatest evidentiary record of any research site. Chapter 8 compares Gombe evidence to the differing theoretical expectations detailed in Part I. It gets complicated, but the essence of science is evaluating theory against evidence, and neither is simple. We start, however, with a couple of simple points. Then I go by the numbers to evaluate adaptive expectations. They do not go well. Gombe, it is said, provides the best evidence in all field observations that sequential killings confer adaptive benefits. The claim of adaptation is carefully scrutinized, which brings in hunting, nutrition, and reproduction. The rest of Chapter 8 summarizes findings from my own perspectives, beginning with human impact on resource competition. Extensive discussions to finish the Gombe narrative focus on status-related display and payback violence, mostly internal, which brings in belligerent personalities, how they got that way, and the destabilizing impact of the intensifying human impact described in Chapter 7.

The Simple Points

One original claim of the Gombe paradigm is that internal violence is relatively mild, compared to between groups. So it once seemed, but no longer. "Though worries continued that males from the large Kasekela community would attack and kill members of other communities, the most violent attacks actually observed took place within communities" (Wilson et al. 2005:17, and below).

Another simple point is that females can be as deadly as males. They do not lead attacks on adult males, but assault other females and sometimes kill their infants. "[O]ur observations show that female chimpanzees can exhibit severe aggression, similar to that of males" (Pusey et al. 2008:970). It remains true, however, that males far more frequently inflict severe violence.

The IoPH, RCRH, and Demonic Expectations

Does the IoPH Explain Behavior?

A core claim of the imbalance of power hypothesis (IoPH) is that when multiple males encounter an outside male alone, that is both *necessary* and *sufficient* for them to kill. That was based on the Four Year war. It was not supported thereafter.

The 1976–2007 data records 360 intergroup interactions (Gilby et al. 2013:65). Projecting that up to 2017, when the record of killings ends, encounters might approach 500—plenty of opportunity for killing. After the 1970s "War" years, there is only one certain (Patti) and two possible intergroup adult killings (Kalande juvenile and Rusambo), even as group sizes were very unequal. Killing is not an automatic response to opportunity.

A tenet of the IoPH is "larger communities have a competitive advantage over smaller communities" (Wilson 2013:374). That smaller parties give way before larger ones is ethologically normal. But do greater numbers lead to territorial *acquisition*? Sometimes yes, but more often no. Yes, Kasakela eliminated smaller Kahama and then moved into its range. Then larger Kalande temporarily displaced Kasakela.

But no, in the early-mid 1970s Kalande did not move into greatly outnumbered Kahama's territory. After 1983 Kalande returned to its old haunts, although they still outnumbered Kasakela. From 1987 Kalande did not encroach on Kasakela after the latter lost many to a respiratory infection. In the late 1990s after Kalande numbers crashed, Kasakela moved into their vacated northern territory, but with little conflict. Kasakela did incur into Mitumba territory after the latter lost numbers, but contrary to expectations Mitumba also frequently went into Kasakela range, even though outnumbered. Numerical advantage only sometimes coincided with territorial acquisition.

RCRH, Reducing Relative Size of Outside Male Coalitional Strength

In the rival coalition reduction hypothesis (RCRH), "[t]he primary benefit of intergroup killing is thought to be the reduction of the coalitionary strength of rival communities. By reducing the fighting strength of a given community, males increase their chances of success in future battles with that community" (Wilson and Wrangham 2003:381). A given side's advantage in group conflict over food depends on how many males each side has.

That logic seemed compelling for the War and Invasion, two likely kills of outside adult males and three possibles (plus five hypotheticals), and none internal. But this imbalance reversed thereafter. From 1984 to 2017, for certain-to-possible grown males killings, Kasakela and Mitumba racked up 2 external and 11 internal. That makes the total of possible-to-certain adult male kills at Gombe, 7 between group vs. 10 within. What makes this more remarkable is that extreme internal attacks on Goblin, Vincent, and all the Mitumba males came when their groups were challenged by external encroachment. Kasakela males did not take advantage of their numerical superiority to kill Mitumba males (except possibly Rusambo), even though Mitumba males' own actions greatly reduced their power of males against Kasakela.

The IoPH/RCRH, however, might be buttressed by infant killings. "The imbalance-of-power hypothesis predicts that a primary benefit of intergroup infanticide is to reduce the future coalitionary strength of rival communities. To ensure the killing of future rivals rather than potential mates, attackers should kill male rather than female infants" (Wilson and Wrangham 2003:382). Facts contradict that. The three external infant killings (plus one suspected) post 1983 are *all* females. For all years at Gombe, there is one certain-to-possible male infant killing between group, and five within group.

Combining all ages and all times, certain-to-possible male killings are 8 between and 16 within group. Contra adaptationist theory, killings of males diminished the "home team" compared to rivals, by two to one.

The RCRH predicts that only males will be killed, while the resource competition hypothesis (RCH) expects both male and female victims (Wilson et al. 2004). For all times, certain-to-possible intercommunity killings are 8 males and 11 females. There were many additional severe attacks on foreign females. External attacks were not directed primarily at males.

All told, none of the RCRH expectations are supported by the total Gombe record.

Recruiting Females

Female acquisition is a central point in *Demonic Males*. This hypothesis requires emphasis here, because it is forgotten in later assessments (e.g., Wilson et al. 2014a).

> For a male-bonded chimpanzee community, conquered land can include not only a larger foraging area, but also new females.... So males of an expanding community can gain females, which means that male chimpanzees should want to expand their territory to the largest area they can defend. Evidence that they do so comes from Gombe, where the territory size of the Kasakela community varied in proportion to the number of adult males. (Wrangham and Peterson 1996:166)

With more data, not so. "There was no significant relationship between the number of adult males each year and community range size"; and "There was no relationship between community range size and either the number of resident adult females or the number of encounters with stranger females. Thus, males did not immediately gain access to more mates by expanding the size of the community territory" (Williams et al. 2004:529). After evaluation of various ideas of how external violence might augment male access to females, they conclude: "In fact, there is little evidence to support any of these hypotheses" (2004:524). (The later immigration of Kalande females was not a result Kasakela aggression, but of the collapse of Kalande itself). At Gombe violence was not used to gain females from outside, but to kill them or drive them away.

Across the board, expectations of the demonic perspective generally or of the IoPH/RCRH specifically, are either unsupported or contradicted by the total Gombe record. The next discussion goes to the fundamental neo-Darwinian question about lethal violence.

Is Gombe Killing Adaptive?

That, of course, is the big idea of adaptationist explanations of killing. Yet in all of field research on chimpanzees, *only two* times and places are claimed to show adaptive benefits resulting from external violence: the Ngogo expansion (Part IV), and post-Four Year War Gombe (e.g., Wilson 2012:374; Wilson and Wrangham 2003:380). The Ngogo claim is based solely on the fact that new rangeland was acquired and used.

Only Gombe provides before and after data series relevant to adaptation. It is intuitively plausible that expanded rangeland provides food benefits that elevate reproduction, especially in a drier and open environment like Gombe. If killing is adaptive, evidence should show up here. But going by evidence rather than intuition, that is not so clear.

Territory and Body Mass

Recapping territorial history, Kasakela lost southern rangelands when Kahama split off and closed them out around 1971. As Kahama numbers shrank, by 1975 Kasakela began using most of their range. By 1977 Kasakela had it all, though Kalande began encroaching northward in 1978. After Kasakela retreated, by 1981 their territory was the smallest ever. They began regaining southern range in 1982, and were back to their old maximum, including the Kahama area, in 1984. After that there is no narrative indication of territorial change until Kasakela expanded into ex-Kalande lands in the late 1990s, and started walking into Mitumba areas shortly thereafter.

Illustration 2.5 (Gilby et al. 2013:66) of range from 1976 to 2007 coincides with this narrative through the Invasion years, although it begins after the initial territory loss c. 1971. From 1986 to 1996, rangeland fluctuates above the 1977 level. It sharply increases in 1997, after Kalande and Mitumba's numbers dropped, and then generally remains greater than earlier years until data stops in 2007. Did expansions of range size result in measurable increases in health and reproductive opportunity?

Body mass was measured, with breaks, from 1968 to 2000 (see Illustration 2.4). Comparison of range size with body mass is possible from 1976 to 1985, and from 1991 to 1999. Only for 1976–1985 can this relationship be tied to territorial changes and intergroup conflicts.

Body mass spiked in 1976 as Kasakela used more Kahama range. Then it fell to previous levels in 1977, even though range size topped out in 1978. Body mass dropped from 1980 to 1983, which coincides with range retraction in front of encroaching Kalande. Mass rose a bit in 1984–1985, after Kalande went back south. Thus, 1976 to 1985 fairly matches body mass and range size, with noted exceptions. Then it gets confusing.

There is no body mass data 1986–1991. In 1992–1994, Kasakela seemingly enjoyed unobstructed access to the old Kahama range, yet contrarily, its measured range dropped into a trough, and contrary to that, body mass hit its highest plateau since the unrestricted provisioning years. Body mass fell off for 1997–1999, though slightly rebounding, even as Kasakela absorbed Kalande's rangeland and reached the largest territory ever recorded. So 1992–1999 shows little correspondence between known history, range size, and body mass.

In the whole record combined, there remains a statistically significant correlation of territory and body mass. "There is still considerable lack of fit around the linear regression, but ample evidence that annual body mass effects vary with range size," "the null hypothesis of no relationship . . . is soundly rejected, but the data do not fit a linear pattern well" (Pusey et al. 2005:19–20). Range size and body mass are related, but not tightly related, close from 1976 to 1985, not for 1992–1999.

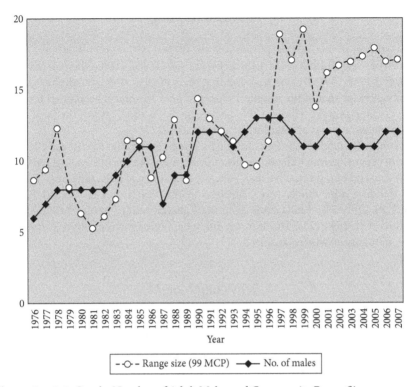

Illustration 2.5 Gombe Number of Adult Males and Community Range Size
Source: Gilby, I., Wilson, M., & Pusey, A. (2013). Ecology rather than psychology explains co-occurrence of predation and border patrols in male chimpanzees. *Animal Behaviour, 86*, 61–74.

Territory and Reproduction

Another data set is critical for adaptive claims. Williams et al. (2004:525, 528) cover 1975–1992, or the War/Invasion years and nearly a decade after that. They found a significant correlation of larger territory size, *three years after a mother gave birth*, with shorter interbirth intervals for females. The trend line among the scattered points goes from a roughly 6-year interbirth interval with a 5 km² range, to about 4¼-year interval with 13 km². More rangeland goes with shorter time between births. "By defending a large territory and excluding feeding competitors, males therefore appear to improve the reproductive success of resident females" (2004:530). They also found that with a larger range males pass more time in mixed-sex parties and are more likely to encounter a sexually swollen female.

This is *the strongest evidence in the entire observational record* that range increase through conflict, with or without killings, has a positive adaptative impact on reproduction. Unfortunately, the issue is not that simple. Another factor may affect body mass and reproductive health, which is not due to territorial expansion.

Increased Hunting

During the reproductively propitious years of 1975 to 1992, red colobus kills increased from 20 per year in 1982–1984, to 35 per year in 1987–1989. Then they soared to 90 in 1990, and 49 in 1991. During peak hunting years of 1990–1993, the number of hunts was about twice that of the middle 1970s, and *back then* meat accounted for 12% of hunters' caloric intake. Hunters killed between 16.8% and 32.9% of the local red colobus population per year (Stanford et al. 1994:218–225).[1]

The intuitive inference is that hunting increased in the later 1980s–early 1990s because of expansion into Kahama rangelands. Intuition may be misleading. Up through 1992—the end of reproductive data—the great majority of kills came from Kasakela's long-standing core range, (even during the Invasion from the South) (Goodall 1986:229). Only 7% of kills came from the Kahama valley (Stanford 1995:579, 586; Stanford et al. 1994:225). This hunting surge happened mainly *within Kasakela's old range*, not range newly (re)acquired.

Why Hunt More?

I argued that the 1970s surge of red colobus hunting was spurred by provisioning cutback with System E. But I don't suggest that nutritional shortfall is the *only* reason for surges in hunting behavior. Several factors can affect rate of hunts and kills. A factor of particular importance is the contribution of individual "impact hunters."

Gilby et al. (2015), using data from Kasakela, Mitumba, and Kanyawara of Kibale Park, show that when red colobus are encountered, specific individuals are most likely to go for them, which makes others more likely to join in. More hunts, more meat. At Kasakela, Figan and Apollo were impact hunters, but Frodo stood out among all.

Of 46 hunts in which he participated, Frodo initiated 40, or 87%. He had higher success in capturing monkeys than either Figan or Apollo (Gilby et al. 2015:8–9). Frodo would wade into a charging mob of colobus monkeys that sent other chimpanzees running (Boesch 1994:1142, 1147; Stanford 2001:101). Stanford et al. (1994:225) elaborate:

> [T]he most proficient hunter among the males in 1990–1991, the young adult male Frodo, reached adolescence and became a regular member of hunting parties since 1987. In 1990 and in 1992 Frodo was estimated to have killed nearly 10% of the entire red colobus population within the range of the Kasakela chimpanzees (estimated 40 kills per year) (Stanford et al. 1994:225).

Frodo hunted up to his death in 2013 (Gilby et al. 2015:7). That covers six years of the good reproduction period (1975–1992), four of the top five largest territory years

---

[1] Fourrier et al. (2008:506) calculate that this rate of hunting was unsustainable, and could extirpate red colobus where targeted.

(Gilby et al. 2013:66); and the second half of the high body mass measures (1991–1999)—a lot of covariation with the good adaptation years.

By catalyzing so many hunts from 1987 onward, Frodo probably elevated the nutritional level of Kasakela females. 10.6% of 1982–1991 kills were by females, compared to 4% in the 1970s. Even though a third of their kills were "immediately stolen by males" (Stanford et al. 1994:221; and see Gilby et al. 2017), females consumed more meat than previously. Meat consumption affects reproduction.

> [A]vailable data for Gombe support the meat-scrap hypothesis, in which the consumption of even small amounts of animal prey serves as a source of macronutrients such as fats, as well as vitamins and minerals that are limited or absent in most plant foods. Given the well-established effects of prenatal nutrient deficiencies on health outcomes in humans and in other animals, we hypothesize that pregnancy may be a critical period for dietary intake of nutrients such as omega-3 fatty acids, vitamin B_{12}, and minerals such as haem iron, sodium and zinc. (O'Malley et al. 2016:22, references omitted)

This suggests a connection between hunting and quicker return to estrus cycling—*coincident with but not due to range expansion*. This could be self-reinforcing. More swollen females mean more males in larger parties, and more hunters participating means more kills (Stanford et al. 1994:223–225).

It is common sense that larger territory—>more food—>increased reproduction. Common sense is not always wrong, but in this—the #1 demonstration of the adaptive killing—it does not carry the day. Evidence for adaptation is Frodo-related, not a clear outgrowth of territory expansion.

Internal Sexual Competition

Yet Gombe researchers recently undercut that common sense. The internal killings especially at Mitumba gave rise to a contradictory alternative. Massaro et al. (n.d.:3) endorse the generalization, and record that Mitumba had a larger range with more males. But then males killed several males. They have a salvage hypothesis.

"Because killing male group members reduces ability to hold territory, such killings must be offset with substantial reproductive benefits to be adaptive." In support, they find that male killers especially at Mitumba had a greater monopoly on mating and paternity after killing other males. It was Edgar in 72% of observed mating. That is not surprising when there is often just one sexually available female, and a *pan*icidal alpha male.

They note, however, that such killings also occurred in the large communities of Ngogo, Mahale, and Budongo, and suggest that other factors may be involved there (Massaro et al. n.d.:7). Other questions arise if one considers cancelling out the posited increased reproductive health of females with larger ranges; that (as will be seen) parous females often abandon groups with very few males; and that solo males are theoretically very vulnerable to outsiders. If evidence flatly contradicts one hypothesis, there is always another reproductive conjecture that could fit.

Resource Competition and the Human Impact Hypothesis

HIH Predictions Confirmed

Turning to my own hypothetical expectations, the RCH + HIH holds that intense, immediate conflict over preferred foods fosters deadly intergroup violence; and that such intensified competition is usually because of human impact. Gombe in the first half of the 1970s is Exhibit A. Outside deforestation and bananas increased numbers and competition, which went critical with drastic curtailment of provisioning, followed by separation and "war."

And conversely, if human impact *did not* lead to severe intergroup food competition, *deadly intergroup violence is not expected*. From the early 1980s to the early 2000s, resource competition did not increase because Park habitat loss was outpaced by demographic decline, from 120–150 in the 1960s to less than 90 after 1996 (Pintea et al. 2011:239; Wilson et al. 2005:9, 37; Wilson et al. 2015:10, 37). If Kalande and Mitumba had stayed at their old numbers while losing so much territory beyond Park boundaries, the later history of Gombe "war" might be very different. By 2010, the total Park population recovered to 101–105 (Wilson 2012:360). Good news, but it suggests some, but not severe, food competition between groups. As expectable then, hostile intergroup encounters happened, "violence between two communities that otherwise would not have come into contact with each other, but are now competing over the same area of forest. *Stress has also become an issue*, making the chimpanzees even more susceptible to conflict and disease" (Thaxton 2006b:2–3, my emphasis). But most killing was *internal*.

Disturbed and Dangerous?

In bloody 2004–2006, external kills were roaming Patti and her infant (with Fifi and her daughter hypotheticals); inside killings were Vincent, Ebony, Tofiki, and Kipara's infant (plus two hypothetical infanticides in 2007). A total of six killings ("1–3") in three years makes this one of the highest rates of *pan*icide in all panology. Is human disturbance implicated?

Starting in the late 1990s but intensifying by the middle 2000s, Gombe chimpanzees lived in a human-impacted pressure cooker. Their heightened violence followed anthropogenic habitat, food, and population losses. Gombe chimpanzees had to cope with drastically changed demographic balances, more disease, and more direct human intrusion by researchers, staff, tourists, and locals. We cannot gauge the psychological effect of all this.

When in 2004 Freud killed his grooming partner's son with a bite to the head, Murray et al. (2007:32, 34) dismiss pathology, yet found no adaptive explanation, since the 3½-year-old could not possibly be a reproductive competitor. Seven years after his fall from alpha, this does not even make sense as display violence. If that sudden outburst is not abnormal, what would be? With the tightening screws of anthropogenic changes, psychological disturbance is a reasonable background supposition from the early 2000s onward, although potentially explanatory contextual description drops to nil long before 2017. But what a stunning contrast to the chimpanzees Goodall encountered in the 1960s.

That's one thing—in what may be *overdetermined* internal violence. Another thing is the developed personality of Gombe's adult male generation, particularly the leaders.

Leaders, Learning, and Violence

Social theory gravitates to properties of social groups, yet small group dynamics are greatly affected by individuals. Much later Gombe violence revolves around Goblin and Frodo. We saw Goblin's penchant for violence develop during the Four Year War. But Frodo's life history opens a fascinating possibility: transgenerational effects of human disturbance. The Four Year War generation grew up with violence. This is imaginable only because Goodall's holistic and humanistic descriptions allow us to follow individuals over time.

Bad Frodo

How bad? In May 2002 alpha Frodo encountered a local woman with two children on a public footpath through the Park. He seized the 14-month-old girl, killed and partially ate her (Kamenya 2002).

Media went wild, debating whether Frodo should be killed, or "tried for murder" (BBC 2004). BBC's "The Demonic Ape" dramatizes the attack, twice. Fallow (2003) suggests it was just an extension of normal hunting behavior. After all, Frodo was the greatest red colobus hunter of all time. But Frodo's hunting prowess itself reflected his personality: Frodo was exceptionally aggressive.

Chimpanzees vary greatly in personality (Freeman and Gosling 2010; Massen et al. 2013; Weiss et al. 2015; 2017), with genetic and neuroanatomical substrates, but affected by early childhood experience (Latzman et al. 2014; Latzman et al. 2015a; 2015b). Some individuals are much more aggressive than others. That affects status competition and domination.

Chimpanzee studies emphasize agonistic dominance and display (de Waal 1982; 1989b; and see Goodall 1986:425–429). Yet affiliation with mutual grooming and sharing is another way of building support. Comparing Gombe's three alphas from 1992 to 2001—Wilkie, Freud, and Frodo—Frodo was unusually belligerent (Foster et al. 2008:137).

> By 1995 he was the second-ranking male behind his elder brother, Freud. Frodo was noteworthy in part for his size. Even as a 14-year-old he was the largest male in the community, dwarfing Wilkie and Goblin.... When displaying he charged into, rather than around, researchers and brutalized the easily dominated younger chimpanzees in the community. He was nicknamed *jambazi* (the rogue) by the Tanzanian researchers for his tendency to hit, kick, and charge them. (Stanford 1998a:48)

The BBC paints a vivid picture of Frodo.

NARRATOR: Of all the demonic males there have been at Gombe, the most demonic is Frodo.

GOODALL: Frodo was aggressive from a very small age. When he was about three years old he started throwing rocks ... Frodo was a real bully.

A favorite target was Goodall herself.

NARRATOR: In 1998 Frodo deposed his own brother, and became the dominant male. From the start it was clear that Frodo would rule through brute force. (Pause) There was a twist to his aggressive strategies that impressed all the other chimps. He attacked Jane Goodall herself.

GOODALL: Frodo singled me out. None of us know why. But from very early on he singled me out, and he didn't just push me over, he would come back and then stamp on me again, maybe three times in a row. And sometimes he dragged me. He's dragged other people. He's stamped on other people. But he had this special expression on his face for me. We've all noticed it. And we don't know why. (BBC 2004)

One of his human victims was visiting *Far Side* cartoonist Gary Larson. (Not funny.) "A year later Frodo jumped on Goodall and thrashed her head so thoroughly that he nearly broke her neck. In the wake of that incident Goodall has consistently refused to enter Frodo's territory without a pair of bodyguards along for protection" (Fallow 2003:2). That bad.

Why So Bad?

Frodo's great size enabled his brutality. Larger alphas rely more on coercion, smaller ones are more tolerant (Foster et al. 2008:143). But was there anything in his upbringing to make him so mean?

Frodo was born in 1976, during Passion and Pom's infanticidal streak. No report says that Frodo himself was attacked in that period, but it was only in late 1976 that observations revived after the rebel kidnappings. A reasonable supposition is that during his first two years, one way or another, baby Frodo experienced Passion and Pom's snatching and eating infants.

Does it push credulity to suggest early encounters with adult abuse could have lasting effect on a 2-year-old chimpanzee? No. This *precise* situation is the probably the best-known example of gene–environment interactionism in humans. One genetic variant (MAOA-L) correlates with overly aggressive, even violent adult men—but *only if* they experience abuse as a child (Caspi et al. 2002). Humans share that allele with great apes (*Science* 2004; Brune et al. 2006). We know from captive research that early trauma can have lasting consequences in abnormal psychology and behavior (Bradshaw et al. 2009). Thus it is a reasonable inference that chimpanzees exposed to extremely traumatic incidents during early development might grow up to be relatively violent adults.

Frodo's violent education did not end with infancy. He matured under Goblin—13-year-old Frodo was making subservient pant-grunts to Goblin at the very moment when all the adult males ganged up and nearly bit and beat Goblin to death (Goodall 1992:136). Frodo was a close-up witness to what was then the most brutal internal attack in chimpanzee field research. Perhaps this made an impression on the teenager.

Children of Violence

Wrangham and Wilson (2004:248) reject Frodo's aggressive character as responsible for the violence, because almost all grown Kasakela males are counted in at least one intergroup attack between 1993 and 2002. Frodo, like Goblin, was more than a participant. He was leader, just as in monkey hunting. But true, Frodo did not act alone.

Let's consider the participation of others. Seventeen adult or adolescent males are counted among four external attacks (Wilson et al. 2004). In addition to Goblin (b. 1964) and Frodo (b. 1976), which males inflicted the most damage?

In the 1993 killing of the Mitumba infant, Apollo, Gimble, and Tubi started the attacks, Freud, Prof, and Pax held the mother down, Prof killed the infant and along with Patti beat on the body, and Goblin grabbed the dead infant from Apollo and ate its flesh. In the 1998 Kalande infanticide, Tubi and Wilkie followed Frodo and Goblin's violent lead. The 1998 assault on the Kalande juvenile was mostly a solo assault by Frodo, although stunted Pax picked up beating the dazed victim after Frodo left.

Wilson et al.'s total of attackers is expanded greatly by adding in *all* males that were seen in the northward traveling Kasakela party, which they suspect killed Mitumba's Rusambo. But that attack was not observed. It is not clear that chimpanzees rather than a leopard killed him, and if so whether it was Kasakela, and if so which led and which stood back (Wilson et al. 2004:528, 530–544).

In *witnessed* attacks, the chimpanzees most involved were: ex-alpha Freud (b. 1971)—the killer of young Tofiki, Prof (b. 1971), ex-alpha Wilkie (b. 1972), Pax (b. 1977), Tubi (b. 1977), Gimble (b. 1977), and Apollo (b. 1979). With Goblin and Frodo that makes nine, only about half the total grown males.

Almost all severe violence witnessed was carried out by chimpanzees born between 1971 and 1977—the older Goblin excepted. These come in two clusters, born 1971–1972 and 1977, all births in between killed by Passion, except for Frodo. All were present during the time of maximum violence, much of it by adults directed at infants. Prof, son of Passion, was present at three infant attacks in 1975 and 1976, and joined in the cannibalism (Goodall 1986:284, 351). Freud, at four years old, was there in 1977 when Kasakela chimpanzees captured an outside infant. He tried to rescue the infant, only to have it snatched back by the adults (Goodall 1977:266). Infant Tubi was attacked by Passion and Pom in August 1977, and barely saved by his mother—hence the name, "To be or not to be" (1986:355). More infant disappearances occurred during the time of the "Invasion from the South." In 1979, chimpanzees unknown inflicted a severe wound to Pax's groin and penis, leaving him effectively castrated and stunted in growth. Freud also was wounded by an adult male in 1980, when he interfered with his copulation (Goodall 1986:100). Only Apollo was born (two years) after the major violence. These aggressive adults also experienced unusual violence as they grew up under Goblin. In 1989, Wilkie single-handedly thrashed Goblin. Soon after, Wilkie, Prof, and probably Freud joined in the second internal gang attack, which nearly killed him. Accompanying Goblin was his 12-year-old brother Gimble, who had licked his elder's wounds after the first assault (Goodall 1992:134).

The pattern is striking. The "war" generation of 1971–1977—born into deadly danger, witness or victim of extreme assaults, coming of age under a bullying alpha—were responsible for the severe external violence observed from 1993 to 2002. If we were talking about humans, the inference would be obvious—those socialized into violence become violent adults. If the violence of the 1970s is seen is seen that way, it represents *intergenerational transmission of human-induced propensities toward violence.*

That's a second thing, another consideration possibly overdetermining the extraordinary rate of killings from the early 2000s. A third may be status-related violence, consideration of which enlightens the timing, the history, of internal killings.

Status-Related Killing

This book is primarily concerned with "war" between chimpanzee groups, as a template for human war. For that, human impact leading to intense resource competition is the main, though not only explanation. Display violence against helpless outsiders is also important in external killings. But as years of observation passed on, killings within groups grew in importance. More intense resource competition may be a factor there, especially in female violence. Internally, status-related violence gains importance.

Theory for that is that within male competitive chimpanzee social organization, a combination of belligerent personalities and status turmoil can foster display killings to intimidate competitors; and payback violence, piling on when a once-dominant bully falls or is weakened. These may or may not be connected to human impact and or anthropogenic resource competition, which may be accompanied by intensified psychological disruption.

We saw a elements of display violence externally in the 1970s: in 1971 when ascendant but insecure Humphrey "bizarrely" smashed an outside infant he caught; in 1974, when recently deposed Humphrey initiated the Four Year War by attacking helpless Godi; and his deposers Figan and Fagan led aggressive moves against Kahama while the hierarchy was in flux; and in 1975, when weakened Figan carried out two theatrical infant killings. Paranoid Passion's infant-killing streak may be related to general disturbance, along with increased resource competition, though it may not count as display. There was great and protracted status turmoil coincident with the Invasion from the South, when there was unwitnessed or suspected violence against some Kasakela infants and adults. Since weakened Kasakela was in no position to make deadly moves against Kalande, if these were violent attacks, they may have been internal. In 1984 Goblin firmly secured the top (see Goodall 1986:424–425). There was one hypothetical internal infant kill that year, which was the last violence for several years.

For several years, belligerent Goblin was on top, while human impact stabilized at less disruptive levels. In 1989, Wilkie thrashed and deposed alpha Goblin, followed soon after by the second "great attack." Payback. Goblin disappeared for a while. Wilkie, relatively small (37.0 kg, vs. 51.2 kg for Frodo), relied more on politically astute grooming than physical intimidation of rivals (Foster et al. 2008:138, 143). "He ruled confidently with guile and political savvy rather than by brute force," cultivating important allies (Stanford 1998a:45). In a well-fed and comparatively undisrupted time, no external display violence accompanied Wilkie's ascendance to alpha. It was not needed, and it was not his style.

The "bad patch" starting in 1993, though not yet within the high disruption years, coincides with renewed status turmoil, among males that had grown up in violence. In February 1993 Freud deposed Wilkie through repeat challenges over weeks, with Wilkie eventually backing down (Stanford 1998a:47–48). Wilkie stayed around. Fraught.

The next month came the first of the four intergroup incidents discussed by Wilson et al. (2004:532–533), the attack on a Mitumba mother that killed her infant. This attack was chaotic, with all of the "war" generation joining in. Goblin, deposed four years earlier but back from exile, ran around, kicking and displaying at others. Ultimately he got the prize, the dead infant, which he ate, sharing with Gimble and Pax. Goblin, down but not out, like Humphrey before him, seized the chance to show that he was still a player. That same year ex-alpha Evered died from an infected, internally inflicted scrotal wound. Also possibly payback. Yet Freud remained alpha, human impact was not yet malignant, and conflict settled down.

Increasing Human Disruption, Status Turmoil, and Internal Violence

Rather arbitrarily, 1997/1998 is noted as the turn from lesser to intensifying human disruption. One marker was the 1997 sarcoptic mange infestation thought to come from nearby cattle that debilitated many, leading to three infant deaths (above). The status hierarchy became unstable. When Freud took ill, his brother Frodo seized the top position (Fallow 2003:2). New at the top and with several challengers, Frodo led the 1998 attacks on Kalande. In the infant killing, both he and Goblin grabbed an infant, though Frodo's got away (Wilson et al. 2004:534–535). Display.

As different measure of disturbance intensified, Frodo's violent displays peaked in mid-2002. He killed the human infant in May. In June, virtually alone, he carried out a theatrical display on the Kalande juvenile.

> In the thick vegetation, Frodo sat over the top of a small chimpanzee, ca. 10 yr old.... Frodo pounded on the victim with feet and fist while the other males made intermittent waa-barks and roars.... Frodo then dragged him into a clearing and sat over him roaring. While the other males emerged from the bushes, Frodo jumped up and down on the victim. During the next 14 min, Frodo continued his attack, repeatedly beating and stomping on the victim, slamming him to the ground, dragging him during displays, and biting his back, abdomen and groin. Frodo punctuated his

attack with ≥ 11 bouts of intense stomping and pounding, usually at the climax of pant-hoots and charge displays. Intermittently, Frodo usually rested, holding the victim by the scruff of the neck, but sometimes continued to crouch over him, biting. Throughout the attack, the victim screamed and whimpered.... The other males gave frequent charge displays, waa-barks and pant-hoots and sometimes hit or bit the victim but generally kept their distance from Frodo.... Frodo still crouched over the victim, biting the back of his neck. Frodo then rose up and displayed at Kris, which backed away with a fear grimace. (Wilson et al. 2004:537)

With his mouth fixed on the back of the prone juvenile's neck, he surely could have killed him. Ten minutes after the attack began, high-status Kris and Wilkie just walked away. His main audience gone, Frodo continued for a few minutes, then left. If these males had any question about how bad new alpha Frodo could be, now they knew.[2]

Payback Ascendant

But belligerent rule grows enemies. Six months after killing the human infant, in December 2002, Frodo took very ill with skinny male syndrome. "'When he was in pain he would lie on the ground with his knees drawn up to his chest, panting quietly'" (Fallow 2003:2). Other males repeatedly attacked him, so he went off by himself. "'When Frodo was at his worst,' recalls biologist Pintea, 'it was crucial for him to avoid a large party of males long enough to recover. Otherwise he could have been badly wounded—or even killed in an overthrow'" (Fallow 2003:3). Payback.

Sheldon attacked Frodo the most. He became alpha in 2003, but then disappeared for much of 2003–2004. The year 2004 was a parade of disturbance, including skinny male syndrome and the great blaze. Goblin died from that combination. With Sheldon absent, near peer Kris rose to the top. Then Frodo recovered from his two-year illness and semi-exile, and by June 2004 was back displaying. When Sheldon came back in November 2004 after the big fire, he was gang attacked by three Kasakela males, and chased out for some time (Wilson et al. 2005:7, 13–15). Freud killed young Tofiki with a head bite, and an internal infant killing was suspected. Mitumba alpha Vincent was injured in a fall, disappeared, came back, and was killed. Great disruption, political tumult, and deadly violence.

The same applies through the decade after that, which includes another peak of bloodshed in 2012–2013. But with so little information there is not enough to draw firm inferences. Yet *all* reported killing was within-group.

---

[2] Perhaps display violence provides insight into Goblin's and Frodo's attacks on Jane Goodall: doing that "impressed all the other chimps." Perhaps chimpanzees can recognize dominant individuals within a group of humans. No doubt Dr. Goodall was treated with deference when in the camp. Probably cartoonist Gary Larson too. "Humphrey ... nearly killed Dr. Wrangham by hurling a large rock at his head. 'He was just showing off.' Dr. Wrangham says indulgently" (Wade 2003). Yes, showing off, and polishing their violent credentials.

We should know more about chimpanzees' displays or attacks directed at human observers across research sites. What is the status of the aggressors, and what is the political situation at the time? See Mahale.

Ferdinand, son of Fifi like Freud and Frodo, seems cut from the same cloth. He drove out Kris, and during his bullying five-year reign without allies, he both monopolized mating and led at least five infanticidal attacks. Don't mess with Ferdinand. Yet in 2016 he barely escaped death by fleeing when males ganged up on him. Frodo wasn't so lucky, dying in 2013 from an infected bite to his genitals. Several other deaths or suspected deaths as in late Mitumba could be display violence—too little known to speculate about Rudi and Edgar. That is where the Gombe story stops, for now.

The Gombe Paradigm Found, and Lost

The Four Year War is the type case for the Gombe vision of human nature and war. From 1973 to 1978, bounded group separation, patrols, penetrations, attacks, killings, and finally territorial acquisition by Kasakela males, seemed to exemplify a sociobiological calculus of maximizing inclusive fitness. The burgeoning paradigm elevated suspicions of intergroup killings at Gombe and Mahale to evidence, and naturalized territorial conquest. In subsequent training of primatologists, this became common wisdom, which shaped understanding of observations. Intergroup killing became "species-typical" behavior. It's just what chimpanzees do. Normal. Natural.

But in Part II's long panorama of Gombe history, the atypicality of the mid-1970s stands out. With Invasion from the South highly questionable for intergroup killings, and Mahale intergroup killings about to be similarly deconstructed, the Four Year War is highly exceptional for sequential extragroup attacks. In all chimpanzee studies, only the Ngogo expansion is comparable. Even at Gombe, if 1974–1977 were excised from the 1960–2017 record, no *pan*ologist would imagine the Gombe paradigm, nor envision the roots of human warfare. Of course, those four years should not be excised. But the other half century of observation should get at least equal attention.

PART III
MAHALE

9
Mahale: What Happened to K Group?

The demonic perspective was forged from the Four Year War, seemingly replicated by the Invasion from the South. Almost immediately came support from intergroup conflict at Mahale, seemingly the same thing all over again.

Chapter deconstructs this confirmation. It examines interpretations and assumptions applied to 1970s Mahale: how group-on-group killing and extermination was accepted on the flimsiest of evidence; why the assumption that an adult male which disappears is dead and probably killed by outsiders is invalid; and that the widely held notion of M-group wiping out K-group was quietly dropped by Mahale researchers. There was no "war" at Mahale.

But there *was* intergroup conflict in the 1970s. Chapter 10 starts by showing that came from provisioning. Next discussed is an extraordinary sequence of display infant killing with M-group. Chapter 10 then carries on with history. Human impact got much worse, but with a single exception, did not lead to intergroup conflict. The Mahale narrative ends with a rare event, the internal killing of M-group's reigning alpha.

Mahale and Its Investigators

In the history of science, independent investigators often arrive at the same point at the same moment. Well, chimps were in the air in the late 1950s. Goodall arrived at Gombe in 1960. Junichiro Itani made a brief visit to Budongo in 1960, and Vernon Reynolds began to work there in 1962. Adriaan Kortlandt went to the Belgian Congo in 1960, and would soon check out other places (Moore and Collier 1999). After Gombe, the biggest research development was Mahale.

The Kyoto School

Kinji Imanishi and his student Junichiro Itani founded the Kyoto School of field primatological studies (Nakamura et al. 2015:21; Takasaki 2000). In 1961, they organized the Kyoto University Africa Primatological Expedition to study chimpanzees along Lake Tanganyika (Izawa and Itani 1966). Two research sites were started but soon abandoned. In October 1965 Toshisada Nishida began work in the Kasoje area, about 170 km south of Gombe along the same Tanganyika lakeshore. Like at Gombe, terrain is cut by steep stream valleys from the highlands to the Lake. The principle study site was a 20 km strip, extending from the shore a few kilometers up the low slopes of the Mahale Mountains. Most was in tropical semi-evergreen forest, recovering from farming.

At Gombe provisioning developed gradually. Mahale was different. The first researchers knew that local chimpanzees "sometimes raided sugarcane fields" (Nakamura et al. 2015:22). So they planted sugarcane to attract chimpanzees and soon added bananas. The principle researcher was Nishida (2012), with many colleagues. Fieldwork began with 19 months from 1965 to 1967, and continued thereafter interrupted by gaps of several months (Nishida 1979:121). At least one scientist was present most of the time after 1975, and by the 1980s sometimes five at once. With more investigators in place, focal follows of specific chimpanzees were added to ad libitum practices. John Mitani, who later studied chimpanzees of Ngogo, often worked alone to maintain data collection from 1989 to 1994. Tanzanian field assistants monitored chimpanzees at feeding locations during researchers' absences (Kano 1972:62–63; Mitani 2020:4–5; Nishida 1979:121; 1990; Nishida 2012:2–4, 8–20, 27; Nishida et al. 1985:286; Nishida and Nakamura 2008:173).

Japanese primatology followed a distinctive course from Euro-American research, more descriptive and less theoretical. Nakamura et al. (2015:27, references omitted) put it this way.

> Japanese primatology could not present a theory ... allowing its followers to investigate and mass-produce articles within the framework, without considering the validity of the framework itself. In particular, stemming from the rise of sociobiology/behavioral ecology, Japanese scholars barely followed the transitions in theories and instead were content to continue with field work. Interestingly, although Nishida, Hiraiwa-Hasegawa, and Hasegawa were the earliest to accept sociobiological theory, even they did not always develop theoretical works.

Yet Nishida's initial field observations broke new ground in understanding chimpanzee social life: that chimpanzees live in distinctive, antagonistic communities or unit-groups; and that maturing females usually transfer from one group to another. Both concepts are now axiomatic in chimpanzee research (Itoh et al. 2011:251; Nishida 2012:29–30).

Nishida's surveys indicated six unit-groups in or around the study area (Nishida 2012:15; Zama 2015:38). His initial focus was on K-group (Kajabara), and secondarily on the larger M-group (Mimiriki) to its south. In 1974 K-group had 7 male and 22 female adults and adolescents (Kawanaka and Nishida 1974:180). M-group numbers were unclear, but it was probably about twice the size of K (Nishida et al. 2003:103). B-group just to K-group's north and N-group overlapping with M-group on the south, are little known; H-group, separate from K-group in mountains to its northwest even less so; and L group not at all (Sakamaki and Nakamura 2015:129).

The People and the Park

At the start of fieldwork, human settlement was much lighter than around Gombe, only about 200 people. Nevertheless,

[s]lash-and-burn agriculture by local people created continuous disturbance of the lowland forest, except in a small patch where a burial ground for traditional chiefs of the Tongwe villages still exists. However, because the Tongwe tribe had sustainable farming practices with cultivation cycles covering a period of 30 to 50 years, coexistence of humans and wild animals was possible. (Itoh et al. 2011:255, references omitted)

In 1973 Mahale researchers began discussions with government officials of Tanzania and Japan to increase protection of chimpanzee habitat. In 1974 a government edict moved some villages out of the research area, but seven hamlets remained along the lakeshore. Creation of the Mahale Mountains Wildlife Research Center in 1979, was followed by the Mahale Mountains National Park in 1985, which at 1,613 km² dwarfs the protected area of Gombe. That led to further reduction of human population after the mid-1980s—though refugees from Zaire, established as fisherman along the shore, remained. Inside the Park, former slash-and-burn fields regrew. Protection led to recovery of some wild animal populations (Itoh et al. 2011:255; Nishida et al. 2001:46; Nishida and Nakamura 2008:174–175; Matsumoto-Oda and Kasagula 2000:148; Uehara 1997:201). Relevant conclusion: habitat loss near studied chimpanzees was not a factor over the first decades of Mahale research.

The Gombe Paradigm Shapes Interpretations

Nowhere is the Gombe paradigm more apparent or significant than at Mahale. Extermination of K-group males by M-group males seemed to confirm that the Four Year War was no aberration. It *became* expected, natural behavior for our phylogenetic cousins.

Applying the Gombe Model

The substance of this Mahale confirmation was seven adult male disappearances, over 13 years from 1969 to 1982 (Nishida et al. 1985:287). At first, these raised no questions. There was no hint of any violence between groups, which avoided each other without direct interaction (Nishida and Kawanaka 1972:131). Nishida noted the first four Mahale disappearances without a hint of foul play—one in 1969, one in 1971, and two in 1975. That left K-group with three adult males. One of those disappeared in 1978, and another in 1979. The last adult male, plus one now-young adult male, went missing in 1982—eight all together, but the young male disappearance is attributed to illness. In 1983, only Limongo, an 11-year-old, motherless male remained within the K-group range.

Soon after news of the Four Year War got out, in a brief newsletter piece Nishida (1980:21) wrote that the violence at Gombe made him *rethink* the Mahale disappearances. He was pleased that his idea of mutually hostile unit-groups was finally taken seriously by "Western primatologists." Yet "it was far beyond my expectation for chimpanzees of the bigger group to search for and kill chimpanzees of the branch group. In this essay I am willing to explore the biological bases of such murderous events." Enter sociobiology.

Nishida invoked the standard precept of that time, that philopatric males shared genetic interests against less related victims. Since four of the disappeared were prime, healthy males, had no obvious problems with others of K-group, and most of all because they were gone, he reasoned: "It is plausible that at least some of these males were killed by chimpanzees of the dominant M-group that consisted of 16 adult males in 1974 and that occasionally invaded even the core area of the K-group" (Nishida 1980:21–22).

Itani (1980:37) took a similar turn. "Then what has happened to the males that have disappeared? There is no certain answer, but there is a clue"—the intergroup killings at Gombe. "This is nothing but speculation at present." After the other disappearances, "circumstantial evidence" led Nishida et al. (1985:258) to "speculate that at least some adult males were killed by M-group's chimpanzees." "Since no male transfer between unit groups has been confirmed at either Gombe or Mahale, some of them may possibly have been killed by the males of M-group" (Itani 1982:366) (Count 5-O-A-M 1969, 5-O-A-M 1971, *two* 5-O-A-M 1975, 5-O-A-M 1978, 5-O-A-M 1979, 5-O-A-M 1982—*all hypotheticals*).

Besides the disappearances themselves, circumstantial evidence is simply that relations between K and M grew more conflicted. Each year, in September–November, M-group moved north to forage. K-group regressed before them, and returned when M went back south in January–February, much like Kasakela's oscillation with Kalande during the Invasion. Over time M-group extended its seasonal movements farther north, shrinking K-group's range.

In 1974 intergroup relations involved more contact—mostly acoustic, a few visual, and a very few with violence. In 1974 and 1976, cross-group attacks on females killed two infants. In 1979 many K females left, five or six going to M-group, four for parts unknown. After the last K-group adult males disappeared in 1982, M-group roamed mostly in K-group's old range, and "rarely returned" to its former habitat. Remaining adult K-group females later began to associate more with M-group, eventually becoming part of it (Kawanaka and Nishida 1974:174; Nishida et al. 1985:289–292, 297; Takahata 2015:121–124; Uehara et al. 1994a:277). K-group was gone.

With news spreading about the Four Year War (1974–1977), it was reasonable to "speculate" on the base of "circumstantial evidence," that "at least some" of the missing adult males were killed by M-group. That may be true. A killing is possible, given the intensified conflict over provisioning (Chapter 10). Yet other possibilities as or more likely to explain the disappearances, were screened out by the post-Gombe demonic paradigm. There is *no direct evidence that any adult killing occurred.*

Suspicion Becomes Certainty

Nishida and Itani's speculation got a lot more conclusive as others told the story. Wrangham (1999a:8, 10; 2006:47) remained cautious, counting six males as "suspicious disappearances" (and Wilson and Wrangham 2003:373–374; Wilson et al. 2014a:EDT 1; Wrangham and Peterson 1996:19). Other less constrained scholars went with what became the received wisdom: M-group killed off K-group males, period. The following compilation of quotations is necessary to establish the spell of the paradigm, and highlight how received wisdom—in this Exhibit B for the Gombe perspective—is built on evidentiary sand.

"[I]n the Mahale Mountains, a smaller group has been all but exterminated by a larger group. This apparently took place through recurrent attacks by larger groups on one or a few strangers" (Boehm 1992:142). Furuichi in 1999 compared Mahale to Gombe, writing "similar intergroup conflict was observed between Mahale M and K groups. Here again, males of smaller k group were killed or disappeared . . . [Chimpanzees are] experts in eliminating other group members" (in Nakamura and Itoh 2015:381). At Mahale, like Gombe, "individuals from a larger community systematically tracked and killed members of another, resulting in its extinction" (White and Tutin 2001:457). After Gombe, a "similar group extinction was later documented in Mahale" (Muller 2002:122). "[A]ll but one of the K-group males had disappeared, and had presumably been killed by M-group males" (Williams et al. 2004:529). "[A]ttacks by males from a neighboring group are also presumed to have caused the extinction of a group in Mahale" (Yamakoshi 2004:46). "[A]t Mahale, prolonged conflict between the K and M communities appears to have been responsible for the annihilation of the K community, its males were probably killed and its females moved to join the M community" (Reynolds 2005:106). "At least twice, whole groups have been eliminated by systematic, one-at-a-time killing combined with female transfer" (Konner 2006:3). Crofoot and Wrangham (2010:185) abandon the latter's earlier caution to assert that K-group went "extinct, apparently as a result of aggression from dominant neighbors . . . almost all males died." Newton-Fisher and Emery Thompson (2012:47) follow suit with "males of Mahale *M-group* community in Tanzania are thought to have systematically killed most if not all of the males of the neighboring *K-group* community." "At three different sites—Gombe, Mahale, and Ngogo—repeated killings result in substantial territorial expansion" (Arcadi 2018:69). There was "systematic killing of K group males at Mahale" (Stanford 2018:81). Even the *New York Times* reported, twice, that Mahale paralleled Gombe in that "a chimp community has wiped out all of a neighbor's males" (Wade 2003:F4; Stevens 1997).

Ghiglieri's *Dark Side of Man* (1999:173), however, takes the cake.

> Chimps in the Mahale Mountains (less than one hundred miles south of Gombe) launched a war a decade later. Toshisada Nishida and his colleagues concluded that males of Nishida's huge M-Group (more than eighty chimps) systematically stalked and murdered the six adult males of the smaller, neighboring K-Group, which contained twenty two chimps at the onset of hostilities. Their violence, too, was shockingly brutal, premeditated, and deliberately lethal.... Both defeated communities ceased to exist, having been wiped out by genocidal warfare. Tanzanian chimps, like Hitler's storm troopers, had fought for lebensraum.

This solid consensus that M-group killed off K-group males is a pillar of the claim that intergroup *pan*icide is normal. Given this common wisdom, it must be fact, no?

No, no, no. Nothing like the Four Year War was seen at Mahale. Yes, M-group gradually assimilated K-group's range and many of its females, but nothing indicates they did that by killing K-group males. The notion that any K-group adult males were killed by M-group, *or even physically attacked*, is entirely unsupported by direct evidence. The killing off of K-group is a projection of Gombe-vision.

War at Mahale?

Boundary Patrols and Incursions

What evidence supports this "war"? Were there boundary patrols and incursions? "Border patrols have not been described in detail from Mahale, but key elements of border patrols have been reported—including scouting, and silent and cautious travel, mainly by males, in border areas" (Wrangham 1999a:6–7).

The main pattern of territorial jostling at Mahale is more group excursion than stealth patrol, with the smaller group clearing out ahead of the larger (Kawanaka and Nishida 1974:175–176; Nishida and Kawanaka 1972:140–142). A pre–Great Revision study of "Inter-Unit-Group Relationships" makes no suggestion of patrols. "No direct encounter between the unit-groups was observed . . . the subordinate group detects the approach of the dominant by vocal outburst [and] avoids contact with the latter" (Nishida and Kawanaka 1972:145). "Generally, chimpanzees of the K-group retreat rapidly and avoid making any calls, when they hear calls from the M-group . . . [although] adult males have been observed to show scouting behavior, or to engage in charging displays toward enemy groups" (Nishida 1979:85). Antagonism, advertisement and avoidance, but not stalking.[1]

The strongest testament to Gombe-like patrolling is one incident in early 1981. M-group was in the core of K-group range, the Mpila Valley between the two feeding stations. They made their nests without any calls. The next day four grown males and three adult females surrounded, and the males attacked, K-group female Wantendele and her infant, 20 times. Both were hurt so badly that researchers intervened, fearing they would be killed. "As the number of mature males in the K-group was decreasing, the M-group began to visit the Nkala Valley and further north more frequently than ever.... It is quite likely therefore that the mother and son accidentally encountered the M-group in the course of the M-group's range-patrolling of the border area" (Nishida and Hiraiwa-Hasegawa 1985:4).[2]

Yet the mixed-sex subgroup came from the entire body of M-group moving together toward a known feeding area. Neither looks like a patrol. Nor is it known how

---

[1] Decades later, Nishida seemed more supportive of patrols. "Adult males and a few females occasionally patrol the periphery of the group range," let out a "hearty pant-hoot chorus," and run back to the center if they hear a response. He cites Nishida (1979) as substantiating (Nishida 2012:182). What does that study say? One time, "seven chimpanzees slipped off quietly and moved eastward" (1979:90). One time, "M-group penetrated the boundary and approached secretly far northward" (1979:86). In a table listing the repertoire of behaviors "in response to strange calls or to approach of strangers," it includes sniffing, listening, looking around, and "patrol the area" (1979:84). Yet nothing suggests a pattern of border patrols. The silent foray just noted is exceptional ("a subgroup of the M-group was once seen to penetrate the exclusive area of the K-group"). Nishida (1979:82, 86) attributes this act to curiosity about a new feeding station.

[2] Note that this interpretation is from the two researchers most associated with sociobiology, just as they went to that paradigm.

Wantendele happened into harm's way. Later that same year, Wantendele *traveled with* M-group in that same area before returning to K, once being severely attacked again by M-group males (1985:6–10). Thus, how the first incident occurred, through patrolling or by Wantendele trying to associate, is speculative.

If evidence of boundary patrolling is highly ambiguous for the years of M-group vs. K, it is nearly absent thereafter. Summarizing half a century of Mahale studies, Sakamaki and Nakamura (2015:131) note group expeditions to peripheral areas, and one "notable case" in 2000 that "was suggestive of a boundary patrol" (Chapter 10). "Mahale chimpanzees rarely conduct boundary patrols . . . they generally avoid encounters, or their intergroup interactions are in the form of displacement."

Wild chimpanzees sometimes stop their quotidian activities, and move off in a line in silent, directed, maximally attentive travel. They do so when they hear strange chimpanzees, or "raid" human crops, or move through open savanna. They do so when apprehensive about what is "out there." In the January 1981 incident, M-group entered K-group's range, heading for the feeding station. They had reason for apprehension. That is not boundary patrolling, much less seeking a chance to kill.

Fighting

Except for once, there is no published evidence of a physical attack of adult males from either K- and M-group on adult males of the other. When Nishida et al. (1985:288) first posited intergroup killings, they noted: "Severe fighting was occasionally witnessed between males of K-group and M-group in the overlapping area of two unit-groups ranges"—citing Nishida 1979. But that article (1979:85–90) reports loud, thrashing displays, *without* physical violence, all of it happening around the feeding station (Nishida 1979:85–90; Takahata 2015:122). In February 1974 came the only "direct inter-unit-group quarrel" observed (1979:79), when a bold *M-group* male snuck into the feeding station while K-group was there, and was chased and attacked by the K alpha Kasonta (1979:89).

None of these encounters approach the level of brutality of Four Year War. (All are described in historical context in Chapter 10). In the feeding station clash, if the other K-group males joined in the assault they could have killed the lone intruder. They refrained. In Itani's (1980:38) retrospective of all intergroup relations through 1979, these 1974 clashes are the only clashes noted. (Other intergroup attacks on females with infants are discussed later.) Neither in patrolling or fighting is there observational evidence suggesting M-group males were looking to kill K-group males. The case for "war" comes down to the supposed killings themselves. That case is extremely weak.

Intergroup Killings?

Mahale researchers identified three males from 1978 to 1982 as the most likely victims. Earlier cases have other explanations. In 1969 Kasagula, "the oldest and most dominant male" disappeared and, it was thought, "died of old age." In 1970, Kaguba, the "youngest and lowest-ranking male" went missing (Nishida 1979:79). "Nishida believed that he had become a solitary, or had transferred to another group" (Itani 1980:37). In April 1975, Kasanga, "then the prime-adult male," vanished. In September 1975, Kajabala, "the past-prime male, also disappeared" (Nishida 1979:79). Kajabala was formerly alpha, and the namesake of K-group (Nishida 2012:22). Referring to Kasanga and Kajabala, Nishida (1979:119) concluded, "it is plausible that these males are living singly or with one or several females in the high altitude of the Mahale Mountains or far from the study area, independent of any unit-groups." We will see that ex-alphas at Mahale often self-exile.

Kasonta

The strongest circumstantial case for killing is fallen Kasonta, in 1978. He had a long reign, beginning in 1969 (Nishida 2012:227-236). Nishida portrays him as a "tyrant" and a shrewd tactician. Unusually large and aggressive within the group, he was leader or active participant in all the intergroup clashes described in Chapter 10.

But when K-group got down to three adult males in 1976, Kasonta's dominance over Sobongo hinged on Kamemanfu's support. He fell when Kamemanfu switched sides. For about 15 months Kasonta avoided the other males, ranging with K-group females or alone in higher ground. In September 1977 he came back, and Kamemanfu once again provided support. Without much serious fighting Sobongo was down, and self-exiled from M-group. In January 1978, Kasonta disappeared for good (Nishida 1983:321-323; 2012:227-236; Uehara et al. 1994b:50).

Kasonta's disappearance is critical for the Mahale war story. Wrangham (1999a:8-9), cites personal communication from Nishida: "In one case, M-group males were known to be very near to K-group males; there were many outbursts of calls; and the next day another K-group male was missing." Uehara et al. (1994b:50), however, say Kasonta was last seen three days *before* what they refer to as "a suspected fight." Much later, Nishida (2012:186) went to this as the best evidence of killing: "Shigeo Uehara confirmed that a ruckus was heard coming from the foothills of upper Miyako, although the steep terrain prohibited him from approaching the chimpanzees."

Whether this ruckus involved M-group is conjectural (Nakamura and Itoh 2015:372-373). Maybe M-group killed Kasonta. Or maybe the old tyrant had a run-in with self-exiled, young and brawny Sobongo. In 1976 a fight with Sobongo left Kasonta "limping, with eight severe lacerations" (Nishida 2012:228). A repeat thrashing could make Kasonta return to his solitary ways. After all, he spent 15 of the previous 19 months absent from M-group, and was 36 years old or older when he vanished. "If individuals estimated to be 40 yr or older disappeared, they were categorized as having died of old age, even if they were in good health when last seen" (Nishida et al. 2003:102). Kasonta was getting close.

If not senescence, maybe a leopard got him. Leopards were common. They ate one adult female, are suspected in three other attacks, and are met by chimpanzees with a lot of ruckus (Nakazawa et al. 2013). Once chimpanzees dragged a cub from a den and killed it (Hosaka and Ihobe 2015:214). Lions are not resident, but occasionally pass through. In 1989-1990, one "chimpanzee killer" may have killed up to eight (Nishida 1994a:373; 2012:81-83; Tsukahura 1993). Kasonta would not put up much of a fight.

No one knows what befell Kasonta. As ambiguous as this is, Kasonta offers the *only observational* evidence for intergroup adult male killing. He is the best case for "war" at Mahale.

Sobongo and the Rest

Sobongo went next. Shortly after Kasonta was last seen, Sobongo ended his exile, and once again performed dangerousness over old Kamemanfu and subadult male Masisa. Meanwhile K-group's cycling females were bugging out. They began the complicated transference to M group in 1977, and were all gone by the end of 1979 (below). K-group was falling apart.

Sobongo was last sighted in May 1979. "As no scientist was present to study K-group from December 1978 to June 1979, this disappearance remains a riddle." But going with the Great Revision, Nishida suspected an intergroup killing (Nishida et al. 1985:287–288). "The riddle was not solved as to why Sobongo dropped out of sight, but there is a strong likelihood that he also was slain by the M-group" (Nishida 2012:236). Takahata (2015:125) is more cautious—"the possibility that some of them, particularly Sobongo, were killed by M-group males, cannot be denied." But the case for killing by M-group is not based on any evidence except his disappearance.

With Sobongo gone, Kamemanfu was "alpha by default" (Nishida 2012:236), over Masisa. He was last seen in September 1982, at 43 + years old (Takahata 2015:123). Given his age, he is the weakest suspected case of *pan*icide.

Masisa was gone in December 1982. Last seen at the feeding station alone, he "appeared to be seriously ill, suffering from both physical and mental depression. It is likely that he died of illness" (Nishida et al. 1985:296; Takahata 2015:124). Mahale researchers never counted Masisa among the suspected killings.[3]

That is the sum total of direct evidence that adult males of K-group were killed by M-group, far from the certainty of extermination so commonly and confidently expressed. Yet the friction between K and M-group indeed *may have* included lethalities.

Intergroup Killing of Infants

In 1974, M-group was moving around the feeding station while K-group was in the area. Three adult K males were seen eating an unidentified infant. No K-group infant was missing and an M-group female was observed without her male infant, Shigeo. In 1976, when M-group entered further north than previously, Wantendele was seen with wounds and without her male infant, Lukanda (Nishida et al. 1979:17–18; also Nakamura and Itoh 2015:373) (Count: 2 O-I-M 1974; 4 O-I-M 1976).

---

[3] Wrangham et al. (2006:22) and Wilson et al. (2014a:EDT 1) include Masisa in their tables of intercommunity adult and adolescent killings, as "suspected" (Count: 5-O-A-M 1982).

The End of K-Group

In 1982 the last K adult male was gone. But even three years earlier, post Sobongo and with only one fully grown male remaining, K was hardly a bisexual group at all. Most of K-group were females and immatures, and they were leaving, sort of.

Between-Group Transfers of Females and Sons

The year 1978–1979 began a then-unprecedented process, large-scale transfer of K-group females to M-group. It was complicated, with visits, returns, and alternations.

In 1978, K-group was down to two adult males, squeezed into their northern range and excluded or threatened at feeding stations. Reproductively active K-group females began to associate more with M-group males, some exclusively (Nishida et al. 1985:289, 292, 294, 296, 298). Immigrants were sometimes attacked, sometimes collectively and severely, but were also protected by males and females (Nishida et al. 1985:295; Nishida 1989:75, 83).

Cycling females transferred to M-group, but in a food-resource sense they stayed in place. Although they roamed with M-group, "[i]t appears that the core areas of these prime females (both ex-K-group and resident) have changed little throughout the whole study period" (Nishida 1989:70–71). By staying put as M-group moved in, they *retained access to provisioning*.

Making this transfer even more remarkable, several females brought along sons, which were accepted by M-group. Masisa, ultimately the last adult male of K-group, went with his mother to M-group in 1976 at age 9. Although treated well, he returned alone to K-group a month later (Itani 1980:38). Masudi went over with his mother at age 5, Dogura at 7, and Hit at 8. Fanana appeared in M-group in 1988, around 10. His "supposed mother" had transferred to M-group earlier. Another K-group transfer, Lulemyo, stayed with M-group 5 years, then was gone (Nishida 2012:258; Takahata and Takahata 1989:218).

It is axiomatic in *pan*ology: no adult male ever transferred permanently into a new group. Yet younger males have. Four juvenile and one adolescent male immigrants became members of M-group. By sociobiological expectations of males promoting their common genes by killing outside males bearing competing genes, none should have been let live. Beyond remarkable is the story of Fanana. He suddenly appeared, by himself, already an adolescent. In November of 1997 he became alpha (Nishida et al. 2003:108; Nishida 2012:257–258, 266). An alien, probably a son of K-group, rose to be lord of M-group!

The Slow Fade-Out of K

The paradigmatic image is that M-group wiped out K-group. That image is distorted by focus on *adult males*. Bring in females and their offspring, and K and M groups *merged*.

With these transfers from K-group, M-group reached prodigious size. By the beginning of complete identification in 1980, M-group at 88 members was the largest chimpanzee community yet observed. The provisioned group continued to grow, peaking at 105 in 1982 (Nishida et al. 2003:104; Takahata 1985:162).

In 1980 K-group consisted of Kamemanfu, 13-year-old Masisa, an old female and her 8-year-old son Limongo, another old female (in her thirties) and her 2-year-old daughter, an adult female (21) and her infant daughter (1), and a 29-year-old female and her 3-year-old son (Uehara et al. 1994a:277). This K band could offer no resistance to M-group. If M-group members felt an urge to kill off or drive out the remaining K-group, they could have easily. They did not. The extinction of independent K-group (at least within the research area), was a drawn-out process.

Over 1981, researchers reduced provisioning to "only one or two sticks of sugar cane given to 20 to 40 chimpanzees a day" (Nishida 1989:70). That year the oldest K-group female disappeared, Limongo's mother. Wantendele and Masudi began to associate temporarily with M-group, in the process enduring the two fierce attacks previously noted. From September 1982 to March 1983 M-group ranged almost entirely in the northern area, around the main feeding station, and "rarely returned to the southern part of its range" (Nishida et al. 1985:297). The two remaining adult males, old Kamemanfu and sick, depressed Masisa, disappeared in 1982. In 1983, Wantendele and Masudi permanently transferred to M-group as did the remaining older female, an adult female, and her son.

Limongo

The last adult male was gone, but a remnant of K-group kept on: one adult female with a 4-year-old daughter, a 5-year-old female, and 11-year-old Limongo. Meanwhile M-group kept growing, supplemented by an additional nine female immigrants from unit-groups unknown, between 1981 and 1985. In 1987 the last K-group females joined M-group. Limongo, fully adult at 15, was left to himself (Nishida 1989:69; Uehara 1994a:277–278).

Limongo stayed on in his old haunts. Between September 1987 and December 1992, this adult male (20 in 1992) was seen nine times within the absorbed K-group range, five times alone, three times with ex-K-group females or the young male Masudi. His sightings during this period were closer to the center of the M-group's range, and *closer* to groups of M-group males, than for 1983–1987. "Limongo has recently begun to dare, on occasion, to approach or not to excessively avoid M-group" (Uehara et al. 1994a:277–278). In 1994 he walked alone down a path, calling attention to himself by pant hooting (Hosaka 2015a:50). In 1998 he was thought seen with two unhabituated females along the lake shore in old K-group territory (Sakamaki and Nakamura 2015:129).

If researchers saw Limongo, so did M-group males—yet they did not kill him. His presence, even consorting with M-group females, was tolerated. But M-group has a record of tolerating outside junior males, and Mahale males have a record of roaming alone.[4] This could be called normal behavior for Mahale. The waning years, the extinction of K-group was not violent.

---

[4] "The present case is the first record of a lone chimpanzee in the wild. However, a very similar life style was observed when some alpha male chimpanzees were defeated and became peripheral, spending much of their time alone" (Uehara et al. 1994a:279).

Disappeared Does Not Mean Killed

The only observational evidence of intergroup adult killing—ever—at Mahale, is merely a distant ruckus. The claim of group extermination rests on the assumption that disappeared means dead, which in the context of K vs. M-group friction, was inferred to mean killed. This assumption is foundational for the idea that intergroup killing is normal for chimpanzees. The assumption is untenable.

Disappeared chimpanzees might be dead but not killed by other chimpanzees. Big cats and falling from trees take a toll, especially of old or infirm solitaries. Disease outbreaks, mostly anthropogenic, claim many.[5] Because disease also strikes single chimpanzees, deaths may be undercounted. "Sick individuals, particularly those that are seriously ill, are more difficult to find, because they tend to spend more time alone or only with their dependent offspring. Therefore, researchers cannot always notice sick individuals, or their symptoms" (Hanamura et al. 2015:354).[6] Totaling known cases from 1980 to 1999, 56 of K and M-groups died of illness, and 24 from senescence (Nishida et al. 2003:106). Dead, not *panicide*.

Moving Out?

Not only do chimpanzees die variously, disappeared males may yet live. At Gombe, some of Kahama maybe moved into uninhabited higher lands to their east. K-group had similar options. In November and December 1979, B-group to the east encroached just as M-group made its deepest incursion to date, "with the result that K-group no longer had any area for its exclusive use." Then came a striking parallel to Kahama of Gombe: "For about 10 days after the invasion, K-group chimpanzees, male and female, disappeared from their usual range, possibly retiring deep into the eastern mountainous area which they had rarely used before" (Nishida et al. 1985:287–288, 297). They had somewhere to go.

Two surveys around Mahale, taken long apart, indicate big spaces between chimpanzee populations, even along Lake Tanganyika (Izawa and Itani 1966:123–139; Shimada 2003). The Mahale research site was selected because of its comparative density of chimpanzees. They were scarce in the less hospitable high land to the east (Kano 1972:44–50; Nakamura and Fukada 1999), where no unit-group appears on any research maps (e.g., Nishida 2012:32). Yet beyond the research area at Mahale,

---

[5] In 1977 chimpanzees showed signs of a cold at the same time local villagers did, though none died (Nishida 2012:283). In 1984–1987 "several" M-group chimpanzees died or sickened and recovered from an "AIDS-like disease" (Hanamura et al. 2008:77; Hanamura et al. 2015:357–361). Flu-like symptoms appeared every year, usually in the July–October tourist season (Hosaka 1995a:3). Eleven died in 1993 and 1994. In June–July of 2006, 23 of the 65 M-group members showed symptoms. Twelve and possibly more died (Hanamura et al. 2006; 2007; Wallis and Lee 1999:815).

[6] In 1980 the 6-year-old Katabi, abandoned when his mother transferred to M-group, seemed seriously ill then disappeared. In 1982, Masisa looked sick, then disappeared (Nishida et al. 1985:296). In 1991, M-group beta male Shike was seriously ill and disappeared (Nishida 2012:247).

"tracks and signs of chimpanzees were found on all survey routes," even if sparsely (Zamma et al. 2015:34). Densities varied 3.43–0.09/km² (Chitayat et al. 2012:1). Bad environments are not rich enough to support a sizable group, but they do allow smaller groups and individuals.

Even if male chimpanzees do not like to live solitary, there is no reason to think they wouldn't encounter other loners, maybe from back home, out in the chimpanzee wilderness. Do the mysterious "peripheral females" stop at group peripheries? Or do they keep on going, free of frequent male harassment but sometimes mating? Limongo shows that adult males *can* live alone and still have access to females. We know virtually nothing about how chimpanzees live in areas beyond unit-groups. There may be a different chimpanzee world out there, of which we are ignorant.

The Great Disappearance

In 1995 and 1996 M-group experienced a wave of disappearances. From mid-December to early January, four adult high-status males and one adult female went missing. By the end of 1996 the alpha female was gone, along with her daughter and grandson. Then alpha male Nsaba vanished. "We lost as many as 15 chimpanzees within about 13 months" (Nishida 2012:254), which "included most of the high ranking adult males (the reason for their disappearance is unknown)" (Itoh et al. 1999:1). Looking back, Nishida (2012:254) wrote "we could only speculate that something like an epidemic had afflicted M-group."

But neither Nishida et al. (2003) or Itoh et al. (1999) reported any signs of disease. Nor are these disappearances mentioned in overviews of infectious disease tolls at Mahale (Hanamura et al. 2008:77; Kaur and Singh 2008:731). Nor is there any indication of a passing lion, or of external conflict, no push and pull between two unit-groups. At the time, Mahale researchers suspected that M-group fissioned, "that M group might have split up. Observers consequently traveled around the periphery of M group to look for a 'branch' or 'splinter' group, but the search was in vain" (Nishida et al. 2003:105).

What happened is a mystery, but may be related to a major shift in M-group ranging immediately after these disappearances (Chapter 11). Regardless, over 13 months about 15 of M-group disappeared without a clue, 5 of them within a few weeks. Compare that to the seven males that disappeared from K-group from 1969 to 1982. This is powerful evidence that individuals may move away.

Is it conceivable that so many chimpanzees could relocate so far away that researchers could not find them? That is known to happen. In the 1980s, north of Mahale along Lake Tanganyika, an entire population of some 70 chimpanzees "vanished" when deforestation began nearby. A later survey rediscovered this group, "shifted inland in response to human pressure on the lakeshore" (Turner and Nishida 1994). In Chapter 10, many unknown chimpanzees suddenly show up within M-group rangelands. Yes, chimpanzees sometimes move out of established territories, and in number.

Deposed Alphas—Exiled or Killed within Group

Another pattern of disappearance pertains specifically to the most-suspected *pani*cides of K-group. Kasonta and Sobongo both disappeared after being deposed as alpha, later returned, and then vanished. Of M-group, Kajugi, alpha from 1976, was beaten by Ntologi in 1979 and acted much like Kasonta: avoiding most males though occasionally associating with others, ranging in remote areas, and finally disappearing in April 1982. K-group was down to two fearful adult males by then, so it is unlikely they killed him—though other members of M-group could have (Nishida 1983:332; Takahata 2015:125; Uehara et al. 1994b:52–53).

Ntologi is the preeminent alpha of Mahale history (Nishida 2012:236–254). Kalunde deposed him in early 1991. From then, he "roamed alone, keeping a safe distance from the rest of M-group," though maintaining contact with one senior male (Nishida 2012:241). Once, Kalunde and other males found Ntologi and attacked, but he got away. A few months later, Ntologi took advantage of a political deadlock to return, emerging as alpha. (How did he know?) In April 1995, another fight made him flee again. Four months later he was back, though of low status. In November 1995, Ntologi was found lacerated and dying, probably killed by other M-group males (Kitopeni and Kasagula 1995; Nishida 1996; cf. Nakamura and Itoh (2015:379) (Count 3-W-A-M 1996).

Other alphas disappeared. Nsaba was among the Great Disappearance. Fanana, alpha since 1997, was mostly absent in 2003, seen only occasionally with a couple of M-group males—though he eventually reintegrated. "Fanana spontaneously chose the solitary life for more than 3 years" (Hosaka and Nakamura 2015a:394). Not only alphas were sent packing. In October 1991 eight of M-group attacked mid-ranked Jilba, and he disappeared for 50 days. With support from Ntologi, Jilba rejoined the group. Five years later, he disappeared for good. Wrangham (1999a:9; Wrangham et al. 2006:23), citing a personal communication, counts him as a "certain" kill by others of M-group, although that is far from certain (Nishida 2012:246; Nishiba et al. 1995:210)[7] (Count 4-W-A-M 1996).

Nishida (1979:258, 260) discerned a pattern: "A defeated alpha male does not pant-grunt to the victor, but runs away to the periphery of a group's range and has a lonely life, until he finds the chance to come back for a rematch," but only returns if he maintained some contact with adult males (and see Uehara et al. 1994b; Hosaka and Nakamura 2015a:393–394).

The pattern is strong. At Gombe, there were disappearances and severe attacks on ex-alphas Goblin, Vincent, Sheldon, Frodo, Kris, and Ferdinand. At Mahale, ex-alphas Kasagula and Kajabala vanished. Kajugi went into local exile for a few years, then was never seen again. Ntologi had two stretches of banishment and then was likely killed. Nsaba disappeared with others while on top; Fanana went missing and

---

[7] During the Great Disappearance, a decaying corpse was found. Based on its teeth, Nishida (2012:254) concluded it was probably Jilba, without suggestion of *pani*cide. Despite their earlier certainty, Wilson et al. (2014a:EDT 3) do not include Jilba as even a suspected killing. Nakamura and Itoh (2015:377–379) are skeptical that he was killed by chimpanzees.

came back. Non-alpha Jilba was driven out once or more, or killed. The bloody fate of alpha Pimu can wait until Chapter 10.

The three most suspected K-group killings, Kasonta, Sobongo, and Kamemanfu, were alphas before or when they vanished, Kasonta and Sobongo disappeared and returned before they were gone for good. The exiled-or-killed ex-alpha pattern is more reason to doubt killings by M-group.

Revisionism Revised

Second Thoughts at Mahale

In the early wave of sociobiological enthusiasm, what were originally considered unremarkable disappearances by Mahale males were reinterpreted as the result of Gombe-like intergroup killings. But with time, reasons for doubt increased. Many additional disappearances were plainly unrelated to intergroup conflict, and little group conflict occurred at all. Since the later 1980s discussions that *should* refer to the possibility of killings notably make no mention of it (Nishida 1989:69; 1990:26; Nishida et al. 2003:106; Uehara et al. 1994a:275, 277). In 1998, when unknown chimpanzees appeared within the old K-group range, researchers initially thought it was *K-group returning*—although they later concluded it was a new group (Itoh et al. 1999; Sakamaki et al. 2007, and see Chapter 10). Despite the frequent, confident assertions by non-Mahale writers that M-group killed off K-group—go back and read them!—that claim largely disappeared in publications by Mahale researchers just a few years after it was first raised.

However, contrary to my assertion here, in his final work Nishida (2012:186) briefly restates his original suspicion, but in *stronger* terms than previously.

> We deduced that at the very least, M-group had killed most of K-group's adult males. The reasoning behind this was that the males who vanished were in good health whenever we observed them, but that every time K-group and M-group had an encounter, adult males from K-group vanished.

That claim is entirely inconsistent with the published evidentiary record, except—approximately—for Kasonta. That is not what happened.[8]

---

[8] What to make of this discrepancy between Nishida (2012) and earlier publications? Nishida was stricken with cancer after he began this crowning account of his work. William McGrew, who did extensive field research at Mahale, stepped in and made it a publishable book (Nishida 2012:xvi). Thank goodness both did what they did. Nishida passed 12 years in Africa (2012:281), and knew as much about chimpanzees as anyone. *Chimpanzees of the Lakeshore* is one of the most interesting and refreshing reads in this field. His account of complex behavioral areas such as growth and development, play, status politics, and female-male interaction is superlative. Nevertheless, given the circumstances of this book, his final endorsement of his most famous assertions does not weigh strongly against the established Mahale evidentiary record.

Rejecting Gombe-Vision

Since Nishida's death, other Mahale researchers openly challenge the intergroup killing scenario. Nakamura and Itoh (2015:380) question the evidence of K-group killings, and make a series of observations close to my argument about the spread of Gombe-vision.

> Researchers at the time faced a shocking and unbearable phenomenon that, at that time, the main study group was becoming extinct and they observed several incursions by the M group into the range of the K group. They might have also heard of the Gombe "war" that was going on in the same period. Under such circumstances, it is understandable that they strongly suspected that the decrease of the K group was because of the killings by M group. (2015:377)

We agree on the importance of Mahale for clinching the Gombe perspective on intergroup relations.

Thus, in order to generalize the case, the extinction of the Mahale K group was often referred to. If the extinction of the K group was the result of coalitionary killings, then the Gombe case is more generalized than it is a special case accompanying the unusual event of group fission (2015:376).

We agree on the power of the Gombe paradigm to shape interpretations of events. Based on the perception that coalitionary killings were common,

> the leading academic opinion is that it has been significant in the evolutionary history of humans as well.... Therefore, scientists should carefully scrutinize the rare cases of coalitionary killing. When one hypothesis is dominant in an academic domain, incomplete information may easily be interpreted as *for* the hypothesis rather than *against* it. (Nakamura and Itoh 2015:381)

Finally, we agree on the broader implications of this old revisionism, newly revised.

> We can conclude that both chimpanzees and humans, under certain conditions, kill members of their own species, sometimes acting as a group. On the other hand, we are yet to conclude that both species are prone to kill others regularly for maximizing their reproductive success.... We need further careful investigations of limited observations in order to understand what types of situations and conditions result in such rare events of conspecific killings in these species. (2015:381)

Bad Demographics

But if M-group did not wipe out K-group, why did it disappear?
Nakamura and Itoh (2015:377) advance a new explanation.

> The number of males that disappeared for unknown reasons in both groups are about the same ... [but] about the same number of adolescent males in the M-group

became adult males, thus maintaining the equilibrium in the total number of adult males. However, in the K group, only one adolescent male [Sobongo] became an adult in 18 years ... there were only one adolescent and two infant males in the group in 1968 (3 years from the start of the research), that is, before the number of individuals in the K group started decreasing. The youngest infant died the next year, and the K group, from the start, did not have enough younger males to cover the losses of adult males.... [W]e cannot rule out the possibility that the number of males in the K group first decreased ... and then as a result of this decrease the M group was able to make more frequent incursions.

"The age-sex pyramid of the average age-sex throughout this periods shows an unhealthy group structure, at least for males.... In retrospect, it appears that the K group never had a demographic structure to maintain itself for a long period of time" (Takahata 2015:121).

No "War" at Mahale

After this deconstruction of serial killings at Mahale, I repeat that it is *possible* that an adult male of K-group was killed by K-group. Chapter 10 starts with K- and M-group's contest over the feeding stations. But there is *no evidence any were killed*. Nor is there a pattern of boundary patrolling, stealthy entries, or physical clashes between neighboring groups. The notion that an imbalance of power is both necessary and sufficient to kill a member of another group is contradicted by the acceptance of young K-group males into M-group, and toleration of Limongo. The assumption that a disappeared adult male is dead and likely killed by outsiders is contradicted in multiple ways by the entire Mahale record.

The case for "war" at Mahale is little more than a reflection of the Gombe paradigm.

10
Mahale History

Chapter 9 addressed the big question: did M-group kill off K-group? (Answer: no.) Mahale offers much additional information on concerns central to this book. Chapter 10 covers all of Mahale chimpanzee history. It shows why M- and K-groups had territorial issues in the 1970s. (Answer: artificial provisioning.) It then examines a series of infanticidal attacks across the 1980s. (Explanation: display violence.) Different modalities of disruption increased from the 1990s onward, with diverse consequences for M-group living and fighting.

The Expansion of M-Group

Initial Observations and Provisioning

Provisioning was central to Mahale research. Starting in October 1965, the "bait" was planted and scattered sugar cane. When scarcity of cane led to "a high frequency of aggressive behaviors," with the less pugnacious getting none, cane was cut into smaller pieces and scattered to prevent monopolization. As at Gombe, provisioning increased internal aggression. Later, bananas were added (Nishida 1979:77).

They gave cane to chimpanzees in the bush, but most feeding was at Kansyana, in the overlap zone of M- and K-group. Initially K chimpanzees were the regular visitors, with some of M coming occasionally. Special efforts to attract M-group included a temporary feeding station in the center of their range. In 1968 more of M-group came to Kansyana, and by 1970 most of M-group ate cane. In 1975, chimpanzees at the "plantation" received 10–30 bananas and/or 5–10 pieces of cane (for detail, see Nishida 1968:172–173, 204–208; 1979:76–83; 1990:20–21; 2012:20–29; Nishida and Kawanaka 1972:133–140; Uehara et al. 1994a:276).

Intergroup relations changed quickly. In 1966, when provisioning was just beginning, K- and M-groups spent about two months (September and October) simultaneously using Kansyana valley around the feeding station (Nishida 1968:204–205). But during September,

> The Kajabara group at the feeding place gradually decreased, and in the mean time the Mimikire group began to move about the vicinity of the camp, only to pass the feeding ground. When large subgroups of the Mimikire group were not near the feeding place, the Kajabara group appeared there ... At the end of September, 1966, one more group besides the Kajabara and Mimikire groups was found within a distance of 2 km from the feeding place. The co-existence of three groups in close proximity suggests that temporary movement of chimpanzees from one group to another may occur. (Nishida 1968:208)

In 1967 territorial occupation got more exclusionary. In seasonal alternation, K-group retreated a few kilometers and three valleys north to Miyako valley as M-group moved toward Kansyana around September. Both returned to their previous areas with ripening fruits around February. Overlap at that time was roughly one third to one quarter of M-group's total range and half of K-group's (Nishida 1979:82). But earlier coexistence was not eliminated entirely. "[D]epending on the year, there were occasions when K-group did not evacuate to Miyako Valley. During these periods, both groups were sometimes within 500m of each other, but as K-group avoided encounters at all costs, usually nothing happened" (Nishida 2012:184).

In 1973, after sustained efforts to draw them in with cane, M-group begin feeding at Kansyana, regardless of season. The "number of days of occupation of the area by the M-group increased remarkably, while those of the K-group decreased accordingly" (Nishida 1979:83).

A second feeding station for K-group was established at Miyako, where M-group had never ranged. In January 1974, M showed up there as well (Nishida 1979:86). K-group was in an increasingly tight spot, because two km further north began the overlapping ranges of B and P-groups (Kawanaka and Nishida 1974:174; Nishida and Kawanaka 1974:134–137).

"Severe Fighting"

The year 1974—coincidentally the first year of Gombe's War—is the time of "severe fighting" between M- and K-group males (Nishida 1979:85–90; Kawanaka and Nishida 1974:179). Contact occurred on 37 days. Of these, 29 were acoustic and others involved K-group meeting former K chimpanzees that had transferred to M. "[S]tranger-to-stranger visual contacts were only observed in three cases" (Takahata 2015:122). The six encounters they describe are summarized here to show their nonlethal character, and the centrality of competition over feeding sites.

Case 1. On January 21, M-group chimpanzees quietly approached the new feeding site at Miyako—their first time that far north—while K-group was there. Reciprocal calling erupted. A few minutes later, M-group chimpanzees appeared at the fringes of the feeding area, calling, breaking branches, and slapping the ground. K-group vacated the station, and M-group also withdrew, calling. K-group returned to the station and resumed feeding. This is the case noted in Chapter 9, involving a rare stealthy penetration by M-group. "[I]t is reasonable to speculate that the M-group chimpanzees were very curious about what was happening around the temporary feeding area" (Nishida 1979:86)—like the Kalande "invaders" at Gombe.

Case 2. In late January, most of M-group went back to their southern range, but individuals remained around Kansyana station. On the 30th, the core of K-group moved south, returning to Kansyana for the first time in 5 months. The next day, one M-group adult male entered the feeding area, but ran away as K-group returned to it. Over the next 2 hours, three M-group females (including two former K-group members) came into the station, and were tolerated.

Case 3. The following day saw the *only* reported incident of intergroup violence between adult males. Mimikire, namesake of M-group, stealthily entered the banana

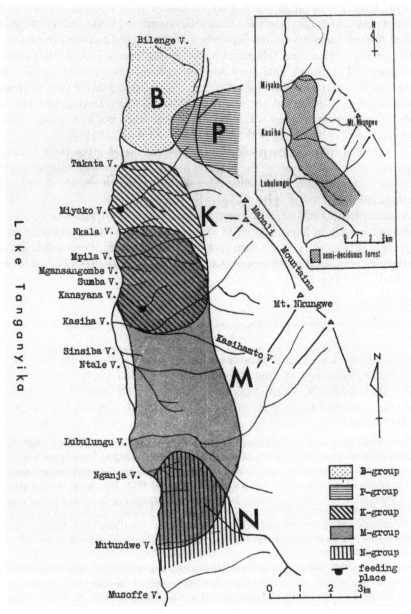

Illustration 3.1 Mahale Territories and Feeding Stations

Source: Kawanaka, K., & Nichida, T. (1974). Recent advances in the study of inter-unit-group relationships and social structure of wild chimpanzees of the Mahali Mountains. *Proceedings from the Symposia of the Fifth Congress of the International Primatological Society.* International Primatological Society.

plantation while K-group males were there. Spotting them, three gave chase. Two quickly gave up, but Kasonta pursued the intruder for 200 m and caught him. "Kasonta and Mimikire wrestled together in upright posture . . . until Kasonta forced Mimikire to the ground and bit him on the right thigh. Mimikire retreated little by little on his buttocks, continuing to scream weakly, when Kasonta stamped on his back. Mimikire finally managed to flee and ran away southward." Kasonta, "swaggering," led K-group back to the station, all calling, dragging branches, and slapping the ground. It was violent, but tepid compared to coalitional attacks elsewhere. K-group males had numerical superiority over a solo male from another group, but passed up the opportunity to kill.

Case 4. On April 27, M-group chimpanzees called from nearby while K-group was at the main feeding station, and K returned calls.

Case 5. On July 7, once again K-group at the station responded in kind to calls from M-group.

Case 6. On Sept 15, seven of M-group were at the main feeding station when K-group burst into calling from just outside. M-group slipped away, and K-group entered. Reciprocal calling and scouting around by K-group followed. All told, this is a benign record, territoriality by advertisement and avoidance.

Besides those intergroup clashes, attacks on alien mothers with infants—two lethal—were also tied to provisioning, at the same high-conflict time. A K-group female and her infant Limongo "once failed to escape from the provisioning site and were beaten to within an inch of their lives" (Nishida 2012:185).[1] As counted in Chapter 9, when K-group males ate a suspected M-group infant, M individuals were "in the vicinity of the feeding station"; and when M-group was lured into Miyako valley with cane, wounded and infant-less Wantendele was spotted among them (Nishida et al. 1979:17–18; Takahata and Takahata 1989:210).

It Was Human Impact

There is no question that provisioned food drew in M-group. Goodall (1983:53), while discounting provisioning as affecting movement or conflict at Gombe after the switch to System E, wrote that Mahale was different. "At Mahali the feeding system has remained unchanged and, apparently, continued to exert pressure on the movements of both study populations." Without doubt, K vs. M conflict centered on provisioning. Except for one fight in 2000, there is *no report of intergroup violence after provisioning ended.*

After absorbing many of K-group, M-group hit a demographic peak, around 100 individuals in the early 1980s. Addition of K-group's rangeland raised M-group territory from 13.4 km^2 to 20 km^2 (Nishida 1979:76, 82), but they did not use it all. For 6 months in 1982–1983 M stayed around the feeding station, and rarely returned to its southern rangelands (Nishida et al. 1985:297).

---

[1] Limongo was born in 1972 (Uehara et al. 1994a:277), which puts the undated attack at 1972–1974.

Then provisioning changed. "Almost no provisioning was done in 1983–84 and 1985–86" (Nishida 1989:70). After 1987, it ended completely, "for fear that poachers might take advantage of this method and because of the possibility of the transmission of human disease to chimpanzees" (Nishida 1990:21). With provisioning curtailed, M-group numbers started to fall, to 90 between 1985 and 1988 (Nishida et al. 2003:103). With eight or more suspected killed by lions in 1989–1990, it hovered around 81 from 1989 to 1992. That is still big for a chimpanzee unit-group, but given its large territory there shouldn't be pressure on natural food resources.

We will come back to this moment, the early 1990s, in the later history of M-group. But before that comes a topical switch, to within-group infant killings. The large number of Mahale killings weighs heavily in any discussion of infanticide by chimpanzees. These attacks provide powerful evidence against an adaptive explanation, and for the display violence hypothesis.

Inward Violence against Infants and Display

In the heyday of sociobiology, Takahata (1985:161) broke new ground by suggesting the infant killings of 1974 and 1976 could be aimed at *rival reduction*. "Intergroup infanticide might result in improving reproductive success by eliminating a future competitor." After that, however, most Mahale killings were *within* rather than between groups, contradicting demonic expectations.

Observed or Suspected Infant Killings

The first task in addressing infant killings is establishing an empirical record. The two comprehensive lists of suspected to certain intraspecific killings at Mahale (Wilson et al. 2014a:EDT 4; Nakamura and Itoh 2015:Table 26.1), largely coincide with my count, though with some technical adjustment.[2] Details come from several publications. In this presentation, cases that do not offer sufficient information for further discussion are in endnotes. Post-1976 incidents are in chronological order, with initial letters added for subsequent reference.

(A) In January 1977, Kagimimi was encountered holding and eating male infant Humbe of Ndilo. Others shared in the eating (Norikoshi 1982:68–69) (Count

---

[2] If a chimpanzee is found eating an infant, I usually label that as "3," a very likely killing, given the general rarity of scavenging (Muller et al. 1995). But at Mahale, scavenging of dead bushpigs or duikers is documented (Hasegawa et al. 1983; Muller et al. 1995:43). In the 1992—case (O)—an infant that was wounded in unknown circumstances and died, was snatched by an adult male and eaten. "Non-mothers generally paid no attention to dead infants but some adult males inspected and tried to snatch them away, possibly motivated by cannibalism" (Hosaka et al. 2000:15). Scavenging an infant that died is thus a real possibility at Mahale. Wilson et al. and Nakamura and Itoh label cases where an infant is already being consumed as "suspicious," and I classify them as "4's," possible killings.

Those two tallies differ in how they categorize seven incidents where killings were not witnessed. Nakamura and Itoh do not sort these as either intra- or intercommunity killings. Wilson et al. have them all as internal. I side with Wilson et al. here, because there is no suggestion of intergroup contacts over these years.

4-W-I-M 1977). (B) In June 1979, observers found alpha Kajugi eating the son of Wakasunga, sharing the meat (Kawanaka 1981:70–76) (Count 4-W-I-M 1979). Next come two attacks, already noted in Chapter 9, where researchers intervened to prevent killings. (C) In January 1981 Wantendele may or may not have been roaming alone when attacked; in (D) November 1981 she was with M-group.[3]

(G) Poor Wantendele. After transferring to M-group in July 1983, her infant was killed and the meat shared (Takahata 1985:165) (Count 1-W-I-M 1983). (H) In December 1983, with no other males present, young male Kasangazi was found eating Chausika's dead son, with the mother walking behind him (Nishida and Kawakana 1985:275) (Count 4-W-I-M 1983). (I) In July 1985, alpha Ntologi seized Tomato's infant and bit him in the face. His mother got him back, but he soon died (Count 1-W-I-M 1985).[4]

(M) In October 1989, after an unsuccessful red colobus hunt, beta (and future alpha) Kalunde started to attack Mirinda. He pulled her son away, but it ended up with alpha Ntologi, who killed it and began the shared eating (Hamai et al. 1992:156) (Count 1-W-I-M 1989). (N) In July 1990, Ntologi was found holding Betty's infant, with nearly 20 others present. He killed it and shared the meat with his allies (Hamai et al. 1992:153) (Count 1-W-I-M 1990). That is the last clear-cut infant killing of this series. There were none after 1990.[5]

The 7 of these 17 counted instances described in footnotes—E, F, J, K, L, O, Q—do not offer enough to work with. Attackers if any are unknown. Three of those are *possible* and four *hypothetical* kills. Of the remaining 10 dead infants, three are likely scavenged rather than killed, A, H, and P. From 1979 to 1989, that leaves seven cases, with good information, where deadly or potentially deadly attacks are very-likely-to-certain: B, C, D, G, I, M, N.

And the bottom line? Subtract the research interventions without killing (C and D), and add the *possible* but undescribed (F, J, and O), makes *eight possible-to-definite infant killings* 4-1), from 1977 to 1993. This is an extremely high rate of killing, .47 per year over 17 years. *All victims are males*, possibly offspring of attackers themselves, future "warriors" of M-group, at a frequency of nearly one every 2 years. This weighs

---

[3] Then come two very ambiguous and lightly sourced cases. (E) In 1981, Wakasunga's infant was found dead with a scar suggestive of an earlier attack (Hiraiwa et al. 1984:409) (Count 5-W-M 1981). (F) Wally disappeared that same year, and his mother's face was "mauled" (Hiraiwa-Hasegawa et al. 1984:409; Nakamura and Itoh 2015:Table 26.1) (Count 4-W-I-M 1981).

[4] Three others lack even that much information (Nakamura and Itoh 2015:Table 26.1). (J) In 1987, Gwamwami's baby was not seen after a loud disturbance was heard off in the distance (Count 4-W-I-F 1987). (K) Sometime in 1988, Fanta's baby was gone, yet she was not observed carrying the body, as Mahale mothers often do (Count 5-W-I-M 1988). (L) In 1989, Juno's infant also disappeared and also was not carried (Count 5-W-I-M 1989).

[5] (O) In September 1992, infant female Garbo died from a stomach wound of uncertain origin, and (future alpha) Nsaba snatched and ate it (Count 4-W-I-F 1992). (P) In October 1993, mid-rank Bonobo carried a dead newborn with umbilical cord still attached, bleeding around the head. Another adult male grabbed it and ran away (Nakamura and Itoh 2015:376) (Count 4-W-I-M 1993). In May 1998 the two highest-status males, Fanana and Kalunde, repeatedly charged and displayed at Ruby and infant daughter Rubicon, and once reached for the infant, leading observers to suspect infanticidal intent. But other females intervened, and in the end only Fanana was bleeding (Nakamura and Itoh 2015:Table 26.1; Sakamaki et al. 2001:360–362) (Not counted). (Q) Sometime in 1998 Pinky disappeared, and her mother had a wound (Sakamaki et al. 2001:364) (Count 5-W-I-F 1998).

heavily against the rival coalition reduction hypothesis (RCRH), and an adaptive perspective.

Is there any other explanation? Mahale researchers recognized another factor coincident with most of these killings.

> All the victims in the 1980s were killed by the M-group males, which might be explained by some kind of social instability.... Another notable detail is that during 1980–1993 ... Ntologi was the alpha male.... After Ntologi fell from the alpha status, infanticides did not occur under other alpha males. Thus it is necessary to consider the possibility that the personality of the alpha male may influence the occurrence of infanticides. (Nakamura and Itoh 2015:376)

That brings us to display violence.

Ntologi

Ntologi was huge, possibly 60 kg. (K-group's brawny Sobongo was about 47 kg.) Ntologi was born around 1955, but we know nothing about his formative years or interactions with local people, although he "was afraid of humans." In 1979 he displaced Kajugi as alpha, the latter going into permanent exile. His time as alpha was the longest known—12 years without interruption, then 3 more years in a comeback. His status was secured by a very stable alliance with Lubulungu and several other senior males. "Ntologi always enjoyed being at the centre of a big grooming cluster.... Ambitious but young, high-ranking males were so much overwhelmed by the senior male club that they would not even approach their grooming cluster" (Nishida 2012:237–239).

Meat sharing was a big part of Ntologi's portfolio.

> Ntologi was not only one of the best hunters but also could snatch a carcass from other chimpanzees. During the 1980s, more than 30 per cent of the carcasses hunted by M-group's chimpanzees went to Ntologi ... he shared meat with senior males.... He never shared meat with his rivals. (Nishida 2012:240; and see Nishida et al. 1992)

So were innovative and protracted intimidation displays.

> Ntologi had great stamina for intimidation displays lasting as long as several minutes at a stretch, where other males usually stopped after 10–20 seconds.... Ntologi was strong enough to lift up heavy rocks and throw them into a stream with both hands. The high splashing water and sound were enough to intimidate other chimpanzees.... Moreover, he was the only male to visit and drum on two metal houses in each display bout. Of course, staging intimidation displays is a much less risky, though perhaps no less energetically expensive, way to maintain alpha status than directly attacking rivals. (Nishida 2012:239)

His displays also targeted humans.

Male chimpanzees sometimes deliberately charge past human observers or lightly slap the humans knees or hips . . . such behaviors may be motivated to display "boldness" to other chimpanzees. . . . Ntologi's displays were sometimes dangerous to humans. . . . One reason why Ntologi was more dangerous . . . might be that Ntologi actively used tools such as stones and boughs in his intimidation displays against humans. The other reason might be that he intended to show "ruthlessness" as the alpha male rather than "boldness," although such an argument has not been elaborated in conventional ethology. (Hosaka 2015b:443–445)

Conventional ethology hasn't, but I have, regarding Goblin and Frodo. It could even be that humans are drawn into chimpanzee politics. "Recently a female chimpanzee at Mahale . . . attacked and severely wounded two researchers whom she considered to be allies of males that had killed her infant" (Wade 2003). Display violence may solve the riddle of internal infanticides at Mahale.

For Gombe, extreme violence against defenseless individuals both within and outside the group could intimidate internal rivals, especially in times of social instability. During most of Ntologi's time on top (1979–1995), M-group had few contacts with any other group. If a status-conscious male intended to impress potential rivals, the victim could only come from within.

Status Display

Consider Ntologi's place in the seven incidents that have good information. The June 1979 killing (B) was not by Ntologi, but by failing alpha Kajugi. His displacer Ntologi was present, watching (Kawanaka 1981:72). If that was display violence to intimidate Ntologi—as I suspect—it failed. Ntologi toppled Kajugi the very next month. Yet it may have taught Ntologi a lesson. From 1979 on, Ntologi was central in every infanticide, with theatrical dangerousness.

Recently ascendant as alpha, he led the two severe assaults on Wantendele and her son Masudi (C, D). At that point in time, he and ally Lubulungu were under challenge by Bakali and Kalunde, with both sides wooing supporters. In January 1981 (C), Ntologi and Lubulungu (and Musa) attacked. In November (D), with many males present, rival Kalunde made an initial charge and a few others joined in, but Ntologi and Lubulungu commandeered the aggression, (Nishida and Hiraiwa-Hasegawa 1985:3, 4, 8–10). Kalunde was trumped.

(G) In 1983, amid a large crowd with lots of noise and charging, Ntologi took Wantendele's infant into his mouth (Hamai et al. 1992:156). Ntologi ate and shared meat with his favored partners (Takahata 1985:165). (I) In 1985, again amid other males, Ntologi seized Tomato's infant and bit it in the face. Though the mother got him back, he died (Hamai et al. 1992:156). (M) In the 1989 attack on Mirinda, beta and rival Kalunde initially grabbed the infant, but lost control of it. After a scramble it ended up still alive, with Lukaja. In a remarkable scene, "Lukaja handed the infant to the alpha male Ntologi, who dragged, tossed, and slapped it against the ground. Ntologi climbed a tree with the infant in his mouth. He waived it in the air and finally killed it by biting it on the face." He shared meat (Hamai et al. 1992:152).

In July 1990, with his position on top under mounting pressure, came Ntologi's last killing (N). He was found with Betty's infant still alive in his mouth, with four adult males watching. "Ntologi began to bite on the fingers of its right hand. He struck the infant against a tree trunk, and also dragged it on the ground as he displayed. As a result the infant was finally killed" (Hamai et al. 1992:153).

Put these scattered reports together and that is a lot of intimidating violence, all involving and most done by Ntologi. Political intent is unmistakable in the flamboyant display and meat sharing with his supporters.

Context

A basic condition of the display violence hypothesis is active status context near the top. *Sometimes* this is related to human disturbance. On status contestation, reports note active turmoil at the moment of attacks B, C, D, N, there is nothing specific pertaining to 1983, 1985, and 1989 incidents (G, I, M). Yet Ntologi always had rivals.

Human impact is even less described. Provisioning was curtailed from 1983 and halted in 1987, with no information about repercussions. By 1989, disruptive tourism picked up (below). Whether that human impact somehow contributed to display violence by Ntologi, the master of intimidating display, simply cannot be assessed.

Across Africa, Ntologi and late Gombe's Ferdinand stand out with a penchant for *internal* infant killings. Like Ferdinand, Ntologi was the most proficient reproducer, siring a disproportionate number of offspring (Hosaka and Nakamura 2015a:391). It is quite likely that Ntologi like Ferdinand killed his own offspring. Yet he stayed on top, and built up a lot of ill will. (Late Budongo offers additional but complicated data internal infant killings by high-status males.)

Ntologi as Target

Ntologi expands the record of severe violence on fallen, overbearing alphas after their fall. In March 1991 longtime rivals Kalunde and Nsaba bested him, forcing him into temporary exile. But he stayed close, sometimes seen with obstreperous young Jilba. In January 1992 Kalunde was threatened by Nsaba, and Ntologi came back, with Jilba. Ntologi skillfully played off the two top males, and by March was back at alpha. Although old, he stayed there until beaten in a fight with Nsaba in April 1995. He disappeared again for a short time, then returned at low rank. In October 1995, Ntologi was found in a coma, covered with 10–20 wounds, with a young adult male and some females around him. He died shortly (Nishida 1996; 2012:240–241, 247–251).

Nishida surmises that he was "subjected to a gang attack by his groupmates, such as Nsaba . . . Ntologi had reigned selfishly over the group for 15 years, and thus other members may have held grudges against him" (Nishida 2015:252–254). Nakamura and Itoh (2015:379–380), noting his age, about 40, and the shallowness of most wounds, caution that it is not certain the attack killed him. Yet surface wounds may

Illustration 3.2 Chimpanzees Surrounded by Tourists at Mahale
Source: Nishida, T., & Mwinuka, C. (2005). Introduction of a seasonal park fee system to Mahale Mountains National Park: A proposal. *Pan Africa News, 12*(2), 17–19.

not reflect internal injuries, and circumstantial evidence is strong (Count 3-W-A-M 1995). An overbearing alpha may be paid pack when he loses his grip.

M-Group History Post K-group

Tourists and Disease

M-group's history did not end when K-group was gone. Increasing tourism brought more exposure to anthropogenic disease. Classic ecotourism—few, wealthy visitors in tents—began in 1987. From about 50 tourists in 1989, it surpassed 300 in 1993, then fluctuated between 200 and 300 until 2001. "Outbreaks," more than 10 chimpanzees coughing within a month, occurred during the dry season when most tourists came (Nishida and Nakamura 2008:176–178). In 1993, some tourists arrived with bad colds, and a severe respiratory infection killed up to 11 of M-group (Hosaka 1995b:5).

Tourism went out of control in the early 2000s, with the advent of two commercial tourist companies. "Competition between tourist agencies results in better service for tourists, including longer observation hours and closer access to chimpanzees" (Nishida and Nakamura 2008:178). Purcell (2002), who worked with one of the tourist agencies, describes the combined human pressure on M-group, from researchers, tourists, and film-makers. All brought attention and funds that help protect the Park and promote conservation.

> However, they all also comprise a threat to the chimpanzees and the project. This can be simply described as that of stress and infection.... We now rigidly restrict to a maximum six tourists per group from our camp, but frequently meet many, many more people when viewing, whether these are other tourist groups, or those connected with research and park maintenance. Furthermore, we require a park ranger plus a tracker and our own guide, and often, a trainee, swelling our numbers in a group immediately to 10.... We currently have to negotiate amongst ourselves to avoid bumping into other visitors. This is not always successful.... Efforts should be made on the part of rangers and tourist trackers to follow individuals not being followed by the research.... Some allowances should be made for the fact that tourists get their most exciting viewing when observing the high-ranking males, more specifically the alpha male.

Baboons

Humans were not the only bothersome primates. In 1973–1974, two baboon groups overlapped with the M-group range, though not by much. The baboons stayed along the lake shore. They first started foraging inland in 1990. In 1991, chimpanzees were barking and chasing baboons. Baboons eat almost all of the main chimpanzee foods, and by 1992 they were causing "a drastic decrease in some food plants" (Nishida 2002:2). In 1995, baboons entered Kansyana camp itself,

> and began to feed on the fruits of a giant tree of *Pseudospondia microcarpa*, which had been previously monopolized by M group chimpanzees. By that time, the fruits of mangos and guava had already begun to be eaten by baboons. Since they can eat the unripe pulp of these fruits, chimpanzees have scarcely any opportunity to eat these favorite fruits. Apparently, feeding competition has become severer between these baboons and chimpanzees. (Nishida 1997:1)

By 1997 four baboon groups regularly used a substantial part of the M-group range. By 2002 baboon groups were larger (50–60 compared to 40 earlier) (Itoh et al. 2011:265), five or six baboon groups were in the area, and chimpanzees had not eaten mangos for 5 years. That year the baboons went even deeper into M-group range, where they consumed the fruit that was M-groups' staple in the late dry to early rainy season. "It is likely that baboons are winning the competition with chimpanzees" (Nishida 2002:2; cf. Matsumoto-Oda and Kasagula 2000:147, 152). Chimpanzees began to prey on young baboons, with one or two cases in 1997, 2001, 2003, and 2004. This is the only recorded chimpanzee predation on baboons outside of Gombe (Hitonaru 2004:3; Hosaka 2015c:276; Nakamura 1997).

How did baboons come to compete with chimpanzees? "I speculate that the recent invasion of the chimpanzee range by baboons has been facilitated partly by the widening of observation paths for the convenience of tourists. The park tourism strategy

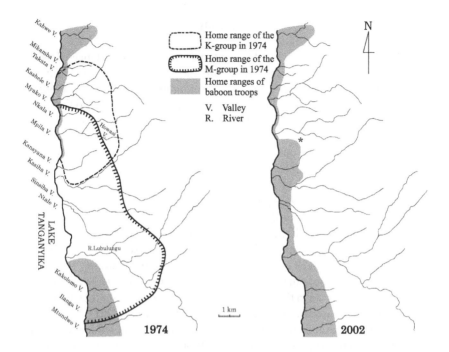

Illustration 3.3 Map of Baboon Invasion, Mahale

Source: Nishida, T. (2002). Competition between baboons and chimpanzees at Mahale. *Pan Africa News*, 9(2): 23–26.

appears to have provided an opener and dryer environment that is more conducive to baboon survival" (Nishida 2002:3). Baboons that previously kept to the lake shore now followed 3 m wide highways (Nishida 2008:4) into chimpanzee resources, picking fruits clean before they ripen.

Landscape Transformation

Other anthropogenic changes impacted M-group foods. *Senna spectabilis* was planted for shade at the research camp and in nearby villages in 1967. In the later 1980s it was spreading rapidly, choking off chimpanzee food trees. Efforts to eradicate it began in 1995, but it is very hard to expunge (Nishida 1996b; Nishida and Nakamura 2008:181; Wakibara 1998). Another negative for chimpanzees was continuing regrowth of farm fields of lakeside villages after 1985 relocations. That reduced human crops and transitional growth fruits that chimpanzees ate (Nakamura et al. 2013:179–180). "Vegetation in the area has been continuously changing since the site became a national park and slash-and-burn farmlands were abandoned. We do not yet know what the forest will look like without major human activity" (Itoh et al. 2011:255).

These anthropogenic changes reduced chimpanzee foods during the early 1990s. Was it just coincidence that simultaneously, M-group dramatically increased hunting red colobus monkeys?

Hunting

From 1966 to 1981, hunting was infrequent, only 50 observed instances. Target species were opportunistic, with red colobus only the third most popular. From 1983 to 1989, with M-group at its most numerous, hunting increased to 103 instances, with red colobus counting for 58 of the kills. More males may contribute to that increase, but it may also reflect increasing red colobus numbers as Mahale forests recovered from land clearing after 1978 (Hosaka et al. 2020:392, 399).

In 1990–1995, while the number of adult males *declined*, hunting soared upward to 295 instances and 245 red colobus kills. For that period, Nishida (2012:65) guesstimates that "adult males of M-group eat about 50 kg of meat per year." Researchers were stumped by the early 1990s jump (Hosaka et al. 2001:113–114, 122–123; Uehara 1997:195). Recently they argue that it just took time for the newly reinvented practice of hunting to spread through the population (Hosaka et al. 2020:339).

I suggest instead that it happened because of increasing scarcity of other preferred foods, due to human-linked changes. But sharply intensified hunting of red colobus was more sustainable here than at Gombe and Ngogo. At Mahale, when the red colobus population declined in the north, hunting shifted to more abundant prey in their southern range, and northern red colobus revived (Itoh et al. 2011:265). At Ngogo pursuit of red colobus outside their old, depleted hunting range led to intergroup violence. Not at Mahale, where downstream effects of human impact did not cause intergroup resource competition.

Range Changes

Another indicator of localized food problems came in May–June of 1994, when M-group's ranging shifted dramatically into higher slopes to their east. "This shift of the ranging might have been caused by the invasion by baboons into the forested lowland area" (Nishida 1997:2). A new observation trail, "the skyway," had to be cut. "From May to July 1994, it was impossible for us to study chimpanzees without this new trail" (Nishida 2002:2). This persisting shift away from lower lands entailed a major expansion of M-group's total territory—not by encroaching on other groups, but by incorporating unused areas. The change was so pronounced that a long-term study of ranging patterns was initiated in 1994 (Nakamura et al. 2013).[6]

Just after this range shift, in December 1995, began what I called the Great Disappearance. About 15 chimpanzees including most of the high status males, were suddenly gone, with no signs of conflict or disease. Now the *historical context* of the Great Disappearance is evident. Losing favorite foods and staples in lower lands to baboons, *Senna*, and regrowth, surrounded by tourists, having already shifted away

---

[6] This study documents major departures from the Gombe perspective. Observations from 1994 to 2009 (Nakamura et al. 2013:172, 176, 179, 180; Nakamura et al. 2015) do not support "the male-defended territory model," of females foraging inside a larger space used by widely roaming males, and so protected from interlopers. Mixed foraging parties commonly went up to territorial edges. Neither was there any correlation between the number of adult males and total expanse of territory. Mahale also undercuts the generalization that natal females emigrate at maturity, as only 24 out of 32 did (Itoh and Nakamura 2015:76).

from their old main range, I submit that many of M-group may have continued outward and upward, beyond the range of tourists, baboons, and researchers.

Y-Group

M-group were not the only ones on the move. In June 1998, M-group went to its far northern range to feed on a fruit never eaten before. An unknown group of chimpanzees, estimated at about 50, from higher land to the east entered the vacant center of M-group range, and ranged across it for five days (Itoh et al. 1999). They had no contact with M-group, and this mystery group was not seen again.

That same year, another and more permanent intrusion occurred in the Miyako area, part of K-group's old range—though upland, not in the lower realms that M-group was now avoiding. After first suspecting it was K-group returning, researchers did not recognize any of its members (although 20 years had passed), and concluded it was a new entry. They called them Y-group. In 2001 habituation commenced for research and tourism, to alleviate the stress on M-group (Nishida and Nakamura 2008:179; Sakamaki et al. 2007; Sakamaki and Nakamura 2015:130–131).

Why did Y-group (and the mystery group) show up and push in? What was happening on the outside? Little is known about the Mahale Mountains east of the Park, except for a brief survey in 1996, when Nakamura and Fukuda (1999) trekked along the very dry eastern slopes. They found signs of chimpanzee inhabitation, but not many. Vast areas were burned over, probably by shifting cultivators (1999:2). From Mahale, the fire glow behind the mountain ridge was sometimes visible at night. The ridge is no barrier for chimpanzees, which have been seen even at the highest peaks (Kano 1972:60).

Researchers thought that Y was a group or a splinter from higher elevations, because they found a well-worn chimpanzee trail between its new range and the mountains (Sakamaki and Nakamura 2015:131–132). That fires and forest clearing pushed Y-group toward the protected area around Mahale is speculation, but entirely consistent with effects of habitat loss elsewhere.

The Big Clash

The arrival of this new group caused tension. In 1999–2000, calling and counter-calling between M and Y was heard on 11 days. Throughout this time,

> M-group chimpanzees occasionally conducted mass expeditions to the peripheral areas of their range, but did not conduct the typical boundary patrols observed at Gombe. In a notable case, on May 8, 2000, six adult males and one estrous adult female traveled silently to the northern boundary. The other M-group chimpanzees remained behind. While traveling, the seven occasionally sought physical contact such as extending a hand or embracing. The volume of pant-grunts directed to the alpha male was low and apparent only as panting. This was suggestive of a boundary patrol. (Sakamaki and Nakamura 2015:131)

Then an event breathed life into the RCRH for Mahale: the only reported intergroup violence since the 1981 attack on Wantendele (Katsukake and Matsusaka 2002).

In December 2000, a group including all M-group adult males heard strangers' calls. Researchers did not know then who they were, but since the Mpila valley where it occurred became Y-group range, it was probably them. The males rushed off silently toward the calls. When observers caught up, four adult males were assaulting a 2.5-year-old stranger male infant. Its mother tried ineffectually to defend it. The infant's body was not found, but the severity of its wounds made death very likely (Count 3-O-I-M 2000).

Later, several M-group males had small wounds, including individuals not present during the infanticidal attack. Researchers concluded that there had been a between-group clash that was not witnessed. They (2002:175) speculate that the violence against the infant was to reduce future male rivals, thus supporting the RCRH. That is a reasonable inference, taking this incident alone and ignoring all the internal infanticides.

No further clash with Y-group or border patrolling is reported. Although M-group outnumbered Y, M did not go into the overlap area when Y-group was present. That is nonviolent avoidance. Researchers infer that M already had enough food in their southern ranges (Nakamura et al. 2013:175, 179). Relations with other, long-term neighbors also seem calm. The only reported contact came in 2001, when M-group exchanged calls from over a kilometer's distance with N-group to its south, then went back north (Sakamaki and Nakamura 2015:132).

The simple fact that M attacked Y-group with uncharacteristic violence suggests that arrival of unknown strangers may initially cause extreme stress, leading to violence. That simple idea is relevant for understanding captive release experiments at Conkouati-Douli and Mt. Assirik, and playback experiments of stranger chimpanzee calls at Kanyawara and Tai.

Later Mahale, Not as Bad as Late Gombe (Yet)

The Rising Tide of Settlers

In the early 21st century, habitat loss outside the Park to regional migrants and refugees got worse and nearer. Forests that in the 1990s surrounded lower-lying eastern Park borders were cleared for cultivation. Local people respected Park regulations, but ground-clearing fires from outside swept in. The research area was near to Park borders, but from maps at my disposal, fires may have reached as close as 5 km.

Confronting these trends and the importance of tourism, the Tanzanian government and NGOs developed a Greater Mahale Ecosystem Action Plan (Itoh et al. 2011:256–257, 267; Nishida et al. 2001:46–47; Nishida and Nakamura 2008:178, 181). Researchers got more deeply involved with local outreach and conservation (Hosaka and Nakamura 2015b; Nishida and Nakamura 2008:180–182). A sustainable solution was urgent, with obliteration of chimpanzee habitat already critical throughout much of western Tanzania (Pintea 2012).

The loss of nearby habitat may explain an unusual occurrence over 2010. One after another five stranger adolescent females appeared within M-group, compared to a total of 17 female immigrants in the previous 19 years. Researchers thought this could be due to "the extinction of a nearby unit-group," although no parous females arrived (Hayakawa et al. 2010). This *could be* the second instance of multiple female transfer at Mahale, not from war but from human disturbance.

More and More Tourists

Tourism, already disruptive, got much more so. From 2002 to 2005 visitors zoomed to over a thousand. Soon it neared 1,200. Tourists became "the heartbeat of the national and local economies." This commercial value contributes to preservation of the Park and its fauna. Nevertheless, chimpanzees pay a price. In May 2006, another flu-like epidemic struck M-group, killing about 12, mostly infants (Hanamura et al. 2008). Two males that allowed tourists to come the closest were believed to be the vector of infection (Lukasik-Braum and Spelman 2008:735). The pathogen was a Japanese strain of human metapneumovirus (Hanamura et al. 2015:364).

Researchers proposed new rules including obligatory face masks. On themselves, they imposed a one-week quarantine before observing chimpanzees. That did not constrain tourists (Hanamura et al. 2006). Revised rules still allowed up to 39 people to visit chimpanzees per day, including tourists, guides, and up to 9 researchers and assistants. Yet in the popular dry season, from June to October, up to six tourist groups may visit on one day. Trackers follow chimpanzees constantly to know where tours should go. Visitors may arrive at the same time by different trails, so chimpanzees have people on both sides. Tourists especially want to see infants or the alpha male, and sometimes come between mothers and offspring (Nakamura and Nishida 2009). In 2008, despite new rules, tourists were found in the Park without guides, without face masks, coughing, disturbing chimpanzees, going off trails into the bush, using flashlights, leaving belongings, and defecating.[7] Recently tourists surpassed 2,000 per year (Nishida 2012:286). Those bad "behaviors are still observed, and no improvements have been made" (Nakamura 2015:666).[8]

This is *massive* disruption. But after all the changes of the 1990s, *food was not scarce*. Going from a population of about 100 with a territory of 19.4 km² in 1980–1982, to 50–60 with 27.4 km² in 2009, (Nakamura et al. 2013:173–174), density dropped from roughly 5.2/km² to 2.2/km². By 2000, that "reduced feeding competition considerably" (Nishida et al. 2003:116). By the resource competition plus human impact hypothesis (RCH +HIH), intergroup violence is *not* expected. Other than the initial intrusion of Y-group, none is reported. But one extraordinarily violent internal incident did occur.

---

[7] Analysis of YouTube videos from mountain gorilla tourism found they received more views and likes if including tourists and gorillas in one shot, with many at just arm's length distance (Otsuka and Yanakoshi 2020).

[8] What happens when a chimpanzee displays at, charges, or attacks a tourist? With so many intrusive visitors, it surely happens. Do guides and trackers defend? If so, how? What consequences follow?

Pimu

In 2011 Pimu was the alpha, since 2007 (Inaba 2009). In October, 2011, he attacked the beta, Primus, and both were seriously injured in a short, intense fight. Primus ran off. Then four senior males including ex-alphas Alofu and Kalunde, attacked, beat, and bit Pimu for nearly 2 hours, right in front of picture-snapping tourists. As described by Steve Ladd, camp manager for Greystoke tours (https://vimeo.com/40444106), at the end of the assault, Alofu bit into the back of Pimu's skull, leaving him quivering. Then old Kalunde picked up a large rock, and repeatedly bashed it into Pimu's head. Pimu was quite dead (Count 1-W-A-M 2011).

This is a killing of superlatives, "the only certain case of conspecific killing of an adult male at Mahale" (Nakamura and Itoh 2015:380). It is the only certain internal killing of a current alpha in the wild, although Gombe's Goblin almost certainly would have died without medical care, Ferdinand barely escaped, and Luit was killed in Arnhem Zoo. The biggest superlative of all is that *Pimu was killed with a tool*—if the report is to be believed.[9]

Kaburu et al. (2013:791, 795) are puzzled by this attack, since it does not fit the model of male coalitional aggression to reduce the strength of rival groups. They suggest it may represent internal reproductive competition when outside chimpanzees are not a threat. Or maybe it is a nonfunctional byproduct of an evolved tendency to kill with numerical advantage. Whichever, for them it is somehow explained by evolution. They do not mention tourism except to acknowledge their eyewitness sources (also see Wrangham 2019:240–242).

This attack came at the tail end of the peak tourist season, when rains increased and chimpanzees begin to congregate in larger groups (Nishida and Mwinuka 2005:3). Probably *hundreds* of *groups* of tourists followed high-status males over the previous four months, on top of the regular compliment of researchers and trackers. For nearly a decade before this killing, with Pimu on top for half that span, increasing numbers of tourists were appearing every day for months, watching the alpha, reacting to aggression, and being watched by the chimpanzees themselves. In captivity, more strange watchers means more wounding attacks. Did the tourist surge elevate levels of aggression, and contribute to the killing of Pimu?

That would fall within the wider pattern of deposed alphas suffering severe, even lethal attacks by males of their own group. That commonly targets older, fallen alphas that are no longer physically threatening. Pimu does not fit that description. He was however, a particularly obnoxious alpha. He would leave a red colobus kill on the ground and then display charge at others to keep them from getting it, "as if to pronounce the meat was inaccessible even when he was not holding it." He slapped females before mating with them, and mated with his mother. "Some researchers speculated that his stint as the alpha would last as long as Ntologi" (Hosaka 2015a:54). But Ntologi had the gerontocracy on his side, and Pimu was alone. According to camp manager Ladd (2012), Pimu was "an aggressive, nasty chimp, particularly

---

[9] Ladd's detailed description is convincing, but given the extraordinary nature of this incident, photographic evidence would be good. I contacted Greystoke to see if photos were available. For the tracker that day, his camera battery was dead, and the enterprise was no longer in contact with Ladd.

disagreeable... nobody liked him, and when I say nobody, no other chimpanzee liked him... they hated this guy because he was such a bully."

Pimu beat beta Primus in the fight he picked, but it left Pimu wounded and weakened. In a social world with tensions heightened by incessant tourist intrusion, four senior males saw the opportunity pay the bully back, and took it.

Even Weirder

The last report from Mahale dates to 2014 (Nishie and Nakamura 2017:195–198). On December 2, 21 chimpanzees including alpha Primus were together. Suddenly female Devota crouched down and delivered an infant. This is highly unusual, as females typically seclude themselves for birth. Immediately, third-ranking Darwin, sitting behind her, grabbed the infant and ran off. Its sex and whether it was born alive are unknown. An hour later Darwin had it up a tree, and ate the entire thing (Count 4-W-I-? 2014). No display of fierceness or status contest is noted. Tourists, if present, are not mentioned. Darwin might have been the father, but probably not. Researchers consider various theories of infanticide, but favor none. They do not consider another possibility: that this is aberrant behavior among disturbed chimpanzees, like Freud killing Tofiki.

Lessons of Mahale

In the article reporting Pimu's killing, the authors open with the standard model of intergroup behavior.

> Adult males pursue an aggressive, collective, territoriality that contests intercommunity dominance and secures access to food resources. Individuals isolated in the periphery of their home range risk becoming victims of violent, potentially lethal, assaults by coalition gangs of aggressors (typically adult males) from neighboring communities. When lethal violence occurs, deep bite wounds are common. Some more specific injuries are also reported: traumatic damage to the throat, removal of some or all of the genitalia, disfiguring of the face and, more rarely, broken bones. There are now multiple reports from across the species' geographic range of such violence. (Kabura et al. 2013:789, references omitted)

This is entirely unlike the empirical record of intergroup relations at Mahale, demonstrating the power of the Gombe paradigm.

The extermination of K-group is devoid of observational support. The positional contest between K- and M-groups, which resulted in one or two infant killings, was caused by artificial provisioning. Encourage two groups to come to the same feeding station, and serious antagonism may ensue. Halt provisioning, and no more intergroup conflict.

If killing neighbors were an evolved chimpanzee predisposition, it was not expressed again, except perhaps the 2000 Y-group infant killing. Moreover, after the disappearance of adult K-group males, M-group accepted young K males into their own. They tolerated Limongo within their range for many years. If it is true that between chimpanzee groups, "When the killing is cheap, kill" (Wrangham 2005:18), one would expect more evidence than three outside infant killings in over 50 years of observation.

The RCRH is supported only if one believes that K adult males (eight hypotheticals) were killed by M-group. Otherwise it is falsified. The total killings of infant and adult males is: *within group*, six likely, six possible, and five hypothetical; *between group*, two likely, and one possible, plus the eight hypotheticals. Counting all certain-to-possibles, Mahale chimpanzees killed their own current and future defenders at 4:1 over outside males. Even if all hypotheticals are added in, internal male killings still dominate, 17 to 11.

The entire Mahale record during and after provisioning shows that intergroup territorial relations are characterized by *avoidance*, with smaller groups getting out of the way of larger ones. After K was gone M-group still had neighbors, but except for the arrival of Y-group, they did not fight. From an RCH + HIH perspective, post-provisioning there is no reason to expect serious territorial clashes with neighbors. By the RCRH, by demonic expectations, there is: it is chimpanzees' nature to seek opportunities to attack and kill.

Politics

At Gombe anthropogenic disturbance, tense intergroup relations, sharp internal status competition, and personalities of individual males were involved in attacks on helpless adults, females, and infants of neighboring groups. The Ntologi case (and one time, his predecessor Kajugi) was different. In a group without external conflict or even much contact, display violence targeted defenseless individuals inside M-group. With Ntologi intense status conflict was present for at least some of the killings, but other political or human disturbance context is missing.

Mahale also parallels Gombe in showing severe attacks on ex-alphas, with losers going into exile, and Ntologi probably killed. Pimu did not have the option, whacked in his prime while being a bullying alpha. Perhaps the high-status Mahale males had been pushed toward hyper aggressiveness by the ceaseless disruption.

Paradigmatics

For the founders and followers of the Gombe perspective of intergroup relations, Mahale was the deciding case. The sensational Four Year War made seemingly innocuous, theoretically inconsequential male disappearances at Mahale were a key part of another earth-shaking discovery, like tool making and hunting. Chimpanzees made war! For the Mahale research community in the 1980s, interpreting events that way validated Nishida's neglected hypothesis of closed, antagonistic unit-groups. The conflict between K- and M-groups was due to chimpanzee nature, rather than to what the researchers were doing. It seemed like a good idea at the time.

But the Mahale record is extraordinarily different from the often told tales of deadly "warfare." It gives negligible support for the idea that males are predisposed to kill neighboring males; and strongly supports Power's claim that the Gombe Four Year War paradigm overwhelmed evidentiary reality in the chimpanzee literature. Yet by the 2000s, from the demonic perspective, Mahale was expendable. By then there was a new, better confirmation of Gombe-vision: serial killings at Kibale's Ngogo. And the Ngogo chimpanzees were never provisioned.

PART IV
KIBALE

11
Kibale

Kibale National Park (KNP) provides the most compelling evidence of chimpanzee "war" in all of Africa, by never-provisioned chimpanzees. At two research sites, Kanyawara and Ngogo, about 27 individuals were killed in intergroup fighting, with up to 10 more possible. Twenty-five come from Ngogo, and the attackers appropriated the killing ground into their rangeland.

At face value, Kibale provides the strongest support of the demonic perspective. One intergroup killing at Kanyawara may be the most famous of any. In this book's conclusion I show that without Ngogo, adaptationist predictions about chimpanzee violence have very little support. Kibale is the adaptive lynchpin and so requires careful and detailed empirical and theoretical consideration. In Part IV I show that these killings are attributable to human impact, albeit in a complicated way.

Did Ngogo chimpanzees kill because of an innate propensity to slay strangers when killing is cheap—the rival coalition reduction hypothesis (RCRH)? Or due to immediate competition for basic resources—the resource competition hypothesis (RCH)? After discussing killings at Kibale (and elsewhere), Wrangham (2006:51–52) concludes:

> In theory, killing might be a response to competition: but there's no indication that it happens more when resources are in short supply—more likely it happens when food is abundant ... Nor is there any short-term benefit in the form of access to contested food supplies. In contrast to those [and other] ideas, there is one explanation that fits the data well. This is the hypothesis that chimpanzees kill rivals whenever they can do so safely, because killing raises the likelihood of winning future battles.

Part IV weighs in for RCH contest over food, but attributes those conflicts to a history of habitat modifications. RCH + HIH.

Chapter 11 introduces the area, the research, and the history of habitat disturbance in and around the Park. Chapter 12 lays out the record of inter-group conflict and killing at Ngogo. Chapters 13 and 14 then link human impact to that violence. Chapter 13 investigates Ngogo's extraordinary size and density and the differing relationships with its neighbors, all in connection to prime foods grown within old farm clearings, and to more recent and extensive forest loss nearby. Chapter 14 relates that context to direct competition over preferred foods—the immediate sources of intergroup contention and violence. Chapter 16 closes Kibale with wide ranging discussion of the Kanyawara research site: its disconformity with demonic expectations, why its history differs from Ngogo's, the impact of a particular research technique, and finally some additional gender essentialisms.

Kibale and Its Primates

Kibale National Park in western Uganda is (as expanded—below) 795 km², (compared to 32 km² Gombe and 1,613 km² Mahale). Gazetted as a Crown Forest in 1932, and a Central Forest Reserve in 1948, it became a National Park in 1993. KNP ecology has been studied for decades, led by Thomas Struhsaker, starting at Kanyawara in 1970 and Ngogo in 1973. These efforts through the New York Zoological Society (later Wildlife Conservation Society) and the Makerere University Biological Field Station (MUBFS), including Kanyawara and Ngogo, and produced extraordinary research with hundreds of scientific publications. Kanyawara is now a research center with labs, apartments, and dormitory space.

The undulating hills of Kibale rise from 1,100 m in the south to 1,590 in the north. Two rainy seasons are March–May and September–November. The south is drier and hotter than the north. Vegetation is a mosaic of tropical forest (about 58%), anthropogenic grassland, papyrus swamps, and secondary regrowth bush and forest. Fauna is diverse, including 12 species of primates.

Estimates of Park chimpanzee population of the Park vary widely, but 1,200–1,400 is a central range. Overall density is unusually high. In 1976–1978, Ghiglieri (1984:57) figured from 1.45 to 2.38/km². Estimates from the late 1990s and early 2000s are slightly higher, from 1.5 to 3/km². In a survey of all Uganda chimpanzees Kibale came out at the top, with 2.32/km², almost twice the 1.17/km² average of all other sites (Plumptre et al. 2003:27). Local densities also vary greatly.[1] But there may be surprises to come.[2]

Chimpanzee Research

Michael Ghiglieri (1984:14–31) initiated research on chimpanzees with 488 hours of direct observation from December 1976 to May 1978, plus additional study in April–May 1981. Mostly he stayed at Ngogo, but 6.6% of his time was at Kanyawara. Although I am critical of many sweeping assertions in his *Dark Side of Man*, *The Chimpanzees of Kibale Forest* (1984) is careful research, cautiously interpreted. His pioneering fieldwork was almost heroic.

Worried about the effects of provisioning on behaviors, he had planned to go to Gombe to study unprovisioned Mitumba. The kidnappings quashed that plan. Thomas Struhsaker suggested Kibale as a research location. Unable to get funding, Ghiglieri scraped together enough resources to begin the project. The chimpanzees

---

[1] On the Park itself, see Chapman et al. (2011:75–76); Southworth et al. (2010:125); Struhsaker (1975:114–117; 1997:13–15; 2008); Wanyama et al. (2009); Watts (2012:319–320). On Park chimpanzee numbers, see Chapman and Lambert (2000:178); Plumptre et al. (2003:27); Plumptre in Wrangham et al. (2007:1609); Wanyama et al. (2009:957); Wrangham (2001:231). On density, see Chapman and Lambert (2000:177–178); Plumptre in Wrangham et al. (2007:1609); Wrangham (2001:232).

[2]
> [U]sing a novel genetic capture-recapture methodology, Kevin (Langergraber] has shown that there are many more chimpanzees in Kibale than anyone would have ever imagined. Many of them are likely to live in communities that exceed 100 individuals. This is an astonishing result given the fact that so many researchers have been working in the Park for such a long time (Mitani 2020:8).

were not impressed. "My initial contacts with Ngogo chimpanzees left me with the unequivocal conclusion that they had no tolerance for humans" (1984:21). Eventually, many became accustomed to his unobtrusive presence around major core feeding areas or on ecologists' transects (1988:5–10). Ghiglieri's 1970s observations provide important contrasts with research beginning in the 1990s, when nearby habitat loss was greater.

After Ghiglieri, Gilbert Isabirye-Basuta (1988) began observations at Kanyawara, with 30 months between 1983 and 1985. Little is published from that. In 1987, he passed research on chimpanzees to Richard Wrangham and Mark Hauser (Struhsaker 1997:4), and the Kibale Chimpanzee Project (Wrangham et al. 1996:48).

At Ngogo (and Kanyanchu, below), Bettina Grieser-Johns and assistants began habituation efforts in 1991 (Grieser-Johns 1996; 1997). David Watts visited for 2 months in the summer of 1993, and in 1995 returned with John Mitani—deeply experienced at Mahale——to begin long-term observation. From 1997 they collaborated with Jeremiah Lwanga, who became director of Makerere University Biological Field Station (Mitani and Watts 2003; Watts 2012:321). Field seasons varied from 2.5 to 10.5 months, and by 2008, totaled 47 months (over 11 years) (Watts 2008a:85–86). Both Kanyawara and Ngogo are covered with grids of observation trails.

Local Humans

Contact with people is nothing new for chimpanzees of Kibale. For thousands of years, western Uganda had complex, iron-working societies, growing and consolidating or declining and dispersing. The heavily forested Kibale region was peripheral in these developments (Taylor et al. 2000:529), but grain storage pits, potsherds, and grinding stones are found even within "undisturbed forests" at the center of Ngogo studies (Chapman et al. 2011:81; Chesterman et al. 2019). What is different about recent years is the sheer number of people pouring into the area, the rate of forest clearing, and hunting with wire snares. This surge came after decades of human retraction.

Early in the 20th century, sleeping sickness forced the Batoro people out of Kibale forest (Ghiglieri 1984:13). Gone, but not without a trace. Open areas of old farm clearings continue to shape the forest mix, with one fig tree particularly important for Ngogo chimpanzees. Some clearings became grasslands, maintained by fires and elephant uprooting. Grasslands and papyrus swamps offer little food for chimpanzees, and in places are quite extensive (Lwanga 2006:235; Mitani et al. 2000:284). Throughout the Park region, human settlement was still low in the 1940s.

Change began in the 1950s with Batoro population growth, and immigration of Bakiga people from southwestern Uganda (Hartter et al. 2015). More rapid growth began in the 1970s, and continued thereafter. The Kabarole District surrounding Kibale went from 519,821 people in 1980, to 746,800 in 1991, to 944,600 in 2000, with an annual growth rate of 3.3%. District population in 2000 averaged 117/km^2, but in some parishes adjacent to the Park, exceeded 300/km^2 (Goldman et al. 2008:133; Southworth et al. 2010:125; Struhsaker 2008:28).

Human disruption had four modalities: logging operations, especially in the northern Park; agricultural invasions and logging in the southern extension of the

Park; clearing of forest all around the Park; and use of Park edges for both legal and prohibited activities. Within the Park itself, about 79 km² of the original reserve, 19% of its total forest, was lost to (mostly) recent human activity (Chapman and Lambert 2000:178), though new clearing ended in the late 1980s. Habitat loss outside the Park boundaries made it an island in a sea of settlements. In coming chapters, my argument is that habitat destruction was a driver of chimpanzee population growth and increasing density in undisturbed areas, which ultimately contributed to intergroup killings in and around Ngogo.

Habitat Loss within the Park

Logging in the North

The Kibale forest originally was gazetted for sustained timber extraction. Mechanized hardwood logging began in the north at Sebitole around 1950. Peak harvest years were 1954 to 1978, curtailed though not prohibited after that by the general economic collapse of Uganda (Lwanga and Isabirye-Basuta 2008:63; Struhsaker 1997:8–9; and see Southall 1980).

Logged areas lack the tall trees and relatively open ground of mature forest (Struhsaker 1997:93–124). Elephants prefer clear areas, and their uprootings impede forest regrowth (Struhsaker et al. 1996). "Heavy logging in Kibale has resulted in a major transformation of the forest habitat into a dense thicket interspersed with small groves of trees or isolated emergents. Forest regeneration was not apparent in Kibale more than 25 years after heavy logging and it may never recover" (Struhsaker 1997:296). Wildlife was commensurably impacted (Chapman et al. 2005; Sekercloglu 2002:229–235).

In 1970 the Kanyawara area gained protection through a field station of the New York Botanical Gardens, under Struhsaker, who in 1977 personally prevented cutting through the last remaining corridor between Kanyawara and the forested center Park. Through the chaotic 1980s Struhsaker worked with the Uganda Game Department to prevent now illegal logging and poaching (Struhsaker 1997:9–15; 2008:28–29). Major habitat destruction around Kanyawara ended around 1978, but great damage was already done.

Chimpanzees were especially but variably effected (Skorupa 1986:58, 62, 64, 67; Struhsaker 1997:198, 203). In the Kanyawara range only about 30% of the land is "relatively undisturbed" (Wrangham et al. 1996:48), whereas Ngogo was not logged at all (Ghiglieri 1984:16). Ngogo has "a high abundance of food for chimpanzees" relative to other areas (Isabirye-Basuta and Lwanga 2008:38)—1,748 fruiting trees per km², compared to 878 per km² at Kanyawara (Teelen 2007:1041). In 1996–1997 chimpanzee occupation of two Kanyawara areas that were harvested in 1968–1969 was less than half that of undisturbed forest (Chapman and Wrangham 1993:268; Chapman and Lambert 2000:172–173, 177). Females with core ranges in heavily logged sections had lower ovarian hormone levels, longer interbirth intervals, and higher infant mortality than females in lightly or non-logged areas (Emery Thompson et al. 2007:508). Yet, confusingly, other work suggests that logging *did not* negatively impact chimpanzee food availability.[3] Food and nutrition is a difficult topic, but chimpanzee spatial choices support the conclusion that forest cutting did cause long-term damage to the resource base for Kanyawara chimpanzees.

Farmers in the South

The most destructive time for Kibale was the 9-year rule of Idi Amin, up to 1979. In 1971 small farmers invaded the southern extension of the park.[4] Habitat destruction did not end with Amin's fall in 1979. Struhsaker characterizes the years of civil war up to consolidation of the Museveni government in 1986 as "chaos."

The south Corridor saw multiplying plantations of tea, cypress, pine, and eucalyptus, and proliferation of schools, churches, and markets (Land Tenure Center 1989:12). Only narrow forest strips, at points less than a kilometer wide, connected the central and southern parts of the Park. Stricter protection followed, culminating in the compulsory relocation of southern farmers out of the Park in 1992. After 1989 new forest loss within the Park was minimal (Berkhoudt n.d.; Chapman and Lambert 2000:171; Naughton Treves 1996:17, 22–23; Struhsaker 1997:9–15; Van Orsdol 1986:116; Whitesell et al. 1997:67, 69; Wrangham 2001:235).

Some improvements in the southern extension were dramatic. From 1989 to 2003, 137 km^2 converted from grassland to bush or forest. By one estimate, forest regrowth there could support approximately 347 chimpanzees within 20 years (Laporte et al. 2008:44)—suggesting how many had lived there prior to deforestation. Other work is less optimistic about regrowth (Bonnell et al. 2011:863; Omeja et al. 2011:704; Southworth et al. 2010:131; Watts 2012:319–320). How many chimpanzees survived in degraded habitat and how many may have returned since then is unknown, but one hopeful note is a transect survey in 2005, which found high nest density in reforested and policed parts of the southern extension (Wanyama 2009:959).

Referring to the devastating loss of forest cover in the southern Park, Chapman and Lambert (2000:181) wonder if the numbers of primates found in nearby viable habitats "represent elevated densities resulting from immigration of animals into the remaining forest from degraded forest." They wonder if those densities will be sustainable over the long run. Excellent questions, and they can be expanded.

---

[3] Potts's (2011) comparison of 18 food trees used by both Kanyawara and Ngogo chimpanzees "suggests that commercial timber harvesting has had relatively little influence on the critical components of the resource base of the chimpanzees at Kanyawara. This is a surprising finding" (2011:262). However, "[t]he most frequently consumed dietary items at Ngogo and Kanyawara overlapped very little" (Potts et al. 2011:680)—so what does this 18-tree comparison actually tell us? Adding to the confusion, in the new Sebitoli site, also logged like Kanyawara and with food availability falling between the two older sites, chimpanzees were most often observed in the *disturbed* areas. Some kinds of figs seem to grow better there (Bortolamiol et al. 2014:2–3, 7–8; 2016:931).

[4] A major part of what became Kibale National Park in 1993 previously was not part of the Forest Reserve, but rather a theoretically "protected" Game Reserve/Corridor linking Kibale to Queen Elizabeth National Park. Human settlement in the Corridor began in the 1950s, grew in the 1960s, and exploded in the 1970s. By the late 1980s, 100% of arable land in the Corridor was cleared, and farms were cutting into the Kibale Forest Reserve itself. Within the Corridor estimates of human population vary widely, but center around 45–60,000, with some 3,500 extending into the original Forest Reserve (Chapman et al. 2011:76–77; Land Tenure Center 1989:xi, xiii, 17–11).

What happened when chimpanzees displaced from the southern extension met those of the more protected forests of the main Park? Was population impaction—increased density and crowding—occurring around Ngogo? Centripetal pressure would come not just from damaged land inside the Park. Kibale chimpanzees were losing rangeland all around it.

The People Outside

Islandization

No habitat protection exists outside Park borders. Not long ago, Kibale was part of a much larger forest expanse. It became an isolate circumscribed by human cultivation and settlement. Ecologists call this "islandization" (Southworth et al. 2010:123). There is no clear chronology of habitat loss. Some happened in the 1950s (Gillespie and Chapman 2006:443), but in the 1970s farming expanded dramatically. By 1984, after the chaos of Amin and the war, "much of the land outside the park had been converted to agriculture" (Southworth et al. 2010:129, 133). By 1995 most forest patches were devoid of resident chimpanzees (Onderdonk and Chapman 2000), as they got smaller, more fragmented, and more isolated (Hance 2010; Hartter and Southworth 2009:649-650). All that new farmland had been chimpanzee rangeland.

Even those mostly within the Park were hurt. Wrangham (2001:231) estimates that 60% to 80% of Kibale group territories crossed Park boundaries. If 60% of Kibale groups lost an average of a quarter of their former rangeland, that would amount to 15% of Park chimpanzee habitat.

Despite risks, chimpanzees still visited the dwindling forests that once were theirs, or the cropland that replaced the wild. In the late 1990s many people living around Kibale encountered chimpanzees "frequently" (Adams et al. 2001:310)

> Edge-living chimpanzees move between Kibale and the surrounding farmlands, using strips of valley forest and patches such as crater forests as travel routes and food sources. They also use these forest patches as bases from which to enter village areas, to harvest crops such as banana and sugarcane. Some chimpanzees appear to live wholly outside the park, migrating among such forest patches. Within a decade or two, all such forest patches will likely have been converted to fields. (Wrangham 2001:231)

Forays outside the Park coincide with low food availability: "during periods of fruit scarcity Kanyawara chimpanzees regularly raid village crops" (Wrangham et al. 1996:48). Occasionally they found and consumed fermented banana beer, which made them especially aggressive to people (East African 2004:2; Wrangham 2001:236). (Now *there* is a human parallel!)

Along the western Park border from 1992 to 2002, chimpanzees attacked human children 18 times, killing and eating three, some not far from Kanyawara (Wilson 2001:86). Local farmers were up in arms. Wrangham's (2001) team concluded that eight serious attacks "were carried out by a single male living largely alone in the affected area. We named this putative killer 'Saddam'" (2001:236). A decision was made to prevent villagers' retaliation against blameless chimpanzees by killing Saddam, but villagers got him first, in September 1998. All that was left to do was the *coup de grâce*.

Conservation ecologist Michael Gavin (2004) went to Kibale and interviewed researchers, officials, and local residents about the attacks on humans. His conclusion: "Squeezed into this diminishing forest resource, chimps are finding it increasingly difficult to locate ample food and have adapted accordingly, seeking out what food they can in the new human-dominated ecosystems."

Snaring

As the Park developed in 1995 local people retained specific use rights, such as collecting medicinal plants, crafts materials, or harvesting wild coffee within a 1 km band inside the boundary. That area could be expanded, sometimes greatly, by negotiation. Prohibited were grazing, firewood or timber or pole collection, charcoal making, and hunting, yet these were common within 5 km of the Park boundary (or even deeper) despite efforts at enforcement (Solomon et al. 2007:82; Wanyama et al. 2009:953; Whitesell et al. 1997:68). Since unhabituated chimpanzees flee at the sight of humans, this usage added to inward pressure.

The worst is snaring. Batoro and Bakiga do not hunt primates, but use wire snares to hunt bushpigs, duikers, etc. Chimpanzees are unintended victims. Wire twists and cuts deep, commonly leading to loss of a hand, digit, or foot. "[T]o chimpanzees, they are land mines in the forest. Striking without warning, they cause terror and suffering, and frequently leave their victims mutilated or dead" (Muller 2000:45). At the end of the 1990s, 15,000 snares could be in KNP at any time (Wrangham and Mugume 2000:1).

In the late 1970s, Ghiglieri (1984:62-63; 1988:171) saw 10 to 13 Ngogo chimpanzees with snare wounds. Exposed Kanyawara had even more. "Of fifty-nine adult Kanyawara chimpanzees observed between 1988 and 1999, four had lost a hand, and another twelve had noticeable wounds ranging from lost knuckles to bent wrists and crippled feet. Several others, with no signs of aging or illness, had disappeared" (Wrangham 2000). From 1995 to 2006, 29% of chimpanzees older than three had snare injuries at Kanyawara, and 10% at Ngogo (Wood et al. 2017:52). Around 2015 it was 28% at Sebitole (Cibot et al. 2015:892). Kibale is not unique. "[A]cross Africa tens of thousands of great apes are likely to be suffering crippling wounds" (Wrangham 2001:234).

Kibale investigators took the lead in fighting this scourge. In 1999 Wrangham initiated a program of snare removal. First around Kanyawara and later expanded to almost half the entire Park, local assistants cleared 2,290 snares in three years (Wrangham and Mugume 2000). Patrolling by rangers of the Uganda Wildlife Authority continued to clear snares and suppress other prohibited activity (Muhabwe 2008:13). Much chimpanzee mutilation was prevented by all their work, (and by the Jane Goodall Institute's Project Snare Removal).

It is impossible to guess the lasting psychological impact of snares. Chimpanzees that endure trauma in captivity, once returned to more naturalistic sanctuaries display clinical signs of PTSD and depression (Bradshaw et al. 2008; Brune et al. 2006; Ferdowsian et al. 2011; Lopresti-Goodman et al. 2012). I know no study focused on lasting psychological effects on wild, mutilated chimpanzees.

Chimpanzees understand the danger of snares, and try to spot and avoid them, but still fall victim (Wrangham 2001). One way to avoid snares is to avoid border areas with higher infestation. A study at Tai in Ivory Coast found a clear association: the frequency of snares in a particular area was a "major predictor" of fewer chimpanzees (Kondgen et al. 2008:263). High frequency snaring may push chimpanzees inward, adding to the centripetal pressure of islandization.[5]

All told, habitat disturbance displaced great numbers. Chapter 12 supports Chapman and Lambert's insight with evidence that high densities in healthy habitat may reflect movement of chimpanzees away from human degraded environments, both within and outside the Park. This is a foundation of my explanation of Ngogo "war."

Other Impact, Differing Effects

Tourism and introduced disease losses were major factors in Mahale and Gombe violence, but effects differed in Kibale. General parameters of human impact play out according to local specifics.

Tourism

Kibale ecotourism developed within a larger international effort of forest conservation, management, research, and education, riven with competing visions and administrative conflicts (MSI 1994). Around 1990, Richard Wrangham wrote a proposal for ecotourism at Kibale, and the Wildlife Conservation Society commissioned a feasibility study. Soon habituation efforts began among the Kanyanchu group (below). Trackers and field guides were trained by the Kibale Chimpanzee Project. Procedures were casual and rules laxly enforced.[6]

Kibale illustrates the pros and cons of ecotourism (Macfie and Williamson 2010). Dozens of trailing tourists are a disturbance, and a potential conduit for disease. Wrangham (2001:239–240) discusses ethical dilemmas.

---

[5] However at the new study site Sebitoli chimpanzees did not avoid the edges, they just go where food is. "Sebitoli is essentially a cul-de-sac surrounded by tea plantations and crossed by a road," roughly four kilometers from Park edge to edge. Thus constricted, protective avoidance may not be an option (Bortolamiol et al. 2014:7; 2016:925, 930–931).

[6] At Kanyanchu, 1,297 visitors in 1992 rose to 4,017 in 1996, but fell off after that, following an outbreak of Ebola and the immediate threat of the Lord's Resistance Army. An option of "an all-day chimpanzee follow" was offered after 2001, and visitors increased to 7,700 in 2008.

This project currently attracts substantial attention and appears to be contributing importantly to local and governmental support for conservation of the forest ... apes desperately need allies, even if those allies are in it for the money. ... Is it too much to require 10 percent of the ape population to be endlessly visited by tourists, even at the risk of occasional epidemic? What about 20 percent or 50 percent? An argument can be made that although we should do all we can to minimize the disease risks, we should promote a substantial flow of tourists wherever the market can sustain it.[7]

That view prevailed. The new research site of Sebitole was intended as a tourist destination. Several locations along the western side of the Park were developed for tourism (Mackenzie 2012:120). Their impact on chimpanzees is unreported. However, neither Ngogo or Kanyawara became designated tourist destinations, even if some showed up anyway. The intensity of daily disruption documented and psychological disturbance inferred later at Mahale was not a factor. But Ngogo may have been affected by tourism, indirectly via Kanyanchu.

Kanyanchu

Kanyanchu group has been large, perhaps 100 chimpanzees, maybe more (Wrangham et al. 2007:1610), even though they experienced respiratory infections possibly associated with tourists (Negrey et al. 2019:145). Kanyanchu rangelands face the Park border on their south, and abut Ngogo on their north (Johns 1996; Plumptre et al. 2003:70). There was intense territorial conflict along that frontier (Chapter 16).

Although it was intended that Kanyanchu provide recorded observations by trained guides for comparison with other Kibale chimpanzees (Mugisha 2008:119), little is published about them. It is not even clear if it is one group, or more than one.[8] The only description of Kanyanchu chimpanzees I found is a demonic portrayal by a visiting news reporter.[9] Whether the constant flow of tourists contributed to

---

[7] Tourism provides local communities with conservation incentives: 20% of gate receipts were to be returned to local communities. Benefits are substantial for Bigodi, the jump-off point for Kanyanchu tourists. They developed tourist services including eating places, accommodations, a women's cooperative selling handicrafts, and an additional destination for ecotourists in a swamp outside the Park (Mugisha 2008:122). Revenue paid for local school development and a maternity clinic (Kasenene and Ross 2008:104; cf. Lepp 2008 for a more critical assessment).
 The Kanyawara research center also provides local jobs in construction, housekeeping, trail cutting, and as guides and collectors. Community projects guided by expatriate researchers, and work with Ugandan scientists and students, all have substantial impact at and around KNP (Kasenene and Ross 2008; MUBFS n.d.). Tourism will shape the future of Kibale and its chimpanzees (Hartter and Goldman 2010:61; MSI 1994:37–40; Mugisha 2008:119, 122–124; Kerbis Peterhans et al. 1993:488; Uganda Wildlife Authority, n.d.).
[8] Wilson et al.'s (2014) tally of killings does not note "Kanyanchu," but "Kanyantale." A tourist website refers to "Kanyantale-Kanyanchu" (Far Horizons 2011). Perhaps there is some separation of chimpanzees in this area, which has not been explained. I will stick with Kanyanchu.
[9] In *The Sunday Telegraph*, Madden (2002) projects the demonic perspective. His guide was Julia Lloyd, who ran the project for the Jane Goodall Institute and the Uganda Wildlife Authority.

> Our final day in the forest revealed that darker side at first hand. After tracking the group of dominant males all morning, we realised they were moving towards an area of the forest we had never been in before. Julia was intrigued: "You guys are luckier than I could ever imagine. Unless I'm very much mistaken, this is a border patrol." Suddenly we found ourselves on the set

Kanyanchu's push inward to Ngogo cannot be inferred. But push they did—and just as Ngogo expanded outward in the opposite direction.

Disease

Also different is the impact of introduced diseases. Initial studies of intestinal parasites at the two sites found the chimpanzees to be in generally good health (Krief et al. 2005; Muehlenbein 2005), albeit with some bacterial spread from guides or field assistants (Golberg 2008:82). But Kanyawara suffered respiratory infections of uncertain origin in 1998, 2006, and 2013. The first claimed three adults, the next one adult and one infant, and the third four adults and one infant (Emery Thompson 2018:3, 14), including the Kanyawara alpha (Sabbi and Enigk 2015). "In the Kanyawara community of wild chimpanzees, respiratory illness has been the leading cause of mortality over 31 years, contributing to 27% of deaths" (Emery Thompson 2018:1). Outbreaks are not associated with any changes in territorial relations with neighbors (Chapter 12), but they may have curtailed Kanyawara population growth.

Incidence of respiratory infection at Ngogo is unclear until recently. In 2014, a male died which "had been suffering from a respiratory infection.... A few individuals who died around the same time also had respiratory infections.... Other chimpanzees were noticeably ill when last seen, and we assume that disease [is a common source] of mortality" (Wood et al. 2017:51).

From December 2016 to February 2017, highly infectious respiratory illness hit both Kanyawara and Ngogo, killing none in Kanyawara, but 25 in Ngogo—*twenty five*. Despite their similarity and coincidence, these were due to entirely different pathogens, metapneumovirus (MPV) in Ngogo and human respirovirus 3 (HRV3) in Kanyawara. Both were genetically close to globally circulating human viruses. No comparable illness was seen among Kanyanchu chimpanzees, or in villages around the Park (Negrey et al. 2019:140, 143, 145). "The pathways by which these viruses entered chimpanzees from humans remain vexingly obscure." Investigators recommend "broad sampling of people (especially research staff) and wildlife during future outbreaks" (2019:145, 146).

The outbreak occurred long after Ngogo's expansion against neighbors (Chapter 16). Even so, since they numbered 205 before the infection, a loss of 25 should would not leave them vulnerable. But then, nothing is published about violence in recent years, except that Kanyawara males attacked one of their own females weakened from

---

of 2001, A Space Odyssey. All around us chimps were "buttress-banging," aggressive display behaviour designed to intimidate the neighbouring community. Crouching low with their fur standing on end, the chimps broke into a demonic screeching before standing up and charging at a tree... These were "our boys" and we began willing them on against the invisible enemy. If it had come to a fight to the death, I know whose side I would have been on. Six million years down the track, no doubt the chimps would have been fixing bayonets ready to go over the top. Not for the first time during our magical interlude with the Kibale chimps, I realised that I had learnt as much about the origins of our own behaviour as I had about our long-lost cousins in the forests of Africa.

The opponents are not identified.

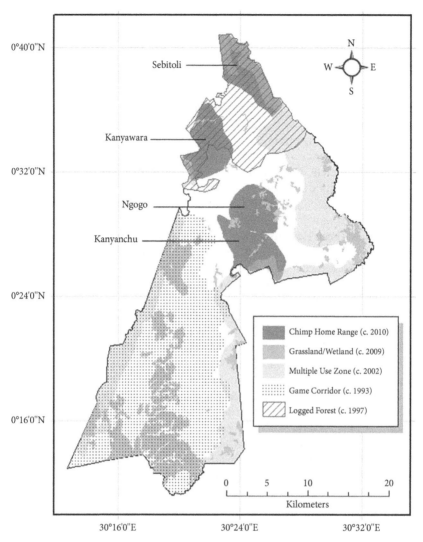

Illustration 4.1 Composite of Habitat Loss and Chimpanzee Groups
Caption: Historical land use impacts on chimpanzee habitat in Kibale National Park. The home ranges of the Kanyawara, Ngogo, Sebitoli, and Kanyanchu chimpanzee communities (dark gray) were extrapolated and generalized from data corresponding to the period around 2010, using the minimum convex polygon method with smoothing. Areas of formerly logged forest (hatched) and a game corridor (stippled) existing prior to its 1993 incorporation into the national park were digitized from maps published by Struhsaker (1997). Regions of grassland and wetland (medium gray) were derived from the Uganda National Biomass Study (2009). The multiple-use zone (light gray) was digitized from the depiction of collaborative resource management areas in the Kibale and Semuliki Conservation and Development Project Report (Chege et al. 2002).

Source: Map created by Jillian Rutherford. Data is from Struhsaker, T. (1997). *Ecology of an African rain forest: Logging in Kibale and the conflict between conservation and exploitation*. University Press of Florida; Chege, F., Onyango, G., Drazu, C., & Mwandha, S. (2002). *Kibale and Semuliki conservation and development project end of phase III/End of project evaluation Report*; Diisi, J. (2009). *National biomass study technical Report*. Uganda National Forestry Authority.

the infection, which died (Negrey et al. 2017:147) (Count 1 W-A-F 2017). (But see Chapter 14 Postscript.)

Human Impact

Violence by Kibale chimpanzees, especially those of Ngogo, is portrayed as illustrating normal evolved tendencies among chimpanzees unaffected by human activity. "The most frequently violent chimpanzees that we know of, at Ngogo in Uganda, live in one of the most pristine habitats in which chimpanzees have been studied" (Stanford 2018:68). Ngogo chimpanzee habitat is not pristine, if pristine means unaffected by people. In the northern Park logging from 1954 to 1978 destroyed much of the forest and recovery has been slow. In the south habitat destruction up to 1986 eliminated natural cover from arable land, and was not reversed until 1992. Around the Park, spreading farms created a sharp boundary for chimpanzees, pushing outsiders inward, and reducing ranges for unit-groups that crossed Park borders. Multiple-use areas and illegal snaring reached inward, maiming a tenth even of protected Ngogo.

This outline of disturbance is greatly out of date. Except for disease mortality, almost no new information about human impact on "protected" Ngogo is available for more than a decade. But it does not seem to have gone well for Ngogo. During final edits, I came across a Ngogo update in *The Atlantic* (Yong 2019). "This year, food has been scarce, and so have chimps." Kevin Langergraber found a mixed party of 30 and followed them. Ahead he heard a scream. Racing forward he found Kidman fatally speared by two hunters with dozens of dogs. The hunters fled but not all the dogs, and Langergraber killed several with the spear.

That is the historical context of observations at Ngogo, and deadly conflicts with neighbors. Chapter 13 and 14 argues that this habitat degradation directed migrating females into Ngogo, leading to major population growth, which led to intense intergroup competition, which led to intergroup killing and the Ngogo expansion. But before that explanation, Ngogo's relations with its neighbors must be described in detail.

12
Ngogo Territorial Conflict

Chapter 12 presents what needs to be explained for Ngogo: intense border patrolling, then lethal clashes with outsiders, culminating in a widely noted "conquest" of new rangelands. In all of chimpanzee observations, this is the best evidence for "war," even better than that of Gombe.

Discussion here gets (again) a little dense and numerical, but necessarily. For either adaptationist or historical theory, this is the behavior that must be accounted for. It is no exaggeration to say that the fundamental idea of chimpanzees revealing humanity's inborn tendency to war stands or falls on the Ngogo expansion from 1999 to 2009.

The Record of Conflict

Boundary Patrols

A cornerstone of the imbalance of power hypothesis is that chimpanzees patrol territorial borders and make stealthy penetrations into neighbors' territories, seeking opportunities to kill. Both are prominent in Ngogo research findings. But *initially*, they weren't.

Ghiglieri in 1977–1978, saw not a single territorial confrontation, or any meeting between two groups. But he did not follow chimpanzees as later researchers did. "Perhaps this was because the study areas I used were not in regions of overlap between adjacent communities. Perhaps instead, Kibale chimpanzees were not territorial" (Ghiglieri 1984:184). After the post-Gombe reinterpretation of Mahale disappearances, he concluded that Kibale chimpanzees were ready for war, especially in the bonding of adult males. "But I must still admit I was hoping to witness a serious clash" (Ghiglieri 1988:258). That is what I call Gombe-vision.

In the mid-1990s, Mitani and Watts guessed there were two to four groups around the Ngogo community, maybe more (Watts and Mitani 2001:304). Frequent patrols were distinguishable by "silence, cohesive and directed travel, frequent attentive pauses, and sniffing of the ground, vegetation, for signs of chimpanzees" (Amsler 2010:95). Was this contrast in observations due to limitations of early observation, or had Ngogo changed?

From 1996 to 1999, 52 boundary patrols were followed, during 1998–1999 averaging one patrol every 9.7 days. That is more frequent and with more males than at Gombe or Tai. Although researchers did not document expeditions into neighbors' territory, they suspected them (Watts and Mitani 2001:305–310, 318). Thirty patrols were followed from 2003 to 2006, with a minimum of 9 and a mean of 16 males (Amsler 2010:98, 101–102). Over both periods, patrols oriented toward territory fringes in the northeast, northwest, and south.

The years 1996–1999 recorded 26 interactions with neighboring communities. Nineteen happened while patrolling, and seven while foraging. Interaction usually was limited to calling. Four times Ngogo males fled and eight times they attacked the strangers, five of those involving physical aggression. "All attacks were on parties that included females with or without accompanying immatures, but no adult or adolescent males" (Watts and Mitani 2001:310)—similar to many attacks at Gombe. There was no danger of serious injury to the attackers, yet neither were there any killings until 1999. In another cumulative data set, extending from 1997 to mid-2004—including most of the expansion killings—they observed 95 patrols, 68 intercommunity encounters "in other contexts," with 12 and 8 acts of direct physical aggression, respectively (Watts et al. 2006:165, 175).

Killings

Ngogo killings of outside chimpanzees began in April 1999.[1] Note the date. I number them here as in the Mitani et al. (2010), my primary source unless otherwise noted. (#1, #2) In April and June, border patrols at the eastern periphery of Ngogo territory snatched infants from unaccompanied stranger females, and ate them (Watts and Mitani 2000) (Count, *two* 1-O-I-? 1999).

(#3, #4) In July 2000, a patrol broke off from a larger feeding group at the northeastern fringe of the Ngogo area, killed two more stranger infants, and engaged with stranger adults (Watts et al. 2002:265–267) (Count, *two* 1-O-I-? 2000).

(#5) In July 2001, a juvenile of unspecified sex was recorded killed to the northeast, but this has not been described (Count 2-O-J-? 2001) (Mitani et al. 2010, supplemental 1). In no case was the infant's sex identified. In August, a foraging party of Ngogo males and females encountered a large party (unidentified), with charges and countercharges, and at least one male bitten (Watts et al. 2006:176).

Then came bloody 2002 (Watts et al. 2006), when Gombe-vision came true. (#6) In June, an eastward patrol entered a neighbor's range without any encounter. Two days later, another patrol on that border came across a feeding party of five strangers. Fifteen adult and adolescent males gave chase, catching one stranger male. Five pursuers beat, bit, and stomped him for 20 minutes, until he lay dead (Count 1-O-A-M 2002).

(#7) In August, a large Ngogo feeding party in their northern periphery heard strangers calling, and several males broke off to approach. After reassurance embraces, they charged down into a valley, their opponents fleeing up the other side. They caught and severely attacked a male about 6 years old, whose condition was so severe he is presumed to have died (Count 3-O-J-M 2002).

In September 2002, foraging males and females of Ngogo twice encountered a large party of outsiders, with physical contact and biting. In October, researchers observed

---

[1] Or *maybe* a few months earlier. Wilson et al. (2014a:EDT 1), include one intercommunity killing, from unpublished data from the Kanyanchu tourism center. On December 5, 1998, an adult male, possibly from Kanyantale (Kanyanchu), was "suspected" killed, by chimpanzees possibly from Ngogo (Count 5-O-A-M 1998).

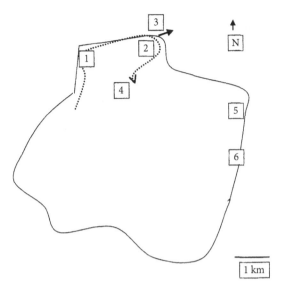

Illustration 4.2 Ngogo Range with Infant Killings c. 1999
Caption: Route followed by patrolling males on July 5, 2001, and location of infanticide sites. (1) Location of papyrus swamp where a large party of chimpanzees had been feeding and where males started the boundary patrol; (2) Location of attack site; (3) Arrow indicates direction that members of the neighboring community took when they fled from the site; (4) Area where Ngogo males resumed feeding after they fled the infanticide site and then moved southwest away from the boundary; (5) Site of infanticide of June 28, 1999; (6) Site of infanticide of April 3. 1999.

Source: Watts, D.P., Sherrow, H.M., & Mitani, J.C. (2002). New cases of inter-community infanticide by male chimpanzees at Ngogo, Kibale National Park, Uganda. *Primates, 43,* 263–270.

a classic deep stealth penetration by 14 adult males beyond its eastern boundary—without contact (Watts 2004:510–511). On November 9, another Ngogo foraging party battled with a large group of outsiders (Watts et al. 2006:176).

(#8) On November 23, 2002, a large, mixed feeding group in their far northwest, where Ngogo range overlaps with others, found and caught a stranger male. For 10 minutes, 16 adult and 3 adolescent males pummeled and bit him until he died (Count 2-O-A-M 2002). On December 4, a patrol of Ngogo males encountered a small party of unidentified outsiders, with a prolonged attack on a female, and possible infanticidal attempt, but no deaths (Watts et al. 2006:176).

In between the two 2002 outside killings, another striking event occurred. In October, a large number of Ngogo males from a mixed feeding party pursued and savagely attacked a male of their own group (Watts 2004).[2] GRA (Grapelli) was socially ambitious, mid-ranked, and without major allies. He and a frequent associate (OR) had been attacked by multiple males at least twice before. This time, GRA managed

---

[2] The attack on GRA can be seen at http://www.youtube.com/watch?v=CPznMbNcfO8.

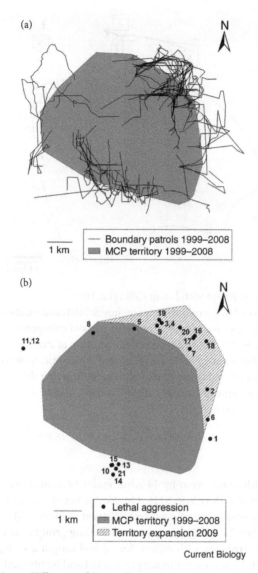

Illustration 4.3 Ngogo Killings and Range Expansion
Caption: (A) The Ngogo chimpanzee community territory, 1999–2008. The 100% minimum convex polygon (MCP) territory shown in the shaded region excludes observations on days the chimpanzees conducted boundary patrols. Tracings of 114 territorial boundary patrols observed during 1999–2008 are also displayed. (B) Territorial expansion in 2009. The area excised from a neighboring chimpanzee community to the northeast is mapped in relation to the 1999–2008 MCP territory. Locations of lethal attacks made by the Ngogo chimpanzees on neighboring individuals are shown.

Source: Mitani, J.C., Watts, D.P., & Amsler, S.J. (2010). Lethal intergroup aggression leads to territorial expansion in wild chimpanzees. *Current Biology, 20,* 507–508.

to leave, but was never seen again. A skeleton picked clear by safari ants was found shortly thereafter, near where he was last seen. It seems beyond reasonable doubt. In a time of high conflict with neighboring groups, Ngogo males killed one of their own (Count 2-I-A-M 2002).

The year 2003 was not as bad. In June a Ngogo patrol attacked an unidentified adult female, again going after the infant. In July, a foraging party encountered strangers foraging in a ficus grove, and Ngogo males drew blood (Watts et al. 2006:176).

The year 2004 was as lethal as 2002. (#9) In August, a mixed feeding party in their northeastern range heard stranger calls a kilometer away. Several males went north toward them for about an hour, then heard the strangers nearby. After embracing in reassurance, they attacked, first a group of females, next moving on to catch a lone male. The attack lasted about 8 minutes, until the severely wounded victim stumbled off. Wounds were so severe "we consider it unlikely that the stranger survived" (Watts et al. 2006:171–172) (Count 3-O-A-M 2004).

In October, 2004, three more outside infants died. (#10) On October 6, 27 adult and adolescent males and 5 females went to their southern periphery, in the Kanyanchu area. Males continued south on patrol for over an hour. They heard a small cry and rushed toward it. Seven-plus males attacked a female with clinging infant. One male got the infant, then the alpha took and killed it. Three males shared the meat (Count 1-O-I-M 2004). An hour later, the group rushed toward another noise. The two groups called and drummed from a distance, until five Ngogo males moved off to engage. A general battle ensued, with at least a dozen males on the other side. They chased each other in waves, fought, and bit. Finally both moved off, several with visible injuries (Sherrow and Amsler 2007:12–15).

(#11, #12) A week later, a huge party of 31 adult and adolescent males and 5 females moved far to the west of their normal range, looking for red colobus they heard. It turned into a patrol, moving closely and silently onward. They heard a chimpanzee to the southwest, embraced, and approached. At 13:32, they heard a soft vocalization, charged, and found four stranger females, some with infants. The males began beating and kicking the mothers. One infant was pulled off, fought over, killed, and apparently lost (Count 1-O-I-? 2004). During the same melee, males and a female concentrated their fury on a mother, trying to pull off her infant. The infant seemed so badly injured that it couldn't survive (Count 3-O-I-?, 2004) (Sherrow and Amsler 2007:15–18).

That ends detailed reports of killings. Tallies and a map of killings add 13 more, with some information for a few (Mitani et al. 2010). (#13) In November 2004 an adult male was killed in the Kanyanchu area (Count 2-O-A-M 2004). (#14) In February 2005 a patrol well into the Kanyanchu range found trees of two favored fruits. Near one they encountered and attacked a female, without any witnessed offspring. But the next day a Ngogo attacker had chimpanzee bones and hair in his feces, leading to the inference that he ate an infant (Mitani et al. 2010:186) (Count 2-O-I-? 2005). In March 2005 a patrol toward fruit trees in its northern overlap zone, found and beat a female, with no killing (Mitani et al. 2010:187). (#15) In October 2005, again in the Kanyanchu area, an unsexed infant was killed (Count 1-O-I-? 2005).

(#16) In February 2006 another unsexed infant died (Count 1-O-I-? 2006). This was to Ngogo's northeast, as were the next four cases. (#17) In February, a dead adult male was found where Ngogo patrolled a few days before, with wounds consistent with a chimpanzee attack (Count 2-O-A-M 2006). (#18) In August a patrol formed out of a large group ranging within its northeastern territory, went to two important fruit trees in the overlap zone, then continued deeper into foreign ranges to three other fruit trees. There they encountered an adult male, and killed him (Mitani et al. 2010:187) (Count 1-O-A-M 2006). (#19) In July 2007 an unsexed infant fell victim (Count 1-O-I-? 2007). (#20) Two-days later in the same area, Ngogo males responding to an outside call were seen eating an infant (Count 3-O-I-? 2007). (#21) In August 2009 an adult female was killed in the Kanyanchu area (Count 1-O-A-F 2009).

Finally, the tally in Wilson et al. (2014a:EDT 1, 2) contribute three more infants and one adult victims of Ngogo, all unsexed. In April 2010, an external infant killing was inferred to the northeast (Count 4-O-I-? 2010). In February 2011 another was observed in the northeast (Count 2-O-I-? 2011); and one more in June in the southwest (Count 2-O-I-? 2011). An adult male is inferred as a victim in March, also in the northeast (Count 4-O-A-M 2011).

This death list does not include any within-Ngogo killings—except the noteworthy Grapelli—nor the three and possibly more Ngogo males killed by outsiders. Both are covered in Chapter 15. Taking just Ngogo's external killings, it is an *astonishing* record—far, far beyond anything witnessed anywhere else. All told, from 1999 to 2011 Ngogo killed 25 neighbors: 8 adult or juvenile males, 1 unsexed juvenile and 1 adult female, and 15 unsexed infants, or 1.9 per year for 13 years. Five of the outsiders seem to be from Kanyanchu, and 16 from the community to Ngogo's northeast.

Mitani et al. (2010:R507) try to gauge the population loss for the northeastern group, up through 2009, using different assumptions about neighbor community size.[3] "These values are extremely high ... *23–75 times higher than the median rates suffered by individuals in nine well-studied chimpanzee communities*" (my emphasis). But 2010–2011 raised the northeastern *panicides* by 23%, which would make it something like *28–92 times* higher than external kill rates of any other community. This is truly a singular string of killings. This outlier is a *primary evidentiary support for adaptationist explanations*.

Conquest

Territorial acquisition followed the killings.

Recent observations of the Ngogo chimpanzees reveal that they have expanded their territory considerably to the northeast into the area previously occupied by their neighbors. Large, mixed-sex parties of Ngogo chimpanzees started to use this area regularly in June 2009, spending 43 of 132 observation days (32.6%) in the newly acquired territory over the next 5 months. They traveled, fed, and socialized in this region in ways similar to that in the central part of their territory. During this same time, neighboring chimpanzees were not observed in the area. This new area,

---

[3] If its size is similar to those of chimpanzee communities studied elsewhere (X = 46.6, SD = 18.7, n = 8 communities), the 13 fatalities represent a mortality rate of 2,790 per 100,000 individuals per year. Alternatively, a rate of 867 per 100,000 individuals per year if one assumes the northeast community is as large as Ngogo's (150 individuals).

equaling 6.4 km² and excised from their neighbor's former range, represents a 22.3% increase in territory size. (Mitani et al. 2010:R507–508)

Territorial acquisition was part of the Kasakela story at Gombe and of M-group at Mahale, but those were both situations of artificial provisioning. The Ngogo expansion appears to be under "natural" conditions, seemingly clinching the point that this is normal, adaptive behavior for chimpanzees. It made headlines.[4] It was a focus of *Rise of the Warrior Apes* (Animal Planet 2017). Why did this extraordinary streak of *panicides* happen?

Ngogo Researchers' Theory

Ngogo researchers see these actions as consistent with a position they developed from first infanticides in 1999 (Sherrow and Amsler 2007:20; Watts and Mitani 2000:361–362; Watts et al. 2002:268; Watts et al. 2006:163, 177–178; Mitani et al. 2010:R5080). However, their theoretical positions do not discriminate between the resource competition and rival coalition alternatives discussed in Chapter 3.

Ngogo researches see killings as supporting the "food defense," "resource acquisition," or "range expansion" hypothesis. Killings led to more territory and so more food resources, which they expect will increase reproductive potential. "By acquiring new territory through lethal coalitionary aggression, male chimpanzees improve the feeding success of individuals in their own community, which in turn can lead to increased female reproduction" (Mitani et al. 2010:R508). "This finding supports the hypothesis that the main function of coalitionary aggression is to defend access to food that females need for successful reproduction, and if possible to increase food availability" (Watts 2012:331).[5]

Ngogo's expansionist attacks support an imbalance of power perspective in a broad sense: great numerical superiority makes attackers more likely to inflict severe damage. All concerned agree that superabundance of prime males enabled Ngogo's deadly "conquest." "These findings are consistent with the hypothesis that lethal-intergroup aggression reduces the coalitionary strength of opponents living in adjacent groups, leading to territorial expansion by the aggressors" (Mitani et al. 2010:R508).[6]

[4] In the *New York Times* (Wade 2010), "Chimps That Wage War and Annex Rival Territory." In *The Economist* (2010), "Killer instincts: Like humans, chimpanzees can engage in guerrilla warfare with their neighbours. As with humans, the prize is more land." In *The Independent* (McCarthy 2010), "Chimpanzees launch murderous sprees to expand their territories." In *U.S. News* (Moore 2010), "Chimpanzee Gangs Kill for Land, New Study Shows." On the World Science (2010) web page, "Chimps Kill Each Other for Territory, Study Finds." On CBS News web page (CBS 2010), "What Drives a Chimp to Murder? Experts Say Chimps Will Murder Each Other for Access to Land." On the MSNBC page, "Chimps Kill Chimps … for Land" (Moskowitz 2010).

[5] Unasked is Wrangham's question. Are attacks a situational response to an active contest over scarce critical resources? Or is it a normal, natural, evolved tendency to kill, ultimately to gain or protect resources but not contingent on immediate resource scarcity?

[6] Yet Ngogo researchers also question the imbalance of power hypothesis proper, as a necessary and sufficient explanation for deadly violence.

> [T]he possibility of making low-risk attacks does not explain why they occur, nor is the "rival reduction hypothesis" (Wrangham 1999a), which holds that lethal attacks on males reduce the strength of neighboring male "coalitions," an ultimate explanation for cooperative male aggression against neighbors. Coalitionary aggression is not risk free and patrolling has time and energy costs. (Watts 2012:330)

The take home of our paper was that patrolling seems to be part of a long-term strategy to dominate neighbors. If successful, chimpanzees can acquire more land. All chimpanzees will do this if they can. The Ngogo chimpanzees have been particularly successful because they have an in built competitive advantage. That advantage is due to the extremely large size of the community. (Mitani in Smells Like Science 2010)

Ngogo attacks undercut the foundational idea that range expansion gains more females. Mitani et al. (2010:R508) note none were acquired. Later, however, three parous females "immigrated into Ngogo as adults following a territorial expansion to the northeast." But that support for female acquisition was transitory. "[T]wo females disappeared after spending several years at Ngogo, but genetic and camera trap data indicate that they emigrated back to the northeastern community" (Wood et al. 2017:44). That left just one possible female acquired from this unmatched string of killings.

Ngogo researchers also step aside from *Demonic Males*'s dark vision. They emphasize instead the cooperative nature of attacks on outside groups, and caution about extrapolating from chimpanzees to humans.

> Human warfare is a heterogeneous phenomenon that varies with respect to who participates, what is involved, and why it occurs. Because of this, whether chimpanzee intergroup aggression can be employed to provide insights into the origins and causes of warfare is likely to remain moot. Using our results to address an enduring question about why humans are an unusually cooperative species may prove to be a more productive line of inquiry. (Mitani et al. 2010:R508)

However, they decisively reject human impact explanations of such intergroup killing, such as Margaret Power's.

> Power left open the possibility that between-group violence would eventually occur at Ngogo because habitat loss and heavy feeding competition with cercopithecines would exacerbate contest feeding competition between chimpanzee communities and limit dispersal opportunities. No habitat loss has occurred in Kibale since 1978, nor do we have any reason to suppose that interspecific feeding competition has a negative impact on the chimpanzees; in fact, the Ngogo community seems to have grown considerably. Inter-group aggression characterizes all populations of forest-living chimpanzees where researchers have habituated groups without provisioning, and seems to be part of the species-typical behavioral repertoire. (Watts and Mitani 2000:363, references omitted)

Muller and Mitani (2005:298–299) broaden this out. After saying that attribution of violence to provisioning is refuted by facts from nonprovisioned sites, they claim that critics—Robert Sussman and myself—are stretching for "alternative forms of human interference as hypothetical causes of chimpanzee aggression," forms which have not been substantiated. "The underlying motivations driving male chimpanzee behavior are clearly not the result of such interference."

Supposedly, the issue has been laid to rest. "The suggestion that such aggression is an incidental by-product of human intervention is no longer viable. Instead our findings support the hypothesis that killing neighboring conspecifics is adaptive" (Mitani et al. 2010:R508; Watts 2012:330). It's not because of their history, it's their nature.

I beg to differ. Except for cercopithecine competition, Margaret Power was prescient. The next two chapters show that the history of human impact is essential for understanding Ngogo killings and expansion.

13
Scale and Geopolitics at Ngogo

Anthropogenic habitat loss within the Park did not end in 1978, and it was not reversed until 1992, not long before observations resumed in 1995. Islandization continued without restriction. This may not be fully appreciated by later researchers. The long-experienced ecologist Struhsaker (1997:9–15), pointedly comments: "During my visits to Kibale in the 1990s, it was apparent that many of the students and other scientists working there often had little understanding of what the conditions were like in the previous two decades."

I foreground those conditions. Habitat modification in and around Kibale National Park (KNP) is essential for understanding territorial violence. To broadly invoke human disruption would be a hollow point, a vague invocation of unspecific "stress," unless habitat change can be tied by clear evidence and deduction to circumstances affecting chimpanzee life at Ngogo, and to intergroup violence. That is done in Chapters 13 and 14.

Chapter 13 argues that human habitat modification led to a sharp increase in Ngogo numbers and density to exceptional levels, which enabled and led up to external killings. It then makes a geopolitical tour around Ngogo's edges, demonstrating territorial pressure from southern and western neighbors which are more exposed to recent habitat loss. Chapter 14 then takes these findings into severe intergroup competition for preferred resources. That led to intense intergroup conflict and killings.

The Mega-Group

Besides killing, Ngogo's other superlative is that it is, by far, the largest chimpanzee group ever studied. Researchers clearly recognize that is what enabled them to kill neighbors and expand. I ask: *why* so many?

Large and Dense

By mid-1999, when killings began, researchers identified 146 Ngogo members, with 24 adult males and 47 adult females (Watts and Mitani 2001:304). From 2003 to 2006 population varied from 137 to 155 (Amsler 2009:18; Potts et al. 2011:670). Before disease struck in 2016, they numbered 205 (McGrew 2017:239; Negrey et al. 2019:140). Except for Mahale M-group's short-lived, provisioned peak of 105 in 1982, and perhaps Kanyanchu, Ngogo during its expansion was more than twice as populous as any enumerated group.[1] It also had a very high population density.[2]

In mid-2000, Ngogo had about 150 members, and a measured range of 35 km^2, which produces a density of 4.3/km^2 (Watts et al. 2002:264), or "roughly four/km^2" (Wilson et al. 2001:1213). In 2005–2006, Ngogo's calculated density was up to 5.1/km^2—*very* high (Potts et al. 2011:672). Yet their number increased only slightly, to perhaps 155 (Potts et al. 2011:670, 672). Then why the density change? Because measured territory shrank.

In Amsler's (2009:30) 19 months of observations in 2003–2006, by two common methods Ngogo had 27.7 or 29.3 km^2. Taking the average of 28.5 km^2, compared to the 2000 territory of 35 km^2, suggests a territory loss around 18.6% in roughly five years. In comparative perspective, the mega-group range was small for its numbers. "Ngogo's territory size is not nearly as big as it would be if either community size or male numbers predicted territory size across sites" (2009:76).

Although Ngogo researchers do not call attention to this apparent territorial compression, I do. Those published figures are consistent with other evidence to come. As Ngogo expanded to its northeast, it was losing rangeland in its south and perhaps west, to groups that were closer to the human frontier. Following Chapter 11's discussion of habitat loss, this inward push from edge groups could date back to the 1970s and continue forward from then, just as Ngogo group itself was growing.

Evidence of Population Growth

During his 23 months of field observations from 1976 to 1981, Ghiglieri estimated Ngogo community numbers and density, while acknowledging (1984:38) limits to his observations, which concentrated in the central part of their range. He recognized 46 individuals, saw 8 to 12 others he could not identify reliably, and "estimated the Ngogo community to contain about 55 members." That is a little large, but in line with group size across Africa. Although Ghiglieri may have missed many individuals, he (1984:53–54) also used nest counts along established observation transects to calculate density. That came to 2.4/km^2 for a home range estimated of 23 km^2—both *far* below later figures.

---

[1] Across Africa the median size of eight communities is 46.6 members (Mitani et al. 2010:R507). Groups vary from 20 to 76 (Sanz 2004:75). The average number of adult males for 11 groups is 7.3 (Watts and Mitani 2001:304). Unit-group population numbers run high in KNP. Although Kanyawara is normal sized, 39 to 52 individuals over time (Potts et al. 2011:671), recently surveyed Sebitole is larger, with 72 (Bortolamiol 2016:926). Kanyanchu is probably even bigger (below), but numbers are not precise.

[2] Calculating density is difficult, and methodologically complicated (Ghiglieri 1984:41–56; Kouakou et al. 2009; Morgan et al. 2006; Strusaker 1975:185–186; Wanyama et al. 2009). Standard techniques of walking marked forest transects to spot chimpanzees or their nests can produce major differences in estimates (Mitani, Struhsaker et al. 2000:281; Plumptre and Reynolds 1996:96–98). For chimpanzees, the very lengthy approach of getting to know them all may be the only definitive way to know their abundance (Mitani, Struhsaker et al. 2000:282).

The denominator of a density calculation is total area, which can be measured in different ways. For 2003–2006, four different methods applied to the same data gave Ngogo a range of 19.5 to 29.5 km^2 (Amsler 2009:76). In several African research areas, territory, as the total area in which group members are seen (other than on patrol) is distinguished from home range or core, the area they use more intensively. That can add confusion in comparing densities.

Crucially, Ghiglieri also counted the number of males in a moving group. From December 1976 to May 1978, he (1984:125) observed 667 "traveling parties." The average number in male-only parties was 1.7. The maximum number in male-only parties, seen only twice, was eight.

Twenty years later, in 1996–1997, Watts and Mitani (2001:308) witnessed 52 boundary patrols. One female joined two patrols, but "[o]therwise, females did not participate in patrols." "Patrols were almost exclusively male activities." Patrols had a mean of 9.4 adult and 3.6 adolescent males, or 13 males all together.

Ghiglieri saw a *maximum* of eight males traveling together, Watts and Mitani saw patrols with an *average* of 13. Web videos of Ngogo patrols and attacks (cited in Chapter 12), show masses of males that no observer could miss. The average of Ngogo attacking parties is 17.4 individuals (Wood et al. 2017:53). The eight males Ghiglieri reported, or even four or five traveling without females, might have been patrols—labeled "male traveling parties" before the concept of "patrolling" was widespread in the literature. I expect inward pressure began before the late 1970s. But if they were patrols, they were *less than half* the numbers later seen, consistent with major population growth in the two decades preceding the second phase of Ngogo research.

Other evidence of growth is from forest ecologists' methodologically consistent surveys from 1975 to 2007 (Lwanga et al. 2011). Despite fluctuations, this solid long-term data shows a pronounced upward trend in chimpanzees, with encounter rates more than doubling from 1979 to 2000.

A third line of support for dramatic growth in the Ngogo community is documented in Chapter 13. Hunting of red colobus—which is strongly influenced by how

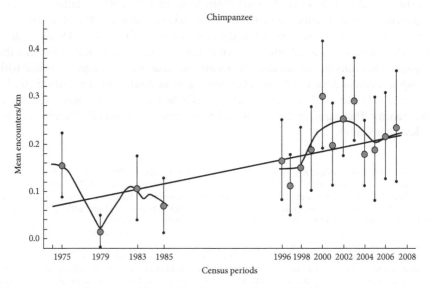

Illustration 4.4 Chimpanzee Population Change at Ngogo 1975–2007, by Encounters along Observation Transects

Source: Lwanga, J.S., et al. (2011). Primate population dynamics over 32.9 years at Ngogo, Kibale National Park, Uganda. *American Journal of Primatology, 73*, 977–1011.

many adult males are together—intensified to the point of virtually extirpating the prey community. In the 1970s, hunting was scarcely seen. A lot more hunters produced a lot more hunting.

Thus, three independent sets of data—Ghiglieri's counts, more than 30 years of transect censusing, and extreme intensification of numbers-dependent monkey hunting—all support the same conclusion: the exceptional size and density of the Ngogo chimpanzees at the start of their expansionist killing spree is the result of rapid growth in the preceding quarter-century. That is the time of population impaction due to habitat loss. It was already a large community in 1976, and it doubled or even tripled by 2000.

Why So Big?

Watts and Mitani (2000:363) themselves conclude that "the Ngogo community seems to have grown considerably," but without a time frame. Looking back from more recently, Wood et al. (2017:51) observe that the "Ngogo community has been growing at a rate that could not represent a long term average for the species." Both publications conclude that reason Ngogo group is so numerous is that their habitat is rich enough to support them. Even with great numbers, Ngogo chimpanzees indisputably are well nourished.[3]

But why are they so well nourished, while so numerous? Watts et al. suggest an historical ecological answer: the abundance of *Ficus mucuso*, which is absent for Kanyawara. Fruiting all year long, this fig is both a staple and a reliable back-up when other fruit is scarce, "quantitatively the most important food" at Ngogo (Watts et al. 2012a:114). "Stems of *F. mucoso* are relatively abundant at Ngogo; each stem can produce an enormous fruit crop and might do so at any time of year" (Wood et al. 2017:52). "[T]he relatively high density of *F. mucuso* gives chimpanzees at Ngogo a particularly abundant and reliable maintenance food source that is probably a major reason why population density is so much higher at Ngogo" (Watts et al. 2012b:141). The question then becomes: why are these critical food trees abundant at Ngogo, while absent in Kanyawara?

Mitani, Struhsaker et al. (2000:284) have a solid hypothesis: it is due to farming at Ngogo before it was gazetted as a Crown Forest in 1932. "[A]lthough there is an abundance of extremely large trees of *Ficus mucuso* in the Ngogo study area, no seedlings, saplings, or poles of this species have been found there. Typically, this is a species that appears to require very open conditions for establishment." This open area was provided by farmers who were ejected 70 years before.

---

[3] Ngogo chimpanzees spend more time feeding and less time resting than those of Kanyawara, which may contribute to higher fecundity or offspring survival (Potts et al. 2011:684). Preliminary data, including 20 interbirth intervals at Ngogo, suggests those are months shorter than at other locations (Watts 2012:325). Measured foraging efficiency was higher at Ngogo than Kanyawara, and temporal fluctuation lower (Potts et al. 2015). C-peptide levels, good indicators of energetic balances, are significantly higher for Ngogo than Kanyawara males (Emery Thompson et al. 2009:302). "Life expectancy at birth for both sexes combined was 32.8 years, far exceeding estimates of chimpanzee life expectancy in other communities," which Wood et al. (2017:41) attribute to "a food supply that is more abundant and varies less than that of Kanyawara."

All agree that Ngogo's killings were enabled by their great number of grown males.[4] If Ngogo researchers are correct, (1) that *Ficus mucuso* made that number possible; and (2) that abundance of the tree is due to old farming, then the Ngogo expansion is predicated on human impact.

However, this aspect of human impact is a *necessary condition* enabling large numbers, but not a *sufficient condition*. *Ficus mucoso* goes back too many decades to explain why Ngogo grew so dramatically in a short period. To address recent growth to its overpowering size, we turn to nearby habitat destruction.

Possible Sufficient Causes

There are three ways that habitat degradation within and around the Park could lead to growth in numbers and density of the Ngogo group. First, it could happen by changing female migration.

Ngogo has had an unusually large number of females, and Wood et al. (2017:43) attribute the community's growth to that factor.[5] The axiomatic female life trajectory is to migrate to another group soon after reaching sexual maturity. Axioms must be questioned. Both Gombe and Mahale deviate from this pattern, with many females staying in their natal group. Now unprovisioned Ngogo is another exception. "Many natal females have remained at Ngogo as adults and reproduced there" (Wood et al. 2017:44).[6]

Female *immigration* is clear. Earlier genetic work found that "the vast majority of females at Ngogo are nonnatal" (Langergraber et al. 2009:846). Wood et al. (2017:44, references omitted) confirm an *unusual level* of female immigration, 31 recognized, (vs. 18 emigrants).[7]

Extensive habitat loss within and around the Park, peaking in the 1970s and early 1980s, left nulliparous females only one way to go—into still forested areas of the Park. Gombe's Kalande, Mahale's K-group, and possibly Budongo's Sonso, to come, show that when a group breaks down under human disruption, parous females with offspring move, substantially increasing the receiving group's numbers.

---

[4] E.g., "The unusually large size of the community, including its exceptional number of males, likely explains the frequency and potency with which it was able to attack its neighbors" (Arcadi 2018:72).

[5] In 1999, the enumerated population was 24 adult males and 47 adult females (Watts and Mitani 2001:304). Several peripheral females were not identified for several years (Wood et al. 2017:43), so that is an underestimate. In May 2016 young had matured to make 35 adult males and 68 adult females (Wood et al. 2017:44). Although an adult sex ratio of 1:1.9 is on the low side compared to other groups, in total that is an unprecedented number of fecund females (Stumpf 2011:347; Wilson et al. 2014:Extended Data Figure 1a).

[6] This "non-dispersal of natal females," is to be addressed in a future publication (Wood et al. 2017:43). At present, it is an inscrutable contribution to population growth (Negrey et al. 2019:140).

[7] Langergraber et al. (2009:846) speculate on its causes. "This increase is higher than found in the female life tables of Gombe and Kanyawara ... [which] probably results from several factors, including higher and less variable food production at Ngogo (which presumably acts as a 'pull' on females in neighboring communities), the success of Ngogo males in inter-group competition and the recent expansion of the community's territory." The pull of abundant food resources is my position exactly. But if the northeastern expansion led to nulliparous female immigration, that would only relate to population growth since the later 2000s.

With islandization, within-Park groups to the south and west of Ngogo, such as Kanyanchu, lost a whole side for potential emigration. Migrating nulliparous females from those could move toward other disturbed groups along the Park edge, or avoid those disturbances by moving inward. Because of habitat loss, female migration from both outside and just inside the Park, probably shifted in the general direction of Ngogo. Especially through the 1970s up to 1986, but continuing since, human-induced habitat loss provides a sufficient condition for great population growth.

Speculation? Sure, as is any explanation of why Ngogo is so large. But consider a comment by John Mitani in *Rise of the Warrior Apes* (Animal Planet 2017). When research began in the later 1990s, there was a surprisingly large number of late adolescent and young adult males, an "unusual demographic blip, of all these males, coming into their prime, all at once. And maybe it was that, that created the situation for all hell to break loose." If late adolescent/young male is pegged at 13–22 years old around the time of the first patrols in 1996, those males were born roughly 1974 to 1983. Ngogo's "Warrior Ape" generation was born during the period of great habitat destruction—consistent with displaced females moving in.

Other Possibilities

Human impact could also induce population growth by restricting exit. At Gombe, after banana feeding was reduced, males and females removed themselves to the south. At Mahale, after the baboon and tourist invasion of the mid-1990s, over 20% of the large group disappeared one by one. At both places, adults had open space nearby. Not for Ngogo, which seems mostly surrounded by other chimpanzees.

Or, growth in population density could occur by compression of distinctive social networks. Ngogo males from 1999 to 2002 had two stable subgroups (Mitani and Amsler 2003). They overlapped through most of the Ngogo range, but A-subgroup leaned to the east and south, and B-subgroup to the central west. "Members of the same subgroup maintained proximity to each other and jointly patrolled their territory." "Determining the factors that permit this community to maintain its unusual demographic size and structure remains a central challenge for future research" (Mitani and Amsler 2003:879, 881). But I found little more about "A" and "B."

This sounds much like the joined Kakombe community at Gombe. One explanation is suggested by Gombe. The joint Kakombe community had "northern and southern 'subgroups'" (Goodall 1986:503), with different ranging orientations and internally directed associational patterns, just like Ngogo. Geographically distinctive networks fused into one because of the lure of bananas. At Ngogo, similarly distributed chimpanzees could be compressed by inward pressure of hostile neighbors.

Ngogo Geopolitics

If Ngogo's numbers and density relate to pressure from areas of habitat loss, then there should be evidence that neighbors more exposed to human impact pushed inward at its borders. There is. Amsler mapped patrolling and intergroup encounters from 2000 to 2006, by quadrants (e.g., 2009:139, 140, 142, 153). Encounters are categorized as *active*, occurring during a Ngogo patrol; and *passive*, when they encounter outside chimpanzees during normal activities. She also walked transects outside Ngogo territory, counting nests to estimate neighboring populations. This data indicates inward pressure from the south and west, just as Ngogo pushed outward in the opposite direction, the northeast.

The East

We start in the middle of the eastern boundary. The first two infanticides (#1, #2, 1999) and one adult male killing (#6, 2002) happened there, but it seems quiet in later years. Except for 2002—who knows why—there are few patrols or encounters. This area has much swamp and grassland (Mutai 2011:6) not good for chimpanzee use. Nest counts due east are light (Amsler 2009:142). Red colobus hunts that went farthest outside the Ngogo home range are in this area (Teelen 2007:1031)—as if there was little to worry about.

Continuing clockwise, the southeastern corner of Ngogo territory may be the best for assessing "normal" intergroup relations. It continues into solid undegraded forest, with a high concentration of nests, and a handful of passive encounters (Amsler 2009:84, 139, 140, 152, 153). Chimpanzees are numerous, but this corner is roughly 10 km from the Park border. That is much farther than in contested areas to the south and west, so they are less likely to be displaced by human disturbance.

The Kanyanchu Front

The broad diagonal that is Ngogo's south/southwestern territorial periphery is very different. This is where Ngogo rangelands abut those of Kanyanchu, (and/or Kanyantale), and perhaps other groups—although for lack of clarity, I stick simply with Kanyanchu. Five, hypothetically six, of Ngogo's extraterritorial killings occurred there.

Here distance to the Park border—the width of chimpanzee rangeland—is about 3 to 5 km. In places it is effectively less, since much of this area was cleared for farming (Mutai 2011:6), besides being a multiple use zone for local people. The westernmost Kanyanchu tourist road (Great Lakes Safaris n.d.) runs within a couple of kilometers of forests degraded by human activity up to 1992 (Whitesell 1997:67, and see illustration 4.3).

Bigodi villagers, just outside the border, had frequent contact with chimpanzees inside and outside the Park, including crop raiding (Adams et al. 2001:310). This extra-Park foraging suggests that Kanyanchu lost a substantial part of its former range land to islandization; and/or that they sometimes experienced food shortages. From its south and its west, human pressure on Kanyanchu is palpable, without even considering the impact of tourism. To Kanyanchu's north lies Ngogo.

Kanyanchu like Ngogo is exceptionally numerous. By the middle 2000s, it could surpass 100 members (Wrangham et al. 2007:1610). In Plumptre et al.'s (2003:70) survey of chimpanzee density, Kanyanchu is *more* dense than Ngogo. Amsler's

(2009:158), nest counts indicate that it "may be even larger than, or at least as large as, Ngogo." Nest density here is far greater than in any other area around Ngogo (Amsler 2009:145).

With Kanyanchu squeezed between Ngogo, the Park border, and degraded land to its west, by the human impact hypothesis and the idea of population pressure pushing inward on Ngogo—intergroup conflict is expected. It happened.

Southern Encounters

Territorial pressure from Kanyanchu was apparent in early observations.

> We often followed Ngogo chimpanzees to the west in 1997 and early 1998, but by mid-1999 most males rarely traveled near or across apparent boundaries to the west, and neared those to the southwest and northwest much less often than more easterly boundaries. They might have shifted their activities to avoid the Kanyanchu community, which is also unusually large, in the south and southwest. (Watts and Mitani 2001:309)

This was not an area to be abandoned lightly, even if it entailed risk, as "the southwest portion of Ngogo territory [compared to other areas] has a high concentration of many of the chimpanzees' favorite food trees" (Amsler 2009:84–85). From December 1998 to February 1999, five of the six hostile encounters observed while Ngogo chimpanzees were foraging (rather than on patrol), involved chimpanzees from Kanyanchu, with calls, counter-calls, flight, avoidance, charging, and counter-charging (Watts and Mitani 2001:312–313). In December 1998, a suspected adult male killing, *possibly* of Kanyanchu (or Kanyantale), *possibly* by Ngogo, could be the first noted killing by Ngogo (Wilson et al. 2014:EDT 1) (already counted).

From 1999 to 2008 Ngogo's patrols in the southwest were second only to those in northeast (Mitani et al. 2010:R508). Yet the overwhelming majority of encounters in the southwest were *passive* (Amsler 2009:153), not while patrolling. The evidence shows that from 1998 and for at least a decade after, southwestern chimpanzees were pressing in on Ngogo. Three Ngogo males were killed by outside chimpanzees in 2004–2005, and others suspected killed (Mitani et al. 2010)—although whether by Kanyanchu or more northwestern neighbors is not clear (below).

Ngogo killed four outsiders on this front in 2004 and 2005, three infants and one adult male (#10, #13, #14 [inferred], #15); and an adult female (#21) in 2009 (Mitani et al. 2010). Only the first infanticide is described, in the overlapping use zone with southern neighbors (Sherrow and Amsler 2007:13). It happened when a large mixed foraging party turned into a patrol and encountered stranger chimpanzees. They heard a cry, found a stranger female with infant, and killed and ate the latter. Then the Ngogo and Kanyanchu main parties collided.

> The males from both sides chased each other in waves, moving back and forth. Several of the males from both communities physically fought during the battle, hitting, kicking, and biting each other, while others called and buttress drummed. The

fighting took place between individuals and groups and there did not appear to be a pattern to the number of males involved. (Sherrow and Amsler 2007:15)

This grand battle is unlike Ngogo's common trouncing of one or a few chimpanzees to its northeast. Kanyanchu was formidable.

Comparing data from the southwest to the expansion area to the northeast, Amsler (2009:146, my emphasis) notes:

> These differences suggest that in the northeast, Ngogo chimpanzees may be taking advantage of numerical superiority to push the territory boundary in that direction . . . In contrast, *the Ngogo chimpanzees may patrol in the southwest simply to try to maintain their territory there against a stronger community, trying to push its boundary into the Ngogo territory*.[8]

By the numbers, Ngogo's total rangeland shrank by about 6 km^2 in the first half of the 2000s. Comparing maps of Ngogo territory around 2000 (Watts et al. 2002:265) with the mid-2000s (Mitani et al. 2010:R508) shows a decided compression of the southwest.[9]

The West

I found no clarification of unit-groups beyond Kanyanchu, also called Kanyantale (or is that a different group?); which has Buraiga as a neighbor (but on which side?) Moving northwesterly along Ngogo's southwestern diagonal, there is nary a clue about group distinction. Nest counts vary by individual observation transect from high to low (Amsler 2009:142). Group definition is simply unknown.

Still, *all* those neighbors fronted on habitat loss to the west and south. The Park border due west of Ngogo and the deforested southern Park extension to their southwest, leaves a habitable band some four to six kilometers, and some of it grassland (Amsler 2009:6; Mutai 2011:6). Beginning with the fuzziness of Kanyanchu/Kanyantale/Buraiga, the expanse can only be characterized as a span that had many chimpanzees, of unknown grouping. The outer edge of this span is where habitat loss pushed on chimpanzees. The inner is where they pushed on Ngogo.

Within Amsler's northwest sector is another concentration of Ngogo patrols (Mitani et al. 2010:R508). Two infanticides by Ngogo (#11, #12), occurred far west of Ngogo's normal range in 2004 (Sherrow and Amsler 2007:16–18). Despite this "offensive" clash, the northwestern quadrant, like the southwest, has mostly passive encounters, hostile meetings during feeding (Amsler 2009:153).

---

[8] Amsler, however, then discounts that possibility for a narrow statistical reason. It is not supported by comparing regression slopes of nest counts vs. patrol rates in all four quadrants of Ngogo's neighborhood.

[9] For the record, three more incidents must be noted, from Wilson et al.'s (2014) extended data tables, labeled Kanyantale instead of Kanyanchu: in March 1999, an inferred within-group infant killing (Count 4 W-I-M 1999); in 2010, a suspected killing by Kanyantale from "Buraiga" group (Count 5 O-A-M 2010); and in September 2014, a suspected killing by Kanyantale of a juvenile of unknown sex, from an unknown group (Count 5 O-J-? 2014). More cannot be said about such bare notations.

The northwest sector... had the highest passive to active intercommunity encounter ratio. This could suggest that both the Ngogo community and the community to the northwest use the overlap zone regularly *or that the northwest community moves into the Ngogo territory more often than the reverse.* .... An adult male from Ngogo was found dead from wounds inflicted by other chimpanzees in the northwest sector in February 2006. Two other Ngogo males were killed just south of the northwest sector in the southwest sector in July 2005. Since my sectors are arbitrary and do not reflect knowledge of where other chimpanzee communities actually range, at least one, but maybe all three, deaths could have been perpetrated by a community to the northwest. (Amsler 2009:157–158, my emphasis)[10]

There's more, but it is vague. Two adult and two adolescent Ngogo males disappeared between 1999 and 2002. In *Animal Planet*, researchers note that Ellington was the most important initiator of patrols, and he disappeared (Chapter 14). They speculate he was caught while scouting for enemies. Gloom deepened. Wood et al. (2017:51) "suspect that seven or more adolescent and adult males, who often ranged in peripheral parts of the Ngogo territory, likewise were victims of such attacks." On camera, Mitani surmises that Ngogo was now "getting as good as they've given."

None of these appear in the Wilson et al. data tables, even as suspected killings. Some may be too recent for that. I count them as hypotheticals, though they could merit upgrading with more information (Count, *Seven* 5 O-A-M, no date). From researchers' suspicions, it is clear that the mega-group, recently, has been under substantial pressure from its neighbors.[11]

The Expansion Area

With this context, we approach the main concern, the realm of the Ngogo Expansion. Intergroup relations due north are separated by "an extremely large swamp" (Amsler 2009:128). The adult male (#8) killed in 2002 is set apart from all others along the northern frontier. He was "presumably" a member of "the Wantabu community, to the north of Ngogo" (Watts et al. 2006:168). Wantabu is the unit-group imagined between Ngogo and Kanyawara group. But it was not an area of much other Ngogo activity, so we move on.

To Ngogo's northeast is an outward expanding funnel of forest, bracketed above and below by swamp and grassland (Mutai 2011:6). Within this chute happened Ngogo's "war of conquest." Besides all the killings, there were more patrols in that

---

[10] Wilson et al. (2014:EDT 1), indicate the attackers were from the west-southwest (Count *two* 1 O-A-M 2005). They do not include the 2006 incident, so that one I count as a possible (Count 4 O-A-M 2006).

In *Rise of the Warrior Apes* (Animal Planet 2017) researchers emotionally describe finding one of the 2005 victims, Branford, barely alive, then rushing forward toward the sound of another chimpanzee fight, to encounter Waller's body. Two adult males killed at once is unprecedented, and suggests a very large number of adversaries.

[11] Similarly unclear, there is another possible kill, without any other information, an adult female received light wounds while in a peripheral area. Her infant was missing and presumed to be a victim of infanticide (Wood et al. 2017:51) (Count, 4 O-I-? no date).

direction than anywhere, and the highest ratio of active to passive encounters (Amsler 2009:140, 157; Mitani et al. 2010:R508). With some qualifications, it was Ngogo pushing outward without major resistance.[12]

What Does "Conquest" Mean?

Much of the 2009 expansion area was already used by Ngogo. The center of the expansion area was not previously included as part of Ngogo's range, but hunting of red colobus within and beyond it increased after 1998 (Teelen 2007:1031, and Chapter 15). Regarding the first four killings—#1, #2, #3, #4—all of infants: "this inter-group aggression and the high frequency of patrols in the general area of the infanticides make us think that the infanticides occurred in areas of range overlap with at least one neighboring community or across boundaries in areas more typically used by those neighbors" (Watts and Mitani 2000:361). After those killings, by 2001 researchers noted a shift of large mixed parties feeding on key foods further north and east than previously witnessed. They invoked the possibility of range expansion (Watts et al. 2002:268).

What changed in 2009 was *further* northeast expansion into an area previously used mainly for monkey hunting and patrols. Large mixed-sex parties behaved in this new range as they usually did in the center of their territory; and outside chimpanzees were no longer seen there (Mitani et al. 2010:R507).

One could call this conquest, though of course territorial data from more than one field season is needed. Yet, in another sense, Ngogo was regaining lost ground. Pushed across their southern-western borders by groups on the front lines of human disruption, Ngogo bulged out in the opposite direction. From 2000–2005, Ngogo went from about 35 km^2 to about 28.5 km^2, a range loss of 18.6%. The 2009 expansion added 6.4 km^2, increasing Ngogo's territory by 22.3% (Mitani et al. 2010:R508). Doing the math, that gives them an expanded territory of 35.09 km^2. The northeastern expansion just brought Ngogo's territorial size back to about what it was a decade earlier.

And then what happened? In all field observations, *only* mid-1970s Kasakela and 2009 Ngogo stand as examples of adaptive gain through a sequence of external killings. At Gombe the case for adaptation is made with longitudinal measures of body mass and of reproductive health, (which on close inspection is not as clear-cut as it seems). At Ngogo, other than the simple fact of range gain, statistics consistent with adaptation suggest that *male participation in patrolling* correlates with having more living offspring, or higher rank, or good physical condition, although other factors may be involved in those associations (Langergraber et al. 2017; Mitani 2020:7), (such as the connection between more frequent patrolling and hunting, below). Not compelling evidence of adaptation through conquest.

---

[12] Not considering the seven hypothetical killings just noted—which have no geographic specification but *could be* northeast—there was little push back from northeast neighbors. The exception is an adult Ngogo female, Dani, and her infant, inferred killings by the northeastern chimpanzees in April 2004 (Wilson et al. 2014:EDT 1). The mother showed up with severe wounds, the infant with light wounds, and both then disappeared (Wood et al. 2017:51) (Count 3 O-A-F 2004; 3 O-I-? 2004).

Despite its theoretical importance, the Ngogo Expansion is described in just four columns of text, published over a decade ago (Mitani et al. 2010) without major follow-up. Detail is lacking for killings #13 to #21 up to 2011, plus other infanticides and Ngogo victims of outsiders. How did the occupation of northeastern land work out? What about the southwest? More information is needed to carry Ngogo's history from conquest, through "getting as good as they've given" just a few years later, up to the surprising denouement of 2015–2018 (see Chapter 14 Postscript).

Conquest with an Asterisk

There is another human impact factor that must be added. Unlike Gombe and Mahale—where chimpanzees on both sides of conflict were all familiar with following humans—chimpanzees to Ngogo's northeast were not. Ngogo researcher William Wallauer told Arcadi (2018:177 n.59) about "the flight of unhabituated chimpanzees from patrolling Ngogo males followed by himself and other human researchers."

> Unhabituated chimpanzees are extremely fearful of humans and flee when they see them. Consequently, researchers closely following a group of habituated chimpanzees that come into contact with unhabituated neighbors could affect the outcome of the encounter in at least two ways. First, they could simply scare the unhabituated animals into flight, facilitating territorial encroachment by the study animals. If contact with humans also inhibited the neighboring chimpanzees from frequenting the area in the future, a more long-term boundary shift could ensue. Second, fleeing animals could become separated from their group and more vulnerable to attack by the patrolling animals.

This same concern applied at Kanyawara.

> It is unclear how important observer effects are. The presence of observers might partially protect study chimpanzees from aggression by unhabituated Kanyawara neighbors. For example, in January 2004, an adult male Kanyawara chimpanzee who was being attacked by a group of males from a neighboring community escaped after his attackers fled on seeing a human observer. (Wrangham et al. 2006:21)

This wasn't an isolated occurrence. "In 11 of the 18 observed cases of visual and/or physical contact, the unhabituated foreign chimpanzees fled soon after seeing researchers" (Wilson et al. 2012:283).

Besides having overwhelming numbers, Ngogo chimpanzees had a trump card over their unhabituated northeastern neighbors. When feeding, hunting, or on patrol, they brought chimpanzee-frightening people with them. Arcadi (2018:78) suggests this effect may be an important factor behind Ngogo's expansion, and calls for "systematic analysis of the impact of human observers on intercommunity interactions." Since this range acquisition is one of only two claimed cases of adaptive gain through "war," this asterisk is theoretically important.

Setting aside historically changed infrastructure of habitat, ecology, demography and food, this lynchpin of adaptive arguments (see Chapter 28) is obviously affected by human impact, with this clear-cut observer effect. Notably and in contrast, the inward-pushing Kanyanchu chimpanzees were long habituated to trailing humans. People would not scare them away.

14
The Ngogo Expansion, RCH + HIH

So there is human impact. But is there heightened resource competition? If there is plenty of food, why should southern/western impingement lead to expansion in the other direction? Did Ngogo experience some sort of food scarcity? Not in terms of nutritional shortfall. They were well nourished. But if scarcity can be *demonstrated* by intense conflict over increasingly scarce *preferred* foods, then yes they did.

Preferred Food Scarcity

The late 1990s clashes over preferred fruits with Kanyanchu continued.

> [M]ost encounters in the southwest have happened while chimpanzees from both communities were feeding near each other during major fruiting events by *C. albidum*, *U. congensis*, or *Aningeria altissima*, three of the most important food species at Ngogo. The high frequency of such intergroup feeding contests is also consistent with the food defense hypothesis. Feeding parties on both side are typically large, so power imbalances are slight at most encounters. (Watts 2012:331, references omitted)

This was not just to the populous southwest, but in the northwest too.

> Valuable food resources occasionally become available in abundance near territorial boundaries, and during these times, chimpanzees use these areas intensively. At Ngogo, chimpanzees appear to increase their patrolling frequency before such seasonal periods of food abundance, perhaps to assess the safety of the area. (Mitani and Watts 2005:1084)

They have plenty of food, they are well nourished, yet they fight over food. Ngogo researchers conceptualize this as the "resource acquisition hypothesis. By acquiring new territory through lethal coalitionary aggression, male chimpanzees improve the feeding success of individuals in their own community, which in turn can lead to increased female reproduction" (Mitani 2010:R508).

I propose that Ngogo and neighbors sustained the *substantial* costs and risks of patrolling and fighting (see Watts 2012:330), because they experienced scarcity of key, *preferred* foods, due to human-impacted growth in numbers and density, and constriction/displacement of ranging areas. Compounding that, killing may have gotten a jump start because of drought.

Drought

Park vegetation took a major hit just when intercommunity killings began. In 1999 a tree-killing drought struck Kibale. Rainfall was low in March, and far under half of normal from April through July (Lwanga 2003:195).

> The first half of 1999 was unusually dry at Ngogo, and caused leaves to dry on most trees throughout the study area. With the return of the rains in the second half of the year, trees on deeper soils recovered. In the year following the drought, massive tree mortality occurred along ridges and on hill-tops that happened to have shallow soils. (2003:194)

Since the beginning of Struhsaker's research in 1970, "mortality of this nature had not been observed anywhere in the forest" (2003:196). In March 2000 (in a patch chosen specifically for severity of drought effect), 19% of all trees were dead, actually dry, and many more moribund. Several major chimpanzee food trees suffered (Lwanga 2003:195; Mitani and Watts 2001:917). One graph (Mitani et al. 2002a:106) shows Ngogo food availability dropping sharply from June to August, where data ends. However, this drought does not register in long-term aggregate data (Chapman et al. 2005).[1] There is no indication of how much of Ngogo's range was heavily impacted, but it is hilly and ridge tops were hit the hardest. The situation is anything but clear.

Uvariopsis congensis

Nevertheless, Struhsaker—the long-term forest observer—never saw anything like it. And it especially killed one of Ngogo's preferred food. *Ficus mucuso* is the most common food at Ngogo, but next most consumed is the drupe *Uvariopsis congensis* (Watts et al. 2012a:119).

The importance of drupes is described for Kanyawara:

> [T]he Kanyawara chimpanzees preferentially consume ripe arboreal drupes, or "non-fig fruits" (NFF), when available. This indicates that NFF are high quality food items. Indeed, at Kanyawara, intake of lipids, simple sugars, and nonstructural carbohydrates was positively correlated with ripe fruit abundance, which was driven by variation in NFF. The benefits of elevated NFF intake are striking. NFF consumption at Kanyawara was highly positively correlated with several energetically expensive factors associated with increased fitness including ovarian function, likelihood of sexual swelling, and probability of conception. (Gilby and Wrangham 2007:1773, references omitted)

---

[1] A long-term study of fruit production around Ngogo shows a drop in early 1999, but nothing remarkable. By their methods, tree mortality *would not show*. "If an individual tree died, it was replaced by one of the same species and similar size" (Potts et al. 2020:523, 526).

Before the drought, *U. congensis* around Ngogo declined by 6.6% from 1975 to 1998 (Lwanga et al. 2000:243), while the Ngogo population more than doubled. Per capita, this most consumed of the most nutritionally important type of fruit, was probably less than half what it was in the mid-1970s, *and then* the 1999 drought hit it worst of all. In the post-drought survey, of 170 *U. congensis* trees, 68 were dead, and 11 moribund (Lwanga 2003:195).

Availability of *Uvariopsis* was a clear factor in some of the first killings.

> [W]e note that the attacks in 2000 occurred during a mast fruiting by *Uvariopsis congensis*, an extremely important food species for chimpanzees at Ngogo, and that this tree species is common in the area of the attack. *U. congensis* fruited again in June–July 2001. The fruit was available in much of the Ngogo community's territory, but in July it was particularly abundant towards the northern extreme of the territory, in the general area of the infanticides reported there. [Also, killing #5, of an unsexed juvenile, occurred in this area in July 2001.] The chimpanzees spent far more time in that area than in previous *U. congensis* seasons and were often farther to the north and east than we had been with them before except during patrols. They usually went there in large parties that included many females with immature offspring. Whether this apparent change in their habitat use patterns reflects a long-term range expansion remains to be seen, but their heavy use of the area is consistent with the range expansion hypothesis for infanticide. (Watts et al. 2002:268)

An already limited, nutritionally vital and preferred food was suddenly reduced to an unknown degree from April 1999 onward—right when killing began in northern peripheries abloom with *Uvariopsis*. This is immediate, direct competition over key resources. If instead Ngogo numbered, say, 80 individuals; and southwestern neighbors weren't pushing in on food rich borders, maybe northeastern *Uvariopsis* availability would not have been a killing issue.

Hunting

The importance of *Uvariopsis* in nutrition, diet, and conflict is all clear. Evaluating another preferred food is a more complicated issue, bringing us back to comparative questions about hunting. Points to come are: (1) red colobus hunting firmly substantiates population growth from the late 1970s to mid-1990s; (2) for Ngogo as elsewhere, major surges in hunting reflect anthropogenic resource stress; and (3) intensification of hunting is behaviorally linked to intergroup violence (see Watts 2012:328–329).

When observation began in the 1990s, Ngogo males were avidly hunting. From 1998–1999 they caught prey once per 6.6 days, with hunters averaging 1.8 kg of meat per hunt (Watts and Mitani 2002:16–17). Four pounds per week! Why hunt so much?

Ngogo researchers recognize the nutritional importance of meat. But they conclude that nutritional shortfall cannot explain short-term variations in hunting, being more frequent during times of higher fruit availability. What predicts the likelihood of a hunt is more males being together at one time (Mitani and Watts 2001:922–923; Watts and Mitani 2002:16–17; Watts 2007:131; 2008:92; Watts 2012:328–329).

My concern is not short-term variation but major intensifications over time. At Gombe a jump followed sharp reduction in banana provisioning. At Mahale it followed anthropogenic food competition with baboons. Budongo will provide another example. For Ngogo, we return to the human impact hypothesis (HIH) demographic motor: major population growth since the 1970s, and centripetal pressure from islandization.

Early Nonhunting

Initially, observers did not find monkey hunting (Ghiglieri 1984:111–117). "During thousands of hours of observation in Kibale Forest, neither T. Struhsaker nor L. Leland have seen one killed by a chimpanzee [though both] have seen probable attempts which failed, possibly due to their presence." Neither did Ghiglieri in 1976–1978, though he witnessed an attempt to capture a mangabey monkey, and two chimpanzees chewing on a fresh red colobus hide.

Ghiglieri's finding was dismissed as due to lack of habituation. "This argument has merit but does not explain why I only once saw evidence of predation during nearly 488 hours of observations of the predators. During several of the chimpanzee-red colobus interactions, none of the primates were aware of my presence" (1984:116).

Later researchers continued the same dismissal (Boesch and Boesch 1989:570; Mitani and Watts 1999:450; Stanford 1998a:9, 90). Yet Mitani and Watts (1999:446–447) witnessed red colobus hunts just 5 months into their fieldwork in 1995. Even if Ghiglieri, Struhsaker, and Leland missed many hunts, it is inconceivable that hunting in the 1970s was anything like the 1995 rate.

Later Intensification

Over summers from 1995 to 1998, Mitani and Watts (1999:446, 448) saw 62 hunts, or one per 7.6 days. 91% targeted red colobus, usually very young ones. A second study, October 1998 to August 1999, saw 59 hunts, making one every 6.6 observation days. The second period saw a "striking" increase in red colobus *adults* taken, going from 2% to 11% of victims (Watts and Mitani 2002:1, 16). Those kills amounted to a perhaps unsustainable rate of 15% of the prey population (Teelen 2008:46).

Then hunting shot upward from 102 estimated kills in 1995–1998 to 258 in 1998–1999—the drought year—224 in 2000, 228 in 2001, and 322 in bloody 2002 (Teelen 2008:45, 47). For 5 months of that year, "[m]eat accounted for 12.3% of feeding time" (Watts 2020:6). As red colobus numbers declined, predation rate reached 40%–50% of the total colobus population per year (Teleen 2007:1042).

Primate surveys from 1975–1976 to 1997–1998 (Lwanga et al. 2011:11–12) showed a "significant" decline in the red colobus population over those 23 years (Mitani, Struhsaker et al. 2000:283–285). Teelen's (2007:1035) re-analysis of data with additional surveys, characterizes this decline as "steep."[2] By 2002, red colobus population in Ngogo territory was down by 86.8% compared to 1975–1976 (Lwanga et al. 2011:7). Local extirpation was foreseen (Teelen 2008:45–46; Watts et al. 2011).

Watts and Amsler (2013:934–335) bring the data through the time of the Ngogo Expansion. Red colobus were first depleted in the center of Ngogo rangelands, and subsequently in its peripheries. Hunting rates and offtake fell off after the hunting peak of 2002, because there were so few left to hunt. No signs of red colobus revival are apparent.

For some years there were few indications of switching prey, but then that changed. By 2015 red-tailed monkeys were targeted, and mantled guerzas were hunted so often that they too became less common. Quoting David Watts, "I've been here a little over a month. The chimpanzees have hunted quite often in that time. They've hunted black-and-white colobus eight times. I've never seen anything like that before." And, "My subjective impression this summer is that they are getting better at hunting black-and-white colobus" (Marshall 2015). However well-nourished they may be in general, Ngogo males want that meat![3]

Ngogo Population Growth, Again

The extirpation of red colobus is a qualitatively unnatural event. "The Ngogo study is the only one to our knowledge providing strong evidence that predation other than by humans has resulted in a pronounced decline in the population of a non-human primate species" (Lwanga et al. 2011:11).[4] This level of hunting *could not* have occurred in the 1970s or 1980s, or the monkeys would be long gone. What changed? The size of the Ngogo community.

Ngogo researchers stress the relationship between successful predation and community size: "high hunting success is a near inevitable consequence of the large number of males and community size at Ngogo" (Mitani and Watts 1999:451). "We agree with Teelen that this unsustainable level of predation was likely the consequence of the extremely large community of chimpanzees at Ngogo" (Lwanga et al. 2011:11).

Chapter 10 gave direct evidence for population growth in chimpanzee numbers from the 1970s through the 1990s. The intensifying pressure on red colobus, attributed by Ngogo researchers to the number of hunters, is decisive support for great Ngogo growth from the time of nearby habitat loss.

---

[2] The dramatic effect is clear in mean number of colobus groups observed per censused kilometer: 1975–1976, .53; 1978–1984, .41; 1997–1998, .30; 2001–2002, .07; 2002–2003, .06 (Teelen 2007:1037; Lwanga et al. 2011:6).

[3] In contrast, red colobus though abundant are not hunted at Sebitoli, where guerzas are the primary target (Watts 2020:5).

[4] The Fourrier et al. (2008) study of red colobus decline from hunting at Gombe was a projection, not a count.

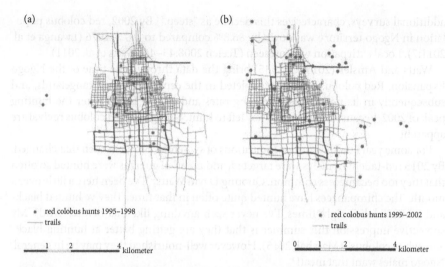

Illustration 4.5 Red Colobus Hunts around Ngogo, 1995–1998 and 1999–2002
Caption: Locations of hunts by chimpanzees on red colobus monkeys at Ngogo in (a) 1995–1998 and (b) 1999–2002. Census routes are marked with thick lines. The traditional census route is located in the center of the grid-system, the newly established routes are surrounding it (maps by S. Amsler based on Mitani & Watts, unpublished data).
Source: Teelen, S. (2007). Primate abundance along five transect lines at Ngogo, Kibale National Park, Uganda. *American Journal of Primatology*, 69, 1030–1044.

Hunting and the Expansion

Whatever the nutritional needs behind it, red colobus meat is a highly preferred food. The extraordinary numbers of the mega-group made monkey meat scarcer and scarcer. Ecologically, Ngogo chimpanzees exceeded the environment's carrying capacity and degraded their resource base. *Perhaps*, somehow the 1999 drought contributed to that. No matter—red colobus hunting is clearly implicated in Ngogo's northeastern offensive.

Geography of Hunting

The orientation of hunting maps on to the geopolitics of intergroup relations. Overpredation pushed Ngogo hunters to peripheries. Comparing hunts in 1999–2002 with 1995–1998, fewer occurred in the center of Ngogo territory, and many more in the north-through-eastern periphery—but *not* in the dangerous south and west (Teelen 2007:1031).

> [T]he habituated Kanyanchu community has over 100 members and an unhabituated community to the west/southwest is also very large and has many adult males. In recent years, red colobus encounters where its home range overlaps that of the Ngogo

community have been strikingly rare and several groups seem to have disappeared. This is consistent with the hypothesis that Ngogo chimpanzees have caused a decline in the red colobus population throughout their home range, but hunting by members of the neighboring communities might have exacerbated the decline. (Amsler and Mitani 2013:935)

Ngogo did not hunt in its northeast prior to 1999. In 2002–2003 red colobus were more abundant there than anywhere else around Ngogo territory (Teelen 2007:1035, 1038). The connection between expansion and hunting is clear:

> [A]s the red colobus population declined, the chimpanzee community there expanded its territory and took over part of the range of another chimpanzee community to the northeast. This expansion resulted in a 22.3% increase in their territory size, where they preyed upon red colobus. (Lwanga et al. 2011:12, references omitted)

And,

> The 2009 increase [in red colobus encounters] coincided with a major expansion of the chimpanzee territory to the east and northeast after years of intense boundary patrolling and many fatal attacks.... [Conflicts at Ngogo, Gombe, and Kanyawara] strongly implicate competition over plant food resources as the main instigator of intergroup encounters in chimpanzees and maintaining or increasing access to food as the main function of lethal coalitionary aggressions. Increased access to vertebrate prey—notably red colobus—may be a side benefit (if perhaps a short-term one) of territory expansion. (Watts and Amsler 2013:935)

Or there could be a more direct connection.

Hunting and Intergroup Conflict

A stealthy, usually all-male patrol is different from a mixed and less quiet red colobus hunt. But "males skilled at hunting may also be particularly inclined to engage in patrols, and others may be most inclined to go on patrols when good hunters are present" (Watts and Mitani 2001:305). Hunting parties are large, with a mean of 13 males, compared to 4 for normal foraging groups (Mitani and Watts 1999:444). More hunting means more groups of more males, and thus more parties capable of attacking strangers. "Pursuing prey is a dangerous activity... and likely to give others an indication of a male's willingness and ability to take risks in intercommunity aggression" (Muller and Mitani 2005:308). A party that begins as a colobus hunt can easily turn into a party chasing strangers.

Most described external killings were connected to hunting. In #2, June 1999, a mixed feeding party in Ngogo's eastern periphery, the vicinity of two recent red colobus hunts, tried to capture a black and white colobus monkey before encountering a stranger female with infant, which was eaten (Watts and Mitani 2000:359). The next two infanticides (#3, #4, July 2001) began with a mixed feeding party in Ngogo's northern periphery, observing red colobus. Some males went for the monkeys, but others seemed uninterested. 15 minutes later, the males formed a patrol, and hearing outsiders, rushed to attack, killing two infants, which apparently were not eaten (Watts et al. 2002:266–267).

A possibly deadly attack on a juvenile male (#7 August 2002) in the northeast started as a mixed feeding party then turned into a search for red colobus. Yet they passed by a small group of red colobus, turning into a patrol. They heard chimpanzees from the north, and caught a male alone (Watts et al. 2006:173). The killing of an adult male (#8 November 2002) happened in the north, by males who were on a red colobus hunt, but made only desultory efforts when they found them. They ran into a few outsiders, surrounding and killing the male (Watts et al. 2006:168).

Another infanticide began with a large mixed party in the southwestern Kanyanchu area (#10, October 2004). They found red colobus, but again registered limited interest, and no hunting occurred. Instead the males began a patrol to the south, which eventually encountered a female with infant. They ate the infant. In the last two killings described, both infanticides (#11, #12) started with a large mixed party, trying to locate red colobus they had heard. Not finding them, they caught two chimpanzee mothers with infants, though the infants apparently were not eaten (Sherrow and Amsler 2007:12, 15–18).

Thus, 8 of 11 well-described killings followed on some level of monkey hunting. The pattern is chimpanzees interested in hunting let that go when alerted to outsiders. But it can go the other way, e.g., #1. In April 1999 as the drought began, a patrol from the center of Ngogo territory to its eastern border, snatched an infant and ate it "enthusiastically, as if they were eating meat from red colobus" (Watts and Mitani 2000:359). Not a hunt but predation, just as predation on monkeys was increasing.

There may be other, unreported examples, such as an encounter incidentally noted in a paper about scavenging (Watts 2008:128–129). In September 2002, a large mixed party somewhere in the northern territory was successfully hunting red colobus. They heard chimpanzee screams to the north, and silently rushed toward them. They charged a party of outsiders, who fled with no physical contact. If they'd caught one . . . ?

Only two killings do not involve hunting or meat eating: #6, June 2002, where an adult male was found and killed by a border patrol; and #9, August 2004, where a mixed feeding party responded to outside pant hoots and killed an adult male.

Although competition over preferred fruits is clear, access to prey seems more than a "side benefit" of the attacks that expanded Ngogo territory. There is a clear behavioral connection of hunting in peripheries as red colobus declined in their central territory, leading to intergroup killings.

Display Killing

Chimpanzees use meat sharing politically, to build alliances and exclude rivals. Political reputation and status are acted out in patrols. With all the hunting and patrolling 1999 to 2011, much political maneuvering can be assumed. My argument for display killing requires substantial political turmoil. It also involves as status hierarchy determined by male on male competition, often coalitional and often violent.

Ngogo males are status strivers (Sherrow 2012:68). Despite their numbers, they can be arranged in a steep, linear status hierarchy, with dyadic association reflecting age and status similarity (Mitani et al. 2002b:734; Watts 2018:988).[5] For adolescents, rising rank goes along with participating in patrols (Watts and Mitani 2001:320–321) and attaching themselves to dominant adults (as a Kanyawara [Enigk et al. 2020]). Dyadic alliances can last for a decade (Mitani 2009:639).

> [M]ales show reciprocity in grooming, coalition formation, and meat sharing and interchange between grooming and coalitionary support, grooming and meat sharing, and coalitionary support and meat sharing. Males also engage in boundary patrols most often with others who are their main grooming and coalition partners and with whom they most often participate in hunts. (Watts 2012:326, references omitted; Mitani and Watts 2001:920–922; Watts 2002:354, 360; Watts and Mitani 2002b:253)

It all goes together. Males that co-hunt and share meat, also groom, bond, mutually support, and look for outsiders together.

Ngogo displayed much internal violence. "Given the extremely large size of the Ngogo community, aggression between males was a regular occurrence. We recorded 1184 acts of aggression between community males" over roughly 2,500 hours, or almost one aggressive incident every two hours (Mitanie and Amsler 2003:875). In some intracommunity fights, multiple males (up to 10) attacked and wounded single males (Watts 2004:517). Up to five infanticides are passingly noted,[6] but no other information is available.

This social fabric seems well suited to display violence. A major complication however, is the number of grown males, 24 adult and 15 adolescents in the late 1990s (Watts and Mitani 2001:313, 315), further complicated by two distinctive associational networks. This opens possibilities unlike when one or a few belligerent males intimidate half a dozen potential challengers, which greatly complicates evaluation of the display violence hypothesis. Moreover, very little detail on specific political alignments and contents are published.

Nevertheless, display violence seems important in the initial outside killings, 1908–2001. That can be reconstructed using commentary in *Rise of the Warrior Apes* (Animal Planet 2017). Remember that killings began with infanticides in April 1999. The context of intense political turmoil is reminiscent of episodes of infant killing elsewhere.

---

[5] Females do not have a measurable hierarchy, and agonistic episodes between them are rare. Contrary to the idea that females are asocial, female-female association with strong social bonds is comparable to Tai and even bonobos. Females stay close to home foraging areas, and form enduring associational cliques with neighboring females (Langergraber et al. 2009; Wakefield 2008:920–921; Watts 2012:327). Langergraber et al. (2013) found long term association of males with particular females, when both selectively range in the same local space, males "inheriting" them from their mothers. This is not our concern, but very different from the standard model of bonded males and atomistic females.

[6] Watts (2012:325) notes three. Wilson et al. (2014a:EDT 4) tally two observed (Count 2 W-I-? 2005; 2 W-I-? 2009) and one suspected (Count 4 W-I-? 1999). Wood et al. (2017:51) note that *five* infants "have been victims of withing-community infanticides (which adds *two* 4 W-I-? no date).

The Shift to Killing

Mweya, strong and smart, was alpha at the start of research in 1995. Bartok supported Mweya as beta. He came under prolonged challenge by Lofty—an aggressive bully. From January 1998 to August 1999:

> Long-time alpha MW put surprisingly low effort into patrolling.... Most of the patrols that we observed occurred during a period when male LO reversed rank with several other top-ranking males and then made a prolonged and successful challenge of MW and replaced him as alpha. As his hold on the alpha position became tenuous, MW might have refrained from patrols to avoid situations in which he could have faced challenges. BA, who had been MW's main ally for several years, refrained from several patrols that LO joined after LO had become alpha; BA seemed not to want to associate with LO. (Watts and Mitani 2001:321)

(Mweya calls to mind Humphrey at Gombe, who ceased patrolling toward Kahama in 1973 as his alpha position became unsteady, and was soon deposed by Figan).

Sometime in early 1999 Lofty supplanted beta Bartok. Without Bartok's support Mweya was vulnerable. Lofty beat him up and became alpha. But Lofty was inept in building support. On top he was mostly alone. Bartok then made his own move, besting Mweya who fell to number three. Still, they remained allies. This was Bartok's strength, cultivating support from many prime males, (as Ntologi did). One day, about a year and a half after Lofty became alpha (so in early 2001?), these males jumped Lofty and thrashed him. Bartok emerged as alpha, and would stay on top for 9 years, until 2009 (Watts 2018:994). So there was turmoil at the top, and at least one very aggressive male.

However, the principle actors in the first four infanticides do not include those top three contenders. Instead, fourth ranked Ellington stands out. Well-liked by many males, Ellington initiated many patrols and kept them going if they stopped (Watts and Mitani 2001:320). Observers dubbed him "the Commander." In three of the infanticides, he led, attacking with his close grooming partner Hare. In the first outside adult killing (June 2002), Bartok and Lofty were involved, but Ellington led the patrol and chase, and did most of the killing. Other participants in mass attacks include many across status middle ranges. Along with co-patrolling, grooming, meat sharing, and being at the center of large groups of males, Ellington repeatedly demonstrated exceptional violence (Watts and Mitani 2000:359–361; 2001:313; Watts et al. 2002:265–266; Watts et al. 2006:166). It seems like he was moving decisively toward alpha, using display violence as a prominent tactic. But Ellington disappeared without a clue in late 2002 (Yong 2019), still early in the expansion. End of that story.

The significance of display violence or of payback cannot be assessed after that. Bartok reigned from c. 2001 until he was deposed by Miles in 2009 (Watts 2018:994), which covers the expansion years. In the few well-described attacks up to 2004, and the internal killing of Grapelli (Chapter 12), Bartok was sometimes involved but not outstanding (Sherrow and Amsler 2007; Watts 2004; Watts et al. 2006). Then the detailed record of attackers ends. But commentators in *Rise of the Warrior Apes* do not see Bartok as patrol leader. He relied primarily on grooming and meat sharing to hold his senior male support. They call him "the President." Display violence depends on personality, and alpha styles differ. How it may have played out in status rivalry through the middle ranks and if it contributed to outside killings is unknown. It did not come from the top down, but it may have been a way to step up.

Understanding the Ngogo Expansion

Ngogo is the capstone case for war as an evolved species proclivity. From 2001 to 2006, Ngogo males very likely to certainly killed *seven* outside juvenile to adult males and one adult female. They suffered at least two and possibly three adult males killed, and one adult female. Other adult male Ngogo losses are suspected. Over a longer span, 1999 to 2011, they killed 13 or 14 outside infants, and lost one to outsiders. This is by far the greatest between-group death toll in the chimpanzee record, and it happened without artificial provisioning.

What explains this record? Evolved adaptive predispositions to kill outsiders when it can be done with little risk? Or situational responses to intensified resource competition generated by human disturbance? Ngogo researchers' propose competition for resources, and rule out human impact (Mitani et al. 2010:R508). But findings from and around Ngogo demonstrate that *both* are involved.

RCH + HIH

My explanation is constructed on the conclusions of Ngogo researchers. They make clear that Ngogo's proficiency at killing derived from its great numbers, which they attribute to a staple fig present because of earlier farmers. They agree that violent clashes occur over particularly valuable foods, particularly a drupe which was made more scarce because of population and drought, as noted in by forest ecologists. Expanded hunting for red colobus nearly extirpated by a swollen population's overpredation, is repeatedly connected to descriptions of expansionary violence.

They acknowledge that Ngogo had grown prior to research and continued to grow at a probably unsustainable rate. They agree that Ngogo's great size was largely due to having so many adult females, both unusual numbers of immigrants and natals that do not emigrate as expected. They note the killing was done by a large cohort of males born during the years of great nearby habitat destruction. Three different sources of data—Ghiglieri's numbers, ecologists' repeated transect censuses, and plummeting red colobus population—indicate Ngogo's number doubled or even tripled from the mid-1970s to mid-1990s. On each point, my analysis agrees with Ngogo researchers' findings. So what do I add?

Historical contextualization brings in all the observations of surrounding habitat loss, eliminating rangeland for uncounted nearby chimpanzees, which also affected some 60% of Park populations directly. I proposed that this loss directed female immigrants toward Ngogo, and possibly compressed and constricted more separated chimpanzees as hostility increased. This centripetal pressure intensified in the 1970s before the main Ngogo research project began. I propose, based on evidence of patrols, active/passive encounters, and violent clashes, that those groups to Ngogo's south and west, more directly exposed to habitat destruction, pushed in on Ngogo coincident with Ngogo's push outward in the less populated or disturbed northeast. Also, that this expansion was driven by increasing scarcity of highly nutritious and *preferred* food sources, even though they were still well nourished. Finally I add a reported though not emphasized point, that trailing researchers gave Ngogo great advantage over unhabituated neighbors, which fled on sight.

Historical contextualization puts all the factors in motion, explaining why things went as they did at Ngogo, and (we will see) why the same variables but with different values led to very different results at Kanyawara. But politics must be considered. Status-related display violence may have triggered Ngogo's "war," beginning with attacks on mothers, and the killing and sometimes eating of infants, by the coalition of Commander Ellington and ally Hare. This extended into the first adult killings. Beyond that it is too complicated and too underreported to speculate on political factors.

RCH + HIH. Why rule out a historical perspective that unifies so many field findings, centers on primatology's focal concern with food resource competition, and connects all that to the habitat destruction that researchers' conservation efforts labor to reduce?

The Latest News

During final editing, dramatic news came from Ngogo (Mitani 2020; Yong 2019). After growing from around 180 in 2011 to about 205 in 2016, *Ngogo fissioned* (Sandel and Watts 2021). The fission corresponds to the A and B subgroups described earlier. It began with reduced association spanning those divisions in 2015. Peaceful interactions stopped by the end of 2017. This is rightly compared to the fission of Kakombe into Kasakela and Kahama at Gombe, by extension lending support to my idea that the mega-group represented two distinct populations pushed together. What they now call the Central group greatly outnumbers the new West group. Two killings were observed, young Erroll in January 2018, and mature Basie in June 2019, plus one suspected (Orff) from a disappearance in November 2017 (Count 1-O-A-M 2018, 1-O-A-M 2019, and 5-O-As-M 2017).

This important development offers several unusual features: males in lethal confrontation with immediate male kin or a long-term grooming partner ("Many males are now fighting with their paternal brothers and fathers" [Mitani 2020:8]), females joining in the deadly attacks, members of the much smaller West group attacking those of the much larger Central. One deadly attack began when local parties were evenly matched, but Central made no attempt to reinforce the one male left alone. These points would be relevant for many discussions in this book—but they are too late to incorporate, or to redo all the calculations from my count. They are included in my tally, and will be noted where relevant in Part IX conclusions.

Explanatory speculation is impossible, as so much remains to be revealed about the context, everything that happened in all the years since the conquest. As previously noted, these included (1) unusual numbers of females not emigrating at maturity;

(2) Ngogo getting as good as they gave from outsiders in the mid-2010s; (3) 25 disease deaths in 2016–2017, contemporary with fissioning; (4) a paucity of chimpanzees and scarcity of foods in 2019; (5) along with men hunting with dogs and killing them. Between the disease losses and a unitary status hierarchy simultaneously being ripped in two by fission, status chaos and conflict in the new divisions should be intense, encouraging display violence. And if there is merit to my argument about Kasakela chimpanzees having learned violent ways leading up to and through the Four Year War, that could apply equally in post-Conquest Ngogo. Killing adversaries may have become a local tradition.

Hopefully future discussions will include holistic and historical context.

15
Kanyawara

This final chapter on Kibale National Park (KNP) moves to its northwestern edge, Kanyawara, less than 10 km away from Ngogo. Kanyawara too is extremely important for establishing—and countering—the demonic perspective. Two male deaths are spotlighted in *Demonic Males*. Richard Wrangham and Marc Hauser initiated new research there in 1987.

Kanyawara's chimpanzees are very well studied, being observed daily by teams with highly developed protocols (Emery Thompson et al. 2020:3–4). Michael Wilson earned his doctorate with field research investigating patrolling and imbalances of power. One intergroup killing 2 years after publication of *Demonic Males* is probably the most publicized *pan*icide of all.

In its broad characteristics, Kanyawara is rather ordinary. If it were a normal, evolved pattern for chimpanzees to patrol borders, penetrate territories, and kill vulnerable outsiders, that should be evident at Kanyawara. But in over three decades of study, there is only one very likely killing—with no context provided; and one definite killing—in the context of a research experiment designed to increase intergroup antagonism. The expectations of deadly "war" and the rival coalition reduction hypothesis (RCRH) fail for Kanyawara.

Historical explanation works from material conditions of habitat, demographics, and food, through the structure of intergroup relations, to explain the presence or absence of intergroup killings. Uniformly applying the same explanatory logic and variables as at Ngogo (and elsewhere), it explains the very different outcomes at Kanyawara. Comparative historical materialism documents generalizations in the specifics of situations. Also of interest is how the demonic paradigm shaped interpretations of deaths; a new and deadly example of observer effects; and critical deconstruction of two gender essentialisms.

An important note to readers: though this history goes up to 2020, the main acts of violence occur in the 1990s. That is when comparison and contrast is the most important, with the two decades since establishing that intergroup violence is not normal.

The Land and Its Chimpanzees

Habitat Loss

Kanyawara range goes up to and beyond the Park border. Land clearing outside KNP was intensive into the 1990s (Whitesell et al. 1997:68). The Park border and active cultivation cut a wedge into Kanyawara's core, the area they most use and where they nest at night (Wilson et al. 2012:284), although substantial patches of forest remained

(Struhsaker 1997:24). Wilson (2001:37) counts 19% of Kanyawara's total range as actively farmed. But chimpanzees did not give it up entirely.

Into the 1990s, chimpanzees traveled up to 3 km outside the Park to visit forest patches and "raid" village crops (Emery Thompson et al. 2020:8; Wilson 2001:13, 33). There is danger of snares or worse. In 1997–1998, a Kanyawara female was killed while raiding bananas (Wilson et al. 2007:1627), Kanyawara's alpha male was speared during a crop raid, and recovered with medical treatment (Hyeroba et al. 2011). Observations within areas of human habitation accounted for 6.5% of all chimpanzee sightings in 1996–1998 (Wilson 2001:56–87, 71). Snares mutilated up to 16 out of 59 adults from 1988 to 1999 (Wrangham 2000), or 29% of chimpanzees older than 3 (Wood et al. 2017:52). Later excursions were briefer and closer to the Park border (Emery Thompson 2020:8).

Kanyawara's usable landscape is more complex than Ngogo's. Commercial logging occurred in the late 1960s and early 1970s (Potts 2011:257). How many local chimpanzees died then is unknown. Around Kanyawara less than a third of chimpanzee habitat is "relatively undisturbed." Of two logged "compartments," one lost about 50% of its trees, and another 25% in 1968–1969 (MUBFS n.d.:2). Post-logging growth is dominated by dense, low vegetation, with fewer and patchy canopy trees (Potts 2011:257; Struhsaker 1997:157).

In contrast to Ngogo, Kanyawara experienced habitat degradation within and lost lands outside the Park. If females move to escape extreme human disturbance, Kanyawara was not an attractive place to settle. They, and maybe even adult males, could have moved on through to better land. Unlike Ngogo, Kanyawara is not hemmed in by neighbors all around.

Demographics

During his 1983–1985 research, Isabirye-Basuta (1988:50) put Kanyawara population at "about 50 individuals." When the Harvard researchers arrived in 1987 Kanyawara had 41 individuals (Chapman and Wrangham 1993:264–265, 272; Wilson 2001:22). Wrangham reports Isabirye-Basuta's conclusion, that "[i]n 21 months from 1986 to 1987 when Kanyawara community was not observed, almost half of its members disappeared, for unknown reasons, while no more than two died in any subsequent year" (Wrangham 2001:240). The arithmetic is unclear, but nine or more chimpanzees were gone without a clue.

Counting Kanyawara numbers is complicated by the large number of peripheral females only weakly attached to the group.[1] Going with what is published, by 1996–1998, Kanyawara had grown to 49–53 individuals, with a range of 37.8 km², producing a density around 1.3/km² (Wilson 2001:22, 30). From the late 1980s to 2008, it

---

[1] From 1987 to 1993, "The community had eight resident adult females, compared with a conservative count of 12 peripheral females who shifted their core areas for a week or more at a time, sometimes within their own community's range and sometimes to another community's range" (Wrangham et al. 1996:50). Perhaps they originated outside the Park. They showed up inside Kanyawara when drupes were plentiful. Chapman and Wrangham (1993:265) specifically exclude three adult females who range in the north, but other population estimates do not indicate whether peripheral females are counted or not.

fluctuated between 40 and 51, the latter (in 2005-2006), with a density of 1.4/km^2 (Potts et al. 2011:671), implying a territory of 36.4 km^2 (and see Potts et al. 2011:670-671). In 2013 population reached 56; before four adults and one infant died in a respiratory infection (Muller and Wrangham 2013:108, 110). In 2020 it hit an all-time high of 57 (Emery Thompson 2020:6). Additional complication is added by variation in reports of territory.[2]

This complicated record establishes that Kanyawara's population density is comparatively low: "estimated at 1.4 chimpanzees/km^2. This is lower than the estimated average density of 2.3 chimpanzees/km^2 for Kibale forest as a whole and that for Ngogo specifically (5-6 chimpanzees/km^2)" (Emery Thompson et al. 2009:301, references omitted). Kanyawara has a range about as big as Ngogo's, but with under a third of its numbers and density. Is that connected to scarcity of food, and if so, is food scarcity related to human activities? Hard to say.

Food

At Kanyawara, only 30% of land is "relatively undisturbed" by logging (Wrangham et al. 1996:48). Yet a 1992-1993 study concluded that they had a "very healthy diet" (Conklin-Brittain et al. 1998:1993). Kanyawara chimpanzees appear healthier than those in Gombe's more marginal environment, exhibiting no seasonal variation in weight or loss of hair sheen (Wrangham et al. 1996:50). Potts (2011:262) comparison of Kanyawara and Ngogo food trees came to the "surprising finding" that logging had little impact on the former's resource base. That seems to answer my question: no. But most evidence leans strongly the other way.

The center places of principle foods are within unlogged land (Wilson et al. 2012:284). In unlogged land, chimpanzees are seen more than twice as often. Fecundity was higher for females with individual core ranges in unlogged areas (Emery Thompson et al. 2007:508). Overall, Kanyawara food availability is well below Ngogo, with a lower percentage of fruit in their diet (Potts et al. 2011). "[T]he average monthly density of trees bearing ripe fruit at Ngogo (1748/km^2) substantially exceeded that of Kanyawara (878 tree/km^2) (Emery Thompson et al. 2008:301).

Kanyawara lacks fruits that are staples for Ngogo, the drupe *Chrysophyllum albidum* and the fig *Ficus mucuso* (Emery Thompson et al. 2009:301). *Ficus mucuso*, of course, is the foundation of Ngogo's huge size. Other figs are present but not as bountiful as *mucuso*. Preferred foods, however, are "non-fig fruits." High drupe consumption leads to elevated energy balances, ovarian function, likelihood of sexual swelling, and probability of conception. When drupes are not available, chimpanzees fall back to figs

---

[2] "The Kanyawara chimpanzee community ranges over an area of approximately 32 km^2" (Gilby et al. 2008:353). "Kanyawara community's range contracted from a peak of 29.5 km^2 in 1998 to 13.8 km^2 in 2006" (Wilson 2012:286). There are other discrepant numbers. The discrepancy between a reported peak of 29.5km^2 and another report of about 38 km^2, both around 1998, might be because there are different ways to figure range size. From 1992 to 2006, "[t]he total area used by Kanyawara chimpanzees... covered 41.1 km^2. Night nest locations occurred within a smaller area of 25.4 km^2. In a given year, the chimpanzees used a subset of this total area, with a median annual home range of 16.4 km^2 (range 10.8-29.5)" (Wilson et al. 2012:282).

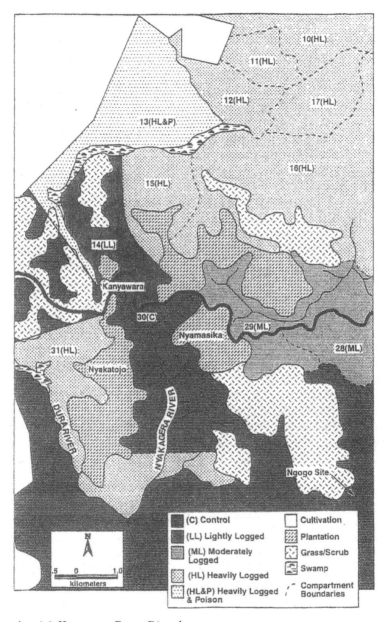

Illustration 4.6 Kanyawara Forest Disturbance
Source: Struhsaker, T. (1997). *Ecology of an African rain forest: Logging in Kibale and the conflict between conservation and exploitation.* University Press of Florida.

(Emery Thompson et al. 2008:303; Gilby and Wrangham 2007:1773). Drupe ripening is when the peripheral females show up.

The most important drupe is, once again, *Uvariopsis*. When fruiting it accounts for 76% of diet. Yet it fruited during only 40 of 180 months of observation, with peaks from 5 months to 3 years apart (Wilson et al. 2012:283). In 78 months between 1998 and 2005, the two most preferred drupes, *Mimusops bagshawei* and *Uvariopsis congensis*, each had two seasons of fruiting peaks (Emery Thompson et al. 2009:301). Abundance is interrupted by longer fallow. *Uvariopsis congensis* was particularly hard hit by habitat destruction, declining by 84% even with moderate logging (Struhsaker 1997:110–111). Effects of the 1999 drought are unknown, but could differ because of Kanyawara's higher altitude and rainfall.

Negative nutritional consequences of food limitations are documented. Foraging efficiency, C-peptide levels, and life expectancy at Kanyawara are significantly lower than at Ngogo (Emery Thompson et al. 2008:302; Potts 2015:1112; Wood et al. 2017:41). "[I]nterbirth intervals at Kanyawara are longer than at any other site for which comparable data are available." Compared to Ngogo, "Kanyawara chimpanzees apparently experienced relatively more intense periods of low food abundance" (Potts et al. 2015:1113).[3]

In sum, the effects of human induced habitat modification for Kanyawara had very different consequences than for Ngogo. It did not include the demographic platform of *Ficus mucuso*, but instead led to nutritional shortfalls that negatively affected reproduction. (That may have changed with fruit availability increasing in recent times.)[4]

Around the 1990s, Kanyawara was not an inviting place to settle for displaced, emigrating females from outside or elsewhere in the Park. This shows in adult/subadult sex ratio. In 1997, compared to Ngogo's 1 male to 1.9 females, Kanyawara was 1:1.5, and 1:1.36 in 2006. Besides that, there were population losses between 1985 and 1987 and possibly earlier during logging. In sum, human impact did not lead to an unusually large group, or high density as it did at Ngogo. This is reflected in another contrast.

Hunting

Kanyawara chimpanzees hunt red colobus, 152 recorded instances from January 1990 to December 2003 (Gilby and Wrangham 2007:1775). These findings are not comparable to the detailed statistics for Ngogo, but hunting clearly *did not* have a similar impact on the prey population. By the late 1990s, red colobus density at Kanyawara, which has many fewer red colobus food trees, was almost an order of magnitude

---

[3] "[D]uring periods of fruit scarcity Kanyawara chimpanzees regularly raid village crops" (Wrangham et al. 1996:48). They "rarely raid crops unless natural food supplies are low" (Wilson et al. 2007:1627; Wilson et al. 2012:285).

[4] Emery Thompson et al. (2020:6–7) propose increasing food availability from the 1990s onward. They infer this from beneficial maturation of some old regrowth forest and replacement of exotics with fruiting fig trees; and also what seems to be a long-term increase of fruits in Kibale (Potts et al. 2020), possibly linked to increased rainfall and temperature. Better health is indicated by an interbirth interval of 5.8 years prior to 2004 and 4.8 years after.

greater than at Ngogo (Teelen 2007:1041). In contrast to Ngogo, most Kanyawara hunting continued near the center of their range, rather than at the edges (Wilson et al. 2012:284-285).

If, as I argue, sharp intensification of hunting reflects increasing scarcity of preferred foods, one might expect even more hunting at resource-challenged Kanyawara. Why didn't they deplete prey? One answer is obvious: scale. Although hunting at Kanyawara depends more on the presence of particular "impact hunters" than total number of males together (Gilby et al. 2008:355, 358), the total number of hunters was about a third of Ngogo, in a similarly sized territory.

Another factor is more inferential. *Short-term* increases in hunting do not reflect scarcity of prime foods, but rather abundance. More hunting follows availability of energy rich food, particularly ripe drupes (Gilby and Wrangham 2007). Less dedicated pursuit of red colobus at Kanyawara may be partly because they lack the energy for it. Maybe they're too tired. This could also inform the finding that Kanyawara chimpanzees spend considerably more time resting than those at Ngogo (Potts et al. 2011:679).

Fewer males and lower drupe availability meant less hunting pressure. Consequently, the quest for prey did not pull Kanyawara males to the edges of their range, as it did at Ngogo. That lowered the probability of finding or being found by antagonistic neighbors.

Applying the resource competition + human impact hypothesis (RCH + HIH) perspective requires historical specificity, and attention to interaction of variables. Although Kanyawara is separated from Ngogo by only about 12 km, human impact is very different in ways that affect likelihood of deadly intergroup resource competition.

Intergroup Relations

Little is known about Kanyawara's neighbors. Based on years of observations "we believe there is one community to the west, one community to the north, one or two communities to the east, and one community to the south and southwest" (Wilson et al. 2007:1630). "During the 15-year study period intergroup encounters occurred relatively infrequently, and when they did occur, they mainly involved vocal encounters between parties separated by hundreds of meters" (Wilson et al. 2012:286). This tour of intergroup relations begins in the west and ends in the south, where the greatest potential for intergroup conflict exists.

Geopolitics

Kanyawara's western range goes up to and beyond the Park border (Wilson et al. 2012:283). Their western neighbors live mostly outside the Park, using the forest fragments and cropland. They make up "Gusazirre's Community," two adult and one adolescent males, and two to four females (Wilson et al. 2007:1645). Demographically similar to Mahale's K-group after 1976, they might be a fragment or coalescence of chimpanzees that lost their lands to islandization.

Although greatly outnumbered by Kanyawara's two dozen grown males, Gusazirre's group still entered deep into Kanyawara territory, several times "starting to the west of the park and progressing toward the center of the Nesting Range. Gusazirre's community made their deepest incursion 500 m from the park boundary and 980 m within the Nesting Range, in January 1996" (Wilson 2001:24). They usually appeared when no Kanyawara chimpanzees were around (Wilson 2001:26), but from 1992 to 2006 there were a dozen encounters in Kanyawara's southeast (group not identified), all acoustic except for one visual and one physical (Wilson et al. 2012:283).

The northwest quadrant of Kanyawara is devoid of external contacts, since at the Park border begin large tea plantations (Wilson et al. 2007:1630; Wilson et al. 2012:283). The northeastern quadrant fronts on heavily lumbered Park lands, former plantations, and grasslands lacking chimpanzees' major foods. Formerly logged areas are used by males, and peripheral females may inhabit them primarily, but males use them *less*. Sightings in areas harvested in 1968–1969 are under half that of undisturbed forests (Chapman and Lambert 2000:172–173, 177). I found no information about the "one or two" groups thought to live east of Kanyawara.

About 5 km northeast of Kanyawara's periphery (Emery Thompson 2020:2) begins the rangeland of the Sebitole (or Sebitoli) group, recently habituated for tourism and research. It ranges the northern tip of the Park, surrounded by tea and eucalyptus plantations and bisected by a high speed road (MUBFS 2011). Although Sebitole had been the center of timber extraction, local chimpanzees consume key foods not found at Kanyawara, *Ficus mucuso* and *Chrysophullum albidum*. *Uvariopsis congensis* is absent (Bortolamiol et al. 2014:7–8; Bortolamiol et al. 2016:925). The group is large and dense, about 80 in 25 km^2, or 3.2/km^2 (Krief et al. 2020:16).

Sebitole group exists in "spatial isolation" (Krief et al. 2017:648). Degraded land between it and Kanyawara appears to be an effective separator. Kanyawara's northeastern encounters from 1992–2006 are few and far between. Of 120 total, only 8 are in their northeast quadrant. Five are acoustic, two visual, and one *famous*, for a very thorough killing (Wilson et al. 2012:283). The victim was called the Sebitole stranger, although his origin was unknown.

Conflict to the Southwest

South of Kanyawara is unlogged forest, the last corridor to the center of the Park, toward Ngogo. This forest was occupied. The great majority of Kanyawara's 120 intergroup interactions occurred here. Most just calling, but 12 were visual and 3 physical. That is where Ruwenzori died (Wilson et al. 2012:283).

Wrangham and Peterson (1996:20) call them "the Wantabu community." Ngogo killing victim #8 was thought to be from Wantabu, suggesting that it spans the area between the two research sites. These neighbors are more numerous than Kanyawara's 50 chimpanzees (Wilson et al. 2012:289). Beyond that nothing is known.[5]

---

[5] In later tables (Wilson et al. 2014:EDT 1; Wrangham 1999:9; Wrangham et al. 2006:22), the supposed killers of Ruwenzori are called "Rurama," not Wantabu. Other studies simply refer to chimpanzees to Kanyawara's south.

South is where action was. It centered on *Uvariopsis congensis*, which is concentrated toward the south of Kanyawara's range (Wilson et al. 2012:284).

[I]ntercommunity interactions are strongly tied to the consumption of ripe fruit from a single tree species, *Uvariopsis congensis*. These synchronously fruiting trees produce high-quality fruits in large groves clustered along the boundary with a neighboring community. Consequently, more than 75% of intergroup interactions at Kanyawara occurred when chimpanzees are eating *Uvariopsis*. (Muller et al. 2013)

Nevertheless, encounters while eating *Uvariopsis* were uncommon, only 45 of 414 occasions (11%) (Wilson et al. 2012:285). Kanyawara's average rate of outside encounters, .33/month, was far below Ngogo's in the late 1990s, at 1.1/month (Wilson et al. 2007:1647), although rate of encounters increased from 1992 to 2006 (Wilson et al. 2012:283).

Possibly connected to that increasing rate was the northward retraction of Kanyawara. From its maximum range in 1998, it shrank 47% by 2006. Pressure from Wantabu seems implicated. "In Kibale one of the study community's most productive fruit-groves lies in the south of its range, and in recent years the community has left the area immediately after its annual defeats in battle by a large neighbouring community" (Wrangham 2006:51). "[A]nnual defeats in battle" is hyperbole.[6] There were only two physical encounters and one presumed killing, in all the southern research follows. In most of the close encounters, southerners *fled when they caught sight of researchers* (Wilson et al. 2012:283).

Kanyawar abandoned the southern peripheral feeding range (Wilson et al. 2012:282, 286–287). "This contraction included a shifting of the southern boundary a full kilometer north from 2004 to 2006" (Wilson et al. 2012:286). Wantabu outnumbered Kanyawara. The rule of chimpanzee territoriality is that parties with fewer retreat before larger parties. However, even with this retraction, the measured centers of most fruits were still within Kanyawara's territory (Wilson et al. 2012:284).

Intergroup Conflict

Superficially, developments on Kanyawara's south resemble those on Ngogo's northeast, but seen from the other side. Wantabu pushes into prime fruit areas, Kanyawara gives up territory. Yet here there is no indication of killings during the time of expansion/retraction. What was going on? Was this "war"?

---

[6] In that same article, Wrangham said (2006:47) that Mahale's K and M-groups "battled every year."

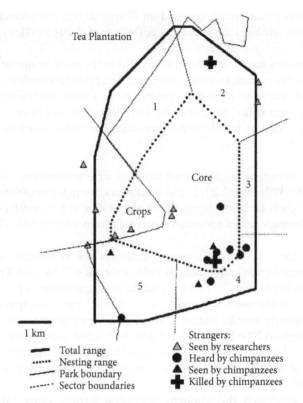

Illustration 4.7 Kanyawara Territorial Encounters and Kills
Caption: Kanyawara community range and location of intergroup interactions and sightings of stranger chimpanzees, 1996–1998, showing the park boundary (solid gray line), nesting range (inner polygon with dotted line), total range (outer polygon with solid black line), and the locations of Core, Crops, and Periphery, including the five different sectors of the Periphery (separated by dashed lines). Gray triangles indicate sightings of stranger chimpanzees seen by researchers when Kanyawara chimpanzees were not present. Black circles indicate locations in which Kanyawara chimpanzees appeared to hear and respond to the calls of stranger chimpanzees. Black triangles indicate the locations where Kanyawara chimpanzees saw stranger chimpanzees. Crosses indicate locations of chimpanzees killed during intercommunity conflict in 1991 (in the south) and 1998 (in the north).

Source: Wilson, M., Hauser, M., & Wrangham, R. (2007). Chimpanzees (*Pan troglodytes*) modify grouping and vocal behaviour in response to location-specific risk. *Behaviour*, 144(12), 1621–1653.

Patrolling

Given that Kanyawara is the focus of research for Wrangham and his students, and the fact that patrolling looms so large in the demonic perspective, Kanyawara is surprising. Patrolling is ambiguous.

Chapman and Wrangham's (1993:265, 267) study of range use notes that males are much more likely seen than females in boundary areas, consistent with Wrangham's proposition that males range more widely. But their analysis excludes peripheral females, which live closer to or across the range boundary. They make no mention of patrols per se, or any clash with another group. Wrangham, in his paradigmatic formulation of the imbalance of power hypothesis (IoPH) (1999a:7–8) checks off Kanyawara for having "border patrols . . . involving parties of males intermittently checking their territorial boundaries"—but that's all. Border patrols are noted in some incident descriptions below. Yet systematic research on border behavior is inconclusive.

The doctoral research of Wrangham's student Michael Wilson (2001; and Wilson et al. 2007) was designed to test aspects of the Imbalance of Power hypothesis. His team logged 7,385 observation hours from 1996 to 1998 (2001:31). Consistent with the IoPH, they found more males per party near borders compared to core ranges (2001:47). But again, this leaves out peripheral females, which spent more time near borders than males did (2001:18, 40–43).[7]

Male behavior near border confounds IoP expectations. Border patrolling is characterized by nearly-all-male parties, silence, and not feeding. At Kanyawara, parties visiting the edges were mixed and spent as much time feeding as they did in the core (2001:49). There was only a slight, statistically nonsignificant diminution of pant-hooting (although they were quite silent when raiding crops) (2001:78–80; and Wilson et al. 2007). Male chimpanzees out on the edge could be looking for food or searching for peripheral females, as well as checking for intruders (2001:41, 54).

"Distinguishing patrols from excursions [loud mixed-sex feeding parties] proved to be beyond the scope of this study, so I considered all border visits together" (Wilson 2001:62). "A more detailed examination of behavior in peripheral areas is necessary to distinguish patrols, in which chimpanzees are expected to be silent, from excursions, in which chimpanzees might be expected to advertise their presence to claim territorial ownership" (2001:80). This does not suggest there were no border patrols at all, but that there was no *pattern* of patrolling as at Gombe, Ngogo, or Tai, and as thought to be normal in contemporary *pan*ology.

From 1992 to 2006, parties moving toward peripheral areas, and specifically toward the fraught southern area, were bisexual feeding groups. Those that moved further south tended to have more males, and more of higher status (Wilson et al. 2012:282, 286). That does not make them patrols.

---

[7] "Central females spent a median of 13% of observations in the Edge, in contrast to peripheral females, who spent 31% of observations in the Edge. These observations probably underestimate the percentage of time spent in the Edge by peripheral females, as these females were infrequently observed. Males spent a median of 17% of observations in the Edge" (Wilson 2001:18, 40–43). Not a big difference from Central females.

Deaths

In *Demonic Males*, three adult males provided much needed support for the claim that killing "is characteristic of chimpanzees across Africa. It looks like part of a species-wide pattern" (Wrangham and Peterson 1996:20–21).

Ruwenzori

The first death described is Ruwenzori, a small 15-year-old of Kanyawara.

> In the second week of August Ruwenzori was killed. No humans saw the big fight. We know something about it, however, because for days before he went missing, our males had been traveling together near the border, exchanging calls with the males from the Wantabu community to the south, evidently afraid of meeting them. Four days after he was last seen, our team found his disintegrating body.... The trampled vegetation bore witness to a struggle.... Ruwenzori's body was bitten, bruised and torn. He died healthy, with a full stomach, on the edge of adulthood, on the edge of his range.

That is the sum of information about this theoretically significant death (Count 3-O-A-M 1992). It is not clear whether these were all-male patrols.[8]

For the HIH, there is no information to work with. Kanyawara was disturbed long before 1992, with islandization, lumbering, and human settlement reaching into their core range. But without detail, that cannot be *specifically* linked to the killing. In my final tally, this decontextualized, barely described event stands out as a rare instance across Africa of likely intergroup killing that cannot be directly connected to human impact—due to lack of information.

Grasping for Killings

The other two cases prominently presented in *Demonic Males* are without substance.

> In 1988 another apparently healthy chimpanzee died in the same border zone as Ruwenzori. At the time it seemed odd. We didn't know then where the border was. It seems less odd now. And three years after Ruwenzori's death, from only a couple of hundred meters away, we saw four Wantabu males stalk and charge a small Kanyawara party, but this time they caught no one. And then in 1994, one day after

---

[8] The year 1992 also records the first "unambiguous encounter between Kanyawara chimpanzees and members of another community"—although that observation may be due to increasing habituation rather than a change in behaviors (Wilson et al. 2012:278).

Kibale workers witnessed a violent attack on a male, tourists found the dead body of a prime male, probably the same victim. (Wrangham and Peterson 1996:21)[9] (Count 5-O-A-M, 1988, 5-O-A-M, 1994)

Ghiglieri (1999:174) spins these, including Ruwenzori, into solid proofs.

Significantly, all three Kanyawara males were killed in combat, all three died in the same border region between [Kanyawara and the southern Wantabu] communities' territories, and at least two died within hours of prolonged territorial pant-hooting and displaying by males of both communities along this border. No reasonable doubt exists today that the natural strategy of common chimpanzees is to establish, maintain, defend, or expand a kin group territory via lethal warfare.

That seems pretty definitive. Except, there is little reason to think either is a *pan*icide.

For 1988, Kerbis Peterhans et al. (1993:494, 498) describe the remains: about a week dead, partly disarticulated, apparently scavenged by bushpigs. There is no hint of cause of death. Wilson (2001:23) includes the 1988 corpse in his list of killings, explaining: "evidence including the location and apparently full stomach at the time of death suggests it may have been killed by chimpanzees." A full stomach means nothing. Well-fed chimpanzees can die in accidents, such as Kanyawara's Teddy, which fell out of a tree in 2011 (Wrangham and Otoli 2011). This case was thereafter dropped in all tallies of killings.[10] The 1994 case, Julian, is counted in two tallies, omitted in three.[11]

Wrangham et al. (2006) and Wilson et al. (2014) also add two more adult males as suspected killings: Badfoot in 1998, and Light Brown in 2001. No other information is provided (Count 5-O-A-M 1998, 5-O-A-M 2001). Were they just disappearances? An epidemic killed at least two adults in 2001, close to when Light Brown was last seen. Julian, Badfoot, and Light Brown could have died at human hands, or by snares. Adult male disappearances at Kanyawara carry no evidentiary weight for intergroup killings. None of these need further consideration.[12]

---

[9] Tourists had been showing up at Kanyawara, "mostly uninvited and unexpected" since the mid-1980s. That was part of the impulse behind creating the Kanyanchu tourist program (MUBFS 2011).

[10] It does not appear in Wrangham's (1998:9) table of "All reported intraspecific kills of adult chimpanzees"; *or* in Wrangham et al.'s (2006:22) list of intercommunity killings, which includes "suspected"; *or* in Wilson et al.'s (2007:1630) discussion of Kanyawara killings; *or* in Wilson et al. (2012:283); *or* in Wilson et al. (2014:EDT 1).

[11] Julian is tallied in Wrangham et al. (2006) and Wilson et al. (2014) as a suspected killing, but is omitted in Wrangham (1998), Wilson et al. (2007), and Wilson et al. (2012:283).

[12] To complete suspected cases before turning to the big kill, in 1996 a Kanyawara male and female (with her own clinging infant), together attacked another Kanyawara female and her infant, which was not seen again (Arcadi and Wrangham 1999) (Count 3-W-I-M 1996). This is "the first time a male and female chimpanzee have been observed cooperating closely in an infanticidal attack" (Arcadi and Wrangham 1999:337). Killing a male of one's own group contradicts RCRH, so will not be considered further here. It comes up again in Chapter 29, on infanticide.

"War?"

Regarding intergroup conflict on the southern periphery, human impact is implicated, but the implications differ from Ngogo. Human impact did not permit (no *Ficus mucuso*) or foster (female immigration) Kanyawara's growth to mega size. Reduced resources were accommodated with lower density. *Uvariopsis*—especially depleted by forest cutting and perhaps by drought—was like at Ngogo a cause of contention, but only one of 10 feeding bouts involved contact with southern neighbors, and Kanyawara typically withdrew before greater numbers. When Wantabu encroached, Kanyawara coped by retreat, as had Kasakela before Kalande, and K-group before M-group. A serious loss, but despite much fruit to the south, their main feeding areas were in the central range. When experiencing shortage they tapped into human crops. Their smaller size and perhaps lack of energy reduced hunting pressure on red colobus, so prey decline did not push them into far peripheries where outsiders might lurk.

Kanyawara chimpanzees did not regularly patrol their borders nor stealthily penetrate neighboring lands. Lacking great gangs of males, Kanyawara did not enjoy Ngogo's ease of killing. But with more than 10 adult males they still had more than enough to kill a solo stranger. Over 15 years, 5,527 research follows, and 120 encounters—except for one case to come—they never did so. If Kanyawara chimpanzees had an innate urge to kill, they were not trying very hard.

Competition for limited resources, yes. RCH + HIH, yes. But conflict did not rise to lethal intensity. Rather, it fits established ethological parameters of nonviolent territoriality. Then along came the Sebitole stranger, and Kanyawara suddenly became the exemplary case of male demonism.

Rasputin

On August 25, 1998 (Muller 2002:118):

Kanyawara males were followed by observers to the fresh corpse of an individual from a neighboring community (Sebitole) who had apparently been killed by chimpanzees the previous evening. There were numerous wounds on the front of his body, his trachea had been ripped through, and both testicles had been removed. Nine Kanyawara males had been patrolling the border on the previous evening, all of whom were present the next morning (17 hours later), and several of whom beat on the victim's body and dragged it about. (Wrangham 1999a:9)

He had compound fractures in four ribs. "Five fingernails and one toenail had been torn from the digits, with significant portions of flesh attached" (Muller 2002:118). In death, he was dubbed Rasputin (Wrangham 2006:49).

This is an intergroup kill without reasonable doubt (Count 2-O-A-M, 1998). But in this instance unlike the others of Kanyawara, we do know its context. If human impact is brought in, this no longer seems an expression of innate demonism.

Playback

From June 1996 to July 1998—the same period when border behavior was studied—researchers led by Mark Hauser conducted an experiment in eliciting aggressive territorial defense (Wilson 2001:96 ff.; Wilson et al. 2001). Earlier studies of monkeys (Cheney 1986:272) and lions (Heinsohn 1997; McComb et al. 1994), investigated territorial behavior by watching reactions to recorded playbacks of the calls or roars of strangers. Now this method was applied to chimpanzees.

A National Science Foundation proposal (Hauser 1998:6-8) asks whether response to strangers is determined primarily by the benefits of protecting territory; or by expectable advantage based on numerical superiority. If territorial defense is paramount, greater response is expected if calls were in the center vs. the fringe of the Kanyawara range. If numerical advantage ruled, reactions should be determined by how many Kanyawara males were together when they heard the solo playback, regardless of its source location. The theoretical point is that a response determined by numerical superiority would support the IoPH/RCRH (Wilson et al. 2001:1205).[13]

Method

The experimental method was for some researchers to locate Kanyawara chimpanzees when they were calm and at rest, usually early in the day within their nesting range. A team member would radio that information to colleagues, who then set up a speaker some 300 m away. The experimenters would play a recording of a single, stranger male pant-hoot, from different individuals recorded at Mahale. (Chimpanzees seem able to recognize individual calls [Kojima et al. 2003]). They removed the speaker, and everybody watched the reaction. Experimenters took pains to ensure that the chimpanzees never figured out that this wasn't a genuine challenge. "Relative to the subjects, the speaker will be placed close to the nearest boundary to realistically suggest an intrusion" (Hauser 1998:10).

Responses were dramatic. "Adult females unaccompanied by adult males often showed signs of fear, including fear grimaces. Males showed signs of aggressive arousal, including piloerection" (Wilson et al. 2001:1209). Kanyawara chimpanzees were repeatedly put in fear because an unknown chimpanzee had entered their range. Yet no intruders were found. They were phantoms, leaving no traces chimpanzees could detect.

The experiment worked. "[O]nly the number of defenders significantly affected the response. Male chimpanzees counter-called and approached when the costs

---

[13] The NSF proposal led with the mantra used to obtain research funds since the early days of field research. "Funding agencies were assured that anything we learned about the behavior and ecology of our relatives, the primates, would better our understanding of ourselves and our antecedents" (Ghiglieri 1988:3). So the NSF was informed: "This study will provide an important contribution to understanding the evolution of a behavior pattern which profoundly affects the lives of several species, including our own" (Hauser 1998:1; and see Wilson 2001:1-2). It will help answer, why war?

of aggression appeared to be low" (Wilson et al. 2001:1212). "Parties with three or more males consistently joined in a chorus of loud vocalizations and approached the speaker together. Parties with fewer adult males usually stayed silent, approached the speaker less often, and traveled more slowly if they did approach" (2001:1203). Thus the hypothesis is well supported.

As stipulated in Chapter 2, I agree that for chimpanzees (and humans) numerical advantage is a very important consideration in the decision to engage. It is not surprising that this overrides location within the territory or the value of localized food resources, as Wilson et al. (2012:286) find. My issue here is not the advantage of numbers, but the possible role of the playbacks in the 1998 killing of the Sebitole stranger.

The Experiment

There were three series of playbacks, over three research seasons (Hauser 1998:3, 8). The first five were in June and July of 1996. The next 15 came from April to November 1997 (Wilson 2001:16). In the NSF proposal for the third round, Hauser (1998:3, 12) explained that the planned multivariate analysis necessitated 15–20 *additional* playbacks, which appeared feasible at a rate of two or more per month from March to December 1998. The minimum statistically required was 15, making a total of 35. However, the experiment ended after just 6 new playbacks, for a total of 26. The last playback was in July, even though research continued until December. The cessation of playbacks far below the minimum required number is not explained in the published report (Wilson et al. 2001:1205–1206).

On August 12, 1998, five Kanyawara males encountered a stranger nulliparous female and subadult male near their southern boundary. The male got away but they caught the female, and three struck her. She escaped as others from her community approached, and the Kanyawara group retreated.

The killing of the Sebitole stranger on Kanyawara's northern periphery where encounters were rare, happened on August 25 (Muller 2002:118). I do not know of any other killing when the assault continued so long, 17 hours, after the victim's death, except for the ex-alpha killing of Froudouko at Fongoli. Eventually other outside males approached from that direction, and after an hour of counter-calling Kanyawara males withdrew.

Ethical Notes and Explanations

No one can say what "caused" this killing, or that the stranger would not have been caught, or killed, or abused so relentlessly, without the playbacks. But it is reasonable to conclude that two years of stimulated territorial fear would intensify the reaction to actual strangers. That danger was well recognized in advance by the researchers themselves.

The NSF-funded proposal was a revised resubmission. In it, the principle investigator (Hauser 1998:3, references omitted) responds to a previous evaluator:

This reviewer's second concern was that the experiments may increase stress levels and even lead to intercommunity violence. This is a valid concern. Nevertheless, playback experiments have been used extensively to explore territorial response in birds and mammals, including species in which lethal intergroup aggression occurs, such as lions. In no case that I am aware of have these experiments resulted in increased levels of aggression between experimental subjects and their neighbors. Lions in particular experience very high rates of injury and mortality from intergroup aggression, yet playback experiments conducted at a rate similar to those in this study have not resulted in any apparent increase of intergroup conflict. The call of an intruder makes for a powerful stimulus; but in all likelihood, the decision to attack depends on more concrete factors, including the balance of power at the time of the encounter. In any case, neither the rate nor the nature of meetings between Kanyawara and neighboring chimpanzees appears to have changed since the initiation of the playback experiments. Indeed, while the field assistants and I observed occasional counter-calling between Kanyawara and neighboring communities, we witnessed no direct intergroup encounters during the 1997 series of playbacks.

Encounters occurred in 1998.

In the published report (Wilson et al. 2001:1208), a section titled "Ethical Note" retains verbatim (up to "intergroup conflict") the discussion of playbacks among other species, but drops the point about no intergroup encounters being recorded. In its place is the following: "One lethal intergroup attack did occur after the completion of the foreign male playback series (Wrangham 1999a), but such attacks also occurred before this study began."

No other reference is made in that article about playbacks to the killing of the Sebitole stranger. As for this occurring "after the completion" of the experiment, it happened just weeks after the last playback. As Hauser described research plans for the NSF, July was not to be the end of project, but the middle of it.

In published discussions, the killing is never put in context of the playbacks. Neither Wrangham (1999a) nor Muller (2002) make any reference to playbacks when they highlight this incident. Both present the killing as confirmation of wild chimpanzees' evolved propensity for lethal intercommunity aggression. Wilson and Wrangham (2003:374, 381) discuss both topics—the killing and the playbacks—in the same article, but in sections separated by many detailed pages, without cross-reference. It is left to the reader to figure out that playbacks continued to just before the situation turned deadly.

In a paper presented at the 2002 meetings of the American Anthropological Association, I called attention to this temporal connection. That, I later realized, was a mistake. I should not have made this point so long before publishing about it (though I had no idea then that this book would take another 20 years).

Word spread, and Mark Muller eventually responded in print, with John Mitani, where they challenge all human impact explanations of intergroup killings.

With the provisioning hypothesis convincingly refuted, critics have increasingly focused on alternative forms of human interference as hypothetical causes of

> chimpanzee aggression. Ferguson, for example, recently suggested that experiments in which calls from strange males were played to chimpanzees at Kanyawara were responsible for the lethal attack observed there in 1998. This scenario is unlikely, for at least three reasons. First, as described previously, similar attacks have been observed at Ngogo, where chimpanzees have never been subjected to playback experiments. Second, long-term data from Kanyawara indicate that the rate of intergroup encounters during 1998, when playbacks were conducted, was indistinguishable from those of previous years. Third, long-term data from Ngogo indicate that the rate of territorial boundary patrolling by chimpanzees is not affected by the rate at which chimpanzees encounter their neighbors, either vocally or visually. (Muller and Mitani 2005:298–299, references omitted)

For point one, see Chapter 13. For the others, they refute claims I never made. My point is quite simple: the only intergroup killing *ever* attributed to Kanyawara chimpanzees in more than three decades of observation, occurred in what was planned to be the middle of an experiment designed to simulate strangers repeatedly entering, sometimes deeply, into their territory. In the debate about whether intergroup aggression among chimpanzees is a normal, evolved, adaptive tendency, or a behavior responding to human impact, this is an obviously relevant fact.

Politics

Another consideration is display violence. Since 1994, 32-year-old Big Brown was alpha, with beta Tofu his ally. In mid-1997, 18-year-old Imoso and his ally Johnny began challenging the top two. "Imoso was clearly the most aggressive member of the community," its leading red colobus hunter. By the end of 1997, he was number one, Tofu number two, Johnny number three, and Big Brown down to four (Gilby and Wrangham 2008:1833–1834; Muller 2002:116). For an alpha, 18 or 19 is young.

The second round of playbacks ran from April to November 1997. Their rise took place during the experiment. Imoso and Johnny were on top when the next round of playbacks began in March 1998, and when the Sebitole stranger was killed. Since the killing was not observed, and individuals the morning after are not identified, their specific role is unknown. Going from other better-described situations, it seems likely they played a leading role.

This could be dismissed as a meaningless coincidence if it was the only time it happened. However, something similar happened at Tai (see Chapter 21). There, the first ever killings were carried out by two young, very aggressive males who surged to alpha status during or shortly after playback experiments. My argument there is that fear-inducing playbacks can be politically destabilizing, and create a status opening for aggressive individuals, which display their fierceness by killing outsiders. Two playback experiments followed by the rise of two exceptionally aggressive young males, were followed by the first *pan*icides ever recorded for that group. Human impact relating to intergroup violence comes in varied forms.

Males Behaving Badly, and Females Cutely

The demonic/dark side perspective is not restricted to war. It brings in several other unsavory behaviors. Most fall outside the scope of this book, even though they provide ancillary support for the central idea of males being evolutionarily wired for violence. Two however, received extensive publicity based on observations at Kanyawara, and will be evaluated here because they are so significant for popular attitudes about human nature.

"Wife Beaters of Kibale" (Linden 2002)

Male "battering" of females is part of Wrangham and Peterson's (1996:143–146) portrait of male demonism. Somehow it transpired—as yet there was no published report—that a *Time Magazine* writer heard about a shocking new discovery, embodied in the "wife beaters" headline. Linden (2002) went to Harvard's Peabody Museum to meet Wrangham and his student Carole Hooven. He saw what he came to see: an apparently ordinary stick, retrieved in the Kibale forest by Hooven.

> [I]n January 1999 in Uganda's Kibale forest, it was in the hands of a big male chimp called Imoso who was using it to beat mercilessly a female named Outamba. As a woman, Hooven felt sick at heart at the violence directed at the smaller chimp. But as a scientist, it exhilarated her. She had never read about anything like this. Trembling, she rushed back to camp to report to Wrangham. He listened in silence and then shook her hand. This was a historic moment. While there are a few scattered accounts of chimps wielding sticks against prey or predators, no one before had ever seen a wild animal repeatedly, unambiguously—and with malice and forethought—use a tool as a weapon against its own kind. (Linden 2002:56)

Imoso "had been trying to get at Outamba's infant Kilimi, but Outamba fended off his efforts. This seemed to enrage Imoso, who began kicking and punching Outamba." He also hung from a branch and stamped on her.

The finding seemed so momentous that Linden went to Uganda in 2001. He saw no violence but did see Imoso, "the top dog" of Kanyawara. A tracker told him "Imoso is just a mean chimp." That he was, "clearly the most aggressive member of the community" (Muller 2002:116). Rising to alpha in 1997 during playbacks, he kept firm control. He monopolized access to females with maximally swollen sex skin, but allowed copulations by allies in an "exchange of political support for mating opportunities" (Duffy et al. 2007).

Linden heard that the stick beating was not an isolated event. "Imoso's behavior was observed by other chimps in the community, and he may have inspired imitators." Between the first attack and June 2002, five more stick-attacks were observed.

> The behavior is new to science and raises intriguing questions. Why have all the victims been female? And why sticks, why not stones? Imoso could have killed Outamba by slamming her with a heavy rock. That may be precisely why they use

sticks, Wrangham and Hooven speculate: to inflict hurt rather than injury. Most of the attacks have been directed at sexually active females. Whereas the males might intend to do real harm to the babies, they have nothing to gain by killing their mates. Brutal as it seems, could it be that the use of sticks signifies restraint? That is one of the mysteries Wrangham and his colleagues are trying to solve, in what they view as a snapshot of the evolutionary process in action. This may be a mirror of how we evolved culturally—by the spread of ideas that moved through our early ancestors in fits and starts. (Linden 2002:57)[14]

A New Behavior?

Male chimpanzees sometimes use coercion to make females more likely to mate with them, as discussed in Chapter 4, and well documented for Kanyawara (as in the expressively titled "Sexual Coercion by Male Chimpanzees Shows That Female Choice May Be More Apparent Than Real," Muller et al. 2011). What is remarkable about this incident is the ballyhoo as a "historic" discovery about chimpanzees and use of weapons.

Goodall (1986:549–559) discusses extensively, with statistics, chimpanzees using sticks and stones as weapons against other chimpanzees (and baboons and other species).[15] A cross-field-site tally of variations in learned behaviors, using data from the late 1990s, codes "stick club" at five out of seven sites, and "aimed-throw" of rocks and other objects at seven out of seven (Nakamura 2002:72).

Goodall (1986:531) sees the use of weapons as one of chimpanzees' preadaptations for war. But should this really be seen as the same kind of thing as when a human

---

[14] The *Boston Phoenix* (Wright 2002) reports that Wrangham presented the stick, to the opening chords of *Also Sprach Zarathustra*—invoking the opening of *2001, A Space Odyssey*—at Harvard, characterizing it as a "'startling' new development in weapons technology." "'This is the first time any animal other than humans has been seen to pick up clubs as weapons and use them against others of their own species.'"
"Despite being a groundbreaking, even historic, development, the discovery of weapon use among chimps garnered little in the way of press coverage," perhaps because at the time of the Harvard presentation, the country was commemorating the first anniversary of the September 11 attack.
Yet Wrangham is brimming with theories about September 11 and its aftermath—many of them founded on what he has seen in the forests of Kibale. "It seems to me that the most important contribution I can make is to add to the sense of danger, the sense of realism," he says. "What the chimpanzee studies are telling us is how easily natural selection can favor these sorts of patterns of violence and how ridiculous it is to think that if we can just persuade humans to be nice to each other, then they will be. You have to take a very hard-headed approach to it."

[15] To quote:
Whipping occurs when a chimpanzee takes hold of a growing branch or sapling and
> swings it vigorously up and down, hitting the victim....The term *flailing* is used when a chimpanzee picks up a stick or palm frond, or actually breaks one off a tree, and, usually in an upright position, brandishes his weapon at the opponent....When a detached stick or frond is used to hit or beat an opponent, this is referred to as *clubbing*. Over a six-year period (1977 to 1982) 22 percent of 188 observations of flailing ended in clubbing...In addition to the generalized hurling of objects during displays, chimpanzees throw stones, rocks, or sticks at definite objectives such as conspecifics, baboons, humans, or a variety of other species....True, weapons are seldom used in serious fighting (the chimpanzees usually inflict punishment by biting, hitting, and stamping), but there are undoubtedly occasions when the use of sticks or rocks, by intimidating the victim, prevent aggressive incidents from becoming more violent. (1986:449–552)

attacks with a weapon? An even earlier intensive study of chimpanzee stick-beatings addresses that question, and answers no.

Chimpanzees sometimes attack leopards with sticks (McGrew 2010). Perhaps the most famous film footage of wild chimpanzees is from Kortlandt's 1960s experiments in western Africa. When concealed researchers ran out a stuffed leopard on a rail, some chimpanzees struck it with sticks, along with the full range of displaying, flailing, and throwing. Detailed analysis of clear film of 56 incidents from two sites shows that these actions were very different from the way people use clubs to cause injury (Albrecht and Dunnett 1971:112–114).

> The style of wielding the stick varied greatly, but at the climax of many attacks was seen a movement, of either the arm or the whole body, which pulled or tended to pull the stick *away* from the leopard....On only five occasions (three at Kanka Sili, two at Bossou) was a chimpanzee seen to use a stick in a nearly "human" beating fashion—that is, holding it approximately in line with the arm, and swinging it down from overhead.... In other stick attacks the stick appeared to be incidental . . . the path the stick followed appeared to be determined by the way in which it was lying when picked up and its position in space at the moment it was released by the chimpanzee, rather than by any deliberate intent of the chimpanzee.

They conclude that the words "weapon" and "attack" are both "unsatisfactory" for getting a sense of these actions. Yet what Albrecht and Dunnet describe sounds exactly like what Hooven recorded at Kanyawara (Linden 2002).

> MS (Imoso) first attacks OU (Outamba) with one stick for about 45 seconds, holding it with his right hand, near the middle. She was hit about 5 times . . . he beat her hard. (The stick was brought down on her in a somewhat inefficient way . . . MS seemed to start with the stick almost parallel to the body and bring it down in a parallel motion. There was a slight angle to his motion, but not the way a human would do it for maximum impact.)

The theoretical *in*significance of Imoso's action is underscored by later publications on male coercion of females at Kanyawara (Muller et al. 2007:1010; Muller et al. 2009:186–187). Although they focus on physical attacks, including "hits, kicks or slaps delivered in passing, as well as extended episodes of pounding, dragging, and biting," the supposedly historic discovery of weapon use just blends into a broader pattern male-on-female violence.

Nevertheless, notably and against adaptive expectations, in 2017 Kanyawara males attacked one of their own females, "for unclear reasons." Still weakened in recovery from the respiratory infection, she died. (Previously noted and counted.)

"Chimp Girls Play with Dolls" (Handwerk 2010)

Kanyawara's implications for human gender essentialization do not end there. "Sex differences in children's toy play are robust and similar across cultures," Kahlenberg and Wrangham (2010:R1067) begin. Although some try to explain this by socialization, "[e]vidence for biological factors is controversial but mounting." Kanyawara juveniles seemed to show sex-specific predispositions: young female chimpanzees play with sticks as if they were dolls. "Our findings suggest that a similar sex difference could have occurred in the human and pre-human lineage at least since our common ancestry with chimpanzees, well before direct socialization became an important influence" (Kahlenberg and Wrangham 2010:R1068). This inference is highly questionable.

In the routine observational records of daily behavior, under the category "stick use" is a subcategory, "stick carry." Stick carry occurs "when an individual gathered an unattached stick or broke off an attached one and transported it from one site to another" (Kahlenberg and Wrangham 2010:supplemental material 2). It could also be "pieces of bark, small logs, or woody vine, with their hand or mouth, underarm, or most commonly, tucked between the abdomen and thigh." Among juveniles and younger, this behavior is more common among females than males. Stick carry is what Kahlenberg and Wrangham interpret to be "play-mothering."

Another observational category for sticks is "solitary play," which presumably includes playing with a stick like a doll (2010:supplemental material 2). Although this would seem to be the most relevant measure, no statistics about solitary play are presented. Instead, the data presented is that eight individuals—six females and two males—sometimes carried a stick into day-nests, and there "were sometimes seen to play casually with the stick in a manner that evoked maternal play" (2010:R1068). Only females played? How often?

Kahlenberg and Wrangham (2010:R1068) also note two well-described cases where juveniles play with a stick as if with an infant. One at Kanyawara in 1993 is the lead for the closing chapter of *Demonic Males* (Wrangham and Peterson 1996:252–255), "Kakama's Doll." On at least two occasions, the 6-year-old was seen to carry a small log everywhere, including into the day-nest, playing with it as mothers' play with infants. Kakama was *male*.

Across Africa at Bossou, 8-year-old female Ja at least once carried a stick around after her mother. "Ja seemed to actually manipulate the rod as if it were a doll" (Matsuzawa 1997). This is a strange situation. While Ja was following her with the stick, her mother was carrying and caring for a slowly dying, eventually immobile 2-year-old infant. After its death, the mother continued carrying it until it mummified, and a young male once played with the corpse.

Goodall, again, discusses playing with objects, including particulars noted at Kanyawara, but with a very different interpretation.

> Youngsters utilize many objects during solitary play.... Fruit-laden twigs, strips of skin and hair from an old kill, or highly prized pieces of cloth may be draped over the shoulders or carried along in the neck or groin pocket (that is, tucked between the neck and shoulder or thigh and belly)...Sometimes a large stone or a short stout stick is used in self tickling—a performance that *can* be labeled tool use. Juvenile and adolescent females are particularly apt to show this behavior: the object is pushed and rubbed into those especially ticklish areas between neck and shoulder and in the groin. The activity may last for up to ten minutes and is often accompanied by loud

laughing. Sometimes these tickling tools are carried up into a nest and the game proceeds there. Two young females (an infant and a juvenile) tickled their own genitals with sticks while laughing. (Goodall 1986:559)

This discovery is no more substantial than that of wife beating. Yet "Chimp Girls Play with Dolls" was an even bigger story, repeated in dozens of web and other outlets around the world (e.g., Bower 2010; Keim 2010; Vergano 2010; Whitty 2010). Though maybe one should not complain. Considering Goodall's observations, the headline might have been "Chimp Girls Play with Dildoes."

PART V
BUDONGO

16
Budongo, Early Research and Human Impact

Roughly 200 km northwest of Kibale is Uganda's Budongo Forest Reserve, "a medium altitude, moist semi-deciduous forest, covering an area of 825 km² of which about 50% is forest and the rest is grassland" (Babweteera et al. 2011:32).[1] Budongo breaks the Gombe mold in many ways.

This chapter introduces the site and its two phases of research. Early findings on intergroup relations at Busingiro flatly contradict the demonic view of natural lethality. Then it describes how human impact worsened for chimpanzees through the research hiatus, and during the second project at Sonso. This record of human impact contextualizes developments within the Sonso community, the focus of Chapter 17.

Early Research and Human Environment

Junichiro Itani reconnoitered the Budongo forest, followed by Vernon and Francis Reynolds in 1962. The Reynolds logged 170 days, with about 300 hours of direct observation of unprovisioned chimpanzees in the Busingiro area, on the southwest neck of the reserve between Siba Forest and Budongo Forest proper. The two forests were divided by a major road, so these chimpanzees were familiar with people (Reynolds 1965; Reynolds and Reynolds 1965). They were followed in 1966 by Yukimaru Sugiyama and then Akira Suzuki, the latter leaving in 1968 (Sugiyama 1968; Suzuki 1971). Then came a gap of more than two decades and a shift in study location.

The second phase of research started with a 1989 news article reporting the sale of young chimpanzees, apparently from Budongo (Reynolds 2010:3 ff.). V. Reynolds reasoned that the best way to protect Budongo chimpanzees was to establish a research station, which could help monitor poachers and other encroachments. In 1990 with seed money through Richard Wrangham, and subsequent start-up funds through the Jane Goodall Foundation, Reynolds returned, recruited local field assistants, and initiated the Budongo Forest Project. He was soon joined by long-experienced forest ecologist Andrew Plumptre and others.

Their main chimpanzee research site was the Sonso community, a few kilometers east of the earlier research focus, on the southern edge of the Forest. After habituation without provisioning, study began in 1994 and 1995, with an extensive grid of observation trails. Research and conservation efforts continued ever since (Babweteera et al. 2008; Reynolds 1994; 2005:1, 22, 145, 182; n.d.).

---

[1] In other studies, Budongo Forest is reported at around 428 km². The larger figure includes a northeastern extension of grass, scrub lands, and relatively pristine forest.

People and Nature

Human presence in 1960 was limited. Density was much lower than elsewhere in Uganda due to 19th-century wars around the Bunyoro kingdom, and later rinderpest and tsetse fly, with consequent relocations after 1912. The area became a de facto game reserve with some 5,000 elephants, which prevented significant expansion of forest cover. Surrounding land was a sea of elephant grass, broken by gallery forest. "The forest is completely surrounded by grassland, with native cultivation nowhere extending to the forest's edge" (Eggeling 1947:32–34; Reynolds 2005:11).

Kibale Park suffered active islandization and all that entailed. Budongo was not recently islandized—it began as a forest island (Eggeling 1947:22). "Unlike Kibale ... Budongo was not settled at the time it was gazetted as a forest reserve and has not been encroached" (Olupot and Plumptre 2010:18).

Another contrast is that timber cutting within Budongo Park began earlier and continues to this day—although early and later logging had radically different implications for chimpanzees. In 1932 Budongo was gazetted as a Crown Forest, with lumbering strictly managed within designated tracts, providing for regrowth. About 100 ha was set aside as a permanent Nature Reserve, and remains so today (Eggeling 1947:32–33).

After 1936 human population increased for work in the sawmills. More came in the 1950s. In 1962 people concentrated around the main mill, with farming villages scattered amid the elephant grass. Still, even in the 1960s the forest was slowly expanding (Reynolds and Reynolds 1965:370, 376; Reynolds 2005:11).

Helpful Habitat Impact?

At Budongo early regulated logging unintentionally promoted chimpanzee food sources (Babweteera et al. 2011:32; Plumptre 1996:102, 105, 107, 109). "What they in fact succeeded in doing was to increase a variety of species of fruiting trees such as figs, with very good results for the forest's fruit-eating animals" (Reynolds 2005:18, reference omitted). Comestible alien species were introduced, such as *Broussonetia papyrifera*, "from which all parts are being eaten" (Gruber et al. 2012:453). "Budongo is rich in tree species, having the highest (449) number of any forest in Uganda" (Olupot and Plumptre 2010:19). The preferred habitat for feeding at Sonso is the *logged* area, and the forest edge (which encompasses human crops). Least preferred are the pristine Nature Reserve and broken canopy forest (Tweheyo and Lye 2005:285–286).

Sonso was last officially logged in 1947–1952 (Newton-Fisher 1999a:345). Compared to Ngogo and Kanyawara, "Sonso chimpanzees have the most diverse food availability, with no record of food scarcity during 15 years of observations ... Sonso chimpanzees appear to have the least demanding habitat" (Gruber et al. 2012:453). Food was ample, even in the two dry seasons (Newton-Fisher 2006:1596; Reynolds 2005:65–67, 94–95). I argue that intense resource competition is a primary cause of intergroup conflicts; *and* that intense resource competition is usually associated with human impact. Since here human impact increased food, no intergroup violence is predicted. Which bring us to 1960s Busingiro.

Busingiro and Intergroup Interactions

Early observations starkly challenge the Gombe paradigm of violent territorial defense and exclusion. Over four years, researchers from England and Japan established fundamentals of chimpanzee sociality, but they also found that chimpanzees of separate local groups *mixed*.

Reynolds and Reynolds

In the time before paradigms and procedures were fixed, Vernon and Frances Reynolds developed their own method of assessing territorial behavior. They went into the forest themselves, logging about 300 hours in direct observations. They also recruited assistants to map the location of chimpanzees in an area of 16 mi^2 (41 km^2). For 3 months local observers worked for 3 hours after dawn, and from 4:00 pm until dusk. They noted identifying characteristics in sightings, but mainly tried to locate parties and track their movements. They counted them when they crossed roads or tracks, and noted the direction and estimated distance of any vocalizations. The goal was to record location and movement. Through this process they identified spatially localized groups (Reynolds and Reynolds 1965:371). One party crossing a road had 40 individuals, which, based on its demographic composition, researchers extrapolated to a total group of 70–80. A traveling band from a different area was counted at 30, for an estimated total of 60 (Reynold and Reynolds 1965:402).

The Reynolds established aspects of chimpanzee sociality which would become Chimp 101: a fission-fusion pattern of parties;[2] that individuals spend most time in a "central portion of the home range" and less toward their peripheries; that females with offspring roam less widely than males and females without offspring; and that "despite the 'looseness' and 'instability' found in chimpanzee groups .... one may entertain the hypothesis that chimpanzees possess a social organization so highly developed that it can persist in the absence of immediate visual confirmation" (Reynolds and Reynolds 1965:398–400, 423). All are obvious now, but not then. They *figured out* what would later be seen as the basics of chimpanzee sociality and ranging.

They also recognized that chimpanzees separated into geographically distinctive groups. Yet these groups occasionally mixed without violence.

> After following band movements in the forest and plotting all known routes and movements on large-scale maps, we found it convenient to divide the study area into three "regions" of about 6–8 square miles each [roughly 15–21 km^2] .... bands within each of these regions had a higher frequency of interactions among one another than with the bands beyond. (Reynolds and Reynolds 1965:400)

---

[2] They credit earlier recognition of that to Kortlandt.

"Bands" frequented three areas, the northern Bubwe River, the Eastern Valleys, and southeastern Kamirambwa. Seen through Gombe-vision, such recorded movements and interactions are impossible. Extended quotation is appropriate, given the significance of what they observed.

> During early *Maesopsis* season bands from neighboring regions congregate and there were bands feeding on *Maesopsis* patches at Game, Kasenene, Busingiro and Eastern Valleys region, and at this season it seemed they were being used by both. On six recorded occasions a band from Eastern Valleys traveled fast and noisily right up into the Bubwe River region, and at other times similar movements occurred in the opposite direction.... On the other hand, on all except two nights during the early *Maesopsis* seasons, when bands from both regions had been feeding in the same area, groups tended to move apart at dusk, and nesting bands were heard calling from within the two regions, only to unite again early the next morning.... During this early *Maesopsis* season there was an extraordinary frequency and volume of calling and drumming throughout the day and sometimes at night. This region resounded with prolonged choruses and long-repeated rolls of drumming for two to three hours on end, with chimpanzees coming and going in all directions, some to and some from the centers of hubub. Later in August, when bands began to move off toward other *Maesopsis* patches along their usual routs, the amount of noise decreased. There were no boundaries within the study area where bands of chimpanzees were not known to cross in both directions. (Reynolds and Reynolds 1965:401)

One meeting is described in detail:

> We were watching a group of chimpanzees on the fringe of a swampy river in the Siba and had noticed that a new group was moving in closer from the north, calling and drumming as it came. There were about a dozen chimpanzees in our group and perhaps the same number again suddenly climbed up into the igeria trees with the first lot, whereupon *all* of them began the wildest screaming and hooting, swinging about, running along branches at top speed, leaping down branch by branch to the ground, climbing up again, shaking branches wildly, and occasionally coming up close to each other to meet briefly and part again, stamping on branches and slapping them, and behind all this confusion a steady undercurrent of drumming resounded. I think on this occasion the performance lasted for fifty-five minutes...
>
> We suspected it was a greeting display when two groups met, although we had watched many utterly uneventful meetings between groups of chimpanzees as big as these, and knew that there must be other reasons for this display. Could it be that there was a latent hostility between the groups, which had to be worked off? We didn't know enough about either lot to say. When the carnival was over, however, they all seemed to be feeding very peacefully beside each other and they all moved off in the same direction. (Reynolds 1965:158)

These "band" movements are quite similar to Goodall's early observations at Gombe (see Power 1991:60–67). Large parties from territorially distinctive groups met over a major stand of fruit, displayed wildly, then settled down to feed.

The Kyoto Researchers

The Reynolds ended Busingiro research in 1962. From September 1966 to March 1967, Yukimaru Sugiyama (1968) of Kyoto University resumed work with some of the same chimpanzees. He was followed by Akira Suzuki (1971) from May 1967 to September 1968. This work confirms that distinctive local groups in an area not suffering major negative human impact can meet, mix, and accept visiting neighbors.

Sugiyama aimed to identify individual chimpanzees and follow them. He focused on chimpanzees that were already habituated to nonthreatening local people and had been followed by the Reynolds. Logging 360 hours of direct observation, he recognized more than 46 adults or near-adults (Sugiyama 1968:226, 228, 230, 241).

Sugiyama (1968:243) identified four "regional populations:" A, B, C, and D. RP-A was the most studied. Between Sugiyama and Suzuki (1971:31, 37–38), they were estimated at up to 85 individuals (though Sugiyama thought fewer), with a total range of about 6–8 mi^2 (or 15–21 km^2). At maximum numbers, that would be about 4.0/km^2. Dense, but food was plentiful.

All Busingiro researchers recognized that interactions were far more common within rather than between groups. Reynolds and Reynolds (1965:402–403) and Suzuki (1971:37–38) mapped foraging parties within regional populations that resemble those of any other chimpanzee community. They seem like standard unit-groups—yet they mixed, especially RP-A and RP-D.

> Some individuals were observed to be with members of RP-D in an overlapping part of the ranges of RP-D and A in November and December and were later seen in the proper range of RP-A with members of RP-A. Some chimpanzees were observed in a mixed party comprising parts of RP-A and D, but they never advanced into the proper range of RP-A. (Sugiyama 1968:242)

Sugiyama rejected the idea that RP-A and RP-D were in fact one population, with two regional orientations. Many chimpanzees of each never moved beyond their central range, while others regularly interacted without aggressive displays in a broad overlap zone. Five adult males were seen in both the A and D core areas (1968:541). "Even in the overlapping area of both populations, other observations stressed that they were separate social units (Example 6). Although they exchanged members and mixed with each other in a friendly manner, there might be a vague social border between social units RP-A and RP-D" (1968:245).

Example 6 describes one morning's observations, accompanying a mixed sex party of about thirty of RP-A.

> As soon as they began to run about and make a booming noise at about 07:30, the same sound was heard from the east of the Biiso block and it gradually approached. At about 8:30, 14 adult males and one subadult of RP-A climbed down from the tree and began to move to the east, crossing the road, but the females and their children did not join this movement; instead, they retreated into the interior of the Siba block. The males met a party that came from the opposite direction at the fruit-bearing *Syzygium guineense* No. 53. Chimpanzees of both parties ran about here and there,

barked vigorously, beat the buttresses excitedly, and ate fruit in an exaggerated manner. Each individual moved independently, and direct social interaction between individuals was little observed. Though few were identified due to their quick movements, chimpanzees of the part from the east were more shy than the others and were presumed to be a part of RP-D. At 09:55, the party from RPD moved quickly to the north and the males of RP-A moved to the southwest, but with less excitement. (1968:245)

What about RP-A and RP-B? When they met, there was similar commotion: "two medium- or large-sized parties came to touch, run and jump about, uttering a heavy booming noise and beating the buttresses of both parties, but moved separately to the southeast and northwest." RP-C was the most distant from A, so they rarely met; plus RP-C "sometimes formed particularly large parties, and more leading and warning behavior could be seen in this population than in others" (Sugiyama 1968:243, 244). Maybe they were less accustomed to people.

Sugiyama (1968:249) also believed that regional populations were open to outside visitors. "Observations of the strangers who appeared occasionally or for only a few days in the main study area tell of this phenomenon. Even to those strangers little antagonistic behavior from the residents was seen."

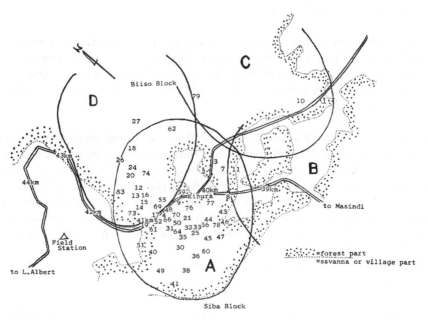

Illustration 5.1 Busingiro Ranges
Caption: Study area and ranges of regional populations. The kilometric distance starts from Masindi. A, B, C, and D show the rough range of each regional population and small figures important food trees.

Source: Sugiyama, Y. (1968). Social organization of chimpanzees in the Budongo Forest, Uganda. *Primates, 9*, 225–258.

All of this closely resemble Goodall's early observation of northern and southern groups at Gombe. These combined observations in all particulars look like agitated but nonviolent meetings between males of two local communities. They stand as a direct challenge for the post–Four Year War consensus, that adult males of different groups *cannot* interact peaceably. In a debate with Robert Sussman, Wrangham (2010:35) comments: "I look forward particularly to the discovery of peaceful association between members of neighboring communities, because such novel data would raise fascinating questions about behavioral variation and its causes." Peaceful association was documented more than four decades earlier. As with Goodall's early observations at Gombe, the record from Busingiro may be ignored but it will not go away. The only reason to discount these detailed reports is Gombe-vision—the fixed opinion that chimpanzees simply do not act that way.

The First Infanticide?

Yet there is one incident from these early years pertinent to chimpanzee killing, in an entirely ambiguous way. Budongo in 1967—the time of getting along—has the first recorded instance anywhere of what seems to be chimpanzee infanticide and consumption. "Observers witnessed a male slowly consuming a newborn infant, umbilical cord still attached, of unknown sex, and unknown origin" (Suzuki 1971:31–34). How he got it is unknown. Thinking of Mahale, scavenging a dead infant is a possibility (Count 4?-I-? 1967). Suzuki (1971:36–41) struggles to make sense of this. I won't.

The Human Touch Becomes Malignant

At this point, Chapter 16 switches gears to bridge between the first and second research periods. In between the 1968 end of Busingiro studies and 1990–1995 habituation of Sonso, human impact turned bad, and worsened severely during the second research project (Paterson 2005).

With work in sawmills, local population was already growing during the early research. Some immigrants settled close to the forest edge (Babweteera et al. 2011:46). A bigger labor magnet followed. In 1976, a 32,000 tons/year sugar mill started up nearby, drawing new immigrants to settle south and east of the Park (Olupot and Plumptre 2010:90).

Then Uganda imploded: Idi Amin in 1971, war with Tanzania in 1979, and civil war until 1986 (Kasozi 1994:88–144; Southall 1980). This same turmoil shut down timbering in Kibale, and allowed farmer invasion of "protected areas." But around Budongo open land was plentiful outside the forest. There was no need to cut trees.

Political upheavals closed sawmills (Babweteera et al. 2011:32). Logging interruption "stimulated the growth of trees that provided food to chimpanzees" (Tweheyo and Babweteera 2007:543). The chaos greatly curtailed sugar production, deflating the migrant draw.

Timber

In 1986 lumbering resumed. Two sawmills opened, though eventually failed in competition with pitsawing. Pitsawing is a nonmechanized way of cutting wooden planks. A two handled saw is guided through the trunk of a felled tree, with one cutter below ground level in a ditch. Pitsawing means than men camp in the forest, sometimes for long periods, instead of felling trees and then removing them with carriers. That earlier timber extraction was closely regulated to encourage regrowth (and inadvertently of chimpanzee food trees) (Plumptre 2001). In contrast, pitsawing is wasteful and inefficient, going for immediate return, cutting only the largest hardwoods and processing them poorly. Pitsawing looms large in recent Sonso history.

By 1992 forests 5 km to Sonso's southeast and east were already "heavily logged by pitsawyers" (Plumptre and Reynolds 1994:634). In some forests, half of standing mahoganies fell to pitsawyers between 1992 and 1996. Where close together, "the resulting gap was so large that the amount of light entering caused a tangle of vines and herbs and shrubs and creeper to come up, so dense that no tree sapling could survive, so the area remained permanently deforested (Reynolds 2010:273; and see Babweteera et al. 2000). By 1996 pitsawing outpaced sawmilling by more than four to one (Muhumuza et al. 2007:15). Since the late 1990s, all timber extraction has been by pitsawing, some legal but most not (Babweteera et al. 2011:32, 49; Reynolds 2005:182). "[O]ver the last 20 years" illegal pitsawing of mahoganies so depleted that species that the overall value of Budongo Forest in the Ugandan national economy is in question (Babweteera et al. 2011:49; Reynolds 2005:182).

While earlier timber extraction benefited chimpanzees by increasing their foods, pitsawing poses an existential threat. Nests are never found near active pitsaw operations (Reynolds 2010:273). Besides chasing chimpanzees out of their ranges, camping pitsawyers are dedicated hunters, for food and sale (Reynolds 2005:182). "Chimpanzees may leave or avoid areas that are being exploited, particularly for timber" (Newton-Fisher 2003:155). Pitsawing can lead to the disintegration of entire chimpanzee communities (Reynolds 2005:106). If snares are land mines for chimpanzees, pitsawing is a big bomb.

In 2000 in the northern Park, far from settlements and pitsawing, chimpanzees abounded. Not so in pitsawed parts of the south, closer to Sonso.

> Here the forest was, in a word, depressing. Snare after snare after snare. Huge patches of forest, quite simply gone, replaced with vast stretches of impenetrable creeper vine. The well worn paths of pitsawyer and poacher ran like a network branching out in all directions. A whole day in this nightmarish place revealed only a snared tree hyrax, and two very old chimp nests—the most common noise being that of axe against wood. (Donne 2001:10–11)

Sugar

In 1989 the Kinyara sugar mill was rebuilt. Production began in 1996 and expanded in 1997. By 2002 land planted in cane was 17 times that of the 1980s. Expansion relied on "outgrowers," local farmers who plant cane (McLennan et al. 2012:602). By the end of the decade, Kinyara was the hub of regional economic development, unlikely to be constrained (Sanya 2012).

By 1999 cane grew up to the edge of the Forest (Reynolds et al. 2003:311; 2010:458). Chimpanzees eat cane, though they do not eat much. In 1999 a Sonso chimpanzee was believed killed by an outgrower. In 2003 a Sonso adult male was speared and killed by a sugar guard. Elsewhere along the border, "it is highly likely that many chimpanzees become victims of similar killings" (O'Hara 2003:2; Reynolds 2005:173–174).

In 2000 and 2003 conservation efforts to create a buffer zone had no effect (O'Hara 2003; Reynolds 2005:174, 237–238; 2006). "[A]ll the cane guards we encountered were in possession of bows and arrows, and coincidentally, behind every one of their huts, a long line of snares stretched deep into the forest" (Donne 2001:11). Sugar cane meant Sonso chimpanzees were more likely to be killed by people.

More People, More Problems

Work opportunities promoted strong population growth. For 1991–2002, Masindi District grew 3.6% annually (Babweteera et al. 2011:32). Most cane growers keep some land in food crops, and some migrants live mainly as subsistence farmers (Mwendya 2010:36). This sharpens the issue of crop raiding, although chimpanzees account for a tiny percentage of losses (Babweteera et al. 2011:47–48). Snares in and around gardens are common. Far worse are "man-traps," large steel spring-loaded clamps. In August 2010 an adult Sonso female stepped in one not far outside the Park. Her cadaver was found up a tree, trap attached, its chain entangled in climber. Her 4-year-old daughter looked on from a nearby tree (McLennan et al. 2012:599, 601).

Wire snares are set inside the forest to capture game. Local people try to put some meat in their diet, but by 2000 there was a bushmeat trade along the Masindi-Butiaga road (Reynolds 2010:470). Most snaring is done by the poorest recent immigrants, whose subsistence plots can suffer the most from a crop raid. They cannot afford to buy meat, and money from bushmeat sale can be crucial (Reynolds 2006:392; Tumusiime et al. 2010:134–139, 142).

Snaring mutilated Sonso (Reynolds 2006:393, 400–401). In 2000 10 of 52, or 19.2% were deformed by snares (Waller and Reynolds 2001:138). A few years later, it was 28% of noninfants (Reynolds 2006:393). Around 2008, it was 30% or 36% of the adults (Amati et al. 2008:1; Tumusiime et al. 2010:129). Healthy males disappeared. "We were losing chimps too fast. Our community's survival was being jeopardized" (Reynolds 2010:468).

No *fatal* epidemic is reported within the Reserve. Partly, that is thanks to researcher's precautions (Reynolds 2006:397). Tourists are not allowed "to visit our chimpanzees at Sonso and this has probably saved them from a number of disease outbreaks" (Reynolds 2005:50–51). But researchers are not the only humans in the forest. In September 1999 the adult male Andy disappeared after a period of coughing. In November 1999, 68% of Sonso was coughing, though all recovered (Reynolds 2000; 2010:431, 491).

Conservation

Budongo researchers took action to clear snares from the Forest, in 2000 hiring two local hunters to search for them. Despite local resistance, even threats and sabotage, thousands of snares were removed, 220 per month in 2005-2007. Because of these efforts fewer snares are planted close to the Sonso research station than elsewhere. Still, in 2007 three of the community were newly mutilated (Amati et al. 2008; Reynolds 2005:170-185, 224; 2010:467-468, 478).

Sonso researchers working with the Jane Goodall Foundation tried to educate local people about chimpanzees, while addressing concerns about crop raiding. The task has been very difficult (Babweteera et al. 2008:148-150; Reynolds 2005:172-173, 215-218; Sowter 2007; Webber et al. 2007). One obstacle was fear created by chimpanzee attacks on people. In November 1995 a human infant was killed just outside the reserve, possibly by one of Sonso (Anonymous 1996). Yet there are signs of progress and hope for the future (Darwin Initiative 2016; Tumusiime et al. 2010:139-140; Zuberbuhler 2007).

Because of the research operation, Sonso has been a protected zone compared to Forest areas just beyond it (Reynolds 2005:26-27, 45-46, 49, 51; see McLennan et al. 2020), which is a big factor in discussions to come. Nevertheless, the disappearance of any Sonso chimpanzee cannot be attributed to the malevolence of other chimpanzees. Unless there is some specific reason to reach that conclusion, humans are more likely culprits.

Tourism

With the Ugandan government pushing increased sugar production and pledging to make more land available (Naturinda 2011), the diminishing value of Budongo timber is ominous for the Reserve. That made a compelling case for tourism to generate revenue, involving locale people, and so fostering antisnaring sentiment.

A 1993 study on tourism possibilities focused on Busingiro. A second site to the north, Kaniyo Pabidi, was added. With funding from the European Union, some 200 km of viewing trails were cut, and visitor accommodations built. Both sites opened in 1995 with 253 visitors in July 1997 (Langoya and Long 1997:7-8; Zeppel 2006:153). In 2006, Jane Goodall Institute Africa Programs began working with the Ugandan National Forest Authority, developing regulations to prevent disease transmission or excessive disturbance, and educating and involving local workers and guides (Cox et al. n.d.). Yet a web posting from the Budongo Conservation Field Station (n.d.) features a photograph of tourists, without face masks, in close proximity to chimpanzees.

Tourists did not get near to Sonso, so that it receives no further discussion. But other human disruptions attained deadly intensity by the early 2000s. Of all Ugandan chimpanzee habitats, Budongo was at the top for timber harvesting, charcoal production, and hunting. The highest disturbance is in its south, bracketing the Sonso site on the east, north, and west (Plumptre et al. 2003:36, 39, 42). Sonso chimpanzees had intensifying habitat destruction all around them within the Reserve.

A Fragmentary Existence

As bad as human disturbance became from the later 1990s onward, it was far worse for chimpanzees in diminishing patches of forest south and east of the Reserve. Kasokwa group in 2000 had 13 individuals plus passers through, in a shrinking strip of gallery forest recently cut off from the Reserve. Bulindi in 2008 had about 25, moving between patches among farms. Conflict with humans was intense, with hungry chimpanzees raiding for crops and even chickens, and attacking people. People set snares and man traps, threw rocks, and sometimes speared them. Although there are suggestions that chimpanzees and humans may coexist even in massively altered landscapes (McClennan et al. 2020), broadly the prognosis is grim (McClennan and Hill 2010; 2012; McClennan and Hockings 2016; Reynolds 2005:212–216; Smith and Marsh 2003). These besieged survivors provide insight into the fraught lives of chimpanzees in disappearing habitats across Africa, as around Kibale. However, they do not enter into the Sonso story, which starts now.

17
Sonso

Sonso group roams around an old sawmill, roughly 6 km east of Busingiro. There "may be one community between the Busingiro and Sonso communities" (Newton-Fisher 1997:2.20). Habituation efforts began in 1990, and in August 1994 Nicholas Newton-Fisher was able to approach and follow chimpanzees, beginning a new period of study (Newton-Fisher 1997:3.2).

The historical narrative of Sonso encases thick theoretical issues—on sudden immigration of parous females with male offspring, on subsequent infanticide by females, and finally on an astounding string of Sonso males killing Sonso infants. That caps off a historical trajectory starting with relatively undisturbed peace and plenty around 1990, through anthropogenic scarcity and social disruption, to deadly violence by the 2010s.

The Pre-Great Revision Alternative, Unconsidered

In 1994 the Four Year War was the archetype of intergroup relations. In his dissertation, Newton-Fisher (1997:2.21–2.22) mentions the Reynolds' findings, noting that subsequent research elsewhere "cast doubt on some of the earlier conclusions." The noisy Busingiro gatherings "may in fact have been encounters between large parties from different communities, converging independently on the same food source.... Such a contest would be highly vocal and involve many displays and associated buttress drumming." Yes, it does indeed look like two groups meeting. But repeated observations established that they *settled down to feed together*—impossible from a demonic perspective; *and*, other meetings between regional populations were *not* marked by loud commotion. The matter was left at that, "no direct reevaluation has been made of the early claims for the chimpanzees of Budongo." The Great Revision ruled unchallenged.

If those early observations were accurate, wouldn't mid-1990s field observers see signs of group flexibility? They did, in movement of individual males. Nik, an older juvenile male, showed up after habituation passed into full research (Newton-Fisher 1997:2.17). According to unpublished Budongo data sheets of all identified chimpanzees, "Sonso Community Chimpanzees" (Newton-Fisher and Davis/[also Hobaiter and Muhumuza] 2004/2013/2018) (a great data source, relied on often in this chapter, hereafter SCC), another juvenile (about 6), Jake, appeared in September 1994 and disappeared 6 months later. Gashom (about 7) showed up in July 1994, and became one of Sonso. A fully grown male, Mukono (about 25) appeared in 1992 and was gone by early 1994. Jogo, a juvenile male identified in November 1992, disappeared in October 1993, reappeared in April 1994, disappeared again in October, reappeared again in

March 1995, and disappeared for good in 1997. Reynolds (2005:31) suggests he may have been "following a strategy of belonging to two communities."

True, Sonso observers never saw two groups meet and mix. But at Busingiro the studied chimpanzees were long accustomed to people. Not so in the Sonso peripheries. Trailing humans frighten away unhabituated chimpanzees. At Busingiro, RP-C was the farthest from the main study group RP-A. Those two rarely met, and RP-C exhibited more "warning behavior" than others. By location, Sonso's western neighbor, the Nature Reserve community, could be Sugiyama's RP-C.

Within a few years human disruption intensified and intergroup relations became more charged. There is no way to revisit conditions of the past. Although the second phase of Budongo research did not confirm earlier claims of nonviolent interactions between groups, neither do initial observations contradict them.

Numbers, Territory, and Intergroup Behaviors

From August 1994 to December 1995, Sonso grew from 38 to 46 from births and young female immigration. Their core range, where males spent 80% of their time, was just under seven km^2, and total range was 14.51 km^2 (Newton-Fisher 2003:151–153). At 46 individuals, that makes a density around 3.2/km^2. Up to 2001 Sonso varied from 48 to 54 individuals (Fawcett and Muhumuza 2000:244; Reynolds 2005:30). Range area is not provided, but 54 chimpanzees in 14.5 km^2 implies a peak density around 3.7/km^2. (Sonso density will be significant in Part IX.) Newton-Fisher (2003:154) believes this high density was sustainable because of local food abundance. Sonso was particularly favored by early logging. The introduced *Broussonetia papyfirera* was planted around the old sawmill, and gradually colonized forest gaps. *Broussonetia* produces food all year round, in leaves, flowers, and fruit (Newton-Fisher 1997:6.34).[1]

Sonso had four groups around it: Waibira/Kasenene Hill to the northeast and east, Nyakafunjo to the south and southwest, Nature Reserve to the west and northwest, and unnamed chimpanzees to the southeast (Emery Thompson et al. 2006:1604). Sonso group was large, with a small territory for its numbers. This seems like a laboratory model for Gombe-like intergroup behaviors. Were they found?

Patrolling

In his table on territorial behavior, Wrangham (1999:6, 9) puts question marks under "border patrols," "deep incursions," "coalitionary attacks," and "border avoidance," citing a personal communication from Vernon Reynolds. Some patrols with fearful

---

[1] Findings about ranging 1994–1995 did not fit the model of females staying in small individual areas within an interior core, with males roaming widely around them. Budongo males too spend most of their time within the community core, and have their own individual areas for foraging. Resource abundance makes these small individual ranges possible (Newton-Fisher 1997:5.24–6.3; 2002:302). Later findings at Gombe (Murray et al. 2008) and Ngogo (Mitani 2008) suggest that such pocket ranges may be common, contrary to established views that "male ranging is typically explained in terms of mating access to females" (Murray et al. 2008:20).

and aggressive behaviors were seen in the northeast and southwest, near where other chimpanzees were (Emery Thompson et al. 2006:1604; Newton-Fisher 2003:153–154). "Range defense is typically by means of loud vocal advertisements of male presence and strength" (Newton-Fisher 2002:304). There are no reports of any physical clash or violence between groups, although Sonso had unspecified "hostile interactions" with Nyakafunjo, and one close encounter near the Nature Reserve (below) (Reynolds 2005:107).

As with Kanyawara, focused study in 1994–1995 reveals a very different pattern than the boundary patrols of 1970s Gombe. Newton-Fisher cautions that patrols should occur only occasionally. Territorial defense is accomplished by noisy advertising in occasional visits. Neighboring groups should rarely clash physically, and avoid each other through "mutual respect" (Newton-Fisher 2002:287–288, 293, 304).

Border behavior in 2002–2003 (Bates and Byrnes 2009:251–253) was not patrolish. Daily, foraging males kept moving in a linear trajectory, while pregnant or lactating females turned around after a while, thus males more commonly reached the periphery. Once there, however, males behaved as they behaved in their core. Of 37 male movements followed to the periphery, *only one* "was indeed suggestive of a border patrol" (2009:253).

This nonpatrolling is said to represent "a novel form of territorial defense" by combining the normal food search with "border checking," thus "generally avoiding the explicit boundary patrols observed at other chimpanzee study sites" (Bates and Byrnes 2009:255, 247). Not so novel. It seems like Kanyawara—just another variation on flexible territoriality.

Newton-Fisher went to Budongo to investigate male ranging patterns, and found mutual respect. (There will be more serious territorial jostling in later, more impacted times.) Thus we see again how the Gombe paradigm shaped perceptions, in Budongo researchers' general portrayal of relations between chimpanzee neighbors.

The Power of the Paradigm

Newton-Fisher and Emery Thompson (2012:48) fully endorse the rival coalition reduction hypothesis (RCRH). "[T]he lethality of aggression functions specifically to slowly reduce the relative coalitional power of neighboring groups, thus increasing the probability of winning future encounters," and so identifying "guiding principles and common patterns than can inform the study of human violence" (Newton-Fisher and Emery Thompson 2012:41). Their theoretical discussion begins with two paragraphs graphically detailing the brutality of attacks at Gombe and Tai, claiming "dozens of similar events have been documented from chimpanzee communities throughout Africa" (2012:46).

Then follows the standard line (2012:46–47). References are omitted, but all refer to cases *other than* Budongo.

> Across the geographic range of chimpanzees, the pattern of violence is the same. The vast majority of attacks involve a group—or gang—from one community targeting a

lone member of a neighboring group for a sustained attack.... Wounds are typically so severe that deaths cannot be viewed as merely incidental but as the intended outcome of the attack ... the violence and range expansion has been targeted and directional.... As part of territorial defense, groups of males engage in patrolling behavior both along and beyond territorial boundaries ... such patrols are a common aspect of chimpanzee behavior.... Boundary patrols sometimes develop into raids, in which groups of males make incursions deep into neighboring territories. These males do not typically exploit resources found in the rival territory but instead appear determined to locate and attack isolated rivals.

This portrait is utterly unlike what these researchers saw with their own eyes at Budongo.

Infanticide, Disappearances, and Territorial Pressure

In February 1995 new alpha Duane and ally Vernon ate an unsexed infant, acquisition unknown, but suspected as from a peripheral female of Nature Reserve group (Newton-Fisher 1999b). In September 1995, very close by, Black—third ranked, but moving up—found a female with a tiny male infant, and displayed aggressively. Other males joined in, Duane taking the lead. The alpha got the infant, killed it, and passed it around for small nibbles. Newton-Fisher speculates that the mother was known to the attackers, returning after a visit to another community with a child.

In "Infant Killers of Budongo," he (1999b:169) interprets these infanticides as reducing *future* competitors. "Reducing the number of males reaching adulthood in a neighboring community reduces its territorial 'strength,' which, for the infanticidal males, should make range expansion, recruitment of females and ultimately extinction of the neighboring community more feasible" (1999b:169). These killings are the closest that Budongo ever comes to supporting the RCRH.

It is far from clear that these infants were from another group. Researchers were still identifying local females up to 1996 (Reynolds 2005:106). In more recent times, there've been *many* internal infant killings at Sonso. So why label the 1995 infanticides as between- rather than within-group killings? The Gombe paradigm (Count 2-?- I-? 1995; 1-?-I-M 1995).

An alternative explanation is display violence, stemming from contemporary political instability (Reynolds 2005:127–129, 155–157, 162–167). Duane deposed Magosi in 1994–1995. Magosi remained high status, with allies. Duane's dominance was neither obvious nor secure. Magosi had allies, and other males were unaffiliated. "[T]he social hierarchy was in turmoil" (Newton-Fisher 1998:3); "rates of agonistic interactions were higher than they were a few years later" (2004:85).

At first Duane relied on Vernon so much they could be co-alphas. Duane led the first (unsuccessful) monkey hunts seen at Budongo, in 1996 (Reynolds 2005:76–78). Over months, "Duane eventually became alpha and under him the hierarchy settled down" (Newton-Fisher 1998:3). The coincidence of intense political jockeying and two infanticides suggests they were display to intimidate rivals.

Disappearing Adult Males

From 1997 to 2001 six Budongo males disappeared and three died of known causes.[2] Other adult males would die or disappear after 2001 of course, but nine males lost in 5 years is unusual, and a major diminution of Budongo's strength. This worried Budongo researchers (Reynolds 2010:491).

> [T]he Waibira community to the north was making raids into Sonso territory and our chimpanzees appeared frightened of them. We feared at that time that all our males might be killed, and the females taken over by the Waibira males from the north, as happened at Gombe. (Reynolds 2005:30–31)

Haunted by the paradigm. What actually happened from 1997 to 2001?

Pitsawing

Why did Waibira push in? In October 1996, forest rangers made a (rare) move against nearby pitsawyers. This pitsawing worried Reynolds, who was "certain that [chimpanzees] did not remain in or near an area where logging was actually taking place ... [and] they cannot just move out of an area into surrounding forest–chimps have well defended territories."

Threat of Waibira invasion ended when Waibira group *disappeared*, due to the "considerable amount of illegal logging in the area between Sonso and Waibira," which pushed the latter "north, away from the loggers and away from our study community" (Reynolds 2005:31). "[E]ver-increasing number of illegal pitsawyers" set up a big camp between Sonso and Waibira, reaching 100 men. It was not until 2011, when researchers cut new observation trails in Waibira territory, that they realized "the sheer scale of the snare and pit-sawing problems in the areas outside of our main research zone" (Budongo Weblogongo 7/31/2011).

There were no signs of chimpanzees around Waibira for about a year. That community's fate is unknown. When the loggers left, *some* chimpanzees re-inhabited the degraded area. These chimpanzees soon "encroached on the Sonso range" (Reynolds 2005:108). I refer to this group as "neo-Waibira" since it is not clear if it is the earlier inhabitants, refugees from elsewhere, or some mix. We should be theoretically open to the possibility of large survivor fragments coalescing.

---

[2] Budongo data sheets (SCC) provide dates, names, and estimated ages, with occasional annotations. In 1997, Chris, 30, disappeared. In 1998, Zesta, 28, killed by other Sonso chimpanzees. In 1998, Kikunka, 22, disappeared. In 1999, Vernon, 34, disappeared, possibly speared by a cane guard (Reynolds 2005:174). In 1999, Magosi, 50+, body found. In 2000, Muga, 23, disappeared. In 2000, Andy, 18, body found, had been coughing (Reynolds 2010:491). In 2001, Bwoya, 36, disappeared. In 2001, Nkojo, 31, disappeared.

Rival Coalition Reduction?

Advocates of the RCRH can imagine support in Sonso disappearances. Between 1997 and 2001 five adult males disappeared without a clue, three during friction with Waibira. But there were many ways to die at this time. Two of those disappeared in 2001, *after* Waibira was gone but when pitsawyers were most active. And of course, males could just walk away, especially if they had experience and perhaps mating beyond group boundaries (below).

Against the RCRH, there are no reported intergroup clashes despite Reynold's mention of "raids"—which he contemporaneously called "exploratory forays" (2010:491). Only one direct intercommunity encounter was observed, not near Waibira but on the west near the Nature Reserve community. Two unknown males charged out of the bush towards Sonso chimpanzees, and split when they saw humans (Reynolds 2005:107).

Killings are possible according to the resource competition and human impact hypothesis (RCH + HIH). If pitsawing pushed Waibira toward Sonso, that might lead to violence. Another factor could be the 1997 drought that struck Kibale. In March 1997: "We have a real drought situation. Even the chimps are suffering" (Reynolds 2010:326). But there is no evidence that any violence actually occurred, then.[3]

Discounting those suspicions however, Reynolds (2005:107) observes, "the lives of the Sonso chimpanzees appear, during the years we have been observing them, to have been peaceful ones. There have been no examples of inter-community killing as far as we know."

An Internal Killing and Politics

The only documented adult male killing at Budongo directly contradicts the RCRH. In November 1998, researchers rushed toward loud and long fear screams (Fawcett and Muhuza 2000; Reynolds 2005:154–163). They found young (about 18) male Zesta down and severely wounded, still screaming. The attackers were Magosi, the deposed alpha, and ambitious Black. Wounds on Duane, the current alpha, and chimpanzee hairs in his feces indicate that he too was an attacker. Observers saw Zesta die (Count 1-W-A-M, 1998).[4]

By the logic of the RCRH, "[m]ales facing greater risk should be less violently aggressive toward one another, while increased levels of intracommunity violence would

---

[3] Although these disappearances do not appear in Wilson et al. (2014a), Emery Thompson et al. (2006:1605) mention them as possible intergroup killings, so they join the count. They are Chris (Count 5-O-A-M, 1997), Kikunku (Count 5-O-A-M, 1998), Vernon—the possible spearing victim (Count 5-O-A-M, 1999), and Muga (Count 5-O-A-M, 2000). Since the two in 2001 occurred after Waibira was gone, and no one has labeled them suspicious, they are not counted. Wilson et al. (2014a:EDT 2) add one "inferred" killing, by Sonso of an infant of an unknown community, with no other information (Count 5-O-I-F 2000).

[4] Postmortem examination shows how much it takes to kill a chimpanzee: lacerations to ears, face, and cranium; deep cuts and punctures in the thorax and pectoral muscles; both arms and hands severely mangled, both legs and feet almost as bad. After cleaning the skeleton, both hands and his right humerus had visible bite marks. "[H]is face was torn apart and most of this body was bitten, ripped and lacerated" (Reynolds 2005:161).

be expected where risk of lethal intercommunity violence is decreased" (Newton-Fisher and Emery Thompson 2012:49). Zesta was killed when Sonso seemed under outside threat, when they were visibly frightened, when theoretically they needed every single "warrior."

Why kill Zesta? There must be a fitness reason. "The lethal attack is interpreted as an act of intra-community male sexual competition resulting in the complete exclusion of one male from estrous females" (Fawcett and Muhuza 2000:243). Zesta was the youngest and lowest status of adults. By paternity assignment he never fathered a child, whereas Magosi, Duane, and Black by 1998 had nine between them (Newton-Fisher et al. 2010:422). What sexual competition could Zesta represent?

"Sexual" or "reproductive competition" is a label that with a little ingenuity can be applied to almost any situation. The display violence hypothesis has more defined conditions and processes.

Politically, Black was ambitious, angling for number two. He initiated the 1995 attack which led to infant killing by Duane. In late 1998 he waged a campaign to replace Vernon, Duane's ally, as beta. Vernon was not present when Zesta died, possibly due to a leg wound, possibly inflicted by Black. Zesta, young and low status, was a minor player, peripheral. In the month before his death, he did not groom with Duane, Vernon, or Black, the three aggressive males that were in direct competition.

Which brings Reynolds close to my position on display killing. He speculates that Black initiated the attack on Zesta, which in a sexually charged and politically fraught situation, led to other political animals piling on. "Whether DN or BK or both made the initial attack on ZT is not known, but each would have had his own motives: BK's sexual and to consolidate his political ambition, DN's sexual and to emphasize his alpha status" (Reynolds 2005:163). Magosi, aging but still high in status, had similar interests.

Once again, politically ambitious individuals in a politically unsettled time take the lead in ostentatious violence–even against one of their own. If one cannot communicate "don't mess with me" by attacking a defenseless outsider, an inconsequential, friendless insider could do.

The Great Immigration—That Didn't Happen, or Did It?

Shortly after pitsawyers chased away or killed Waibira chimpanzees came a "startling" (Mitani 2006:1492) development. "During 2000–2003, Budongo Forest Project field researchers observed 10 new parous, adult females, in addition to 5 nulliparous females, in association with the Sonso community" (Emery Thompson et al. 2006:1605). Three showed up in just 2 weeks of October 2001. Some seemed to know each other. Five parous and one nulliparous so regularly associated with others in the center of Sonso range that it was clear they joined the community. Other females were seen that may have been passing through. Some fled on seeing humans, some not.

> Having considered various options, those who observed these events have concluded that this influx of females and young may have been the outcome of the disintegration

of a neighboring community, perhaps as a result of human activity such as intensive pitsawing. (Reynolds 2005:106)

If some newcomers were habituated to people, how could they be? Possibly through habituation around Busingiro; *or*, researchers thought, some were among Sonso during habituation efforts pre-1994, moved away as they matured, and now returned. In contrast to patterns elsewhere, no violence was directed at the newcomers by resident males or females, at least at first (some came later). Even more startling, among the offspring brought by these immigrants were juvenile or subadult *males*. Squibs, about 13, and Simon, about 11, both appeared suddenly in 2004 (Emery Thompson et al. 2006; Langergraber et al. 2014:5; Reynolds 2005:105–106).

Such immigration has major theoretical implications. A fundamental tenet of the Gombe perspective is that no adult male can enter another group. At Mahale, Fanana broke that rule. At Sonso, Squibs and Simon weren't fully adult, but close. If near-adult males joined Sonso group, that confirms group boundaries can be porous, as reported earlier for Businigro. My scenario for Ngogo—of parous and nonparous females being directed into a safer area by habitat destruction—is here exemplified in recorded practice. And so for Gombe-vision, there is a compelling reason to dispute the conclusion that these were immigrants. And so it was disputed, with genetics.

Did It Really Happen?

In "Genetic Analyses Suggest no Immigration of Adult Females and Their Offspring into the Sonso Community of Chimpanzees," Langergraber et al. (2014) challenge the factuality of this great immigration with seemingly unassailable DNA evidence. They conclude that these were not immigrants at all, but peripheral members of the Sonso community all along. Here we come to one of those deep dives into specifics. It matters for big issues, so this must be done, but I will stick to essentials.

Of nine immigrant offspring that were genotyped (from feces), four males could *not* be assigned to a Sonso father. Rather than admitting extragroup paternity, researchers counter that four possible fathers in Sonso when these offspring were conceived (1991–1999) were never genotyped (Langergraber et al. 2014:3).[5] They claim within-group paternity on another basis. It gets technical.

Y Haplotypes

Among the four paternity-unassigned immigrant offspring were two Y chromosome haplotypes (genetic markers passed from father to son) that are common among Sonso males. These specific haplotypes have not been found among four other Budongo groups: Businigro, Kaniyo-Pabidi (in the north of the Reserve), Kasokwa

---

[5] Which seems a little dodgy. Another study of reproduction within Sonso over this 1982–2002 period, assessed paternity for 21 of 24 offspring (Newton-Fisher et al. 2010:419, 421). That is a non-paternity-assigned rate of 12.5%, vs. 44.4% for the immigrants in question—quite a difference.

(in gallery forest south of the Reserve), and Waibira (Langergraber 2014:4). However, that "Waibira," may not be the original neighbors. The original Waibira, the one that disappeared, was not genotyped. Neither were other neighbors.

Generally, neighboring groups commonly share Y haplotypes, as at Mahale (Inoue 2015:632) and Kibale (Langergraber et al. 2014:4). Sometimes, so do groups separated by distance, as at Tai (Schubert et al. 2011:6), or neo-Waibira and Kasokwa of Budongo (Langergraber et al. 2014:4). Shared Y haplotypes do not demonstrate within-group paternity.[6]

Odd Fathers

Those Sonso males that were genotyped as fathers of the five other immigrant offspring raise additional questions. Four fathers—Chris, Vernon, Nkojo, and Bob—eventually disappeared (Langergraber et al. 2014:5 Reynolds 2005:174; SCC). Maybe they went elsewhere, to a place they had been before, a place with females.

Too speculative? Consider this. Father Bob was born in 1990, his immigrant daughter TP in 1999 +/- 2 yr. BG, born in early 2004, was sired by another immigrant, Fred, himself born in 1994 +/- 1 yr. Both Bob and Fred impregnated females when they were roughly *9 or 10 years old*. Either could qualify as the youngest father *ever* recorded among wild chimpanzees.[7] Also strikingly odd, except for Nkojo, none of the six Sonso males that fathered offspring *within* the group, a total of 18 between them, fathered *any* of the "immigrant" offspring (Newton Fisher et al. 2010:422).

It seems there were two populations of females, those within Sonso receiving the attention of Sonso's male reproductive winners, and other females somewhere else, visited by those males not breeding within the Sonso. Recall those roaming young males seen during Sonso's habituation.

Genes vs. Observations

Langergraber et al. (2014:6) argue that newly seen "females were actually long-term Sonso residents who escaped previous identification due to their peripheral or unhabituated status." Sonso field observers firmly reject that:

> Could it be that we have actually missed seeing these females, that they are not in fact new arrivals but had hitherto successfully evaded detection by our field assistants and

---

[6] Fall-back defense on this point is that nowhere else have different groups been shown to share *two* Y haplotypes, as the immigrant offspring do in this case. This case "would involve a previously unknown pattern of between-community haplotype sharing" (Langergraber et al. 2014:6). Previously unknowns become known. Two neighboring groups in Kalinzu share five Y haplotypes (Ishizuka et al. 2020:2).

[7] Testes do not reach full size until the age of 12–14 years, and it is unlikely that males are fertile before age 10 (Constable et al. 2001:1280). It was thought that "no males at Gombe ... sired infants prior to their fourteenth year" (Goodall 1986:84), but one at 11 is now recognized (Walker et al. 2018:4). A 10-year-old sire is known at Tai, with the next youngest 12 (Boesch et al. 2006:108; Newton-Fisher et al. 2010:419). At Sonso, "the mean ages of first and last reproduction are 16 and 25 years" (Lowe et al. 2019:11).

students? This is extremely improbable.... We were finding and naming new *adult* females until 1996 (Harriet was the last), after which there were no new *adult* females found until the three who arrived in 2001. Added to this, recognition of the new females was made easy by the fact that both Wilma and Flora were missing hands, while Melissa was quickly and easily identified by her resemblance to the adult male Jambo. [Others had visible snare wounds.] [W]e can be 99% certain that these are immigrant adult females. (Reynolds 2005:105–106)

Where does that leave things? Very uncertain. "Immigrant" females and offspring could be peripheral members of Sonso, or from a disintegrated bisexual group, or females formerly living independently—visited by Sonso and/or other males that roamed outside their own home range (and may eventually have returned there).

Critically, however, there is *no dispute* that they previously *did not live within the Sonso home range*. They moved in. The *only* hypothesis offered for their sudden appearance is habitat destruction around Sonso. Nor is there dispute that their arrival greatly elevated population density in the Sonso home range. Resource abundance enabled high density, but it was human impact that elevated it. That had serious consequences.

Infant Killers, Both Male and Female

Sonso had up to eight infanticides from 1991 to 2000 (Reynolds 2005:146–150).[8] In 1991 as habituation began, chimpanzee dung was found with hair, bone, and cartilage from a chimpanzee of under 3 years (Count 4-?-I-? 1991). In 1993, a Sonso female and male fought over a screaming infant, origin unknown, which was never seen again (Count 2-?-I-? 1993). In 1995, came the two infant killings, by Duane and company, previously discussed. (That's four.)

From 1997 to 2000, the time of adult males losses and outsiders pressing in, several infants died under strange circumstances (Reynolds 2005:146–151). In August 1997 a Sonso female with her own infant carried an infant carcass with deep lacerations, sex and origin unknown. The corpse was taken by a male, groomed repeatedly, then discarded. Since no females were missing an infant, it was classified as an outsider (Count 2-O-I-? 1997). (That's five.)

Later that month a Sonso female was seen with a screaming infant. Others tried to grab it, and it was not seen again (Count 5-?-I-? 1997). (Six.) In December 1999 an adult male carried and cuddled a recently born male infant, believed from a Sonso female. Eventually it starved to death, and he carried it for 2 more days (not counted). (Seven.) In February 2000 an adult Sonso female with her own infant carried and groomed a dead infant. (Eight.) Wilson et al. (2014a:EDT 4) note a 2000 inferred killing of an outside female infant, and I assume these are the same (Count 4-O-I-F, 2000). That makes three cases where adult *females*, not males, are implicated in infant killings.

---

[8] My record of infant killings differs from the graph in Lowe et al. (2019:7). When those graphed incidents are noted in previous publications, I stick with that information.

Population Pressure

Food abundance buoyed Sonso in the 1990s. But the sudden influx of females and offspring dramatically increased population pressure in the center of their territory. Sonso went from 54 in 2000–2001 (Tweheyo and Lye 2005:283), to 65 in 2005 and 75 or 78 in 2007 (Slocome et al. 2009:443; Townsend et al. 2007:R356). That doubled the August 1994 population of 38.

In Chapter 14, I argued that Ngogo population doubled or more from the 1970s to the 1990s. Budongo population doubled in 14 years. "Such an influx of additional females should increase feeding competition, but there is no evidence to date" (Emery Thompson et al. 2006:1611). Between March 2004 to July 2006, violence at Sonso provided that evidence. Not, however, violence by males.

Three infants were likely killed by Sonso females. Once, several Sonso females attacked an unknown mother and pulled away her clinging infant, which wasn't seen again (Count 2-O?-I-? 2006). If done by males, this would be called a *coalitional killing*. In March 2004, several females fought over the carcass of an unknown infant with head wounds. A recently arrived female may have been the mother (Count 3-O?-I-? 2004). In July 2006, researchers found agitated females with what was left of an infant, thought to be newborn of a *resident* Sonso female (Count 3-W-I-? 2006). Wilson et al. (2014a:Extended Data Table 2) also note one inferred intercommunity infanticide, sex of killers not mentioned (Count 4-O-I-? 2006).

Interpretation was straightforward: "Our observations test and provide support for the hypothesis that increased pressure on resources precipitate severe female aggression, as females compete for limited foraging areas" (Emery Thompson et al. 2007:R356). Given their small core range, that is persuasive. The only causal explanation of this immigration and resource pressure is human destruction of one or more nearby community of chimpanzees.

Muller (2007:R366) comments: "This raises the troubling possibility that human activity may have indirectly contributed to the killings. No clear anthropogenic influence has been identified, however, and similar demographic shifts in chimpanzee communities are known to occur in the absence of human interference."

Not really. The only comparable transfers of parous females are from dwindling Kalande to Kasakela at Gombe, and from K- to M-group at Mahale. Human interference was very present in both.

Demonic Females?

Lead investigator Emery Townsend spelled out the implications of these infant killings:

> There is a widespread belief in scientific literature that male and female chimpanzees differ greatly in their nature. It's true that males are much more often seen to engage in extreme physical violence than females, and this has led to the notion of violent and demonic males in contrast to quite peaceful females. However, our research shows that under the right socio-ecological circumstance, these chimp gender

stereotypes collapse completely. If their resources are under threat, females can become just as violently aggressive as males. (University of St. Andrews 2007)

Budongo females seem comparatively aggressive in another way. Twenty times in 2003, females joined together to respond aggressively to male aggression. More coalitions. Five instances included physical attack on the males (Newton-Fisher 2006). Coincidentally, Sonso lacked intense male violence toward females (back then). Budongo males seemed comparatively *non*aggressive in general (back then). So Reynolds and Reynolds (1965:416) found; and so too Newton-Fisher (2004:85), "the adult male chimpanzees of the Sonso community are less likely to initiate agonistic interactions than are males in some other populations." That would soon change.

Newton-Fisher (2006:1596) suggests that this pattern of more aggressive females and less aggressive males derives from resource abundance, which allows for gregariousness among females; which enables them to form coalitions; which curtails male aggression against females. "Under appropriate ecological or demographic conditions, female chimpanzees may be able to use cooperative social strategies *comparable to those of bonobos* and achieve a similar result" (Newton-Fisher 2006:1597, emphasis added). Agreed, like bonobos—which suggests behavioral plasticity. But the implications of females killing would be marginalized in later discussion which swerved back to demonic males.

Accelerating Change from 2008

In the later 2000s, published scholarship relevant to this book falls off. Research continued, but focused on other topics, such as a finer understanding of chimpanzee vocalizations. But pertinent information appeared on the blog Budongo's Weblogongo (cited here as BW followed by dates of postings, up to May 2014). Following Weblogongo, 2008 appears as a tipping point for stress and violence.

Hunting

Francis and Vernon Reynolds thought Businogiro chimpanzees were pure vegetarians. Suzuki (1971:31–34) twice saw meat eating (besides the infant chimpanzee in Chapter 16). When research resumed after 1990, Sonso chimpanzees were infrequent and indifferent hunters, and consuming much less meat than those elsewhere (Reynolds 2005:73–78). Rather abruptly, that changed in 2008.

> The chimps at Sonso have been observed over the years to feed on several species of monkeys as well as some of the other small mammals ... but this seemed to be a relatively rare occurrence, only reported once or twice a year. However, over the past year the Sonso chimps seem to have developed a taste for the Black and White Colobus monkeys, at times hunting them on a daily basis.... It's definitely the younger adult males who are doing all the hard work.... The group also seems to be getting more proficient, at times even taking on the larger adult monkeys. (BW 2/11/09)

(There are no red colobus monkeys in the Budongo forest.)

By October 2009 an 18-month trend toward hunting produced its star, 16-year-old Hawa, who correspondingly rose from low to high status (BW 10/21/09). In 2013 there were 17 hunts, 19 in 2014, and 11 in 2015, compared to 2.1 hunts per year in the first 8 years of study (Hobaiter et al. 2017:7). For Gombe, Mahale, and Ngogo, I argued that an abrupt intensification of hunting reflects a major problem with preferred foods. Sonso makes it four cases.[9]

Death, Politics, and Sex

Many adult males died 2003–2010.[10] *Pan*icide is suspected in no case. In late 2008 that left three prime males in a group of 70 chimpanzees: Nick, Zefa, and Bwoba (BW 2/21/09). Bwoba was last seen in 2009 with what looked like a bite mark. In mid-March a skeleton with facial features like his was found in the forest (BW 3/17/09, 5/22/09). If, how, Bwoba died is unknown. It might have been political.

Death of so many senior males intensified status competition. Nick deposed Duane in late 2006, but his position was shaky. He was surrounded by seven adolescent and five young adult males (SCC) vying for position (BW 1/27/09, 5/22/09, 10/21/09). Status contests between Nick and Zefa hinged on Bwoba's fickle support. Then Bwoba began to act more independently. Nick a had a reputation for severe violence within the group (BW 1/27/09), and would remain alpha until 2013 (SCC). Nick or Zefa could not kill big Bwoba alone, but young males may have been recruitable. However, since no suspicions of *pan*icide are published, Bwoba is not counted.

These were tense times, violent times, unlike before. Really unusual are killings of *adult females within Sonso*. In 2007, Zana's inferred. In 2008, Lola's observed (Count 4 W-A-F 2007; 3 W-A-F 2008). In 2009, a combination of male and female attackers within Sonso killed Juliet's infant (Count 2-W-I-? 2009) (Wilson et al. 2014a:EDT 3)—a bisexual coalition.

In September 2009 alpha Nick and a lower ranked male attacked young Sonso female Zimba, and tried to grab her recently born son. While other males defended the mother, a female grabbed the infant and killed it with a bite to the neck. She and Nick ate it (BW 9/14/09) (Count 1-W- I-M 2009). This could reflect resource scarcity like other infant killings by females; but could also be Nick intimidating young contenders.

Intergroup Tension

The elimination by late 2008 of all but three prime males meant there was little pushback against exploring outsiders. Prior to 2005 Sonso was gradually shifting and

---

[9] See Hobaiter et al. (2017), for a different sort of human impact explanation.

[10] A sugar guard killed Jambo in 2003. Black fell out of a tree in 2005. Young male Bob disappeared in 2007. Duane "[d]ied a sudden death (within 20 minutes)" in 2008 (no explanation); and Gashom was seen near his body, then never again. Old Maani, very weak, disappeared also in 2008 (SCC).

slightly extending its range to the south and west (Emery Thompson et al. 2006:604). In 2008 the tide turned, with encroachment from their east, which probably means neo-Waibira. Meeting little resistance, those made bolder forays deeper into the Sonso range.

After years of Budongo research, *intergroup clashes finally appear*, with "lots of screaming, stamping and branch shaking; and they can get very aggressive." Alpha Nick generally ran away and others followed. In February 2009, "for the first time it was the Sonso chimps who succeeded in driving away the Eastern group." An eastern female was caught and attacked by Sonso *females*, until Nick came to the outsider's rescue (BW 2/21/09).

This merits emphasis: in Sonso's *only* described intergroup clash, females led the charge. Female aggression against immigrant females is common, but this was something different: a violent attack by females, on one outside female, during an intergroup clash. The demonic image, but with females.

In 2010 outside territorial pressure displaced Sonso's ranging. They moved into swamp lands to their southeast, beyond the network of observation trails, where research follows are extremely difficult. Although hunting was good in the swamp, fruit was scarce. Researchers surmise the move was due to "pressure from their neighbors to the north" (BW 1/19/2010), which then moved in. "[T]he Sonso community has in recent years shifted its range *in the absence of lethal violence*, with areas previously part of its range now home to chimpanzees from another community" (Newton-Fisher and Emery Thompson 2012:48, emphasis added).[11]

After 2010 territorial encroachments eased as subadult males matured into strong adults (BW 1/25/11). (Note that maturation for the following discussion.) Yet *the first probable intergroup adult killing in Budongo history* occurred on May 6, 2011. The adult *female* Zimba was "severely injured" in "an intergroup encounter," and disappeared in a few days. Her 10-year-old son Zak died from his injuries (SCC) (Count 3 O-A-F 2013; 1 O-As-M 2013).

The Deadly 2010s

Almost no detail is available about intensifying human disturbance over this period, but the screws kept tightening.[12] A fire started by people raced through Sonso rangeland in the dry season of 2011 (BW 2/17/2011). "Human pressure on the forest increases with each year" (BW 7/31/2011). I found no descriptions of human impact after that except one telling indicator.

---

[11] These cascading developments led to a decision in January 2011 to habituate a second community. They picked those to the northeast, called "Waibira South" (BW 11/17/2013)—an unclear specification. Waibira South is a very large group. Initial estimates in 2017 put them at about 100–120 individuals, compared to Sonso's 69 (Hobaiter et al. 2017:3).

[12] In an unsolicited e-mail to me, Filippo Aureli disputed my argument about external killings being tied to human disturbance. "At Budongo there is disturbance (school in the middle of the field site), but no intergroup lethal killing" (Aureli, October 23, 2010). I found no other information about a school, but that does suggest intense human impact.

An important part of Sonso diets is decaying pith of raphia, which is high in sodium. By 2009 it was becoming scarce due to harvest for string by local coffee growers (Reynolds et al. 2009). By 2015 it had "all but disappeared from the forest"—meaning local people were all over the Sonso habitat. Simultaneously, Sonso chimpanzees took to eating clay solutions (Reynolds et al. 2015:2).

By 2010 human disturbance was severe, and worsening yearly. The year 2011 was the start of an astonishing wave of internal infant killings that continued until 2018 (where the record ends). By 2013, this propelled Sonso to #2 in total killings (Wilson et al. 2014a:415), and more followed.

A "Highly Infanticidal Population of Chimpanzees"

In Lowe et al.'s long-term study of Sonso (2019:70), there were 46 infant deaths. Fourteen were not from infanticides or were simple disappearances with no indication of violence, leaving 32 "candidates" for killing. Of those, five are categorized as probably *inter*group infanticides, and three of ambiguous origin, (including the two in 1995 that I classified as of unknown origin).

Their focus is on the remaining 24 candidates for *intra*community killings, of which 11 were definite, 4 "almost-certain" with attack seen and infant subsequently died or disappeared, and 9 "suspected" because of observed wounds or other behaviors. I count these as respectively as (1) certain, (2) beyond reasonable doubt, and (4) possible, although two of those I categorize as (5's) hypotheticals, because they are just disappearances. Additionally, they count nine "failed attempts" at infanticide (which do not enter my tally), bringing the total to 33 internal-infant deadly events (2019:73–74).[13] But I also count two internal infanticides that occurred after the after the study closed in 2017 so are not graphed (2019:80). Those deaths are counted here as two (2's).[14]

That makes 26 possible-to-certain internal infanticides over the entire 24 years. Attackers (when seen) were both males (16), females (4), and both in one attack. Over the entire 24-year study period, "[o]f 103 known births, 23% became victims of infanticide" (Lowe et al. 2019:74, 77).

Having already discussed the earlier infanticides, attention here is on late Sonso, 2011–2018, with cases as listed in Lowe 2018, Appendix 2.[15] Over 8 years from 2011 to

---

[13] "30 victims total despite 33 attacks as three infants survived only to be killed in a subsequent attack" (Lowe et al. 2019:8).

[14] A very young within-group male was killed with theatrical violence by a large number of chimpanzees, including a female, in July 2018 (Leroux et al. 2021). The reason this incident merited its own publication is that the infant was albino, and seemed to elicit fear reactions before it was killed, so there might be others. This report comes too late to enter into my tally or any calculations.

[15] Here is the 2011–2018 count, with two-letter codes of mothers replaced by names from Sonso Community data tables. Rose's 5 W-I-F 2011. Oakland's 1 W-I-F 2012. Kalema's 4 W-I-F 2012. Janie's 2 W-I-F 2012. Kutu's 4 W-I-F 2013. Kalema's 2 W-I-M 2013. Oakland's 1 W-I-M 2013. Kewaya's 4 W-I-F 2013. (Up to end of Wilson et al. 2014a coverage.) Janie's 5 W-I-F 2014. Melissa's 4 W-I-F 2014. Katia's 2 W-I-? 2015. Coco's 1 W-I-F 2015. Irene's 1 W-I-M 2016. Mukwano's 1 W-I-? 2016. Deli's 1 W-I-F 2017. Upesi's 1 W-I-F 2017. Mukwano's 4 W-I-? 2017. Ramula's 1 W-I-? 2017. (After study ended:) Unidentified 2 W-I-? 2018. Unidentified 2 W-I-? 2018.

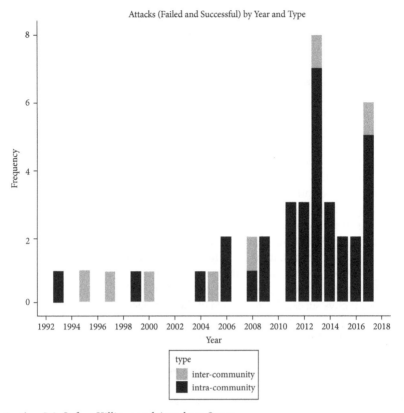

Illustration 5.2 Infant Killings and Attacks at Sonso
Source: Lowe, A.E., Hobaiter, C., Asiimwe, C., et al. (2020). Intra-community infanticide in wild, eastern chimpanzees: A 24-year review. *Primates, 61,* 69–82.

2018, Sonso males likely killed about 18 of their own offspring—three boys, 11 girls, and four of unidentified sex. Based on the Sonso community data tables, for 2011–2018 that looks more like 40%—while human impact got progressively worse, Sonso was displaced into swamp, and took to eating monkeys and clay.

Is It Adaptive?

Lowe et al. (2019) say yes, could be. They disregard the earlier argument (Newton-Fisher 1999) that infant killers reduced the relative strength of neighboring males, and set aside the earlier killings by females after the female immigration, to focus on within-group killing by Sonso males. That is a conundrum for sociobiology, seemingly contradicting increased reproductive success. They consider and reject three adaptive hypotheses: resource competition, meat acquisition, and mate competition. (See them for that.) Better supported they argue, is the sexually selected infanticide hypothesis (SSIH).

Sexually selected infanticide gets direct consideration in Chapter 27. The fundamental idea is that it may be adaptive for males to kill offspring of other males, if that means that mothers come more quickly into sexual receptivity, and then are likely to mate with the killers. The SSIH has a strict condition that "must" apply: "the probability that the male had sired the infant(s) is zero or close to zero" (Van Schaik 2000:35).

Their position rises upon facts consistent with SSIH: most killers are male, most victims are very young, usually the mothers are not seriously injured, and on average conceived about seven times more quickly than if the infant survived (Lowe et al. 2018:77). But there is no data on the two central issues: could the killers be victims' fathers; and were killers more likely to sire subsequent offspring? Regular paternity assessment for Sonso ended by 2008, and young carcasses were rarely if ever genotyped. So Lowe et al. make their argument by going to the paradigm.

They start with the broad generalization that male rank correlates with reproductive success. (True, but with many variations and exceptions—see Part IX, note 8 in Chapter 27). They posit that infant killings could be consistent with SSI if: the male breeding hierarchy is very steep; and there is much political tumult and turnover at the top (Lowe et al. 2020:79). Formerly shut out but newly risen males might increase their reproductive success by getting rid of their predecessors' newborns and quickly impregnating newly cycling females—and speed would be essential if another turnover is likely. They formulate this as P_I being greater than p.[16]

In the absence of direct evidence supporting this calculation, the theory itself becomes the evidence. "Unfortunately, we do not have the necessary long-term data on male hierarchy" to test this proposition (2018:79). But the "high rates of infanticide at Sonso suggest that these males experience steeper or more unstable hierarchies than do those in other communities" (2020:7). It *should* be so.

There is no reason to expect a particularly steep hierarchy within Sonso.[17] In an earlier study, paternity was widespread, not limited to those at the top. Six adult males fathered 18 offspring (Newton-Fisher et al. 2010). If the "odd fathers" previously discussed are added in, the spread of sires is much greater, down to young males with newly descended testicles. Because of "female dispersal" there was "low paternity certainty in this community—even for an alpha male" (2020:77). Under those circumstances—and nothing indicates they changed—any attacker would risk killing his own offspring, yet remain in great competition to sire the replacement.

During the infanticidal period, attackers were not confined to top ranks, but included most adults, 10 out of 12 adult males, 2011–2018 (SCC).[18] Moreover, there is

---

[16] "A male rising in rank increases P_I and, where hierarchies are steep (Kaburu and Newton-Fisher 2015) and high ranking males effectively lower-ranking males' mating access, a male who rises rapidly in rank will experience a large increase in P_I relative to a small value for p, and thus have a high resultant $P_I - p$. (Lowe et al. 2020:79).

[17] Kaburu and Newton-Fisher (2015:3, 67–68), analyzing directionality of grooming—*not mating*—in 2003–2004 when males were *not* infanticidal, found the hierarchy was relatively steep, and predict it would be shallower with a great number of males. During the infanticidal time, there were more adult males than earlier (11 v. 8).

[18] By age and number of observed attacks: Nick (b. 1982, 1), Squibs (b 1991, 1), Musa (b. 1992, 2), Hawa (b. 1993, 3), Kato (b. 1993, 1), Simon (b. 1993, 1), Kwezi (b. 1995), Zalu (b. 1995, 3), Pascal (b. 1998, 1), and Frank (b. 1999, 4) (Lowe et al. 2019:8; SCC). Two adult males, Zefa (b. 1982) and Zig (b. 1997) were not identified in any attack. Note that 13 attacks were not seen, so this record is incomplete.

no pattern of new alphas killing predecessors offspring. Only 2 of 10 well-described, possibly deadly attacks are by newly ascendant alphas.[19]

Nothing here suggests that "the probability that the male had sired the infant(s) is zero or close to zero." Although "we cannot entirely rule out the possibility that males are killing their own offspring," it would be "highly maladaptive for males to practice infanticide if they were regularly killing their own infant and the behavior would be selected against" (Lowe et al. 2020:63). The theory is the evidence. But males killing their own offspring is known at Mahale and Gombe. With most of Sonso's adult males involved in killing 23%–40% of the groups' infant over 8 years, how could it be otherwise at Sonso?

A Display Violence and Human Impact

The display violence hypothesis is that within a strong male hierarchy, exaggerated and even deadly violence against nonthreatening individuals, may be *displayed* to intimidate status rivals. Two facilitating factors are turmoil near the top, and the presence of particularly aggressive males. Either may or may not be connected to human impact.

Broadly, the 2011–2018 killings fit that profile. The very young victims could not harm the attackers. In 15 of 20 witnessed attacks, it was not defended except by the mother (Lowe 2020:Appendix 2). Continuing to assault the mother could risk injury, but mostly they were not hurt.

Turmoil? Yes. After years of relative stability—Nick had been alpha since 2006—many immature males were newly prime, a recipe for vying and conflict. Hawa deposed Nick in March 2013; Musa deposed Hawa in December 2016 (and was still on top at least a year later) (see note 20).

Particularly aggressive individuals? Yes. Those participating in multiple infant attacks otherwise were noted among adults for aggressiveness (see note 19). Nick (five attacks) compensated for his fear of outsiders by being especially violent inside the group (BW 1/27/09). Hawa (six attacks) pioneered monkey hunting (BW 10/21/2019). I found no description of Musa, though he did topple Hawa.

Young Frank (five attacks) by age 13 had a reputation for trouble (BW 2/5/2012). In one of only two described attacks (Lower et al. 2019:5) he exhibits the theatricality found in other display killings. "The infant's belly is ripped open. At 10:50, Frank begins to eat the infant. After a few minutes, he swings the carcass against the undergrowth and throws it from him. No other individuals intervened or became involved."

Thus the infant killings broadly align with display violence.

Yet in the number of participants and killings, it seems beyond display violence seen elsewhere. Mahale had eight possible-to-certain infant killings from 1977 to

---

[19] Nick was alpha until March 2013, Hawa from July 2014 to December 2016, and Musa became alpha in January 2017 (SCC). While alpha, Nick joined in the 2009 infanticide, but also participated in one after being deposed as alpha. Hawa had one during his reign and two after, Musa one before and one as alpha. Frank had four although he was never alpha.

1993, about 16 years. Sonso had 20 in just 8 years.[20] Which brings us back to the great unknown of anthropogenic psychological disturbance. That seems likely in highly disturbed late Gombe, with multiple infanticides and other attacks by alpha Ferdinand; or in tourist-inundated Mahale, with the killing of alpha Pimu, and Darwin snatching and eating Devota's infant at birth.

Given the all-encompassing and multiplicative manifestations of human impact—all very poorly described—it is impossible to draw any *direct* connection between disturbance and infant killings. But can that context be ignored?[21]

Which perspective seems more plausible? That an evolved reproductive strategy led to Sonso's unprecedented infanticidal streak; or that it expressed vying for status in an environment churned by increasingly impactful human disturbance?[22]

Adaptationism and Historical Disruption at Budongo

Answering that question has implications beyond SSI or Budongo. In the proadaptationist/anti-human impact statement of Wilson et al. (2014a), their strongest evidence for adaptation correlates frequency of all killings and population density (Chapter 29). They assume population density reflects resource abundance, and is unrelated to human disturbance. After Ngogo, the weightiest case in this correlation is Sonso, with density in 2013 up to a towering $9.2/km^2$ and killings at .8/year (Wilson et al. 2014a:Extended Data Figure 1a). Add in 12 more Sonso infant killings from 2014 to 2018 (2.4/year) and the association of density and killing would be stronger. On the other hand if both population density and frequent *pan*icides reflect human disruption, this strong support for adaptationism would instead be powerful support for the HIH.

Budongo is bad for the demonic paradigm of violent males attacking neighbors. While some Sonso researchers endorse it, their own findings challenge it. Take pioneer Vernon Reynolds. He acknowledged the consensus that emerged after his early field work. "Fierce community hostility has now come to be recognized as a standard feature of intercommunity relationships in chimpanzees" (Reynolds 2002:88). Still, after more years of field observation, he stayed skeptical. "What really seems to happen if food is artificially provided is that increasing competition leads to outbreak of violence, as Power suggested" (Reynolds 2005:25–26). From what he saw, males might follow "a strategy of belonging to two communities" (2005:31)–contrary to the demonic perspective.

---

[20] And there was more strange behavior. In September 2017, as neo-Waibira comes into research focus, female Monika and the group alpha ate Monika's infant—though nothing indicates they killed it. (Not counted). Fedurek et al. (2020) discount human disturbance because both chimpanzees were already habituated. (So?) Their explanation is "maternal detachment."

[21] An apt comparison is the stunningly aberrant violence of elephants, when their exquisite sociality is atomized by poaching, culling, habitat destruction, and relocation. In one place, intraspecific killing "accounts for nearly 90% of all male deaths, compared with 6% in relatively unstressed communities" (Bradshaw et al. 2005:807; and see Bradshaw 2009; Siebert 2006).

[22] A late entry: in September 2017 in (neo-)Waibira, a recently born infant was seen in the mouth of a juvenile male. The alpha took and began to eat it. The presumed mother Mon begged for meat, and ate some. The authors suspect infanticide, so it is included (Count 4 W-I-? 2017).

His and others' pre-paradigmatic observations of different groups meeting and mixing were never reevaluated and rejected for Sonso–just ignored. Even so, in Sonso for years non-violent avoidance, vocalization, and mutual respect ruled inter-group relations–standard ethology. After years, heavily impacted neo-Waibira encroached on Sonso range and eventually moved part way in, without killing. The *only* adult male killing ever was internal, just when Sonso should need defenders against neighbors, contrary to the RCRH.

Many outside females came to Sonso but none due to intergroup violence. Some brought along mostly-grown males of ambiguous natality. Females were widely ranging, gregarious, and aggressive. They cooperated in coalitional attacks on infants, on Sonso males, and in leading the only intergroup clash described. Early on, males were comparatively non-aggressive, except for a few status contenders. In more disrupted times, males killed their own young and within-group females.

The RCRH is flatly contradicted by killings of males. Between-group is adolescent Zak. Within group are adult Zesta and seven possible-to-certain infanticides—8:1 against the RCRH. The RCH is well supported. Early on with food abundance and without centripetal pressure, researchers found openness and nonaggression. With rising density in curtailed habitat, females killed infants, groups clashed on edges, young males became avid hunters, and older males turned highly infanticidal.

Human impact shaped all these conditions. Early on, Sonso enjoyed food abundance increased by old regime regulated lumbering. That gave way to the nearby habitat devastation and displacements of pitsawing. Snare poaching and killing chimpanzees at forest edges claimed many. Disruption kept getting worse, but in undescribed ways, which is the largely unreported historical context for Sonso's unprecedented infanticidal streak. Although associated with political instability and particularly belligerent males, as in display violence, its duration and scale—23%–40% of all births over 8 years—suggests psychological disturbance as well. After decades of worsening human damage, the peaceable chimpanzees of early Budongo became murderous.

Isn't it time to merge history with theorization of violence?

Postscript

In February and March 2019 a respiratory infection of unknown origin hit both Sonso and Waibira, affecting all ages, visibly sickening 59 of Sonso's total of 67, and 67 of Waibira's 94. At least three Sonso adult males and one female infant succumbed. Fecal samples of affected chimpanzees with visible helminths suggest they were already immune-compromised before the outbreak (Asiimwe 2019).

PART VI
ELEVEN SMALLER CASES

18
Eastern Chimpanzees, *Pan troglodytes schweinfurthii*

Prologue

The principle chimpanzee research sites are Gombe, Mahale, Kibale, Budongo, and Tai. Part VI passes quickly through 11 more research sites across Africa, garnering pertinent information. The central question, as always, is whether chimpanzees are naturally prone to kill outsiders when they can do so with impunity. Part VI documents *variation* in ecology, demography, human impact, social organization, territorial orientation, intergroup relations, and violence. Combined with the five major sites, this tour documents chimpanzees' situationally flexible *adaptability*, rather than one chimpanzee pattern, Gombe or otherwise.

Subspecies and Geography

McGrew (2017:239–240) counts over 120 field study sites, excluding bonobos (and see Nishida et al. 2010:13–14). Most produced little or no published information relevant for this book, but 11 locations have enough to discuss. Narratives for each will vary according to available evidence. Order follows geography and phylogeny.

Estimates of total chimpanzee numbers vary greatly (Butynski 2003:8; Oates 2006:104). The World Wildlife Foundation (n.d.) put it at 150,000–250,000. Chimpanzees were classified into three subspecies (Bjork et al. 2010; Gonder et al. 2006). East African chimpanzees, *Pan troglodytes schweinfurthii*, live north and east of the Congo and Ubangi Rivers. Gombe, Mahale, Kibale, and Budongo are East African. So are four locations with limited information, Kalinzu and Toro-Semliki in Uganda, Kahuzi-Biega in the Democratic Republic of Congo, and Ugalla/Filabanga in Tanzania, all discussed in this chapter. West of the Ubangi River is the much less studied subspecies, Central African chimpanzees, *Pan troglodytes troglodytes*. Usable reports come from Conkouati-Douli and Goualougo in the Republic of the Congo, and Lope and Loango in Gabon, all in Chapter 19. West of the Niger are West African chimpanzees, *Pan troglodytes verus*. This includes four important research sites, Mt. Assirik (Niokola Koba), Fongoli, and Bossou in the Republic of Guinea, and Tai in

Ivory Coast. Those are covered in Chapter 20, except for Tai, which gets its own Part VII.[1,2]

The genus *Pan*'s second species, *Pan paniscus*—bonobos—are located south of the great bend in the Congo River, with ancestors possibly crossing during exceptionally dry periods (Takemoto et al. 2015). A conventional separation date of *paniscus/troglodytes* is 2.5 myr, but newer estimates whittle that down considerably, with a range as old as 2.6 million and as young as 810,000 (Bjork et al. 2010:619; Cassell et al. 2008; Langergraber et al. 2012:15718; Lobon et al. 2016:2027; Won and Hey 2005:304).[3]

A relative comparison may be helpful. Very roughly, the chimpanzee last common ancestor (LCA) is a little less than half the age of the chimpanzee/bonobo LCA (Prado-Martinez et al. 2013:474). For reference, the *Homo/Pan* divergence is currently pegged at anywhere from 4.6 to 13 million years ago (Caswell et al. 2008; Chen and Li 2001:452; Langergraber et al. 2012:15718; Patterson et al. 2006). Take your pick.

Kalinzu

Measuring 137 km^2, Kalinzu Forest is southwest of Kibale in Uganda. Contiguous with the Maramagambo Forest, the two amount to 580 km^2, the largest forest block left in Uganda. Kalinzu was surveyed in 1992 by Chie Hashimoto, Takeshi Furuichi, and colleagues. Habituation began in 1997, and research in 2001. Three, then four groups were identified. Most of the 50 or so members of the focal M group were known by 2001 (Hashimoto 1998; Hashimoto and Furuichi 2006:247–249).

Like Budongo, Kalinzu is a Forest Reserve, and more or less open for exploitation. Most of Kalinzu has been logged since the early 1970s, but as at Budongo, regrowth includes many chimpanzee food trees, thus providing a more solid and stable year-round food base in disturbed compared to undisturbed forest (Furuichi et al. 2001). About 100 people lived around a sawmill in the western part of the forest. Pitsawing occurs in many places. Chimpanzees and humans have had contact for decades (Hashimoto 1998; 1999). Nest counts in 1992 produced a density estimate of 2.4–4.7/km^2, with higher densities in regrowth areas (Hashimoto 1998).[4]

Kalinzu chimpanzees suffer greatly from snares. By the mid-1990s, 56% of adult males had missing or paralyzed hands, feet, and digits (Hashimoto 1999). Kalinzu researchers and others began a snare removal program in 2005 (Hashimoto et al.

---

[1] A fourth subspecies barely survives between Western and Central chimpanzees, the east Nigeria/west Cameroon chimpanzees, *Pan troglodytes ellioti* (originally *vellerosus*) (Bjork et al. 2010; Gonder et al. 2011). This is the most endangered, with 3,000–8,000 survivors scattered in dwindling patches of forest, targeted by hunters (Beck and Chapman 2008; Fowler and Summer 2007; Ghobrial et al. 2010; Greengrass 2009; Hughes et al. 2011). They do not yield information for this book.

[2] Genetically, Eastern and Central African chimpanzees are closely related. The *schweinfurthii* clade is nested within a broader *troglodytes* lineage (Bjork et al. 2010:621). Those two and *verus* are farther apart. Different methods and assumptions put the east/west split—the LCA of all chimpanzees—from 422,000 to 1,026,000 years ago (Becquet et al. 2007:623; Gagneux et al. 1999:5081; Goldberg 1998:238). More recent findings put that LCA at 410–780,000 (Lobon et al. 2016:2028).

[3] de Manuel et al. (2016) suggest limited gene flow from bonobos to ancestors of Central and Eastern chimpanzees 200,000–550,000 years ago.

[4] 15 years later that was revised downward, to 1.67/km^2, but M group's numbers counted at 68 (Hashimoto et al. 2007).

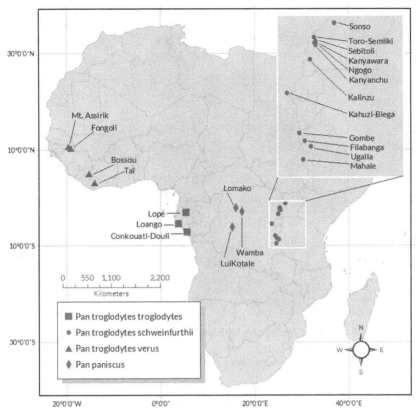

Illustration 6.1 Chimpanzee Subspecies and Bonobo Research Sites
Caption: Current and former chimpanzee and bonobo field research sites across Africa. Site coordinates were determined through self-reported locations drawn from publications produced by each site.
Source: Map created by Jillian Rutherford.

2007); and an outreach program through local schools, promoting the value of conservation (Kuhar et al. 2010).

Like Sonso, Kalinzu's M group subverts the Mars vs. Venus dichotomy of chimpanzees and bonobos. Like bonobos, females range as widely as males do (Hashimoto and Furuichi 2015). Kalinzu females copulate *a lot*, more frequently than at other chimpanzee sites, or even bonobos. One female copulated 39 times in 343 minutes.

Among males there is little internal aggression, and a weak status hierarchy.

> Adult males did not interact aggressively, except when young males approached the estrous females and were chased away by older ones.... There seemed to be no relationship between dominance rank and copulation rate of males.... [T]he dominance rank among males was unclear except that DO was the alpha male.... DO did not

Illustration 6.2 Kalinzu Chimpanzee with Snare Injury
Source: Hashimoto C., Cox D., & Furuichi, T. 2007. Snare removal for conservation of chimpanzees in the Kalinzu Forest Reserve, Uganda. *Pan Africa News,* 14(1), 8–11.

copulate so frequently as compared to other males, and some young adult males copulated more frequently than DO did. (Hashimoto and Furuichi 2006:252–253)

Kalinzu is a caution against generalizations.

An Adult Male Killing

Despite this resemblance to bonobos, in September 2003 the western group killed an adult male of the eastern, M group. One day researchers heard much pant-hooting and screaming for 10 minutes—the kind of ruckus that accompanies severe violence. Two weeks later near that spot researchers found a mostly skeletalized adult male carcass. A male, Nui of M group, was never seen after the commotion.

> In 2003, the M group home range was narrower than in the previous year, and we frequently observed a neighboring group in the area from which the M group had retreated. The carcass was found on the boundary of the M group home range in this area. We also observed three agonistic encounters with a neighboring group near the boundary. One case occurred on the same day that we observed the carcass, 100 m away from it. We also observed patrolling by the M group males more often than we had in previous study periods. Based on these circumstances, we postulated that

Nui had been killed in an agonistic interaction between the groups. (Hashimoto and Furuichi 2005:1)

Agreed (Count 3-O-A-M, 2003).

This is one of few between-group adult male killings reported outside of Gombe and Kibale.[5] Why did it happen? Hashimoto and Furuichi (2005:2) provide the critical context: "The neighboring group appears to have shifted its home range eastward, following deforestation in their home range" where the sawmill is located. "Our study also suggests that a territory shift or expansion caused an inter-group killing in chimpanzees." Resource competition hypothesis + human impact hypothesis (RCH + HIH).

Toro-Semliki

Another project began in 1996 at arid Toro-Semliki Wildlife Reserve in Uganda. Sleeping sickness between 1898 and 1915 and subsequent evacuation depopulated the area. Gazetted as a game reserve in 1929, most of its 548 km^2 are grasslands, but there are swamps and riverine forests where chimpanzees spend most time. From the 1950s villages grew around and even inside the Reserve. One on a peninsula into Lake Albert today has thousands of residents, working in commercial fishing.

The Reserve was a battlefront in the 1978–1979 Uganda/Tanzania war, with great slaughter of wildlife. Into the early 1990s poachers had free rein. Environmentally degraded, the Reserve would have been de-gazetted if not for the forerunner of the Uganda Wildlife Authority, working with the Semliki Safari Lodge. Poaching declined. Kevin Hunt was given the opportunity to survey chimpanzees in 1996.

Then more human war—the Ugandan army against guerrillas—erupted unpredictably over the years, fueled by the discovery of oil reserves. For research the disruption of war was compounded by off-and-on funding, and the unsurprising fact that local chimpanzees were extremely wary of people. In 2005 Hunt established his research camp, and observation times increased from minutes to hours per month, though still little compared to some other sites (Hunt 2000; Hunt and McGrew 2002:37, 41, 44, 46, 48; Patrick et al. 2011:56–58, 65–68; Semliki Chimpanzee Project n.d.a). Given this heavy human impact, what seems surprising is that "we have observed no chimpanzees with snare injuries" (Hunt 2000). Perhaps soldiers do not need snares with all their guns.

Regional Groupings—How Separate?

Early surveys suggested four chimpanzee groups within the Reserve. The principle study group was along the Mugiri River. Their home range was about 72.1 km^2, and

---

[5] A decade later Kalinzu researchers infer that M group killed a foreign adult male in February 2013 (Wilson et al. 2014:Extended Data Table 2). With no details or context, nothing more can be said (Count 4 O-A-M 2013).

they were an estimated 30 males and total community of about 104 (Samson 2012:358) (producing a density of 1.4/km²). Also visited were those of the Wasa River.

Notably, "all injuries, ear bites, facial scars, missing digits and other healed wounds are inexplicably rare at Mugiri" (Hunt 2000; Hunt and McGrew 2002:46). In 2002 I e-mailed Dr. Hunt to ask about the evident lack of violence. He replied, on the record:

> I think some pant-hooting we have heard is back-and-forth between the two nearest communities, the Wasa and the Mugiri that is typical of territorial calling of chimps elsewhere. We have not yet habituated the Mugiri community, much less the Wasa, so this is mostly speculation. However, the behavior of males I've seen pant-hooting in this circumstance, including piloerection and anxious embracing suggesting exactly the same sort of territorialism seen at Gombe. I think the lack of scarring of Mugiri chimps is related to their large community area and low population density.... Mugiri chimps, then, are an exception.

A subsequent study connected low population density and low levels of internal aggression. "Male chimpanzees at Semliki seem to experience less frequent aggression (charging, displays, chases and attacks) than do males" than at Gombe and Kanyawara (Samson and Hunt 2014:16). I don't doubt that high dispersal and lower direct resource competition associates with less internal aggression. More interesting is the difference between the 2002 understanding of intergroup relations and what developed later about Mugiri and Wasa, raising the possibility of peaceful interaction between local groups.

> Chimpanzees are seen sporadically near the lodge, in the Wasa Riverine forest. We once thought that this was a separate community.... We have long known that these chimpanzees disappear for months at a time. For years we thought they were disappearing to the west, but after years of tracking we have concluded that they are actually the same chimpanzees we see in the Mugiri, or at least some of them are.... Still, we are not absolutely certain the Wasa chimpanzees are part of the same community as our study group. They appear rarely enough in the Wasa that we have never gotten a positive ID on any individual there. (Semliki Chimpanzee Project n.d.b)

A combined community would number about "150 individuals, among the largest known"—or enough for two or three normal sized unit-groups.

This raises once again the possibility of peaceful interactions between local populations. Were it not for the Great Revision, Mugiri and Wasa would be seen as geographically separate clusters that sometimes mixed, as at early Gombe and Budongo. They were reinterpreted as one mega-group because of the paradigmatic assumption that chimpanzee groups *do not* mix.

The Gombe paradigm shapes perceptions. On a blog, Hunt (2011) responded to another blogger who questioned the violent proclivities of chimpanzees, under the title "Is Lethal Violence an Integral Part of Chimpanzee Society? Like it or not, yes."[6]

---

[6] Not far from Kalinzu is Uganda's Kyambura Gorge, called in tourist promotions the "Valley of the Apes." I found next to nothing about its chimpanzees, but Wilson et al. (2014) include them, and code them as the

Kahuzi-Biega

Arid Toro-Semliki expands the ecological spectrum of chimpanzee habitats. So does high-altitude Kahuzi-Biega National Park in eastern Democratic Republic of Congo. Officially gazetted in 1970 and expanded in 1975 to 6,700 km^2 Kahuzi-Biega is montane forest at 1,800 to 3,308 meters (Spira et al. 2019:137; Yamagiwa et al. 2011:204). Really upland. Kanyunyi Basabose spent 60 months in the highlands from 1991 to 2000, observing chimpanzees on 729 days. He found three chimpanzee groups, with 13, 20, and 27 individuals. "They were located in different regions and their home ranges did not overlap" (Basabose 2005:34). His focal community had a very low density of about .13/km^2, consistent with environmental limitations and scarcity of fruits (Basabose 2004:218; 2005:37, 48; and see Yamigawa and Basabose 2006).

> It seems that Kahuzi chimpanzees form small communities with few adult males and avoid each other, being separated by unusable areas that mostly contained bamboo forests or swamps. The limited number of adult males per unit-group at Kahuzi may account for this avoidance strategy. (2005:50)

With that information, little can be surmised about relations between these small, ecologically distributed clusters.

Human fighting disrupted research in 1996 (Inogwabini et al. 2000:275; Prunier 2009; Yamagiwa et al. 2011:206, 217). Bushmeat hunting by artisanal miners, together with militia activity, eliminated many Kahuzi Biega chimpanzees and gorillas by 2014 (Spira et al. 2017:5). Apes accustomed to people were often killed, so when research resumed it did not habituate, but relied on indirect approaches such as nest counts and feces analysis—which may soon be the norm in *Pan* field studies. That data on one local group 2011–2013, found a population of about 32 individuals, with 13 males. Y haplotypes of males match (Basabose et al. 2015). But the other two montane groups were not sampled, so whether they shared that haplotype is unknown. Intergroup relations remain an open question.

Ugalla and Filabanga

Ugalla is a recently surveyed site (Moore et al. 2015) in Tanzania, in arid interior lands between Mahale and Gombe, with an estimated density of .25/km^2 over a hypothesized range of 268 km^2. Male haplotypes and autosomal genotypes garnered from fecal samples indicate 67 males, which researchers assign to at least three communities. Their theoretical point is that males are philopatric and divide into distinct, hostile groups, even in very dry environments—antagonistic group separation is a phylogenetic inheritance.

---

fourth most disturbed *Pan* study location. The local group has just three adult males, but in 2011 one adult male is tallied as an observed within community killing (Extended Data Table 3) (Count 2 W-A-M 2013). With merely that to go on, this case is more consistent with HIH than RCRH.

That's one possibility.

> Another possibility is that geographic clusters of Y-chromosome haplotypes do not represent different communities, but instead represent male neighborhoods within a single community.... However, this "reproductive neighborhood" explanation is unlikely to explain the geographic pattern of Y-chromosome variation we observed at Ugalla, where haplotype clusters were much too geographically distant from one another, e.g., 20 km between haplotypes C and D, to represent male neighborhoods within the same community, unless community home range was exceptionally large. (Moore et al. 2015:391–392)

A very large range is very possible. Mt. Assirik and Fongoli, to come, both show one group using a very large territory. Toro-Semliki and Kahuzi-Biega show the possibility of distinct local subgroups within a much larger area. No theoretical conclusions can be drawn.

Near to Ugalla is arid and seasonally parched Filabanga, intermittently observed in the 1960s dawn of field *panology*. By ecology and phylogeny, Filabanga and Ugalla should be similar to each other. Early observations support the position argued here, that chimpanzees are very flexible and *adaptable*, rather than manifesting a specific inherited *adaptation* toward violent exclusivity.

Within a space of some 450 km^2 (Itani 1980:36), "[a]reas where food is plentiful are shared by two or more unit groups of chimpanzees" (Kano 1971:229). As seasons changed major group migrations occurred, with 43 chimpanzees once counted traveling along a ridge. After a group migration, entire areas were left with only a few resident chimpanzees for months at a time (Itani and Suzuki 1967:357–365; Kano 1971:238–242).

Of course, early Gombe and Budongo also indicate that geographically separate (but nearby) neighborhoods of philopatric males sometimes coalesced. It seems unwise to project hostile, exclusive local groups into areas like Ugalla where so little is known.

19
Central Chimpanzees, *Pan troglodytes troglodytes*

The Ubangi River in the northwestern Democratic Republic of Congo is an impassible divide, *schweinfurthii* to its east and *troglodytes* to its west. Known populations are dwindling through disease, hunting, and deforestation. But the good news is that total numbers are greater than originally estimated, rising considerably to 128,700 (Strindberg et al. 2018:1, 6).

Behaviorally, "studies of *P.t.t.* continue to play catch-up to longer-running studies to the east and west, in terms of social relations and ranging" (McGrew 2017:239). But great discoveries may be expected from the vast Bili-Uere "behavioral realm in the Northern Republic of Congo" (Hicks et al. 2019). My own review of published findings from there was dropped for length, and because they weren't pertinent to this book's main themes—other than to further demonstrate great behavioral plasticity.

But four *troglodytes troglodytes* research sites include reports of intergroup relations that well-frame the extremes of the disturbed and the pristine. In the Republic of Congo is Goualougo, nearly pristine; and Conkouati-Douli, a totally unnatural captive release experiment. In Gabon, chimpanzees of Lope were in flight before an advancing timber line, but Loango is advertised as an untouched ecological paradise. Loango is especially important because early reports seem to provide an example of an intergroup adult killing in an undisturbed context. I argue instead that this killing was by a leopard. Very recent findings indicate widespread violence, including attacks on gorillas, which seem related to global climate change.

Goualougo

The Goualougo Triangle is within the Nouabale-Ndoki National Park (NNNP), established in 1993. The NNNP is part of the Sangha River Tri-National Conservation Area, including 36,236 km² spanning Republic of Congo, Cameroon, and the Central African Republic. The expanse is lightly populated by humans. The Kabo Logging Concession allowed lumbering since the 1970s, and the Goualougo Triangle was part of that Concession, but separated from the rest by rivers and swamps. Demonstration of its special conservation value resulted in the Triangle being added to the Park in 2003, yet some annexed area remained scheduled for timber extraction (Gillespie et al. 2009:558–560; Morgan et al. 2006:154).

Primate research began in 1999 when NNN Park director, ecologist J. Michael Fay, invited experienced field investigator Dave Morgan to document the importance of the Triangle (Quammen 2003:95–102). In 2000, Crickette Sanz joined Morgan (Sanz 2004:59). The Triangle had little human presence for many years. The closest village is about 50 km. away. There were no campsites or paths, not even machete cuts on trees. Since watercourses circumscribe long approaches to the forest, new entry could be monitored (Sanz 2004:57–61).

A research goal was to estimate chimpanzee and gorilla densities for four areas: before and after, next to, and protected from projected logging, plus one area geographically insulated from scheduled logging (Morgan et al. 2006:154). These chimpanzees were "naive," not afraid of people. Some ran away, but more were curious about the people in their midst (Morgan and Sanz 2003; Sanz 2003). In one early encounter the chimpanzees intently observed the observers, building night nests directly over the camp, and descending in the morning to watch the people build a fire and make breakfast (Foer 2010:1). They had not been taught what other chimpanzees learned the hard way: humans are bad news. They also have an exceptional repertoire of tool making and use. These qualities were so remarkable that Jane Goodall trekked in to see these chimpanzees firsthand (Quammen 2003), a visit that "was the first at another study site other than her own in the forests of Gombe National Park" (Washington University 2003:5).

Moto

From February 1999 to December 2003, Morgan and Sanz booked 911 hours of minimally disturbing observation, identifying 198 individuals in seven communities. Their focus is the Moto community, about 54 individuals, with 10 adult males, 18 adult females (Sanz 2004:59–73; Sanz et al. 2004:569), and a density of $2.23/km^2$, which makes it middling size and density, but high for central African forests (Morgan et al. 2006:172).

Moto offers more nondemonic sociology. Individual associations split into northern and southern neighborhoods. Three pairs of dyadic associations cross between them, and one individual has multiple connections to the other half (Sanz 2004:92). This evokes early Gombe and Busingiro, but goes directly against the post-Revision Gombe model of complete separation.

Not Demonic

Undisrupted Moto was generally unaggressive. Within groups, "Aggression was rarely observed in the Goualougo Triangle (n = 47) and most consisted of directed threats (72.3%) [by males at females]. It is interesting to note that in 911 hours of observation, only four agonistic interactions were seen between adult females and one between adult males. None of these contests were over access to food" (Sanz 2004:142). Between groups:

> We have not seen any instances of severe inter-community aggression and identified individuals in the main study community have been accounted for at regular intervals since 1999 (with the exception of two very elderly adults who presumably

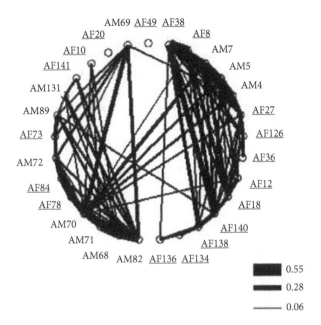

Illustration 6.3 Goualougo Sociogram of Individual Associations
Caption: Sociogram for all adult dyads in the Moto Community with minimum association level of 0.10.

Source: Sanz, C.M. (2004). *Behavioral ecology of chimpanzees in a central African forest:* Pan troglodytes troglodytes *in the Goualougo Triangle, Republic of Congo*. Washington University in St. Louis ProQuest Dissertations Publishing.

died from natural causes). Minor injuries have occasionally been observed, such as torn ears, puncture wounds on the foot, and scrapes on the mouth. These could have resulted from either conflicts within or between communities, but we have no direct evidence of intercommunity agonism or raids from direct observations. Border patrols consisting of the community's prime adult males have occasionally been observed, but the most common inter-community interactions consisted of vocal displays or volleys across community boundaries. (Sanz 2004:137)

Moving Forward, Ambiguously

By 2006 observations surpassed 2,000 hours (Sanz and Morgan 2007:421–422), and Moto was up to 71 individuals (Sanz and Morgan 2013:5). There is no further discussion of aggression or intergroup relations, but Wilson et al.'s (2014) Extended Data Tables list a killing of a Moto infant by outsiders (Count 4 O-I-M 2005) and one suspected internal infanticide (Count 5 O-I-? 2006).

By 2010 logging cleared much of Zone D across a river. A *National Geographic* reporter came to see these still undisturbed, peaceable apes. "What if everywhere scientists have thought they were observing chimps in their natural state, they've actually been studying behavior distorted by the presence of humans?" Then he ambiguously suggests times were a'changing. "Humans don't necessarily have to be clear-cutting forests for our presence to distort primate behavior. Even selective logging and casual hunting can throw chimp society into disarray if it pushes groups into conflict or decreases the number of termite mounds where they can fish" (Foer 2010:3). End of story, so far.

Conkouati-Douli

The second *troglodytes* research site in the Republic of Congo exemplifies an enormous challenge to chimpanzee conservation: what to do with captured wild chimpanzees, many young orphans. One response was by HELP, Habitat Ecologique et Liberte des Primates (Farmer et al. 2006; Goosens et al. 2005; Tutin et al. 2001). They gradually prepared young wild-born chimpanzees for independence, and released them into Conkouati-Douli National Park, an expanse of over half a million hectares managed by the Congo government and the Wildlife Conservation Society. Most were 6 to 10 years old, and project managers hoped their youth would buffer them from attacks by resident chimpanzees. The release area—The Triangle—was about 20 km^2 mostly bounded by water, and lightly used by resident chimpanzees. Starting in 1996, in stages over 4 years, 37 individuals were released and monitored daily using radio collars.

Some females associated with local chimpanzees, and four may have joined them. A 9-year-old female was killed by other released females (Goosens et al. 2005:469) (Count 1-W-J-F, 2002). A released female disappeared after a group clash (Count 3-O-I-F 1999). The 10 released males fared worse.

A 6-year-old fled on release, his collar found 3 weeks later near a skull and nests a few weeks old (2005:466) (Count 3-O-J-M 1997). A male was attacked by wild chimpanzees in 1999, leaving part of his anus missing. He required surgery. A second attack in 2000 was followed by a third, which killed him, at 9 (Count 1-O-As-M 1999). A 10-year-old male disappeared shortly after a group attack by wild chimpanzees (Count 4-O-As-M 1999). An infant male is reported killed (Count 4-O-I-M 2002). A 12-year-old suffered so many wounds in five attacks, by both released and resident chimpanzees, he likely would have died without surgery. A 10-year-old also recovered after surgery (Count *3-O-As-M 1997–2002, *4-O-As-M 2002).

> [A]ll but one of the 10 released males were attacked by wild chimpanzees.... In contrast, no females are known to have been seriously injured or killed by wild chimpanzees. However, three of six babies (one male and two females) born to released females disappeared during interactions with wild chimpanzees, and seem likely to have been victims of infanticide. (2001:467) (Count *one* 3-O-I-M, *two* 3-O-I-F, 2002–2004?)

Citing Gombe and Mahale, Goosens et al. believe these events support the rival coalition reduction hypothesis (RCRH), since more males were victims than females.

Yet direct resource competition is suspected. Because of elevated population density brought by the releases, the area might be "saturated" (2005:471).

This is the most artificial situation imaginable—albeit undertaken with the best intentions. A large number young individuals were dropped into a group's range. They had not formed a community themselves. Many additional attacks occurred *among* those released, and increased over time. Earlier "releasees" attacked later "releasees," with females doing much of the damage (2005:469). This highly unnatural situation is unmistakably the result of human activity.

Thankfully, the released group and other added individuals to a total of 53, eventually stabilized. Relations with neighbors are not further described, but those introduced developed a fission-fusion pattern, with association frequencies derived from batches and places of initial release (Le Hellaye et al. 2010). They diversified their diet (Renaud et al. 2013). It seems to be working.

Lope

Our tour now goes to Gabon, and first to Lope National Park, a highly disturbed area. Around Lope humans and chimpanzees (and gorillas) coexisted for some 60,000 years (Tutin and Oslisly 1995). *Recent* human activity is not coexistence, but assault.

For 6 years beginning in 1983 researchers contacted chimpanzees 791 times, mostly fleeting encounters. Most data came from vocalizations, feces, and nests (Tutin and Fernandez 1991; Tutin et al. 1991:180). From this limited information, chimpanzee warfare was inferred.

Logging had been practiced for decades. An area cut 10–15 years earlier had far fewer chimpanzees than undisturbed areas. A 1987 rail line increased lumbering. Selective harvesting occurred along a front 5 to 10 km long, with the noise heard 5 km in advance. White and Tutin (2001:450–457) conducted nest counts along transects from February 1989 to June 1991.

As the front slowly approached, "large, excited groups of chimpanzees were frequently encountered, or heard pant hooting, screaming, and drumming. After the fifth month of the study, logging was under way about one km from the transect, and the number of nests (and individuals seen and heard) decreased" (2001:454). Before logging, density was about $1.1/km^2$. After logging, in Site A it stabilized around $.2/km^2$, the same as Site B logged 3 to 5 years earlier. Those are the facts. How was this interpreted, and reported in the *New York Times* (Stevens 1997)?

> It is not unlikely that the advancing chaos could displace entire chimpanzee communities. The high chimpanzee density of this study could reflect such a displacement, and the general excitement might have been the result of two communities coming into contact. The displacement of an entire community of chimpanzees would probably never occur naturally. However, observations from such long-term field sites as Gombe and Mahale suggests that it could result in violent conflict, which could cause high mortality and the eventual disappearance of one group, likely the smaller. This rather disturbing scenario would explain the changes caused by logging. (White and Tutin 2001:457)

But there is no direct evidence of any intergroup violence or killings. Heightened territorial signaling is unmistakably due to human impact, and "would probably never occur naturally." By 2000, apes across Gabon were decimated by logging, hunting, and Ebola. Lope is within that zone of devastation (Walsh et al. 2003:612), but I found no more recent studies of Lope chimpanzees.

Loango

A few hundred miles northwest of Conkoati Douli and southeast of Lope is Loango, also in Gabon. An adult male killing in 2006 is claimed to demonstrate that a widely noted intergroup killing is normal in chimpanzees, in an area without obvious human disruption. Critically examined, more evidence supports a killing by leopard. But there were many later killings at Loango, which implicate global climate change.

Loango National Park is a mix of rainforest, ocean coast, swamp, and savanna. It is remote from population centers, with protection varying over many years. Villages around and a few inside the Park are oriented to traditional subsistence, with minimal roads or land connections to the outside (Lee et al. 2006:230, 234). Loanga has the reputation of a jewel of ecological diversity, "Africa's Last Eden" in tourist promotions, with "surfing hippos" yet. (They sometimes wade at the beach.)

Habituation under the Max Planck Institute for Evolutionary Anthropology (also running the study projects in Tai and LuiKotale) began in February 2005, with two habituation teams; Josephine Head and Nikki Tagg, with one field assistant each. They surmised two chimpanzee groups in the area, with a boundary zone near the research camp. The northern chimpanzees were afraid of people, perhaps related to their nearness to a village. The southern were curious about humans (Boesch et al. 2007:1028; Head 2011:111).

The Killing

Six months into the habituation project in August 2005, while settling down for dinner in camp, researchers heard vocalizations. They observed two separate parties of chimpanzees heading southward. After the second party passed, came 45 minutes of nearly continuous vocalizations from about 300 m south of the camp, trailing off sporadically for another hour. "Vocalizations included pant-hoots and screams, but were not remarkable in any way other than their duration. We noted no alarm call, such as waa-barks" (Boesch et al. 2007:1029; Head 2011:101).

Bright and early, more vocalizations drew researchers to a cluster of new nests. About 50 m away they found disturbed and disturbing ground, with broken saplings and shrubs, tufts of hair, pieces of intestine, chunks of flesh, and testicles. Searching around they found "more tufts of hair, and then a trail of intestines leading behind a large tree." Behind the tree, to their shock, lay a dead, torn-up, adult male chimpanzee, "his chest and throat ripped open, and his entire face and body covered with dozens of cuts and bruises" (Head 2011:105).

Soon nine chimpanzees approached and viewed the corpse, without signs of aggression, agitation, or display. One sat down beside it. Noticing the humans, they departed silently to the north. From inferred fear of people, observers think they were from the northern population. Genotyping suggested that the nest makers and the victim were from different groups. No member of the presumed southern, supposed victim group were seen, though a few were spotted days later, coming up from further to the south (Boesch et al. 2007:1029–1032; Head 2011:102–106). Very murky.

Whatdunnit?

Researchers know that leopards live in Loango, and that leopards kill chimpanzees, but conclude that the weight of evidence indicates a chimpanzee attack (Boesch et al. 2007:1032). Leopards are indeed common. Loango is within the equatorial rainforest belt that has highest leopard density in all Africa. Mineral prospectors in the early 1970s sometimes heard "grunts and coughs from more than one leopard at once; in an environment where sound travels poorly, this suggests a high density" (Myers 1976:59–62). Leopards kill and eat large primates.[1]

Loango leopards eat chimpanzees. In 1995 Takeshi Furuichi and colleagues were in southern Loango for just over a month, doing nest counts (Furuichi et al. 1997).[2] Four days after arrival, Furuichi found a dead chimpanzee in pieces scattered over a couple of dozen meters. Apparently a 12- to 13-year-old male, it seemed dead for just a day or two. Leopard dung and tracks were close by. Since leopards eat dead animals they find, including putrid ones (Bailey 1993:214–220), scavenging can't be excluded. But combining advanced consumption with little decomposition, death by leopard is likely (Furuichi 2000). Given all of that, a killer leopard would seem to be the prime suspect in the 2005 death. Instead it was ruled out.

The expert on chimpanzee–leopard interactions is Christophe Boesch, lead author in the decisively titled paper, "Fatal Chimpanzee Attack in Loango National Park, Gabon." He investigated numerous leopard attacks on chimpanzees at Tai in the Ivory Coast. But Boesch was not at Loango, not a witness. As reported, the weight of Loango evidence leads to a different conclusion. A leopard did it. Since this is the *only* alleged killing by undisturbed chimpanzees in all Africa, the reported facts require careful scrutiny.[3]

---

[1] Including people (Brain 1981:97–98), baboons (Brain 1981:95–96; Busse 1980), gorillas (Fay et al. 1995; Schaller 1976:303–304), bonobos (D'Amour et al. 2006; cf. Corredor-Ospina et al. 2021), and Mahale chimpanzees (Nakazawa et al. 2013). In Lope, chimpanzee and gorilla remains were found in leopard scats (Henschel et al. 2005:24).

[2] Their overall estimate for chimpanzees is .78/km^2 (Furuichi et al. 1997:1033). Recent work farther north in the Park using remote cameras produced a much higher density, 1.72/km^2 (Head et al. 2013:2909–2910).

[3] Six months before this killing the first observed *pan*icide occurred at Tai. This prompted Boesch's reformulation of chimpanzee intergroup behavior as the evolutionary precursor of human warfare (Boesch 2009:1, 79). Perhaps that influenced his reaction to the Loango corpse.

CSI Loango

Multiple sources document the wounds multiple chimpanzees inflict on single victims.[4] In most cases the cause of death appears to be internal injuries from massive pummeling. They were beaten to death.

How does the Loango victim compare?

> He had suffered multiple injuries on his exposed ventrum. His testicles and penis and much of the skin from the groin and right thigh had been torn off, and both testicles were 20 m from the corpse. His throat was torn open, leaving a hole $\geq$15 x 10 cm. There were 7 large lacerations to the chest and stomach, exposed internal organs and several smaller puncture wounds. (Boesch et al. 2007:1030)

Puncture wounds were on the limbs and head. They saw no injuries on the back, but in the attack area saw many tufts of fur and four chunks of flesh.

> The chimpanzee's corpse was undisturbed and uneaten, which is inconsistent with a leopard attack, and no sign of leopards, e.g. tracks or feces, were in the area. Instead the injuries are consistent with a chimpanzee attack: removal of the genitalia, the large opening in the throat, and the presence of many small wounds on the body. (Boesch et al. 2007:1032)

Inconclusive. A spread of small wounds can also be inflicted by a leopard. In leopard attacks at Tai, two *survivors* had 19 and 18 small wounds, one with 13 just on the head (Boesch 1991a:225). Seemingly more telling is the absence of perceived claw marks. Of the two chimpanzees killed at Tai, one had "23 claw cuts all over her body." In the other case, "[e]ight claw stripes covered her trunk" (Boesch 1991a:226-227).

But claw marks may not *look* like claw marks. Leopards use their claws to grab prey and hold it for biting. "The forelimbs of felids are used solely for seizing prey and play no direct role in actual killing" (Bailey 1993:208; and Kruuk and Turner 1967:9; Turnbull-Kemp 1967:114). In one well-described attack on a human, there were punctures and big bites to the head and neck, but no raking (Bahram et al. 2004). In an attack on a hunter, the victims arms were clawed, but many claw injuries looked like puncture wounds (Walker 1935). At Tai a male victim had "one neat little hole in his side" from a claw that penetrated the pleural membrane and did not heal (Boesch 1991a:225).

Absence of tracks or feces means nothing. Sometimes they are left, but mostly not (Boesch 1991a:239; D'Amour 2006:214). More supportive is the apparent absence of wounds on the victim's back. That could be from chimpanzees pinning the victim down. But it also could be from a leopard, which usually attack from behind, this time attacking from the front. And how close was the back inspection, with whatever did it still out there?

---

[4] Including, Boesch 2009:80-82; deWaal 1989a:65; 1986:243 Goodall 1986:506-514; 1992:139; Kabaru et al. 2013:793; Pruetz et al. 2017:47; Reynolds 2005:161; Watts 2003:515; Watts et al. 2006:167; Wilson et al. 2004:537-542.

The neck wound is not probative. Neck wounds occur in some chimpanzee killings (Boesch 2009:80–82; Watts et al. 2006:162; Wilson et al. 2004:541), but major tracheal tears are common in leopard kills. They typically dispatch with a suffocating neck bite, then drag the corpse by the neck to seclusion (Schaller 1972:293; Smith 1977:13; Kruuk and Turner 1967:9). In one study 13 of 50 large prey had holes in the neck (Bailey 1993:208).

Seemingly the strongest evidence for a chimpanzee killing is the loss of the victim's penis, testicles, and part of the scrotum. In Chapter 7's discussion of Rusambo, that was noted as a distinctive marker of *pan*icide. If those facts were the only evidence, the conclusion would be simple—chimpanzees did it. However, there *is* more evidence.

Why Not Chimpanzees?

The victim had its chest "ripped open" (Head 2011:105), with "7 large lacerations to the chest and stomach" that "exposed internal organs" (Boesch et al. 2007:1030). *By far*, that is more massive injury than in *any* adult chimpanzee killing. It is quite consistent with a leopard attack. Of the two leopard killings at Tai, one had the viscera exposed; the other's "left chest looked awful as the leopard had bitten her there, compressing all the ribs which now formed a blood-stained protrusion" (Boesch 1991a:226–227; 2009:22).

Another major wound was a continuous loss of tissue from the remaining scrotum down the right thigh, halfway to the knee (Boesch et al. 2007:1031). That too is beyond anything reported in chimpanzee killings, which involve genitalia only.

A big point against killing by leopard is that the body was not eaten. Yet feeding may have begun. "Leopards frequently fed on the groin or anal region first." Of 34 kills in one study, "leopards had already eaten the groin on all" (Bailey 1993:212). They also pull off fur with their teeth before feeding (Brain 1981:92, 99; Schaller 1972:294; Smith 1977:13). At Loango, tufts of hair were all over the attack site.

Why not eat more? Leopards don't necessarily consume prey right away, or eat without interruption (Schaller 1972:294). In Kruger National Park a cat started to feed on an impala it cached in a tree. For about an hour, it plucked out hair and fed on the groin, anal region, and thigh down to the knee. Then it jumped down and walked away. Leopards may take several days to finish off a large carcass (Bailey 1993:213–215). In both Tai killings the leopard initially left the corpse. Also at Tai, leopards sometimes move off when they hear several chimpanzees nearby (Boesch 1991a:223, 226–228; Zuberbuhler and Jenny 2002:877). Many chimpanzees arriving from the north could have that effect. An undevoured corpse the morning after fits a leopard killing. Uneaten days later doesn't. What happened to this corpse?

Other evidence is leopard-like. The body was dragged 20 m from the attack scene to behind a large tree, the path marked by a trail of intestines (Boesch et al. 2007:1030; Head 2011:104–105). Leopards drag their prey to a secluded area.[5]

---

[5] Where terrestrial predators or scavengers are present, they cache prey up a tree, but none are reported at Loango, except crocodiles by the water (Bailey 1993:208–210). On the ground, out of sight behind a tree is good.

Pieces and a trail of intestines is strong evidence of a leopard attack. In one Tai leopard killing, the intestines were extruding (Boesch 2009:52). Extruding intestines are so common in leopard kills that there is scholarly disagreement about how often, how, and why it occurs (Bailey 1993:212; Brain 1981:92; Turnbull-Kemp 1967:117). "At least in the case of larger prey animals, these were frequently moved some distance to cover from the site of the killing.... About 70% of the prey were eviscerated en route, or near the kill if the carcass was not moved" (Smith 1977:13). A trail of intestines is not quite a smoking gun, because in later killings intestines protruded (Martinez-Inigo et al. 2021:7), but the partial evisceration weighs in for a leopard.

Calls

Another sort of evidence contradicts the chimpanzee killer theory. Vocalizations "were not remarkable in any way other than their duration" with "no alarm call, such as waa-barks" (Boesche et al. 2007:1029). "The excited pant-hoot vocalizations continue until 8 p.m. that night, which is unusual, since chimpanzees usually settle down to sleep by about 6:30 p.m., and only call at night *if they are disturbed by something on the ground like an elephant or a leopard*" (Head 2011:103, my emphasis).

After finding the corpse, Head comments (2011:106), the "excited calls of last night suddenly sound like bloodthirsty cries of victory, and it is impossible for me to reconcile the 'high spirited' sounds we heard with the vicious attack ... how could they sound so carefree and joyful [?]" Good question. There is no known chimpanzee attack that does not include prolonged, intense, agitated cries. It is inconceivable that the suspected culprits at Loango could have carried out the most damaging assault on an adult ever inflicted by chimpanzees, without any vocal hint being heard by attentive observers just 300 m away.

Taken together, evidence tilts strongly against killing by chimpanzees. (1) Some physical signs are consistent with a chimpanzee attack, but do not preclude a leopard. (2) Some are equally expectable in chimpanzee and leopard attacks. (3) Some physical clues are characteristic of leopard predation, not of violence by chimpanzees. (4) Acoustic evidence is consistent with a leopard presence, and entirely inconsistent with an assault by chimpanzees.

Given Boesch's credibility regarding leopard attacks, and later observations of *pan*-icides at Loango, I count this a possible killing (Count 4-O-A-M 2005). Based on facts as reported, it could be counted as hypothetical, more influenced by expectations than evidence. And that is important.

"[A] lethal attack in unhabituated chimpanzees directly addresses the question of human influence on chimpanzee lethal violence and how widespread such violence may be" (Boesch et al. 2007:1026). The Loango killing is held to prove that intergroup killing occurs *independently of human disruption*. If a leopard did it, never mind.

Subsequent Violence

In 2006, pant-hoots and alarm calls drew observers to a spot where they "found a heavy trail of blood and diarrhea leading away from an area of trampled vegetation.

A week later, we found the dead and heavily decomposed body of an adult male chimpanzee about 200 meters from the site" (Head 2011:111). The implication is that this is another casualty of chimpanzee "war." But these events refract differently by one's perspective. If the orienting position were: "leopards kill chimpanzees in Loango," the inference could be: a chimpanzee survived a leopard attack, but died later (Count 4-?-A-M 2006).

Another time Head (2011:110–113) "witnessed two parties of chimpanzees displaying aggressively at one another and vocalizing loudly." That happens. More intriguing, in June 2007 (?), less than 500 m from the 2005 killing, researchers saw six adult males harassing a female in a tree. She did not appear badly hurt. As mixed parties left heading north and south, researchers found blood, diarrhea, and a tiny infant's foot. An infant killing seems certain (Head 2011:110–113). Head assumes this to be an external killing, and puts it in the context of the RCRH.

> Not only are they weakening the potential strength of the neighboring community by reducing its numbers and thus protecting themselves against future attack, they are also encouraging the bereaved female to join their community, since succeeding in killing her infant proves to the female that her own community is not strong enough to protect her and her offspring. (Head 2011:113)

Yet across research sites, within-group infanticides are as or more common between-group (see Tables 3 and 4), and some later Loango *pan*icides were group unknown. Since the sex is unknown, even if it were an outsider, it could have been a future female immigrant (Count 2-?-I-?, 2007).

Two more are noted but not described. Also in June 2006, an infant of undetermined sex was found with injuries consistent with a chimpanzee attack, but so was the possible leopard killing (Count 4-O-I-M 2006).[6] In December 2008 an adult male was found killed, but nothing suggests it was an external rather than an internal killing (Count 4-?-A-M 2008). This was before habituation was achieved, so animals fled on sight. But camera traps showed up to nine adult males of what became identified as the Rekambo community, which individuals later were gone (Martinez-Inigo 2001a:6–9).

Head (2011:114) strongly endorses the demonic perspective.

> So perhaps we should not be so quick to condemn the chimpanzees for their behavior, and should instead look at their actions from a different perspective, one that can teach us more about ourselves than perhaps we would like to admit. Perhaps we humans are not so very different from our chimpanzee neighbors, but have just learned to control our aggression in certain situations, and perhaps our different social models have resulted in different moral codes.

Reporting this event in *New Scientist*, and quoting Head, "Is our 'moral code' nothing more than a controlling system that humans have invented to keep some order in society?," Hooper (2011) responds, "The answer is surely yes."

---

[6] This is of unclear categorization. Table 3 in Martinez-Inigo et al. (2021a:6) has it a juvenile of undetermined sex, while Arandjelovic et al. (2011:5) call it a "probable infanticide."

This evidence is consistent with a high rate of killing, but given multiple uncertainties about incidents, group definition and ranging, and increasing food competition, internal killings are also possible.

Territoriality

During the habitation period, in 2005-2008 noninvasive genetic study of feces addressed range use, with puzzling results. Nine Y haplotypes from 58 males suggests six groups with some overlap, four with very small distributions. It was unclear if these were hostile groups, local neighborhoods, or a very recent spatial separation. One male's feces was found along with feces of three different haplo-groups. Thirty-eight percent of females could not be associated with any single group (which harks back to the old but now neglected question of whether females are distributed across the landscape and males form the groups). From very close similarity in Y haplotypes, the authors infer a very recent immigration of a small number of chimpanzees which spread out, perhaps after a previous population crashed because of hunting or disease (Arandjelovic et al. 2011) (Ebola?).

Fully habituated study began in 2017, sometimes with three teams of followers (Martinez-Inigo 2021b). They observed hunting, with coordination comparable to that discussed for Tai. As elsewhere, hunting is higher in times of greater fruit availability (Klein et al. 2021). Consumption also includes smashing open ground tortoises (Pika et al. 2019).[7] Loango promises to be a major source of chimpanzee information going forward.

Illustrating the difficulty of calculating home range, the Rekambo group came between 27.64 and 59.03 km². For 44-47 individuals and a low number of 8-9 adult males, this is a very large territory (although researchers believe it had been even larger before). There are three to five communities around it (above). Group foraging extends through other groups' ranges, and encounters are more often in Rekambo's central core than at its peripheries. Researchers surmise that Rekambo is expanding to its south while being pressed on other sides (like at Ngogo).

Two reasons for big ranges and high intergroup pressure are large areas of food-poor swamp and savanna; and "intense interspecific competition for food resources" with more numerous gorillas and abundant forest elephants (2021b:8). Loango and Lope 200 km northeast, show substantial interspecific food overlap and competition, along with different specializations, particularly in times of fruit scarcity (Head et al. 2012; Oelze et al. 2013; Tutin and Fernandez 1993a). But interspecifically, they do compete—and elephants go first.

For chimpanzees alone "our camera trap data revealed that other communities visited areas that individuals of the Rekambo community also frequently used at the

---

[7] This is the first observation of tortoise smashing by chimpanzees, but the practice was reported based on local knowledge and found shells in the northern Democratic Republic of Congo. Other vertebrates are there reported as prey of chimpanzees, including—quite astoundingly—killing and eating leopards (Hicks et al. 2019:11-27).

same time" (Martinez-Inigo 2021a:9). Rekambo patrolled, and patrols *always included females* (as if their own food depended on it). In 2017–2019 there were 16 acoustic, visual, or deadly encounters with other groups, but only five while patrolling—i.e., they *were* encountered by others (as in southwestern Ngogo).

Killing

And they killed—four infants and one juvenile (Martinez-Inigo 2021a). Since not all of Rekambo was habituated, "[i]t is possible that victims, whose community could not be assigned were indeed from the Rekambo community." All but one witnessed attack were on females with infants; no victim parties had an adult male (as noted at Gombe in the "War" years as counting toward the resource competition hypothesis [RCH] over RCRH). Two of those five were within the core area, only the last was preceded by a patrol (Count 4-?-I-? 2017; 2-?-J-M 2018; 2-?-I-? 2018; 2-?-I-? 2019; 2-?-I-F 2019).

One remarkable patrol killing involved a juvenile male that was with two females and an infant. The infant was killed, and partly eaten.

> When the Rekambo chimpanzees had the infant's corpse in permanent possession, they started traveling while forcing the unidentified juvenile and his supposed mother to accompany them.... The attacks on the juvenile male became more frequent and violent.
>
> The remaining unidentified female attempted to protect her supposed juvenile and was charged several times.... The males continued attacking the juvenile. One of them hit him with a branch, tore a piece of flesh out of the juvenile's leg, and ate it. The juvenile female of the Rekambo community used her fingers and leaves to collect blood from the unidentified juvenile chimpanzee and lick it.

Finally, they stopped attacking him, two and a half hours after they began. He was lethargic, and his corpse was found the following day (Martinez-Inigo et al. 2021a:8). Again, this could not be classified as an internal or external killing.

Then come witnessed killings identified by group. In March 2018 within their core area, nine of Rekambo, including four females, attacked an unknown male for 20 minutes. He seemed to be dead after 15. He had bite marks all over, a torn throat, with intestines protruding from a deep cut in the abdomen (Count 1-O-A-M 2018). (Score a point for killing by chimpanzees in 2005.) In June 2019 a patrol with 14 individuals including 5 females, encountered 3 stranger adults, one with a female infant. The adults fled, but the patrol captured the infant, and pounded it to death against the ground and trees. It was not eaten (Count 1-O-I-F 2019). (Note: none of these killings involved dragging a body behind a tree, or scattered chunks of flesh.)

That study went up to June 2019. "[B]etween July 2019–September 2020, individuals killed three additional individuals of other communities." Sex, age, or certainty of kill are not reported, so those will *not* be entered into the Count. Also, in August 2018 one Rekambo adult male was "severely injured" by wounds consistent with a chimpanzee attack (Martinez-Inago et al. 2021a:5–11).

Gorillas

The year 2019 also saw something unprecedented—chimpanzees attacking and killing gorillas (Southern et al. 2021). Gorillas are more common in Loango than chimpanzees, 1.2–1.4 compared to 0.8–1.1/km². Nine peaceful interactions were recorded from 2014 to 2018, including feeding within the same tree. But in February 2019, battle broke out. Twenty-seven of Rekambo went on patrol out of their territory. After no encounters, 18 of them ran into a silverback, 3 females, and an infant.

> A first chimpanzee scream was followed by a succession of chimpanzee screams and barks, and gorilla barks and roars.... At 7:13, the silverback charged an adolescent female chimpanzee, Gia, knocking her into the air. At 7:15, a group of approximately nine male chimpanzees (adults and adolescents), and at least one adult female chimpanzee surrounded the silverback, and repeatedly jumped down on and hit him whilst screaming and barking. The silverback retreated to a distance of approximately 30 m with all other members of his group. (Southern et al. 2021:3)

The infant gorilla was left behind and killed, though not eaten.

In December 2019, 27 of Rekambo seemed about to start a patrol, but they saw 7 gorillas in a tree, including a silverback. The chimpanzees began to climb that tree. After more up and down, the silverback, having seen human followers, fled. One female with infant descended and was surrounded, until finally the chimpanzees got the infant, killing and eating it (2021:4–5). (Not being chimpanzees, neither gorilla is counted.) "[W]e cannot rule out that the presence of human observers, in both events, may have had an effect on the unhabituated silverback's departure and may have tilted the imbalance of power in favour of the habituated chimpanzees" (2021a:6).

Why So Violent?

In terms of direct human contact, Loango seems much less disturbed than most places in this book. But from 2017 to 2019, they killed five infants, one juvenile, one adult, three unspecified outsiders, and two gorilla infants at sizable risk to the attackers. (In 2006–2008, certain-to-possible were three infants and one adult.) That makes 12 deadly attacks in under 4 years. "[W]ith some of the killings being intracommunity and the others intercommunity, [Rekambo] would still rank . . . as one of the most lethal chimpanzee communities studied so far" (Martinez-Inigo et al. 2021a:12). Does this provide the ultimate proof that chimpanzees are natural killers? Or could this be resource competition + human impact hypothesis (RCH + HIH)?

Stiff resource competition is evident in hostile chimpanzees regularly foraging in each others' rangelands, even Rekambo's core. That might be related somehow to the suspected recent "colonization" of this area. "Consequently, the present study may portray a period of unusually intense territorial behavior" (Martinez-Inigo et al. 2021a:9). "[I]intense interspecific competition for food resources" is perhaps a greater factor. "Elephants and gorillas could be lowering the density of food available to chimpanzees"; "elephants competitively exclude chimpanzees when fruit are scarce";

"interspecies competition between elephants and chimpanzees may also have a crucial impact upon home range size" (Martinez-Inigo et al. 2021b:8). "The two lethal encounters [on gorillas] occurred at times characterized by food scarcity and a period of high dietary overlap (for fruit resources)" (Southern et al. 2021:6). Still, that seems a lot for normal food competition. Southern et al. (2021:7) suspect something more is involved: "analysis of long-term phenological data could aid in investigating if potential high levels of feeding competition may be a more recent phenomenon caused by a collapse in fruit availability as observed in other tropical forests in Gabon" (Southern et al. 2021:7).

Global Warming

Southern et al. refer to findings from Lope National Park, 200 km northwest in the same forest (above), site of the longest study of fruiting in all of Africa (Bush et al. 2020). From 1986 to 2018, *fruits of all types declined by 81%*. The study's main concern was elephants, and an archive of camera trap photographs was coded to quantitatively evaluate elephant's apparent physical condition. In the decade from 2008 to 2018, it declined by 11%. In the longer term, in 1987 one in 10 trees provided food for elephants, but fewer than one in 50 in 2018. All types of fruit showed comparable decline. By 2018, the monthly availability of fruit at Lope was starkly diminished, without seasonal ups and downs, and all months below the months of lowest productivity in 1986.

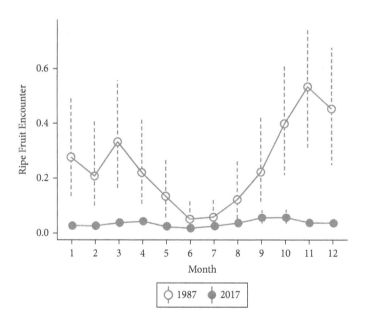

Illustration 6.4 Lope Fruiting Levels 1987, 2017
Source: Bush, E. et al. (2020). Long-term collapse in fruit availability threatens Central African forest megafauna. *Science*, 370, 1219–1222.

A possible explanation of drastic and long-term decline in fruiting is the minimum temperature hypothesis (vernalization) (Tutin and Fernandez 1993b:244). Temperate zone fruiting is highly sensitive to environmental cues. Tropical fruits may be too. Specifically, fruiting may need a sufficient number of dry season days when the temperature is below 19 degrees Celsius (69° Fahrenheit). With Lope temperatures warming by .25 Celsius° per decade (Bush et al. 2020:2), that could drastically undercut the basic food of elephants, gorillas, and chimpanzees. A prognostication from three decades ago now seems prophetic:

> a small permanent increase in minimum temperatures resulting from global warming, would have dramatic consequences: not only would certain tree species in the Lope forest cease to reproduce but also the quantity of food available to frugivores would be drastically reduced. (Tutin and Fernandez 1993b:247)

Bush et al. (2020:1) warn: "Fruit famine in one of the last strongholds for African forest elephants should raise concern about the ability of . . . fruit-dependent megafauna to persist in the long run." In that global warming would join other global trends leading toward widespread extinctions of primate populations. "[C]limate change is likely to be the principle driver of species range change in coming decades, equaling or surpassing the potential effects of land use change by 2070" (Carvalho et al. 2021:1665).

The central question of this book is whether chimpanzees kill because of an evolutionary legacy of killing outsiders. If they are plunged into a human-induced, accelerating crisis of food availability, is that qualitatively different from islandization? This book focuses mainly on the immediate, "micro," effects of human disruption. On the macro scale, climate change joins other global changes threatening the existence of primates around the world (Estrada et al. 2017). An obvious implication is that researchers at other sites concern themselves with possibility of climate change affecting chimpanzee foods throughout Africa.

20
Western Chimpanzees, *Pan troglodytes verus*

West African Chimpanzees suffer the same existential hazards as other subspecies, but more so (Campbell et al. 2008; Fleury-Brugiere and Brugiere 2002). A survey across the subspecies range found an *80% drop from 1990 to 2014* (Kuhl et al. 2017). Chapter 20 includes two populations in Senegal—Niokolo Koba and Fongoli—and the long-term research site of Bossou, in the Republic of Guinea, Conakry. All are impacted by recent human actions, but so far endure. Part VII will continue with *verus* separately in the major research project at Tai, in Ivory Coast.

Niokolo Koba (Mt. Assirik)

Better known as Mt. Assirik, Senegal's 8,130 km^2 Niokolo Koba National Park is "perhaps the hottest, driest, and most open environment inhabited by chimpanzees today" (Pruetz et al. 2002:36; Baldwin et al. 1982:368–371). Importantly for *Demonic Males*, released captives in the mid-1970s were severely attacked, seemingly confirming its perspectives.

From 1976 to 1979, P.J. Baldwin, W.C. McGrew, and C.E.G. Tutin worked in Niokolo Koba, logging 358 hours of nondisturbing observations over 44 months (Baldwin et al. 1982:372).[1] There research reports end, except for nest surveys in 2000 (Pruetz et al. 2002) and 2012 (Pruetz et al. 2012). (That is not the release program.)

In the 1970s, other than the release project, human impact was minimal and chimpanzees fairly well protected. Total population was estimated at 25–30, and range at 278–333 km^2, for a density around .09/km^2 (Baldwin et al. 1982:375–379), (similar to Kahuzi-Biega). Density from the 2002 nest count was .13/km^2 (Pruetz et al. 2002:39).[2] People were not a deadly danger.

> Where traditional subsistence is based on game species (e.g. ungulates) taken for village consumption and not for sale in markets, primates such as chimpanzees may be able to survive in sympatry with humans. It appears that although humans in southeastern Senegal consume bushmeat, primates such as chimpanzees are able to live sympatrically with humans in these areas. (Pruetz et al. 2002:41)[3]

---

[1] "The site is undisturbed and our methods of research were designed to minimize our influence on the surroundings. The camp was small and unobtrusive, and we did not provision chimpanzees with food. We wore camouflaged clothing and most observations were made from hiding" (Baldwin et al. 1982:369).

[2] The brief 2012 survey suggests a big increase, to 1.28/km^2—although researchers caution about reliability (Pruetz et al. 2012:9).

[3] But things were changing for the worse. 2012 surveyors encountered commercial bushmeat hunting, once in a run-in with hunters that made researchers flee (Pruetz et al. 2012:9–10).

Territoriality

Mt. Assirik's ecology shapes their use of territory.

> 55% of the study area (plateau and grassland) was very open with only isolated trees, 37% was woodland of variable density, and only 3% was closed canopy forest.... Not only is the habitat very open at Mt. Assirik, but there are four species of Carnivora which can be considered as potential predators of chimpanzees, [lion, leopard, wild dog, and spotted hyena]. All these species are relatively common, and chimpanzees are particularly at risk when moving or feeding in areas with no, or few, trees. (Tutin et al. 1983:164)

Water is critical. "[V]ery large parties were more often seen in the dry season.... These large parties often involved chimpanzees arriving at, or leaving, one of only two areas of gallery forest where flowing water was still available by the end of the dry season" (1983:167).

Assirik offers the major territorial variation of "occasional bivouacs and massmigrations from one part of the home range to another, especially in the dry season" (1983:154).

> [A]ll, or most, of the community moved together from one part of the range to another. These movements appeared to be prompted by food or water becoming scarce in the area left behind. Thus, chimpanzees seem to congregate and then move long distances in a burst of rapid, directed travel.... The few observations of large traveling parties showed that, once formed and traveling, a party moved rapidly and remained silent. (1983:169)

This resembles a patrol in silent directed travel, but unlike patrols, everyone participates.

Researchers first thought theirs was the only community in the Park, "single, small and probably isolated" (Tutin et al. 1983:157, 166). The 2000 fieldwork found chimpanzee signs to their south and east; and a visit in 2012 found nests 20 km north (Hunt and McGrew 2002:39; Pruetz et al. 2012:10)—not so far for trekkers. Other chimpanzees live around them, but no patrolling is found. Do these local groupings ever come together? We have no idea.

Comparing Assirik with Toro Semliki, another dry open environment: "Although there are some predictable patterns, we cannot yet generalize about The Savanna Chimpanzee as an ecotype, any more than we can generalize about The Chimpanzee as a species" (Hunt and McGrew 2002:48).[4] Variation is the rule and unanticipated patterns are expectable.

For instance, Mt. Assirik chimpanzees had more physical marks of violence than at Toro-Semliki (Hunt and McGrew 2002:46–47, 48). "Patterns of aggression appear

---

[4] Although a "forest" vs. "savanna" chimpanzees is widely used, van Leeuwen et al. (2020) clarify that dichotomy is misleading. A gradient of chimpanzee habitats exists between the two, with "forest mosaic" a useful intermediate category.

to differ across habitats. Like Gombe, Mahale, and Kibale, Assirik chimpanzees show damaged ears and fingers attributable to fighting, but Semliki chimpanzees are largely unscarred." Seven out of 13 Assirik adults had visible ear damage.

Was fighting internal or external? "One-Eyed Sam was severely attacked at least twice, suffering a ripped scrotum and bitten-off finger. He died shortly after the last attack." Since no external encounters were seen, these could only be from internal attacks. This incident does not appear in any tally of killings, but it counts in mine (Count 3-W-A-M, c. 1978).

Demonization

Assirik chimpanzees appear in *Demonic Males* as much-needed evidentiary support confirming deadly propensities. In their foundational overview of intergroup violence, Wrangham and Peterson (1996:19–20) turn to Mt. Assirik right after Mahale and before the first, dubious Kanyawara deaths.

> On the other side of the continent things look much the same. In West Africa the first hint of intercommunity violence came in 1977, within Senegal's Niokola-Koba National Park, when conservationist Stella Brewer brought a group of ex-captive chimps into the forest with hopes of reintroducing them to a wild existence. But repeated attacks by native chimpanzees, including a terrifying nighttime raid of the camp by a gang of four adults, finally forced Brewer to shut her experiment down.

Brewer was an animal protectionist dealing with the same problem that drove the Conkouati-Douli experiment: ever more captives filling sanctuaries. She released an 8-year-old female and two 7-year-old males around 1972. They disappeared between visits. Then Brewer corresponded with Jane Goodall and spent 2½ months at Gombe in 1973, learning about wild chimpanzees. For the next release of two young males, Pooh and William, in 1974, she stayed longer and mentored. The previously released female Tina reappeared, and regularly joined them (Brewer 1978:xiii, 22, 105–116, 127–128, 134–143).

Brewer and colleagues walked with their charges, often carrying them, showing them what to eat, trying to teach them to fear snakes, lions, and leopards. One day Tina began termite fishing, Brewer did too, eating termites to show the newcomers. When wild males chased Tina, Brewer "stood up on a rock in full view and pant-hooted..... The wild chimps seemed shocked into immobility by the sight of me standing on a rock with Pooh on my shoulders. Pooh followed my pant-hoot with two aggressive whaas" (1978:211). Once Pooh—with Brewer behind him—aggressively challenged the locals. Other times newcomers subserviently but successfully approached the wild ones. Still, to Brewer it was clear: Assirik chimpanzees associated the releasees with humans (1978:168–169, 185, 213–215, 219–227)—a very unnatural situation.

Five years into it, Brewer (1978:296–298) felt things were going well. The releasees might never join the wild chimpanzees, but repeatedly were tolerated. They matured and Tina gave birth, but remained around the rehabilitation center, now considerably built up for people. The attacks of 1977 came too late for Brewer's optimistic book, but she told Goodall what happened.

As related by Goodall (1986:521–522), local chimpanzees began chasing the aliens into camp, and displaying aggressively nearby. One night four adult males came into the camp itself, and attacked. Tina "almost certainly would not have survived without medication" (Count 3*-O-A-F, 1977). Goodall asks:

> Why these violent incidents after several relatively peaceful years? The rehabilitant group was located in part of the home range of the wild chimpanzee community. The year of the raids there was a drought, and at the height of the dry season the only known source of running water was that close to Brewer's camp. This, moreover was one of the few locations where *tabbo* trees produced fruit that year, a particularly important resource because many fruit crops had failed or yielded poorly.

Far from confirming demonic tendencies of wild chimpanzees, this attack clearly demonstrates human impact leading to violent conflict. Resource competition hypothesis + human impact hypothesis (RCH + HIH).[5]

Fongoli

Fongoli is about 45 km. southeast of Assirik in Senegal, outside the protected Niokolo Koba Park. It too is extremely dry and hot, with mixed woodland, grassland, bamboo, and gallery forest. Habituation began in 2001, and systematic data collection in 2005. From then until 2014 group numbers varied from 29 to 36 (Pruetz 2010:365–366; Pruetz et al. 2015:2). With greater study than Assirik, Fongoli chimpanzees greatly expand our knowledge of chimpanzee behavioral plasticity.

They adapt to the blistering heat physiologically (Wessling et al. 2018) and behaviorally, taking shelter in caves (Pruetz 2007), "soaking in pools of water during the early rainy season, and moving and foraging at night during maximum phases of the moon" (Pruetz and Bertolani in Hawks 2007). They maneuver with aplomb around the fires that burn their range every year, and adjust foraging accordingly (Pruetz and Herzog 2017). With seasonally scarce food, they dedicate more time than other chimpanzees to termite fishing (Bogart and Pruetz 2010:17).

Remarkably, male chimpanzees but more often females, fashion a "spear," sharpening it with bites, and forcefully jab it into hole where bushbabies (gallagos) nest, extract, and eat them.

Bushbaby remains are common in feces (Pruetz and Bertolani 2007; Pruetz et al. 2015:5). Overall males hunt more, outpacing females in capturing vervets, bushbucks, and baboons. But using tools, females racked up 30% of total Fongoli kills (Pruetz et al. 2015:5–6, 9–10).

---

[5] That ended the Assirik release experiment. Happily it was not the end for those and other captive chimpanzees. In 1979 they went with others to islands without resident chimpanzees in the River Gambia National Park. By 2006 they grew to 113, in four groups over three islands. They adapted, matured, reproduced, and outpaced wild chimpanzees for life expectancy (Brewer et al. 1990; Brewer et al. 2006).

The behavior of these chimpanzees demonstrates that hunting is less adult male-biased among our closest living relatives than previously believed, when tools are used, and emphasizes the need to take into account the range of behavioural variation within a species, specifically when findings are applied to attempts to understand evolutionary adaptation (Pruetz et al. 2015:10).

"'It doesn't fit the old paradigm of Man the Hunter,'" comments Pruetz (Gibbons 2007).

Sociality and Human Impact

Fongoli chimpanzees are very cohesive. "On average, almost one-half of the Fongoli community is together at any given time, which is approximately three times greater than the level of cohesion reported for chimpanzees at other sites," and more like bonobos (Pruetz 2010:367). They regularly share plant foods and tools (Pruetz and Lindshield 2012:133). Like at Mt. Assirik they use their large range cyclically, moving collectively from place to place (Pruetz and Bertolani in Hawks 2007).

The closest neighbors are 15 km to the northwest, between Fongoli and Mt. Assirik (Pruetz 2006:164). There are few interactions and "this chimpanzee community has not been observed to exhibit boundary patrolling behaviors that is typical of chimpanzees elsewhere" (Pruetz et al. 2017:51, 54).

Adding Fongoli to Semliki, Assirik, Kahuzi Biega, and Ugalla/Filabanga, that makes five low-density populations where territorial defense does not seem to be at issue. These are no more exceptional than high-patrol-and-conflict groups. Territoriality is flexible and situationally adaptive.

Human coexistence is long-standing (Waller and Pruetz 2016). "Anthropogenic factors that shape the Fongoli chimpanzees' >85 km home range include permanent and seasonal settlements, cropland, roads, foot trails, annual bush fires, wood collecting for timber and fuel, free ranging cattle, seasonal sheep herding, and artisanal gold mining" (Lindshield et al. 2017:3). Yet as elsewhere, human impact is changing for the worse.[6]

An immediate threat is "rare but opportunistic hunting of female chimpanzees.... to obtain infants for the pet trade" (Pruetz et al. 2017:51). In early 2009—amazingly—researchers found and rescued a captive infant for sale, and returned it successfully to her Fongoli mother (Pruetz and Kante 2010). Pruetz et al. (2017:51) surmise that similar attempts have killed mothers. That, combined with Fongoli being closed to immigration on two sides by a town and highway (and a third by a river), accounts for the group's extraordinarily high ratio of adult males to females, 1.7:1. (See Wilson et al. 2014:Extended Data Figure 1.) This human-impacted sex ratio may be involved in an internal killing.

---

[6] In arid Fongoli, where food is limited (Pruetz 2006:164), probably the most important food is *S. senegalensis*. Local people increased extraction of this fruit from the study area at an alarming rate, and the end is not in sight (2006:177; Hockings 2010:349). Small-scale gold mining is also increasing, but with limited fallout for chimpanzees, so far (Boyer Ontl 2017).

Killing an Ex-Alpha

At habituation in 2005 Foudouko was alpha. Soon after a severe injury hobbled his beta ally MM in 2007, YO deposed Foudouko. In March 2008, others chased Foudouko away from a dry season water source. For 6 years he appeared only occasionally, but then with increasing association in 2012–2013.

In June 2013 between 2:00 and 3:00 a.m.—they forage at night—observers heard loud cries, moving in location, indicating "extensive agonism." Going out before dawn, they found Foudouko's body, with many small wounds and a mangled foot. Death seemed due to internal injuries. As day broke, the chimpanzees returned. Both males and females beat and bit the corpse, even eating small pieces of flesh (Pruetz et al. 2017:37, 42–45, 47, 53) (Count 1 W-A-M 2013).

Researchers suspect this killing was due to sexual competition—a claim made plausible here because of the highly skewed sex ratio, and because Foudouko copulated in his moments of return. "Therefore, we cannot reject the hypothesis that anthropogenic disturbance is a contributing factor of lethal aggression at Fongoli" (Pruetz et al. 2017:53).[7]

The authors see this as very unusual. "The peripheralization of an adult male is rarely reported in the literature," citing Mahale's Ntologi as exceptional (Pruetz et al. 2017:50). But we've seen exile of ex-alphas and severe violence against them several times at Gombe and Mahale. Foudouko's successor also disappeared after being deposed. Foudouko is no outlier, it illustrates a previously unrecognized pattern.

Bossou

Bossou is a village surrounded by low hills in the Republic of Guinea-Conakry. Lower land is cultivated, in regrowth, or natural savanna. About 6 km^2 of evergreen forest on hilltops is the principle chimpanzee habitat, although they move and forage beyond the trees. Bossou is full of surprises.

Study began with short visits by Adriaan Kortlandt from 1966 to 1969, which included well-known filming of reactions to stuffed leopards. In 1975 Yukimaru Sugiyama, previously at Busingiro, visited and began research the next year. He observed chimpanzees in three stays from 1976 to 1980, for a total of 15 months. By 1976 all 20 chimpanzees were habituated. In 1986 Testuro Matasuzawa joined Sugiyama, initiating a second more intensive period of research. Bananas or oranges were provisioned from 1990 to 1995, not otherwise (Albrecht and Dunnett 1971:10, 14; Sugiyama 1994; 2004:156, 160; Sugiyama and Fujita 2011:23–24; Sugiyama and Koman 1979:324–325; Yanakoshi 2011:37–38).

---

[7] Foudouko may not be the only within-group victim. An adolescent male, Frito, was listed as a suspected internal killing in 2010 (Pruetz et al. 2017:55; Wilson et al. 2014a:EDT Table 3) (Count 4 W-As-M 2010).

Chimpanzees and People

Bossou exemplifies long-term coexistence of humans and chimpanzees, a classic case for ethnoprimatology. Among the approximately 2,500 local Manon people, the apes are understood as reincarnations of ancestors, associated with village founders (Matsuzawa and Humle 2011:5–9). An elderly villager said in 2005:

> The Bossou chimpanzees will never leave the forests surrounding our village; they are our ancestors and are different from other chimpanzees. They come to the forest edge and scream to us when an elder in the village is about to die. They are very intelligent and like us; the males protect the females and young from danger. They often visit the village and fields where we cultivate, forming an orderly queue when they enter. We let them feed from our fields so they will never go hungry. (Hockings 2010:347)

The hills themselves are sacred, having served "as a refuge for women and children during periods of tribal conflict. The current peaceful coexistence between man and chimpanzee ... is 'firmly embedded in the political and environmental history of the village'" (Yamakoshi quoted in Hockings 2010:351). In 1976 when a soldier shot a chimpanzee, village protest got him transferred. When refugees from the Liberia civil war poured in during the early 1990s and began cutting trees, the government cooperated in demarcating chimpanzee habitat by planting bamboo around 12 km^2 (Humle 2003:148).

Human-chimpanzee relations are not all smooth, however. About a quarter of their feeding is on 17 different crops (Hockings 2011; Hockings et al. 2009; 2012). People don't always tolerate them, and chimpanzees "are often chased away by angry or scared farmers, sometimes with the use of stones and noise" (2009a:644). Chimpanzees also attacked human children 11 times from 1995 to 2009. Most attacks were mild and none lethal, though some might have been without intervention. Although people say chimpanzees frighten them, they draw on local beliefs to explain attacks, such as that the culprits are not real chimpanzees, but malevolent were-chimpanzees.

Crop raiding behavior resembles hunting and patrolling (Hockings 2011:217–218; Hockings et al. 2012:807–808). (Hunting is not reported for Bossou, although there are not many vertebrates to hunt.) Crop incursions are often male-only, though sometimes females go along. Raiders appear nervous, scanning for people. While not silent they vocalize less than normally. More males being together increases the likelihood of forays into fields. As in hunting and patrolling, raids have a political dimension. "Crop-raiding certainly provides energetic benefits, but as has been proposed for hunting, it might also provide males with opportunities to 'show off' their boldness" (Hockings 2011:217).

Local people set forest snares for other animals, yet very few snare wounds are seen. Though chimpanzees elsewhere recognize and avoid snares, Bossou chimpanzees dismantle them, breaking the arched stick or sapling used as a spring.

> Long-term exposure to snares may have allowed Bossou chimpanzees to learn about the dangers associated with them, and possibly how to interact safely with and eventually deactivate them. It is also possible that these initial active responses to snares

have been passed down through the generations and carried down in the group as culture. Indeed, when the adult male broke the snare in case 1, another juvenile male closely observed the situation and subsequently also interacted with the snare. (Ohashi and Matsuzawa 2011:4)

Partial Social Isolation

Bossou chimpanzees are mostly isolated by extensive forest clearing and savanna. One long southeastern extension of their peripheral range allows some access to chimpanzees of the Nimba Mountains of Liberia, about 6 km southeast of Bossou (see Koops et al. 2010; Matsuzawa et al. 2011).[8] The closest group is at Seringbara, just 4 km away (Matsuzawa and Kourouma 2008:204). That distance is through dry savanna and gallery forests. One time, six Bossou chimpanzees were followed to the national border, and continued beyond unobserved (Ohaski 2011:313–315). No intergroup contact has been seen, but one paternity is clearly extragroup (Humle and Matsuzawa 2000:60; Sugiyama 1999:62–63; 2004:163).[9]

Despite Bossou's very high level of human impact, conditions did not create resource, social, or psychological disruption that has encouraged violence elsewhere. This illustrates the fallacy of evaluating any simple index of disturbance on induced violence. The connection must be approached with historical specificity.

Demographics

Bossou numbers fluctuated around 20 from the late 1960s to 2001. About 20 may be the carrying capacity of local forests (Sugiyama 2004:156–157, 162; Sugiyama and Koman 1979:324). In 2003 a flu-like epidemic, possibly from tourists, killed five. This catastrophe brought them down to 13 (Humle 2011:329; Sugiyama and Fujita 2011:24–25).

All females born in Bossou emigrated. One female is suspected but not confirmed as an immigrant (Humle and Matsuzawa 2000:59; Sugiyama and Fujita 2011:27, 30). Researchers surmise that surrounding people scare off prospective immigrants. With

---

[8] Nimba provides a somewhat horrifying note about human impact and violence. In the 1940s and '50s, a Methodist missionary sent 246 skulls of "wild-shot" chimpanzees from Nimba and nearby, to Ernest Hooten at Harvard. Recent study found the skulls had an exceptionally high rate of healed trauma, (over 56%), compared to chimpanzee skeletons from other sources.

> The incidence of healed trauma in the Liberian crania suggests an extremely high level of violence ... To account for these regional differences, we would have to examine the ecology, demography, and history of each of the skeletal populations. In northern Liberia, at least, the situation is clear enough. By the 1940s, trees were being extracted on a massive scale.... Habitat destruction probably intensified competition among all the remaining chimpanzees, and human predation would have disrupted the hierarchies of specific chimpanzee communities. (Novak and Hatch 2009:339)

[9] Beginning in 1997, interrupted by war, conservationists and researchers worked to plant a 300-m-wide corridor of chimpanzee food trees to link Bossou and Seringbara (Kormos et al. 2003:72; Matsuzawa and Kourouma 2008; Matsuzawa et al. 2011). Although Nimba chimpanzees face their own serious human threats (Granier and Martinez 2011; Humle and Kormos 2011), this effort is imperative for the survival of Bossou chimpanzees.

the home grown females and several males leaving, and no new blood coming in from outside, the population got not just smaller, but much older. About 2/3 were over 36 in 2006 (Matsuzawa and Kourouma 2008:204). Then in 2011, 100% of Bossou caught a respiratory infection. Three adults and two infants died (Emery Thompson et al. 2018:3). Nothing further is reported.

In earlier observations, the Bossou community had a social organization strikingly different from other chimpanzees, usually with just one resident adult male (Albrecht and Dunnett 1971:32; Doran et al. 2002:31; Sugiyama 1999:66; 2004:157; Sugiyama et al. 1993:545). After 1991, there were two, or later three or four adult males (Sugiyama and Fujita 2011:25). Sugiyama's interpretation of the early pattern was that with ecological limitations on total numbers, and the absence of predators or rival chimpanzee groups posing a threat, dominant males drove out subdominants, similar to Mountain Gorillas (Sugiyama 1999:66–67; 2004:162–163). This led him to another conclusion: "some males of this subspecies do in fact migrate" (Sugiyama 1999:61).

Male Emigration

As young males matured, they disappeared without apparent cause. From 1978 to 1988, 4 adult and 10 adolescent males went missing (Matsuzawa et al. 1990:639; Sugiyama and Fujita 2011:29–30). There is no possibility of intergroup violence, since there were no neighboring groups. Sugiyama (2004:164) notes that this gradual imbalancing of sex ratios, leading to substantially more adult females than males, is not appreciated as *the statistical norm across Africa* (see Wilson et al. 2014a:Extended Data Table Figure 1a). This species-wide, female-skewed adult sex ratio suggests that male emigration is actually *common*, and that chimpanzees are not as male philopatric as assumed.[10]

Sugiyama's second type of evidence for male emigration is three stranger males that entered the community. In 1977 two showed up, to great clamor but no hostility. The older male and Bossou's alpha frequently embraced, although the adolescent did not interact with others. The youth was gone after a day, the older male stayed for 3 weeks. Then he went away with a Bossou male and adolescent female. Those two came back, but the stranger did not (Sugiyama 1984:397; Sugiyama and Koman 1979:324, 327–328). Another adult male arrived sometime during the researchers' absence in 1980–1982, ranged with the community during the 3 months of study, and was gone by their next research (Sugiyama 1999:64–65; Sugiyama and Fujita 2011:30–31).[11]

---

[10] This idea led to a dust-up with Tai researchers. Sugiyama (1999:67) questions Boesch and Boesch-Achermann's assumption that males which disappeared at Tai, died. They in turn (2000:39, 46), doubt that Bossou males emigrate, suggesting instead poaching or capture for sale. Those are possibilities, but while Liberian poachers have operated in the area (Sugiyama et al. 1993:547), they were not present during the four most notable disappearances (Sugiyama and Fujita 2011:30). Killing or capture for sale by a local Manon seems unlikely.

[11] Boesch and Boesch-Achermann (2000:46) again register skepticism. They note that the first immigrants arrived 3 months after field research began, and conclude that they might be natal members returning after an absence. Sugiyama et al. (1993:551) considered that possibility.

> Although cultivated fields are scattered around the home-range of the Bossou group, no information about peripheral resident chimpanzees, other than those of the group, was available from villagers. Therefore, it is probable that they came from a more distant habitat, rather than

All of the visitors left, never seen again (Sugiyama 1984:1994). Even if they were born at Bossou, rather than among some foreign community, they lived their lives apart. Meaning at a minimum, that some males do move away from their natal group. Some males emigrate. Disappeared does not mean dead.

Across Africa, Variation and Devastation

Yukimaru Sugiyama—whose 1960s observations from Budongo still challenge the later consensus of invariable hostility—was a pioneer in recognizing chimpanzee behavioral diversity (Stanford 1998b:401). More than two decades after his initial field work, Sugiyama (1984b:399) emphasized unanswered questions about "the adaptive variability of chimpanzee behavior and ecology." He kept on (1999:67) arguing against explaining "away behavior that does not fit the pattern of animals living in different social and ecological environments."

This cross-continental tour highlights behavioral plasticity of chimpanzees, and the variability of territorial and intergroup behaviors. Part VII, on *verus* at Tai, extends this range of variation, and Part VIII on bonobos takes it even further. Looking back, border patrolling and/or deadly intergroup violence occurred Kalinzu, in context of major territorial loss due to lumbering; and was suspected at Lope under similar circumstances. At Loango, a claimed intergroup kill more likely is the work of a leopard; and later violence seems related to intensified hunger and competition due to global warming. At Conkouati-Douli, there was plenty of killing, in the highly artificial situation of released young captives. Mt. Assirik was similar, with much less bloodshed. There is no support in these locations for intergroup killing as a normal, evolved, predisposition, even though that notion arises. The Gombe model is a distorting lens. But there is plenty of evidence that human disturbance can lead to deadly attacks.

This tour also highlights the terrible human threats killing countless chimpanzees. "The stark truth is that if we do not act decisively our children may live in a world without wild apes" (Walsh et al. 2003:613). It is only getting worse. If more protection is not implemented, a "Planet without Apes" (Stanford 2012) is all too foreseeable.

Many *pan*ologists argue that chimpanzees have "culture." Although I do not go that far, it is crystal clear that different chimpanzee groups include unique ways of living, with distance from Pleistocene forest refugia exhibiting more behavioral diversity (Kalan et al. 2020). The massive population losses of recent decades have destroyed hundreds, probably thousands of local groups. Craig Sanford (2012) made the case: if we were speaking of humans, these could be called ethnocides. Of course if we were talking about humans, there would be no ambiguity in naming the totality of this process: genocide (and see Kuhl et al. 2019).

---

the periphery of Bossou, though it cannot be established whether those visitors and immigrants had passed before the 1982 visitor appeared.

PART VII
TAI

21
Tai and Its Afflictions

Tai National Park in Ivory Coast provides the only long-term study of Western Chimpanzees where relations between neighboring groups are well investigated. The Park is 435,000 hectares of dense evergreen rainforest. After an initial visit in 1976, long-term observation began in 1979 by Christophe Boesch and Hedwige Boesch-Achermann. Research initially focused on nut-cracking, which had not been observed elsewhere. No provisioning. By 1984, habituation of North Group allowed follows, although the thick vegetation made it difficult, and study often relied on sound rather than sight.

In 1988 habituation began of South Group, with follows by 1993. Smaller Middle Group was habituated by 1995. After these groups lost numbers, habituation of East Group began in 2000, and by 2005, 13 adults were identified. With some variation and interruptions, all have been observed regularly since habituation, with day-long focal follows of individuals (Boesch and Boesch 1989:549; 1994:2–3; Boesch et al. 2008a:185–186; 2008b:521; Herbinger et al. 2001:145–146).

Research findings from Tai expands the ongoing variation demonstration, with distinctive use of territory and intergroup clashes more sophisticated than any previously discussed. Yet for decades, they did not kill. That changed, with three deadly intergroup assaults in 2002–2007, two on adult males. By then, Tai chimpanzee communities were greatly disrupted. Two very young males fought their way to the peak, and led the killings.

Chapter 21 provides the historical context. Chapter 22 describes a complex, collective, nonlethal form of territoriality, before population losses. Chapter 23 focuses on the killings, and demonstration violence.

The Devastation of Tai Chimpanzees

Islandization

Tai National Park was created by a presidential decree in 1972, out of a Forest Refuge since 1926. In 1982 it became a World Heritage Site (World Heritage Center n.d.). But around the Park, what had been a broad band of forest fell to agriculture at a rate "among the fastest in the world." The Park region swelled with settlers and refugees, going from 23,000 in 1965 to 375,000 in 1988. Simultaneous with observers' initial habituation effort and first glimpses, in the middle 1980s, about one-third of nearby forest was cleared (Boesch and Boesch-Achermann 2000:9, 11). Not far from the research area, "the northern part of Tai National Park, which comprises 21% of the total park area, was temporarily de-gazetted and is now heavily impacted by human agricultural activity" (Chapman and Lambert 2000:170), though subsequently most farmers were removed (Boesch 2019:14).

Deforestation continued in the early 1990s. Area population doubled with refugees from war in Liberia, only 20 km to the west (Boesch and Boesch 1994:4–5), with more war refugees in 2002 (Boesch 2019:10). "Since the start of our project, the Tai National Park has become an island within a rapidly growing agricultural landscape" (Boesch and Boesch-Achermann 2000:11; Christie et al. 2007). Later immigrants flooded into the forest of southern Ivory Coast from the north and Sahel (Yao et al. 2005), and suitable environment for chimpanzees declined by 18.34% after 2000 (Tweh et al. 2015:710). Apparently, small farmers were replaced by large commercial production. Writing in 2018, Boesch (2019:24) describes the area as "a huge cocoa plantation in which the Tai National Park is a small island." Large NGO conservation agencies left "to concentrate their efforts where more could be saved."

Following discussions will document the anthropogenic destruction of Tai chimpanzee populations. But first comes a natural killer, leopards.

Leopards

Most reports about leopard predation come from 1985–1990, when there were an estimated seven leopards per 10 km^2, with 29 observed or inferred chimpanzee–leopard interactions. Leopards strike from ambush and can kill quickly (Boesch 1991a:224–225, 235–239). Over those 5 years of North Group observations, two adults and three juveniles were confirmed killed, and nine wounded. Injured were cared for by others of the group, and those in danger supported by group-mates rushing to assist (Boesch 2009:52–53). Boesch (1991a:230) suspects that as many as 17 chimpanzees (out of 48 disappearances) fell prey.

But there were many causes of death, and considering the evidence others register skepticism that predation approached those numbers (McGrew 2010; Muller 2011:525; Zuberbuhler and Jenny 2002; Jenny and Zuberbuhler 2005). Details on leopard killings are lacking in later years (cf. Coscolla et al. 2013:970), but Boesch's summary table up to February 2011 puts total killed at 11, and injured at 9, all from North and South groups (Boesch 2012:91). Klailova et al. (2013:316) puts total deaths at six. Predation by leopards is of course natural. Other causes of death are not.

Bushmeat

Hunting by people poses a much greater threat. "An estimated 895 tons of wild meat were extracted from the Park and surrounding forests in 1999, including >68 tons of protected species" (Kouassi et al. 2017:293). Here, local people do eat chimpanzees, which "stands very high on the preference list" (Boesch et al. 2008a:188). Researchers in 1987 ran into poachers shooting at chimpanzees (Boesch and Boesch Achermann

2000:35). Bushmeat markets sprang up in villages around the Park, sometimes with smoked chimpanzee meat.[1]

The Tai research area is on the western side of the reserve. Chimpanzees just west of the original (North) study group—between it and the Park boundary—were eliminated, presumably by nearby farmers. "It is intriguing that the study community did not expand westward" into this empty space. Researchers infer they kept away from the border area to avoid poachers (Boesch and Boesch-Achermann 2000:136). As at Kibale, the islandization effect extends inward. Snare wounds were seen in 1983 (Boesch 2019:13). A minimum of nine of North Group were snared, with at least one dying. Areas with more snares had fewer chimpanzees (Kondgen et al. 2008:253).

Farmers cut new fields within the Park close enough for studied chimpanzees to forage on their crops. Catching chimpanzees still sleeping, farmers "can kill up to 9 chimpanzees in a row" (2000:34, 35; Boesch 2019:13–14).[2] To combat poaching, Boesch worked with several agencies to foster conservation attitudes, with advances and setbacks.[3] Efforts continue (Kouassi et al. 2017).

Ebola and Anthrax

Ebola was the great killer from 1992 to 1994. This mystery disease is hard to pigeonhole as natural or anthropogenic.

> The emergence of infectious diseases has often been linked to ecological changes. The environment and climatological perturbations recorded in Tai could have combined to change the demographic parameters of the EBO reservoir or some aspect of its behavior.... Crop activities have developed on the edge of the park and in the park itself. Illegal plantations and poaching into the Tai National Park have increased from 1985 to 1995 and led to the existence of a large area of farmland and broken forest. This area was only 2 km from the home range of the chimpanzees that were studied. (Fomenty et al. 1999:S125, order reversed)

Boesch and Boesch-Achermann (2000:37–38) suggest a possible vector of transmission, beginning with decreased precipitation beginning in the late 1980s, leading to

---

[1] Near the Sapo National Park, 70 miles from Tai in Liberia, 58 chimpanzee carcasses were found at one hunting camp (Tweh et al. 2015:711).

[2] In Sierra Leone, a previously unknown group of chimpanzees was discovered. During 3 weeks of observation, two chimpanzees were hunted and killed because they raided local farmers' crops (Halloran et al. 2013:519).

[3] Their Wild Chimpanzee Foundation (http://www.wildchimps.org, accessed March 4, 2020) develops awareness activities, monitors chimpanzee populations, works with local school children, and promotes forest protection and antipoaching agreements. With a local theater company, they produced a play on the similarity of chimpanzees and people. Three months after performances in villages around the park, 27% of those surveyed responded that they stopped consuming chimpanzee. "[C]hildren were said to refer to their parents as 'man-eaters' when they ate chimpanzee meat" (Boesch et al. 2008c:133). But the following September, when political violence in Ivory Coast closed out research for 6 months, six habituated chimpanzees were killed by poachers (Boesch 2011:82–83; Boesch 2012:239; Boesch et al. 2008a:197). From 2008, the research group, working with Park administration, hired local men to patrol against poachers; and developed an ecotourism project, which recently opened (Boesch 2019:15).

local habitat changes, with more bats and rodent carriers infecting seemingly healthy red colobus monkeys, which were eaten by chimpanzees. Thus, all the animals of Tai "might be affected by global ecological changes due to human activity."

Another killer in 2001 was anthrax, which is assuredly anthropogenic at Tai. Spread by spores associated with livestock, it was never seen in any ape population prior to the outbreak at Tai. In 2002 the healthy leader of Middle Group dropped dead from it within 20 minutes of acting normally (Boesche 2019:19). At least two adults died from it in or around 2008 (Boesch et al. 2010:3). It now seems endemic. Study from 2012 to 2014 found anthrax DNA in large numbers of carrion flies. "We predict that this pathogen will accelerate the decline and *possibly result in the extirpation of local chimpanzees*" (Hoffmann et al. 2017:82, my emphasis). Anthrax came to Tai with cattle transported from areas where anthrax is common. "[O]wing to deforestation, in recent years cattle transports from Mali and Burkina Faso have passed close to the border of the Tai National Park" (Leendertz 2004:451).

Whatever connections are ultimately established between Ebola or anthrax and human activity, the multiple deaths they caused cannot be taken as "normal." Both are recently arrived.[4]

Anthroponotic Disease

People brought other infections (Patrono and Leendertz 2019:387–389). Disease events with four or more deaths were common in North and South groups after 1984, which had high subadult mortality typical of respiratory infections, (unlike adult-biased mortality with Ebola) (Kondgen et al. 2008:260–261; Kuehl et al. 2008:1–3). In 1999 an acute respiratory infection spread through North Group. Tissue analysis suggested human origin, "either by people working in the park or by outside visitors" (Formenty et al. 2003:172). From 2004 to 2006, four respiratory outbreaks hit South Group, killing 8 of 44 in 2004, and 1 of 34 in 2006. East Group too was struck in 2006. Fifteen died in these five outbreaks, most infants or juveniles. Pathological studies "strongly suggest that humans introduced the two viruses directly and repeatedly into wild chimpanzee populations in the recent past," and the record of proximity points to researchers rather than poachers (Kondgen et al. 2008:260–261). In 2009, 32 of 37 chimpanzees in South Group developed severe respiratory symptoms with possible human origins, and 14 died (Kondgen et al. 2017:2). "[A]t least six major respiratory disease outbreaks of human origin [claimed] up to 19% of the chimpanzee communities" (Grutzmacher et al. 2016:2).[5]

Elevated infant deaths have unexpected consequences.

---

[4] Simian immunodeficiency viruses (SIVs), common in *troglodytes* and *schweinfurthii* subspecies, have not been found in *ellioti* or *verus*. SIV levels are high in Tai red colobus monkeys, which are avidly consumed, but apparently the local chimpanzees are not susceptible (Leendertz et al. 2011:2).

[5] Given the human role in transmission, decision was made to give visibly sick individuals long-lasting antibiotics by dart. Some sick chimpanzees could not climb trees and slept on the ground, making them vulnerable to leopards. When possible, researchers kept vigil with them in shifts, lamps on (Boesch 2019:18). Standards to prevent anthroponotic transmission tightened greatly in steps, followed by reduction but not elimination of respiratory outbreaks after 2008 (Patrono and Leendertz 2019:390).

Infant abundance and mortality rates at Tai cycled regularly and in a way that was not well explained in terms of environmental forcing. Rather, infant mortality cycles appeared to be self-organized in response to the ontogeny of social play. Each cycle started when the death of multiple infants in an outbreak synchronized the reproductive cycles of their mothers. A pulse of births predictably arrived about twelve months later, with social connectivity increasing over the following two years as the large birth cohort approached the peak of social play. The high social connectivity at this play peak then appeared to facilitate further outbreaks. (Kuehl et al. 2008:1)

Human impact unfolds in complex ways. The authors surmise that retrospective examination of mortality across Africa would show a similar pattern.

From this perspective, Boesch (2010:132) has ample reason to concur with one of my main points: "sudden disappearances of healthy individuals could have many causes besides chimpanzee violence.... The assumption that the disappearance of a healthy adult individual is a sign of violent death through intergroup hostility is tenuous, and will lead to an over-estimation of the frequency of intergroup killings."

Tourism

The World Wildlife Foundation got involved at Tai in 1988, working with other NGOs to combat poachers and educate neighboring people about the economic benefits of a sustained chimpanzee population. In the later 1990s the WWF helped develop nine ecotourism sites around Tai (Zeppel 2006:225). Measures to prevent human–chimpanzee contagion increased after 1999, including an eight-day quarantine for international visitors imposed in 2008 (Boesch 2008:725). After 2006 only one outbreak occurred, in 2009 "when the quarantine was ignored" (Grutzmacher et al. 2016:5). That one was disastrous. Enforced quarantines are essential for chimpanzee survival.

The costs and benefits of tourism and research come into focus, once again. "Our results suggest that the close approach of humans to apes, which is central to both research and tourism programs, represents a serious threat to wild apes" (Kondgen et al. 2008:262). Yet proximity to the research and tourism sites correlate with *more abundant* signs of chimpanzees. That reflects almost unimaginable losses for the Tai National Park chimpanzees overall. Those not being directly observed suffered even more than those that were.

Demographic Decline

Group Numbers

Tai groups suffered drastic population losses during study (Boesch and Boesch-Achermann 2000:21–38; Boesch et al. 2008b:521; Wittig and Boesch 2019). From 1982 to 1987 North Group hovered around 80 individuals. In February 1984 seven adult and adolescent males disappeared. Supposition was they died, probably by human hunters. From 1988 to 1991 it dropped from 74 to 50. Five or more seem due

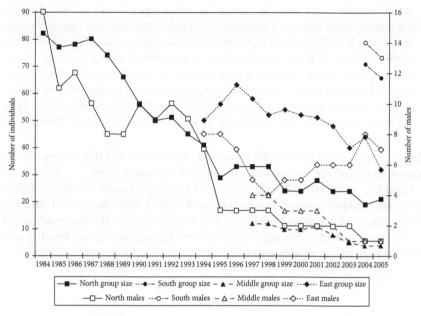

Illustration 7.1 Tai Community Numbers
Source: Boesch, C., Boesch, H., Goné Bi, Z., Normand, E., & Herbinger, I. (2008). The contribution of long-term research by the Taï Chimpanzee Project to conservation.

to leopard predation. In 1992 and 1994, Ebola hit North Group. Along with other diseases, that reduced them from 51 to 29, with two adult and one adolescent males.[6] In October 2001 four healthy individuals succumbed rapidly to anthrax (Leendertz et al. 2004:451). All told, over 15 years, North Group lost 66 individuals, including infants that starved after mothers died (Boesch et al. 2008b:522). After 2001, population level roughly stabilized.

South Group lost 43 over 7 years, with a similar mix of causes. Their head count begins in 1994 with something over 50 individuals. Ebola had taken its toll *before* this first count. It dropped to the low 30s in 2005, with 7 males. After some rebound, a respiratory outbreak in 2009 killed 14 of 37 (Kondgen et al. 2017:2). It recovered substantially after that.

Third-habituated Middle Group was small, around 12 individuals in 1997, also post-Ebola, and dropped to 5 by 2004, with 2 adult males. Four died from anthrax in June 2002, including its alpha in 2 hours (Leendertz et al. 2004:451). In 2007 two adult females, one with a son, transferred into South Group, "after the MG had basically dissolved" (Wittig and Boesch 2019:131). After that, Middle Group was just one adult male and one female (Max Planck Institut 2017).

---

[6] It took courageous work for Tai researchers to diagnose Ebola. One was infected but recovered (Boesch and Boesch-Achermann 1995; Boesch 2019:17).

East Group came under study in 2004–2005, and was habituated by 2007, when it numbered in the high 40s. In 2011 that dropped (somehow) into the mid 20s (Wittig and Boesch 2019:129). Then it stabilized.

In 1989–1990, the entire Park was estimated to contain 4,507 chimpanzees. In 2007, "only about 480 individuals survive, a tenth of the assumed population size" (Campbell et al. 2008:R903; N'Goran et al. 2013:330). Take that in. Nearly 90% drop in under 20 years. Without doubt, increasing human presence decimated the chimpanzees of Tai National Park.[7] Studied groups' losses were terrible indeed, yet not as horrible as losses overall.

> The Tai chimpanzee communities have suffered huge declines.... The NG has declined to a fourth of its original size, the SG to a third, and the EG has been reduced by half.... These declines were caused by disease outbreaks throughout the populations, many of which were related to zoonotic transmission from humans to chimpanzees.... Since 2010, it seems that the habituated communities have stabilized and mortality rates have reduced to the level of birth rates. (Wittig and Boesch 2019:136)

Islandization, but with Different Consequences

For Kibale, I argued that islandization pushed more chimpanzees inside Park borders, and directed nulliparous and parous females into Ngogo group, which increased group size and led to intergroup resource competition and killing. Tai was different.

It is possible that habitat loss outside and even inside the Park did stimulate individual or group relocations, contributing to the large (but not mega) size of North Group as first counted in 1984. But death by leopards, poachers, farmers, and disease quickly brought numbers down, even before the first count for all but North Group. Any influx of migrants could not outpace those losses. The population between North Group and the Park border did not swell up like Kanyanchu, but disintegrated under this onslaught. That later happened to Middle Group, but it had few left to transfer.

This is the overarching context. What began as large groups suffered severe population loss throughout the time of study. That demographic crash is necessary for understanding the shift from nonlethal territoriality to killing.

---

[7] In this depleted field, a new group, North-East, appeared and "started to drive North group out of their original territory and set a lot of pressure on South and East group." North-East Group may have 60–70 members. They are being habituated for research (Max Planck Institut 2017).

22
Sociality and Intergroup Relations

Chapters 22 and 23 take up the behaviors central to this book. Chapter 22 describes the Tai way of territoriality: sophisticated, coordinated, and nonkilling. Chapter 23 is what happened next: killing. The earlier record at Tai exemplifies a developed system of nonlethal territoriality, which was rendered inoperative by drastic population losses. With additional disturbance, that created the conditions for deadly demonstration violence. Not incidentally, Tai subverts the male-centered sociology of Gombe vision.

Ranging, Associating, Hunting, and Patrolling

Tai rangelands and density vary considerably from 1982 to 1995, from 4.1/km^2 to 1.9/km^2. Fluctuation was greatest for peripheries. The heavily used core area hardly changed at all (Boesch and Boesch-Achermann 2000:130–135). Overlap in rangeland is perhaps the greatest on record, excepting bonobos. For North Group: "In 1989, 53%, and, in 1995, 56% of the territory formed part of an overlapping zone" including "important parts of the territory" (Boesch and Boesch-Achermann 2000:135). In 1996–1997 "less than two-thirds" of the *core* areas of North, Middle, and South groups were used exclusively by that group alone (Herbinger et al. 2001:155). This extensive overlap underlies a pattern of territoriality that enables *mutual usage*, including *by* females.

Gender

Tai deviates from the standard donut image of males roaming about a protected female core. North Group females ranged over 93% of the space used by males. This goes along with greater female affiliation than in the Gombe model.[1] In some ways, Tai is closer to bonobos (Boesch 1996:111). Although Tai female bonding remains less than Tai males, "as more data on female relationships accumulate, it becomes evident that chimpanzee female sociality can vary dramatically between populations" (Lehmann and Boesch 2008:78). Although they visit the most peripheral areas less

---

[1] [T]he tendency for males to associate with females seems to vary, with Tai males the most inclined to do so and Gombe males the least so. This supports the idea that the grouping pattern of chimpanzees differs in the sexual bonding tendency. Tai chimpanzees are characterized by strong bisexual bonding, Gombe chimpanzees are male-oriented in their bonding, and Mahale chimpanzees show an intermediate tendency (Boesch 1996:111).

"[T]he view of chimpanzees as a purely male oriented society does not reflect the social life in Tai chimpanzees" (Boesch and Boesch-Achermann 2000:127; and see Riedel et al. 2011), (or of Sonso).

often than males, "females in Tai have repeatedly been observed to patrol together with the males in border regions" (Lehmann and Boesch 2005:532).

Tai females exert considerable selectivity in mating partners. They resist unwanted advances, have favorites, and even leave their group for up to 2 months and mate elsewhere (Boesch et al. 2008b:526–527; Stumpf and Boesch 2006; 2010). Of Tai offspring, 6%–10% have extragroup paternity (Schubert et al. 2011:7; Vigilant 2001).[2]

That, and transfer of females with male offspring, go against the foundational notion of genetic competition between groups of closely related males. Tai males show nearly as much genetic similarity across local groups as females do (Lukas et al. 2005). Within groups, higher male relatedness was determined by how many maternal and paternal siblings happen to be resident, but other males were not genetically close. Conclusion: "levels of average male relatedness significantly higher than zero are only to be expected in very small chimpanzee groups" (Vigilant 2019:73–74). So much for the genetic implications of male philopatry.

Hunting

From the first observations, Tai chimpanzees hunted red colobus (Boesch and Boesch-Achermann 2000:158–190; also Boesch and Boesch 1989, Boesch 2009:41–44; Boesch 2012:81–91). For Gombe, Mahale, Ngogo, and Sonso, I argue that *surges* in hunting coincided with sharpened scarcity of preferred foods. At Tai hunting rates were always high, and demonstrated a level of cooperation unreported from any other site. When Boesch explored Tai in 1976, in the center of the Park he saw three chimpanzees feeding on a large red colobus (Boesch 2012:81). For Tai, *I do not claim* that frequent hunting reflects human pressures. It may be better taken, consistent with Boesch, as showing the great variation in socially learned behaviors among different chimpanzee populations.

In the middle 1980s before the population crash began, North Group had nine adult males and averaged 2.62 hunts per month, mostly of red colobus. As elsewhere, larger parties increased success. Unlike other chimpanzee hunters specializing in infants and young, at Tai they often went after adults, which fight back. Females hunted with males, although at a lower frequency and in roughly the same proportion as at Gombe and Mahale. On three occasions three females alone took on larger prey, adult black and white colobus monkeys.

Boesch and Boesch-Achermann (2000) portray extraordinary cooperation in hunts (and see Samuni et al. 2018). Silently finding their prey high in a tree, a "driver" slowly climbs the tree, as those on the ground move to anticipated escape routes. The climber rushes upward, sparking colobus flight, moving prey along but not trying to catch one himself. Those on the ground follow, sometimes blocking escape. Now

---

[2] An initial study, when some research complexities were not yet appreciated, found that 7 out of 13 individuals had extragroup paternity. It was retracted, and a later study found only one of 41 offspring was not sired within the group. Study to date of paternity of 117 Tai births found that for "14 offspring, no fathers could be found, but one or more potential sires were not sampled" (Vigilant 2019:72–73).

blockers and pursuers can alternate. Eventually colobus are trapped and the catching begins. Meat is shared according to "rules" (2000:180) among hunters. "Each individual may change strategies during a hunt, and group members adjust the amount of meat an individual receives according to its contribution to the hunt" (2000:175). With this complexity, learning to hunt begins when males are 9 or 10, and it takes about 20 years of practice to become a master (2000:185).

These assertions of exceptional sophistication have been questioned (Muller 2011:527; cf. Boesch 2012:105). They are comparable to claims about exceptional sophistication in war (below).

Much meat is consumed (Fahy et al. 2013). From 1987 to 1991, male adults averaged 186 g (6.56 oz) per day, and females 25 g (.88 oz). In comparison, a long-term estimate of Gombe consumption is 55 g for males, and 7 g for females (2000:165). But this high intake was before the population crash. In this cooperatively hunting population, "as the number of males dropped from seven to two . . . the hunting frequency diminished dramatically" (2000:165).

By 1990–1991, as North Group fell from 80 to 50, one chimpanzee responded to the lack of hunting partners through a cruder and costly technique of hunting alone. He would slowly move through trees near groups of red colobus, provoking a mob attack. "When that happened, Ulysse would invariably try to capture one of the males. Thus for the first time a single Tai hunter was very successful"—albeit at physical cost (Boesch 1994:1147). This foreshadows changes to intergroup confrontations when group numbers dropped.

Patrolling

Another collective activity is patrolling, also evident early in research. From 1984 to 1991—as Tai Park chimpanzees were losing outside rangelands—the North community patrolled about once every 2 weeks, often into ranges where neighbors also foraged (Boesch 2009:85–87; Boesch and Boesch-Achermann 2000:135–136). North Group had 137 encounters with neighbors from 1982 to 1996, about nine per year, or one in three patrols. Encountering outsiders was *routine* in their islandizing world (Boesch et al. 2008b:523; and below).

From 1982 to 2005, 485 intergroup encounters were recorded by all four groups. Most were calling only; 118 (25%) were visual, but 47 (10%) involved physical contact. In many later clashes, observers were present on both sides (Boesch et al. 2008b:521–524). What happened when they met depended on how many each group had left at that time.

Patterns of Intergroup Conflict

If clashes between groups were first known from Tai instead of Gombe, we'd have formed a very different impression of chimpanzee "war." Early on, Boesche (1992:163–168) discounted comparison of Gombe raiding to human war, because unlike war it lacked coordinated group confrontations. With more observation, continuities with war seemed stronger. Group clashes as reported were elaborate and coordinated, more so than anywhere else. But for years, the intent to kill seemed absent (Boesch and Boesch-Achermann 2000:140–156).

Tactics

According to Boesch and Boesch-Achermann, as a patrol line of Tai chimpanzees got close to neighbors, they fanned out. They seemed to assess numbers, and if

> they estimate them as numerous, they start the charge from farther away and make aggressive waa-barks earlier than if they have estimated them as being small in number, in which case they then go in much closer, start the attack silently, and try to catch them.... The surprise effect is impressive and attacked individuals always retreat at first. These initial attacks are also the ones in which physical contacts are most frequent. Bad bites can be suffered within a minute. (Boesch and Boesch-Achermann 2000:140)

Extended battles could ensue—with surprises.

> In an extreme situation, one can observe two lines with all the adult males and some females facing one another, the attacks alternating from one side to the other. In other situations, they are more spread out in the forest, and we have seen parties of two to three males attacking the other side. These attacks seem to be coordinated vocally through attack calls. In two of these back-and-forth attacks, lasting over twenty minutes, the opponents calmed down, just facing and threatening each other. Five young oestrous females quietly crossed the lines to join the males on the other side, mated with one or two of them, and returned calmly back to their community. (Boesch and Boesch-Achermann 2000:141)

Clashes are opportunities for females to cross-over and mate with the enemy (Boesch 2009:89)!

Exposed individuals were taken "prisoner" and assaulted, on 18 occasions through the late 1990s. Most "prisoners" were female, and were approached with sexual interest (Boesch et al. 2008b:523). "[I]n 11 of 13 cases sexual activities were observed between the female and her male aggressors, whether or not they had sexual swelling (Boesch 2009:92, 94; also Boesch 2009:91; Boesch et al. 2008b:525). Prisoners or any individuals under attack were usually rescued quickly by reinforcements from their own group (Boesch 2009:128). In almost a third of all visual encounters males rushed to support others in a difficult situation, and that rose to three-quarters when females were threatened. Doing all this requires a sufficient numbers of males.

Yet Tai raises doubts about the importance of an imbalance of power. "[S]mall communities do not refrain from attacking larger communities ... even when in very small parties" (Boesch et al. 2008b:530–531). When outnumbered—and as numbers dropped—North Group developed a tactic of advancing obliquely to catch the end of the opposing line.

Once the [North] study community had less than nine adult males, Brutus, at the time alpha male and clear leader in most inter-community encounters, started to lead lateral attacks instead of frontal ones. A lateral attack occurs when the advancing and strictly silent males aim their progress not straight towards the audible opponents but laterally. In this way they avoid the noisiest and possibly also largest party and looked for individuals in smaller parties that they might defeat. (Boesch and Boesch-Achermann 2000:142)

Still, a major loss in numbers compared to neighbors led to changes in intergroup confrontations.

When the overall number of males at Tai decreased after 1990 . . . they became more careful when facing strangers. . . . When the group declined further to four or even two adult males, they started to avoid confrontation. The higher frequency of avoidance tactics by small groups illustrates how the territory size reduces, and how neighbours progressively extend their territory without encountering resistance. (Boesch and Boesch-Achermann 2000:145)

Much of that decline in adult males was due to poaching and anthropogenic disease. It calls to mind Kasakela's move into ranges of depleted neighbors after the middle 1990s.

As population decline continued, even lateral attacks were no longer feasible. Yet the imbalance of power hypothesis (IoPH) remained in question. In May 2000, when deaths reduced North Group to two adult males, and Middle Group chimpanzees repeatedly entered their range, North males waited quietly in ambush, charging out to chase the interlopers away (Boesch et al. 2008b:524). In 2007 Porthos of North Group had adopted an orphan, Gia. He heard the cries of Bamu, a one-armed North female, surrounded by five males of South Group.

Porthos on his own, with Gia on his back, charged the South Group males through the thick undergrowth. The loud aggressive calls of Porthos were, however, impressive enough to deter them and so save Bamu. It was breathtaking to see this adult male with a baby clinging to his back charging five male opponents. (Boesch 2009:51)

This would provoke a deadly reaction (Chapter 23).

Females and Males

Tai females participate in clashes (Boesch 2010:144–145), 91% of all incidents in one sample (Samuni et al. 2017:271).

Female involvement in territorial encounters has been proposed to be rare in humans and in chimpanzees. Tai chimpanzees are an exception to this statement, for females are part of the attack parties in more than two-thirds of the cases, and 35% of the members of such parties are female. They are significantly more often in parties going to make a frontal or rearguard attack than for a commando or a lateral attack. Thus their contribution seems to be specially important for certain strategies, and males attack more readily when females are present. Females may, however, lag behind during the last minute of the attack.... In a low visibility environment, vocal display is important, and females always contribute by aggressively barking and frequently drumming, making it quite impossible for strangers to estimate the real power of the opponent community. (Boesch and Boesch-Achermann 2000:150, citations and statistics omitted)[3]

Tai females are bold. One Middle Group female with two offspring heard an infant to the west. For 4 hours she took her baby and juvenile and stalked, sniffed, watched, and listened. When she heard chimpanzees nearby, both daughters climbed on her back as she advanced. Spotting two West Group females with offspring up a tree, she barked and displayed. The startled intruders ran off.

Perhaps most impressive, in January 1991, North Group's Goma and her 5-year-old daughter were traveling with male Macho. She stopped to feed, he went ahead. Soon she heard loud cries from his location. Goma, daughter on belly, charged Macho's adversaries, barking. As the attackers paused, Macho ran off (Boesch et al. 2008b:525–526; Boesch 2009:94–95).

Strategy

Boesch and Boesch-Achermann (2000:153–156; also Boesch 2010:154) discuss leadership, rapid evaluations, decisions, and collaborations they see in confrontations, and "strategic planning" in deciding which neighbor needs more aggressive attention—up to nine patrols in a month.

> At Tai, chimpanzees used four strategies to react to the presence of strangers and used five different strategies when attacking strangers. The use of these strategies was not random, but context-dependent, demonstrating a dynamic decision-making process among the males of a given coalition. The strategic planning of attacks in chimpanzees includes a precise evaluation of the forces present, and a precise collaboration between the males when applying these strategies. (Boesch and Boesch-Achermann 2000:155)

Tai chimpanzees are claimed to recognize neighbors' calls and base decisions to attack on knowledge of the number of males and females in a neighboring group relative to their own group. "All this suggests a precise and long-term memory-based knowledge of neighbors in chimpanzees" (Boesch 2009:98–102).

---

[3] In intergroup conflicts, Tai females experience a rise in oxytocin levels similar to that of males (Samuni et al. 2017:271).

Most Sophisticated Apes

Claims of extreme Tai sophistication in confrontations, hunting, patrolling (and other behaviors not relevant here), elicited skepticism. Reviews of *The Real Chimpanzee* were unusually harsh, suggesting Boesch overstated findings with weak evidence (Gilby and Connor 2010:226–228; McGrew 2010:190; Muller 2011:525–527; Pusey 2010). I mention this because I too am skeptical, especially given the limits on observation in Tai's dense foliage.[4]

For instance, Tai chimpanzees are said to engage in intentional cooperative deception, far beyond anything reported in any other intergroup confrontation.

> This strategy may be intentionally deceptive when some males remain at the back, drumming and repeatedly calling loudly, while other males move silently towards the opponents. There, the front males may wait silently for the strangers advancing to surprise the noisy rearguard, unaware of the close presence of the silent males who may then attack unexpectedly. (Boesch and Boesch-Achermann 2000:141)

This tactical sophistication is beyond that reported for many human warriors.

Even if overstated, Tai confrontations are sophisticated practices involving mutualistic actions and coordination of numbers of males and females. Over many years of observation and 485 group encounters, there was another thing noteworthy about Tai intergroup relations: they did not kill.

Nonkillers

Until September 2002 Tai stood in contradiction to the idea that killing outsiders comes naturally to chimpanzees. "In Gombe chimpanzees, the physical attacks were much more violent than at Tai." When isolated individuals were surrounded and attacked, the violence included hitting and biting, but not with the "intent to kill" inferred at Gombe (Boesch and Boesch-Achermann 2000:149). One time an infant was consumed by females, but the researchers did not know if adults had killed it, or whether it came from within or outside the community (Count 4-?-I-?, no date). "[W]e never witnessed any sign of aggression aimed at infants in all the intercommunity encounters we observed" (2000:33–34).

Interviewed for the BBC (2004), Boesch compared clashes at Tai to Gombe.

> I have not seen this kind of killing in Tai Forest. This violence is not always present. Wrangham's ideas originate from his observation in Gombe, and its's obviously something extremely worrying to see chimpanzees killing other chimps. But I also

---

[4] Tai was the location of Disney's film, *Chimpanzee*. But the plot theme of aggression by "Scar's gang," uses footage of intergroup aggression by Ngogo, because of restricted visibility at Tai. "The directors felt there was nothing to be gained by showing the audiences pictures of a brush rustling in the darkness while the narrator described a fight no one would be able to see!" (Boesch and O'Connell 2012:38).

think we need to take in account in this thinking the huge behavioural diversity that exists between chimpanzee populations.

The contrast in killing between Tai and Gombe seemed clear and categorical.

[A]fter more than 18 years of observations of the chimpanzees . . . initially of one community and then of three neighboring ones, no lethal violence was observed despite regular aggressive interactions between communities. . . . Especially striking is the fact that observers had not seen infants of stranger mothers to be killed nor to be subject to intense aggressions by the attacking males and the injuries suffered by the females were minor compared to the reports provided from other chimpanzee populations. (Boesch et al. 2008b:520)

For the three groups up to 2002, that totaled about 37 years of direct observation (Boesch et al. 2008b:521), without a single intergroup killing.

Tai thus offers a distinctive pattern of territoriality: intensive patrolling and sophisticated, *nonlethal* intergroup confrontations, with females as active participants. This chapter considers that pattern in terms of local ecology and subsistence, then closing with human impact.

Competition for Scarce Resources

Boesch and Boesch-Achermann (2000:146 and Herbinger et al. 2001) discount food scarcity in intergroup conflict between groups, because food is abundant all year. Edible plants are widely distributed, no more common in the core area than the peripheries (Anderson et al. 2002:93–95).

Adequate food is not the same as *preferred* food. Measurably, some fruits are preferred, some neglected, and consumption varies between North, South, and Middle groups. Boesch et al. (2006:197–198) call these "cultural" preferences. But overall, nuts and meat are preferred over fruits. For those and more, scarcity is evident. Females actively compete over monopolizable food resources involving "meat, stone hammers to crack nuts, water holes in trees, eggs of ants, honeycombs" and certain plants, especially "crowns of fruit trees" (Wittig and Boesch 2003:855, 860).[5]

Nuts? Tai chimpanzees crack nuts open with hammer and anvil stones, and eat them in abundance. Over a four-month season, cracked nuts are a major source of protein and calories, providing about 3,450 calories on an average day. This entails competition. It is hard to find a good nut tree, anvil stone, and hammer together. "Hammers are the factor limiting nut cracking." "Good quality hammers tend to be quickly monopolized by those who find them first." Females put more time into this solitary activity, so they consume more (Boesch and Boesch-Achermann 2000:202–205). Nuts are a foundation of female nutrition.

---

[5] Female competition is more frequent than at Gombe or Mahale. Researchers infer that this strong competition led to an unusually clear linear dominance hierarchy among Tai females, which mitigated direct aggression (Wittig and Boesch 2003:858, 862).

But the prime monopolizable food is meat. Males eat more meat, but high-ranking females eat a lot. "[D]ominant females may access 500 g of meat per successful hunt, a substantial benefit compared to 80 g obtained by average females" (Wittig and Boesch 2003:860). Meat was at stake in 42% of time spent on monopolizable foods, but in almost 70% of the *conflicts* over monopolizable food (2003:855).

Protein comes from many sources, but all protein is not equal. Given the major dietary contribution of nuts and meat it is reasonable to surmise that they fulfill some important nutritional needs. Without doubt they are greatly preferred. That brings us to back to territoriality.

Meat, Nuts, and Territoriality

Tai is exceptional, both in how much group ranges overlap, and how active are females in the outer ranges. I suggest that is because females' preferred foods are there. About one-quarter of all patrols turned into red colobus hunts (Boesch 2009:87). Given the difficulty of finding a good nut tree, hammer stone, and anvil together, much nutting must be done in overlap zones as well.

Hunting and nutting in overlap zones entails risks. Tai chimpanzees search for neighbors by listening for them. Normal hunting is usually raucous, yet in patrols-turned-hunts, "they remain silent throughout the hunting episode and if a squabble breaks out between them, the screams that normally are so loud are totally suppressed" (Boesch 2009:87). When neighbors may be around, hunters keep mum. But the noise of nut-cracking cannot be eliminated, and carries over a few hundred meters (Boesch et al. 2008a:185–186).

Why are females so active in patrols and intergroup confrontations, and why do they assault vulnerable outside females? Females actively compete for monopolizable food. With nuts and meat, females have a direct stake in intergroup contests over overlap areas. And it makes a difference. Group size and lessened neighbor pressure is better explained by total adults, not just males (Lemoine et al. 2020).

Nonkilling

"From our long-term observations, chimpanzees seem to pursue some specific aims when fighting strangers and these can be achieved often without killing" (Boesch 2009:104). Since two groups cannot hunt red colobus or crack nuts in the same place and time, "specific aims," I suggest, included temporarily clearing outsiders from shared peripheral areas with preferred foods.

Before the population crash, the sophisticated pattern of patrolling, defense, and surprise attacks appears to include *expectations* of limited, nonlethal interactions. Often the attackers were themselves outnumbered.

> It seems that the goal of patrols is not to win battles against the neighbours, but rather to gain information about their location and, if they find them, to try to unsettle them.... they would make a surprise attack, and pursue the strangers, but when

counter-attacked, they simply run away without putting up any resistance, until they are no longer pursued and return to their territory. (Boesch 2009:87)

They were finding where they would be safe in foraging—where neighbors were and weren't—and by being really obnoxious, making it uncomfortable for neighbors to browse around. It worked. "[T]erritory size shows a tendency to correlate negatively with encounter rate.... Thus, territorial encounter risk, not food distribution or abundance, appears to explain the variation in territory size used by chimpanzees over short periods of time" (Boesch and Boesch-Achermann 2000:132).

The evidence from the early years of observations suggests a well-tuned, socially adaptive territoriality, enabling exploitation of dispersed resources in ranges *too big to monopolize*, with individuals safe from serious danger.

Human Impact and Territoriality

Did human impact play any role in this territorial jostling? For Ngogo, islandization contributed to major population growth, which led to deadly intergroup conflict. Tai also islandized, but human impact crashed group numbers, the opposite of Ngogo. Increased pressure on preferred food is not expected.

Displacement however could be an element. Even as overall chimpanzee numbers started downward, massive disruption to their north and west could shift chimpanzees away from farmers and poachers, thus increasing boundary tensions in the study area. Human impact possibly increased the frequency of patrols and intergroup contacts, but it did not change the nonlethal character of territoriality—for a while.

Tai chimpanzees before demographic collapse displayed a highly developed, *learned*, pattern of resource competition without deadly violence, which secured access to preferred foods. As with sophistication of hunting and nut cracking, this could be an ancient pattern. Then in a generation, massive population losses, much directly or indirectly related to human contact, rendered those sophisticated intergroup tactics inoperative—as it did with earlier forms of monkey hunting. Yet even through the demographic crash of the 1990s, territorial clashes were still not deadly. That changed after 2002.

23
Killings and Explanations

Three Brutal Incidents

In September 2002 five adult males and nine adult females of South Group moved into the western range of Middle Group. They encountered strangers and chased them off. South Group male Sagu, young but already alpha, noticed an infant left behind in a tree. On prior occasions females were taken "prisoner" without any effort to harm their infants. This time was different. Sagu caught the baby, bit it multiple times, then dropped it. Gogol, Sagu's young ally, picked it up, and bit its throat. They ate none of it. The three other adult males and nine adult females were bystanders, except for one that dragged the corpse. As no Middle Group infants were missing, the victim was thought to be from an unhabituated group to the west (Count 1-O-I-M 2002) (Boesch 2009:90; Boesch et al. 2008b:523). Given the devastation to chimpanzees beyond research purview, the westerners' recent history was probably pretty bad.

In March 2005 a South Group party of six adult and adolescent males and four females heard chimpanzees to the east and ran toward them. The Southies caught a young adult male of East Group and enveloped him in a furious mass, all except one female biting and hitting him. After 22 minutes, they rushed off toward buttress-drumming to the east. The victim managed to sit up, cuts visible around his face. Five minutes later, Sagu, Gogal, and another adult male came back and killed him. Sometime during all this, the testes and penis were ripped off (Boesch et al. 2008b:524; Boesch 2009:79–80) (Count 1-O-A-M 2005).

In March 2007 East Group male Porthos, carrying an adopted infant, rescued a female and singlehandedly chased off five South Group males (Chapter 22). This humiliation was followed by a burst of calls from the west, while East Group kept drumming and barking. Rushing to the scene, the observer found a mass of South Group beating and biting an East Group male. Present were all four South Group adult males, four adult females, and three adolescent males. Fewer than half of the males were in extreme attack mode, but all three females were. Sagu and Gogol had bloodstained mouths from biting deeply, as did the female Zora. Sagu killed him with bites to the throat.

After 15 minutes the attackers backed off. Then Gogol and Zora went up and pounded on the corpse. The observer noticed that the genitals were gone. Female Zora had them, and ate them with fresh leaves from a nearby sapling. This is extraordinary. Cannibalism of killed infants is not unusual, and ripping skin or licking blood was witnessed in some attacks at Gombe. But other than little bits of Foudouko at Fongoli, this is the only cannibalism ever reported in the killing of an adult—and by a female. The whole assault took an hour and a half (Boesch 2009:82) (Count, 1-O-A-M 2007).[1]

---

[1] For reasons unknown, this definite killing does not appear in the tables of Wilson et al. (2014a:EDT 1).

All these attacks were by South Group, two against East Group and one (infant) from unknown chimpanzees to the west.

Wow. What a difference from earlier portrayals of Tai chimpanzees! And all are consistent with the imbalance of power hypothesis: multiple males encounter and kill a solo outsider.

An End to Exceptionalism

"I was very intrigued and thrilled when early in 2005 Emmanuelle Normand told me about her observations of the killing of an East Group male by the South Group chimpanzees . . . the ambivalence between violence and cooperation I have always seen in male chimpanzees was reaching higher levels of complexity than I had expected" (Boesch 2009:81).

Boesch still sees the *frequency* of killing as a major difference between Tai and East Africa.[2] But the 2002–2007 Tai killings and those suspected at Loango brought him over to the position that intergroup killing is "a typical aspect of chimpanzee sociality," not due to "increased human encroachment" (Boesch et al. 2008b:520).

> Long-term studies of different chimpanzee populations have revealed that warfare is present in all of them and that it can lead to the extinction of whole communities.... At first, the descriptions of warfare in the Gombe populations were greeted with skepticism, as if seeming to imply that the observation of warfare in the wild chimpanzees gave some moral justification for going to war! Consequently, it was dismissed as a result of the artificial provision of food that occurred in Gombe in the early days of the study. However, the observation in the Tai forest and then in other chimpanzee communities, where none of the individuals were provided with food or even before they were habituated to humans, removed any doubt that such behaviour is natural and part of the repertoire of all known populations. (Boesch 2009:127–128)

But this was not a simple switch to Gombe-vision.

A New Hypothesis

Boesch does not suggest a dominance drive. His (2009:102–103) theory begins with the existential threat posed by leopards. This, he hypothesizes, fosters intense in-group loyalties so individuals risk injury to themselves in rescues. "Under these circumstances, xenophobia can develop, whereby outsiders are violently ostracized." A dark lesson for humanity, and it gets darker.

---

[2] "[F]atal violence is less common than documented for other chimpanzee populations" (Boesch et al. 2008b:520–521). He calculates rates of intergroup killings as Tai 0.08 kills/yr, Gombe 0.83/yr, Mahale 0.3/yr, and Ngogo 1.83/yr (Boesch 2012:90).

Reproductive Competition

"[E]limination of rivals, sex and food competition as related to density all coincide to make chimpanzees attack their neighbours. Chimpanzees take into account the two main driving forces for survival and reproduction to make decisions about conflicts" (Boesch 2009:101). Of the two, Boesch emphasizes competition for sex, discounting direct resource competition over food—which of course I stress. What is the evidence that patrolling and intergroup hostility increases male reproductive opportunities?

Chimpanzees attempt sex even with nonovulatory female prisoners, but capturing a female is a rare event—11 instances out of 485 observed encounters. On the other hand, five estrous females mated with foreign males in just one intergroup clash, and similar crossovers happened other times. Intergroup encounters seem to give outside males a shot at paternity, more than the reverse.

Boesch revives an abandoned theory from Gombe. "Killers might be rewarded by attracting females."[3] But advertising strength can be done without killing, as *any* territorial encounter could be a form of self-advertisement to attract future mates (Boesch and Boesch-Achermann 2000:146). Moreover, any witnesses from the other groups were gone before Sagu or Gogol did anything exceptionally violent. If they were advertising, it was for the home-town crowd.[4]

For a quarter-century of study, or 46 observation years if counting time spent with each group, 331 months of continuous group observations, and 485 recorded encounters, involving something like 50 adult males (Boesch et al. 2008b:521, 523), the only three killings ever seen were led *by the same two males*, Gogol and Sagu of South Group.

Death and Politics

Boesch (2009:100) clearly explains why South Group turned deadly:

> The group had become exceptionally aggressive since the young males, Sagu and Gogol, had gained the two highest positions in the hierarchy. It was the conduct of these two ambitious males that started the South Group's terrible violent encounters with their neighbours. It was the first time in 25 years of the Tai project that we had this pairing of young dominant males, whereas up until then there had only been prime males, around 25 years of age, taking up the alpha position.

3

> The example of the South Group suggests that this may be the case.... It is especially relevant for this discussion that at the end of January 2007, for the first time since 1995 when we had started to follow the South Group, two new immigrant females integrated into the community.... Were these females attracted by the strong young males of the South Group? Difficult to draw firm conclusions, but the coincidence is informative. (Boesch 2009:100, also Boesch et al. 2008b:530)

The year 2007 is elsewhere (Wittig and Boesch 2019:131) noted as the year two females transferred from disintegrating Middle Group.

[4] Boesch also notes that in the two adult killings, victims had their testicles and penis ripped off, which he takes as an indicator of sexual competition. However in the second, a female ate the genitals (Boesch 2009:82).

South alpha Sagu was 13 when the first killing occurred. Gogol, the beta, was 11 (Blasse et al. 2013:5194). That young an alpha is exceptional not just for Tai, but across Africa. The only precedent is superaggressive Goblin at Gombe, temporarily reaching alpha status before being deposed and nearly killed in "the Great Attack." Sagu and Gogol remained on top. Understanding why South Group turned to killing requires asking why Sagu and Gogol rose to dominance.

I found just two comments about their rise. Gogol "fought his way up the social ladder through many fights" (Boesch 2009:80). Sagu, alpha by the first killing in September 2002, in August 1999 was third ranked (Boesch et al. 2006:106). This establishes a time frame for the pair's unprecedented, fighting ascendance: sometime between August 1999 and September 2002. That brings us back to human impact.

The Political Milieu

Chimpanzee politics are transacted, negotiated, and tested in continuous flow. A chimpanzee group is a web of constructed and often contested relations. A political rise or fall takes time, and sometimes coalitional attacks by multiple males (Boesch 2009:78).

Thirty different coalitions were recorded prior to 2000, 18 involving status inferiors pushing against higher ups (Boesch and Boesch-Achermann 2000:124). At Tai, unlike Gombe and Mahale, females are assertive political actors. They participate in coalitions and join in attacks on males. The support of a dominant mother affects the status aspirations of sons—as it is with bonobos (Boesch and Boesch-Achermann 2000:72–75, 124–127).

Within a web of dyadic connections, death of key players can destabilize the status order and shake or break coalitions. Prior to 2000 that was apparent in the only major status change resulting from two males working together. In the North Group, the disappearance of four adult males, probably due to poachers, opened the hierarchy to great contention. Two young males combined to attack the alpha Brutus, weakened by a snare wound and having lost an ally. Intense fighting went on for months. Brutus remained on top, but the two challengers rose to second and third rank (Boesch and Boesch-Achermann 2000:71–72). Human impact caused demographic disruption, followed by the rise of two young contenders.

That was with four deaths. Between 1996 and 1998, South Group dropped from just over 60 to just over 50 (Boesch et al. 2008b:521). Then it got worse. Using data that ends in 2005, the losses spiked.

> In the last seven years in the South Group, 43 individuals died. Eleven individuals, including three adults disappeared for unknown reason. Five were killed by leopards and eight by poachers, whereas 13 from disease, five starved after the deaths of their mothers, and one died from injuries. (Boesch et al. 2008b:522)

Those 1999–2005 losses and attendant social disruption led up to and through the rise of Sagu and Gogol and the killings that followed.

Playback

From July 1999 to June 2001, teams of observers played chimpanzee calls to members of North, Middle, and South Groups (Herbinger et al. 2009). Methods were similar to Kanyawara, with an important difference. At Kanyawara all calls were recorded elsewhere, so every playback was of a complete stranger. At Tai they used calls recorded elsewhere, but also calls of neighbors and from within the group.

Recognition of group-specific calls is suspected at Tai (Crockford et al. 2004; and see Kojima et al. 2003), and even of individuals (Boesch 2009:101). Over two years, 20 times parties heard calls of strangers, 22 times of neighbors, and 11 times of their own group. Neighbors' calls came from normally expectable directions to simulate a real intrusion. Within-group calls were played only when the recorded caller was not seen in the target group for at least an hour (Herbinger et al. 2009:1390–1392).

At Kanyawara target chimpanzees stayed quiet or retreated when they did not have a numerical advantage. At Tai, for calls of neighbors, even single individuals countercalled. "[S]tranger calls soon led to retreat in contrast to responses to neighbours" (2009:1394). Strangers are scarier than familiar adversaries, as with newly appeared Y-group at Mahale.

Researchers acknowledged that playbacks might worsen relations between groups, but discounted that danger if "they simulate a natural situation and give individuals the opportunity to select an appropriate behavioural strategy" (2009:1395). They claim their experiment fulfilled the first condition because playbacks were "comparable with the naturally observed frequency of the event." But if neighbor playbacks are added on top of natural ones, that increases the total rate. To sophisticated Tai chimpanzees, it would seem that neighbors were unusually intrusive.

Playbacks of strangers are not "natural situations." "It is important to point out that encountering a group of strangers must be a rare event in chimpanzees.... In more than 30 years of observation in Tai ... we never observed a natural encounter with a group of strangers" (2009:1394). Thus, on top of the apparent increase in assertiveness of neighbors, all three groups experienced an apparent intrusion of strangers, like never heard before. These two years of playbacks represents a major psychological disturbance.[5]

Elevated tension is documented; 23 of 42 calls of strangers and neighbors directly triggered patrols (2009:1392). During the 2-year experiment, there were 121 intergroup encounters, versus 41 in a 2-year follow up (2009:1396). The May 2000 ambush of three Middle Group males by North Group (Chapter 22), occurred during playbacks.

Because responses to playbacks were like those to natural calls, and because the number of encounters decreased in the follow-up period, researchers were "confident that our study has had no unacceptable negative impact on our study animals" (Herbinger et al. 2009:1396). However, North and Middle group lost four members

---

[5] Playbacks of in-group members also might unnerve. If Tai chimpanzees recognize specific pant hoots, how would they comprehend a situation when they just saw an individual an hour ago, but hear that same chimpanzee calling from way over there? Or when he is with others in a nontargeted group, but heard calling from a distance?

each to anthrax during the follow-up period, including the Middle alpha (Leendertz et al. 2004:451). Those losses should depress patrol and encounter rates, so the researchers' follow-up measure is inconclusive about the degree of experimental disturbance.

Internal Politics and External Killings

The killings that came after the playbacks, researchers portray "as part of the natural social changes within the community." Rather than the playbacks contributing to those killings, "[a] much more likely explanation is that changes in intergroup interactions were the result of ongoing changes in the social and demographic variables of these communities" (Herbinger et al. 2009:1396). Those changes were substantially though not entirely due to human impact, and a critical outcome was the rise of Sagu and Gogol. Unlike Kanyawara, where killing of the Sebitole stranger occurred mere weeks after a playback, at Tai the first killing, of the infant, happened 15 months after the experiment ended. The first adult killing was more than three years after playback ended, and the second more than five. Playback cannot be held directly responsible for any killing.

My hypothesis is this: human augmented social fragmentation from population losses, plus an induced psychology of fear, was conducive to the unprecedented rise of two belligerent adolescents. They used violence to consolidate and maintain their position, and then led their group into deadly confrontations with outsiders, which then did not display the sophisticated, numbers-dependent defenses, mutual support, and rescues of earlier years.

Display Violence

During the killings, South Group had six to eight adult/adolescent males, plus many assertive females, enough for upstart coalitions. In my hypothesis, violence intimidates potential challengers while on the rise or on top. In disrupted Tai, where chimpanzees had never seen a killing, young Sagu and Gogol displayed extreme violence to an audience of their own South group. Their fight to the top during playbacks is comparable to the rise of "mean chimp" Imoso and ally Johnny at Kanyawara.

The first killing, of a stranger infant left alone, is instructive. Note the performative quality, as with Goblin and Ntologi.

> Sagu climbed the tree with the infant and hit it against the branches, while some South Group members looked on. At 16:39, Sagu started to bite the infant and the sound of breaking bones could be heard, then he twisted one foot of the infant, who screamed loudly. In response, the two groups exchanged calls. At 16:50 Sagu let the infant fall to the ground and seven adults of the South Group looked carefully at him for 12 min. At 17:12, Gogol bit the infant in the throat, probably killing him, then broke the infant's fingers, feet, and some articulations and extracted some foot bones without eating anything. (Boesch 2008b:523)

Sagu and Gogol made it clear to all in South Group that they could be very, very violent, without risk to themselves.

In the later deadly attacks on adults, others participated, but Sagu and Gogol still exceeded all others (except Zora) in violence. In the 2005 attack on an adult, all the males and most females joined in the attack. But after they moved on, Gogol came back and broke his arm with a bite (Boesch et al. 2008b:524; Boesch 2009:79-80).

In the third attack, 2007, when others immobilized their captive, Sagu bit its throat "for prolonged periods of time, which appeared to lead to the victim's death." Gogol, Sagu, Zora, and two others continued beating the corpse. When some of the group started to leave, Sagu, Gogol, and two others struck and bit the body for 4 minutes. Gogol kept on, bending back the arms and legs, biting the insides of elbows and knees, finally biting all the fingers and toes, one by one. "Sagu and Gogol pant-hooted, drummed and then left the site" (Boesch 2009:81-82).

That third attack happened just minutes after Sagu and Gogol were chased out by Porthos, with other males there to see (Chapter 22). In human terms, we would call that a massive loss of face. Well, they straightened that out fast. If others of South Group followed the lead of its two precocious leaders, that is no surprise. Deadly aggression can be shaped by dominant personalities, as when Kasakela was led on by Goblin and Frodo.

Conclusion

Can the three killings be *directly* attributed to human impact? No. Can they be said to happen under "natural conditions"? No. Conceivably a Sagu/Gogal alliance could rise and kill for political effect without human disturbance. But because of population losses and playback experiments, the context of their rise *was* disturbed—very.

Regardless of their individual dispositions, within the framework of earlier intergroup interaction, it seems unlikely that any of these killings would have happened. Back then, adult males were rarely caught alone, infants were never attacked even when captured with their mothers, and those in danger were quickly rescued.

In the first two killings, there is no hint of the formerly sophisticated territoriality of Tai chimpanzees. The 2007 South vs. East group confrontation most resembles earlier group confrontations, but for reasons unknown, East did not come to the rescue, leaving the "captive" to Sagu and Gogol, learned in killing and publicly humiliated by Porthos. If these killings are consistent with the imbalance of power hypothesis, they are also inextricably embedded in a context of massive human disruption.

Postscript

Tai still produces detailed field observations. Samuni et al.'s (2020:344) study leads off with the standard image of killer chimpanzees.

> Chimpanzee intergroup encounters are highly risky, at times resulting in severe and lethal injuries. Power asymmetries between rival groups directly influence the

likelihood of suffering costs, as lethal violence occurs at times of power imbalance in favor of attackers. Collective group defense in chimpanzees is essential for maintaining a territory, and if successful it may increase the group's access to valuable resources. (2020:344)

However, their own observations suggest something quite different.

Over about 16 months in 2013–2015 followers observed South Group (5 adult males and 12–15 females) and East Group (5 adult males and 15–18 females)—the attacker and victim groups in two of the *pan*icides (2019:345).

> During the study period we observed 34 border patrols and 39 intergroup encounters in East group, and 6 border patrols and 27 intergroup encounters in South group. Although 9 encounters (6 in East and 3 in South) involved an attack on a few isolated outgroup individuals, we did not observe any cases of killing or severe injuries during the study period. Furthermore, we did not observe any cases of immediate retreat of group members to core areas after detecting neighboring groups. In all border patrols or intergroup encounters at least one male was present in both East and South groups. Females participated in 91 of the 106 documented territorial activities, with a range of 0–11 females per event. The number of participants per territorial activity event was (mean $\pm$ SD) 4.59 $\pm$ 0.82 for males and 4.62 $\pm$ for females. (Samuni et al. 2020:351, references omitted)

That doesn't sound very dangerous. There is no mention of Sagu or Gogol. There is not enough information to speculate further.

PART VIII
BONOBOS

24
Pan paniscus

Ruminating over chimpanzee's significance for assessing human nature, bonobos provide the great contrast. Back when behavioral reports about bonobos began to accumulate in the 1970s and 1980s, chimpanzees provided a "coherent picture of human social evolution ... one emphasizing meat, violence, and male superiority" (de Waal 2008:11). "There was now a coherent, irrefutable view of humanity. Look at the chimpanzee, the argument went, and you will see what kind of monsters we truly are" (de Waal 2005:25). "Then the bonobo came along" (de Waal 2008:11).

Bonobos exhibited broad behavioral contrasts to chimpanzees. By the 1990s the difference between the two species seemed profound, and gave rise to the popular image of bonobos as female-centered, peaceful, "hippie apes." Chimpanzees were from Mars, bonobos from Venus—not killing, and having sex in almost every possible way (de Waal 1997:2; Parker 2007).

Bonobos do not form aggressive male coalitions, patrol territorial boundaries, stealthily penetrate neighbors' ranges, or kill outsiders. They often mix across groups, and even accept outside adult males into a group. *Demonic Males* asserts that bonobos cleave off from both humans and chimpanzees by lacking the suite of behaviors that constitutes male demonism, even hunting, and that these are evolved, innate differences (Wrangham and Peterson 1996:210–216; Wrangham 1996:6, 17–18). Seen that way, the bonobo/chimpanzee contrast reinforces his case that human males are born to kill. Bonobos are the exception that proves the rule.

Are the chimpanzee/bonobo differences innate, the result of long-term natural selection? Or are they explained by different resource and impact situations, channeled through a distinctive social organization, and perhaps temperamental differences from nature/nurture interaction? Part VIII examines these alternatives. If there are evolved adaptive predilections to kill or not to kill, that is consistent with the idea that men also are genetically inclined to kill outsiders. If acquired, responding to circumstances, that weighs against innate human propensities for war.

Chapter 24 introduces the species, and presents field observations on aggression, territoriality, and intergroup relations. Chapter 25 builds a model of bonobo social organization, which contrasts strongly with that of chimpanzees and greatly affects the likelihood of male violence in the two species. Chapter 26 critically evaluates alternative evolutionary scenarios and biobehavioral investigations for the options, and what they mean for chimpanzee, bonobo, and human natures. In many discussions, sex is a critical dimension.

The Species

Bonobos were recognized as a distinct taxon by 1928 (de Waal 1997:6; Kano 1992; Susman 1984; Wrangham and Peterson 1996:202-204). They were called "pygmy chimpanzees" by Schwartz in 1929, who studied museum specimens and found that they were "dwarfed, paedomorphic" compared to chimpanzees (Badrian and Badrian 1977:463; Shea 1983:521). Coolidge (1933:56) noted "the paniscus, a true paedomorphic species, shows definitely juvenile characteristics in an adult state." Although they are more slender, there is considerable overlap in body mass between the two species. Visibly, bonobos have pink lips, a smaller, darker face, hair parted in the middle, smaller ears, less sexual dimorphism, a smaller skull, and smaller teeth (White 1996a:11-12).[1]

Chimpanzees and bonobos are branches of the same evolutionary line that split from human ancestors, which means they are equally related to *Homo sapiens*. A conventional branching date is 2.5 million years ago, though recent studies put it from 810,000 to 2.6 million years (Chapter 18). Bonobos inhabit the huge basin south of the Congo River, and do not overlap the distribution of chimpanzees or gorillas (Stanford 1998b:399; Thompson 2003).

Reviewing new evidence on the biogeography of the Congo Basin, Takemoto et al. (2019:241) argue that bonobos are an offshoot of the broader *Pan* line, from a small founding ancestral population that crossed shallow stretches of the Congo during a period of reduced flow, possibly around a million years ago (but also possibly 1.8-1.7 myr). Consistent with a recent bottleneck event followed by dramatic expansion (Clay et al. 2016:24), there is little genetic divergence among geographically distant bonobo populations, indicating uninterrupted gene flow across the entire population (Pilbrow and Groves 2013).

Estimates of bonobo numbers vary but center around 20,000-50,000. Long-term coexistence with people is possible where locals do not hunt bonobos (Hart et al. 2008:245-246). Still a 1973 survey suggests that fewer humans in an area means more bonobos (Kano 1984a:46-48). More recently a high toll has been taken by farming, lumbering, bushmeat hunting, and human wars (Grossmann et al. 2008:189; Reinartz et al. 2006:623).

---

[1] Though different species, the species designation is itself ambiguous. The meaning of "species" was debated before Darwin, and at least 20 definitions are recognized (Hey 2006). Of the two big variants, the biological species concept is defined by the inability of populations to interbreed and produce fertile offspring. Chimpanzee-bonobo hybrids exist, two males and two females in the Antwerp zoo in 2004 (Vervaecke et al. 2004). If they procreated (oy!), then chimpanzees and bonobos would not be different biological species. The other main variant, the phylogenetic species concept, refers to populations that share some unique characteristics and a clear line of descent (Agapow et al. 2004:162-163). By that, chimpanzees and bonobos are different species—though by the same token, some think Western Chimpanzees should be too (Fischer et al. 2006:1134).

Bonobology

Bonobos have been much less studied than chimpanzees. Although chimpanzees are studied in captivity, those findings are eclipsed by observations in the wild. For bonobos, much of our knowledge has come from small, captive groups. Main research colonies are the San Diego Zoo and Arnhem Zoo in the Netherlands (de Waal 1989a; 2001a). More recent work includes colonies such as Wuppertal (Germany), Apenheul (the Netherlands), Twycross (United Kingdom), Planckendael (Belgium) (e.g., Stevens et al. 2007), and the Lola ya Bonobo Sanctuary for rescued animals in the Democratic Republic of Congo—a situation between zoo and wild.

It is often questioned whether captive bonobo behavior and social patterns represent bonobos in the wild. Definitive answers were thwarted by "the lack of wild data" about more subtle behavioral interactions (Sherrow 2009). Recent years have seen great improvement.

But wild study is indeed difficult. Much bonobo terrain has thick vegetation and limited visibility. The two most productive research sites have been Wamba and Lomako, both in Equateur province, with similar low, wet, swampy environments. Most land is in climax forest, though Wamba has substantial secondary regrowth from earlier clearing. Wamba was provisioned with sugar cane and sometimes pineapples from 1976 to 1996, while Lomako was never provisioned (Furuichi et al. 2012:415; Idani et al. 2008:291; Kano 1979; Kano and Mulavwa 1984:255; White 1996a). These two sites make a total of 39 years of intermittent observation before Zaire's wars broke out in 1996, interrupting research (Wrangham 1999:17).[2]

By 2002 conditions around Wamba calmed enough to allow work to resume, this time without provisioning. Work at Lomako resumed in 2005 and intensified in 2007 (Furuichi 2009:198). A new, major research initiative began south of Lomako and Wamba, in and around Salonga National Park. Particularly important is long-term study begun at LuiKotale in 2002, with its Bompusa community habituated by 2008 (Fowler and Hohmann 2010:509; Parker 2007). Other new study sites are coming online.

Contrasting Types

Without sweating the details (until later), here are the behavioral contrasts that initially emerged from captive and wild studies (see de Waal 1989a; 1995; 2005; 2008;

---

[2] Other research sites are Lake Tumba, Lilungu, Yalosidi, and Yasa (White 1996a:12). In 1992, Jo Myers Thompson (2002) began research with bonobos at Lukuru, in higher southern lands, with a dry forest/savanna mosaic habitat. Bonobos crossing open areas of short grass, standing and silently picking ripe fruits from bushes (Thompson 2003:195), or wading waist deep into water to gather algae and subaquatic plants (Thompson 2002:66), shake the standard image of bonobos as rainforest canopy feeders. Exploratory studies report bonobos in even higher altitude mosaic forest (Malebo-Nguomi-Northeast Mbanzi)—with the highest density and largest groups ever reported; and in seasonally flooded forests with islands of terra firma (Bonginda-Gombe, Botuali-Botola, and Mbala-Donkese)—where bonobos dig in the mud for worms (Inogwabini et al. 2008:280). These tantalizing observations suggest that adaptive flexibility of bonobos in the wild is comparable to chimpanzees, and Equator-based understandings may need major reevaluation as more geographically diversified studies publish more.

Kano 1992; Stumpf 2007). Bonobos use few tools, and hunt much less. Their vocalizations are different. Sexual contact occurs in many circumstances and same-sex combinations. Daily parties involve greater portions of the total community, and are made up of more females than males. Female range lands are as extensive as males'. Although bonobos like chimpanzees are male philopatric, the pattern of individual bonding is different. Females groom and bond with males, but also bond and form alliances with females. Males infrequently associate with other males, and (generally) do not form coalitions.

> Roughly speaking, chimpanzees are characterized as violent apes. Their competitions are aggressive both within and across groups. By contrast, bonobos are characterized as peaceful apes. Their competitions are relaxed both within and across groups. In particular, infanticides and lethal raids have been reported several times among chimpanzees but never among bonobos. (Horiuchi 2004:65, references omitted)

"Obviously, the virtual absence of hunting and 'warfare' in this ape, combined with its relative peacefulness and female dominance, should raise questions about earlier scenarios of human evolution built around themes of violence and predation" (de Waal 2008:11–12).

That is the general image. Chapter 24 focuses on observed bonobo–chimpanzee contrasts in aggression, hunting, territorial behavior, and intergroup relations. Observations from Wamba, Lomako, and LuiKotale document the interspecies contrast, but also problematize it in two ways: showing behavioral variation among bonobos; and behavioral overlap with chimpanzees. For this book, what needs to be explained is the difference in violent behavior. Is it due to situational and social adaptation and learning, or innate tendencies toward violent aggression? But first some fundamental background is needed, which involves additional physical differences.

Sex

Among bonobos sex is not an act set apart, but casually engaged to dissipate tension in situations of competition for food, and for reconciliation after conflict (de Waal 1987; 1997:109; Savage-Rumbaugh and Wilkerson 1978:327). "Often sex is used to defuse tension that arises from aggressive encounters at the onset of feeding. Indeed, sex is invariably seen when food is present; food is often presented by males to females in exchange for sex" (Parish 1994:161, references omitted).

> [T]he more one watches bonobos, the more sex begins to look like checking your email, blowing your nose, or saying hello. A routine activity. We use our hands in greetings, such as when we shake hands or pat each other on the back, while bonobos engage in "genital handshakes." Their sex is remarkably short, counted in seconds, not minutes. We associate intercourse with reproduction and desire, but in the bonobo it fulfills all sorts of needs. Gratification is by no means always the goal, and reproduction only one of its functions. This explains why all partner combinations engage in it. (de Waal 2013:70)

"The chimpanzee resolves sexual issues with power; the bonobo resolves power issues with sex." "The use of sex to promote sharing, to negotiate favors, to smooth ruffled feathers, and to make up after fights is enough to make it the magic key to bonobo society" (de Waal 1997:32, 112).

Female bonobos are sexually receptive more commonly than female chimpanzees. They are maximally tumescent longer, have sex when not maximally tumescent, and return to sexual activity much sooner after giving birth (Dahl 1986; Savage-Rumbaugh and Wilkerson 1978; Thompson-Handler et al. 1984).

> Whereas the chimpanzee has a menstrual cycle of approximately thirty-five days, the bonobo's is closer to forty-five days, and the period of swelling covers a greater portion of the cycle (75% compared to 50% in the chimpanzee). In addition, bonobo females resume swellings within a year after having given birth—when they are definitely not yet fertile—which further adds to the amount of time when they are sexually attractive to males. These characteristics make for quite a contrast: the chimpanzee female is receptive less than 5 percent of her adult life, whereas the bonobo female is so nearly half the time (de Waal 1997:107; and see Wrangham 1993:56).

Others put the difference in maximal swelling as considerably less (Paoli 2009:412; Takahata et al. 1996:147, 151). Even so with a more rapid return to swelling after birth, the total swelling difference between species remains dramatic.[3]

Takeshi Furuichi (2009), who worked with chimpanzees (at Kalinzu) and bonobos (at Wamba), and others (de Waal 1997:139–140; Kano 1996:135), propose that more females being sexually available at any time reduces sexual competition among males. Furuichi (2011:134–136) calculates an "estrus sex ratio," the number of adult males vs. females showing estrus at a given time: Wamba 2.8, Mahale 4.2, Gombe 12.3. In Wamba's comparatively large daily groups, the presence of multiple estrous females at one time makes monopolization practically impossible (Kano 1996:143). Part XIII has much more to say about sex and social behavior.

But now we go to field observations about aggression, territoriality, and intergroup relations, in some detail. Although bonobo behavior often overlaps with that of chimpanzees, they also expand the range of variation found among *Pan*. If one argues—as many have and I will (Chapter 25)—that whatever bonobos do chimpanzees can do and vice versa, then these detailed behavioral observations drastically alter understanding of chimpanzees as innately predisposed to "war."

Wamba

Toshisada Nishida initiated bonobo field research with a 1971 survey of the Congo Basin. In a 1973 survey Takayoshi Kano found people of the village Wamba to be

---

[3] Why this difference in estrus evolved is anyone's guess. Pronounced female sexual swelling of both species appears to be a derived characteristic, not present in the last common ancestor of Pan and Homo (Vaesen 2014:13). It may be useful to consider it within the framework of extended evolutionary theory (see Chapter 26).

unusually welcoming, and in 1974 sent Suehisa Kuroda there to begin study. He focused on a group that came to cultivated areas to eat sugar cane, naming them E group, after "elanga" or agricultural field. By 1976 all members were identified while they fed on cane. In that year or the next the project set up its own provisioning site in the forest (Furuichi et al. 2012:415; Kano 1984a). Other researchers soon joined in, most notably Takeshi Furuichi.

Prior human impact on Wamba bonobos was substantial. About 34% of the area was cultivated or secondary regrowth (Kano 1984a:48). Local Bongando people had a strong prohibition against killing or eating bonobos (Lingomo and Kimura 2009). But over the years, non-Bongando entering the area ate and sold bonobo meat. Bongando themselves hunted other game, and snare wounds were as common as in afflicted chimpanzee groups—in 1982, 46 of 96 individuals (Kano 1984b:1, 8).

Increased poaching in the 1980s led researchers working with the Centre de Recherche en Ecologie et Foresterie de Mabali to submit a plan for bonobo protection. In 1990 the Luo Scientific Reserve was created, covering 22,700 hectares (87.6 mi^2). It let local villagers stay, but set rules to protect bonobos (de Wasseige et al. 2008:195–196; Idani et al. 2008:294–295). It's been an uphill struggle. But regarding intergroup conflict, Wamba bonobos were disturbed yet still had much forest; and snare mutilation itself does not lead to violence.

Five Groups

Researchers recognized five groupings with extensively overlapping ranges: P, B, K, S (rarely seen), and E.

> During late 1978 and early 1979, Group E comprised two subgroups, one in the north end of the range and the other in the south, but on 3 occasions, part of the northern subgroup was observed to fuse with the southern subgroup. The resulting group of more than 40 members moved about together, until the northern subgroup members returned north. The members of the northern "delegation" were different on each occasion, except for the 3 most dominant males of Group E: these 3 males were frequently observed traveling together [see Chapter 25]. During this entire period, most members of Group E lived in their own restricted areas, and only the 3 dominant males covered the entire range. (Itani 1980:37)

Together E numbered 55, but grew over a decade to about 70. E1, the main focus of study, went from 18 in 1979 to 32 or 33 in 1987. P group was thought to be the size of E combined, with B and K larger (Furuichi et al. 1998:1033; Kano 1992:76).[4] It was later realized those were overestimates, probably from observing temporarily merged groups (Sakamaki et al. 2018:699). Population density for E group from 1975 to 1996 varied from 1.4 to 2.5 km^2 (although the method used to calculate range size

---

[4] P group was pegged at 39 in 1986 (Idani 1990:163), and in 1991 B, K, and S were somewhat under 50 (Idani et al. 2008:296).

differs from that used for chimpanzees) (Hashimoto 1998:1051; Kano and Mulavwa 1984:236).

During research periods (usually two or three months between August and February), individuals got one-to-three meter-long sticks of cane and pineapples at Field Stations 1, 2, and 3. FS 1 and 2 were in E1's range, FS 3 in the center of E2's. E2 feeding was more sporadic than E1. P group began getting cane within its own range in 1980, and K in 1981. For about half the research/provisioning months, bonobos were engrossed with two heavily fruiting species. The time they depended heavily on artificial feeding was usually about a month and a half in the dry season (Furuichi et al. 1998:1031, 1039; Kano 1992:77; Kano and Mulavwa 1984:233). Wamba bonobos were widely but not intensively provisioned.

If my human impact hypothesis is correct, why didn't that lead to increased conflict among the locals? Actually it did—but not to killings. Elevated aggression under provisioning is a neglected corner of the bonobo story.

Aggression

At the start of observation around farmers' fields, aggression was minimal. Over 8½ months in 1974–1975:

> Neither exaggerated threat displays such as "bipedal swaggering" and "swinging and throwing sticks," nor violent physical attacks such as "biting," "rolling," and "stamping on the attacked"—which are often observed among the common chimps—were seen. Therefore, the aggressive behavior of the pygmy chimps appears even lighter and milder than that of the common chimps, in which physical injury rarely occurs. This is supported by the observation that there had been found no wounded pygmy chimps except two juveniles during the whole period of my study. (Kuroda 1980:183; and see Kano 1992:175–181)

Then deliberate provisioning in forest observation camps began, and over 6 years much aggression occurred. In 427 hr in the forest and 165 at feeding stations, *sharing* occurred in about half of interactions at provisioning sites, which is much more prosocial behavior than among chimpanzees. Yet unusual hostility characterized about 1 of 10 interactions (Kuroda 1984:308–313). Intensified aggression was clearly linked to provisioning—like at Gombe although at a lower level.

> Agonistic interaction occurs with a greater frequency during artificial feeding than in the natural state (3.26 versus 0.70 per party per hour).... Under artificial feeding conditions, behavior such as threats, attacks, and chasing was so frequent that some party members were excluded altogether from feeding. Aggression was most frequent between adult males. In almost all cases, such behavior was directed by a higher ranking animal toward a lower ranking one. Aggressive encounters between adult females and adult males were infrequent.... Agonistic interactions between females were also rare. (Kano and Mulavwa 1984:264–265; and see Idani 1990:174, 180)

Provisioning and Intergroup Hostility

As at Gombe, provisioning affected group aggregation. White (1992:211) compares Wamba's large daily groupings to unprovisioned Lomako.

> Larger party sizes at Wamba may result from this artificial feeding. The higher relative frequencies of male-male aggression may reflect these larger parties, or be a direct consequence of increased feeding. Female-female aggression is relatively infrequent at Wamba, which may be a response to relaxed feeding competition due to the availability of provisioned food. (White 1992:211)

Provisioning reduced fission-fusioning.

> At both Lomako and Wamba, peaceful association between members of different communities have sometimes been seen. However, due to the lack of fission-fusion at Wamba, such aggregations appear to be the whole of two communities coming together most often at the artificial feeding site, whereas at Lomako these associations usually consist of only a few individuals of each community. (White 1996b:35, references omitted)

The importance of the feeding stations is clear in early intergroup relations at Wamba. Hostilities resemble K and M groups at Mahale. Although there was some intergroup tolerance,[5] usually "the relationship between unit groups is antagonistic or hostile" (Idani 1991:235).

> Rarely do groups have direct contact, and we have obtained few data about mutual interactions between groups. K-group and B-group have come close to each other ... the smaller group seems to avoid contact and probably keeps the frequency of group contact low. In some cases, the larger group may pursue the smaller group. One evening, for example a small party from E-group went south, but *on their way to the feeding site*, they saw P-group and started to retreat. Even though it was getting dark, P-group followed E-group that day for more than a kilometer. E-group does not always avoid P-group, however. When the northern and southern subgroups of E-group join together and form a large party, they pursue P-group. Occasionally, group encounters develop into conflicts. Kitamura reported that when E-group and P-group met *at the feeding site*, a violent fight occurred, leaving several individuals injured.... When a small party of E-group was *at the artificial feeding site*, another party nearby erupted in chorus. Immediately, the members of E-group responded with loud vocalizations and left the feeding site, heading toward the sounds ... the clamoring voices continued for two hours, with no sign that they would return. I

---

[5] Members of K and E groups sometimes met peacefully over provided food, but when is not specified. "When artificial food (sugarcane) was provided, the peripheral members from the two groups intermingled and fed on it ... one day several individuals, including young adult males of E-group, stayed behind in K-group for as much as 20 minutes, but nothing happened" (Kano 1992:203).

approached the parties and found E-group and P-group close to each other, incessantly exchanging calls, but without apparent aggression. (Kano 1992:203–204, my emphasis)

Like Kakombe at Gombe

Researchers suspected E group was an amalgamation drawn together by provisioning. "There is a possibility that, before their habituation, E_1 and E_2 were not constituents of one unit group but were independent unit groups." They foraged separately, but at times merged.[6] "Between 1976 and 1984, frequent sexual and friendly interactions, as well as agonistic ones, were observed during E_1–E_2 encounters" (Kano 1992:82).

Then came an echo of early 1970s Gombe, but without the violence.

Recently, it appears that E-group has split or is in the final process of splitting. According to Takeshi Furuichi (pers. comm.) the southern (E_1) subgroup and the northern (E_2) subgroup rarely encountered each other during his research from 1983 to the beginning of 1984. When they occasionally did get together, a large dispute would usually ensue, and soon they would separate. Later, during my investigation (from November 1984 to February 1985), the two subgroups did not contact each other even once. Up until about 1982, the subgroups had joined regularly, about once per month… It is noteworthy that almost all the constituent members [excepting two young females] first recognized in 1976 as belonging to either the northern or southern subgroup are being allocated to the present respective groups without an exchange of members (Kano 1992:79).

The two E's kept separate, grew, expanded their ranges, and moved apart. In 1985–86 they shared 21.6% range overlap, dropping to 4.2% in the early 1990s (Furuichi et al. 1998:1031–1033; Hashimoto et al. 1998:1051). There is no hint of serious violence. In 1988 they twice met and mixed without altercation (Idani 1990:161).

Why no raiding after the separation? de Waal (1997:88), referring to the idea that Gombe violence was provoked by provisioning, asks: "If true, then why should bonobos under similar circumstances fight so little?" Wilson et al. (2014b:5) observe "Killings have not been observed at the provisioned bonobo site (Wamba).… But if provisioning causes chimpanzees to kill, why should it not cause other species to kill, especially closely related species." My answer is that it is the *specifics* of human impact which make for violence, or don't.

Circumstances of competition were quite different at Wamba compared to Gombe, or even Mahale. E2 had Feeding Station 3 in its own range, and neither group experienced the favoritism shown to Kahama at Gombe. Bonobos enjoy a more abundant resource base, the two groups were free to move away from each other, and the intensity of provisioning-related violence was nothing like Gombe before the fission.

---

[6] Association of geographically distinct groups probably occurred much earlier in farmers' fields.

New Relations at the Feeding Stations

Beyond those immediate conditions, bonobo social organization impedes formation of aggressive male coalitions to launch external attacks (Chapter 25).

New Relations at the Feeding Stations

After the split as E1 ranged more to the south, relations with evenly matched P group changed for the better (Furuichi 2011:139).

> Both groups approached exchanging loud calls with each other, and then they moved toward FS1 at a short distance. When two groups appeared in FS1 at the same time, though there was a clear boundary between both groups and they were exchanging loud calls face to face, no battle was seen between individuals of the different groups. After about half an hour, a female of P group approached a female of E_1 and they performed genito-genital rubbing (GG rubbing). Then both groups had a peaceful feeding and resting time in FS1 for about 150 minutes.... When both groups had encounters at the feeding sites, male-female and female-female approaches and contacts between the different groups were frequently observed.... On the other hand, there was a clear boundary between males of the different groups, and they never approached over some distance with each other. The males of different groups approached only on the occasions of agonistic behavior. (Idani 1991:235–236)

This resembles *initial* descriptions of mixing at Gombe and Budongo.

P group followed E1 as the latter switched between Feeding Stations 1 and 2. E1 was accommodating, led by their females in sharing the sugar cane. "[I]t cannot be denied that provisioning was one of the factors responsible for the encounters" (Idani 1990:181). On several occasions, after co-feeding, they continued ranging together for a short time (Idani 1990:160–163).

Yet males of E1 and P did not groom each other, as E1 and E2 did. They remained apart, and sometimes actively hostile (Idani 1990:157–162, 169). Then encounters fell off, for reasons unknown. In the next field season, 1988, contact between E1 and P dropped to just one time, and in the forest rather than the feeding station. Two meetings with F2 also happened away from the feeding station, without hostilities (Idani 1990:160). Intergroup dynamics were fluid.

War and Destruction

From 1991 to 1996 as Mobutu lost his grip on Zaire, political instability limited research to short visits, though local assistants continued gathering data. Five years of chaos took a grave toll on bonobos. E1 dropped from 30 to 20, and other groups had similar declines. Total bonobos in the area went from around 250 to just over 100 (Furuichi et al. 1998:1032–1033; Idani et al. 2008:296). Human hunting is the likely cause.

During the First and Second Congo Wars (1996–1999), commercial bushmeat hunting flourished. During the Second War, soldiers posted around Wamba paid locals for bushmeat, and gave them guns and ammunition to get it. When soldiers left much firepower remained behind and the taboo against eating bonobos eroded. Against that, the international interest in bonobos, NGO activities, and tourism possibilities increased local respect for bonobos as a "cultural resource" and encouraged their preservation—though not without local struggles (Furuichi et al. 2012:417; Lingomo and Kimura 2009; Nackoney et al. 2014).

Post-War Wamba

Full-scale research resumed in 2003, *without provisioning*. E1 and E2 had similar or larger numbers than before. E1 had 20 members in 1996, and 25 in 2004/2005. P group seemed stable, S was not seen enough to tell, but B and K groups were gone—poaching suspected (Furuichi et al. 2012:421).

Optimistically, perhaps B and K bonobos roamed away, leaving under pressure as chimpanzees sometimes do. Across the Congo occupation by bonobos is "patchy and discontinuous and often nonexistent in areas where seemingly suitable forests exist" (Reinartz et al. 2006:605). They could easily move away.[7]

Post-war Wamba had as much or more group mixing than before. As E1 moved eastward around 2010 in vacated lands, it encountered a new group and had peaceful meetings with them (Furuichi 2011:139). Males sometimes aggressively challenged out-group males when they met (Tokuyama et al. 2019). Females, especially older females, were more tolerant, and sometimes switched affiliations during an encounter, usually with neighbors which in a range which they already knew (Ishizuka et al. 2020a; Toda and Furuichi 2020). Although intergroup encounters varied and changed over time, "more frequently they approach each other while exchanging intermittent vocalizations" (Furuichi 2020:206, 212).

Post-war and post-provisioning, researchers found striking examples of intergroup acceptance. At least two adult females with offspring, and two *adult males* had joined E1. The males were first seen with E1 when it was in vacated lands east of K group. They remained there when E1 went back west. Observers interpreted this as "aggregation of declining groups" (Hashimoto et al. 2008:111–112; 117). "The two adult males were usually found in the central part of mixed-sex parties" (Furuichi et al. 2012:422). Such acceptance has never been reported for chimpanzees.[8]

Continuing research follows revealed even more mixing and merging. P group turned out to have two distinct parts, P East and West, which often merged but without membership change, as E1 and E2 had once done. Every month or two, some of PW traveled further west to merge with individuals of another group, BI—previously unknown?[9] Researchers following PE for 1,478 days (2010–2015) saw intergroup

---

[7] In contrast to chimpanzees, contagious diseases are not reported as killing bonobos. Two flu-like illness spread from one Wamba group to another in 2013, but the origin is unknown, and no deaths are recorded (Ryu et al. 2020).
[8] Although chimpanzees also incorporated juvenile or adolescent males. At Budongo, Squibs (13) and Simon (11) joined Sonso. At Mahale, M-group tolerated adult Limongo and 10-year-old Fanana rose to become alpha. At Gombe and Bossou, fully adult stranger males associated with local males, but for brief periods. So it is a fine distinction—no *fully* adult joined and *stayed*—but still a significant one.
[9] The designation BI is not explained. Could this be the missing B group?

encounters on 440 days. One association lasted 12 days. Groups PE, PW, BI, and E1 all joined together for 4 days (Sakamaki et al. 2018:689–694). "We occasionally observed ca. 100 individuals of four different groups feeding, resting, and traveling together" (2018:695).

"However, severe aggressive interactions, which resulted in the injuries of several individuals (though no lethal cases), have also been observed during encounters, though they are rare"—just three in 2010–2015 (2018:700 citations omitted). The grievance is unknown. The reason for intergroup aggregation is more clear. First, localized fruit abundance during high fruiting season. Second, presence of maximally swollen females even in low fruiting season (2018:697–698).

"During inter-group associations, infants often play with and are groomed by individuals of other groups, including adult males" (Tokuyama et al. 2021:6). Recent video showed "an adult male surrounded by juveniles from a neighboring group, who were poking him, climbing on top of him, and dangling around him. It was all in fun, without a grain of danger or hostility around him" (de Waal 2013:65). Wamba females adopted two outside females' infants, which could have died without them (Tokuyama et al. 2021:6).

Human war–caused population loss did not result in between-group aggression. With over half the population and whole unit-groups gone, emptied range lands opened and provisioning halted, there was no basis of severe resource competition, nothing to fight over. Here again extreme human impact did not lead to resource competition, and so not to "war."

Lomako

Lomako is 182 km. east of Wamba within similar climax evergreen forest. The area has been uninhabited by people since the 1920s. The nearest village was 35 km away (Badrian and Malenky 1984:276). Timber concessions led to cutting from 1980, but Lomako had much less forest disturbance than around Wamba (White 1996b:34). At the request of the study project, the multinational corporation agreed to set aside 50,000 (193 mi^2) hectares around the research site. But logging was not distant, and logging brought roads, which brought workers and hunters. Twenty-three of 81 bonobos had deformities from snares (Thompson-Handler 1990:169, 198–199).

Research Complications

The Lomako record of observation is complicated. In 1974–1975 Alison and Noel Badrian spent 11 months in Zaire scouting for bonobos. They found a suitable population at Lomako and spent 6 months collecting information (Badrian and Badrian 1977). Then followed intermittent efforts to habituate and identify bonobos by students and colleagues of Randall Susman and later Frances White. The Lomako Forest Project began long-term studies in 1980, but research was not continuous

(Thompson-Handler 1990:158, 169). In the early 1990s, as White (1996a:11) puts it, "we were joined by Gottfried Hohmann." A gossip-filled *New Yorker* article (Parker 2007:54) describes tensions when Hohmann of Max Planck Institute set up camp in Lomako in the absence of Stony Brook researchers. Relations between human groups were not good, producing more disjunction between field research than most other sites. Hohmann and Barbara Fruth gathered information about the Eyengo community from 1991 to 1998 (Hohmann and Fruth 2003a:564).

Without a feeding station to draw them in, and given the bonobos' practice of foraging in the high canopy and moving long distances through the trees, and their quiet vocalizations (Badrian and Badrian 1977:466)—going was very slow. By 1980, 17 individuals could be recognized, within two seemingly distinct groups (Badrian and Malenky 1984:277). The better-habituated group was dubbed Hedons (better known as Bakumba), the other called Rangers (aka Eyengo). Bakumba was guesstimated at about 50 individuals, with a range of about 22 km^2 (Badrian and Malenky 1984:277), which calculates to a density of roughly 2.3/km^2. Later surveys produce density estimates from 1.1 to 3.46/km^2 (Dupain et al. 2000:269).

Complex Social Groups in Flux

In contrast to large daily agglomerations of Wamba, Lomako bonobos followed a more standard fission-fusion pattern (see Hohmann and Fruth 2003a). Foraging parties were much smaller, averaging 6.2 vs. 16.9 at Wamba (Chapman et al. 1994:53; White 1996a:15). Even more than Wamba, unprovisioned Lomako reveals the fluidity of group boundaries and associations. It takes the *Pan* spectrum of intergroup sociality further.

When study began, researchers employed Nishida's concept of exclusive "unit groups" (Badrian and Badrian 1984:326; Thompson-Handler 1990:211–225, 275–276). In 1980–1982, relations seemed tense. One time 15 or more of Eyengo were feeding in an overlap area, when a smaller party of Bakumba vocalized. "The members of the Eyengo community immediately answered and showed evidence of great agitation." Both groups called for 20 minutes, until Bakumba became silent and presumably left (Badrian and Badrian 1984:335). In two close encounters in the overlap area they maintained silence, whereas in the center of home ranges they each made a lot of noise (Badrian and Badrian 1984:340; Badrian and Malenky 1984:292–293).

Blobs

Then came the surprise "Materialization of the Blobs." In 1984–1985 along the southern trail, a previously unknown group was encountered frequently—called Blobs, "for their annoying habit of caching themselves in the foliage" (Thompson-Handler 1990:213). Their party size never exceeded nine, with a mean of 4.8 (Hedon mean 7.9, maximum 26; Ranger mean 10.7, maximum 18) (1990:243). The Blob core was a female, an old male, two young adolescent females, and one individual of indeterminate sex. A second parous female was among them in 1984–1985, never again;

and a few unknown young males frequently associated for a few days at a time (White 1988:187). An odd group, but not without precedent.[10]

Observers (White and Burgman 1990:83–85; White and Wood 2007:841) suspected the Blobs were a splinter off the Hedons, because on several occasions they associated with them, and Hedon parties generally were smaller than in pre-Blob years. Blob-like association clusters were eventually recognized *within* the Hedons. In 1985–1986 the Blobs were seen less frequently, and their two adolescent females went with Hedons (Thompson-Handler 1990:213–218). In 1991 observations, one Blob male was with them too (White 1996b:35). The Blobs dematerialized. Once a concept such as "bonobos live in discrete unit-groups" takes hold, it is hard to shake. But field observations made Thompson-Handler doubt this simple construct. Puzzling information was of many types. In 1987 Rangers traveled with a Hedon male, and a Hedon mother and infant son foraged with Rangers. On several occasions parties beyond expectations for a single group were seen in both Eyengo and Bakumba areas. Hedon, Ranger, and Blob range lands greatly overlapped, without any reports of hostile face-offs. Foraging areas shifted markedly by year. Both major groups fed beyond the research trails, and so could have contact with still other communities. Many individuals were not recognized, but seen in temporary parties with known individuals. Several times small parties were encountered, with up to 14 individuals, where none could be identified. Individual bonobos disappeared for a year or more, then returned (1990:208, 221–225, 244, 275–276). Known females who were "highly peripheral" then became central members of a group (White 1996b:35).

Thompson-Handler came to believe that "our provisional communities will be redefined as partially isolated subgroups of the same large population" (1990:221)—just as Goodall initially surmised about the chimpanzees of Gombe.

Later Eyengo

Hohmann and Fruth worked with the Eyengo (Ranger) community. As at Wamba, intergroup relations changed over time, and tensions seemed more prominent than earlier.

In six field seasons from 1993 to 1998, totaling 48 months (Hohmann and Fruth 2003a:564), Eyengo individuals were within sight of neighbors 23 times (Hohmann and Fruth 2002). Antagonism was the norm.

> All but two encounters ended with spatial separation. In two cases, the two parties nested within 100 m of each other (2002:140).... Aggressive exchanges that involved vocal and gestural signals and motor displays (e.g. branch dragging) occurred in 20

---

[10] In a monkey study at Lake Tumba in the mid-1970s bonobo signs were encountered in 1972, disappeared except for once in 1973, then reappeared in later 1974. That year, along with an individual adult male, once seen with a juvenile male companion, there were two groups spotted several times in the same area. One had an adult male, adult female, and a juvenile male; the other an adult male, adult female with a clinging larger infant, and a juvenile female (Horn 1980:153–154). This seems Blobbish.

out of 23 (87%) encounters, and eight (35%) involved physical aggression between members of different communities. (2002:143)

"I once saw males of different groups wildly chase each other through the undergrowth with all females hanging in the trees, shouting and screaming. It looked so aggressive that I feared for my own life." But no injuries were seen. Later interactions were less aggressive, though still tense. Relations between groups could be tolerant one day, actively hostile another (Fruth in de Waal 1997:82). Still there were no border patrols and ranges overlapped so extensively that no area seemed beyond outside visitors (Hohmann and Fruth 2002:146). Of 10 juveniles, one had extragroup paternity, another possibly (Gerloff et al. 1999:1192).

Later Lomako provides the most detailed direct observations from any *Pan* site of adult males transferring from one group to another (Hohmann 2001:93–94). In late September 1997, two stranger adult males appeared in the center of the Eyengo range. Both showed signs of fear. At first they were attacked.

[October 4] Resident males and females charged the two strangers who responded with submissive vocalizations and retreated. Following a joint attack by three adult females, the older male bled from wounds on one leg and both hands.... [October 13] Again, resident males made agonistic displays and adults of both sexes charged the strangers. Some of the joint attacks involved severe physical aggression. That night the two males built their nests about 200 m from the residents.

By March 1998 they were regularly traveling, foraging, and mating with members of Eyengo. The last published observation (August 20, 1998): "The younger male played with an adolescent resident male." "What remains to be seen is whether or not the two males will become stable long-term members of the community" (2001:96). Then the human war ended research.

Lest too much be made of this apparent contrast to chimpanzees, the adult males with Eyengo were seen through field research that went from September to August. At Bossou, an adult male was present at the start and the end of 3 months of field research. These two cases may not be so different.

Eyengo's acceptance of the males is not startling given the flux and permeability of local groups. Lomako seems at the far end of the spectrum of *Pan* territorial exclusivity. Looked at historically and comparatively, including early observations of chimpanzees at Gombe, Budongo, and Bossou, Lomako seems more like the closing of a circle.

Eyengo, Bakumba, and the Blobs were cohesive but not closed networks within a larger social field of unknown scale. Mixing in were females and males occasionally associating in temporary parties. Both males and females could depart for fates unknown. Within local groups there sometimes were tighter sub-networks, which had the potential to hive off and reintegrate later. Relations between both individuals and groups could be open and accepting, mildly antagonistic/avoidant, or violently hostile.

Aggression at Eyengo

As at Wamba, Eyengo males were often hostile to other males, especially in contexts of mating or feeding. From 1993 to 1998 "the rate of male-male aggression by Lomako bonobos (M = 0.14 per observation hour) was similar to that of Kanyawara chimpanzees (0.15 per observation hour)" (Hohmann and Fruth 2003b:1410). "Groups of bonobos were seen to charge resident or strange males and most attacks were headed by females. In such cases the female aggressor was always joined by females and males. Often males took an active role and their fighting was fierce and violent" (Hohmann and Fruth 2003b:1408).

The most extreme violence ever implied for wild bonobos took place within Eyengo. In 1997 Volcker, the young, ambitious, and aggressive son of alpha female Kamba (see Chapter 25), had challenged his way to number two position among males. One ordinary day, while much of Eyengo fed on a large stand of fruit, Volcker jumped down onto a branch where a young, lower-status female was sitting with her infant. She pushed him off the branch and jumped to the ground in pursuit. Numerous females and males jumped to join in the attack, which was mostly concealed by dense vegetation. The tumult lasted half an hour. All that was found the next day was some small bundles of black hair. Only mother Kamba stayed out of it, high up in a tree. Research continued another year, but Volcker was not seen again (Hohmann and Fruth 2011:70–75).

Of course gone does not mean dead, much less killed. The absence of blood suggests this was less than lethal. Hohmann and Fruth note he might have moved away or died, but Hohmann suspects "that the male bonobo suffered fatal injuries" (Parker 2007:59) (Count 4-W-A-M 1997, *by females and males*). Hohmann and Fruth were stunned by this unexpected behavior, although it has ample precedent in captivity.[11]

Another odd "case involved an adult female that kidnapped the baby of another. Attempts by the mother to retrieve the baby failed. When the mother was seen again one day later she carried the body of the dead baby" (Hohmann and Fruth 2003b:1409). Hohmann suspects it was not fed, so died (Parker 2007:59). This does not register in Wilson et al. (2014a:EDT 4), but to me, the circumstances warrant counting (Count 4 W-I-F, no date).

Destruction and Conservation

Before the first Congo War, human settlement, logging, and bushmeat trade was intensifying not far from the research site (Dupain and Van Elsacker 2001; Dupain et al. 2000). In 2005, when Lomako research resumed (White et al. 2008) (although Hohmann and Fruth had moved elsewhere), the toll of war was evident. Bakumba

---

[11] In zoos, severe female-on-male violence is well known, with more 40 cases of males being severely wounded. "Most often, the attacks have taken the form of several females holding the male down while biting him in the extremities (fingers, toes, ears, and testicles)" (Parish 1996:77). "We observed fierce female attacks against lower-ranking males in Planckendael, Twycross, Apenheul, Wuppertal and Frankfurt Zoo. Often they result in the temporary or permanent removal of the target males" (Paoli and Palagi 2008:34).

was not found. Eyengo had moved outside of their former range, and were fewer in number (Waller and White 2016). Observation was limited (White et al. 2015). In 2014, habituation and nonintrusive genetic monitoring began 15 km away at Iyema (Brand et al. 2016:108).

Positively, in July 2006 conservationist efforts paid off when the DR Congo government announced a new 3,625 km^2 Lomako Yokokala Faunal Reserve (African Wildlife Foundation 2006). There is hope for the future.

LuiKotale

After war halted Lomako research, Hohmann and Fruth began a research project at undisturbed LuiKotale, about 400 km south of Lomako, and away from active warfare, on the southwestern periphery of Salonga National Park (Draulians and Krunkelsven 2002:36). Created in 1970 at 104,144 km^2, Salonga is the world's second-largest tropical forest park, and bordered by even more mostly intact forest.

Surveys produced an estimate of 5,000 to 7,000 bonobos inside the Park (de Wasseige 2008:317–320; World Wildlife Foundation 2006:5). LuiKotale research base was established in 2002, 25 km from the nearest village. Habituation of the Bompusa West community was slow, but accomplished by 2007, and East by 2015 (Fowler and Hohmann 2010; Hohmann and Fruth 2003c; Parker 2007), with 39 and 27 individuals, respectively (Fruth and Hohmann 2018:95–96; Surbeck and Hohmann 2013:1770).

West and East have largely overlapping territories, oriented to two sides of a stream. Over 2015–2016 they met four times, but in 2017 averaged once a month. When they meet, "physical aggression is known from initial stages of intercommunity encounters, although they may diminish as the encounter continues, leading to grooming, sex, and co-feeding." (Fruth and Hohmann 2018:99). Male on male aggression at LuiKotale is lower than at Wamba or Lomako, and about one-third that of Tai (Surbeck et al. 2017a:6).

A notable incident occurred in July 2008. An adult female had a 2.5- to 3-year-old daughter clinging normally to her. An hour and 20 minutes later, she had the infant but it was dead, with no visible wounds. There were no excited calls suggesting an attack. Researchers suspect illness or a fall, not infanticide, so it is not counted. Over the next day the infant was eaten by most present, including the mother. This is the first cannibalism witnessed among bonobos (Fowler and Hohmann 2010:510–512).

Hunting

A standard contrast between chimpanzees and bonobos is that bonobos hunt much less. The contrast was never absolute, with some small kills seen.[12] From a demonic

---

[12] At Wamba, five times since 1973, scaly-tailed squirrels were hunted, and in 2010 once more. In three instances meat was shared (Hirata et al. 2010). In early work at Lomako, three times bonobo males bagged infant duikers, with excited begging by others (Badrian and Malenky 1984:292–293; Hohmann and Fruth 1993).

perspective, the most "war-like" activity—group hunting of monkeys—was not seen. "At Lilungu site, bonobos catch guenons and colobus monkeys but do not eat them, and at Wamba, bonobos and red colobus monkeys have been seen to engage in mutual grooming" (Surbeck and Hohmann 2008:R907). LuiKotale was different.

During habituation, fecal samples indicated frequent meat eating. Between 2003 and 2007, 18 cases of prey consumption were recorded, most commonly duikers. Although meat eating was half again that of Lomako, incidents were consistent with the earlier findings: terrestrial animals were sometimes caught opportunistically by single individuals. Meat consumption was far below Tai or Ngogo, and near that of earlier Sonso at Budongo (Hohmann and Fruth 2007:104–108).

But as habituation improved, predation was observed on four types of *monkeys*. These look like chimpanzee monkey-hunts.

> Bonobos changed their travel direction and silently approached their prey after detecting them through auditory and visual cues. When bonobos were underneath the monkey group, they stopped and several individuals took position at the bases of different trees directing their visual attention towards the monkeys. Twice bonobos were seen to capture prey in a sudden pursuit into the trees while some individuals remained on the ground. (Surbeck and Hohmann 2008:R906)

An important difference from chimpanzee hunts is that female hunters outnumbered males by four to three.[13] LuiKotale hunting transgresses the standard *Pan* sexual dichotomy.

It also challenges the evolutionary contrast of aggressive chimpanzees and pacific bonobos.

> It has been argued that cognitive architecture, uniting predation and "social demonism," evolved in a common ancestor of *Pan* and humans but was lost again with the split between chimpanzees and bonobos. The absence of hunting of highly mobile prey such as other primates has been associated with the lack of social violence in bonobos compared with chimpanzees.... The current finding supports the notion that part of the dichotomy in the behavioral ecology of chimpanzees and bonobos is based on the absence of detailed data from bonobos. (Surbeck et al. 2009:173; references omitted)

With more observation came more surprises. In January 2017 most of East and West groups were joined near the center of West range. The West alpha male caught

---

[13] Why do LuiKotale bonobos hunt more than others? Their "forest productivity is relatively low.... Bonobos forage in open swamp forest and savannah patches to feed on resources such as herbs that are available year round. The use of open habitats may indicate the need for supplementary food sources" (Surbeck et al. 2009:173). However, hunting of duikers and diurnal monkeys is already documented at the newly established research site of Iyondji, just across the Luo River from Wamba but less disturbed (Sakamaki 2016)—and presumably with abundant resources. No explanation of hunting variation is yet apparent.

a duiker, climbed a tree and began eating. Females from both groups followed and begged. He favored the West females, but ceded the whole head to one of the East, who shared with others. This is the first observed food sharing between groups. The alpha was the only male involved in it (Fruth and Hohmann 2018:96–97). Bonobos seem like they are making it up as they go along.

Bonobo Groups and Their Interactions

Even with limited observation, bonobos' intergroup and aggressive behaviors overlap with chimpanzees' in many ways. Much of the difference is quantitative. Tolerant intergroup behavior by bonobos is seen much more commonly. And while chimpanzees have never been known to permanently admit a fully adult outside male into a unit group, immigrant adolescents at Mahale and visiting males at Bossou brush closely against that distinction. The categorical behavioral difference is at the other extreme, of deadly violence between groups—although seasoned observers did not rule out that possibility.

"Intragroup aggression sometimes resulted in scrapes or cuts to one or more of the participants. Actual contact between different unit-groups was generally prevented by group avoidance, but in cases where such contact does take place, fierce fights may occur" (Kano 1984b:4).

> Although the remarkable gentleness of the bonobo species has been noticed by other investigators, we should also realize that, until a decade ago, the same opinion prevailed with regard to chimpanzees and gorillas. Now we know better.... If violence does occur, presumably it is chiefly during territorial encounters. (de Waal 1989b:221)

> It would be wrong, however, to characterize bonobo communities as coexisting peaceably, since half of encounters do involve aggression of some sort. Chimpanzees were observed for more than 15 years and thousands of observer-hours, including many intercommunity encounters, before lethal aggression was seen. We should therefore not assume that lethal or injurious intercommunity aggression never occurs among bonobos. (Stanford 1998b:402)

Kano (1998:410) agrees, adding:

> I once found a severe laceration on the foot of a young adult male of the E1 group on his rejoining the main party after days of separation that might have resulted from intergroup aggression. However, the presence or absence of lethal intergroup aggression does not count for much, as the overall peaceful nature of bonobos is much more important in the social comparison between the two species.

That is the empirical record of bonobo territoriality. There is only one qualitative difference with chimpanzees that is unlikely to be transgressed. If an intergroup killing is ever witnessed, it will not be by an all-male patrol, or a tight male coalition, or a hyper-aggressive male showing his fierceness. Why not? Because even if material circumstances change with increased human impact and/or resource competition, bonobo social organization limits possibilities for violent male coalitions or display violence. Chapter 25 shows why.

25
Social Organization and Why Male Bonobos Are Less Violent

Most of what chimpanzees do frequently, bonobos do occasionally, and vice versa. If both species have equal behavioral potentials, why are they yet so different? Why *don't* bonobo males contend intensely and sometimes violently for status? Why *don't* they bond with male allies to form strong alliances?

In the demonic perspective, patrolling, killing neighbors, violently contesting status, and forming coalitions all express the dominance drive, present in chimpanzees but selected out of bonobos. Chapter 25 offers an alternative explanation of the species contrast.

Instead this duality is explained with the anthropological concept of *social organization*. Frequent behaviors and interactions fit together to make a larger social pattern, which as lived social environment, shapes actions of innately flexible individuals, and so reproduces itself. Get down to detail at the behavioral level, consider how the parts conjoin, and there is no need to invoke differences in evolved tendencies.

Making that case requires great detail. Field observations are largely consistent, but dispersed throughout a large literature. Findings are more complicated than popular images of species difference. Chapter 25 thoroughly describes bonobo social organization, in contrast to that of chimpanzees. It shows, observational brick by brick, a clear contrast in social structure which is not innate, but grounded in elemental behaviors and interactions, themselves grounded in ecology and sexuality. This contrast must be elaborated because it is the basis of my hypothesis of *chimpanzee* display killing. Chapter 26 will put this in motion, considering how it *socially* evolved, compared to biological adaptationist alternative.

The Species Dichotomy Questioned

Ecology and Variation

Early field observers connected bonobo particularities to food abundance (Malenky et al. 1994; Nishida and Hiraiwa-Hasegawa 1986; White 1996a:15–16; 1996b:36–37). In 1998 Sanford published a provocative manifesto, challenging the common Mars vs. Venus dichotomy, and arguing that differences had been exaggerated because of limited study of wild bonobos, distortions related to captive observation, and politicization of the issue of male/female differences. Stanford asserted the two species are more alike than generally imagined, and what differences are real reflect ecological rather than inherited differences.

Many others reached the same conclusion, based on relative resource abundance.[1] "In many respects there is a continuum between the two species, often depending on ecological conditions" (White et al. 1998:414). "We suggest that the proposed dichotomy between bonobos and chimpanzees in these matters is not real, and that it reflects a population difference brought about by different environmental conditions" (Boesch and Boesch-Achermann 2000:263). "[I]t is our opinion that the behavioral diversity of bonobos resembles that of chimpanzees. As behavioral data from hitherto unknown populations become available, the existing gap between the two *Pan* species may close" (Hohmann and Fruth 2002:147, and 138–139). "Many behavioral patterns once thought to distinguish chimpanzees and bonobos, such as their propensity for hunting, consorts, and tool use as well as party sizes and composition vary substantially across *Pan* sites and thus may not support the distinction between these two taxa" (Stumpf 2007:335–336). Yamakoshi (2004) titles an article: "Food Seasonality and Socioecology in *Pan*: Are West African Chimpanzees Another Bonobo?"[2]

Bonobos demonstrate "the adaptive potential" of the species, "the range of conditions to which a species can adjust" (Stevens et al. 2008:20). "The *emphasis* on the kind of behavior, I believe, differs between the two species.... We must keep in mind that what *Pan* offers us is examples of the range of possible adaptations for an intelligent hominoid" (Igmanson 1998:10). Referring to the whole package of contrasts: "bonobos can be seen in some sense as exhibiting an extension of the trend among chimpanzees toward larger, more stable parties in less seasonal habitats" (Moore 1998:412). In "Are West African Chimpanzees another Bonobo?," Yamakoshi (2004) argues that those two show similarities because both lack seasonal fluctuation in food availability. Reviewing 20 years of research since Stanford's provocation, Gruber and Clay (2016:248) find it well supported. "[B]onobos and chimpanzees fit along a continuum rather than appearing as polarized versions of each other." This is very different from the demonic perspective of categorically different evolved behavioral predispositions.

---

[1] There is disagreement about the salient specifics of abundance. Is it the ubiquity of terrestrial herbaceous vegetation (THV) as fallback food, larger patches of preferred food, shorter distances between big patches, the relative lack of dry-seasons, or some combination (Furuichi et al. 2008; Hohmann and Fruth 2002:138–139)? And the food contrast with chimpanzees is not cut and dried. Comparison of Salonga bonobos with chimpanzees at Gashaka in Cameroon puts the chimpanzees ahead in fruit but behind in protein (Hohmann et al. 2006:142, 147, 150). The LuiKotale environment seems less productive than Wamba and Lomako (Surbeck et al. 2009:173). But for Wamba and Lomako abundance is undisputed, and that is where most wild observations came from.

[2] The species dichotomy also eroded in captivity. "In general, it is difficult to maintain clear species differences as expressed levels of sociality, dominance relationships, aggression and playfulness in both species may well lie on a continuum" (Jaeggie et al. 2010:49, references omitted). Contrary to expectations, "the bonobo group studied here exhibited lower social tolerance, measured as the proportion of the group that entered into close proximity to obtain a resource, than chimpanzees tested in the same paradigm" (Cronin et al. 2015:173). "[B]onobo Assertiveness factor was similar to chimpanzee dominance.... This finding calls into question the perception that bonobos are egalitarian, and the prediction made by some that bonobos should not have a dominance or assertiveness dimension" (Weiss et al. 2015:7, references omitted). Yet assertiveness is *expressed* differently.

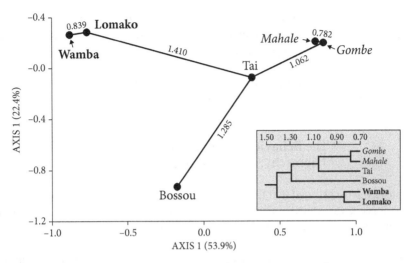

Illustration 8.1 Average Taxonomic Differences between Species and Locations
Caption: Summary of average taxonomic distances generated from BEHAVIOR data subset (*n* = 6 taxa, 57 variables) using *(a)* UPGMA clustering and *(b)* principal coordinate analysis. In principal coordinate summary, taxa are joined to nearest neighbor by minimum spanning trees; average taxonomic distances between taxa are indicated.
Source: Doran, D., Jungers, W., Sugiyama, Y., Fleagle, J., & Heesy, C. (2002). Multivariate and phylogenetic approaches to understanding chimpanzee and bonobo behavioral diversity.

Still Different

Nevertheless, interspecies differences are quite real. In aggregate measures of behaviors, the two species remain markedly distinctive (Hohmann et al. 2006). Statistical comparison of 57 behavioral variables sets bonobos apart—although Tai chimpanzees differ considerably from Gombe and Mahale, and Bossou is farther from Gombe/Mahale than Lomako/Wamba bonobos are from Tai (Doran et al. 2002:20).

They conclude that compared to chimpanzees, wild bonobos have (1) greater female sociality, reduced tendency for females to be found alone, and less sexual disparity in ranging; (2) absence of male dominance and the ability of females to control resources; (3) more varied intergroup encounters, including GG rubbing [below] and mating; and (4) different mechanisms of integrating immigrating females by their association with females rather than males. Chimpanzees, compared to bonobos, (1) have strong male–male bonds and male–male coalitions, (2) male dominance over females, (3) less female sociality, (4) territoriality and aggressive defense of home range, (5) frequent hunting of monkeys, and (6) tool use for food acquisition (Doran et al. 2002:27).[3]

---

[3] Tool use is a complicated subject (Furuichi et al. 2015; Haslam 2014; Koops et al. 2015a). Call (2017:178) summarizes:

> Both chimpanzees and bonobos readily use tools for extractive foraging in the laboratory but only chimpanzees customarily use tools for extractive foraging in the wild. There is no evidence

Together most contrasts relate to stereotypical behaviors of males and females, with greater female status and connectivity among bonobos, and greater male aggression and alliance making among chimpanzees. For bonobos the configuration of female behavior, despite exceptions and local variations, imposes a distinctive social character on bonobo life, limiting intense male aggression and male alliances in pursuit of status. Chimpanzee males don't have that structured female check.

The Behavioral Organization of Sex and Hierarchy: Constructing a Social Niche

Chapter 24 demonstrated that the absence of Gombe-like intergroup conflict among bonobos is consistent with natural resource abundance and HI that did not create severe intergroup competition. That is not a complete explanation. Social organization is must be brought in.

Chapter 25 constructs a model of bonobo social organization from empirical findings on interrelated aspects of social behavior. The through-line goes from female association and bonding, then dominance relations between and within sexes, to the importance of mothers in promoting sons' status and mating possibilities, finally showing how this interlocked system of action makes male coalitional violence a nonstarter. Common bonobo behaviors, although overlapping with chimpanzees, combine on a *social* level to generate a distinctive political system that inhibits male aggression.

Associating

On average bonobo females associate and bond more than female chimpanzees. In the Gombe prototype, ranging of females especially with offspring is restricted by more limited food availability. Males spend more time ranging more widely together, and consequently associate, groom, and form coalitions. Females associate with males but spend more time alone, so not with other females.

With greater food availability bonobo females are as common as males in multi-individual parties. Comparing Wamba to Kalinzu chimpanzees (2003–2005), "[w]hile less than one-tenth of the females were found in parties of chimpanzees on average, almost two-thirds of the females were found in parties of bonobos. Female bonobos do not only attend parties frequently, but usually aggregate in the central part of the

---

that socio-ecological factors such as rainfall, fruit availability or party size explain this difference. Furthermore, detailed tests in the laboratory revealed virtually no differences in the cognitive processes underlying tool use between chimpanzees and bonobos. Both species use multiple tools, solve multiple tasks, encode the same tool and obstacle properties and show the same depth of planning.

He offers some speculative factors for the wild difference, such as bonobos' greater social orientation, but this contrast remains a mystery. Tool use is not an issue for this book.

parties" (Furuichi et al. 2012:425). Within parties, the rate of female–female grooming was much higher than either male–male, or female–male (Sakamaki 2013:356–357). Between parties females associate across groups, know each other and their common rangeland, may switch affiliation during joint encounters, and three out of five times do not emigrate further than next door (Ishizuka et al. 2017). Female bonding seems a strong and continuous network over the landscape, not group-bound.

For Lomako the record on female association is mixed. Females stayed closer together while males moved away from other males (White 1996). Yet frequencies of same- and cross-sex affiliation and aggression was proportional to how many of each sex was present in a given party, not female biased (White 1992:203). Later research with Eyengo and at LuiKotale found much the same (Hohmann and Fruth 2002:142). If the mother–son associations are factored out, then male–male, male–female, and female–female association within parties were equally likely, i.e., random (Surbeck et al. 2017b:15). But even if cross-sex associations are no more than just *balanced*, that is a sharp contrast to the male-centered associations of many chimpanzee groups.[4]

Yet some wild chimpanzee groups are more female connected than in the Gombe model (Tuttle 1986:274–276), as with abundant resources at Tai (Boesch 1996:111; Lehman and Boesch 2008), and at Sonso (Newton-Fisher 2006:1597). Association and bonding of captive female chimpanzees also is common (Parish 1994:159; Stevens et al. 2008:19–20). Thus, the pronounced contrast between female bonobo and chimpanzee associations seems situational rather than a reflection of innate dispositions.

Females Fighting and Rubbing

Females occasionally fight, and fighting can be intense. "There are times when aggression between two females starts silently, but then screams rise as a fight develops and the two combatants begin rolling around on the ground. Other females may join, creating great confusion" (Kano 1992:190).

They also have sex. "Female bonobos, while feeding together, perform GG rubbing with each other and show high tolerance to proximity" (Sakamaki 2013:357). Genito-genital rubbing between females is frequent, though possibly more frequent in captivity. The standard practice is for one sexually swollen female to lie on her back, and invite another to mount her, face to face (Kano 1992:190–196). The "two participants grasp each other and swing their hips laterally while keeping the front tips of the vulvae, where the clitorises protrude, in close contact" (Paoli 2009:411).

GG rubbing is not unknown among chimpanzees. Although regularly practiced among four captives at the New Iberia Research Center (Anestis 2004), in the wild it is rare. "[A] small number of adult and immature females at Tai have made genital contacts, though at low rates" (Anestis 2004:486). One example was seen at Mahale (Zamma and Fujita 2004:3). At Bossou, over 556 hours of female focal follows, 17

---

[4] In three captive bonobo populations, when females were close to another adult, 60% were females, and females preferred females in many interactions (Parish 1996:66–70). Yet in another comparison of four captive populations, in only two did females prefer proximity to females over males (Stevens et al. 2006:210).

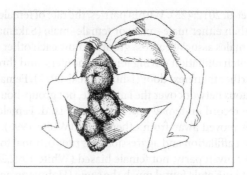

Illustration 8.2A GG Rubbing Positions among Bonobos and Chimpanzees
Caption: Bonobo GG rubbing in typical ventro–ventral position.
Source: Hohmann G., & Fruth, B. (2000). Use and function of genital contacts among female bonobos. *Animal Behaviour, 60,* 107–120.

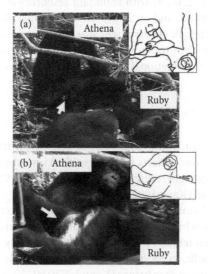

Illustration 8.2B Caption: Chimpanzee GG Rubbing in Mihale.
Source: Zamma, K., & Fujita, S. (2004). Genito-genital rubbing among the chimpanzees of Mahale and Bossou. *Pan Africa News, 11*(2), 5–8.

efforts to rub were witnessed, all within one 7-day period, all involving one female, with two different partners. Female chimpanzees can do it, but rarely do. It might be an impertinent question, but why don't they rub more?

As portrayed at Bossou, sexual contact between female chimpanzees seems decidedly awkward compared to the easy rubbing female bonobos. This behavioral contrast is based on pedomorphism of female genitalia (Blount 1990:707).

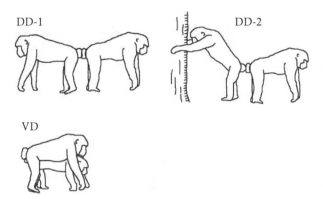

Illustration 8.2C Caption: Chimpanzee GG Rubbing in Bossou.
Source: Zamma, K., & Fujita, S. (2004). Genito-genital rubbing among the chimpanzees of Mahale and Bossou. *Pan Africa News, 11*(2), 5–8.

Retention of the immature configuration of the labia minora into adulthood in P. paniscus becomes functionally significant as a result of tumescence. In adult P. troglodytes the clitoris is maintained in approximately the same plane as the vulval aperture when tumescent, but in P. paniscus it is relocated between hind limbs. This permits pairs of female P. paniscus to stimulate each others' frenulum in the ventro-ventral position. (Dahl 1985:27)

In plainer words, "the vulva is situated between her legs rather than oriented to her back, as in the chimpanzee" (de Waal 2001:133; and Savage-Rumbaugh and Wilkerson 1978:327). This adds a new wrinkle to de Beauvoir's insight that the body is a situation. The bonobo body-situation means that females can readily have sex with each other. They do, and that has consequences.

Why GG?

GG rubbing defuses tensions (see Anestis 2004:478; cf. Hohmann and Fruth 2000). In the Stuttgart Zoo, a feeding mechanism was contrived to resemble fishing for ants or termites. "Dominant adult females were usually first to approach the fishing site on any given day. Other females interested in fishing would approach, give a sexual solicitation, engage in GG-rubbing with the fishing female, and then peacefully begin to cofeed" (Parish 1994:172). When young females entered new groups at Wamba they selected a resident female, and tried to affiliate through grooming and GG rubbing (Furuichi 2011:134). In this GG-rubbing is one expression of a broader pattern of diminishing tension, anxiety, or uncertainty via sex in all possible combinations of individuals, including infants (de Waal 1987; 1990; Kuroda 1984:317–319; Parish 1994; Wrangham 1993; and below).

Sex defuses tension, but does it lead to female bonding, to alliance between particular individuals? Parish and de Waal characterize Wrangham's view that GG rubbing is merely to "regulate competition rather than maintain an actual bond," as symptomatic of unwillingness to recognize females as essential to social formations. "The highly elaborated sexual interactions are very likely a proximate level mechanism for reducing tension among these unrelated individuals and promoting bonds that then lead to cooperation and coalition formation" (Parish 1994:176). "In fact, it is female–female relationships that are of central importance in understanding bonobo social organization" (Parish and de Waal 2000:104; and Parish 1996 65). "[B]onobo females are bonded by any standard; no other term will do" (de Waal 1997:86).

Yes, but the role of GG rubbing in bonding remains unclear. Over six field seasons with Eyengo, Hohmann and Fruth (2000) observed 466 instances of female GG rubbing (vs. 2 between males, and 15 mixed). Rubbing occurred after agonistic encounters or with feeding competition—consistent with tension reduction. But they *did not* find a correlation of GG rubbing and female affiliation. Females that rubbed were not significantly more likely to stay close to or groom each other. In a captive study (Annicchiarico et al. 2020:949), mutual eye contact during GG rubbing and strength of bonding were inversely related—"the more the eye contact, the weaker the social relationship." This is not to dispute that females bond, but it does problematize the tie between GG rubbing and bonding.

Intersexual Dominance, Aggression, and Sexual Coercion

Females bond, but do they dominate males? Among chimpanzees, with a few exceptions (e.g., Nishida 1970:73), adult males are dominant over all adult females. Bonobos are different, even though adult females are about three-quarters the size of adult males (Parish 1996:81; Wrangham and Pilbeam 2001:11). In the popular image of bonobos, females *do* dominate males. It's not that simple (Surbeck and Hohmann 2013:1769).

In Captivity

The idea of female dominance came from captive studies (Parish 1994:174). Even in zoos however, females' dominance was not complete (Stevens et al. 2008:31). In Apenheul, the hierarchy was nonlinear, and female dominance not uniform. In one study period, a female occupied the highest rank, while in a second a male did (Paoli et al. 2006:120).

In captivity, "in coalitions, females supported each other more than male–female or male–male dyads" (Stevens et al. 2006:210).

> [C]aptive adult females are not attacked by males. Even more remarkably, there are more than forty recorded cases of males being severely wounded by one or several females (seven individuals in five institutions). The aggression is absolutely unidirectional. In all cases the females have inflicted the wounds on males. (Parish 1996:77)

Paoli at Apenheul zoo never saw male aggression against a female followed by copulation, and asked other researchers about it. Not a single instance was witnessed in San Diego or Columbus zoos, or in the wild at Lukuru. There *were* instances of females sexually coercing males (Paoli 2009:414).

Wamba

Observations in wild situations are not as tilted toward female dominance (White and Wood 2007:844). At Wamba, in 7 months with E1, "males were dominant over females in 27 cases, while females were dominant over males in 25 agonistic interactions, showing that males and females had relatively equal status." Again the apt word is *balanced*. But females did have priority in feeding: "when females approached males who were feeding in a preferred position at a feeding site, males yielded their positions to late-arriving females. Furthermore, males usually waited at the periphery of the feeding site until females finished eating" (Furuichi 2011:136). Unlike at Gombe and Mahale, males did not take or withhold food from females (Kano 1992:185).

When Wamba males did act aggressively toward females, it was limited to "excited vocalizations, dragging branches, and dashing toward females" (Furuichi 2011:136). A factor limiting male aggression was the "female bond" (Kano 1992:188) and the fact that "[m]ale bonobos rarely joined forces in aggression" (Ihobe 1992:163). "Several examples have been reported in which a male provoked a female and a group of females cooperated in a counterattack. A group of males will not attack a female, but the opposite can occur" (Kano 1992:188). "[A]llied females sometimes chased males, but males never formed aggressive alliances against females" (Furuichi 2011:136).

Lomako

Less cohesive Lomako was different. "[M]ales were consistently dominant in dyadic interactions." "All adult and subadult male bonobos outranked all females, male aggression against females was relatively common and included evidence of sexual coercion, and male submission to female aggression was rare" (White and Wood 2007:837, 846). Lomako females had feeding priority over males in small food patches but not in larger ones, and could control highly valued resources like meat. In other species, such feeding advantage would in itself be taken as establishing dominance (de Waal 2001b:142). With bonobos, it is a bit more complicated.

"Males were often observed to arrive at a food patch just ahead of a party of females. The dominant male would then evict other males and control the main access route into the food tree, and females would mate with this dominant male as they entered the tree to feed." This can be seen not as female domination, but as males being deferential in order to mate. "The difference in feeding may reflect male strategies to increase reproductive success through increased access to females. Males could influence female mate choice by allowing them to feed first. Females would then chose males based on this deference" (White and Wood 2007:846–847).

White and Wood (2007:838–839, 842) distinguish priority in feeding from winning dyadic contests. In the latter, males dominate, in 13 of 16 dyadic face-offs between the sexes. Twice "male aggression against females was followed by matings, as consistent with sexual coercion." Even female feeding priority was partly the result of their leading more feeding parties than males (30 to 7), and so getting there first.

Sex dominance within Eyengo changed over time. Just a few years later, Hohmann and Fruth (2003b:1399) found that females had the edge. Dyadic male-on-female aggression was less than half that of female-on-male. "Aggression by males against females was rare and was almost never [but sometimes?] followed by mating between aggressor and target" (Hohmann and Fruth 2003b:1389).

LuiKotale

LuiKotale complicates issues further (Surbeck and Hohmann 2013:1767, 1773–1775, 1767, 1778). Males often aggressed upon females, but generally females got the better of it. Female attacks were more commonly provoked by male attacks on offspring, rather than on themselves. Of 297 conflicts between females and male, females clearly came out on top 56% of the time, and males 36%. Female advantage reflects sex differences in cooperation in conflicts: 26 female–female coalitions, 25 male–female, and 7 male–male—yet 7 is still 12%. Of 120 intersexual conflicts, 27 were in mating contexts. Males won 9 and females won 12. Whether mating followed is not specified.

From 2007 to 2012 at LuiKotale, over 5,763 hours of observation, 6 adult males attacked immature individuals 60 times, 4 males and 6 females. Of these attacks, 58% were by the alpha male and 23% by another high-ranking male. Six attacks were on their own offspring (by genotype), one reason why these attacks do not support expectations of sexually selected infanticide. Another SSI contradiction is that the infants victims were already weaned, 3–7.9 years old. Some aggression was severe enough to leave visible wounds, and some protracted, but none appear deadly (Gottfried et al. 2017:304–305). Whether mothers were present and if so their responses is not noted.

Lomako and LuiKotale thus establish significant points that go against the common image of bonobos. Males joined in attacking females, and used coercion in mating contexts. They attacked young, but not infants. Bonobo males are not nonaggressive. They just act out aggression far less frequently or intensely than chimpanzee males do, and rarely coalitionally. LuiKotale further problematizes the relationship between GG rubbing, bonding, and coalitions against males. Females commonly joined with regular associates in attacking males, but only because they were more likely *to be with* regular associates in temporary parties. Within any temporary party, however, females were *not* more likely to join with associates than with another female (Surbeck and Hohmann's 2013:1775–1776). "[D]egree of affiliation in female–female dyads is not related to coalitionary support" (2017a:16). Additional study developed even more complications (Muscovice et al. 2017:168). The intuitive line of associating—> rubbing—>bonding—>coalitions against males must have a ? with each of the arrows.

Dominant Females?

Parish and de Waal (2000:99; and de Waal 2001b:140–141) write, "categorization of bonobos as a species with 'female dominance' is resisted in some quarters. The literature abounds with equivocation." But the evidence does vary by how, where, and when it is measured. "In the wild, dominance between males and females is equal or equivocal, but females seem to be dominant over males where feeding is concerned;" and "there really does appear to be a difference in this respect between the social tendencies of wild and captive bonobos" (Furuichi 2011:136–137). Captive females are more dominant than wild ones.

In wild situations, often "males have dyadic dominance over females, but are unable to exert this dominance if females join forces against them" (Surbeck and Hohmann 2013:1769). In captivity female allies are assuredly present, not like in the forest (White and Wood 2007:847). Female dominance? Yes, *socially*, with qualifications. The hinge is that females regularly cooperate in attacks on aggressive males.

Male bonobos do not act like male chimpanzees and coerce females for sex because they usually do not have a shot at it, and also risk being trounced by a female group attack. Being cooperative and empathetic is the way to go. "We suggest that male intersexual aggression is incompatible with intersexual bonding and propose that the potential benefits that males derive from affiliative long-term association with females prevent males from being aggressive against females" (Hohmann and Fruth 2003b:1390). Solidary females choose, and nice guys win. This has major implications.

Males and Status Hierarchy

Male status competition is a key concern for this book. In the demonic perspective, the sometimes violent striving of male chimpanzees grows from a dominance drive that also impels external killings. This drive is said to be shared by chimpanzees and humans, but selected out of bonobos. My hypothesis of display violence invokes no violent drive, but does argue that male competition among chimpanzees sometimes leads to killings. This section shows how bonobo male status competition is channeled by social organization away from rather than toward protracted status conflict or coalition formation—two pillars of male demonism—although not completely eliminating male display aggression.

Individual Ranking

Bonobo status hierarchies are not as well understood as those of chimpanzees, though they can be pronounced. Investigators of captive populations characterized them as despotic (Jaeggie et al. 2010a), semidespotic (Stevens et al. 2007:1417), or hierarchical but tolerant (Paoli et al. 2005:121).

The elevated position of females complicates linear ranking of individuals. "Males and females rather seem to have overlapping ranks, with females being disproportionately represented near the top ... an individual's sex hardly predicts its rank, which is itself a huge contrast with chimpanzees" (de Waal 2008:12–13). The status ladder is bisexual. Ranking can be hard to measure, since in contrast to chimpanzees, bonobos lack "formalized rituals of dominance and submission" (de Waal 1997:72; and see Nishida and Hiraiwa 1986:173; Wrangham and Peterson 1996:211).

At Wamba:

> Even after ten years of provisioning we do not understand how rank is established among males. We find that although dominant-subordinate interactions randomly occur in certain associations, they often do not occur in others.... [S]ome males are very aggressive, and others show little dominant behavior. The breadth of variation and personality among pygmy chimpanzees is so great that a simple graphical representation of the dominant-subordinate relationships between individuals cannot be drawn. (Kano 1992:181–182)

Nevertheless, on the "supposition that E1 males had a linear rank order," and using incomplete dyadic observations, E1's 10 adult and adolescent males could be ranked, though position varied in particular parties (Kano 1996:139–140). Lomako is similar. Forty-nine agonistic encounters were "not enough ... to allow definitive determination of all relative rankings," but male placement was consistent with a linear hierarchy (White and Wood 2007:842–843).

"[A]dult bonobos from LuiKotale form a mixed-sex dominance, like in captivity. Adult females held the highest positions, adult males and some adult females held intermediate ranks, and sub-adult males as well as primiparous and nulliparous females held the lowest ranks." But there is "linear dominance hierarchy and consistent dominance relationships" (Surbeck and Hohmann 2013:1776, 1770). Generally then, males and females mix on the status stairway, but males have distinct interests in this bisexual game. In pursuing those interests, one male–female tie is most important.

Mothers and Sons

The rank and active support of a mother is important for raising the status and mating opportunities of her son (Ihobe 1992:176; Kano 1992:182–183). In captivity, "bonds between mothers and their (sub-adult) sons are very strong" (Stevens et al. 2006:215). A similar bond is found in wild situations. "Adult male bonobos were significantly more likely to co-reside with their mothers than were adult male chimpanzees" (Schubert et al. 2013:7). Sons "are always near their mother" (Kuroda in de Waal 1997:60). "When males are involved in agonistic interactions, mothers sometimes join to support their sons" (Furuichi 2011:137).

Furuichi (2011:137–138) details succession of both top-ranked females and males in E1 group. In this observed usurpation, a mother and son fought with another mother–son pair, both highest ranked, and eventually replaced them. Generally when an alpha female had an adult male son, he became alpha male. Although in captivity dominant females stay on top until they fall ill or die (de Waal 2008:13), wild females sometime usurp the top spot, and bring their sons along with them.[5]

There is a negative side to maternal support. It can be withheld, to the son's peril. In the captive group at Planckendael, a conflict developed between the son and female ally of one high-status female. When the mother intervened, it was usually on the side of her ally (Legrain et al. 2011:241–242). When Volker was attacked by 15 or more males and females at Lomako, his mother, the alpha female, remained aloof up a tree. But Volker had been more attached to his mother than she to him (Hohmann and Fruth 2011:67–68, 73).

> Volker would not spend a single day away from his mother. Preoccupied with raising an infant, Kamba was not a particularly amenable partner for her older son.... [Yet when with her, Volker] was exposed less often to aggression by adult community members, and when other adolescent males were denied entry to a feeding tree, Volker entered the patch in the shadow of his mother. Kamba also took the side of her older son during quarrels with other males. However, most of the time the strong association between mother and son appeared to be due to Volker's attachment to his mother. (Hohmann and Fruth 2011:68)

Thanks, Mom

Furuichi and others proposed that the extended sexual receptivity of females precludes male monopolization. That may be so for the larger groups of Wamba. Yet even there status rank correlated with mating priority (Kano 1996:140–142). This correlation owes more to mother than to dominating other males. Sticking close goes with elevated mating, especially near alpha levels (Ishizuka et al. 2020b:4).

> Adult female bonobos closely associate with one another. A son's close association with his mother will result in closer contact to females in his mother's cluster. Hence a mother may advantage her sons in two ways: (1) in raising his dominance rank; and (2) in facilitating his access to mating partners. Both likely increase the son's chances of mating. (Kano 1996:142, references omitted)

As Volker illustrates, being accepted along with mother also means gaining access to food patches momentarily dominated by females.

At Lomako, the role of mothers in "helping sons achieve social rank and sexual access to other females is less clear" (White 1996a:14). Yet for later Eyengo, sons of high-ranking females had the highest paternity. "[A] high-ranking mother may be the best ally a male can find in his natal community" (Gerloff et al. 1999:1193).

---

[5] As usual, there is some overlap with chimpanzees. At Tai, support of a high-status mother may assist the rise of her son (Boesch and Boesch-Achermann 2000:72–75, 124–127).

At LuiKotale bias in reproductive success is clear. Of 13 offspring over 7 years, the highest-ranked male fathered 62%, which is more skewed than among chimpanzees (Surbeck et al. 2017c:R640). Within mating contexts, males do not act aggressively toward potential mates, but they *do* act aggressively toward other males.

> Within its unusually clear male status ladder, a male's rank has a strong effect on his individual mating success. The alpha male of the community, as well as the highest ranking male in a given party, had the highest mating rates with oestrous females. Given that the copulation rates of the highest ranking male in a party did not obviously depend on the presence or absence of his mother, a large proportion of the observed mating performance seems to reflect dominance status rather than maternal support. (Surbeck et al. 2011:594)

This does not contradict the importance of mothers, since rising to high status itself depends on maternal support, whether she is immediately present at a mating moment or not. At LuiKotale, just having a living mothers made males 3.14 times more likely to sire offspring than males without living mothers (compared to only 1.26 time more among chimpanzees) (Surbeck et al. 2019:R354). But it does suggest that dominant males may have an additional edge. Display violence may also factor in—just not as intense, not deadly.

Display Violence

After rejecting SSI as an explanation of not-infrequent aggression by prime males on young ones, Hohmann et al. (2017) offer another hypothesis. "By directing nonlethal aggression toward young males, older males may reinforce their superior status toward individuals that will soon compete for the same resources" (2017:306). Supportive evidence is that the 16 most violent attacks were against males exclusively, and more likely with older ones (2017:305). Teach them a lesson. But why attack young females at all (36 times) (2017:304)?

The LuiKotale alpha male with great mating success aggressed against other males in mating contexts, although 83% were without physical contact (Surbeck et al. 2012a:662). I suggest adding to Hohmann et al.'s explanation, that high ranking bonobo males may intimidate mating rivals by demonstrating severe aggression against individuals which pose no risk. Individual display violence intimidates rival individuals, although relations with mother come first.

That importance is clear across research sites.

> The most successful sires also have social status in the Lomako bonobos, and male dominance ranks translate into mating success in the LuiKotale bonobo group. In the Wamba bonobo group, the presence of dominant mothers may help to increase the dominance rank of the sons. (Schubert et al. 2013:7)

"Taken together, our results indicate a strong role of mother–son preferences in structuring association patterns in bonobos … these strong associations might promote coalitionary support from mothers, which leads to increased mating success of their sons" (Surbeck et al. 2017b:16). For male bonobos like male chimpanzees, status elevates success in feeding or mating. But unlike chimpanzees, male bonobos' mothers frequently aid in male contests that raise status, and proximate association increases feeding and mating opportunities. The self-interested choice for a young male is obvious: stick close to mother, and get along with her female associates. Whether a male is on top, rising, or even low in rank (Surbeck et al. 2011:595)—success in mating and feeding is enhanced by maternal support. A male hanging on to his mother's coattails cannot hang out much with potential male allies. He may attack male rivals, but individually. Which brings us to the theoretically crucial issue of male coalitions.

Being Coalitional

De Waal (2008:13, references omitted) observes that in captivity there is a "virtual absence of bonding and alliances among adult males." Females do make alliances, which are "directed down the hierarchy. Such alliances reinforce the hierarchy, hence create a more rigid structure than found in chimpanzees, which do show frequent coalitions from below. This may explain the relatively stable hierarchies of bonobos." In contrast, "flexible male alliances in chimpanzees create a rather unstable hierarchy, hence a volatile social environment compared to the predictable social structure of bonobos." Since de Waal literally wrote the book on chimpanzee politics (1989), this assessment carries weight.

With bonobos there is less political space for aggressive males to push their way to the top. If they do it is mainly with help from mothers, not male allies. The social organization that actively fosters demonstration violence among chimpanzees, typically *does not exist among bonobos*. This is a critical point for understanding the contrast between species in killing. In the demonic perspective, evolution selected out bonobos males' intrinsic ability to bond with other males.

Evidence suggests otherwise. Bonobos not only act aggressively against other males, they exhibit behaviors for forming alliances. "[A]dult males groomed each other for the longest period of time. This may reflect the potential male-bonding strategy that is shared with chimpanzee males" (Sakamaki 2013:357; and see Furuichi and Ihobe 1994:226). Small all-male groups are occasionally seen, usually just two but up to six (Badrian and Badrian 1984:332; Kano 1983:9; Kuroda 1979:170). At LuiKotale, 12% of intersexual aggressions involved males acting in concert. The elements of male coalitions are there, but they do not congeal.

Yet a persistent coalition was once actualized, at Wamba. "The term 'alliance' ... may or may not apply to male pygmy chimpanzees. Nevertheless, in the northern (E2) and southern (E1) subgroups of Wamba's E-group, there were eight males that were intimately associated" (Kano 1992:182). An association of three in E1 did not amount to much, but the five of E2 were different.

> [A]t Wamba, five adult males, with one named Kuma at the top, formed a high-ranking group. All five belonged to the northern sub-group, and moved south as a unit. When these northern males merged with the southern subgroup, the unit of

five males from the northern subgroup ranked higher than the males of the original, southern subgroup. But when the fourth- or the fifth-ranking male independently joined the southern subgroup, he assumed a submissive attitude toward a male in the southern subgroup. Their high rank had been maintained by the northern group's "male alliance." (Kano 1992:182)

The E1–E2 contrast is due to differing mother–son cohesion.

> Males of the E1 group were divided spatially into several clusters, while there were cohesive relationships among the adult males in the E2 group. Males of the E2 group participated more frequently in agonistic or affinitive interactions than did males in the E1 group.... [S]trong mother-son bonds in the E1 group caused males to separate from each other into mother-son clusters in the unit-group and the frequency of social interactions among males decreased. By contrast, in the E2 group in which strong mother-son bonds were not detected, several adult males became a core in the proximity relationships and they frequently participated in social interactions among themselves. (Ihobe 1992:176)

It is unlikely that incipient male cohesion of E2 could be reproduced and solidify over time, because in the next generation mothers would be helping their closely bonded sons, thus breaking up the boy gang. The bonobo social pattern would reassert itself.

Bonobo males can and do form alliances, it is within their natural capacities. They also engage in individual status clashes, and even cooperate in aggressive confrontations. Yet bonobos do not have the kind of male status competition common among chimpanzees, or form coalitions to rise in the hierarchy. What prevents that is the female orientation of bonobo sociality.

Why Are Bonobos Different?

Demonic Males is so titled because it is about evolved propensities of *male* aggression. The bonobo contrast as elaborated here provides an alternative perspective on male violence. Understanding the micro socioecology of why bonobo males *do not kill* helps explain why chimpanzee males *do*. But understanding requires a holistic approach.

Switched at Birth

Wilson et al. (2014a:419) challenge a human impact explanation by noting the absence of *pan*icide among bonobos at Wamba, despite provisioning. In a brief blog response, I merely noted (Ferguson 2014:4): "Provisioned bonobos at Wamba have not killed, but bonobos rarely engage in serious violence. They are a different species." Wilson et al. (2014b:5) quite reasonably jump on that.

But if provisioning causes chimpanzees to kill, why should it not cause other species to kill, especially closely related species? Ferguson argues that Wamba should not be included in the analysis because bonobos are a different species. Fair enough.... But we also note that Ferguson has previously written that violence in chimpanzees is the result of social learning, proposing that bonobos would behave like chimpanzees if they experienced similar conditions. "What would happen if a bonobo were raised among chimpanzees or vice versa? I expect their behaviors would reflect the local custom" (Ferguson 2011:255). Following this line of logic seems to us to suggest that exposing bonobos to the same stimulus as chimpanzees (provisioned food) should result in a similar increase in aggressive behavior.

But simple indices like Wilson et al.'s (2014a) provisioned or not provisioned are inadequate for evaluating human impact on violence, which must always be examined in detail and situated in historical, ecological, and social context. Provisioning at Wamba did cause strife, but did not lead to intense intergroup competition because—in its practice and in context—the impact of provisioning was very different from what occurred at Gombe or Mahale.

But let's revisit the thought experiment: would chimpanzee or bonobo infants raised by the other species reflect "local custom." Imagine if a male chimpanzee infant was raised among bonobos. What if he grew up in a community with restrained internal competition among males? What if he rarely if ever experienced severe resource competition with neighbors, and occasionally mixed and mated with them? What if he grew up among female chimpanzees that were actively bonded, and gang-attacked any male that made an aggressive move toward themselves or offspring? What if he had little opportunity to form close bonds with other males, and none in striving for status in multi-male coalitions? What if the status hierarchy was more stable and less susceptible to uprisings, and involved both females and males?

Imagine that. What would *that* chimpanzee act like? If he tried to be a macho male *troglodytes*, how would that likely work out for him, in politics, sex, and food? So yes, it is a reasonable surmise that when grown, this cross-fostered male chimpanzee would act much like the bonobo males all around him.

Or reverse the thought experiment. Consider an infant male bonobo raised in chimpanzee circumstances—say, baby Frodo's natal environment. Provisioned food was of great importance, and had great irregularities and scarcities, leading to great competition. Males often coerced females for mating opportunities. Violence was commonplace, with lots of hunting and including deadly attacks on infants. This cross-fostered bonobo would learn to travel in mostly male groups, often under domineering alphas, within a web of male dyadic relations of cooperation or conflict. He would see his elders show severe apprehension about neighbors, and sometimes attack or be attacked by them. Adult females ranged in smaller home areas, with limited opportunities for association. When they did associate, it was physically difficult for females to have sex with each other, and in practice they did not. In this switched males's world, females bonded little, and rarely attacked males, which dominated them categorically. Adherence to mothers could occur but would not help much in status contests, where male–male challenges were the rule, and male allies crucial.

This infant would mature inside an unstable status hierarchy often contested, sometimes in coalitions, sometimes with intense violence. Imagine that. How would that infant male bonobo turn out? Would it surprise if he was prone to act coercively toward females, join in coalitions with other males to violently advance his status, and exhibit intense hostility to outsiders?

Summing Up and Moving Ahead

Despite behavioral variation between bonobo groups and overlap with chimpanzees, a multifactorial social pattern differentiates the species. Comparative food abundance enables greater aggregation and association of females. Pedomorphic vulvas facilitate sex between females, which dissipates tensions in feeding. In this situation, females make strong alliances, which impart stability to the bisexual status hierarchy. Together females attack and defeat individual males, thus making deference the winning strategy for males wanting to copulate.

In this context of female social dominance male ties to their mothers are key: directly, by gaining access to females and food; and indirectly by elevating the son's rank, which confers advantage over other males in feeding and mating. Pegged to their mothers, males do not have the opportunity to form a strong alliance with other males. That is not how the social game is played.

Combine social organization with relaxed resource competition, and there is no need to invoke innate differences to explain why the two species act differently, why bonobos males are not "demonic," why they do not "make war." Bonobo males do not kill other adults because unlike chimpanzees, they *do not* severely compete for food with neighbors, either naturally or through human impact. Social organization channels self-interested males away from coalitional and/or violent status contest with other males, and precludes attacks on infants. Reverse those conditions, you get the chimpanzee spectrum of behaviors. That is the species contrast as observed today. Chapter 26 considers alternative theories about how it got that way, including 21st-century theoretical developments applicable to the cross-fostering scenario, and new appreciation of how lived behavior can generate biologically differing temperaments.

26
Evolutionary Scenarios and Theoretical Developments

Demonic Males offers a scenario of how the bonobo branch evolved away from the violence of chimpanzees and humans. Chapter 26 evaluates that scenario. But first it offers an alternative of *social* evolution based on sexual physiology and ecological abundance. Guided by Amy Parish, Takeshi Furuichi, and others, this postulates that the species' social organization is self-reproducing. Even though bonobos and chimpanzees vary and overlap in specific behaviors, they remain socially distinct because of these larger patterns. Then comes a substantial discussion of recent changes in evolutionary theory in general, consistent with behavioral plasticity and social inheritance.

Social Evolution

Both Paris and Furuichi posit an evolutionary environment of resource abundance. That assumption seems sound. Whenever proto-bonobos got there, the Congo basin even in the driest epochs, contained vast forest cover along the widely ramifying river system, unlike many chimpanzee areas (Colyn et al. 1991:406–407; Maley 1996:55). "During the most arid periods these riverside forests trailed over a much larger area than the vestigial jungles of Biafra and the central African uplands. At such time riverine galleries became by far the most extensive of all forest habitats in Africa" (Kingdon 1989:191–192).

Beyond this enabling ecology, both emphasize sexually skewed social organization. For Parish (1996:89):

> The key seems to be a distribution of food which allows females to aggregate coupled with an advantage in cooperation. From female-centered association, bonobo sociality could theoretically have evolved in the following way: Female association coupled with defensible resources provides an impetus for females to cooperate. Groups of females begin to defend resources from male encroachment. This provides all females with better access to the key resource (food) on which their reproductive success depends, providing a proximate explanation for evolution of female cooperation. Female cooperation leads to formation of strong and enduring affiliative relationships with one another. Female solidarity allows females to reduce other disadvantages from living with males (such as male domination of females, and male-inflicted aggression in the contexts of feeding competition and sexual coercion). Female power bases even allow them to dominate males and back up their dominance with aggressive attacks to ensure male submission. Females gain an ultimate

payoff from these relationships by reduction of many of the primary costs associated with emigration.

Furuichi (2011:139–140) emphasizes greater female receptivity to sex, which undermines male-male status competition as it exists among chimpanzees. "[I]f genetic changes occurred in the physiology of females, causing them to show estrus during nonconceptive periods, this whole social system may have developed in an environment with abundant and dense food resources without requiring many other genetic changes" (2011:140).[1] To mate, "the most important thing for males is not to dominate other males, but rather to be preferred by females as copulation partners" (Furuichi 2011:135–136).

As he elaborates, food abundance allows these less conflicted and more affiliative populations to stay in larger, more cohesive daily groups. With females having greater affinity than males, and their high status within the group, they set the pace and direction of ranging, and regularly take the lead in mixing when two groups meet. With females more closely bonded, they not only reject male coercion and exercise greater choice in mating, but the mother's support becomes critical for male status elevation and sexual access (also see Ihobe 1992:167, 177; Kano 1998:142).

Chimpanzees and bonobos, he proposes, "evolved different social systems" (Furuichi 2009:197). With the initial kick of differing, physically based female sexual receptivity, in their cohesion-permissive environment, other changes followed socially. "This comparison of the social structures of chimpanzees and bonobos illustrates how the nature of societies may change depending on which sex controls behavioral initiatives" (Furuichi 2011:139–140).

Clay, Furuichi, and de Waal (2016:25–26) sum up:

> a combination of female attractiveness, concealed ovulation, greater initiative of females in social, sexual and ranging behaviors, and ecological factors, such as larger food abundance and shorter travel distance between food patches, appear to act together in order to reduce inter-male competition among bonobos as well as strengthen the value of inter-sexual relationships and those among females, in order to promote the more peaceful nature of bonobos society.

Self-Sustaining

The bonobo pattern of social organization could self-perpetuate over evolutionary time scales.

Once such features were established, female bonobos may have been able to retain their cohesiveness even in drier habitats similar to those in which female chimpanzees range alone or in smaller parties to maintain feeding efficiency. If this hypothesis

---

[1] Genetic changes themselves need not be due to natural selection. Given the possibility of a bottleneck in the bonobo phylogenetic line, unlike chimpanzees, founder effects combined with drift could account for them (Clay et al. 2016:24). And see the EES, below.

holds, the differences in the grouping patterns and especially in female cohesiveness between chimpanzees and bonobos may be substantial differences that have formed through the long process of ecological and behavioral adaptation to the habitats of each species, rather than reflecting merely current environmental differences. (Furuichi 2009:205–206)

There may be specific means of behavioral reinforcement. Estrous females tend to travel together, which attracts both males and nonestrous females to join them. That goes for chimpanzees too, but a female in estrus is a much more common situation among bonobos. Larger parties with more associating and rubbing females promotes greater female solidarity. This party-augmenting attraction occurs even when food is *not* abundant (Hohmann and Fruth 2002:142–143; and see Furuichi et al. 2008:145–146).

Applying evolutionary game theory to competition in the two species' differing environments, Horiuchi (2004) models deadly violence within and between groups in Hawk vs. Dove strategies. Mathematically, if either strategy were established, it would be a robust social order. "In any possible habitat, they could have kept their social structure stable against changes in ecological conditions" (2004:69).

The power of cooperative females could serve a self-perpetuating "policing" function, reproducing across generations a less conflicted, socioecological pattern (Flack et al. 2006).[2] Chimpanzee alphas may "regulate conflicts between group members" by breaking them up (Boehm 1999:26). The downfall of an alpha can leave the larger situation unstable and conflicted. With bonobos, social organization itself prevents broader breakdown. The death of individuals does not overturn the structure of sociality.

Tradition

Along with structural reinforcement, tendencies toward or away from violence may persist as *learned traditions*. I will not dive into the big debate over whether *Pan* or other animals have "culture." Yes, much local behavioral variation is documented for chimpanzees and bonobos. I don't see that constituting culture, for reasons discussed in Chapter 31. But while rejecting the label "culture," I suggest a greatly *expanded* view of the scope and importance of learned *traditions*.

Most literature about traditions focuses on discrete behaviors, usually some manipulation of natural objects or simple actions. These are all easily noted—checked as present or absent in data books—and well suited for cross-group comparison. Is there any reason to expect that learning of local custom is restricted to such discrete actions?

---

[2] Pigtail macaques provide an analogy, despite their very different group structure. "Conflict managers" dampen conflicts and facilitate positive interactions, creating an environment for reconciliation and "the construction of a prosocial niche" (Flack et al. 2005:1097–1098). For that species, "policing" is concentrated in a few dominating males. Remove them, and social networks fragment and aggression increases.

What about learning traditions of social behavior and organization, about bonding, roaming, gender, status, and violence? As young *Pan* join into activities with their elders, are they subject to a continual mix of positive and negative reinforcement, by external circumstances and by others—*socialization*? For all the clamor about chimpanzees being cultural, shouldn't we ask if they learn, growing up in their own group, important aspects of how to behave, or "local custom" as I put it earlier? From that perspective, different tendencies toward *violent aggression* by male or female bonobos and chimpanzees could be learned traditions.

Evidence demonstrates the learning of aggression, in stump-tailed macaques,[3] and captive chimpanzees.[4] But Sapolsky's finding for wild savanna baboons is the most enlightening.

Savanna baboons in Masai Mara Reserve in Kenya were studied continuously from 1978. Unlike male-philopatric chimpanzees, at maturity male baboons migrate to other troops. One troop in the study regularly fed from the garbage dump of a tourist center. So did the most aggressive males of Forest Troop, which managed to push their way in. When in 1982 bovine tuberculosis vectored through the dump, most of the garbage dump baboons died, and so did the aggressive Forest Troop males that fed there. With those individuals dead, Forest Troop developed a "pacific culture." They had more male–female grooming and affiliation, a "relaxed" dominance hierarchy, and physiological measures of lessened stress such as lower glucocorticoids among low-status males. Most remarkably, this more peaceful pattern was still in place when examined in 1993–1996, when no males remained from the epidemic era. The less aggressive lifestyle had been transmitted to and through males that joined the tension-reduced group (Sapolsky and Share 2004).

In Sapolsky's very thorough discussions (and see 2021) he considers if the milding of immigrant males can be explained by observational learning. Yes, but he suggests a different or additional process may be involved.

It involves a cascade: when females are less stressed by the random aggression of males, they are more likely to be spontaneously affiliative to new males: when new

---

[3] Stump-tailed macaques are known for less aggression and more reconciliation behavior than rhesus macaques. When rhesus juveniles were co-housed with stump-tailed juveniles, they gradually trended toward less aggression and more reconciliation than a control group of just rhesus juveniles, raised without stump-tails. This more pacific behavior continued among the rhesus after they were separated from the stump-tails (de Waal and Jahanowicz 1993).

[4] Observations at the Lisbon Zoo from 1993–2005 show the development of a method for coping with human disturbance and aggression that was passed along through three successive alphas. Human visitors in school or tour groups sometimes engaged in very harassing behaviors. Chimpanzees reacted strongly. One time the alpha Buba responded to high visitor density and noise with a charging display. He hit a young female, which screamed. All other colony members began to chase him. Buba grabbed and carried ventrally an infant female that had been adopted by the alpha female, and the others stopped chasing. When things calmed down, he released the infant.
Warding off attack by using an infant shield was an invention that became a tradition, repeated 32 times during three observation periods, and replicated by two alphas after Buba. It never transpired without a very high density of disruptive visitors. It usually involved grabbing the alpha female's infant. "Male chimpanzees not only recognized the status of the alpha female's infant, but also knew how to profit from her/his importance" (Casanova et al. 2007:5–59).

males are treated in this more affiliative manner, they gradually become more affiliative themselves. This is not cultural transmission where males *acquire* a new behavioral style: instead, the social atmosphere of the troop, most proximally mediated by the behavior of females, facilitates the *emergence* of these behaviors from males. Within the limits of baboon sociality, in the absence of Hobbesian treatment, a young male reverts to his inner Rousseau.

This cascade described—more affiliative males resulting in less-stressed females who are more likely to act prosocially toward new males, resulting in new males becoming more affiliative—is self-perpetuating.

(Although this could be reversed by specific circumstances) (Sapolsky 2021:433–434)
A similar perspective may apply to bonobo-chimpanzee differences.

A Kind of Evolutionism

Bonobo and chimpanzee social patterns are alternatives within distinctive social evolutionary frameworks, founded on an infrastructure of ecology and female sexual biology. Individuals of both species are socialized into differing local traditions, and by living them pass them along.

This is an evolutionary perspective premised on plastic, flexible, and intelligent behavioral adaptation, without evolved predispositions in male attitudes toward neighbors and violence. That would only encumber situationally attuned behaviors, and so hinder reproductive success.

As will be shown, this perspective fits perfectly with major recent developments in general evolutionary theory. Before that we examine the old school mainline.

A Demonic Perspective on Angels

That is one evolutionary approach to chimpanzee-bonobo differences. (We will revisit it.) Now we consider the alternative. In the demonic perspective, the two species biologically evolved to be different, with chimpanzees killers and bonobos nonkillers. Bonobos "began with a tendency for lethal raiding which was lost or inhibited" (Wrangham 1999:18, 25). This directs attention to males rather than females (consistent with male-centered early primate research—Harraway 1990).

Evolving Males Out of Demonism

In this view, male chimpanzees like men are demonic. Bonobo males are born to be nice. Not only are they peaceful, no *component* of the imbalance of power hypothesis is present—no aggressive male coalitions, no border patrols and avoidance, no silent deep incursions. The whole demonic suite is absent (Wrangham 1999:6, 17–18; Wrangham and Peterson 1996:210–216).

An emphasized marker of nondemonism is no monkey hunting. *Demonic Males* argues that chimpanzees' taste for hunting monkeys derives from an urge to coalitionally kill neighbors.

> The strongest hypothesis at the moment is that bonobos came from a chimpanzee-like ancestor that hunted monkeys and hunted one another. As they evolved into bonobos, males lost their demonism, becoming less aggressive to each other. In so doing, perhaps they lost their lust for hunting monkeys, too. It could be that they are less readily excited than chimpanzees by blood, by the prospect of a kill. Or perhaps they are more sympathetic to a victim. Or possibly male coalitionary skills have been lost. (Wrangham and Peterson 1996:219)

Now we know that bonobos are capable of hunting and male coalitions. At LuiKotale they hunt monkeys like chimpanzees do, except with more female participation. In Wamba's E2, a male alliance formed in the absence of strong mother–son bonds. Both activities are within bonobo capacities. Still, the species differ in those behaviors' frequency, like many other behavioral contrasts. And so one could still suggest the two species innately tend in different directions, though with flexibility. The question then becomes, is the posited selection mechanism for pacifying males plausible?

Resource Abundance, Again

Wrangham (1993:8–9) hypothesized that a cold, dry period 3 million years ago led to loss of terrestrial herbaceous vegetation (THV) south of the Congo River, and disappearance of gorilla-like apes which depend on THV. When it got wetter and THV came back, proto-bonobos had no ape competition, unlike proto-chimpanzees, which shared ranges with proto-gorillas. Thus when fruit was scarce, bonobos could fall back on THV without breaking up into smaller parties (and see Thompson 2003).

Although the THV hypothesis "was short-lived" (Tuttle 2014:453; cf. Wrangham 2019:106),[5] the broader idea of resource abundance enabling more cohesive parties is generally accepted. Wrangham and Pilbeam (2001:12) turn this to selection for male docility.

> Reduced scramble competition allowed more stable parties, which then made several forms of aggression more dangerous and costly, and less beneficial, to the aggressors. This change in the economics of violence led through various social consequences to female-female alliances, concealed ovulation, and reduced individual vulnerability to gang attacks. All these favored a reduction in the propensity for male aggressiveness.

---

[5] Studies of sympatric gorillas and chimpanzees in Gabon found they overlap and compete in the fruits they prefer, but differ and do not compete in fallback foods during low-fruit times (Head et al. 2001; Oelze et al. 2014; Tutin and Fernandez 1993).

Larger parties enabled females "to develop alliances that inhibited male sexual coercion," and so males "benefitted less from being dominant over other males and more by being socially attractive to females" (Wrangham 1993:71–72; and see 2019:102–104).

Imbalances of Power

Those observations are pretty standard. What the demonic perspective adds is the factor of *inability* to increase genetic advantage by killing outsiders. The key selective condition is party cohesion (Wrangham 1999:18; Wrangham and Peterson 1996:221–227).

> Bonobos nowadays travel in parties that are more stable than those of chimpanzees, a luxury allowed them by the distribution of their unique foods.... Possibly, therefore, a difference in food supply underlies a difference in the stability of parties, which in the case of bonobos means that *individuals are hardly ever forced to travel alone*. Among chimpanzees, by contrast, when food is scarce, parties are forced to break up, leaving lone individuals vulnerable to attack. (Wrangham 2006:54, my emphasis)

This is theoretically critical. Pronounced fission-fusion dynamics shared by ancestral chimpanzees and humans is said to account for both species' evolved predisposition to kill outsiders whenever an individual is outnumbered (Wilson and Pilbeam 2001:13). For bonobos "[s]table parties would also have eliminated extreme imbalances of power in territorial encounters. A plausible result is that selection would no longer favour attempts to attack and injure members of neighbouring communities" (Hare et al. 2012:579). In Wilson et al.'s (2014a:415) collective rejection of human impact in favor of "adaptive strategy" explanations of *Pan* killings, the *only* adaptive explanation of bonobos' nonlethal intergroup relations is: "ecological factors apparently allow relatively high gregariousness, which reduces the risk of experiencing a lethal attack." This postulated selective foundation is repeatedly contradicted by field observations.

Lone Males Common

The idea of reduced fission-fusion was based primarily on Wamba (Wrangham 1999:13, 18). Even there, however, before provisioning young males were spotted alone (Kuroda 1979:171). Later, males disappeared for months at a time, one returning with "a number of new scars" (Furuichi et al. 2012:422).[6]

Lomako bonobos regularly break into smaller parties for daily foraging, and both males and females sometimes set off on their own. Badrian and Badrian (1984:332) spotted lone adult males 24 times. "Males often feed alone" (White and Burgman 1990:200; and White 1988:190–191). Later, solo males were seen 19 times over 6 years

---

[6] Even though Wamba bonobos are relatively cohesive in *the percentage of group members found in any party* (Furuichi 2009:199), in absolute numbers "there is no statistically significant difference in party size between the two species"—as chimpanzee unit groups were on average larger (Furuichi et al. 2012:423).

(Hohmann and Fruth 2002:141). Comparison of party size at Lomako and among Kanyawara chimpanzees found the average of adult males was 2.17 for chimpanzees, vs. 1.85 for bonobos (Chapman et al. 1994:47-48). From 1993 to 1998, parties were even smaller, and "the median for the number of male party members was 1" (Hohmann and Fruth 2002:141).

At Lake Tumba in the central Congo basin, among Horn's (1980:153-154) few glimpses of bonobos, he identified a loner adult male. He was seen once in 1973 while no other bonobos were around. In July-September 1974, when at least seven other bonobos were in the area, he was seen again, alone four times, and once with a juvenile male. Single nests suggested that the male was there by himself for 2 months. At Yalosidi, in the southeastern limit of the bonobo range, in 3.5 months of observation from 1973 to 1975, of 36 bonobo sightings, 5 were of solo males (Kano 1983:9).

A bonobo male foraging alone is not unusual. This posited selection scenario does not work.

However, Wrangham and successive colleagues also developed a different theory on chimpanzee-bonobo evolutionary divergence. Emphasizing the social patterns that lead from female association to their higher status and coalitional resistance to male attack, they argue for another form of selection for less aggressive males. This argument is consistent with behavioral plasticity and social evolution, and with the revolution in evolutionary thinking in the 21st century, elaborated below.

The Self Domestication Hypothesis

Wrangham and Pilbeam (2001:12) lay out an evolutionary scenario constructed on bonobo pedomorphy, including reduced sexual dimorphism compared to chimpanzees and gorillas (Shea 1983).[7] "Here we elaborate Shea's idea with the specific suggestion that reduced sexual dimorphism functioned to reduce aggressive behavior by adult males" (Wrangham and Pilbeam 2001:11). Retention of juvenile characteristics into adulthood is a form of "self-domestication," similar to dogs vs. wolves. "We can be reasonably confident that what has happened to bonobos is something to do with the taming of their behavior. They are strikingly peaceful, they look like domesticated animals" (Wrangham quoted in O'Connell 2004b).

Hare, Wobber, and Wrangham (2012) elaborate the "self-domestication hypothesis." Selection against violent aggression favored juvenile behaviors (2012:573). This drove a trend toward neoteny, setting off a cascade of morpho-neuro-psycho-behavioral changes: reduced cranial capacity, juvenilized cranium, smaller canines, reduction of pigment in lips and tail, altered interactions between the hypothalamus and adrenal and pituitary glands, altered serotonergic system, altered occipital frontal cortex and amygdala, altered androgen functioning, delayed psychological development, increased tolerance, less xenophobic aggression, decreased predatory motivation, and altered emotional reactivity (2012:574).

---

[7] Even that foundational idea is now in question. "Surprisingly, however, the little data available from the wild indicate that difference in body weight between the sexes might be slightly less in chimpanzees (26-30 percent) than it is in bonobos (35 percent)" (Wrangham 2019:92).

This perspective is buttressed by Wilkins, Wrangham, and Fitch's (2014) argument for a mammalian "domestication syndrome" (DS), as proposed by Darwin, and elucidated in Belyaev's well-known experiment in domesticating wild silver foxes (Wilkins et al. 2014). Across several species, an array of seemingly unrelated morphological and physiological traits similar to those distinguishing bonobos, can be connected to a unitary developmental source: mild deficiencies in neural crest cells, which migrate during development to be incorporated in diverse tissues (and see Theofanopoulou et al. 2017). Apparently, selection by humans for tameness or docility leads to developmental changes related to amount or migration of these cells. An end result among domesticates is "a relatively immature emotional response to social threat" (2014:805). Although that paper does not specifically address bonobos (Wrangham 2019:102), it applies, as in Hare and Woods (2017).

A strength of this theory is scope and cogency. The hypothesis consolidates findings from different aspects of chimpanzee/bonobo differentiation into one explanation (Wrangham 2019:77–103). And unlike the original demonic theory of deadly differentiation, it fits well with contemporary trends in evolutionary theory. That takes some explaining, and so we now turn into those new waves in evolutionism.

The Revolution in Evolution

The demonic perspective of chimpanzees and bonobos grew on sociobiology/selfish-gene/inclusive fitness theory, which dominated evolutionary research in the 1970s. That approach "considers only how the behavior tends to maximize genetic success," and "accounts easily for selfishness, even killing" (Wrangham and Peterson 1996:22–23; and see Chapter 2).

Long before the postgenomic era, this perspective had many critics. Out of inclusive fitness theory came multilevel selection theory, including group selection (Sober and Wilson 1998) (which in some ways is more consistent with evolutionary developments about to be described [Huneman 2021]). Then there are long-standing critiques of neo-Darwinist emphasis on aggression and competition, and disregard of cooperation in evolution.[8] Now we turn to how evolutionary theory in general has changed from 1970s into the 21st century. Evolution ain't what it used to be.

---

[8] Two similar but distinct critiques challenging the emphasis on selfishness and killing require special mention. One holds that a focus on conflict obscured those behaviors that are at least as important: reconciliations, or physical gestures and actions to repair momentary ruptures in relationships. In this view, bonobos and chimpanzees are natural "peace makers," models of how to get along in a world full of individual conflict (Aureli and de Waal 2000; Coniff 2003; de Waal 1989a; 2001:43–45).

A second view is even more fundamentally against the emphasis on aggression. In this perspective, reconciliation behaviors among primates are not primarily about repairing relationships, but rather efforts to return to the immediate advantages of cooperation, by reducing uncertainty about the other's hostile intent. It is this more normal *cooperation* that has the big evolutionary payoffs, yet mutualism has been neglected by the emphasis on conflict (Fuentes 2004; Silk 2002; Sussman and Garber 2004). Both variants dovetail with increasing appreciation of the importance of cooperation and mutualism across the living world (Fry 2013; Sussman and Cloninger 2011). (In an earlier plan of this book those topics were examined, but had to be cut for length.)

Missing Heritabilities

There was a time when advocates of diverse biologistic theories of culture and behavior expected validation from deepening comprehension of genetics. Some day, we'll find those genes! Genomics popped that balloon. Very notable initially was the "mystery of missing heritabilities" (Maher 2008). Genome Wide Association Studies (GWAS) in humans proliferating from 2006 on found that for highly heritable polygenic diseases, as well as simple measures such as height, only a small fraction of heritability could be traced to candidate genetic sequences (Danchin et al. 2019:2).[9] Long-practiced gene hunters were driven to distraction (Plomin 2011:589).

A decade or more later it seems clear that even with refined genetic searches and estimates of heritability, much inheritance is not attributable to genetic sequences, but to something other than that (Genen 2020; Trerotola et al. 2015; cf. Wainschtein et al. 2019). "Other" brings in postgenomic evolutionary theory, upending long presumed relationships between genes and inheritance. These advances give substance and clarity to something long recognized in many perspectives: it is not nature vs. nurture, but interaction of nature and nurture.

Standard evolutionary theory, the modern synthesis (MS), combines random genetic variation, subjected to selection by environmental conditions (or sexual preferences), to produce incremental statistical shifts toward more adaptive variants. "Natural selection, acting on the heritable variation provided by the mutations and recombination of a Mendelian genetic constitution, is the main agency of biological evolution" (Huxley to Mayr 1951 quoted in Huneman 2021:12).

This neat package is long challenged, for instance by Gould (2002), who stressed pluralistic means and mechanisms of evolution and speciation. Now Gould seems prophetic (Hall 2012:186). Recent decades have seen proliferation of interpenetrating findings and theory, an "explosive cocktail of fields and subdisciplines [portending] a conceptual revolution" (Abouheif et al. 2014:108). These advances undercut the genocentric framework of most late 20th-century evolutionary theorizing.

Evolutionary Developmental Biology

Evolutionary developmental biology, aka evo-devo, or eco-evo-devo, greatly expands the old insight that ontogeny follows phylogeny, that development of embryos recapitulates earlier evolutionary forms (Gould 1977). Developmental systems in interaction with manifold environmental conditions can evoke phenotypic variations that are neither random, incremental or explainable by DNA sequences alone. This can lead to new phenotypes which are then subject to selection and genetic fixation, and even evolutionary divergence at species levels and beyond (Abouheif et al. 2014:121; Gilbert et al. 2015; Hall 2012).

---

[9] A huge study turned up 40 genes possibly affecting height, but taken together "they accounted for little more than 5% of height's heritability." "Taken to the extreme, practically every gene in the genome could have a variant that affects height" (Maher 2008:18–19).

The field of developmental psychology has for decades experimentally shown that seemingly hard-wired instincts. For instance, newly hatched ducklings' "innate" response to maternal calls, requires specific environmental stimulation at specific developmental moments,

> while still in their shells (Blumberg 2005:97–101). Many behaviors seem to be instincts because they invariably appear under natural conditions. But laboratory work shows that without the conducive developmental stimuli, the "instinct" disappears. (2005:93)

Epigenetics

The most broadly known and investigated aspect of nature–nurture interaction is epigenetic regulation of gene expression (Cech and Steitz 2014; Crews et al. 2014; Powledge 2011; Tammen et al. 2013). Chemical changes to chromosomes that affect gene function without altering the genes themselves are a normal part of the genome's operation. They are responsible for producing cells of the correct tissue type in different organs. In addition to internal determinants of these epigenetic changes, numerous kinds and levels of environmental factors regulate expression of DNA sequences. And they can stick. "Epigenetic changes are defined as alterations in gene expression that are self-perpetuating in the absence of the original signal that caused them" (Dulac 2010:728). "It is now a commonplace that one can hardly study genetics for anything more than highly limited purposes without also studying epigenetics" (Moreno and Schulkin 2019:31).

Extensive research has elucidated molecular mechanisms involving methylation, histone modification, and microRNAs, by which not just physical circumstances such as toxins or nutrition, but countless *social* conditions have pronounced epigenetic effects (Gudsnuck and Champagne 2012; Landecker and Panofsky 2013; Tung and Gilad 2013). Environmentally affected gene expression affects innumerable biological processes in embryo or infant environments, and continue to regulate gene expression throughout the life span. Epigenetic modification continues through adulthood.

The big science surprise was that epigenetic change may be inherited from parent to offspring (conceivably to or beyond 80 generations—Danchin et al. 2019:5). One reason epigenetic changes persist can be that the conditions causing them persist across generations, when the "parental environment predicts the offspring environment" (Herman et al. 2014:632). Persistent epigenetic modification may lead to changes in DNA sequences (Sharma 2015).

Note well: *It should not be assumed that these inheritances are adaptive*, as many are involved in pathology. But others may confer selective benefits. If so, with persisting environmental conditions, natural selection may favor DNA modification facilitating intergenerational epigenetic transmission, while retaining flexibility; or "the evolution of epigenetic marks (imprint control regions) which are heritable and undergo reprogramming in the oocyte to regulate imprinted gene expression according to the parent of origin." So in primates, "[t]he neo-cortex has evolved to be adaptable and while the adapted changes are not inherited, the epigenetic predisposing processes can be. This provides each generation with the same ability to generate new adaptations while retaining a ... predisposition to retain others" (Keverne 2014:207).

Epigenetics have major effects on brain development and functioning (Fagiolini et al. 2009; Hunter 2012; Keverne 2014). This is not just in elemental functions. Epigenetics are implicated in the "coordinated orchestration of multiple highly conserved pathways" in mammalian "social brains" (Bludau et al. 2019:471). Social stress (Dirven et al. 2017; McEwen 2017) and dominance relations[10] have major epigenetic impact. A crucial locus for epigenetic effect is the endocrine systems (Zhang and Ho 2011).[11]

A major area of epigenetic behavioral manifestation is aggression. Yet while "aversive environments" clearly contribute to adult aggression, recent studies also "suggest that the same genetic variants that increase the risk of aggressive behavior in combination with a negative environment, may actually act as plasticity variants, making the brain more sensitive also to *positive environmental* inputs, resulting in *prosocial behavior*" (Palumbo et al. 2018:4, my emphasis).

Plasticity

Variable phenotypic developments in response to diverse environmental conditions are is inherent in organic life, and have long been central ideas in evolutionary adaptation (for instance in norms of reaction to specific environmental variations) (Nicoglou 2015). Research today goes further in examining the mechanisms and significance of "plasticity led adaptation" as itself a factor in evolution (West-Eberhard 2003). This view focuses on phenotypic variations not caused by genetic variation, which may be more or less adaptive, and thus subject to selection. Understanding evolution requires more than DNA sequences, and focuses on the environmental circumstances that encourage particular forms of plasticity (Lema 2020; Sommer 2020; Uller et al. 2019).

> The key finding here is that plasticity not only allows organisms to cope in new environmental conditions but to generate traits that are well-suited to them. If selection preserves genetic variants that respond effectively when conditions change, then adaptation largely occurs by accumulation of genetic variations that stabilize a trait after its first appearance. On other words, often it is the trait that comes first; genes that cement it follow, sometimes several generations later. (Laland 2014:162)

This may clarify the long proposed "Baldwin Effect," that selection may stabilize variations that arise through environmental interactions.

---

[10] Mice with fathers that experienced social defeat exhibited depressive and anxiety behaviors (Tammen et al. 2013:760). Epigenetic silencing of one gene "made the mice more dominant" (Powledge 2011:591).

[11] In laboratory rodents, epigenetic changes in the hypothalamic-pituitary-adrenal system respond to prenatal conditions, maternal care, abuse, living circumstances, and social stress. These can affect adult neuroendocrine functions, from cognitive ability to reproductive behavior (Godsnuk and Champagne 2012).

Niche Selection

Organisms transform their own lived environment, thereby creating different selection pressures that shape ongoing individual coping and perpetuate the constructed socioecological niche over time. Niche construction and selection is a process of nonrandom change that involves behaviors and outputs of multiple species, leading to evolutionary trajectories not derived from genetic sequences (Fuentes 2015; Laland et al. 2015; MacKinnon and Fuentes 2011; Odling-Smee et al. 2003). A pioneer in this area was Darwin himself, whose final book was about earthworms "adapted to thrive in an environment that they modify through their own activities" (Wray et al. 2014:161). Niche construction and selection can include species typical behaviors, as well as symbiotic and mutualistic interactions within and across species in a biome.

Social Behavior as Inheritance

Another widely recognized evolutionary factor is socially learned behavior (Jablonka and Lamb 2008), often labeled "culture," widely documented across species and increasingly recognized as a second system of inheritance that shapes organic evolution (Whitten 2021). As elaborated in Chapter 31, I think this learned behavior is better characterized as "tradition" not "culture," but agree on traditions' great importance in *Panins*, perhaps more than previously recognized.

In the ferment around evolutionary theory, social traditions are seen as key to "extended" or "inclusive" inheritance. Following their own nongenetically specified logics, learned traditions can "relax or intensify selection under different circumstances, create new selection pressure by changing ecology or behavior, and favor adaptions"; and also "shape population genetic structure and diversity" (Whitehead et al. 2019:1).

Revo-Devo?

All of the above go together. For understanding evolution, what it all adds up to is hotly contested. Several theoretical syntheses argue that the MS is inadequate and encumbers theoretical progress, arguing for a new EES, extended evolutionary synthesis (Jablonka and Lamb 2008; Jablonka and Noble 2019). The "Modern Synthesis was founded on tenets that, while useful heuristics for advancing biological theory at that time, are now known to be anachronistic" (Mesoudi et al. 2013:193).

> The Modern Synthesis cannot integrate new findings of developmental and molecular biology and genomics; about the non-genetic forms of inheritance such as parental effects or epigenetics; the role of organisms in shaping their environment (niche construction); and the complexities of genomic systems; or the prevalence of phenotypic plasticity and developmental biases. (Huneman 2021:11, references omitted)

Defenders of the MS agree that this is an exciting time for new lines of study, but assert that they do not invalidate the priority of DNA sequences. They point to genetic constraints on evo-devo, epigenetics, and plasticity, and argue that niche selection and social learning still operate within genetic limits (Wray et al. 2014). MS defenders say all this new ferment can be seen as proximate causation, the working out of the ultimate causality of DNA sequences (Dickens and Rahman 2012). EES advocates see the ultimate/proximate distinction as a convention, and both unnecessary and unhelpful in understanding evolutionary causality (Danchin et al. 2019:10; Laland et al. 2011).

Some elegant efforts try to compartmentalize and combine different evolutionary questions, causalities, and time scales (Danchin et al. 2011; 2019), in which the teleology of inclusive fitness may remain central (Huneman 2021). Perhaps ironically, one challenge for the MS is what it explicitly excised from Darwin's own view of evolution, Lamarckian inheritance of acquired characteristics (Skinner 2015). Lamarck is back! Even Darwin's idea of "gemmules" that originate in the living body and then move to the germline for inheritance may come back as small noncoding RNA (Danchin et al. 2019:8).

The old idea that evolution is a process of inherited DNA sequences that read out to living organisms adjusted for environment, is inadequate for understanding the evolution and production of living organisms. Phenotypes come into being through a dialectic of genes and molecular interaction (epistasis) shaped and channeled by multiple developmental processes. The phenotype results from a multidimensional, pluralistic, interaction of ancestral, embryonic, infant, and life-span environments.

Even if the MS is not fundamentally contradicted by these new understanding, it is still incapable of explaining "how physical development influences the generation of variation (developmental bias); how the environment directly shapes organisms' traits (plasticity); how organisms modify environments (niche construction); and how organisms transmit more than genes across generations (extra-genetic inheritance). For [standard evolutionary theory], these phenomena are just outcomes evolution. For the [extended evolutionary synthesis], they are also causes" (Laland et al. 2014:162).

Evolution involves far more than maximizing reproductive success or inclusive fitness. Especially but not limited to highly intelligent creatures, evolution does not wire fixed behavioral algorithms. Evolution, in pluralistic interactions, produce organisms that are born for life. It programs flexible scaffolds for coping with lived circumstances. It sets the stage for plastic adaptability, which may then shape genetic evolution.

Which brings us back to chimpanzees and bonobos.

Revo-Evo Bonobo: Nature/Nurture on the Species Divide

Wrangham and colleagues theory of self-domestication applied to bonobos, the wide evidence they marshal fits squarely within this seismic shift in evolutionary theory.

For *evolutionary developmental systems*, their foundation in pedomorphy compared to chimpanzees—retaining juvenile characteristics into adulthood—perfectly illustrates the importance of development. Connecting that to an environment of food abundance makes it eco-evo-devo. Altered neural crest cell development and migration, potentially linked endocrinologically to environmental circumstances, provides the mechanism.[12]

Developmental psychologist Mark Blumberg caps off his book about instinct with Belyaev's selection for domesticity in silver foxes. Like Wilkins et al. (2014), he notes all the seemingly unconnected morphological changes. His discussion highlights the contrast to standard genocentric evolutionism, where every physical feature is the result of selection.

> How did Belyaev and his colleagues manage to induce all of these changes—in anatomy, physiology, and behavior—in just forty years? Did they only breed those foxes with smaller heads, floppy ears, curled tails, or unpigmented skin? *No*.... All they did, in fact, was give young foxes a monthly test: "When a pup is one month old, an experimenter offers it food from his hand while trying to stroke and handle the pup.... The test is repeated monthly until the pups are six or seven months old." "Then, the pups are given a 'tameness' score and only those foxes that score high on this score are allowed to breed.... It turns out that by selecting for "tamability" Belyaev was selecting for foxes that developed at different rates than those in the original founder population [and thus] selecting for the *entire developmental manifold*." (Blumberg 2005:220–221)

For bonobos, an evolutionary scale reduction in food competition or periodic scarcity could be an epigenetic developmental kick for juvenilization. If pedomorphic genital orientation is foundational for GG rubbing and greater female association, evo-devo may be foundational for chimpanzee-bonobo differentiation. Perhaps the species difference in female sexual swelling and receptivity is somehow connected.

For *epigenetics*, Wilkins, Wrangham, and Fitch (2014:804) discuss candidate genes possibly involved in a multigenic domestication syndrome, noting gene regulation by conserved noncoding elements, and the possibility that cascading changes may be epigenetically induced. They cite pioneers in experimental domestication who have "long argued that hormonal states in the mother, associated with the less stressful conditions of domesticity, are involved in generating the DS... We suggest that Belyaev's hypothesis, positing inducible epimutations as initiating events in the DS, though unconventional, deserves reconsideration" (Wilkins et al. 2014:804).

Cross-species epigenetic comparison indicates substantial differences between species in methylation, a primary mechanism of epigenetic inheritance. "~800 genes with significantly altered methylation patterns [are found] among the great apes.... Some of these are known to be involved in developmental and neurological features," and

---

[12] Two very different studies offer tangential support for an evo-devo explanation of bonobo differentiation from chimpanzees. Consistent with my idea that developmental differences in female genitals provide a basis for increased female connectivity, Kennedy and Pavlicev (2017) propose that in human females, the location of the clitoris relative to the vagina is an evolutionary development related to female orgasm and prosocial empathy between men and women. Kappeler and Fichtel (2015:11) propose an eco-evo-devo explanation of "the lemur syndrome": "a suite of behavioral and morphological traits characterizing virtually an entire primate radiation may represent an example of adaptive canalization of a developmental process." This is different but comparable to the self-domestication hypothesis.

show very distinctive clustering for humans, bonobos, and chimpanzees (Hernando-Herraez et al. 2013:1, 3).

Plasticity is a main theme throughout this book, and argued specifically for the difference between chimpanzee and bonobo behaviors. Both share the other's behavioral capacities, but systematic frequency differences make for a pattern difference. In evolutionary studies, insects, fish, birds, and rodents typically are used to demonstrate plasticity. With the addition of neocortex, intelligent flexibility is the rule, actively coping with physical and social circumstances. Acted out over generations, this may have led selection for epigenetic control loci.

Niche selection is obvious across primates (MacKinnon and Fuentes 2011). Chapter 25 documented in fine detail the construction and self-replication of bonobos' prosocial niche. This elaborates social organization actively constrains bonobo actions—a perfect example of nongenetic, inclusive inheritance.[13]

Social inheritance is apparent in the socially evolved and transmitted behaviors of the niche. Within but beyond that are inherited traditions that distinguish one bonobo group from another, such as hunting, and probably much else as we learn more about tool use and sociality and aggressiveness by sex. The contrast between chimpanzee and bonobo lifestyle could be taken as a type case for the EES.[14] But connecting that evolutionary theory to burgeoning research on behavior and biology is way beyond complicated.

Nature and Nurture on the Species Divide

Finer Points of Behavioral Comparisons

Detailed studies in behavioral contrasts are daunting. I discussed broad bonobo/chimpanzee differences in intergroup interactions or female/male differences and relations. Going to finer behavioral contrasts, as much work does today, is as or more complex and ambiguous.

While some research indicates that bonobos, as expected, are more disposed to food sharing, and their tolerance enables cooperation in obtaining food (Hare et al. 2007; Hare and Kwetuende 2010; Tan and Hare 2013; 2017); in zoo populations, "chimpanzees share more frequently, more tolerantly, and more actively than bonobos" (Jaeggi

---

[13] Discussion here focused on bonobos, but applying the same perspective to chimpanzees suggests a different lesson. Their self-perpetuating niche could be *mal*adaptive. Kelly (2005:15294) suggested this long before genomics. "If fitness is enhanced by territorial enlargement, then fitness would be reduced by a pattern of lethal intercommunity attacks that curtails resource availability along borders") (cf. Lucchesi et al. 2021:2).

[14] This has implications for assessing chimpanzee-bonobo differences *even in captivity*. Captive populations may retain epigenetically transmitted characteristics of their parents' past. Burggren (2014:687–688) cautions that laboratory experimentation (not referring to apes) may be confused using wild-caught subjects, because of epigenetic patterns acquired in the wild. He recommends using animals that have generations in captivity. "Epigenetic inheritance may best be studied in animal models that can be maintained in the laboratory over multiple generations, to yield parental stock that themselves are free of epigenetic effects from the historical experiences of their parents" (2014:682)—(though wouldn't that experience itself create its own epigenetic transmissions?).

et al. 2010b). (Both species prefer to eat alone [Bullinger et al. 2013].) Three studies demonstrate empathy and consolation among bonobos (Palagi and Norscia 2013; Clay and Norcia Waal 2013; 2013b), something long seen as a species hallmark (de Waal 1997:153–160); but another large study documents consolation and empathy among chimpanzees (Romero et al. 2010; and see Note 13).

If such fine points of behavior are contentious, it is immeasurably more difficult to connect complex social behaviors with biological substrates? Whether MS or EES, trying to tease apart social-biological interaction leads to abstruse questions.

Social Complications in Neurobiology and Endocrinology

Comparing the two species' social cognition and brain organization, Hopkins et al. (2017:209) found:

> The findings showing increased serotonergic innervation of the amygdala in bonobos relative to chimpanzees may play a role in reducing their emotional reactivity to potential threats in the social environment through a relatively lower neuronal excitability in major output nuclei of the amygdala (i.e. basal and central nuclei) that send projections to cortical and autonomic centres.

(That is, bonobos may be less responsive to social threats). The data "are somewhat, though not entirely consistent with the current narrative regarding species differences between chimpanzees and bonobos." However,

> we have previously found that chimpanzees with different early *social rearing experiences* differ significantly on social cognition tasks, and the effects in these studies rival or exceed the between species variation reported here (my emphasis).

The species differ neurobiologically, but measured differences may be less than those produced by differences in rearing.

Then come the multiplying complications of endocrinology.

Because bonobo females demonstrate "partial dominance over males, more overt aggressiveness and a prolonged period of [sexual] proceptivity," researchers expected them to have higher testosterone levels. But testing urine of wild groups, bonobo females are about the same as chimpanzee females, "so high T levels are probably not the proximate mechanism underlying dominance and more pronounced aggressiveness in female bonobos" (Sannen et al. 2003:693).

Male bonobos had lower testosterone than male chimpanzees—which fits the stereotype. But it is well established (in but not limited to humans), that social circumstances greatly affect testosterone levels—"biology itself is susceptible to social determination" (Kemper 1990:2; and see Archer 1991; Book et al. 2001; Sapolsky 1998). "Whether these low T levels in male bonobos are a cause or consequence of the current social system, cannot be determined. We can only state that *under the current social conditions, such T levels seem apt*" (Sannen et al. 2003:693, my emphasis). "Apt" is a good word from an EES perspective.

In another article, authors of the self-domestication hypothesis (Wobber et al. 2010a) find that in experimental food competition, chimpanzees show a rise in testosterone, and bonobos a rise in cortisol. They interpret this as indicating that bonobos have a more passive coping style, consistent with their larger domestication hypothesis. Yet research at LuiKotale in mating situations shows how complex and *socially mediated* are endocrine reactions involving testosterone[15] and cortisol.[16]

All these findings are from particular populations, and cannot be generalized to the two species. As argued above, behaviors differ on a continuum rather than categorically. In some ways Sonso, Kalinzu, and Tai chimpanzees were said to be like bonobos. As field research on bonobos expands, it would be no surprise to find bonobos which somehow resemble chimpanzees. Multiply cases and variations, and hormonal comparisons will be immeasurably complicated. Conceivably, that could apply to anatomical variations as well, such as variations in sexual swelling.

Combining newly appreciated extended evolutionary processes with cross-species differences in behavior, and connecting them to neurological/hormonal differences— is a *distant* prospect. "If research on epigenetics is in its infancy, research on behavioral epigenetics is in embryo" (Powledge 2011:588). A leap to interspecies differences in lifestyle is not even on the horizon.

Eventually, we may learn that features of an intergenerationally transmitted social niche, and socialization into a chimpanzee or bonobo world, are supported by epigenetics and developmental pathways that generate biologically distinctive organisms, with socially well-tuned brains and endocrine systems. In a currently unfathomable n-dimensional dialectic, chimpanzees and bonobos could *develop* different natures, ones that prepare them for the social environments into which they are born.

Conclusions

However—for our question of why bonobos don't kill but chimpanzees do, evolutionary resolution is not necessary. The EES is consistent with explanation of behavioral differences rooted in lived circumstances, ecology, sexuality, social organization, learned traditions, and the history of human impact.

The species may differ broadly in moods or tones of interaction, in emotional reactivity that may change over differing time scales or by current circumstances. Internal

---

[15] Among bonobos:
Aggression and rank were positively correlated, as were aggression and mating success. In the presence of potentially fertile females, male aggression increased but only low-ranking, less aggressive males showed increases in testosterone levels, which consequently tended to be negatively related to rank. High-ranking males who had lower testosterone levels and were less responsive in their testosterone increase were more often involved in friendly relationships with unrelated females. These results suggest that, in bonobos, amicable relationships between the sexes rather than aggressive interactions mediate males' physiological reactivity during periods of mate competition (Surbeck et al. 2012a:659).

[16] [T]hree out of the four highest cortisol levels detected in the samples from the highest-ranking male were collected after he had been attacked by females in the context of mate competition ... aggression from females may have a stronger effect on male cortisol levels than aggression from other males ... close proximity to oestrous females may expose dominant males to an increased risk of aggression from females more often than lower ranking males, which could explain elevated cortisol levels even in the alpha male (Surbeck et al. 2012b:27).

biologies are *apt* for experience, but not *restricting*. And let's not forget individual variation in behavior, and its effect on group processes. Evolved biology *follows* intelligent coping. That is far from the wired-in behavioral programs of sociobiology and selfish-gene theory.

Different innate tendencies are not needed to explain why bonobos *do not* have violent males, patrols, stealth penetrations, "war," and infanticide. What bonobos do or don't do, violently, follows as social elaborations based on an ecological and sexual infrastructure, self-reproducing over evolutionary time scales, and perhaps biologically reinforced in species-specific temperaments.

This book argues against innate predispositions toward or away from demonic behavior. Yet couldn't evolutionarily supported temperaments be considered exactly that? No. An EES perspective is fundamentally different from the paradigm challenged in this book.

In the demonic perspective, chimps inherited from a common ancestor—which they share with us—inborn predilections for intergroup hostility and killing in reproductive self-interest when there is little risk to themselves. Chimpanzees are born with this Darwinian legacy because acting it out weakened rivals and so enhanced acquisition of resources or mates. Over evolutionary time this enhanced inclusive fitness, and led to genetic and hormonal differences that support these predispositions.

Bonobo ancestors supposedly lost their will to kill because of a lack of opportunity to kill defenseless solo males. This led to loss of hunting, and of tendencies for male coalitional bounding. But solo male bonobos are common, and they sometimes hunt and male-bond.

Wrangham, master theory builder, developed the demonic hypothesis in the context of then current selfish-gene theory. In the 21st century, with colleagues, he developed a new theory, consistent with current developments in evolutionism. It could be that *both* are valid. However, the demonic and broader adaptive perspective have specific behavioral expectations. As Part IX summarized, those expectations are roundly contradicted by the observational record.

In an EES perspective, the species' hormonal and neurobiological differences are a product of evolutionary forces that do not begin or end with genetic selection. Rather than the differing emotional tones leading to differences in aggressive behavior, differences in aggressive behavior lead to differing emotional tones. These can vary within and across a species, and change over time. Whether EES represents a transcendence of the MS or an extension of it, bonobos are a perfect example of the new approaches to evolution.

The bonobo contrast spotlights chimpanzee patterns too easily taken for granted. For chimpanzees, status-related killing can arise from a combination of individual personality (hyperaggressive males), circumstances (tumult at the top), and social organization that channels males into direct, often coalitional, sometimes violent competition. Bonobo social organization limits possibilities of fighting to the top, and leads to a male status game played with mothers, not brothers. While males do sometimes aggress on other males and even inflict display violence on young, one can only pity the fool that leaned heavily on intimidation. Kill an infant? Consider Volker. Bully an adult male? Deal with mom and friends.

This book is not against evolution, but rather *for an alternative perspective* on evolution. Chimpanzees were not selected to be killers, or bonobos not to be. Evolutionarily both have been and are shaped by differently constructed social niches and local traditions, but always respond to lived circumstances, ecological and historical. Chimpanzees incline toward male coalitional aggression, bonobos away from that—but they vary and overlap.

Why are bonobos more peaceful? By the resource competition hypothesis + human impact hypothesis (RCH + HIH), they should be. No intense intergroup competition over preferred foods is reported. Human impact could be extreme, but never in a way that pitched one group seriously against another. Circumstantially, there is no push toward intergroup killing. Nor is there a political logic for deadly male display violence.

If seen demonically, as evolved exceptions to the demonic ape rule, bonobos support the inheritance of warlike tendencies in chimpanzees and humans. If bonobos and chimpanzees are not innately different regarding "war," but *constructed* differently, could one argue anything less for *Homo*?[17] I could not say it better than Sapolsky on savanna baboons.

[T]he point of Forest Troop is not that our darkly stained Hobbesian roots contain more Rousseau than 1960s textbooks might have suggested. It is that if the social system of another primate is so malleable and free from assumed inevitabilities, we must be vastly skeptical about the existence of constraints regarding human social change. (Sapolsky 2013:436; and see Sapolsky 2006)

---

[17] Wrangham (2018; 2019; 2021) recently proposed a new evolutionary theory about human self-domestication. My book avoids theory about human evolution, but this one must be mentioned. According to "the execution hypothesis," humans share high levels of *proactive* aggression with chimpanzees but not bonobos, manifested in external attacks and killing. But humans share low levels of *reactive* aggression with bonobos as opposed to chimpanzees, which manifests in little open aggression within the group. Both proactive and reactive had their own evolutionary selection, and consequent developmental, neurological, and behavioral differences. So chimpanzees may reactively but not proactively, kill within their own group, as opposed to the intentional seek and kill with neighbors.

No changes are implied regarding "war" and the imbalance of power hypothesis. "Since there are long-term benefits from killing members of neighboring groups, natural selection has putatively favored this style of pro-active aggression" (2018:249). What is new is the hypothesis about reactive aggression within human groups.

Drawing from Boehm (1999), over evolutionary spans, humans who learned to cooperate and develop cultural norms, ganged up on within-group bullies and deliberately and proactively killed them. This pro-active step cut down on reactive aggression. Deliberate within-group killing—some call it capital punishment—is not rare among nonstate peoples. But overaggressiveness is only one possible reason. Suspicion of witchcraft is far more common (Otterbein 1987:485).

How this articulates with the demonic hypothesis that the within-group dominance drive is extended to external fights (Chapter 2); or the "Fighting for Status" hypothesis about urban gangs (see Chapter 29) is not explained. But the hypothesis has already been extended into a new "targeted conspiratorial killing hypothesis"—founded on language, and responsible for human self-domestication and "groupishness" (Wrangham 2021). It's always about killing, but I'll stop there.

PART IX
ADAPTIVE STRATEGIES, HUMAN IMPACT, AND DEADLY VIOLENCE

Theory and Evidence

PART IX

27
Killing Infants

Part IX evaluates major theoretical positions on *pani*cides and intergroup behavior against everything compiled in this book. Whatever is happening within evolutionary theory, adaptationist perspectives challenged in this book are frequently proclaimed as empirically validated, and the human impact hypothesis (HIH) to be unsupported. Evaluation of both is the object of Part IX. How do they differ in theoretical expectations? How do they fare against observational findings?

Chapter 28 takes on claims specific to *Demonic Males* and broader adaptationist explanations presented in Wilson et al. (2014a). Chapter 29 considers the rebuttal of the HIH, and summarizes the findings supporting a historical approach to resource competition and killing, including display and payback violence. To start, this Chapter 27 focuses on infanticide. But first, some summary points about the empirical record regarding *all* killings, the total tallies.

Tallies

Wilson et al.'s (2014a) summary tables from 18 chimpanzee and 4 bonobo research sites contain *152* entries. My total for all reports is 234. (For clarity, their numbers are italicized throughout Part IX.) My total is greater because it contains individuals reported in primary sources that did not make their list; the highly artificial case they exclude (with good reason) of young captives released at Conkouati Douli; and numerous killings that occurred after their compilation. Every case noted by Wilson et al. is included in my count.

In my running count, a 1 is certain killing, with a witnessed attack and body. 2 is a killing beyond reasonable doubt, mostly where a probably deadly, incapacitating assault is observed followed by disappearance but no body found, or a body found almost certainly indicative of a chimpanzee attack. 3 is a very likely killing, usually where a severe but not necessarily lethal attack is observed but no body is found. For the following discussions, I treat 1 through 3's as kills, and lump them in appendix tables. A 4 is a possible killing, where a severe attack is witnessed but no body found, or a body found that could be a *panicide*, but where there is still substantial room for doubt. To avoid any impression of undercounting, in following discussions I will include 1's through 4's under the general label of certain-to-possible killings, even though many of the possibles (60 in total) are quite questionable as killings by chimpanzees. Although primary reports often lead me to differ in some cases (mainly some of their suspecteds and certains I count as possibles), generally my certain-to-possible basket corresponds to Wilson et al.'s "observed" and "inferred." (More about classifying infant deaths in a moment.)

Wilson et al.'s "suspected" killings generally correspond to my 5's, hypotheticals. These are without empirical support except for a disappearance, which as demonstrated does not necessarily mean dead, and certainly not killed by chimpanzees—though some of them could be. Wilson et al. wisely do not include suspected cases in most of their calculations, only observed and inferred (2014a:415, supplementary material "Methods"). Adding suspected/hypotheticals to grand totals greatly increases the appearance of *pan*icide, amounting to over a third of all in Wilson et al., and nearly a quarter of mine. As these cases are without direct evidence and seem a projection of assumptions and expectations, they are not considered in Part IX as probative of any theoretical position. Eliminating the suspected brings Wilson et al.'s total from *152* down to *98*. Eliminating hypotheticals brings mine down from 234 to 179 certain-to-possibles.

Wilson et al. divide cases into weaned individuals and infants to clarify that some post-infants are not fully grown, but juvenile or adolescent. In my tables there are 6 juveniles, and 7 adolescents. But to avoid a cumbersome construction, I lump weaned individuals as adults, with case-by-case specifics left to the text. Here is my summary.

	Intergroup adult	Intergroup infant	Intragroup adult	Intragroup infant	Unknown group adult	Unknown group infant	Total
Very likely to certain (1–3)	29	35	13	34	1	7	119
Possible (4)	15	6	11	23	2	3	60
Certain to possible combined (1–4)							179
Hypothetical (5)	36	5	0	11	2	2	55
Total	80	46	24	68	5	4	234

Sexually Selected Infanticide

More infants are killed than adults. Omitting hypotheticals, certain-to-possible infant killings number 108 (60%) (or 59% in their count). Wilson et al. (2014a:414, 416) claim this fact validates an adaptationist approach. Yet prior adaptationist hypotheses weren't about killing infants *in general*. Predictions were about killing specific relational categories of infants, in circumstances that hypothetically confer reproductive benefits to killers. Those specific claims are scrutinized here.

Doing so requires bringing in a parallel body of very influential sociobiological theory, sexually selected infanticide (SSI). Sarah Hrdy developed SSI theory from observations of monkeys in India, to explain infant killings as an evolved reproductive practice. From the start, chimpanzees seemed a recalcitrant outlier for SSI. They just did not mesh with expectations.

The Adaptive Infanticide Paradigm

SSI theory began with study of hanuman langurs at Mount Abu, Rajasthan. Before Hrdy's work, infant killing was known but seen as pathological, attributed to human disturbance and/or unnatural crowding. (Sound familiar?) Hrdy (1974) came to a very different conclusion.

> Early on in my study it became clear that assaults on infants were not random acts of violence by stressed animals. Infants were attacked only by strange adult males, never by males likely to be their fathers. These attacks occurred when males from outside the breeding system took over one of the breeding troops and drove out the resident male. Then, in a relentless and goal-directed manner, the newcomer stalked mothers with unweaned infants and attacked them. Once their infants were eliminated, the mothers became sexually receptive and solicited the new male.... Rather than pathological, this infanticidal behavior appeared to be surprisingly adaptive behavior on the part of males. By eliminating the offspring of their predecessors, males induced the mother to ovulate sooner than she otherwise would have. Thus the killer had compressed reproductive access to her into the brief period he was likely to be present in her troop (on average twenty-seven months). From the male's point of view, his behavior was genetically advantageous. (Hrdy 1999:32–33)

In the sociobiological fervor of the time, this interpretive framework spread rapidly across animal research, and went public (Hrdy and Hausfater 1984a:xiv; Rees 2009:10–13). Infanticide in many species was reconceptualized, not as "abnormal and maladaptive behavior" but "normal and individually adaptive activity" (Hrdy and Hausfater 1984b:xi).

The theory has had strong critics,[1] who argue that it is sustained by a narrative structure within the paradigmatic expectations of sociobiology, more than by facts.

> A dependent infant separated from its mother has no chance of survival—but Hrdy was plainly ascribing the cause of death to a male attack rather than maternal abandonment. Her inference and her implication were that social change in langur troops is frequently accompanied by infant death—and she managed to render the potential empirical weaknesses of her account almost irrelevant by her theoretical justification. It no longer matters that she did not see males killing infants, because she has clearly shown the audience how males ought in certain circumstances, to kill infants. (Rees 2009:106)

Spirited rejoinders ensued (e.g., Packer 1999; Silk and Stanford 1999, Sommer 2000), yet work built on adaptationist assumptions progressed unfettered. By 2000 (Van

---

[1] Including Bartlett et al. 1993; Curtin and Dolhinow 1978; Dagg 1999; Sussman et al. 1995. They argue that there were few observations of the whole sequence of events, those are concentrated in a few disturbed places, and the status of an evolved adaptation is attributed to behaviors without addressing selective prerequisites.

Schaik and Johnson 2000a) the adaptive significance of infanticide was considered *settled*.[2] So an absence of observed infanticide was interpreted as compelling *evidence for* the evolutionary significance of infanticide, because "where counterstrategies are quite effective, the rate of infanticide will be so low that infanticide by males may never be observed in the average field study" (2000b:5).[3] Of special importance is a new category of potential adaptive benefit, keyed specifically to the chimpanzee record: "elimination of future rivals" (Van Schaik 2000:48).

Chimpanzee Infant Killings

The strength of the SSI hypothesis is its applicability across many species. Chimpanzees have been "the only fly in the sexual selection ointment" (Rees 2009:135). Nothing exists like the langur (or lion) pattern of hostile outside male takeover. Much mental labor tried to make chimpanzees' infanticide *somehow* seem adaptive, as in the late streak of infanticide at Sonso (Chapter 17 and below).[4]

Getting precise about infant killings proves difficult. First-year infant mortality runs about 20% across research locations (Fedurek et al. 2020:184). In possible infanticides, basic facts are often unknown, and particulars vary enormously.[5] Some are between group, some within—a fundamental distinction for any explanation. Six are group-unknown. Here I discuss internal killings first, then externals. Within groups there are 57 certain-to-possibles, and between groups 41.[6] Many cases lack other information, which reduces greatly the number of cases that can be analyzed for different purposes.

---

[2] By "taking for granted that infanticide is an evolved behavior" the editors "liberate" authors to explore new adaptive angles (Hrdy 2000:xiii). "[W]e encouraged authors to speculate" (Van Schaik and Janson 2000b:5). Presentation of evidence consistent with SSI across species is impressive, and studies have only grown since then (Palombit 2012; 2014). Even so, as Rees (2009:213) concludes: "There is no end in sight for the infanticide controversy."

[3] Van Schaik (2016:7) calls this the White Knight Problem, after the white knight in *Alice in Wonderland*. The Knight's horse had spiky anklets, to avoid shark bites. When Alice mentioned there were no sharks around, she was confidently told that the anklets were extremely effective.

[4] Another example of really trying comes from Gombe: "fathers played with and groomed their own offspring more than expected ... [and] fathers associated more during early infancy with [mother-infant] pairs for whom they were sires," than with others pairs. These observations "suggest that this early association by fathers may provide protection services" against infanticide *by females*. "How fathers recognize their offspring, or vice versa, remains an open question" (Murray et al. 2016:8).

[5] A dead infant may be glimpsed in an adult's hand or mouth without observers knowing its sex, mother, or circumstances of acquisition. There are discrepancies in reports and tallies, especially dates. Many infant killings are suspected because of disappearances. Since an infant without a mother cannot survive, I accept that a disappeared infant truly died, and generally count them as possible killings (4's) if they are accompanied by any suggestion of an attack. Without that, they are hypotheticals. Most attackers are males, but a good number are female. Commonly the victim is eaten as if prey, but often not, or only a few bites are taken (Kirchhoff et al. 2018:119).

[6] Wilson et al.'s tally is: internally, 25 observed and inferred, externally 33.

Internal Killings of Infants

As SSI developed, chimpanzee within-group killings were theoretically problematic. Some "were killed by male relatives" (Fossey 1984:230), including their own fathers. Nevertheless over time it was confidently asserted that internal infanticides by adult males met SSI expectations. (Note their source citations for coming discussions.)

> The facts are consistent with all the elements of the sexual selection hypothesis (see Hamai et al. 1992). The victims' mothers tend to be primiparous females who mated little if at all with the top-ranking males in the community during their conception period.... The killers were parties of top-ranking males who also gained sexual access to the females. (Van Schaik 2000:49)

Or from Wilson et al. (2004:525–526):

> In chimpanzees, intragroup infanticide appears largely consistent with the sexual selection hypothesis (Arcadi and Wrangham, 1999; Hamai et al., 1992). Attacks tend to focus on infants whose paternity is in doubt, either because the mother is a recent immigrant (Nishida and Kawanaka, 1985) or has a peripheral range (Arcadi and Wrangham, 1999). After the attacks, a mother mates more restrictively with the killer of her infant. (Arcadi and Wrangham, 1999; Hamai et al. 1992; Takasaki, 1985)

Compare those confident assessments to the actual record.

The Sexual Coercion Hypothesis

Male chimpanzees sometimes coerce females to copulate (Chapter 4). Hamai et al. (1992:160) extend that toward infanticide. Mothers of Mahale victims had mated with younger males more than mature males. Two victims' mothers, some time after the infanticides, mated with the mature killers. "We suggest, therefore, that one function of infanticide might be to 'correct' a female's promiscuous habit and coerce her into more restrictive mating relationships with adult males, and especially with high-ranking males."

That is the *best* evidence for SSI, and it is not much. But Mahale also offers much evidence against SSI.

> [S]ome males may have killed their own infants. In fact, Kawanaka (1981) observed that a male, who was thought to have killed and then eaten an infant, copulated with the victim's mother at the period of her conception. Also, in this study an immigrant female (CH) had repeatedly copulated (although not at the time of conception) with the male (KZ) who later killed her infant. (Hasegawa 1989:101)

"M group males have killed their own sons four times, and wasted the genes of the infants" (Takahata 1985:168). That was only part way through coercive Ntologi's reign as prime copulator and killer of infants, possibly his own. The Mahale killings present "an evolutionary puzzle because the males who are the real or suspected killers may have fathered the victimized infants" (Nishida 1990:27).

From Kanyawara, Arcadi and Wrangham (1999:348) do not challenge the coercion hypothesis, but neither do they provide much support. In the one internal infanticide, the main attacker SY "was a relatively frequent associate of MU's before the attack, it is possible that he was the father of MD, making his attack on MB genetically costly rather than potentially beneficial." His partner in the assault was a high-ranking female, a strange and until recently unique combination, a bisexual killing coalition. From Ngogo, Watts and Mitani (2000:358) conclude that evidence of sexual coercion through infanticide is "limited and circumstantial." Generally evidence for the sexual coercion explanation got no stronger since. Kasakela's Ferdinand killed Tarime, and attacked three other infants, *after* he had often monopolized mating over years (Mjungu et al. 2014). Some likely were his.

Van Schaik (2000:35) specifies that a "must" condition for seeing infanticide as a male reproductive strategy is "the probability that the male had sired the infant(s) is zero or close to zero." Internal infanticides violate that condition, clearly and repeatedly. So that approach does not work. Perhaps paternity uncertainty can save the SSI hypothesis for chimpanzees.

"Kill the Bastard"

The other supposed fit with SSI is eliminating paternity uncertainty. In Mahale's June 1979 and July 1983 infant killings,[7] the mothers were formerly of K-group.

> [T]ransitional ranging and association patterns may have awakened the M group males' suspicion toward the infants' paternity; then the males may have fostered the erroneous idea that the infants had been sired by the males of other groups, or may have wanted to remove the slightest possibility that infants sired by the males of other groups would remain in their own unit-group. (Takahata 1985:168)

This inference—at the apex of sociobiological fervor—shows the calculation often attributed to adaptive decisions. Reynolds is doubtful.

> [T]he rationale for male chimpanzees to practise infanticide became clearer, if and only if the infant victim had been conceived outside their own community. But first, they must be clear about this fact, so the question becomes: do chimpanzees (and other species practising infanticide) know about the relationship between

---

[7] In Chapter 10, these are infanticides B, by soon to be deposed Kajugi; and G, one of the attacks on Wantendele by Ntologi.

copulation and pregnancy and birth? Do they know about the length of time between copulation and birth? ... Or do they know that a female immigrant into their community who arrives with an infant ... has thus conceived with a "foreign" male? And is this the trigger for their attack on the mother and killing of her infant? (Reynolds 2005:146)

An obvious riposte is that these calculations are not deliberately rational. Evolution programmed the response. That answer jumps from frying pan to fire. It posits an evolved, genetically encoded paternity algorithm, requiring fine-tuning of multiple elements through an entirely unspecified and difficult-to-imagine selection process. How could this calculus evolve?

Time did not favor this hypothesis. While earlier infanticides at Mahale occurred during the K/M group friction, later on there was no competitive group to create paternity doubt. "In other words, 'the killing of the bastard' hypothesis appears less likely to be appropriate than before" (Hamai et al. 1992:159–160). Hosaka and Nakamura (2015:390) conclude "it is difficult to claim that chimpanzees kill infants as such an adaptive mechanism."

Thus the two posited applications of SSI go under. In Lowe et al.'s (2019) argument for SSI at Sonso, these are not a factor. But there SSI is given another try. Despite all the negative findings, maybe chimpanzees could still be brought into the selection mainstream after all.

Steep Hierarchy and Internal Takeover

As detailed in Chapter 17, an astonishing Sonso record of within-group infant killings and unsuccessful attempts from 2011 to 2018 is argued as consistent with SSI. So if siring opportunities were narrowly restricted to the male status pinnacle, then with political instability usurpers might increase their own reproductive success by killing infants sired by predecessors—something not unlike when lions or langurs move in and take over a group of females. Most of the attackers are male, most of the victims very young, and mothers were not injured. All of those fit SSI expectations. But evidence both absent and contrary gives this hypothesis little plausibility.

Absent is evidence on paternity of victims or of post-killing conceptions, the critical points for SSI. Contrary is earlier evidence at Sonso of broad paternity shared among adult males. No evidence suggests major status tightening after that for the high infanticide years. New alphas killed newborns in only one of five cases. With no evidence that male breeding hierarchy is far beyond that of other chimpanzee groups, SSI has no explanation why Sonso males killed from 23% to 40% of group births over 8 years. They may have killed their own offspring.

That is disqualifying for SSI, but not a problem for display violence + HI explanation. Combined with status competition, Sonso males were pushed into violence, possibly "aberrant," by the multipronged human disturbance, which got worse every year.

All told, infant killing is not looking good for sociobiology. But could my own hypothesis of internal infanticides as display violence be exapted to fit with SSI? Could that explanation be turned to the adaptationist cause?

Display Killing and Reproductive Success?

I argue that some individuals use deadly violence, sometimes directed at infants within the group, as display to intimidate rivals for alpha status. Could that have evolved as a reproductive strategy?

At Gombe, Mahale, Budongo, and Tai, paternity assessment gave between 16% and 50% to alphas.[8] Even if not a steep pinnacle like that proposed for late Sonso, in most places being at the top is associated with increased reproductive success. It seems as simple as 2 + 2—alphas killing infants to be at the top is an adaptive strategy. But it does not add up that way.[9]

At Mahale and late Gombe, most internal infant killings were done by only two alphas, Ntologi and Ferdinand. If this were an evolved behavior, why would it appear in so few cases? In contrast, at highly disrupted Sonso but nowhere else, four out of five adult males were infant killers, not just those at the top. More fatal to adaptationism, in all three sites males likely killed their own offspring.

Any way you look at it SSI fails to accommodate internal infant killings by adult males. They remain an exception and challenge to SSI.

Internal Infant Killings by Females

That covers male killers of infants. What about females? For their infanticides, there is good evidence of immediate resource competition, which sometimes traces to human impact. However, there is little reason to believe that that these infanticides represent a reproductive strategy beyond getting enough to eat.

Resource Competition

Pusey et al. (1997:830) suggest that 1970s infant killers Passion and Pom were not aberrant. Rather, their killings expressed female competition over food and rank.

---

[8] Gombe (Constable et al. 2001:1290; Wroblewski 2009:876), Mahale (Inoue et al. 2008:259), Budongo (Newton-Fisher et al. 2010:424–425) and Tai (Boesch et al. 2006:112). But it is not a monopoly. "[L]ow-ranking and even crippled males who have highly developed strategic skills in consort formation are able to sire infants without the need to compete with higher-ranked rivals in the group situation." Young and lower-status males' opportunities increase with larger numbers of competing males and receptive females (Wroblewski et al. 2009). High-status males may be reproductive underachievers (Newton-Fisher 2004:81). Other factors also correlate with reproductive opportunity: political alliance (Duffy et al. 2007), participation in coalitional aggression (Gilby et al. 2013), and sexual coercion (Feldblum 2014). The reproductive success of eight alphas at Gombe varied, connected to differing political styles (Bray et al. 2016). However more recently overall Gombe alpha paternity was put at just 15.9%, 7 of 44 known paternities (Massaro et al. 2020).

[9] Contra adaptive benefit, adverse health consequences also correlate with being at the top: elevated glucocorticoids (Muller and Wrangham 2004:332; Muller et al. 2021)—although the fitness implications of elevated glucocorticoids in primates is not clear (Beehner and Bergman 2017)—foraging costs (Georgieve et al. 2014), and higher parasite load (Krief et al. 2010; Muehlenbein and Watts 2010). Health costs associated with higher status are found among other primates (Anderson et al. 2021; Cavigelli and Caruso 2015; Lonsdorf et al. 2017:3; Sapolsky 1982; 2005; 2021). And alphas, would-be alphas, and ex-alphas can be subject to severe, even deadly internal attacks.

At Gombe female rank correlates with more births, infant survival, and how quickly infants mature. Hypothetically this is because higher-status females occupy prime local ranging land, although evidence of that is not strong (Wrangham 1977:774). They also refer to the initial attack by Fifi with Gigi on Gremlin and her infant; and observation of Mitumba females eating an infant. Theoretically, violence against lower-ranked or incoming females or their infants could protect their own home areas of prime foraging. "These observations suggest that female infanticide may be a significant, if sporadic, threat, rather than the pathological behavior of one female" (Pusey and Williams 1997:829).

That idea was bolstered by findings that females aggressively compete for prime local ranges (Miller et al. 2014; Williams et al. 2002; cf. Markham et al. 2015; Foerster et al. 2015). From Kasakela came additional attacks by Fifi on Gremlin and infants, and others by females in 2012–2013. Among Budongo's Sonso:

> Our observations test and provide support for the hypothesis that increased pressure on resources precipitate severe female aggression, as females compete for limited foraging areas. Recent demographic shifts at Sonso may have produced such socioecological pressures, which may explain the concentration of three infanticides within only 28 months. Since 2001, Sonso has had an influx of at least 13 female immigrants, many with dependent offspring. (Townsend et al. 2007:356)

"These patterns of infanticide by female chimpanzees are reasonably interpreted as an extreme manifestation of competition for space" (Pusey and Schroepfer-Walker 2013:5). Agreed.

But the strength of this association reflects historical developments. Killings by Passion and Pom occurred after reduced banana provisioning, when body mass fell. Goodall said they killed infants for the meat. For Sonso, the ingress of many females was probably due to pitsawing, just as Sonso was later squeezed by neighbors also pushed by pitsawyers. Resource competition hypothesis + human impact hypothesis (RCH + HIH) works for infant killings by females.

Promoting the Genes?

Is there suggestion of an *ultimate* goal of females increasing their reproductive success, beyond the proximate goal of getting enough food? Does the concept of passing along genes add anything to the noncontroversial objective of staying fed? That is the sociobiological question. Hrdy (1999:51–52) answers yes.

Hrdy begins with reproductive history of another Gombe female, Flo. Flo did everything right, building a "dynasty" of gene bearers. While Goodall saw Passion and Pom's killing as pathological, Hrdy suspected something adaptive. With Pusey and Williams' findings (above), she elevated this to a general principle of status-linked competition for reproductive success—SSI for females. "We now know that, *given the opportunity*, a more dominate female chimp will kill and eat babies born to other females" (1999:52). Who ever knew that?

Passion was no dynasty builder, but *measured* as disturbed and paranoid. She exhibited "extraordinarily inefficient and indifferent maternal behavior" (Goodall 1986:78). Pom managed to survive, and eventually bonded closely with Passion, but both then withdrew from social interaction. Passion left few descendants.

Future descendants might be a factor for Fifi, but Gigi, her companion in the first attack, was sterile. "From 1975 on Gigi has shown an interest in infants between one and a half and three years of age, and has become 'auntie' to a succession of them" (Goodall 1986:67). She was allomothering, helping care for unrelated infants, not eat them. Who knows why she participated in the attempted grab? As for Fifi vs. Gremlin, repetition of attacks over years—unique other than for Ntologi's repeat attacks on Wantendele—suggest that this might involve something "personal."

Females clearly can kill. The question for them as well as males is why they kill, where and when they do. For internal infanticides by females, the plausible answer is immediate food competition, traced to human disturbance. Beyond that, internal infant killings by either sex do not support the SSI perspective.

How about *external* infant killings? Are they adaptive? On that point, SSI and the demonic perspective converge.

External Infant Killings

Killing outside infants to reduce rivals was not part of the original imbalance of power perspective. Rival reduction was limited to adult, not infant killings (Manson and Wrangham 1991:370–371; Wrangham and Peterson 1996:151, 159–160, 166; Wrangham 1999:8–10). *Demonic Males* offers a different sociobiological take on infanticide: sexual coercion. "[A] mother whose infant is killed learns that the males of her current community are inadequate as her defenders, so that a strategically sensible move from her point of view would be to move into the killers' community, where her next infant would presumably be safer" (Wrangham and Peterson 1996:289). That idea was floated when it was imagined that external violence served to recruit new females. Chapter 28 shows it does not.

SSI Meets Rival Coalition Reduction Hypothesis (RCRH)

The saving theoretical extension already had been offered by Takahata (1985:167): "intergroup male infanticide may result in more or less improving the reproductive success of killers by eliminating future competitors." A 1995 Budongo killing of an outside male infant seemed supportive. "Reducing the number of males reaching adulthood in a neighboring community reduces its territorial 'strength,' which, for the infanticidal males, should make range expansion, recruitment of females and ultimately extinction of the neighboring community more feasible" (Newton-Fisher 1998:169).

Ghiglieri (1999:216) took this to an extreme.

As observers became more sophisticated and followed chimps into their own terrain and away from feeding stations at human researchers' camps, they watched male chimps kill many infants of their own species. Nearly all of these infants belonged to females from *outside* the males' territory. A few belonged to females residing in the periphery of the killers' territory but adjacent to that of alien males. Hence every infant probably was, or could have been, sired by an alien male. On top of this, most of the murdered infants were males. More to the point, cannibalism was clearly not the primary object of these murders. Murder was. Genocide was. And, ultimately, a reproductive victory of the killers' DNA was. We now know ... that our nearest primate relatives, chimps and gorillas, are wildly infanticidal, but in a strictly genocidal way. That chimps wage genocidal war against adults, too, only deepens the meaning of this knowledge.

Van Schaik and Janson (2000:50) put this idea more soberly, as a permutation on adaptive infanticide. "Killing the male infants of a neighboring community may strengthen the position of the killers' sons in the balance of power with the neighboring community, and may even allow expansion of their territory." "Killing infants directly eliminates competitors, [and] reduces future coalition size of rival groups (if the victim is male)" (Kirchoff et al. 2018:120).

This notion seemed more plausible with additional intercommunity infant killings. When Mahale's M-group killed a male infant from newly arrived Y group (Chapter 10), it was taken to support

> that attacking and killing a male infant reduces the number of future adult males in a neighboring group, and that this may have the effect, in the long-term, of weakening the power of a neighboring group; it may also lead to better access to resources, and to expansion of the group range, thus ensuring their future safety. (Kutsukake and Matsusaka 2002:178)

At Conkouati Douli (Chapter 19), the killing of two released male infants were interpreted in this way, even though three female infants were likely killed as well. The Ngogo Expansion from 1999 to 2011 (Chapter 12), added 12 observed and 4 inferred killings of external infants, but every one was sex unknown (Wilson et al. 2014a:EDT 2).[10]

All told, where the sex and group of victim is known, the balance of external to internal infant *male* killings flatly contradicts the goal of relative reduction of rivals. Combining the certain-to-possibles results in 9 external male infants killed (plus two from Conkouati-Douli),[11] and 21 internals. Where sex is known, chimpanzees kill

---

[10] In the high proportion of external to internal infanticides, Ngogo is highly exceptional. Certain-to-possible killings of male infants are at Gombe, 7:14, Mahale 3:12, and Sonso 6:21. Ngogo is 17:6.

[11] A note on counts as reported in Part IX. So far, my totals included the highly artificial situation of Conkouati Douli. (Wrangham et al. [2014a] do not count these.) From this point on, breaking down cases for discussion produces smaller totals, and Conkouati Douli introduces more distortion. Going forward, totals will *not* include Conkouati Douli, which numbers will be indicated in an initial report by parentheses—so external infant killings as here will be initially tallied noted as 8 (2), and subsequently as 8.

more than twice as many of their own vs. outside infant males. Across the field record, infant killing on average *increased* the relative strength of neighbors.[12]

Killing Infants: Adaptive Strategies and Human Impact

Chapters 28 and 29 consider killings of adults. I began Part IX with infant killings partly because of their importance in SSI theory, but also because of their importance in adaptive claims by Wilson et al. (2014a). In that adaptationist statement, a weighty confirmation is said to be that victims are "mainly young infants (most vulnerable and/or reduced time to mother's next estrus)." A robust pattern shows that "attackers most frequently killed unweaned infants" (Wilson et al. 2014a:414, 416; EDT 6). All the infant killings at Sonso post-2013 would further reinforce that point.

But claiming support by the simple fact of more infants killed than adults changes the predictions after results are in. It ignores previously stated adaptive expectations, for which results are bad. Infant killings by adult males cannot be explained as curtailing mothers promiscuity within the group; nor as "killing the bastard" because of paternity uncertainty; nor as coercing outside mothers to join or copulate with the killers; nor as ascendant alphas eliminating predecessor offspring to themselves breed sooner. Most germane for this book, infanticide does not reduce future outside male rivals vs. defenders of the home gene puddle—quite the opposite. Even early advocates of adaptive infanticide Arcadi and Wrangham (1999), later acknowledged difficulties with subsequent findings.[13] The simple fact that more infants are killed than adults does not validate an adaptationist explanation.

Human impact plus display violence explains infant killing better. Passion began her cannibalistic streak after Kasakela's body weight crash with System E. The two outside infant killings at Mahale came during competition over feeding stations; and the killing of a Y-group infant happened when the intruders relocated out of rangelands diminished by people. Ngogo's many outside infant killings derive from their very large size and consequent expansion, both of which derive from introduced food trees and the fall-out of islandization. Internal Sonso killings by females coincided

---

[12] Wilson et al. (2014a:EDTs 2 and 4) tally 5 external observed/inferred infant killings, and *10* internal.
[13] Wrangham (2019:229) is the more positive:

> The traditional sexual selection theory ... does not apply. Possibly, the killers benefit by intimidating the female into avoiding the area, leaving more food for the killers's community. Alternatively, the attackers might gain by killing male infants that would otherwise grow up in the neighboring community to become future opponents. Further observation will eventually test such ideas.

Resource defense might apply to the Ngogo expansion, but there is more than enough evidence already to challenge the RCRH.
Arcadi (2018:75–77) is more skeptical:

> Lethal aggression toward infants is even more puzzling. Killing infant males from neighboring communities would, for males, eliminate future competitors, but then why kill infant females, future potential mates? Both intra- and inter-community infanticide would increase the reproductive success of killers if they were subsequently able to impregnate the infants' mothers, but evidence for this is scant. (2018:67)

Recent findings from Sonso do not change that.

with pitsawing population displacement and increased population density. Killings at Conkouati-Douli followed release of captive chimps, as did the severe attacks on a juvenile at Mt. Assirik. All were obviously human-impacted.

Bringing in display, Humphrey's outside infanticide was within the hungry, disturbed time of Passion's kills. Later Goblin and Frodo's attacks on external mothers and infants came as they nervously explored the mostly depopulated Kalande range. The first external kill by Gogol and Sagu followed collapse of Tai's sophisticated non-lethal territoriality due to largely anthropogenic population loss, and their rise to the top during playbacks.

Those killings by high-status males mix human impact and display violence, which also seems likely for late Gombe attacks by Ferdinand. But display killing also may possibly occur without any evident connection to human disturbance. The number one internal infant killer was Ntologi. His intended intimidation of others is clear, but a causal link to human disturbance is not. Two infants died during Duane, Vernon, and Black's status jostling in Sonso, again without *connectable* human influence.

Bonobos have no infant killings to consider, but do have adult male attacks on within-group young. These actions clearly fall outside the SSI model, but they work as dominant males intimidating potential rivals within the bisexual, mother-oriented status hierarchy.

Other infant killings do not fit under either human impact or display violence. Some may be textbook aberrant—if not Passion, then Freud suddenly killing his grooming partner's son, or Darwin snatching and eating Devota's just-born infant in tourist-plagued Mahale. Still inscrutable is the recent surge of 19 possible-to-certain killings over 7 years at Sonso. While adaptive explanations are not supported there, the paucity of contextual information prevents any estimate of the respective roles of human disturbance, display violence, and psychological disturbance.

The Bottom Line

Chapter 27 is full of detail, but we should not lose sight of the major findings against adaptive explanations of infanticide. Each of the specific hypotheses about adaptive infanticide may fit a few cases, but each is unsupported or contradicted by much more evidence, with the exception of resource need by food-stressed killing females. In those cases where the big numbers in infant killings rack up, possible-to-certain fathers killed their own offspring, flatly contradicting adaptationism.

Within-group killing of male infants greatly outnumber between-group, *negatively* impacting their future balance of power with neighbors. Almost all killings are situated in circumstances of high disturbance, and/or intense status competition at the top, often by especially aggressive males.

That is infants. What about adults?

28
The Case for Evolved Adaptations, by the Evidence

"Lethal Aggression in *Pan* Is Better Explained by Adaptive Strategies Than Human Impacts" (Wilson et al. 2014a) is state-of-the art adaptationist theory. Signed by 30 *pan*ologists, combining findings from 18 chimpanzee and 4 bonobo research sites, subjected to sophisticated statistical modeling, it is already a benchmark in the field (e.g., Sapolsky 2019:42; Wrangham 2019:233). This and the next chapter hang on that manifesto. Chapter 28 contests in detail their and other claims of killing as evolved adaptive strategies.

Having considered infants, intergroup killing of adults, especially males, is the focus of Chapter 28. My count exceeds the tally in Wilson et al. (2014a). They count *21 adult/adolescent males and 6 adult females* as observed or inferred. For 426 years of observation in 18 chimpanzee research sites, that is not so many. (*Figures from Wilson et al. appear in italics.*) I count 28 adult males and 10 adult/adolescent females, certain-to-possible. But before getting down to cases, an important clarification.

Differing Perspectives

I use "the demonic perspective," or "Gombe-vision" to denote the overarching paradigm that came out of the Four Year War. Not all *pan*ologists subscribe (although there is no sign-up sheet). Most behavioral ecology focuses on how populations adapt *flexibly* to environmental conditions, without grand generalizations about chimpanzee or human natures. So, in lauding Wilson et al., Silk (2014:322) sums their findings.

> The data tell us that there are some ecological and demographic circumstances in which the benefits of lethal aggression exceed the costs for chimpanzees, nothing more. Humans are not destined to be warlike because chimpanzees sometimes kill their neighbors.

If one added that those circumstances are typically due to human disruption, it would be near to my position.

But Silk's "nothing more" isn't the public face of *Pan* field research. The scientific moral is much bigger, and scarier. You've read the claim time and again: chimpanzee (and human) males are evolved to kill outsiders whenever they can. As a refresher, here are a few additional: "No reasonable doubt exists today that the natural strategy of common chimpanzees is to establish, maintain, defend, or expand a kind of group territory via lethal warfare" (Ghiglieri 1999:174). "[T]here can be no questioning ... that lethal aggression occurs between communities and that [is] characteristic of chimpanzees in the wild across the African continent" (Stanford 1998b:406). "A growing body of evidence suggests that lethal intercommunity aggression is typical for chimpanzees across populations" (Gros-Louis, Perry, and Manson 2003:341). "Forty years of observations across Africa have shown that when three or more males from one community find a lone individual from a neighboring community, they kill this individual" (Hauser 2005:60). "Intergroup killing thus appears to be a widespread trait of chimpanzees, rather than the result of circumstances peculiar to one or a few study sites" (Wilson 2013:370). "[B]etween-group violence is pervasive, found in all communities subject to long-term study ... chimpanzee males benefit from exterminating their neighbors, provided they can do so at low cost. Indeed, it seems as though male chimpanzees will engage in this behavior whenever they have weaker neighbors" (Van Schaik 2016:345–346). And Stanford again (2018:85): "After half a century of observation, we can say with certainty today that lethal aggression is a strategic, adaptive, and routine aspect of chimpanzee social behavior." There seems little doubt.[1]

And two more you have not seen, to emphasize the broader implications of the Gombe perspective, by very prominent scholars, two decades apart, in the premier journal *Foreign Affairs*.

Once one views international relations through the lens of sex and biology, it never again looks the same. It is very difficult to watch Muslims and Serbs in Bosnia, Hutus and Tutsis in Rwanda, or militias from Liberia and Sierra Leone to Georgia and Afghanistan divide themselves up into what seem like indistinguishable male-bonded groups in order to systematically slaughter one another, and not think of the chimps at Gombe. (Fukuyama 1998:33)

[On Ngogo] He never stood a chance. His first mistake was looking for food alone; perhaps things would have turned out differently if he'd been with someone else. The second, bigger mistake was wandering too far up the valley into a dangerous wooded area. This was where he risked running into the Others, the ones from the ridge above the valley ... they left him there to bleed to death and later returned to mutilate his body. Eventually, nearly 20 such killings took place, until there was no one left, and the Others took over the whole valley.... Over the course of a decade, the male chimps in one group systematically killed every neighboring male, kidnaped the surviving females, and expanded their territory.... Similar attacks occur in chimp populations elsewhere.... If such is the violent reality of life as an ape, is it at all surprising that humans, who share more than 98 percent of their DNA with chimps, also divide into "us" and "them" and go to war over these categories? (Sapolsky 2019:42)

---

[1] Yet the consensus is not universal. Sussman and Hart (2010:207–211) and Sussman and Marshack (2010:16, 22–23) review field reports, and find that intergroup adult killings are very infrequent. Wrangham and colleagues (2010:32–36; Wrangham and Glowacki 2012:9–10; Wilson 2013:370) took issue, but Sussman et al. were correct. The common wisdom of *pan*ology is mistaken. The numbers show it.

Many *pan*ologists *do not* claim their data supports this inference. It would be nice if they said so explicitly, and directly rejected the demonic perspective. Until then it rules.

Intergroup Killing Is Rare, Not Normal

Chapter 28 begins and ends by going broader than the specific predictions to come. First addressed are two of the most *widespread, important, and unfounded* claims about intergroup killings by chimpanzees.

Two "Wars" Only

Intergroup adult killing is much more rare than totals suggest. Most kills happened in just two times and places. To make without doubt a point that may be met with skepticism—given conventional wisdom—for the following discussion I rely *exclusively* on Wilson et al.'s numbers (2014a:EDT 1), not my own tallies.

The compiled results from so many years and locations document a major point, mostly neglected in the *pan*ological literature. Contrary to received wisdom, across the continent, *there are only two "wars" with sequential adult killings*, plus a scatter of singletons from other situations.[2]

Of their total *21* male and *6* female intergroup adult/adolescent killings,[3] *5* males and *1* female are from the Four Year War at Gombe, 1974–1977. *Eight* males and *1* female come from the Ngogo Expansion, 2002–2006, making *15* total. That leaves just *8* adult/adolescent males and *4* females, *12* total, from all other years.

Thus *15* out of *27* intergroup adult/adolescent killings, both sexes, come from just two locations and 9 years, 55.5% from just 2% of all observations. Limiting this to only adult/adolescent *males*, 61.9% are from the war years. The remaining 98% of observations, 417 years, produce just *12* outside adult/adolescent killings, 8 males and 4 females.

Intergroup killings during the Four Year War and the Ngogo Expansion produce a rate of 1.66 killings per year. The rate for all the other 417 observation years is .029% per year, or one killing per 34 years. That is about once in a chimpanzee lifetime.

If limited to males alone—the focus of rival coalition reduction hypothesis (RCRH)—that is 1.44 vs. .019 per year, the latter about *once in 53 years* of observation. I call that rare. An intergroup adult/adolescent killing during those nine "war" years is 57 times greater per year than during 98% of observation time, or for males, 76 times greater.

---

[2] Before the Ngogo expansion was fully evident, Wrangham et al. (2006:16, 22) tallied killings from five populations over 158 observation years. "Gombe stands out with its high level of intergroup violence." Nothing more is made of that fact. Nakamura and Itoh (2015:381), see it and say it plainly: "To date, certain cases of chimpanzee 'wars' (series of coalitionary killings of other group members) have been reported for only two study groups, Gombe and Ngogo."

[3] In this total of *27* adult and adolescents, I exclude a 6- and an 8-year-old juvenile male, one from the Ngogo expansion and one from Sonso.

External Adult Killings, Observed And Inferred

	Male	Female	All	Adult (weaned) kills per year	Adult male (weaned) kills per year
Gombe, 1974–1977	5	1	6	1.666	1.444
Ngogo, 2002–2006	8	1	9		
417 other observation years	8	4	12	.029 1 per 34.4 yr	.019 1 per 52.6 yr.
Total 426 years	21	6	27	.063 1 per 15.9 yr	.049 1 per 20.5 yr

Source: Wilson et al. 2014a:Extended Data Tables 1–4

If these two violent periods are expanded a bit, they account for an additional 16 cases of intergroup killing (including infants).[4] All told, Ngogo killings of outsiders are "23–75 times higher than the median rate suffered by individuals in nine well-studied chimpanzee communities" (Mitani et al. 2010:507). The Four Year War and Ngogo Expansion are true outliers. Without them intergroup killings of grown individuals are certainly rare.

And to clarify the obvious—while it is common to read that chimpanzee raiders "sometimes exterminate" neighboring groups, that claim is applicable to *only one instance*: Kasakela vs. Kahama. No "war" is evident at Mahale; and no neighbor extermination was implied for Ngogo. Not sometimes. One time, maybe. The common claim of common group extermination is without foundation.

The Two "Wars" and Adaptive Benefits

Their outlier status grows in importance because the adaptationist case rests squarely upon them.

> Whether chimpanzee violence is adaptive or not, is a question for which we do not yet have a definitive answer. Answering this question in full requires information on reproduction and information on individual participation in violence, which is available for only a few sites and which has not yet been analyzed. Additionally, chimpanzees (like humans and other animals) may sometimes make mistakes, participating in killings that result in fitness (i.e. reproductive) costs. Whether a given behavioral

---

[4] Extragroup infant/juvenile killings add *one* to Gombe during the War years, and *six* for the Ngogo expansion. Also, conflict at both sites bled out beyond those boundary dates. Gombe, adds an inferred killing of an adult female in 1973. (In my count, I add two possible outside adult female killings in 1978–1979). Ngogo, adds *six* additional external infant killings in the few years preceding and following the peak of expansionist conflict.

strategy is adaptive depends on average effects of traits. Given these caveats, previous studies provide evidence in support of the view that chimpanzee violence provides fitness benefits to the attackers. Mitani et al. found that the intergroup killings by the Ngogo community were associated with substantial territorial expansion in the area where disproportionately many of the killings had taken place. Studies at Gombe provide evidence that larger territories provide important fitness benefits, including more food, as indicated by heavier individual body weight, controlling for age and reproductive condition and shorter inter-birth intervals for females. Males who enlarge their territory thus provide more food for their mates and offspring, enabling faster reproduction, and thus greater success for the aggressors. (Wilson 2014b, references omitted)

The possible adaptive benefits for both "wars" were analyzed in detail in Chapters 8 and 14. For Gombe evidence is supportive, but with major qualifications. Adaptive measures of body mass and reproductive health correlate with larger range, but not linearly; range expansion reflects anthropogenic population losses among neighbors; and enhanced reproductive variables may be related to intensified hunting largely unrelated to expansion. Ngogo expansion improved access to preferred fruits and hunting space—facilitated by trailing observers who frightened the locals—but without specific measures of reproductive success.

Although adaptive benefits are likely, that says *nothing* about whether either is situational coping within circumstances shaped by human impact, or expressions of evolved adaptive predispositions to eliminate neighbors. If the latter, shouldn't it happen in more than 2% of all field observations? As for single killings conferring adaptive benefits, there is no evidence supporting adaptation except for a few infant killings by females.

Nevertheless, for Wilson et al. (2014a:414, references omitted) killings in general display an adaptive logic. "Kin selection and evolutionary game theory yield a set of specific predictions for how benefits and costs should vary with the context, age, sex, and genetic relatedness of the attackers and targets." Let's see.

The following discussions consider both of the overlapping but not identical behavioral adaptationist claims articulated by Wilson et al., along with the staples of Gombe vision. The first topic, about males as killers and victims, draws on both. Discussion then fans out to two predictions from *Demonic Males* rather than Wilson et al., one about males and one about females. After that we switch to the factors of Wilson et al.'s statistical analysis: clade, number of males, and population density. That will exhaust main claims of adaptiveness.

Is Killing a Male Thing?

In Wilson et al.'s pattern of male aggression sex bias is the strong suit, with two predictions: most attackers will be males; most victims will be males. Both are solid by the numbers. The sex of attackers can be dealt with quickly, but sex of victims gets complicated.

Attackers

Evidence is unambiguous: males do *much* more serious violence than females. "Considering all cases for which the number of attackers was observed (n = 58) or could be inferred (n = 6), males constituted 98% of participants in attacks" (Wilson et al. 2014a:416). But that was obvious from the get go.

Unexpectedly, females also kill. Female coalitional attacks at Budongo led to the conclusion that "lethal aggression is these apes in not a gender-specific trait" (Townsend et al. 2007:356). In their only intergroup clash, females were more aggressive than males. Tai females patrolled and joined in intergroup clashes, though less than males. In the 2007 intergroup killing, three females excelled in violence, with Zora eating the victim's penis. In zoos, females can out-aggress males. Females are potentially as violent as males, but males far more commonly inflict severe violence. *Explaining* that behavioral difference can go in different directions.

In this book, I argue against specific predispositions toward killing outsiders. However, I do not assert there are no dispositional differences between sexes regarding aggression and violence, for chimpanzees, bonobos, or humans. I am agnostic on this issue (Ferguson 2021—see closing comments). Male chimpanzees are larger and stronger. Given sex differences in endocrinology and development—however evolutionarily engendered—sex differences in temperament are certainly possible. Even bonobos, when separate bonobo groups meet, adult males usually remain apart and hostile while others mix. But extended inheritances flow together. Compared to bonobos, chimpanzees are *socialized* into aggressive confrontation against other males.

Victims

Turning from attackers to victims, the sexual angle is more complicated. If the prediction were simply that victims will be mainly males, it is well supported. In my count of certain-to-possible killings when sex of victim is known, 83 (7) are males, and 36 (4) females, 2.3 to 1 (Wilson et al. put all observed/inferred killings at *47* male, *18* female, or *2.6:1*). Males are more than twice as likely to be killed as females. Then come the complications.

The adaptationist expectation in Wilson et al. (2014a:414) is that more males than females will be killed. But all along, without ambiguity, the actual prediction was of *outside* males being killed. Killing males within the group contradicts the theory. Wilson et al. add those in anyway. The big theoretical point was and is: does killing reduce the relative strength of male outsiders?

Outside Males Attacked, Tolerated, and How Does It Add Up?

Males are the focus in Wilson and Wrangham's (2003:372–375) overview of adult killing. "[T]hey direct their attacks almost entirely to males, the sex that alone defends the territory.... Even infants killed by adults are mostly male. Those who die, therefore, are mainly the present and future defenders of the territory. By killing rival males when it is cheap to do so, chimpanzees shift the balance of power between their own community and the neighbours" (Wrangham 2006:52). "If escalated aggression is cheap and serves to increase the future dominance of the aggressors' community, it should be directed towards the most effective fighters among the neighbors. Females are not active aggressors in intercommunity interactions in most sites" (Crofoot and Wrangham 2010:186).

Imbalances of Power—Necessary or Sufficient for Killing?

The imbalance of power hypothesis holds that if multiple males from one group catch a solo male from another, that is *all* that is needed for them to kill. It is necessary and sufficient for killing.

The importance of numerical superiority is uncontroversial. There is strength in numbers, and one does not need an evolved tendency to explain what chimpanzee intelligence easily accounts for. The more of "them" compared to "us", the more likely we can get hurt. One male found alone by several of another group is *potentially* vulnerable.

Far more significant and much more questionable, is whether overwhelming numerical superiority is *sufficient* for killing, that males kill males of other groups *whenever they can*. "Provided that killing is cheap enough, in almost any rivalry killing will pay" (Wrangham and Peterson 1996:165); and "chimpanzees inflict fatal injuries on foreign males whenever they have the opportunity" (Wilson et al. 2002:1108). In their foundational statement, Manson and Wrangham (1991:371) argue that "unrestrained attacks on opponents are favored merely because their cost is low." "Whether chimpanzees forego opportunities to attack vulnerable opponents (i.e. solitaries from neighboring groups) is unclear.... Resolution of this issue awaits further data."

The theoretical claim that male chimpanzees should take every chance they get to kill an outside male is not supported. Beyond the two "wars," an outside male kill rate of one per 53 observation-years indicates that (1) greatly unbalanced meetings are very rare, or (2) killing is not the normal action taken when that happens (and see Sussman and Marshack 2010:19).

Tolerating Outside Males

Since the record of killings is unsupportive, let's approach this question from the other side. Are solo outside male chimpanzees ever encountered by larger numbers, and *tolerated*? Yes.

At Mahale from 1966 to 1984, four juvenile males transferred with their mothers from K- to M-group and were accepted. Another, Fanana, showed up by himself as a 10-year-old adolescent and rose to be alpha. The last grown male of K-group, Limongo, continued roaming inside M-group's new haunts—alone, vulnerable, and tolerated. At Budongo never-seen adolescents Simon and Squibs appeared along with newly arrived mothers. At Bossou two adults and an adolescent male visited. At

Tai a few male "prisoners" were captured and assaulted, but without the intent to kill inferred at Gombe.

Compelling evidence against universal violence against adult outside males comes from Gombe of all places. Not previously noted, in 1974 a juvenile male, "the orphan Beethoven" was accepted into Kasakela (Goodall 1986:71; Pusey 1979:469). In early years of study, known individuals were spotted roaming in rangelands to their north, south, and probably east. Subsequently unhabituated males associated with Kahama males; an unknown male nested near to Figan, and the two may have gone off together. Evered disappeared for long periods toward the Mitumba range, consorting with unhabituated females. Goliath after being attacked was thought traveling with an unhabituated individual.

In some group attacks on solo males, assailants refrained from killing when they could. At Mahale a solo M-group male snuck into the feeding station while K-group was there. The alpha caught the intruder and smacked him around, but no other males joined in this clear opportunity to kill. At Gombe attackers drifted off as Godi "slowly got up and looked after them, screaming." Sniff too was left alive, and got up and walked away. If evolution built in a tendency to kill, why not finish the job? What better opportunity of reducing neighbor-competitors than when a captive is alone and bleeding on the ground. Letting them go fits with the resource competition hypothesis (RCH), not RCRH.

Larger groups accommodated smaller: as when Mitumba was down to a couple of adult males but still went into Kasakela's home range; or when Gusazirre's remnant group penetrated deep into Kanyawara's core area; or when later Mahale's M-group reoriented its ranging away from intrusive, smaller Y-group. Well-documented toleration of outside males occurred en masse when groups met and mixed at early Gombe and Budongo.

Shedding paradigmatic blinkers, the record of between-group *toleration* of grown males is robust, and the adaptive prediction of always kill when can is empirically contradicted. Without the foundational Four Year War at Gombe and the great outlier of Ngogo, would any scholar surveying the entire observational record imagine that to kill males found alone is *standard* behavior?

Tipping the Rival Male Balance?

The sociobiological bottom line is that killing must diminish the relative strength of outside male rivals: the RCRH. That did not add up for infants. What about adults, the main concern in *Demonic Males*? That fundamental prediction loosely connects (i.e., not age or sex specific), to Wilson et al.'s (2014a:414) expectation that killing is guided by "genetic relatedness of attackers and victims: mainly non-relatives," i.e., members of other communities.

In Wilson et al., the imbalance of more outsiders killed is clear, at *1.67* to *1*.[5] But in my count, adding in the recent internal infanticides at Sonso eliminates that gap, with 76 (10) certain-to-possible between-group kills, and 80 (1) within-group. Roughly

---

[5] Like so many elements of the demonic paradigm, actual findings may be greatly exaggerated in retelling. So in *Foreign Affairs*, Sapolsky (2019:42) cites that study to assert "chimps are about 30 times as likely to kill a chimp from a neighboring group as to kill one of their own."

even. Yet Wilson et al. (2014a:416) make a valid point: "chimpanzees could potentially attack members of their own community on a daily basis, but rarely encounter members of other communities" (Wilson 2014a:416). Without doubt, observed chimpanzees *usually are antagonistic to outsiders*, and not to insiders—with important exceptions on both counts. That has been clear since Nishida in the 1960s. The ultimate genetic logic of this is anything but clear.

How Related Are Philopatric Males?

How much does genetic relatedness differ between groups? Demonic theory takes male philopatry to mean that males within a group are more related to each other than to outside males; or compared to the relatedness of adult females which immigrated from other groups. It is this supposition which confers the logic of inclusive fitness on collective hostility toward males of other communities. It makes kin selection sense. The record from multiple studies is mixed, yet tilts strongly against high male relatedness.[6]

Contrary to the demonic model, natal males are not much if at all more genetically related than are immigrant females. Those females bring in the genes of surrounding local groups. Over endless generations of "exogamy," genetic mixing (except for Y chromosomes) should be thorough. External rivals could be gene-sharing cousins, uncles killing nephews. Shouldn't that decrease inclusive fitness? That question was raised in Ferguson (2011), but is not clarified in Wilson et al. (2014a), or anywhere else that I know. Nor have other neo-Darwinian conundrums.[7] Genetic relatedness is hardly predictive of conflict.[8]

---

[6] A study at Gombe (Morin et al. 1994:1194–1195) found support for kin-selection: "males are indeed more related to one another than are females.... The results suggest that males are related at the level of half-sibs" more frequently than females are. But those findings were later "recognized as flawed, making inferences based on that data untenable" (Vigilant et al. 2001:12895). At Mahale mature males were significantly more related to each other than mature females; but take out one exceptionally long lived and highly related male, males were *not* more related to other males than females to other females (Inoue et al. 2008:259). Samples from Sonso from 1995 to 2002 did not find "significantly higher relatedness" among males of the community than among females (Lukas et al. 2005:2188). Among three contiguous local groups at Tai, one study found that "on average, males were not found to be significantly more related than females in the same community" (Vigilant et al. 2001:12895). Another study there found that for males, two groups show somewhat higher male relatedness within the group than between, but a third showed more relatedness between groups than within (Lukas et al. 2005:2185–2186). Finally, although theoretical expectations were that group males should be related at the level of half-siblings, within Tai groups that was found only for actual half siblings, not otherwise (Vigilant 2019:74).

[7] Such as: with pleiotropy—one gene having multiple expressions and so selection pressures—how could a genetic program for the complex suit of demonic behaviors be constructed? Or, why would natural selection fix *this* suit of behaviors, setting the dial to attack rather than in neutral, when so much other behavior is clearly flexible?

[8] A similar sociobiological expectation is also unmet: that more related individuals preferentially associate and support each other. Study at Kanyawara supplemented by data from 14 other groups, found no relationship between maternal relatedness and affiliation (Goldberg and Wrangham 1997:564; 566). At Ngogo maternal kinship was not associated with male cooperation or close association (Mitani et al. 2002). "The results of our analyses are unexpected given the putative importance ascribed to kinship in chimpanzee society" (Mitani, Merriweather et al. 2000:888). A more expansive Ngogo study found that maternal brothers "show clear and consistent biases in their social behavior," yet "males in the majority of highly affiliative and cooperative dyads are unrelated or distantly related" (Langergraber et al. 2007:7788). More recent analysis of Ngogo data concludes, "there remains no clear-cut explanation for partner choice among male chimpanzees." After finding limitations of kinship, age, or rank, they suggest, "dyads may possess some

Inside vs. Outside Killings

A second problem with the early expectation of more outside than inside killing is: so many inside killings. Physical aggression "within the community, although common, seldom leads to serious injury and it is usually rather brief" (Goodall 1988:10). "Male chimpanzees Pan troglodytes have violent aggressive interactions within alliances [inside communities] but do not inflict serious bodily injury" (Wrangham 1982b:282).

If inside vs. outside is taken as distinguishing relatives vs. nonrelatives, then 80 inside to 76 outside, 51% of all instances violating expectations must be taken as falsification rather than confirmation an evolved behavioral logic.

A third problem is that the RCRH does not predict that more outsiders will be killed, but more outside *males*. "A strong evolutionary rationale for killing derives from the harsh logic of natural selection. Every homicide shifts the power balance in favor of the killers, giving them an increased chance of outnumbering their opponents and therefore of winning future territorial battles" (Wrangham 2005:18). By that same evolutionary logic, killing a male from one's own group makes the community more likely to *lose* "future territorial battles." The key for the imbalance of power theory is relative numbers. So we come to the theoretical nub for the RCRH. Empirically on average, does killing tilt the odds toward the home team?

Certain-to-Possible Killings (1–4's)
Conkoauti-Douli not included in totals, but added in parentheses

	External	Internal	Int/Ext killing un-known	Total
Adults, Adolescents, and Juveniles				
Males	28 (5)	21	3	52 (5)
Females	10	2 (1)	0	12 (1)
Unsexed	1	0	0	1
Total	39 (5)	23 (1)	1	63 (6)
Infants				
Males	9 (2)	21	1	31 (2)
Females	5 (3)	18	1	24 (3)
Unsexed	22	17	5	44
Total	36 (5)	56	7	99 (5)
Combined Total	75 (10)	74 (1)	7	156 (11)

distinct quality that engenders strength and stability, such as compatible personalities" (Bray and Gilby 2020:1). They hang out because they like each other! Male chimpanzee behavior has been a disappointment for inclusive fitness theory.

Female chimpanzees bond less often than males, but when they do, "the vast majority of females who form close social bonds are not close maternal or paternal kin" (Langergraber 2012:503). Among bonobos, philopatric males bond less than immigrant females, demonstrating "female bonding without female relatedness, male relatedness without male bonding" (White 1996a:12). "Thus, the high degree of sociality and cooperation between resident females cannot be ascribed to close genetic ties but is more likely the result of mutualism or reciprocity" (Gerloff et al. 1999:1194). More contra-sociobiological: male bonobos are *more closely related* within vs. between groups than chimpanzees, even though it is the chimpanzees which are group antagonistic, not bonobos (Ishizuka et al. 2020b:2–4).

By my numbers, certain-to-possible weaned male killings are 28 (5) external, and 21 internal. As usual, the two "wars" make all the difference, with 14:1 for them. Infant killings when sex is known add 9 (2) external and 21 internal. Combining infants with adult, including the "wars," makes a grand total of 33 (7) males killed externally, and 42 internally. All together, males killed within the group outnumber between groups, a *net loss of nine of their own* against the others. Without the "war" years, the net loss is much greater.[9]

An expected response to this point is that is internal male killings may serve other reproductive logics (e.g., Massaro et al. n.d.a). "When a cabal of male chimpanzees seeks out and gangs up on another male in their community, a biological justification can always be found. He's a genetic rival, a competitor for food resources, or a political rival" (Stanford 2018a:68). With a little imagination, falsification of RCRH expectations by any single case is rendered impossible. But so many?

Attacking or Recruiting Outside Females

The flip side of the prediction that victims are mostly male is that females are killed less often. This too is supported, with (as noted) 2.3 male victims to every 1 female. But this too must be interrogated. Reproductively, why should males *ever* kill females?

Compounding this question is a prediction notable by its absence in Wilson et al., despite its prominence elsewhere: acquiring more females to mate with. Its absence is understandable, because this key hypothesis resoundingly failed.

Recruiting More Females for Mating

Early on Wrangham (1977:536) postulated that "the functional consequence of territorial expansion was the acquisition of females." Goodall (1986:528) argued that violent territoriality, besides acquiring expanded ranges, is "not only to protect the female resources of a community, but to actively and aggressively recruit new sexual partners from neighboring social groups." In the foundational statement of the imbalance of power hypothesis, comparing across the primate order, whether aggression acquires females or of food resources depends on which are "alienable," i.e., acquirable by aggressors (Manson and Wrangham 1991:369). But

> the ultimate benefit of intergroup aggression among chimpanzees is expected to be increased access by aggressive males to reproductively valuable females, via either incorporation of neighbors or encroachment on the territory of neighboring males. As we have seen, such benefits have been observed.... We view chimpanzee community territorial expansion (as occurred at Mahale) as a proximate benefit leading to

---

[9] Using Wilson et al. (2014a), the RCRH does do better. For all ages, they tally *28* external and *19* internal male killings, a net gain of *9* over rivals, or about one every 47 years. Yet without the two "wars," internals outnumber externals by *three*.

the ultimate benefit of increased access to fertile females (Manson and Wrangham 1991:374, 385).

In *Demonic Males*:

> For a male-bonded chimpanzee community, conquered land can include not only a larger foraging area, but also new females.... So males of an expanding community can gain females, which means that male chimpanzees should want to expand their territory to the largest area they can defend. (Wrangham and Peterson 1996:166)

Ghiglieri (1999:173) states that male victors at Gombe and Mahale instantly benefited by taking both females and territories. Muller (2002:122) writes, "[t]he evolutionary benefits of such expansions are clear.... After the group extinctions at Gombe and Mahale, the aggressors appropriated both territory and females from their defeated neighbors." For Langergraber et al. (2014:646),

> The transfers of parous females following severe reductions in community size, known (Gombe) or suspected (Mahale) to have occurred as a result of lethal between-community aggression, show that male chimpanzee communities that successfully cooperate to expand their territory can also increase their reproductive success by attracting more adult females to their community.

For Moore et al. (2015:379, references omitted) "lethal intercommunity aggression is responsible for (Gombe), and likely caused (Mahale), the transfers of parous females into the larger community, demonstrating that successful cooperation among males to expand their territory can also result in increased reproductive success through the addition of more adult females to their community." Stanford (2018a:85) finds clear evidence of adaptive benefits in territorial attacks because the aggressor group "obtains females from those eliminated communities." In *Foreign Affairs*, Sapolsky (2019:42) tells readers that at Ngogo, "the male chimps in one group systematically killed every neighboring male [and] kidnaped the surviving females." Popular tellings of the Gombe story take special flight when imagining the sexual plunder.[10]

It Hasn't Happened

The Four Year War gave little and questionable evidence of violent female acquisition. "[O]nly one female definitely transferred permanently from Kahama to Kasekela" (Manson and Wrangham 1991:385). That was Little Bee, but she went over at the very start of the War. Another fence-sitter (Gilka) went with Kasakela earlier as the two groups drew apart and while Kahama had the upper hand (Pusey 1979:475). Honey

---

[10] "If a single female is sighted, they will generally gang-rape her, and then either leave her for dead or bring her back with them as a concubine" (Meilinger 1997:601). "Groups of half a dozen males are regularly running into isolated females. The males do not always rape the females, but it happens with alarming regularity" (Morris 2014:304).

Bee eventually transferred for a few years then left; and *possibly* a young Kahama female joined Kasakela years later as an adult (Goodall 1986:524). Since females routinely transfer from their natal group at maturity, these moves are normal. In the context of Kakombe fissioning, none can be attributed to violence.

No support came after that. Gombe records from 1975–1992 flatly contradict the expectation of more males leading to more territory, leading to more females. No significant relationship is found between number of males and range size; or between range size and number of females; or encounters with stranger females. "Thus, males did not immediately gain access to more mates by expanding the size of the community territory" (Williams et al. 2004:529). Violent acquisition of females did not happen at Gombe.

At Mahale many females transferred to M-group as K-group lost all its adult males, but that male loss can't be attributed to violence. At Ngogo males were never seen to copulate with mothers after an infant killing (Watts and Mitani 2000:362; 2002:263–264; Sherrow and Amsler 2007:10). Nor was there any immediate female acquisition from their Expansion. Eventually three parous females showed up, but two went back where they came from, and fate of the third is not reported. Besides these there are no intergroup transfers of females after intergroup violence.

On the other hand, human impact contributed to *many* adult female transfers. The 2002 move of females at Gombe was due to the largely anthropogenic population drop of Kalande; as was transfer from a crashing group at Tai. At Mahale the absorption of K-group females occurred as they remained in place around feeding stations when M moved in. Habitat destruction is implicated in unusual female immigration at Mahale in 2010, and Budongo in 2000–2003.

Attacks on Outside Females

Against the idea that violence is an adaptive tool for recruiting females, males brutally assaulted potential mates from outside. From 1971 to 1982, Kasakela on 16 occasions severely attacked stranger females with infants. Six were possible-to-certain adult kills, which could exceed the number of outside adult males killed there.

Females with infants were not immediately available for copulation. Yet "[m]ale chimpanzees are in general less attracted to, and less likely to compete for, females who have not yet demonstrated their reproductive capacity" (Wrangham and Wilson 2004:236). Mothers with offspring theoretically should be recruited. Instead they were fiercely attacked.

Attacks on outside females were and are "an unsolved puzzle" (Goodall 1986:522). "[W]hy would males *ever* kill females, i.e. potential reproductive partners?" (Marchant and McGrew 1991:381). Maybe thought Goodall, "the recruitment of new females into the community at Gombe is facilitated by repeated brutal attacks on their mothers which serve ... to weaken the mother daughter bond or ... to break it altogether" (Goodall 1986:524). Over time at Gombe, no evidence supported that idea (Williams et al. 2004:524).

Considering the total record, Arcadi (2018:72–73) sums it up: "There is little evidence to support the female recruitment hypothesis.... The hypothesis is additionally weakened by observations at all sites of severe attacks on stranger females, which would seem contrary to a strategy of recruitment."

The RCH + HIH on the other hand, fares well. The RCH predicts that both sexes should be attacked in defense of resources; and the HIH connects heightened resource competition to human disturbance. The 1970s attacks on females in provisioning-reduced Gombe are consistent with that. Outside of 1970s Gombe, only three intergroup killings of adult females are reported (Wilson 2014a:EDT 1): Patti at Gombe, Dani at Ngogo, and Zimba at Sonso. Human impact connected to those attacks is more complicated, but as described in those chapters very present.

Models

The adaptationist challenge to human impact explanations offers more than simple percentages about demographic characteristics of attackers and victims. It creates and tests models, looking for statistically significant associations of observed/inferred killings per year, against 16 combinations of 3 variables related to human impact, and 3 variables fitting adaptive expectations. The "variables for the adaptive strategy thesis" are: clade, number of males, and population density. Do these three variables support an adaptive strategy explanation, as claimed?

Clade

The obvious reason for considering the relationship between evolutionary lines of descent and killings is the bonobo/chimpanzee contrast. Maybe Eastern and Western Chimpanzees also evolved different proclivities toward deadly violence. They've been genetically isolated for hundreds of thousands years. Tai chimpanzees have been called "a second bonobo." Their distinctive traditions—some say cultures—are usually attributed to learning. Another theoretical possibility is that they reflect genetic differences.

Langergraber et al. (2014:2) posit an evolved difference in violence between Eastern and Western Chimpanzees. "Despite ample opportunities for observation due to the long-term study of multiple chimpanzee communities only two between-group killings have been observed in west African chimpanzees, compared to dozens in the east African subspecies." The general issue of genes vs. traditions led to a ping-pong match of papers, which probably will continue.[11]

---

[11] "[I]t is plausible that some behavioural differences among chimpanzee sites have a genetic origin" (Laland and Janik 2006:544). Lycett et al. (2007; 2009; 2010) argue back, for learning over genes. Langergraber et al. (2011) (the "et al." including Boesch, Nishida, Pusey, and Wrangham) respond, noting the concordance of genetic similarity, geographic distance, and behaviors such as bee-probe, marrow pick, or leaf clip. Lycett et al. (2011:2092) respond that "genetics plays only a minor role (if any) in determining chimpanzee behavioural variation;" and Langergraber and Vigilant (2011) respond that "[g]enetic differences cannot be excluded from generating behavioural differences among chimpanzee groups." But studies from Tai (Luncz et al. 2012; Luncz et al. 2015) and Kalinzu (Koops et al. 2015b) show that behavioral variations between *neighboring* groups persist even as females migrate from one to the other, which seems a convincing demonstration of their nongenetic basis.

But Wilson et al. (2014a:415–416, EDT 5) find no significant relationship between chimpanzee clade and number of killings per community. "The best model included only males and density." Although it is impossible theoretically to foreclose different tendencies to aggression by clade, given that finding, and the social-inclusive inheritance explanation of chimpanzee/bonobo contrasts, genetic difference by clade can be discounted here as a factor affecting killing. That leaves two adaptive variables to consider.

Male Numbers and Density

What does their best model show?

[I]ncreases in *males* and *density* increased the number of killings; for all other parameters, the 95% confidence intervals included zero. Excluding one community (Ngogo) that had both an unusually high killing rate and unusually many males resulted in similar values for model averaged parameters, but only the estimate for density excluded zero from the 95% confidence interval. (Wilson et al. 2014a:415)

The association of male numbers with killing rests heavily on Ngogo, the great outlier.

By their calculation, the average number of male Ngogo attackers was *17.4*. In other intercommunity adult killings, the average number of attackers was *4.9* (Wilson et al. 2014a:Extended Data Figure 1, Table 7). In attacks on infants Ngogo averaged *14.8* attackers while Gombe, Mahale, Budongo, and Tai averaged *6.5*. (At Mahale it was done by one or two.)

Ngogo became the mega-group because of human impact, and without Ngogo the number of males is not a significant predictor of killings in their best model. Which leaves population density as the most significant adaptive strategy variable. Interpreting that correlation is complicated.

In adaptationist theory about chimpanzee "war," where was population density previously hypothesized as an adaptive consideration contributing to higher levels of killing? Wilson et al. (2014a:415) suggest it "may affect frequency of intercommunity encounter and/or intensity of resource competition." They argue that "[d]ensity was unrelated to disturbance"—meaning by that their own constructed human impact variable of "disturbance," which Chapter 29 shows has no expected relationship to human induced violence. Instead, "[w]e consider density to reflect natural food abundance." Food abundance leads to higher population density, which leads to more killing. To support that crucial assumption, they note food abundance at Ngogo, where density reached $5.1/km^2$.

This must be clear. Their assumption that density is *a function of natural food abundance* and *not reflective of human impact* is all that undergirds the strongest finding of their adaptive strategy model. If this assumption is invalid, then their case for adaptive strategies explaining lethal violence is shaken severely.

Food availability is a critical constraint on population density in all species. But for *actual* population density, i.e., chimpanzees per square kilometer, much more is involved than that. Food availability and density are not associated in a linear way.

Arid areas such as Fongoli and Mt. Assirik, or high-altitude Kahuzi-Biega, have extremely low densities (.09–.13/km^2) consistent with very limited resources. Yet chimpanzees in largely undisturbed central African rainforests have *low* densities, 1.31–1.5 for Conkouati-Douli, 1.1 at Lope before logging, 0.8–1.1 at Loango, and 1.53 for Goualougo. Although their food abundance has not been measured, it is hard to imagine that it is only a third or a quarter of Ngogo's. Bonobos in Wamba and Lomako, with documented food abundance, have estimates ranging from 1.4–3.46/km^2.

High density could result from human-induced population impaction, within the permissive possibilities of local food availability, itself augmented by past human farming. That is my argument for Ngogo. Gombe is similar, where provisioning and outside forest clearing increased chimpanzee density, enabled by their staple of oil palm, also introduced by past farmers. In the only two cases where "war" is related to high density, high density is connected to human impact.

Budongo's Sonso illustrates the limitations of a statistical vs. a comparative historical approach to lethal violence, in the complications of going from a single data point to understanding. Its density in Wilson et al. (2014a:Extended Data Figure 1a), is a towering 9.2/km^2. In total killings per year it comes in at #2 (after Ngogo), at .8/year. For the association between density and killing, Sonso is up there with Ngogo, very important in supporting their adaptationist model.

Sonso's forest productivity is not natural, but the result of earlier managed logging. Its density fluctuated wildly. In 1992 it was estimated at 2.5/km^2. Its later extraordinary density of 9.2/km^2 was because of an influx of females likely due to massive human disturbance, pitsawing. After that frequent killing began, mostly within the group itself. Update to 2018, Sonso was 75 individuals, with a core home range of 6 km^2, making its density 12.5^2, as infant killing continued (Leroux et al. 2021:2).

In killing times at Ngogo, Gombe, and Sonso density is not a simple function of nature's abundance, and cannot be understood without considering human impact. These three places are critical for adaptationist claims. Look at figure 2b in Wilson et al. (2014a:416), which plots the relationship between number of killings per year and population density: the only four data points above .2 per year are (left to right), Gombe's Kahama and Kasakela, Ngogo—the two "wars"—and Sonso. Without those the illustrative diagonal would be a flat line along the X axis.

Adaptive Variables and Models Summarized

"Lethal Aggression in *Pan* Is Better Explained by Adaptive Strategies Than Human Impacts" compiles more than enough evidence to evaluate demonic and broader adaptationist expectations vs. a human impact explanation. Wrangham (2019:233) says that with this benchmark effort, "the debate is now settled ... killing was explicable as a biological adaptation." A confident claim, but what has their effort and evidence actually shown?

Most long-term research sites have coalitional killings of some sort, but 55.5% of all intergroup adult kills come from just two situations, totaling 9 years, or 2% of all chimpanzee observations. The kill rate then is 1.66 per year, vs. .03 per year for all other times and places. Only in those situations, and with even more rare kills of

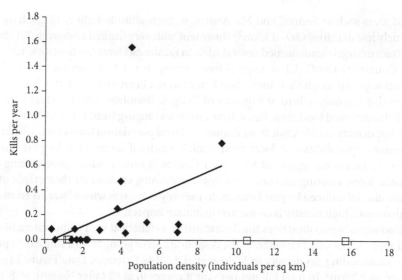

Illustration 9.1 Relation between Density and Kills Per Year
Caption: Number of killings per year for each community versus number of males and population density. Rates for each community are indicated by black diamonds (chimpanzees; $n = 18$) and open squares (bonobos; $n = 4$). Black lines indicate simple linear regression for chimpanzee data for illustrative purposes only; statistical tests were done using Poisson regressions. a. Number of killings versus number of males. b. Number of killings versus population density (individuals per km^2).

Source: Wilson et al. (2014a). Lethal aggression in Pan is better explained by adaptive strategies than human impacts. *Nature*, 513, 414–417.

within-group infants by females, do circumstances support any adaptive benefit from killing, and those must be qualified. Bonobos do not kill—a fact long known, and explainable without invoking differences in inherited predispositions. The posited difference in tendencies toward violence between Eastern and Western clades did not pan out. Across subspecies, lethal attacks are mainly by males—yes, as predicted, and obvious from the start. This sexual difference could have both biological and social bases, interacting. Females kill too—unpredicted. Dead victims are mostly males—predicted; but numerous females are killed—unpredicted. Many male victims are from within the group, sometimes offspring of the killers—all flatly against expectations. Some outnumbered foreign males are not killed, but tolerated—unpredicted.

Relative reduction of rivals by killing more outsiders than insiders, amounts to about one every two generations, and less than zero if the nine "war" years are factored out. The total number of outsiders killed is not greatly more than insiders—not exclusively outsiders as originally claimed—but about equal. Killings typically involve numerical superiority by the attackers—another obvious point. Even so, a significant statistical relationship between number of male attackers and killing hangs on Ngogo. For their remaining adaptive variable, density, the assumption that it reflects natural food abundance is not supported comparatively. Where associated with killings, it reflects long- and short-term human impact. Recruitment of females by killing males, a baseline expectation of adaptive explanation, is decisively refuted.

Conclusion

An adaptationist approach to killings is proclaimed as fully validated by abundant evidence.[12] As scrutinized here—not so much. Instead, Chapter 28 shows the weakness of the demonic/adaptationist paradigm. Sequential killing of outsiders is very rare. In only those cases, and female killing of internal infants at Sonso, are adaptive consequences supported. Yes, most killers and victims are male, and more outsiders than insiders are killed, but often *not* in ways that increase inclusive fitness. Only with the outlier of Ngogo is the number of males present predictive of kills. The "adaptive" variable of *density* is their most predictive, but that was not previously posited as an adaptive causal factor. When a connection of high density and killing is found, that density is connected to human disturbance. If that is instead counted as a human impact variable, Wilson et al. (2014a) is turned on its head. No, killing does not significantly reduce outside rival males compared to inside defenders. No, it does not lead to acquisition of females from outside.

That is one side of the claim that the adaptationist/human impact debate has been settled, for adaptationism. Now let's consider the other side.

---

[12] That conclusion is not accepted by all *pan*ologists. "Because intraspecific killing in chimpanzees occurs in a variety of contexts and involved a range of victims and attackers, it is probable that the evolutionary advantages accruing to killers vary. However, it has been difficult thus far to definitively identify these hypothetical benefits" (Arcadi 2018:66).

29
Human Impact, Critiqued and Documented

As commentary to Wilson et al. in *Nature,* Silk (2014b:321) proclaims victory for adaptationism.

> These results should finally put an end to the idea that lethal aggression in chimpanzees is a non-adaptive by-product of anthropogenic influences—but they will probably not be enough to convince everyone. Perceptions of the behavior of non-human primates, particularly chimpanzees, are often distorted by ideology and anthropomorphism.

Ouch.
Stanford (2018:67–68) is equally dismissive.

> There is a school of thought—a poorly informed one—that holds that chimpanzee aggression is somehow the product of human interference in their behavior.... The argument that extreme violence is an aberration dissolved with more and more field observations of chimpanzee violence. For most of the past three decades there has been a consensus that violence is a normal, adaptive behavior among chimpanzees.... It might have been acceptable in the 1970s or 1980s to be skeptical about the adaptive nature of chimpanzee violence, but with the accumulated observations of wild chimpanzees since, it cannot be written off as "unnatural."

Case closed, and nailed shut.

Well, no. As shown, it is the adaptive explanation, evaluated against nearly half a millennium of field observations, that fails to inform. Chapter 29 turns to the alternative: that ideological, anthropomorphic, uninformed, antique, consensus-rejected, and simply unacceptable human impact perspective. First up is rebutting the rebuttal, countering Wilson et al.'s supposed disproof of human disturbance theory. Then follows historical summaries of exactly how anthropogenic disturbance contributed to killings at particular places and times. Support for status-related killing is also presented.

Their Great Refutation

Wilson et al.'s challenge tests three variables of anthropogenic disturbance: provisioning, size of protected area, and disturbance rating. Of their five models reaching statistical significance, only one consists of these three variables. No wonder. They are plainly inadequate for evaluating human impact on chimpanzee violence.

The Human Disturbance Factor

Wilson et al. is framed as responding to my position on human impact in "Born to Live" (Ferguson 2011). Although I had much to learn back then, it specified the kind of disturbances I was implicating. After discussing the significance of *reduced* provisioning at Gombe:

> Habitat loss in unprotected areas and around or even within protected areas has eliminated chimpanzee rangeland. Snare poaching and retaliation for crop raiding has added to rangeland impaction, even within Parks This has led, I argue, to intensifying territorial competition. Epidemics, some introduced through humans, caused major demographic disruption, and with social consequences we are only beginning to discern. Other huge unknowns are the effects of research and tourism, which are often extremely intrusive. We cannot specify their effects but are unwise to discount them. (2011:252–253)

Wilson et al.'s composite human impact factor is quite different. They use a measure constructed for the sexually selected infanticide debate, about urbanized South Asian monkeys (Bishop et al. 1981). This combines five scales: disruption of home range, human harassment, habituation to humans at the start of the study, and presence of predators (including dogs). Wilson et al. bring it closer to chimpanzee realities by adding in hunting by people. The only variable that gets its own graph to demonstrate *no relation* to kills per year (Extended Data Figure 2b) is "disturbance"—their human impact factor. This method does not come near the historical comprehension required for comparative explanation of disturbance and violence. Here's why.

No simple relationship is expected between disturbance and killing. Zero-killing Bossou, encapsulated for decades by villagers, is rated most disturbed, maxing out every submeasure except for hunting. At Bossou the two species worked it out, with long-term coexistence. Counted second in disturbance is Wamba's E1 bonobos, also with zero killings. Yes, there was forest clearing before research started. Yes, whole groups may have been killed or driven off during the Congo Wars. But during study, with ample open land Wamba was much less disrupted than other places which register lower in disturbance: Tai, Gombe, and Mahale.

One submeasure, disruption of home range is surely important, but requires specification. Lumbering may reduce chimpanzee food (e.g., Kanyawara), or make more food available (e.g., Sonso). Critically what is not included in their combined disturbance measure is habitat destruction *outside* a group's territory. That led to intergroup conflict at Gombe, Mahale, Kibale, Budongo, Kalinzu, and Lope.

The submeasures of degree of habitation when study started, elimination of predators, and harassment by people are significant for the south India infanticide debate, but not for this book, except perhaps excessive tourism at Mahale. Human hunting truly is a great threat to chimpanzees and bonobos, but not implicated in chimp-on-chimp violence. For the human impact hypothesis (HIH), their human disruption variable has no expected relationship to killing.

Provisioning

Six of their 22 groups were provisioned: Kasakela, Kahama, Mitumba, M-group, K-group, and E1. Four were in the top seven killing groups, yet statistical analysis of 22 groups found no significant relationship between provisioning and kills per year—given the weight of Ngogo and Sonso. "Provisioning is thus clearly not necessary for chimpanzees to kill. Nor is it sufficient for killing to occur" (Wilson et al. 2014b:unpaginated). Agreed.

Only in the Four Year War is provisioning, and specifically the *curtailment* of provisioning, responsible for killings. Provisioning might explain the Invasion from the South by Kalande, but those are only hypothetical killings. Later Mitumba and Kasakela both had and lost provisioning at the same time, so that did not pit one group against another.

At Mahale provisioning led to territorial conflict between M- and K-group. That included two likely/possible external infant killings, and conceivably an adult or two—but there is no sound evidence for that. M-Group's kill rate went high because of within-group infanticides, plus one external killing of a Y-group infant. Here, the apparent covariation of provisioning and killing is a spurious connection.

On the bonobo contrast, Wilson et al. (2014b:unpaginated) say that by the HIH, "exposing bonobos to the same stimulus as chimpanzees (provisioned food) should result in a similar increase in aggressive behavior," but it did not. Yet among the E1 bonobos at Wamba, provisioning did indeed lead to conflict around the provisioning station, similar in kind but not degree to Gombe. E1 provisioning was not nearly as important as at Gombe or Mahale, disputants had plenty of open food territory and multiple feeding stations, and they lived within the violence-dampening effect of bonobo social organization. No killing expected.

Provisioning in itself does not cause killing. Whether provisioning creates or intensifies food competition and conflict between groups depends on detail and context.

"Protected Area"

Their last human impact variable is "size of protected area, with smaller areas assumed to experience more impacts" (Wilson et al. 2014a:415). This is the only human impact variable they calculate as significantly associated with killings, although "size of the protected area did not have a consistent effect on rates of violence" (Wilson et al. 2014b:unpaginated). Nor should it. Humans pressing in all around can generate conflict in different ways, but the relationship is not simple, as following cases demonstrate.

Gombe Park is relatively tiny, and a prime case for killings connected to human pressures, exemplifying a meaningful connection. Ngogo has many killings and a large protected area, but Park boundaries did not wall out the impact of islandization. Bossou has no protected area and no killings—but also no neighbors, and long-term coexistence with people.¹ Sonso is within a large Forest Reserve yet has many killings. Those connect in demonstrated ways to habitat disruption within the Reserve. Tai has the largest protected area and only a few killings, so it is good for a statistical relationship. But protection did not keep out hunters, diseases, or playbacks that preceded those few killings. No consistent effect is expected of "protected area" on rate of killings.

Changes over Time

Wilson et al. call me on an earlier prediction. In a paper for a 2009 conference—about the halfway point for producing this book—I (Ferguson 2011:253) went out on a limb: "As human impact intensifies in the future, I predict substantially more male–male intergroup attacks, and more of other sorts of violence, in sharp contrast to field observations from 1983 to 1998." They (2014a:415) respond: "controlling for changes in the number of communities observed per year (communities) the rate of killing has not changed over time (year)."

I was specific in time frame, not asserting a general trend through time as Wilson et al. assess. Gombe in the 1970s and Ngogo in the 2000s were deadly. My prediction looked ahead from the late 2000s. Nevertheless, declining populations and recent killings at Gombe, Budongo, and perhaps Loango require modification of the prediction. It was only half correct. Intergroup killings may be fewer, and within-group violence—"other sorts of violence"—may become the norm.

Conclusion

Wilson et al.'s (2014a) measures are not invalid in themselves. Disruption of home range, hunting, provisioning, and a small protected area are important considerations, but they must be done in detail and with historical context, not reduced to simple numbers. Other important factors are missing entirely: frequent follows by hordes of tourists, introduced and emerging infectious disease, habitat loss or killings by people near to study areas, disturbance by playback, and anthropocene climate change.

Display and ex-alpha violence is not considered in their study. (It was not then a hypothesis). Nor is contrasting chimpanzee/bonobo social organization. Nor is individual personality—but remove a Frodo or Ntologi, or drop an imaginary one into another situation, and the group-by-group tally of killings could be very different.

All these factors interact systemically, understandable in their historical specificity, with variable causes and probabilistic effects. Epistemologically this is a fundamental difference in method. By their methods, human impact appears mostly irrelevant for *pan*icides—although their adaptive factors do not do too well either. My method relies on comparative historical contextualization, with theoretically elaborated hypotheses built into comparison. Specific hypotheses were formulated and evaluated not

---

¹ Wilson et al. (2014a:415) specifically note that although Goualougo has a large protected area, it nevertheless has an inferred intercommunity and a suspected internal infanticide. That sounds like a point against human impact, but both incidents are entirely undescribed, so evaluation should be reserved.

selectively or anecdotally, but against *every* reported killing, in detail. This is science, but science of a different kind than reigns in contemporary *pan*ology.[2]

Human Impact, Politics, and Killings: A Narrative Summary

Case comparison establishes three generalizations about chimpanzees. (1) Demonic, Gombe-like situations are unusual, one of many variations on intergroup relations. Most intergroup contacts between males are antagonistic and avoidant, but some show tolerance and mixing. Territoriality is malleable, not innately determined. (2) Violent territoriality connects to past or current human disturbance. If that greatly heightens intergroup resource competition without options like exit, violence is more likely. (3) Other killings involve male status competition: display killing of defenseless individuals and payback against bullying alphas. The comparative historical method supports all these conclusions, not with aggregate numbers but with detailed documentation across research sites.

Gombe

Gombe is the crucible of the paradigm. In the mid-1970s every aspect was on display: male patrols, incursions, and confirmed killings of Kasakela's Kahama adversaries. Yet Gombe also is the type case for human impact, as Power showed.

At the start of observation, two localized groups often joined to feed, mate, groom, and sometimes travel together. Drawn by banana feeding over the 1960s they merged, still distinct in networks, but all enjoying access to shared rangelands. As more forest turned to farms around the Park, additional chimpanzees appeared inside it and at the feeding station. Banana provisioning led to chaotic violence among chimpanzees and with baboons. System E stopped most of that but drastically reduced caloric intake. At that point red colobus hunting surged and infants were cannibalized, mostly inside Kasakela by females.

With the banana bounty curtailed, Kasakela and Kahama drifted apart as Kahama returned to its southern ranges. When Kasakela went there looking for food, Kahama chased them out. That is the historical moment of the "classic" territorial model of patrols, incursions, and kills. Occasionally enticed back to the station with preferential feeding, Kahama on arrival scattered the locals. Then it lost one of its most imposing males and stayed away, and Kasakela timorously entered the south. Instigated by ex-alpha Humphrey, in need of violent credibility, the Four Year War began. A few Kahama adults were killed, others might have been, or were driven away. Unrecognized outside females were attacked and killed in possibly in greater numbers than males—range defense in this time of anthropogenic resource scarcity.

---

[2] The method used here is similar to that used in *Yanomami Warfare* (Ferguson 1995). That was discussed in *Philosophy of Science* by Steel (1998) and Jones (1998). The debate was not whether it constituted science, but about which model of science is better supported by my method.

With Kahama gone Kalande moved north in Kasakela range, seeming to confirm the normality of "war." Kasakela was apprehensive and patrolled frequently, but killings are hypothetical, based more on expectations than evidence. Kalande earlier had been given bananas, and their northward encroachments headed toward the feeding station, until one day they walked right in. They looked and sniffed around, presumably got no bananas, and subsequently receded to their southern range. After that, territorial interactions fell off for almost a decade.

From 1984 into the middle 1990s, human presence increased around the Park, but within was shielded. Mitumba got its own provisioning in 1992. Gombe's three local groups had no induced reason to fight, and mostly didn't, with just a couple of deadly attacks on infants within or between groups. From the late 1990s, human disruption got much worse. Tourists flocked to Gombe. Farmers cleared around the Park, taking much of Mitumba and Kalande ranges. Killings by people, anthropogenic illness, and emergent diseases of unknown origin, crashed their populations, but differentially by group.

Then Kasakela entered emptied Kalande territory without resistance. Belligerent alphas Goblin and Frodo displayed their stuff with attacks on females, killing an infant. Frodo brutalized a Kalande juvenile male but left him alive. Kasakela jostled with Mitumba along the northern front, with a possible killing, but which could have been by leopard. Yet Mitumba went into Kasakela rangeland, and the frequent encounters usually did not rise above calling and moving apart. Human disturbance escalated through the 2000s and kills did too, most internal. So much diverse violence with so little context makes it impossible to explain individual killings. But in this chaos, human churning seems more likely than evolved, long-term reproductive strategies.

Political violence appears throughout Gombe's record, both display violence on helpless individuals by high-status males, and severe attacks on once overbearing ex- or even current alphas (Goblin, Sheldon, Vincent, Kris, Ferdinand, and Frodo). History played a role. Goblin, Frodo, and their generation learned violence during the highly disrupted 1970s.

Mahale

As first encountered, Mahale groups tolerated proximity. Provisioning started quickly, and so too relations quickly turned more exclusionary. The first feeding station was in K-group's core, but researchers lured M-group to there. K-group retreated north to a new feeding station, and M-group quickly followed. That was the moment of greatest intergroup tension.

But no pattern of patrol or incursion was seen in the mid-1970s, or anytime afterward, although there are instances of each. Hostile encounters centered on the feeding area, with at least one and maybe two outgroup infant killings, but no evidence supports killing of adults. Eventually K was gone, by one way or another. M-group roamed into their territory and feeding stations, and absorbed the K-group females with offspring which stuck around the provisioning. M population peaked. From 1981 to 1987 provisioning drew down and then ended. M population declined. Also ended was intergroup conflict, even though B-group was never far away.

Mahale of the 1980s joins 1970s Gombe and later Sonso as an in-group infanticide outlier, with Ntologi the main killer, including of his own offspring. Although M-group was humanly disturbed in many ways, with available information that cannot be directly connected to Ntologi's display killings. This display violence was part of his very successful domination strategy. Fallen, he exemplifies ex-alpha killing.

As at Gombe, human impact worsened post-provisioning, from the late 1990s with tourist swarms, disease, and landscape transformation. Baboons advancing along wide paths cleared for tourists ate much chimpanzee food, followed by intensified red colobus hunting. But unanchored to provisioning, M-group spread into adjacent unoccupied and less disrupted land, or disappeared. Thus human disturbance did not generate intergroup competition, and no intergroup violence followed.

Except in 1998—when Y-group showed up and stayed in M's range, probably pushed by habitat loss elsewhere. Y's arrival caused fear and agitation, but only one reported patrol, and one group clash which probably killed an outside infant. After that shock the two groups settled into accommodation, even though M greatly outnumbered the newcomers. With ample range and no provisioning to contest, no "war." But the execution of bullying alpha Pimu takes the ex- out of ex-alpha killing, and suggests that a tourist tsunami aggravated within-group tensions.

Kibale-Ngogo

Ngogo is the bulwark against human impact explanations, the lynchpin of adaptationism. What does history have to do with "undisturbed" Ngogo?

Researchers agree that the astonishing number of Ngogo adult males enabled their unprecedented sequence of external killings. The questions are: when and why did Ngogo get so big, what role did human impact play, and did recent growth lead to severe resource competition?

Disturbance was nearby. In the 1970s Kibale became an island amid farmers and roughly 7 of 10 Park groups lost rangeland. Inside the Park, lumbering up to 1978 degraded much northern habitat. Deforestation was worse in south, closer to Ngogo, displacing or killing unknown numbers of chimpanzees. Moving away from disrupted habitat meant moving toward more protected areas, such as Ngogo.

Ngogo researchers propose that Ngogo's size was made possible by food trees planted by farmers long ago. Yet multiple indicators establish that the sharp population growth came later, coincident with nearby habitat disruption. Ngogo numbers doubled or tripled from the 1970s up to the start of killing. Possible human impact factors are compression of territorially distinct networks, and reduction of vacant areas for exit. Probably most important however, was accelerated immigration of fecund females, which had limited movement options.

Even after human impacted population growth, nutritional necessities were more than met. But some *preferred* foods were scarce, notably *Uvariopsis congensis* and red colobus monkeys. *Uvariopsis* had declined per capita as population grew, and was hit hard by the 1999 drought. Huge parties of males overhunted red colobus to local extirpation from the 1990s on. Both foods were also sought by populous southern and western neighbors, which were more exposed to islandization and pushing inward along Ngogo's southwest, just as Ngogo bulged out in the opposite direction. Most of Ngogo's external killings occurred while seeking preferred foods in overlap zones.

In "undisturbed" Ngogo human impact led to very big groups and severe resource competition, which led to "war," which—combined with unhabituated neighbors' fear of accompanying researchers—led to group expansion. The famous conquest was not untouched by humans. As for the status angle, there are strong suggestions of display violence at the start of expansion, but no clarity after that.

Ngogo-Kanyawara

Kanyawara was hit hard by forest clearing, even into its home range. Still, plant food resources were adequate for its numbers and density, at about a third of Ngogo's. Red colobus were not overhunted. Human disturbance did not foster intense resource competition between neighbors. Correspondingly there was no clear pattern of border patrolling. One small group sometimes entered Kanyawara's core range, without much fuss. In unlogged forest in its south, Kanyawara gradually receded before a bigger group, but had enough space and resources to accommodate with avoidance.

Also correspondingly, Kanyawara had few killings, with just an odd internal infanticide, an uncontextualized presumed killing of a young male by outsiders, and the main event, the Sebitole stranger in 1998. That demonically iconic attack happened within a planned sequence of stranger playbacks intended to stimulate territorial fear and hostility. On status politics, the highest ranked chimpanzees at this moment were an aggressive pair that rose to the top during the unsettling playbacks, which may encourage display violence.

Budongo

Chimpanzees of the Budongo Forest Reserve did not experience islandization, it being a forest island for decades. Early research on unthreatened Busingiro group—long acclimated to local farmers—clearly documented temporary mergers of geographically distinct groups, and male cross-group association. Research resumed in 1990 at Sonso, with food abundance due to earlier regulated logging. Sonso was exposed to the Reserve edge on one side, and surrounded by chimpanzee groups on the others. If border patrolling and killing does not depend on immediate resource competition, we should see it at Sonso. But there was no pattern of patrols or stealthy penetrations. Territoriality was by avoidance, some calling, and "mutual respect." Sonso seemed the peaceful alternative to Gombe and Mahale. Then that changed.

Human impact got much worse from the late 1990s. Illegal pitsawing led to vast habitat destruction and displacement or disintegration of local groups within the Reserve. Sugarcane cultivation came right up to its borders, and armed guards and snares killed or mutilated many. In this disturbed atmosphere, political status competition became intense. One adult male and two infants were killed in ways implicating display violence.

External relations heated up. After years without territorial conflicts, in 1998 Waibira group pushed in. Then Waibira vanished, as pitsawyers took over their range. After they moved on, chimpanzees reappeared in the vacated space. Within a few years, they too encroached on Sonso, still without serious violence. Several parous females with offspring came into Sonso, attributed by observers to human destruction of another group (whichever males fathered their offspring). Sonso density skyrocketed, plausibly explaining infanticidal attacks by Sonso females. Consistent with a new food problem, Sonso chimpanzees which had hunted little, took to it with gusto starting in 1998.

When outside chimpanzees again encroached, Sonso didn't fight but avoided, even shifting into inhospitable swamp. In 2013 came the first intergroup killings, of a Sonso female and son. These occurred within widespread lethal violence from 2007 onward, mostly internal killing of infants. Human impact led to resource competition and very high disturbance, and killing followed. Display violence is implicated, which may have intensified due to increasing human disturbance.

Eleven Smaller Cases

Long-studied Gombe, Mahale, Kibale, and Budongo cover most *pan*icides. Until very recent years, the briefly considered sites in our cross-continental tour offered few killings. Starting with Western Chimpanzees, Kalinzu's Forest Reserve is heavily impacted. These chimpanzees patrolled borders and killed, exactly where and when lumbering pushed neighbors into their range.

Of Central Chimpanzees, largely undisturbed Goualougo reports some patrolling and one inferred intercommunity infant killing, but without detail or context. Releasing young captives at Conkoauti-Douli led to several killings, both among those released and by the resident chimpanzees. The latter could be called violent territorial defense, but under circumstances artificial in the extreme. Lope suggests territorial displacements ahead of a logging front, with killings speculated.

Loango's earliest and most widely noted killing of an adult male, may be instead a killing by leopard. Later killings, some possibly internal and others between group, and the stunning attacks on gorillas that killed an infant, may be related to Anthropocene climate changes that greatly reduced fruiting and greatly intensified within and between species competition.

For Eastern Chimpanzees, at arid Niokolo-Koba (Mt. Assirik), released captives were initially tolerated, but later attacked by locals—as they lived with people on the main water source in extremely dry times. At arid Fongoli people were close, but did not displace chimpanzees or foster intergroup competition. The only killing is a typical attack on an ex-alpha. Bossou had long coexistence with humans all around them, but again that did not pit one group against another, and there were no killings.

Tai

Islandization was underway from the start of observation in the early 1980s, decimating a group adjacent to those studied. It cannot be discerned whether two patterns which relate to human disruption elsewhere—frequent territorial friction and hunting—already reflected anthropogenic change, so I accept them as local givens, traditions. Intergroup relations were far more sophisticated than reported anywhere else, with strategic accommodation and no killing.

Human impact inside the Park intensified and many chimpanzees died. As four studied groups' populations crashed, prior nonkilling territorial advertisement and defense, which relied on numbers, became less workable. After that came ambushes and multi-male attacks on solo individuals. Taï's only killings were led by two highly aggressive, very young males, which fought their way to the top during a time of great dying and a playback experiment. Their *pan*icides exemplify display violence, with theatrical brutality.

Bonobos

Bonobo's bountiful ecology and human contact history did not provoke intense competition. The conditions that led to intergroup killing among some chimpanzees did not apply, and their socially evolved organization acted against intense male aggression and killings, perhaps temperamentally reinforced by nature/nurture interactions as in extended evolutionary theory.

Nevertheless, provisioned E Group at Wamba displayed tensions similar to 1970s Gombe, in kind though not degree. Aggression at the feeding station got bad, with both hostility and toleration in intergroup encounters. When the two local networks that mixed at the main station split without violence, each had more than enough food, despite nearby farmers. No reason to fight. Bonobos at Lomako and Wamba were grievously harmed by Congo's wars, but that did not leave post-war groups competing with each other.

Conclusions

Simplistic numbers processed through sophisticated statistics do not support the HIH, but theoretically informed comparative history does. Provisioned food led to intergroup killings at Gombe, and conflict at Mahale and Wamba. Habitat loss led to displacements, circumscription, and altered female residence at Gombe, Mahale, Ngogo, Sonso, Kalinzu, and Lope. All connect to conflict. Earlier human farming enabled larger populations at Gombe, Ngogo, and Sonso. Disease and human killing sharply changed intergroup balances, and/or rendered inoperable nonlethal territorial defense at Gombe and Taï. Violence followed captive release which threatened resources for residents at Conkouati-Douli and Mt. Assirik. Playbacks stoked fears of strangers, and possibly fostered the rise of particularly aggressive young alphas at Kanyawara and Taï, the latter and maybe both killers. Anthropogenic climate changes may have increased within and cross-species competition and violence in Loango, with frightening implications for chimpanzees in otherwise relatively undisturbed environments elsewhere.

Status-related violence can explain many killings. Display violence against helpless adults or infants within or outside the group occurred at Gombe, Mahale, Taï, likely Budongo, and possibly Ngogo. Payback against ex-alphas occurred at Gombe, Mahale, and Fongoli, plus the killing of the reigning bully at Mahale. Status-related violence is structured by social differences between chimpanzees and bonobos, but also reflects individual personality and political turmoil, which may or may not implicate human impact.

The adaptationist perspective leaves most of this out. I don't doubt that the adaptationist variables are significant. But if population density, number of males, and categories of age, sex, and within/between groups do connect to killing, it is only within specific historical and political circumstances. Without that context these variables do not channel deadly violence.

Pan intergroup relations span a great range. At one end is classic demonic behavior of border avoidance, patrol and incursion, and sometimes killings. The big middle ground is calling and avoidance or bluster without violence—an intelligent working out of standard territoriality. Smaller groups get out of the way of larger with or without protest, but larger groups may avoid areas where smaller ones are active. Neighbors accommodate each other in sometimes very sophisticated ways. At the other end of the spectrum, males and more often females associate across groups, individuals and fluid groupings form temporary affiliations, and larger numbers from different locales meet and even travel together.

Pan like *Homo* is socially plastic. Human impact that creates severe competition and/or dramatically destabilizes social relations and balances, can tip actions toward more conflict and violence, between and within groups. We have seen much of that, and will learn of more with greater description of violence and historical circumstances since the early 2000s. The future of human impact only looks worse.

If *pan*ologists became more historical, behavioral adaptation could be approached in new ways. All prior field data could be reexamined—contextualized—bringing in real-life circumstances of human intrusion. By doing so, researchers would imbue with theoretical purpose all the work they have done to protect chimpanzees. The wall between conservation and research would fall. And for conservation in the broadest sense, there may be additional value in recasting the current image of chimpanzees as innate killers. If human disruption made them kill, that is a wholly different story.

PART X
HUMAN WAR

30
The Demonic Perspective Meets Human Warfare

I wrote this book because of claimed applicability of the Gombe paradigm to human warfare. Chapter 30 turns the species corner to examine how the perspective fares when actually *applied* to people. Engaging with human practice leads to major definitional restrictions, analogies contradicted by evidence, and internal inconsistencies. There will be theoretical surprises, resulting in a version of demonic theory that is almost unrecognizable. After those particular applications, Chapter 30 steps back to consider one of the broadest claimed parallels: that chimpanzees and humans share a proclivity for hostile territorial exclusivity. The gulf separating chimpanzees and human territoriality and intergroup relations brings us into the realm of true culture. Culture comes into focus in Chapter 31, laying out two great gulfs that separate what chimpanzees do, including "war," from human existence. That is the foundation for concluding Chapter 32, which lays lay out and applies an alternative anthropological approach to war, my own.

Where Does Demonic/Adaptationist Theory Apply?

In the highly publicized debut of the demonic/dark side view the relevance for modern and future war was the take-away message. National wars are pushed by pride, by the dominance drive. Athens and Sparta were like two male chimpanzees vying for rank. Imperial expansion reflects male reproductive interests. Man's chimpanzee-like nature is why wars happen, and why future war imperils our species (Wrangham 1996:192; Wrangham and Peterson 1996:190–191, 235, 247–251).

Many times since, in articles, grant applications, and interviews, the message has been that understanding evolved predispositions of chimpanzees are necessary to understand the problem of war today. Usually that comes qualified, that the way people fight truly is unique in many ways. Nevertheless—the story goes—evolution gave us deadly proclivities that endanger us today, and can never go away. This chapter considers first where, and then how, chimpanzee intergroup behavior is said to directly apply to human warfare. It starts with a major constriction of applicability.

Not War by States

Crofoot and Wrangham resurrect an old hypothetical divide. The "military horizon" (Turney High 1971 [1949]:21ff.), supposedly distinguishes "primitive" from "civilized" war. The two are held to be essentially different. "Below the military horizon, warfare is conducted anarchically in the sense that individuals cannot be ordered to participate.... Above the military horizon, warfare is practiced by armies" (Crofoot and Wrangham 2010:188). Below the military horizon, combat by surprise raids is similar to chimpanzees. The element of surprise confers safety for attackers, similar to the impunity of superior numbers among chimpanzees (and see Wrangham and Peterson 1996:72–73). Above the horizon, there are deadly battles structured by internally coercive politics.

> We distinguish "simple" from "complex" war. Simple (or "primitive") warfare is a style found in small-scale hunter-gatherer and farmer societies whose communities are not integrated with each other by any political officials. It is dominated by raiding and feuding, is often motivated by revenge, and has few lethal battles, where battles are escalated conflicts between prepared opponents. Complex warfare, by contrast, also sometimes called "real warfare," "true warfare," or "warfare above the military horizon," occurs in larger societies containing political hierarchies. It includes lethal battles fought by soldiers under orders from leaders, and its goals are typically conquest and/or subjugation. It has no known analogues in chimpanzees or other nonhumans. (Wrangham and Glowacki 2012:8, references omitted)

Motivations of soldiers differ strikingly from a pack of screaming chimpanzees, and the enthusiasm of some simpler warfare. Soldiers follow orders and have no taste for killing. In "true warfare," leaders call the shots, and usually don't fight themselves (Wrangham 2006:58).

> The leaders' motivation for fighting includes complex political considerations, and tends to be aimed at destroying or subjugating the opposing army. The soldiers' motivation for fighting varies widely. Individuals may fight from a sense of duty; they may wish to fight out of patriotism or opportunities for loot; or they may fear the consequences of not fighting, such as being killed by the enemy, being killed by their leaders, or letting down their immediate comrades. (Crofoot and Wrangham 2010:189, references omitted)

"The biological propensities resulting from a putative evolutionary history of collective violence therefore have little relevance to explaining the killing behavior of soldiers in confronting armies" (Wrangham 2006:59). War between states is beyond the scope of adaptive theory. Then where does the demonic model apply?

Genocides, Civil Wars, etc.

Collective violence of the modern world is not excluded entirely, however. A page after redlining war by state armies, Wrangham relates "the psychology of chimpanzees" to the "unsolved evolutionary and cultural puzzle" of why "human predatory violence arises easily in rather consistent forms resembling those of chimpanzees, from street gangs and small-scale societies to civil wars and genocides." In Wrangham and Wilson (2004:251): "In general, the kinds of collective violence exhibited by youth gangs are part of a common human pattern evident in societies lacking effective central authority, manifested in ethnic riots, blood feuds, lethal raiding, and warfare." Or: "Similar behaviors emerge among chimpanzees and hunter-gatherers as among freedom fighters, street gangs, or the underworld.... The ultimate example, coalitionary proactive aggression enabled concentration camp employees to shoot or gas millions of Jews, Romanies, Poles, homosexuals, and others during World War II" (Wrangham 2019:259–260). So besides lethal raids and warfare in small-scale societies, chimpanzee behavior provides evolutionary understanding for street gangs, ethnic riots, civil wars, freedom fighters, blood feuds, the underworld, concentration camps, and genocide.

Chimpanzees acting "as a gang committed to the ethnic purity of their own set" (Wrangham and Peterson 1996:14) is a powerful rhetorical hook. *Demonic Males* (Wrangham and Peterson 1996:2–4) and *The Dark Side of Man* (Ghiglieri1998:24) invoke irregular fighters in Africa to draw readers into their arguments. Fukuyama (1998:33) took this view into the premier foreign policy journal, *Foreign Affairs*. Amid the global carnage of the late 1990s, on *ABC/Discovery News*, Wrangham and Ghiglieri spoke persuasively about biology and history combining in genocide (ABC/Discovery News 1999).

But these ideas were left hanging midair, assertions without elaboration or serious application to any cases. I will not try to fill in the absent theory, but it is naive to think genocides and civil wars lack the same disjunction between coercive leaders and soldiers that is found in other state-level mass killing. My own approach to "ethnic" violence is presented in Chapter 32.

City Gangs

Gangs however, are another story. They get a new, named hypothesis, the "Fighting for Status Hypothesis" (Wrangham and Wilson 2004:248–249)—which is pretty much the dominance drive hypothesis.

In that, the ultimate Darwinian cause of gang formation is the evolved male tendency to challenge other males for status. In situations of "anarchy" such as inner cities, males fight for status. One-on-one violent domination—the acts of a "bully"—compels young males to seek alliances. Interpersonal alliances lead to gangs, which then compete violently with other gangs, much as chimpanzees do. Thus violent urban gangs reveal the ape-like demonism within all men.

Yes, protection against neighborhood predators is one reason why some youths join neighborhood gangs—along with broken homes, violent role models, older youth needing legally younger to do crimes, social marginalization, segregation and competition of new immigrants, local cultural values, criminal opportunities, and the instrumental and demonstration violence that goes along with drug dealing and other enterprises, including adoption of the "crazy" persona. Nevertheless, in gang areas many more youths do not join gangs than do join (see Vigil 2003).

That is what is interesting for a social analysis. Simplistic Darwinianisms such as the fighting for status hypothesis only cloud why gangs exist in some times and places, what they are like, and who joins or does not, and obscure the enormous variability, situational determinants, historical specificity, and individual agency of gangs. Nor does it reconcile with Wrangham's recent argument (2019) that humans were evolutionarily domesticated through collective execution of bullies, so that males *do not* engage in violent status competition within a group. Now we turn to the strong suit for adaptive applications.

The Main Application: Band-and-Village Societies

"Simpler" peoples, what anthropologists sometimes lump as band-and-village societies, without local group-spanning authorities, are the main arena where evolutionary continuities are asserted. Supposedly these avoid the confounding factors of civilization. Simple hunter-gatherers, better called egalitarian mobile foragers, (because their ecological, social, and ideational sophistication is anything but simple), offer a plausible through line to the deeper species' ancestries of chimpanzees and humans. Augmented by small-scale horticulturalists who also lack political institutions or hierarchy, they are the cross-species Darwinian sweet spot (Wrangham 2006:60).

What Social Units?

But to make that comparison, what kind of human grouping is analogous to a chimpanzee unit-group? Obviously there is no imbalance of power/rival coalition hypothesis without two separate and antagonistic social groups. Regarding intergroup conflict, an analogy with a hunter-gatherer *band* just does not work.

> [T]he differences between great ape and simple human societies are indeed fundamental and profound.... [A] foraging band ... is strikingly egalitarian, with much less competition among males over females, a uniquely human pattern of food sharing, and a remarkably shifting, open and flexible membership. There is one difference of special interest in the present context: a chimpanzee community, unlike a social band, is a social isolate. (Rodseth and Wrangham 2004:397–401)

In stark contrast, human bands aggregate, socialize, exchange, intermarry, share food, and join in rituals. They are enmeshed in a wider network, a "tribe."

> [T]he local band is not the appropriate social unit to compare to the chimpanzee community, though it has often been treated as such in earlier analysis. With an average size of perhaps 25 members, a local band is somewhat smaller than a chimpanzee community, which averages more than 40 members. Yet the social network of a human forager is much larger than that of any ape.... A tribe in this sense is vast in comparison with any other primate society.... Foraging society, in this perspective, resembles a greatly expanded chimpanzee society with relatively stable parties (bands) that are physically isolated from each other for weeks or months at a time but remain loosely integrated at the regional level. (Rodseth and Wrangham 2004:397; and see Wrangham 2006:55–56)

Thus application of the theory to humans is scaled up from local groups to *tribes*, citing Jones portrayal for Tasmania.

> [A] tribe is an agglomeration of bands with contiguous estates, the members of which spoke a common language or dialect, shared the same cultural traits ... usually intermarried, had a similar pattern of seasonal movement, and habitually met together for economic and other reasons. The pattern of peaceful relations between bands, such as marriage and trade, tended to be within such a tribal agglomeration and that of hostile ones or war outside it. (Jones 1984:40)

But contrary to some uniformed popular opinion—"Tribalism Is a Fundamental Human Trait" (Wilson 2012:57)—we are not born with a tribal instinct.

People Are *Not* Innately Tribal

The concept of tribe provides no load-bearing bridge to chimpanzee unit-groups. It is a vague notion, subject to incessant disagreement within anthropology (Ferguson 1997). Jones's picture is derived from observations during the Tasmanian genocide (below), framed in terms of an old theory of bounded, hostile tribes as a stage in social evolution (Service 1971:104). Fried (1975) refuted that scheme, demonstrating that most ethnographically known tribes were "secondary" formations, shaped by intruding states.[1] Global historical ethnography reaffirms that expanding states generated "tribalization" in areas around but not incorporated within them, called "tribal zones" (Ferguson and Whitehead 1992a, below).

Yes, there were social formations we can call tribes, long before states. Prehistory provides many examples of contiguous populations with cross-cutting social ties and similarity in material culture, apart and different from more distant collectivities. They appear like "smears across the archaeological landscape, with few discernible internal or external boundaries" (Parkinson 2002:8).

Their identity is of internal similarity and connections, not in the key point of demonic analogy, external bounding, and antagonism. Consistent with Fried, the "idea that tribes exist only as a discrete entities, with well-defined social and geographic boundaries ... can be attributed to the skewed temporal perspective offered through the information contained in the ethnographic record" (Parkinson 2002:7)—i.e., following state intrusion. "[T]he very malleability of social boundaries ... is what many archaeologists have found to be *most* characteristics of the tribal type" (Fowles 2002:19).

---

[1] Fried's position was based on ethnographic research around the world. A giant of ethnography, Alfred Kroeber (1955:313), put it succinctly for the Americas.

> The total drift is this. The more we review aboriginal America, the less certain does any consistently recurring phenomenon become that matches with our usual conventional concept of tribe: and the more largely does this concept appear to be a White man's creation of convenience for talking about Indians, negotiating with them, administering them—and finally impressed upon their own thinking by our sheer weight.

Those "smears" are ancient, but even those do not extend backward forever in the archaeological record. "An archaeological perspective of tribal social trajectories [suggests] that tribes were a dominant social form on the planet for several thousand years *following the end of the Pleistocene*" (Parkinson 2002:9, my emphasis). Going back into the Pleistocene, even that kind of tribal differentiation disappears. Upper Paleolithic remains *do not* indicate cultural differentiation across space. Virtually identical lithic traditions are found throughout North America, South America, and from Europe to Siberia. "Everyone, across continental spaces and over long stretches of time, was making the same kinds of tools.... All of the issues of group boundaries, 'traditional enemies,' different ethnicities, and territoriality are simply incompatible with a model of open continent-wide social networks" (Haas and Piscitelli 2013:183).

Application of the imbalance of power hypothesis to "simple societies" does not work for local human bands, and the concept of tribe is no help. Notwithstanding common parlance of today, that "people are tribal," no hint of tribal differentiation is found in the oldest material remains, the locally differentiated cultural collectivities of the later Holocene usually do not suggest bounding or hostilities, and the *sometimes* fraught tribal boundaries of post-contact history are usually the result of state impingement.[2] If there is a valid analogy with chimpanzees, it is that last point.

Flux

Even in recent ethnography however, there may or may not be a tribal level of integration, of amity within and enmity without. Instead band and village peoples have multiple bases and levels of identification, with politically shifting cooperation and conflict pertaining thereto.

Rodseth and Wrangham recognize this flexibility.

> When relations between neighboring groups are openly hostile, any encounter with outsiders may be dangerous. In most ethnographic contexts, however, overlapping social networks and incremental ethnic and linguistic differences make for a broad and shifting gray area between friend and foe. This human pattern contrasts sharply with the pattern of chimpanzees. (Rodseth and Wrangham 2004:400)

Cross-culturally, relations between groups can be amicable, hostile, or ambivalent at any level of social organization. I can only applaud:

---

[2] Under some circumstances, bounded, materially differentiated, warring tribes *did* emerge before any proximate state. In the Kayenta Valley of Arizona from AD 500 to 1250, archaeological remains indicate passage from areal cultural homogeneity, to localized differentiation, to physical distancing, defensive bounding, and finally war (Haas 1990). Haas attributes this to increasing population density combined with worsening extreme droughts. Soon after war began, the whole the area was abandoned. Major climatic reversals may have produced similar results elsewhere as the Medieval Warm developed and flipped into the Little Ice Age, contributing to much warfare late in prehistory, the centuries before European contact. This will be considered in future work.

[T]he openness and flexibility of local bands is precisely what allows members of such bands to unite at higher levels of organization, and thus to wage war, if necessary, over stored food or other concentrated resources. *When this happens*, a boundary sharpens between one band or tribe and another, and their conflict may follow a pattern of raiding not unlike that between chimpanzee communities. As long as this does not happen, however, the level of intergroup violence in simple societies may appear to be much lower than in the case of chimpanzees. (Rodseth and Wrangham 2004:397–398, emphasis added)

How demonic is that? (1) With people there may be no active hostility between groups at any level of group. (2) If war does develop, it is due to resource concentration and competition, which may occur at varying levels of social inclusion. (3) Only when such conflicts develop do boundaries sharpen. Few cultural anthropologists would take exception with those points. It is close to my own position. Rodseth and Wrangham even cite *War in the Tribal Zone*: "an expanding state can introduce violence into an otherwise peaceful population of foragers or horticulturalists (Ferguson and Whitehead 1992[a])." Yay!

This is far from that old time demonism. The demonic saving grace is that when intergroup war breaks out, they raid like chimpanzees do—on which more to come.

How Could That Evolve?

From a selectionist perspective, how could that flexibility evolve? If the Last Common Ancestor practiced deadly male intergroup hostility, what selection scenario could lead to its being replaced by the flexible orientation of humans? Starting off with that lethal predisposition, any male trying to associate with foreign males would be dead meat. How could an evolutionarily stable strategy of killing vulnerable outsiders evolve into openness? How could we get here from there?

Quite easily if one steps away from Gombe-vision, and admits all the evidence of chimpanzee group openness and mixing summarized in Chapter 28. Include that evidence, include bonobos as extending a behavioral spectrum, and recognize the conflict-generating aspect of exogenous impact, then *Pan* mixing and mating foreshadows recent human hunter-gatherer relations, as once argued by Reynolds (1966:444; 1967:302) and Power (1991).

How Does the Demonic/Adaptationist Theory Apply?

Demonism Redux

The ethnographic realism of Rodseth and Wrangham, however, is absent in a return to demonic basics with Wrangham and Glowacki (2012:7). There hunter-gatherers are expected to fit "three expectations of the chimpanzee model: exhibiting continual hostility to other groups, attacking outgroup members only when safe, and benefitting from attacks." They claim ethnographic support from six locales: Australia, Tasmania, the Andaman Islands, Tierra del Fuego, Great Lakes/Central Canada, and Northwest Alaska (and see Wrangham 2019:235–239).

A previous version of this book dove deep into the ethnohistory of those six areas, exceeding 40,000 words. So that's been hived off, destined for another broad study on hunter-gatherer fighting, history, and the much ballyhooed Hobbes vs. Rousseau debate. *This book will have a sequel!* Here only a few broad conclusions are noted.

Wrangham and Glowacki find four evidentiary parallels between hunter-gatherers and chimpanzee "war": #1 "shoot on sight, or trespass as cause of war"; #2 "ambushes and/or raids"; #3 "overt fear of strangers"; and #4 "underused border zone or territory." They find #1 and #2 reported for every case, #3 for five, and #4 for three. Three generalizations can be treated summarily.

Simply put, numbers 1, 3, and 4, express a *condition* of war. *When* a state of deadly animosity exists, when a killing divide between "us" and "them" arises, then, if strangers come into your lands without good reason, be at arms. They may be raiders or spies, and should be feared as enemies unless otherwise known. Don't get close to a hostile border lest you be killed. Elementary. There is no need to posit a phylogenetic inheritance for practical common sense within a situation of war. Parallel #2, raiding, comes up soon, within discussion of their broad "expectations of the chimpanzee model."

"Continual Hostility"

A fundamental demonic proposition is that males of local groups typically are in hostile opposition to other groups. Rodseth and Wrangham's position was a deviation, Wrangham and Glowacki come back to the demonic main stream. They claim this continual hostility is demonstrated in all six cases—each of which had a previously established reputation for war. Hardly a random sample. Even for these six, however, warfare is incomprehensible without bringing in colonial intrusion. That is my cross-species analogy.

In Tasmania, war was not evident in early contact reports. It developed over years of settler expansion and genocide, as hunted and culturally devastated refugees scrambled for survival. In the Andaman Islands, what is portrayed as endless war between tribes was resistance by scattered bands to invasion and counterinsurgency by the British and their local minions. Other tribes lived in peace. For Tierra del Fuego's two hunter-gatherer peoples, the group first contacted and observed while culturally intact (Yahgan, who disgusted Darwin sailing on the *Beagle*), did not wage war. Their upland neighbors, the fabled "warlike" Ona were observed decades later—when like Tasmanians they were driven, hunted refugees, fighting for food.

In the Great Lakes/Central Canada area, hunter-gatherers were sometimes at war and alternately at peace, with permutations following standard dynamics of fur trade frontier conflicts (e.g., Abler 1992). Northwestern Alaska has by far the greatest archaeological record. That shows limited war first arising from AD 400 to 700, connected to developing social complexity. But the intense warfare noted by Wrangham and Glowacki came with the intense conflicts of Russia's Siberia fur trade in the late 18th century.

Australia is the most complex and debated of their six cases, with "dove" (Fry 2006) and "hawk" (Gat 2015) positions. Aboriginal peoples had elaborated cultural means of managing conflict below the level of war; yet also collective killing around the fringes of 19th-century settler expansion. My preliminary research indicates seemingly "precontact" wars are connected to previously unappreciated early disruption, including the often-cited warfare of Murngin and Walbiri.[3] Australian archaeology suggests individual violence and managed group conflicts in prehistory, but not war (cf. Darmangeat 2019).

While debate over Australia continues, it is certainly *not* true that aboriginal tribes lived in "continual hostility." As reported in the classic early ethnographies of central and northern Australian tribes:

> To judge from ordinary accounts in popular works, one would imagine that the various tribes were in a state of constant hostility. Nothing could be further from the truth. In almost every camp of any size you will find members of strange tribes paying visits and often taking part in ceremonies. (Spencer and Gillen 1969a [1904]:31)

> [W]here two tribes come into contact with one another on the border land of their respective territories, there the same amicable feelings are maintained between the members of the two. There is no such thing as one tribe being in a constant state of enmity with another. (Spencer and Gillen 1969b [1899]:32)

Period.

The notion of warlike hunter gatherers is old and popular, as relayed again in Pinker (2011:48–49). Yet beyond Wrangham and Glowacki's chosen six cases, ethnographic and archaeological surveys demonstrate the opposite. True, some settled complex hunter-gatherers make intensive and sophisticated war, with or without colonial disruption (e.g., Balee 1984; Ferguson 1984b). But egalitarian mobile forager bands (simple hunter-gatherers)—as characterized most of humanity's time on earth—are different. They certainly have conflict, and often personal violence and killing, but with some exceptions one group does not set out to kill members of another group (Ferguson 2006; 2008a; 2013a; 2013b; Fry and Soderberg 2013; Haas 2000; Haas and Piscitelli 2013; [Ray] Kelly 2013a; 2013b; Lee 2018; Wilson and Glowacki 2017:478). If mobile foragers make war, typically circumstances of recent historical disruption are implicated (Peterson 1974:57; 1976:355–356; Steward 1955:294).

---

[3] These are the two best-known cases of aboriginal warfare, supposedly beyond colonial influence. In the first decades of the 20th century, Murngin (now Yolngu) of Arnhem Land had large deadly fights with sophisticated tactics (Warner 1958:16–20, 144–165). The desert Walbiri had one bloody clash over a water hole (Meggitt 1965:37–42). Both illustrate the need for careful historical investigation.

Far from undisturbed, Yolngu for at least a century had worked for Macassans from Sulawesi, gathering beche-de-mer for the China trade. That contact led to local "kings," with "great drunken orgies, and much blood was shed" (Warner 1958:449). After the Macassans, from 1903 to 1908 all of the Yolngu area was incorporated in a huge Anglo-Australian ranching enterprise, with ruthless repression and displacement of local people in the way. Then came missions (Roberts 2005:153)—which routinely bring other conflict. Native peoples of the north look back at this as the "killing times" (O'Connor et al. 2013:550–551).

The Walbiri water hole was just beyond demarcated ranch lands (Meggitt 1965:18–20). Lines on maps didn't stop squatters from raiding locals for forced ranch hands (Sharp 1952:17–18); and clearing them away (or just shooting them) to acquire their water holes (Reynolds 1978:56–57; Roberts 2005:160).

In simple human societies, exclusivity and boundedness of social groups are largely precluded by shifting resource availability, fluid population movement, lack of fixed property and need for intergroup alliance and support. Territorial rights, while often formally recognized, are rarely enforced when permission to hunt or forage is requested.... With emphasis on egalitarian access to resources, cooperation, and diffuse affiliative networks, contrary emphasis on intergroup rivalry and collective violence is minimal.... There is some historical evidence of reciprocating collective conflict, sometimes ethnically based, among simple foragers. Feuding or warfare does not, however, appear pronounced except where, as among the Ache, Agta, and Waorani, large-scale intrusion by agricultural societies resulted in conflict over land and internal societal reorganization. (Knauft 1991:402–403)

This broad connection of war by simple hunter-gatherers and disruption by expanding states is discussed in Chapter 31, and the next book. For current purposes, it is enough to reject the claim of continual hostility between hunter-gatherer groups.

"Attacking Outgroup Members Only When Safe"

A second evolutionary expectation in Wrangham and Glowacki (2012), and foundational in the imbalance of power hypothesis, is that attacks happen only when they pose no or little risk of death or injury for attackers. That assurance comes from overwhelming numbers. No chimpanzee has died as part of a coalitional attack. Humans however, often go to war and die. How to reconcile this with ethological expectations? Perhaps by distinguishing two types of combat: open battles from stealthy raids and ambushes.

Raids

Wrangham and Glowacki characterize open battles as risky, therefore unchimpanzee-like, and for people associated with coercive authority. "Lethal battles among humans are an evolutionary novelty among mammals. They appear to have arisen with state-level armies. A strict hierarchy appears to be an important precondition for their occurrence. Lethal battles present a challenging problem for evolutionary analysis" (Wrangham 2006:58). Battles in nonstate societies involve issues that need not detain us, because the posited chimpanzee analogy is in raiding.

All six of their warring hunter-gatherers are checked off for raids and ambushes. Agreed. There is no doubt that the "most common form of combat in primitive warfare but little used in formal civilized warfare has been small raids or ambushes" (Keeley1996:65). But is raiding safe for attackers? Wrangham argues yes. "[P]articipation in warfare was voluntary, but since attackers were rarely killed it was not considered especially dangerous.... [In both species] the killing is overwhelmingly predatory, meaning that it is safe for the killers." Among the Yanomami, only 5% of raiders were wounded during a raid, and most recovered. "[T]he most likely outcome of a raid is total success, because raids are undertaken only when the attackers have overwhelming force" (Wrangham 2019:256). In one study of Waorani, another Amazonian group with a reputation for raiding, there were "no reports of a member of an attacking party being killed" (Wrangham 2006:56–57).

Whoa! Yanomami raiders are acutely aware of the dangers they face, and many back out at the last minute. In one well-described raid that killed a single adversary, a raider was shot "with a bamboo-tipped arrow completely through his chest just above his heart" (Chagnon 1968:128–133). Another raiding party was caught en route, with six men killed (Ferguson 1995:212). Known killers are specially targeted in revenge, so accomplished raiders die early (Ferguson 2015:401–402). For the Waorani, another study includes raiders being killed (Wasserstrom 2016:16), and such deaths are common in historical documents (Wasserstrom, personal communication, 8/22/16).

Accounts of raids ending badly could be multiplied ad nauseam, so just one more example will do. In 1857 in the last major clash between unsubjugated Native American nations, a raiding force of about a hundred Quechans and Mohave were caught en route to attacking Pima and Maricopa, and completely wiped out (Kroeber and Fontana 1986).

Men going off to raid know they may die, completely unlike the bulldozer coalitional attacks of chimpanzees, or expectations from the ethology of territoriality. A hoped-for surprise victory may end in disaster. This chimpanzee analogy too fails when applied to humans.

"Benefiting from Attacks"

Given the inescapable risks of raiding, benefits should be great indeed.[4] What rewards do Wrangham and Glowacki see? Browsing in ethnography, they find a few reports of territory being acquired, but conclude that it wasn't widespread (Glowacki and Wrangham 2013:446; Wrangham and Glowaki 2012:17–18). If human raiders expose themself to deadly risk for limited if any practical gains, how is that like chimpanzees? Apparently it isn't.

The Cultural Rewards War-Risk Hypothesis

Even with the advantages of surprise, Glowacki and Wrangham (2013:444–445) recognize the inescapable fact that raiders get killed. "The voluntary participation of warriors in conflict creates a puzzle: from an evolutionary perspective, individuals should avoid conflict when doing so presents a mortality risk." And no evolutionary existing hypothesis seems able to explain it.[5] This is looking bad for an adaptive strategy perspective. But they have a surprising answer

---

[4] To be clear up front, my theoretical position is that wars happen when those who start them anticipate practical benefits, though usually not something as simple as gaining land. That identifies me as a materialist, as elaborated in Chapter 31 (and see Ferguson 1984:37–42, "The Question of Motivation"). At the moment, the question is not my theory but theirs.

[5] They find against two evolutionary hypotheses: that through group selection, humans have evolved a special adaptation for self-sacrifice; or that negative sanctions within a group compel men to go off to war (2013:445, 454–455).

[T]he difference is cultural rather than biological. We call this inference the "cultural war risk" hypothesis. The cultural war-risk hypothesis conforms to well-established conclusions that cultural norms can promote individual military prowess, and also that cultural group selection can explain how such norms arise and are maintained. It complements those ideas by proposing that *in societies where cultural institutions promoting military prowess are relatively few or weak, human warfare is expected to closely follow the chimpanzee model.* (Wrangham and Glowacki 2012:7, references omitted, emphasis added)

Huh?

Drawing from ethnographies of 21 hunter-gatherers and horticulturalists, they conclude: "a greater number of [cultural] benefits from warfare is associated with a higher rate of death from conflict" (2013:444). More common than practical rewards such as women, slaves, or plunder are symbolic rewards such as a special distinction in dress, or a new name, or spiritual power, or trophies, or prestige (2013:450). Thus *culture* impels men to kill neighbors.

In cultural anthropology, the importance of cultural incentives for fighting is axiomatic.[6] But when the cultural rewards war-risk hypothesis combines with a chimpanzee-based, demonic perspective, the implications are startling. "Thus we expect that when warriors receive rare or no benefits from their participation, warfare will be rare, primarily opportunistic, and less risky, *such as occurs in intergroup violence among chimpanzees*" (Glowacki and Wrangham 2013:449, emphasis added).

You might want to read that passage again. Not just war by states, but *most* tribal warfare is thus ruled *unlike* chimpanzee war. Is there any such case?

How Is That Adaptive?

Behaviors that do not obviously augment inclusive fitness are "puzzles" to be solved. How does the cultural rewards war-risk hypothesis solve the Darwinian puzzle? What is the reproductive payoff, the bottom line? Glowacki and Wrangham (2013:454–455) reach out to another biologistic theory of war: by augmenting social status, warriors enhance their own reproductive success.

The touchstone is Chagnon's (1988) famous claim that Yanomami killers (*unokais*) had three times as many children as nonkillers, a claim so often repeated in neo-Darwinian explanations of war that it seems like established fact (e.g., Diamond

---

[6] Goldschmidt (1988) summarizes, very appropriately for our concerns.

> To say that war is a cultural phenomenon may seem to my fellow anthropologists the belaboring of the obvious. Yet there are those who argue that mankind, particularly *man*kind, fights wars because he is naturally aggressive. What these data clearly show is that this aggressive potentiality—which manifestly is present—must be carefully nurtured and shaped.... I call this the concern with the "symbolic self." The symbolic self is defined—as are all symbols—by the community. It is in the service of this symbolic self that men engage in the actions that the society considers essential or for which it gives rewards in material satisfaction and public influence. It is in the service of this symbolic self in militaristic societies that men seek the bloody trophies of war. That is why men fight. (1988:58–59)

2012:163; Wade 2006:150). No, that claim has been thoroughly refuted, and is without significant defense (Ferguson 2015:399–402; Miklikowska and Fry 2102). *Unokais* probably have *lower* lifetime reproductive success than non-*unokais*. Nevertheless, elevated reproductive success for warriors is the only adaptive game in town.

Glowacki and Wrangham (2015) go that route, employing the former's field data about Nyangatom pastoralists in East Africa. In his reconstruction, historical Nyangatom participated in two kinds of raids: small incursions to make off with some cattle, which involve few casualties; and large battle raids with many casualties. Cattle are coin for marriage bride payments. But the captured beasts are not kept by the younger men who grab them. They are given over to senior relatives. (This is standard practice in the region—see Fadiman 1982.)

What evidence suggests a risk payoff in reproductive success? For 29 elders, their *current* reputation of being prolific raiders when young is associated with more wives and children, as elders.

As with *unokais*, this does not show that raiding contributes to lifetime reproductive success because it excludes men who died during raids. Measuring "only the reproductive success of elderly survivors, their sample does not include those prolific raiders who died in battle. This is likely a large group" (Zefferman et al. 2015). I would add that being a big shot at present may well enhance reputation for past valor.

How does this connect with the cultural rewards war-risk hypothesis? Although "status competition" may motivate men, among Nyangatom there are "few means for status to be converted into additional marriage opportunities." Glowacki and Wrangham (2013:352) conjecture that raiding while young might contribute to later reproductive success, because elders who get the cattle eventually die, and sons inherit. Or, perhaps elders with more cattle take additional brides, who then birth daughters, and bride payments for them could contribute to the family cattle estate. Maybe this expanded patrimony eventually helps young raiders get more wives (2013:353). What if those additional wives instead bore more sons, thus putting more demand on the family herd? Raiding Junior would be less able to make bride price.

Back to the Public

When *pan*ological adaptationist hypotheses are applied to human war they fail to inform, whittled down to increasingly narrow relevance, and even there with serious theoretical and empirical problems. The booming implications of *Demonic Males* come down to this. But no worries. For public presentation, the thunder is still there.

In his new *The Goodness Paradox*, Wrangham (2019:259) breezes past all these restrictions, revisions, and difficulties regarding war by band and village peoples.

> Revenge motivations and moral pressures are only two of many unique features of our species that influence the practice of simple warfare. Others include advanced weaponry, language, social norms, docile psychology, training of warriors, and the ability to devise a shared plan. But the mere occurrence of simple warfare depends on none of those explanations, given that the human pattern is strongly similar to intergroup aggression in some other species. In humans practicing simple warfare,

as is in chimpanzees and wolves, proactive aggression is the norm; the goal is to be safe; and killing tends to lead to long-term benefits for the killer. The traits that decorate human warfare beyond these elements are rococo additions, not necessary features. The essential facts of simple warfare of humans are barely more puzzling than the intergroup aggression of other animals that kill their neighbors when they get a chance to do so.

If that message is not clear enough, Glowacki (2016) took their research into a *Washington Post* Op-Ed, headlined: "How the Tribal Warfare of Our Ancestors Explains the Islamic State."
Familiar positions are strung together.

> In a pattern that disturbingly resembles human warfare, chimpanzees across East Africa regularly kill members of neighboring groups.... Sometimes these attacks cause the extermination of entire communities, a phenomenon akin to genocide in human society. When this happens, the successful group takes over the territory of the defeated group, gaining valuable resources.

Then it jumps to hunter-gatherers.

> [M]y Harvard colleague Richard Wrangham and I found that for most of human history, societies generally carried on some form of war with neighboring groups.... Like the terrorist attacks of today, these conflicts generally targeted members of perceived enemy groups, commonly including women and children. The bodies of victims were frequently mutilated with a creativity that the Islamic State would find astonishing. Entire populations and ethnic groups were wiped out. This type of violence stretches deep into our prehistory.

Then comes the closer, the cultural rewards war-risk hypothesis.

> What explains how people can commit such violent acts? One answer lies in our psychology. Humans are hard-wired to adopt their communities' norms.... When norms provide status, material rewards or membership in a privileged group, they become even more potent. Cultures are able to hijack this psychology for violent ends by providing status, promises of an afterlife and a sense of meaning. People belonging to communities' that advocate violence will adopt norms of violence.

Chimpanzees and tribals are bloodthirsty killers, and so are we, especially if culture hijacks our hard-wiring. That is how the demonic, evolutionary perspective informs our understanding of war and ISIS.

The Territorial Foundation of All Applications

This final discussion of cross-species applicability goes to the foundation of *all* comparisons: territoriality. Notwithstanding elemental differences (such as *families*) demonic male humans and chimpanzees are held fundamentally similar in territorial exclusivity and active defense (see Part 1).

> In both chimpanzees and human foragers, competition over territory plays a central role in intergroup relations. As in many other species, chimpanzees and humans depend for their existence on limited resources associated with specific locations: food, water, and shelter. By defending territories, territory owners prevent outsiders from depleting the resources they need to survive. (Wilson and Glowacki 2017:485–486)

For *Pan*, this book demonstrates great variation in territorial usage related to neighbors, including sharing. When used areas are actively advertised or defended, that may come with mutual accommodation. The Gombe pattern of lethally exclusive territoriality, the standard image in theoretical broadsides and for public consumption, is one extreme of the *Pan* spectrum. But it seemed to fit well with one prominent vision of hunter-gatherers.

The Roots of Forager "Exclusivity"

The demonic perspective built on an old and crumbled anthropological foundation. Kelly (2013b) describes how Frank Speck, working with Labrador Algonquians, theorized a cellular model of defended territories of patrilineally related kin. That model was then extrapolated to hunter-gatherers around the world. Even though Leacock and Bishop showed that Speck mistook fur-trade developments as precontact, the exclusive patrilocal band reigned as the standard model for foragers (Layton 1986:24). This vision of male blood kin aggressively defending group territory reached the public mind via Robert Ardrey in *African Genesis* (1961) and *The Territorial Imperative* (1968). It supported bellicose visions of chimpanzees and human ancestors (Ferguson 2011a:263). "[S]ince humans were innately territorial, the argument went, war and national aggression were unavoidable" (Kelly 2013a:152).

Deeper and wider research overturned this image of mobile hunter-gatherers. Patrilocal (virilocal) bands did exist, sometimes, but more common were ad hoc amalgamations of people connected through both females and males, by descent and by marriage (Fry 2006:166–171; Layton 1986:25–26). That social flexibility is how people coped so well with nature's challenges. "All over the world, societies of small community size were shown to be neither essentially virilocal nor patrilineal in any sense. 'Flux,' 'flexibility,' and 'fluidity' became the new buzz words to describe their social organization" (Barnard 1983:196). Even where male-defined group membership existed as an ideological model, actual behavior was much more labile (Blundell 1980:115).

Sometimes the idea of flux was taken too far, an overcorrection to closed, patrilocal bands. "[I]t seemed that hunter-gatherers went where they pleased, when they pleased, and were welcomed by all" (Kelly 2013a:152). Decades of research supported neither extreme, but something more complex, subtle, cultural, and *human*, going far beyond the flexible territoriality of *Panins*.

What Means Territoriality?

Mobile hunter-gatherers associate with local areas that we label territories. The meaning of territory was thoroughly debated decades ago. Dyson-Hudson and Smith's model (1978:23) associated higher resource density and predictability with greater active defense. That point could be compared to chimpanzees. But they also foreground complexity.

> It is not enough to know if a particular group exhibits territorial behavior. Instead, it is necessary to discuss particular resources and determine if these resources are defended, how they are defended, the circumstances under which access to these resources is restricted, and which people or groups of people are allowed or denied access to resources. (1978:37)[7]

Others found this emphasis of defense an unrealistically narrow approach. Cashdan (1983:49) proposed that territoriality instead involved "reciprocal altruism through controlled access to the social group." Rather than exclusion and hostility, forager territoriality is about managing access, through shared cultural rules (and see Peterson 1974:60). Assured granting of use requests for access to resources is *normal* among simple hunter-gatherers, called "demand sharing" (Peterson 1993)—and at least some complex hunter-gatherers as well (Ferguson 1983:139). "Boundaries often are controlled socially through use-requests and permission-granting" (Fry and Soderberg 2013:271). Both the ask and permission may be implicit, understood without saying (Williams 1983:96).

Commonly territoriality is not about exclusion, but regulated openness, as across Australian deserts.

> [T]he concept of ownership does not denote a real division of resources, but serves merely to effect an ideological separation between "givers" and "receivers" in the case of food-sharing, and "hosts" and "visitors" in the case of territorial admission. This separation is a necessary condition for the expression of generosity, and for the satisfaction and prestige that accrues to those who—from time to time—are in a position to play host to their neighbors. (Ingold 1987:134)

---

[7] Much earlier, Steward (1955:293-294, order altered) put flesh on this bone, about Native North Americans:

> The question is not merely whether an identifiable group or society occupied and maintained exclusive use of a delimitable territory.... The variety of ways in which Indian societies claimed exclusive use of natural resources was enormous. Commonly, eagle nests were claimed by individuals regardless of attitudes toward other resources. Fishing streams might be accessible to anyone, although weirs were used exclusively by their builders. Family or group rights to seed territories did not necessarily imply territorial hunting rights. In much of the Northeast and Canada, family trapping territories involved only fur-bearing animals and co-existed with band hunting territories for large game. Farm land might be family—or lineage—owned while other resources were regarded in different ways.... Occasional skirmishes against alien groups can by no means be taken as evidence that a society has mobilized in defense of territory per se or even of resources on it.

Although hunter-gatherer territoriality is exquisitely attuned to ecological exigencies, it cannot be reduced to that. Continuities in ancestral adaptations frame different possibilities, with choices. That shows by comparing convergent yet very different adaptations of southern African and Australian peoples to extreme aridity, and very localized adaptive variations of a shared tradition in the central arctic:

> the !Kung and Ptijantjatjara participate in cultural communities that have different historical trajectories and have adjusted to the exigencies of their environments by adapting their specific cultural heritages to similar conditions [just as] variations in central Eskimo social structure represent alternative cultural solutions to similar problems in obtaining and distributing food. (Layton 1986:28)

Long-term cultural trajectories and immediate coping entwine resource ownership and sharing with exchange, movement, and layers of identities. Complex understandings about the highly esteemed value of generosity are acted out as individuals play an unending cultural game, invoking sacred truths and the authority of ancestors while cannily giving in order to receive (Kelly 2013b:138, 151).

> [W]e see that no society has a truly laissez-faire attitude toward spatial boundaries. Instead, all have ways, sometimes very subtle ways, of "assigning" individuals to specific tracts of land and of allowing them to gain access to others.... Many foragers do not live their lives on delineated tracts of land that they consider to be theirs and theirs alone, but individuals do have specific use rights or statuses as members of a group that connect them with a particular area.... Understanding land tenure, therefore, requires considering the ways that people related themselves to one another and thus to land. (Kelly 2013b:154)

> The basis for much of the behavior labeled "territoriality," then, is the product of individuals deciding whether and how to share the right of resource use with others. These decisions are embedded in a complex intellectual process whereby people come to share an identity. Through kinship, trade, mythology, and other cultural mechanisms, people construct ways to relate themselves to each other and thus to land. These social relations form the basis for the right to be asked—and the right to ask—to use resources. (Kelly 2013b:156)

All this is alien to the demonic idea of chimpanzee territorial defense. The combination of male philopatry, border avoidance, stealth penetrations, reflex antagonism, and coalitional killings is utterly *unlike* territoriality among most simple hunter-gatherers, outside of some situations impacted by expanding states. Unlike chimpanzees, the materially rational choices of foragers are made within a shared cooperative framework. Territoriality in chimpanzees and mobile foragers is not just different in form and variations, it is different in essence. Human territoriality, essentially, is *cultural*.

31
Species-Specific Foundations of Human War

I share with *pan*ologists the goal of better understanding war, but approach it anthropologically. Up to here, the demonic perspective, broader adaptationist claims, and inclusive fitness theory are repeatedly challenged by evidence about chimpanzees and bonobos. Evolutionary hypotheses sputtered out when applied to people. That's critique. Can anthropology offer anything better?

There are countless anthropological perspectives on war. These concluding two chapters present my own. I started studying war in the Vietnam era, always working toward a holistic, cross-cultural theory. For me, explaining war means understanding why war exists, cultural variations in war, systemic interactions of war and society, and why actual wars happen—all across human experience and applicable to the contemporary world. Chapter 32 lays out my specific explanations, which can be compared to *Pan*ology's efforts to inform our understanding of war. Before that, Chapter 31 provides a species-specific foundation for those theories. This became much more clear to me though my engagement with primatology.

Culture

Anthropologists have debated the meaning of "culture" since the discipline began. It's been so thoroughly picked apart that many today avoid using the term. That has unfortunate consequences. Abandoning "culture" meant that in our zeitgeist, "human nature" was left to zoologists and evolutionary psychologists, who were happy to step in with neo-Darwinian perspectives. Why do people do what they do? Evolution! Culture provides a better answer than biology, as it did a century ago.

"Culture" as used here avoids the difficult conceptual issues by returning to its origins. Franz Boas, the founder of American anthropology, took Edward Tylor's (1970:1) famous description of culture as "that complex whole which includes knowledge, belief, art, law, morals, custom, and any other capabilities and habits acquired by man as a member of society," and stripped of its racialism and progressive social evolutionary stages. All people everywhere equally had their own culture, which determined how they lived and thought. Boas used the term plurally, *cultures*, without implication of separation or bounding. The task of anthropology was to understand them in historically specific terms (Stocking 1966).

Boasian culture is obvious if you step from one into another. *Pan* isn't like that. Local traditions of termite fishing or leaf snapping notwithstanding, one chimpanzee or bonobo group seems much like another. With people, cultural differences smack any visitor in the face. Culture shapes *all* aspects of living for *all* humans, how people eat, sit, walk, have sex, excrete, laugh, show affection, labor and exchange, relate to spirit worlds, practice politics, cooperate, and fight. Compared to chimpanzees, Goodall said it succinctly many years ago.

> There are customs and taboos concerning almost every aspect of behaviour from religious beliefs to menstruation, from the way in which music is made to the manner of weeping and the contexts in which it is permissible to weep. Therefore, in essence, all behaviours observable to the anthropologist studying human beings can be described as a part of their culture. (van Lawick-Goodall 1973b:144)

Including war.

Seen in species contrast, human culture is obviously different from chimpanzee learned traditions. Why? Because of two unbridgeable gulfs between the species: human symbolic cognition and language; and cumulative development of social systems and material technology. These qualitatively separate war from "war," and are implicit in Chapter 31's concrete applications.

Great Divide I: Symbol and Language

Chimpanzees exhibit "socially transmitted behavior," like many species. Human culture exists on a different plane, with our unique cognition enabling equally unique "ratcheting up" of one modification on top of all that came before (Tomasello 1999). Compared to other primates, how we learn, and collectively apply what we learn, is worlds apart. Cumulative ratching is built into our evolved mentality (Tomasello 2016).

> [W]hat most clearly distinguishes the cognition of humans from that of their nearest primate relatives is their sociocognitive adaptations for operating together in cultural groups. Given those adaptations, groups of individuals are able to cooperate to create artifacts and practices that accumulate improvements, or ratchet up in complexity, over time as new environmental challenges arise. Since this process creates ever-new cognitive niches for developing youngsters, human children must be equipped to participate in this groupthink with special skills for collaboration, communication, and cultural learning. As part of this process, children construct cognitive representations of the world that incorporate the perspectives and normative judgements of others, and they learn to symbolically represent those perspectives and judgements for others in acts of interpersonal and intrapersonal communication. Humans are adapted for life in a culture, and the particular tools, symbols, and social practices of the cultures into which they are born enable them to construct further cognitive skills for coping with the exigencies of their local environments. (Herrmann and Tomasello 2012:712)

Cooperation is found throughout the animal kingdom and certainly among primates, contrary to neo-Darwinism's overwhelming emphasis on conflict and competition. But humans take cooperation and altruism to an entirely different level (Sussman and Cloninger 2011).

Symbol and Language

Human learning process depends on language and symbolic thought. "[S]ymbolic culture is redundant, and human culture with no symbolism is an oxymoron" (Tuttle 2014:587). In contrast to chimpanzees, simple human tools derive from symbolic concepts. "In the preparation of a stick for termite-eating, the relation between product and raw material is iconic. In the making of a stone tool, in contrast, there is no necessary relation between the form of the final product and the original material" (Holloway 1992:53). A mental image, a symbol, exists before the tool takes shape. That symbol is one instance of a symbolic category of *tools*, with more specific, more encompassing, and other connected symbolic categories.

Tuttle (2014:585) puts this difference in the center of debates about whether chimpanzees have culture.

> To date, little more has been demonstrated than that great apes have relatively trivial local or demic behavioral practices that are variably influenced somehow by group conspecifics such as variant grooming postures, vocal signals, food handling techniques, and tool behavior. No one has shown that chimpanzees in nature have pervasive shared symbolically mediated ideas, beliefs, and values, the *sine qua non* of culture as understood by most students of culture. Indeed, one rarely encounters mention, let alone detailed discussion, of symbols in the argument for naturalistic chimpanzee culture.

(Cf. Boesch 1991b.)

Language is the medium of symbolically constructed universes. Language is the master ratchet for cumulative cultural development. "[I]t is the capacity to denote and to predict about states of affairs not tethered to the here and now of communication that seems to be unique to human evolution" (Tuttle 2014:571). This communicable symbolic understanding of existence underwrites the cultural diversification of human behavior around the world.

The contribution of language has long been obvious, again as per Goodall.

> [Why] does the chimpanzee in nature not show a *more* advanced level of cultural behavior? [Because] the chimpanzee has not method of communication that can be compared with human language.... It seems very likely that the development of language opened up the evolutionary road leading to the diversity and richness of culture in men. (van Lawick-Goodall 1973b:181)

The medium is the essence.

Meaning Matters

This symbolically constructed, linguistically expressed universe appears in every aspect of hunter-gatherer territoriality. What is good to eat, who it belongs to and who can share, how to get and prepare it—these and other understandings are all engaged before nutrients ever enter a body. They are matters of life-sustaining behavioral adaptation. They meld with each other and everything else in the minds of cultural people. All the micro-ecology of living in an area—this tasty, that taboo—connects with understandings of the person, the world, and beyond. Eve and Adam could naively nosh in the state of nature, but when they woke into knowledge, every bite meant something.

Multidimensional webs of thought inform us on what to do, and what it all means. Culturally patterned social behaviors have their own logics, with elements and aspects that are detached from fitness payoffs, and which mesh in complex systems of systems. Hill (2009:269, 279)—an evolutionary ecologist with extensive field experience among hunter-gatherers—once thought that "the differences between humans and nonhumans in the importance of social learning were simply a matter of degree, not of kind." No longer. "In short, animals show socially learned traditions, but there is no evidence in any animal for socially learned conventions, ethics, rituals, religion, or morality, which are critical and universal components of human culture."

Culture as a whole is the adaptive quantum leap, enabling people to live anywhere, as Ashley Montagu (1968) put it, humanity's "adaptive dimension." Adaptation is coping with practical challenges, *and* it is normative. Cultural evaluations of good/bad, better/worse, right/wrong, inform all human activities. That fact led to lively scholarship on the evolution of morality, and its crucial role in human conduct (see Baumard et al. 2013; Boehm 2012; 2000; de Waal 2016; Hall and Brosnan 2016; Hauser 2007; Krebs 2011; Tomasello 2016). Human life transpires within and according to an integrated symbolic-linguistic sphere, a culture-dome. Other animals do not have that.

Practicality and Symbolic Construction in War

For decades, anthropologists took sides on whether war reflects material interests, or rather is a performance of particular cultures' symbolic scripts. I come from the materialist camp—self-interest drives war. Yet *both* perspectives are necessary. As woven throughout practical interests, cultural beliefs have their own autonomy and integrity. They imbue actions with meaning, and meaning channels actions. The practical constrains the symbolic, but within those constraints the symbolic shapes practicality. Deciding for war is both practical *and* meaningful.

Violence, including war, is symbolically expressive, performative. Collective killing defines an "us" and "them," and the relationship between, laden with powerful messaging for those beyond the immediate fight (see Riches 1986).

> Close ethnographic engagement [with cases of extreme violence] strongly suggests that it is the cultural meaning of the violence that is performed, not just the empirical fact of the act itself, which is a key element in advancing our understanding of these human capacities. The performance of violence, how it is enacted according to cultural codes, is therefore as relevant to our understanding as is the appreciation of its sociopolitical consequences and causes. (Ferguson and Whitehead 2000:xxvi, references omitted)

Deeply meaningful acts of collective aggression shape all the social relations that follow from that.

War is not just about relations between enemies, it reflects and shapes social patterns *within* each group. War is distinguished from homicide in that it is culturally approved and inherently *social*, the outcome of collective social processes. In processes leading to war, both practical self-interests and the ability to influence collective decisions depend on one's situation within a society at a given historical moment (Ferguson 1995a:364–366; 2006b). At egalitarian levels, individual differences include male or female, age status from youth to elder, kinship, marital relations, and more. Particularly important are constructions of masculinity (Chapter 32). With increasing social hierarchy, political position becomes crucial. Within and form-fitted to social placement, symbols and values shape understanding of events, appraisal of situations, and perceived options.

In any complex, fraught situation involving different groups, within the practical/symbolic nexus for any given people, there are always options—to cooperate, to fight, to ally, to submit, or to flee—just to start. How individuals see these options depends largely on their position. Socially structured political voice affects how anyone can influence the social processes, as does their individual personality. This practical, symbolic, and political nexus shapes how people perceive their options. That shapes how collective decisions are made, with choices that mean life or death. Once chosen, they shape future options. This is the realm of agency, where culture, history, and free will come together.

Moral Conversion

Which brings me to a central point in my theory on war. When people with public influence argue for one or another option in a conflict, typically their preferred course is consistent with their own practical self-interest. But they speak and persuade in terms of local perceptions, values, and symbols, of good vs. bad, right vs. wrong, who we are, and who they are. I refer to this as "moral conversion"—self-serving actions which in public advocacy are transmuted into potent cultural imperatives. These common understandings are used to persuade others, but also to justify self.

This is more than patina. Systems of culturally specific cognitions—what I will soon label "Superstructure"—have logic and weight of their own. Certainly there are selfless individuals and leaders, who advocate for what they see as right against what is self-advantageous. Saintly people do exist and can be transformative, but most leaders are not saints.

Those who shape or make the decisions to war typically believe that it will serve their interests, *and* that doing so is moral, good. In both they can be terribly wrong, but that is what they think going in. In my theoretical approach, pan-human interests and local cultural norms combine for war. There is no analogue for all this in *Pan* "war." That is one Great Divide.

Great Divide II: Culture as a Causal System

The other is social causality. Practical interests and symbolic evaluations channel regularities in personal behavior and interactions. These regularities constitute highly patterned social life, as experienced by every person from birth to death. It is the water in which we swim.

These pattern regularities are more than just conditioners and expressions of individual behavior. Social life is an *emergent domain* in itself, of open functional systems within systems, with their own logics of causes and consequences. These social regularities have a life of their own, in the realm of cultural causality.

Pan has something like this in the important social contrast between chimpanzees and bonobos. Yet that is paltry compared to people. Every human society is an elaborate artifice of organization, constructed upon millennia of ancestral practice and innovation.

Cultural norms and practices cover all aspect of life. In the complex organism of any culture, the parts must fit together, mutually accommodate. Change something important and other changes follow. This is the hidden hand of culture. Think of electricity, internal combustion engines, computers, and the internet. Or think of agriculture and the wheel. Exploring cultural causes and results of cultural phenomena is the a,b,c of anthropology.

Social causality is foundational in the anthropology of war. Early findings: when marriage-related patterns such as polygyny and patrilocality combine, "fraternal interest groups" of co-resident male kin develop that make local warfare more likely (Otterbein 1968). Combine fraternal interest groups with a strong ideology of male descent, and "segmentary lineages" enable progressively higher levels of "us vs. them" solidarity, conferring the ability to expand against others not similarly organized. "I fight my brother, but with my brother against my cousin," and so on (Sahlins 1961). If colonial frontiers introduce a strong demand for a commodity that requires extensive female cooperation (e.g., producing manioc flour in Amazonia), patrilocality may give way to matrilocality and village exogamy, thus suppressing local violence and facilitating a tribal level of unity and long-distance external warfare (Murphy 1957).

Those illustrations from the anthropology of war's early days were followed by work on innumerable, mutually conditioning, social connections involving war, with countless arguments over *how* they fit together. To address those findings and debates in the broadest way, I developed a model that is both theoretically inclusive, and opinionated. This paradigm (of one) recognizes the diversity of questions to be asked, and integrates them within a clear causal framework. It offers a stark alternative to the reductionist Gombe paradigm.

A Cultural Materialist Paradigm

My (1995b) broadest theory modifies Marvin Harris's (1979) "cultural materialism." As a first step toward cross-cultural analysis, cultural materialism categorizes social existence into three dimensions. *Infrastructure* encompasses physical production and reproduction, including the environment, demographics, technology, and labor. Within Infrastructural parameters, *Structure* includes all aspects of social organization from kinship to class, economy, and politics. Within Infrastructural and Structural constraints, *Superstructure* is the realm of culturally specific understandings, commonly held symbols, values, even emotions. *All* behavior involves symbolic thought—how to make and use a tool for instance—but Superstructure encompasses *systems of meaning* that guide proper behavior—see Great Divide I.

This epistemological categorization approaches humanity as physical, social, and sentient beings, a three-dimensional framework of culturally lived space. Theoretically, the physical realities of Infrastructure constrain social possibilities of Structure, and both constrain possibilities of Superstructural ideology. Each contains integrated systems—e.g., food quest, marriage, religion—which interact with and constrain possibilities of other systems. All are impacted by changing historical circumstances.[1] Taken together, they probabilistically determine social likelihoods, possibilities, and options. For example, with mobile egalitarian hunter-gatherers, their foraging adaptation (Infrastructure) shapes social patterns of association, cooperation, and territoriality (Structure), which shapes beliefs encouraging interconnectedness and conflict resolution short of war (Superstructure). But Superstructure feeds back to Structure and both to Infrastructure.

Broadly applied to war (Ferguson 1990), Infrastructure is foundational, determining basic outlines of *if*, why, and how war is practiced, the obvious contrasts between war in different kinds of societies. (If you want to understand why modern war in 2020 is different from modern war in 1820, start with infrastructure.) Inside those fundamentals, Structure includes the patterns and processes that define groups in alliance or opposition, ways and means of mobilization, and political processes to make nice or make war. If you want political patterns leading to war, go to Structure. Superstructure infuses all of that with meaning, how people think themselves into or away from war, thus creating actionable situations, where decisions for war or peace are made.

Pan could be said to have Infrastructure and rudimentary Structure, but no Superstructure, and so "war" is essentially different from war. But one *great similarity* across the two species is the need for historical context—bringing in outside disruption to explain conflicts leading up to violence. That is making it real.

The cognitive realm and social causality are two unbridgeable divides between human and nonhuman animals. My approach imputes specific characteristics to both regarding war: the fusion of practical interest and symbolic meaning in moral conversion; and a hierarchy of more limiting constraints beginning with Infrastructure but allowing substantial autonomy; all approached in historical context.

I do not care about theory for its own sake. For me theory must do work, as a set of tools leading to better understandings of realities, in this case the realities of war. Theory has to be flexible and adaptable for different questions and situations. But the applications must come together with consistency within the broader theory. Unification of explanation is how science progresses.

---

[1] Being attuned to history—which I learned from Morton Fried—is one way my model diverges from Harris's (Ferguson 1995b:30–32).

32
Applications
An Anthropology of War

That is the theoretical mainframe. Chapter 32 puts it to work, applying the general perspective concretely to specific topics. As I asked of chimpanzee-based theory, how does it fit, or inform? The exposition hops around, reflecting different studies over many years, my own anthropology of war.[1] All have substantial empirical support (in the cited publications), are consistent with the broad theory of Chapter 31 and with each other, and hopefully tell us something clarifying about war.

Chapter 32 begins close to adaptationist arguments, war by nonstate people and the archaeological record. It proceeds to where the demonic perspective does not tread, with large-scale war in our contemporary world. The goal is to demonstrate a framework for understanding war, without the neo-Darwinism. We begin with an application that is perfect for paradigmatic comparison.

Application: The "Fierce" Yanomami

The Yanomami, shifting horticulturalist-foragers of the Upper Orinoco, became the type case of "primitive war" through the best-selling ethnography, *The Fierce People*, by Napoleon Chagnon (1968). Chagnon portrays them as undisturbed survivors of the Hobbesian stone age, our contemporary ancestors, with endless fighting over women and vengeance (Chagnon 2013).

Not all Yanomami are "warlike," but those he studied in the 1960s were. His Yanomam*o* (a linguistic subtype of Yanomam*i*) around the juncture of Orinico and Mavaca Rivers, became the acid test for developing anthropological theory. Some argued for populations adapting to limited but nutritionally necessary game protein. Some stressed the norms of Yanomami culture (Ferguson 2001). When sociobiology came around in the 1970s, Chagnon jumped on board (Chagnon and Irons 1979).

With that flag raised, Yanomamo became the go-to case for evolutionary explanations of human war. Yanomamo are invoked for biologistic claims, even when Chagnon's own findings *directly contradict* them (see Ferguson 2001:106–111). Case in point: *Demonic Males* (1996:69) says chimpanzees resemble Yanomami local groups made up of "closely related males and unrelated females who have emigrated from other kinship groups." No. Customarily, marriage was between intermarrying lines of cousins living with or near each other (Chagnon 1968:69–73). Females marrying out about came with the missionaries, and their material enticements (Ferguson 2015).

---

[1] All published papers are available as pdf files at https://www.rbrianferguson.com/.

Demonic Males spotlights Yanomami as *the best case* showing chimpanzee–human continuities, the bridge across species.

> No human society offers a better opportunity for comparison in this regard than the Yanomamo.... Do they suggest to us that chimpanzee violence is linked to human war. Clearly they do.... The differences are important, but so are the similarities because they hint at a shared cause and common origin. The Yanomamo suggest to us that as human economic and ecological conditions move closer to those of chimpanzees, so the patterns of violence in our two species start to converge. (Wrangham and Peterson 1996:64, 70–71, order altered)

That flows from the demonic paradigm. How about mine?

Why So Warlike?

My alternative has two sides, systemic and agentic, both historically situated (Ferguson 1992; 1995a; 2015).

Infrastructurally, steel tools transformed hunting and gardening, supporting larger and more sedentary populations. People settled and stayed around missions and other Western outposts to monopolize their commodity trade. Fixity led to local overhunting, eliminating widespread meat-sharing that elsewhere glued Yanomami villagers together. New infections killed so many that families had to be reconstituted from survivors.

All that reshaped Structural patterns, themselves directly affected by Western contact. Intervillage exchange went from balanced reciprocity, which solidified relations between equals, to exploitative extraction of products and labor by middlemen who channeled Western goods. Mutuality became dependency. Marriage similarly changed, from largely endogamous within lines of cousins, to serving male strategic interests, so brides went to trade controllers. These changes in trade and marriage sometimes generated intense personal antagonism. Simultaneously status politics became more fraught because of Westerners' favoritism in handing out steel tools. Some ambitious men played the game with violence, both instrumental and performative. These historical structural rearrangements patterned intergroup antagonisms and alliances. Any major changes in the Western presence, like the opening or closing of a mission, set off dangerous shockwaves.

Superstructurally, new epidemics generated widespread suspicions of death shamanism, which can be grounds for war. Coveted Western goods were thought to give off an invisible fume that caused disease and could be directed against enemies. Women's status in an already patriarchal society was brought lower by sedentism, which made them drudge laborers rather than skilled foragers, and sometimes pawns in men's games. Destruction of families and of reciprocal food sharing led to personal violence, often directed against women—both instrumental and performative. Capture or coerced ceding of women became common. A key masculine value, *waiteri*, went from meaning aggressive and valorous, to meaning proficient in killing. Even myths changed to emphasize a primal origin of impulses to war.

So historical change worked through all of local Yanomami culture, Infrastructure, Structure, and Superstructure, lowering the flashpoint for violence, making them "warlike." That is why Chagnon's Yanomamo seem "fierce." But that leaves the question: why do actual wars happen?

Deciding for War

Particularities of local situations led to variable patterns and intensities of hostility and alliance. Male animosities over trade, women, status, and sorcery sometimes created a milieu of war. Different men were situated differently in the mix of within and between group relationships, and did their best to make things go their way. They orated on how others should see things, sometimes in the middle of the night, about what has been and should be done. They took the lead in galvanizing actions. Discussions seem personal, local, and immediate. But look closer and across Yanomami lands, and a pattern is clear. Practical interests in accessing manufactured goods *explain* when, where, how, and why actual wars occurred—and also long-distance explorations, village relocations, intervillage alliances, and major club fights.

This method to explain Yanomami wars employs a predictive model developed for complex hunter-gatherers of the Pacific Northwest Coast: of mapping historical changes in contact circumstances against each reported war (1984b). For the Northwest Coast and Yanomami both, I situate every war within specifics of changing circumstances of Western intrusion—just as this book contextualizes each and every chimpanzee killing. Antagonisms rooted in conflict over access to trade goods explain times of war, times of peace, what kind of groups attack, and what kind are attacked (Ferguson 2015:392–3932).

Within any context, there are always choices. One influential man is conciliatory, another belligerent. One may be elevated by a new alliance, another by a successful raid. Before any collective action is taken, people talk it over. Values of bravery and cowardice, generosity and stinginess, friendship and malice involving sorcery are invoked to great effect.[2] Acts of war are not by preset groups, but by collectivities of individuals who decide for themselves and their own reasons. Well-argued values—"who here is brave and will avenge their death magic?"—increase social pressure to follow leaders. Within this space for agency, options are both tightly circumscribed and critically consequential. Personal and collective decisions can tilt the social field in different directions, and that shapes future options. In all of this, the Yanomami typify war in a tribal zone.

Application: War in Tribal Zones

Tribal zones are areas affected by but not under control of proximate states or state agents. Transformative impacts of expanding states spread far over land *in advance*

---

[2] For a glimpse into the actual practice of decision-making, unlike the simplistic images typically attributed to tribal warfare, see *Yanomami Warfare* (Ferguson 1995:222–239; also excellent is Weisner 2019).

of literate observers; in new technologies, foreign plants and animals, reoriented trade patterns, diseases, and population displacements (Ferguson 1992c:111).[3] Supposedly "first contact" situations usually incorporate many such changes. Ancient states affected war among peoples around them or along their trade routes, but the oceanic distances involved in Western expansion made it far more disruptive (Ferguson 1993). Western colonialism invariably transformed existing war, frequently intensified it, and sometimes generated warfare where there was none, before and after "first contact" observations.

What seemed "untouched" by outside forces, even to anthropologists, was often already transformed and transforming. As noted previously, Western disruption has been implicated in collective violence across the ethnographic spectrum, including mobile foragers often noted as warring (Ona of Tierra del Fuego, Tasmanians, Jarawa of the Andaman Islands). Similar external stimulation of local war is evident from the beginning of the age of the Pharaohs in modern Jordan (Ferguson 2013b:222–225), up to present-day Highland New Guinea (Ferguson 2019:237).

Ahistorical cultural explanations, common for decades in anthropological studies of war, may radically misconstrue why peoples are "warlike," and why actual wars happen (Ferguson 1990b). To emphasize historical context does not invalidate explanations stressing endogenous social and belief patterns, but can clarify why war breaks out where, when, and how much it does. Around the world and across historical epochs, war in tribal zones reveals pronounced similarities, though always locally specific (Ferguson and Whitehead 1992c). This can be framed in terms of the materialist paradigm.

Infrastructurally, changes in tools, weapons, and other manufactures, means of transportation, demographic disruption through displacement and disease, loss of land or game, and ecological transformations—each with very specific local manifestations and intensities—radically shake up prior ways of life, often pitting locals against each other with new antagonism—just as with Yanomami. Structurally in those shook-up situations, local agents find themselves differentially positioned in relation to the encroaching leviathan, reacting to both coercion and seduction, forced to choose between accommodation or resistance, with placement and posture affecting their relations with those around them, leading to new wars.

Superstructural changes are legion, as when limited practices with heavy ritual meaning, such as taking captives, heads, and scalps, turn into industries. An overarching Superstructural point is that although tribal zone situations display great parallels cross-culturally, local response is always framed in terms of immediate local understandings, values, and symbols—moral conversion on a global scale.

Alien intruders quickly transform indigenous social landscapes. Initial explorers typically note amorphous and open social identities, identified with geographic locations. That sort of messiness does not work for expanding states. They seek *polity*, defined groups and leaders to engage, subjugate, or destroy. Neil Whitehead and

---

[3] Ferguson and Whitehead's *War in the Tribal Zone* (1992a) compared cases from Roman North Africa, early Sri Lanka, the Aztec environment, the West African Slave Coast, northeastern South America, the Iroquois region, eastern Peru around Ashaninka, the Yanomami, and highland Papua New Guinea, but drew on much additional research.

I call these frontier *and beyond* areas "tribal zones." They generate "tribalization," newly demarcated and frequently hostile groupings. Beyond that, often as tribes collapse, comes "ethnogenesis," the development of categorical cultural groupings as devastated peoples move and combine, trying to survive and live in their own way. Those ethnic identities then play out in any later wars and alliances that follow. (See "Identerism," below.)

Application: The Origins and Intensifications of War

Tribal zones are often full of war, which is often mistaken as representing a pristine "state of nature"—as Hobbes himself did in the 17th century. Today tribal zone violence is projected backward forever in imagining tribal warfare. In Hobbesian harmony, tribal war across ethnography combines with war in prehistory, to connect back to a "warring" chimpanzee and the Last Common Ancestor. Critics (Fry et al. 2020; Haas and Piscitelli 2013) including myself, argue that war has archaeologically recoverable beginnings, in skeletal trauma, settlement remains, sometimes specialized weapons, and occasionally art. I published extensively on archaeological issues (Ferguson 1997; 2006a; 2008a; 2013a; 2013b), and will return to ongoing controversies in future work. The relevant point right now is how my general theory of war fits with its origins and intensifications.

For prehistory, we will never know the immediate reason for specific wars. But cross-cultural archaeology suggests a set of *preconditions* that make the onset of war more probable. Infrastructurally: increasing population numbers and density, sedentism and spatial inequality in subsistence resources, such as lagoons or marshes amid areal paucity and aridity. These don't cause war in themselves, but war is more likely when people can't move away and are bordered by have-nots. Livestock and stored food gives people something to fight over, to take or defend through violence. Environmental reverses can increase scarcity to extremes and create or intensify hostility, unless people have a way to cope with it.

With these Infrastructural developments, archaeologically recoverable Structural changes provide more immediate preconditions for war: mainly increased social bounding of groups, and sociopolitical hierarchy. Long-distance trade in high-value goods—when subject to monopolization or predation (not always so)—is an especially potent precondition. Roughly speaking, combination of these social preconditions creates "complexity."

War did not begin with agriculture. Distinct from egalitarian mobile foragers, some complex hunter-gatherers are notable for intense war, such as peoples of the Brazilian Atlantic coast (Balee 1984) or the Pacific Northwest coast (Ferguson 1984b). Mainstream archaeology has long associated complexity with the Mesolithic period—between Paleolithic big game hunters and Neolithic farmers—in a period of highly productive, sedentized broad spectrum exploitation, commonly of shore environments. After the bounty of following and hunting big or abundant game, people found more bountiful and sustainable resources, albeit with more work. *Some*, not most, Mesolithic (or Epipaleolithic) situations have long been argued as the presenting the earliest signs of war (Crevecoeur et al. 2021; Lahr et al. 2016; Vencl 1983; 2016;

Wendorf 1968). There is a great deal more to discuss about war in the archaeological record, but not here.

Application: Comparative Politics

Chimpanzee politics consists of dyadic alliances and oppositions. *Pan*ologists fully understand that human politics play out in a social medium alien to chimpanzees, emphasizing the endless variety of institutions conferring influence or power (Chapais 1991; Lewis 2002), the seemingly unlimited scale and flexibility of social inclusion and cooperation (Cronk and Leech 2013; Leech and Cronk 2017), and all that comes with the foundational medium of language (Watts 2010). Those fundamentals apply across humankind, leading to endless varieties of political systems and stratagems, far beyond primatology. That is grist for anthropological analysis.

Politics, Hierarchy, and War

To address the critical question of why an actual war occurs, one should focus on the political *decision* that starts the war, starting with who decides and how. Cross-culturally addressed, the first concern is social inequality (Fried 1967). In *egalitarian* societies all men are equal, and decide for themselves on matters of war. In *ranked* societies, hierarchy gives some individuals greater influence than others, but without compelling power. In *stratified* societies rulers rule the ruled, implemented through institutions of a *state*. These elementary contrasts matter fundamentally for understanding how and why war happens.

As noted, in war any cost or benefit regarding external interactions refract differently depending on one's social position. Across politics leaders use oratorical skill to invoke higher Superstructural meanings to further their interests. If resolving conflicts without violence is an admired quality for leaders, they act accordingly. Individuals vary, and for some, values themselves trump self-interest. But when war is in the system, external belligerence may be politically advantageous. Even among the relatively egalitarian Yanomami, in violent times war gives aggressive men greater influence over others.[4] War or the threat of war, may reinforce one person or faction over others. In an internal/external dialectic of tensions, framing external enemies often reflects internal political advantage. Often, leaders favor war because war favors leaders (Ferguson 1990:40–42, 47–51)—though often it doesn't work out as hoped.

In ranked societies including complex hunter-gatherers, this is very clear. Big men—self-made leaders with many but fickle followers—can be Machiavellian in persuading and cajoling for war or for negotiation (e.g., Maybury Lewis 1974; Sillitoe 1978). With chiefs—who occupy defined, elevated social positions, often with specific

---

[4] Helena Valero, captive among Yanomami for some 24 years, relates a comment by her husband Fusiwe as he provoked a war with neighbors, and then adds her own suspicion: "'All the Namoeteri live apart; I want to kill the Pishaanseteri so that I can see whether all those who live apart join together for fear, in one single *shapuno*.' Perhaps he wants to go back to being chieftain of them all?" (Ferguson 1995a:238).

responsibilities—war can express chiefly ambitions, and war can give them more authority than in peace time (e.g., Arkush and Allen 2006; Redmond 1998). From egalitarian societies on up, those who see internal advantage in belligerence have their own interest in promoting confrontation (e.g., Kracke 1978; Carneiro 1998). War can be *domestic* politics by other means.[5]

Stratified societies have permanent social inequality in wealth, status, and power. That inequality radically affects differential costs and benefits of war. A state is the institutional system that implements rule. War changes along with hierarchy, but a categorical break occurs with the advent of states, which is one reason why anthropologists refer to "states" not just as governments, but as a type of society.

In states authorities decide and demand compliance, even unto death—as Wrangham rightly highlights. Subjects might or might not gain from a war, yet have no choice but to obey, when rulers command. But since employing power is cheaper than using force, far better to gain willing even enthusiastic support by invoking transcendental values. With Infrastructures producing great surplus, and logistical capabilities for campaigns far beyond tribal peoples, states can field mass and professional armies, plus mercenaries. With the capacity for strategic plans, states can wage war by and for broader political policy extended over time. States more than tribal peoples are obsessed with territory, identity, and borders.

War and Society in Ancient States

Adaptationist approaches rule out application to war by states or in the contemporary world (except for insubstantial rhetorical invocation). For anthropologists of war, that application has always been a central goal (Boas 1912; Malinowski 1941; Fried, Harris, and Murphy 1968). About states and their war, I use the cultural materialist paradigm to synthesize findings on war and society in 13 ancient and medieval states, and to compare those to nonstate warfare, including how war shapes societies (Ferguson 1999).[6] There is way too much to summarize here, but a snippet from conclusions on Structure notes first commonalities across political systems, and then developments particular to states.

> [All] Internal politics thus plays a major role in shaping external policies, indeed, the boundary between the two may fluctuate. On the other hand, internal politics is conditioned by a structured external field of oppositions and alliances. Allies are crucial for success in war, and alliance making intensifies alongside war.... [States] [A]lliance appears to be the end of a continuum that reaches to territorial conquest and incorporation. Alliances or somewhat more permanent confederacies tip from equality to hegemony, and from hegemony to empire, as hegemony grades into

---

[5] One significant comparison between chimpanzees and humans, is that both may use external violence to enhance internal status. Chimpanzee display violence may have a human analogy in leaders who rattle sabers or even use them to impress the home audience.
[6] Early China, Japan to 1300, ancient Egypt, the Achaemenid Empire, Archaic and Classical Greece, the Hellenistic World, Republican Rome, the Roman Empire, the Byzantine Empire, early Medieval Europe, the early Islamic world, ancient Maya, and the Aztec Empire.

conquest and incorporation. In the other direction, regional autonomy can grow within territorial states to the point of independence. In sum, what often exists is a complex and fluid political field, involving varied political relations between varied types of polities. (1999:425)

The internal/external dialectic and pursuit of domestic political interest is clear in ancient empires. As Eric Wolf (1987:142) said well:

> [C]onflicts over rights to succession within the ruling Inca elite of the Central Andes in the century before the Spanish Conquest led to the incorporation through warfare of new territories through which contending claims could be satisfied. Similarly, the Aztec state ... organized itself by projecting internal conflicts into aggressive war, and then widened its ability to co-opt and reward its elite adherents through expansion outside the Valley of Mexico.

But that's ancient history. What about applying anthropology to war in the contemporary world?

Applications: Contemporary War

Asked to summarize my main findings on war, I (2008b) came up with ten points applicable to war *in general*.

#1 Our species is not biologically destined for war.
#2 War is not an inescapable part of social existence.
#3 Understanding war involves a nested hierarchy of constraints.
#4 War expresses both panhuman practicalities and culturally specific values.
#5 War shapes society to its own ends.
#6 War exists in multiple contexts.
#7 Opponents are constructed in conflict.
#8 War is a continuation of domestic politics by other means.
#9 Leaders favor war because war favors leaders.
#10 Peace is more than the absence of war.

Each of these is then applied to US wars in Iraq and Afghanistan.[7] For brevity, here I stick with one main line, which applies the moral conversion framework in the second Gulf War (Ferguson 2006b:59–62).

The US Invasion of Iraq

On both sides, decision-making was highly concentrated.

---

[7] Much earlier I applied the cultural materialist paradigm to the Cold War (1989b), and to our limiting perceptions of the East–West confrontation (1988).

For the cliques around Saddam Hussein and George Bush, the path toward war seemed politically advantageous. Hussein's practical priority was survival in power. He saw two main threats: Iran, which motivated his coyness about having weapons of mass destruction; and restive officers of his own army, to be occupied with external enemies. For Hussein, the United States was not seen as an existential military threat, because until late 2002 Hussein *believed* it would not invade. In the United States, after Republican victories in Congressional elections, it was an open strategy to run on Bush as war commander. Quick and easy victory over Iraq would cement that advantage. Domestic politics shaped external policy.

On each side, self-serving policies were proclaimed in terms of high ideals. Advisers around Bush saw military projection as a righteous way to spread American values, such as the rights of women. Hussein saw himself as restorer of Iraq's Mesopotamian glory and defender of Arab dignity against modern Crusaders. This moralistic combination of interests and values fostered self-delusion, Hussein on his army's ability to resist, Bush et al. on smooth sailing after victory. Both sides saw the other as morally corrupt by association, with Israel or al Qaeda. In all that, this war was like many wars, the internal advantage foreseen for rulers weighing against external risks. (Wrangham argues that such delusions express an evolved tendency.)[8]

What about our subsequent adversaries in Iraq? In 2005, at the height of what was called "the insurgency," politicians, military, and media could not make sense of the incoherent proliferation of leaders, factions, identities, and causes. Different fights involved different religious, regional, ethnic, and tribal identities, differentially connected to power. What *was* the insurgency? In my analysis, it was a proliferation of "identerest" groups (including what became ISIS), like those found in so many violent conflicts around the world (Ferguson 2006b).

Identerism

Primordialism

A crucial difference between the resource competition hypothesis and the rival coalition reduction hypothesis (Chapter 3) is the latter validates "primordialist" explanations of civil wars along ethnic or sectarian lines; people are primed to kill outsiders simply because they are alien. A big selling point of the demonic perspective (Chapter 30) is that it accounts for this seemingly irrational carnage—though just how is left unsaid. That lacuna didn't stop others from taking people-as-warring-chimps into international relations and security studies. Look back at the epigraphs by Francis Fukuyama and Robert Sapolsky from *Foreign Affairs*. Their publication dates of 1998 and 2019 span the work on this book. For decades chimpanzee militancy has been a given in our intellectual universe.

Or consider Thayer's *Darwin and International Relations: On the Evolutionary Origins of War and Ethnic Conflict*, lauded as "a brilliant analysis of how contemporary

---

[8] It should be noted that Wrangham (2018:263–269) proposes that military overconfidence is itself an adaptive tendency. That seems too tangential to give it the lengthy consideration it would need here.

Darwinian studies of evolution and human behavior can provide a solid basis" for international relations theory (Masters 2004). For Thayer (2004:254–261), chimpanzees, ancestors, and tribals show that "[x]enophobic behavior serves as a foundation for ethnic conflict because evolution caused it. There is always the potential it may be triggered." So too ethnocentrism: "masses are well prepared by human evolution to have their ethnocentric strings pulled by the elite." On primordialism: "As with the in-group/out-group bifurcation, this argument improves the paradigm ... scholars in the paradigm will be able to anchor their arguments about ethnocentric behavior in evolutionary theory." The moral of this story is that manipulative leaders may pursue selfish interests, but the will to kill wells up from human nature. As Einstein and Freud agreed.

Structure, Superstructure, and Moral Conversion

In a comparative synthesis of later 20th-century, identity-linked wars and political violence within states (Ferguson 2003),[9] I come to antithetical conclusions. The deadly divides are constructed in the development of conflict. Conflict makes the group.

Social identities shape up and become toxic through politics at multiple levels of context, from globe to neighborhood, all interacting. Salient social/political categories rise on legacies of past empires, morphing and mixing markers of language, religion, ethnicity, "race," tribe, clan, lineage, region, class, subsistence base, country to city, and relation to government. Some conglomerates of identities can be mapped onto perceptions of practical interests, who's done well or badly in popularly understood history and recent experience. What *kinds* of people got richer or poorer, fared better or worse, were respected or disrespected, served or suppressed by existing political arrangements? Here identities and interests fuse.

Some elite—business leaders, politicians, clerics, academics, communicators—gravitate to some common path of self-advantage in this mash of identities and interests, and form up as a political force. They broadcast histories that define and valorize some "us" and demonize some "them." They mine Superstructure for powerful values, symbols, tales, and myths. Young junior men, often rootless and futureless, are the prime medium for recruitment, but always directed toward seniors' goals. The leaders may even believe their own propaganda.

The ideological poisoning proceeds in recognizable phases up to deliberate violence. As it progresses, categorization, moral imputation, and polarization engage powerful biological systems (Sapolsky 2019). An attack on any of us by them elicits passionate emotions beyond rationality. Studies of "ethnic violence" without this emotional side are clearly inadequate (Tang 2015). But these emotional fevers are the symptom, not the cause of conflicts. It may become kill or be killed by simple identity labels, this or that tribe, ethnicity, or religion. But conflicts do not begin so. They are constructed to be that way.

---

[9] The studies were of Peru, India, Yugoslavia, Macedonia, Liberia, Angola, Chad, Somalia, and Papua New Guinea.

Gombe-vision suggests deadly passions erupt from human groups as a primordial, evolutionary heritage. My argument (2003) is entirely different. Any number and configuration of groups can be constituted in "civil" wars, which may then take on passionate loyalty and hatreds. Loaded identities have deep roots, yet they are newly minted. The variability of construction, in which some identities are ignored and others are to kill and even die for, illustrates human plasticity and flexibility, not innate allegiance to a natal group. Everything about local society is involved in that construction, from Infrastructures of putting food on the table, through Structures of kinship, class, and politics, and Superstructures of local identities and imagined histories. Material interests are intertwined with value-laden symbolic social mapping. This is a profoundly *cultural* process, and one where there are choices and alternative directions.

I coined the awkward neologism "identerest" because using labels such as "ethnic," "religious," or "tribal" were *actively misleading* in understanding identity-linked mass violence of the 1990s. This was painfully evident when the US military tried to harness ethnographic intelligence and Pentagon-defined "culture" in the 2000s (Ferguson 2011b; 2013c).[10] "Identerism" avoids misleading common language labels. It directs attention to the fusion of perceived identities and interests, in active construction of new us's and them's, channeled by and for power, all of which must be empirically specified. Identerest groups, identerest leaders, identerest violence. Elaborating the main elements and processes in their construction and weaponization is how understanding is gained. To instead seek guidance from chimpanzee models is looking in the wrong direction.

In *The Goodness Paradox*, Wrangham (2019:258) supports male demonism with examples of beastly men—Japanese soldiers in Nanking and Croatian collaborationists massacring Jews, Serbs, and Gypsies. Similar horrors can be multiplied ad nauseam. I could give you a hundred. In the demonic perspective they are obvious evidence of men's evolved depravity. It is human nature, it's in the genes, it's evolution, it's men. Anthropologically, these horrors are social facts, particular to situations, which require cultural, theoretical, and historical explanation.

---

[10] A final note shows the will to believe in primordial tribalism, and its fallaciousness. US soldiers in Afghanistan kept running into tribal identifications. The Human Terrain System's analytic branch was tasked for guidance. That Reachback Center went to their ethnographic library, and reported out that although tribal labels are ubiquitous, tribe was a variable and layered phenomenon, and mixed with many other identifications. " 'Tribe' is only one potential choice of identity among many, not fixed, and not necessarily the one that guides people's decision making." Tribe could not be employed reliably for military purposes (Afghanistan Research Reachback Center White Paper 2009:2). Kind of a downer.

To the rescue came a Special Forces field commander, styled as Lawrence of Afghanistan, with a strategy for victory "One Tribe at a Time." Forge personal ties and joint military support with tribal leaders against their local adversaries (Gant 2009). Ignoring the HTS advice, the United States decided to implement this "Strategy for Success in Afghanistan." Soon an opportunity appeared. Elders of the Shinwari pledged to unify their 400,000 people against the Taliban, in return for "$1 million in development aid directly to the Shinwari elders" (Filkins 2010). Six weeks later, Shinwari subtribes were at war with rocket-propelled grenades, mortars, and machine guns (Rubin 2010).

Application: Are Men Born to Kill?

A final theoretical application addresses the subtitle of this book. "Demonic *Males*" speaks to an elemental cross-cultural generalization: war is by men. The sociobiological rationale is elementary—making war is a male reproductive strategy. A tendency toward war evolved because it contributed to the reproductive success of males born with those genes.

Across archaeology and ethnography, combat is by men—though with great complications and exceptions. Yet warless societies in archaeology and ethnology clearly show that war is not a necessary outgrowth of male-ness. Our deep forefathers did not wage war. If masculinity does not in itself lead to war, then why is it that warriors so typically are men? What is theoretically called for is a cultural explanation for both this broad uniformity, and for the great variations about it. Inborn predispositions to kill outsiders does not help.

I incorporate Ortner's (1972) and Eagly and Woods's (2003) approach to cross-culture gender specialization within the cultural materialist paradigm, and thus apply it to masculinity and war (Ferguson 2021). In their "biosocial" theory, hormones and such may play some currently undefined role, but are not decisive. Differences in upper body strength are important, but many women exceed many men in that. The categorical difference is that women bear, nurse, and care for babies (and see Goldstein 2001:406).[11] In more traditional societies, tasks that are *not compatible* with those requirements are men's work. Cultural materialistically that is Infrastructural—reproduction and production. But Infrastructure is only the beginning.

Except for the most recent human experience, a family with adult men and women had to be skilled in every task needed to live. Girls and boys are prepared from birth for those tasks. For adults, these weave through the channels and niches of social Structure as prescribed roles of women and men. Wood and Eagly argue that these role sets engender appropriate emotional orientations, "agentic" or "communal." In Superstructural constructions of the world and personhood, appropriate gender schema differentiate masculine and feminine, but all allow choices. Some versions of masculinity are part of social life, even where there is no war.

When and where war developed, masculinity as it existed was "exapted" (put to new function) for war, and they've been fused ever since. That is the cross-cultural commonality. Cross-cultural differences in society and war, all with their own complexity and causation, both enable and constrain cross-cultural exceptions, variations, and options in gender differentiation for war, including many examples of women combatants. Future war may have gender possibilities hardly dreamed of today—for better or worse.

By the principle of holism, military masculinity must integrate with other Superstructural norms, values, and symbols, in motivating men to fight. Militarized masculinity feeds back into other domains of masculine attitudes and actions. Much

---

[11] Consider the 19th-century kingdom of Dahomey (Edgerton 2000:20–26). Athletic women were its shock troops, but had to cut ties to family and forswear children. On parade they chanted they had become men.

comes along with that, starting with greater male dominance, and cross-cultural association with rape. One might call that demonic.

In America today, with each mass shooting, my wife, Leslie, asks, "What is with men?" *I have no theory at all* to explain these killings. Obviously much is involved. I can only speak to why the killers are almost always male.

Where war exists, little boys come to comprehend that men kill, and they may be expected to, by vocation or necessity. That association is all around them, for impressionable boys and seasoned men. Not so for little girls and women, who are channeled away from violence. Killing people—culturally—is men's work, masculine.

Men are not born to kill, but they can be cultivated to kill. Don't blame evolution.

Tables

Table 1. Intergroup Adult Killings

Location	Victim	Certainty of killing	Within/outside group	Age of victim	Sex of victim	Year
Gombe	Stranger	3	O	A	F	1973
Gombe	Madam Bee	1	O	A	F	1975
Gombe	Sniff	2	O	A	M	1977
Gombe	Charlie	2	O	A	M	1977
Gombe	Patti	2	O	A	F	2005
Gombe	Godi	4	O	A	M	1974
Gombe	Goliath	4	O	A	M	1975
Gombe	De	4	O	A	M	1975
Gombe	Stranger	4	O	A	F	1975
Gombe	Stranger	4	O	A	F	1977
Gombe	Stranger	4	O	A	F	1978
Gombe	Stranger	4	O	A	F	1979
Gombe	Kalande juvenile	4	O	Juv	M	1998
Gombe	Rusambo	4	O	A	M	2002
Gombe	Hugh	5	O	A	M	1973?
Gombe	Faben	5	O	A	M	1975
Gombe	Wanda	5	O	A	F	1977?
Gombe	Mandy	5	O	A	F	1977?
Gombe	Willy Wally	5	O	A	M	1977
Gombe	Sherry	5	O	A	M	1979
Gombe	Humphrey	5	O	A	M	1981
Gombe	Prof	5	O	A	M	1998
Gombe	Fifi	5	O	A	F	2004
Mahale	Kasagula	5	O	A	M	1969
Mahale	Kaguba	5	O	A	M	1970
Mahale	Kasanga	5	O	A	M	1975
Mahale	Kajabala	5	O	A	M	1975

(*continued*)

Table 1. Continued

Location	Victim	Certainty of killing	Within/outside group	Age of victim	Sex of victim	Year
Mahale	Kasonta	5	O	A	M	1978
Mahale	Sobongo	5	O	A	M	1979
Mahale	Kamemanfu	5	O	A	M	1982
Mahale	Masisa	5	O	A	M	1982
Ngogo	#5	2	O	Juv	?	2001
Ngogo	#6	1	O	A	M	2002
Ngogo	#8	2	O	A	M	2002
Ngogo	#9	3	O	A	M	2004
Ngogo	#13	2	O	A	M	2004
Ngogo	Nameless	3	O	A	F	2004
Ngogo	Nameless	1	O	A	M	2005
Ngogo	Nameless	1	O	A	M	2005
Ngogo	#17	2	O	A	M	2006
Ngogo	#18	1	O	A	M	2006
Ngogo	#21	1	O	A	F	2009
Ngogo	Errol	1	O	A	M	2018
Ngogo	Basie	1	O	A	M	2019
Ngogo	Nameless	4	O	A	M	2006
Ngogo	Nameless	4	O	A	M	2011
Ngogo	Of Kanyantale	5	O	A	M	1998
Ngogo	Nameless	5	O	A	M	2013–16
Ngogo	Nameless	5	O	A	M	2013–16
Ngogo	Nameless	5	O	A	M	2013–16
Ngogo	Nameless	5	O	A	M	2013–16
Ngogo	Nameless	5	O	A	M	2013–16
Ngogo	Nameless	5	O	A	M	2013–16
Ngogo	Nameless	5	O	A	M	2013–16
Ngogo	Orff	5	O	A	M	2017
Kanyanchu	Nameless	5	O	A	M	2010
Kanyanchu	Nameless	5	O	Juv	?	2014

Table 1. Continued

Location	Victim	Certainty of killing	Within/outside group	Age of victim	Sex of victim	Year
Kanyawara	Ruwenzori	3	O	A	M	1992
Kanyawara	Sebitole Stranger	2	O	A	M	1998
Kanyawara	Nameless	5	O	A	M	1988
Kanyawara	Julian	5	O	A	M	1994
Kanyawara	Badfoot	5	O	A	M	1998
Kanyawara	Light Brown	5	O	A	M	2001
Sonso	Zimba	3	O	A	F	2013
Sonso	Zimba's	1	O	As	M	2013
Sonso	Chris	5	O	A	M	1997
Sonso	Kikunku	5	O	A	M	1998
Sonso	Vernon	5	O	A	M	1999
Sonso	Muga	5	O	A	M	2000
Kalinzu	Nui	3	O	A	M	2003
Kalinzu	Nameless	4	O	A	M	2013
Conkouati-Douli	Dolise	3	O	Juv	M	1997
Conkouati-Douli	Hinda	1	O	As	M	1999
Conkouati-Douli	Mekouto	3*	O	As	M	1997–2002
Conkouati-Douli	David	4	O	As	M	1999
Conkouati-Douli	Bateko	4*	O	As	M	2002
Loango	Nameless	4	O	A	M	2005
Nikola Koba	Tina	3*	O	A	M	2005

(*continued*)

Table 1. Continued

Location	Victim	Certainty of killing	Within/outside group	Age of victim	Sex of victim	Year
Tai	Nerone	1	O	A	M	2005
Tai	of East Group	1	O	A	M	2007

*Recovered with medical attention.

Key

Column 1: Research community

Column 2: Name of victim

Column 3: Status of killing
 1 A certain killing
 2 A killing beyond reasonable doubt
 3 A very likely killing
  1, 2, and 3 unshaded. 1, 2, and 3 referred to in text as "likely killings"
 4 A possible killing
  Light shading. 1-4 referred to in text as "certain to possible killings"
 5 A hypothetical killing
  Dark shading

Column 4: Group of victim
 O Victim from outside the group
 W Victim from within the group
 ? Victim group unknown

Column 5: Age of victim
 A Adult
 As Adolescent
 Juv Juvenile
 I Infant
 ? Unknown

Column 6: Sex of victim
 F Female
 M Male
 ? Unknown

Column 7: Date of killing

Table 2. Intragroup Adult Killings

Location	Victim	Certainty of killing	Within/outside group	Age of victim	Sex of victim	Year
Gombe	Goblin	3*	W	A	M	1989
Gombe	Vincent	1	W	A	M	2004
Gombe	Ebony	3	W	Juv	M	2005
Gombe	Franzi	2	W	A	M	2017
Gombe	Old Huxley	4	W	A	M	1967
Gombe	Pooch	4	W	A	F	1968
Gombe	Mel	4	W	As	M	1994
Gombe	Frodo	4	W	A	M	2013
Gombe	Evered	4	W	A	M	1993
Gombe	Kris	4	W	A	M	2010
Gombe	Forrest	4	W	A	M	2012
Gombe	Apple	4	W	A	M	2015
Mahale	Ntologi	1	W	A	M	1996
Mahale	Pim	1	W	A	M	2011
Mahale	Jilba	4	W	A	M	1996
Ngogo	GRA	2	W	A	M	2002
Kanyawara	Nameless	2	W	A	F	2017?
Sonso	Zesta	1	W	A	M	1998
Kyambura	Nameless	2	W	A	M	2013
Conkouati-Douli	Makabana	1	W	Juv	F	2002

(*continued*)

Table 2. Continued

Location	Victim	Certainty of killing	Within/ outside group	Age of victim	Sex of victim	Year
Niokola Koba	One-eyed Sam	3	W	A	M	c. 1978
Fongoli	Foudouko	1	W	A	M	2008
Fongoli	Frito	4	W	As	M	2010
Lomako	Volker	4	W	A	M	1997

*Recovered with medical attention.

Key

Column 1: Research community

Column 2: Name of victim

Column 3: Status of killing
    1 A certain killing
    2 A killing beyond reasonable doubt
    3 A very likely killing
        1, 2, and 3 unshaded. 1, 2, and 3 referred to in text as "likely killings"
    4 A possible killing
        Light shading. 1-4 referred to in text as "certain to possible killings"
    5 A hypothetical killing
        Dark shading

Column 4: Group of victim
    O Victim from outside the group
    W Victim from within the group
    ? Victim group unknown

Column 5: Age of victim
    A Adult
    As Adolescent
    Juv Juvenile
    I Infant
    ? Unknown

Column 6: Sex of victim
    F Female
    M Male
    ? Unknown

Column 7: Date of killing

Table 3. Intergroup Infant Killings

Location	Victim	Certainty of killing	Within/ outside group	Age of victim	Sex of victim	Year
Gombe	Outside infant	1	O	I	?	1971
Gombe	Outside infant	1	O	I	F	1975
Gombe	Outside infant	2	O	I	M	1975
Gombe	Outside infant	1	O	I	?	1979
Gombe	Rejea	1	O	I	F	1993
Gombe	Kalande Infant	1	O	I	F	1998
Gombe	Andromeda	1	O	I	F	2006
Gombe	Hepziba's	5	O	I	F	1981
Gombe	Dapples'	5	O	I	M	1981
Gombe	Barbet's	5	O	I	F	1982
Gombe	Furaha	5	O	I	F	2004
Mahale	Shigeo	2	O	I	M	1974
Mahale	Wantendele's	2	O	I	M	1976
Mahale	Of Y Group	2	O	I	M	2000
Ngogo	#1	1	O	I	?	1999
Ngogo	#2	1	O	I	?	1999
Ngogo	#3	1	O	I	?	2000
Ngogo	#4	1	O	I	?	2000
Ngogo	#7	3	O	I	M	2002
Ngogo	#10	1	O	I	M	2004
Ngogo	#11	1	O	I	?	2004
Ngogo	#12	3	O	I	?	2004
Ngogo	#14	2	O	I	?	2005
Ngogo	#15	1	O	I	?	2005
Ngogo	#16	2	O	I	?	2006

(*continued*)

Table 3. Continued

Location	Victim	Certainty of killing	Within/outside group	Age of victim	Sex of victim	Year
Ngogo	#19	1	O	I	?	2007
Ngogo	#20	3	O	I	?	2007
Ngogo	Nameless	2	O	I	?	2011
Ngogo	Nameless	2	O	I	?	2011
Ngogo	Nameless	3	O	I	?	2004
Ngogo	Nameless	4	O	I	?	?
Sonso	Nameless	2	O	I	?	1997
Sonso	Nameless	3	O?	I	?	2004
Sonso	Nameless	2	O?	I	?	2006
Sonso	Nameless	4	O	I	F	2000
Sonso	Nameless	4	O	I	?	2006
Sonso	Nameless	4	O	I	?	2013
Sonso	Nameless	5	O	I	F	2000
Goualougo	Nameless	4	O	I	M	2005
Conkouati-Douli	Valentine	3	O	I	F	1999
Conkouati-Douli	Nameless	3	O	I	M	
Conkouati-Douli	Nameless	3	O	I	F	2002–2004
Conkouati-Douli	Nameless	3	O	I	F	2002–2004

Table 3. Continued

Location	Victim	Certainty of killing	Within/ outside group	Age of victim	Sex of victim	Year
Conkouati-Douli	Andreas	4	O	I	M	2002
Loango	Nameless	3	O	I	M	2006
Tai	Unhabituated	1	O	I	M	2002

Key

Column 1: Research community

Column 2: Name of victim

Column 3: Status of killing
  1 A certain killing
  2 A killing beyond reasonable doubt
  3 A very likely killing
    1, 2, and 3 unshaded. 1, 2, and 3 referred to in text as "likely killings"
  4 A possible killing
    Light shading. 1-4 referred to in text as "certain to possible killings"
  5 A hypothetical killing
    Dark shading

Column 4: Group of victim
  O Victim from outside the group
  W Victim from within the group
  ? Victim group unknown

Column 5: Age of victim
  A Adult
  As Adolescent
  Juv Juvenile
  I Infant
  ? Unknown

Column 6: Sex of victim
  F Female
  M Male
  ? Unknown

Column 7: Date of killing

Table 4. Intragoup Infant Killings

Chapter number	Name of victim	Certainty of killing	Within/ outside group	Age of victim	Sex of victim	Year
Gombe	Otta	1	W	I	F	1975
Gombe	Patti's	3	W	I	?	1975
Gombe	Orion	1	W	I	M	1976
Gombe	Genie	1	W	I	F	1976
Gombe	Melissa's	3	W	I	M	1976
Gombe	Banda	3	W	I	F	1976
Gombe	Little Bee's	3	W	I	?	1976
Gombe	Rafiki's	1	W	I	?	1994
Gombe	Tofiki	1	W	I	M	2004
Gombe	Kipara's	3	W	I	M	2004
Gombe	Eliza's	1	W	I	F	2012
Gombe	Tarima	1	W	I	F	2013
Gombe	Sophie's Baby	4	W	I	?	1966
Gombe	Kenitum's	4	W	I	M	1991
Gombe	Gandalf	5	W	I	M	1974
Gombe	Sprout	5	W	I	?	1984
Gombe	Schweini's	5	W	I	M	2007
Gombe	Imani's	5	W	I	?	2007
Mahale	Wantendele's	1	W	I	M	1983
Mahale	Tomato's	1	W	I	M	1985
Mahale	Mirinda	1	W	I	F	1989
Mahale	Betty's	1	W	I	M	1990
Mahale	Humbe	4	W	I	M	1977
Mahale	Wakasunga's	4	W	I	M	1979
Mahale	Wally	4	W	I	M	1981
Mahale	Chausika's	4	W	I	M	1983
Mahale	Gwamwami's	4	W	I	F	1987
Mahale	Garbo's	4	W	I	F	1992
Mahale	Nameless	4	W	I	M	1993
Mahale	Devota's	4	W	I	?	2014

Table 4. Continued

Chapter number	Name of victim	Certainty of killing	Within/outside group	Age of victim	Sex of victim	Year
Mahale	Wakasunga's	5	W	I	M	1981
Mahale	Juno's	5	W	I	M	1989
Mahale	Fanta's	5	W	I	M	1998
Mahale	Pinky	5	W	I	F	1998
Ngogo	Nameless	2	W	I	?	2005
Ngogo	Nameless	2	W	I	?	2009
Ngogo	Nameless	4	W	I	?	1999
Ngogo	Nameless	4	W	I	M	2010
Ngogo	Nameless	4	W	I	?	?
Ngogo	Nameless	4	W	I	?	?
Kanyanchu	Nameless	4	W	I	M	1999
Kanawara	Nameless	3	W	I	M	1996
Sonso	Nameless	3	W	I	?	2006
Sonso	Nameless	1	W	I	M	2009
Sonso	Oakland's	2	W	I	F	2012
Sonso	Janie's	2	W	I	F	2012
Sonso	Oakland's	1	W	I	M	2013
Sonso	Kalema's	2	W	I	M	2013
Sonso	Katia's	2	W	I	?	2015
Sonso	Coco's	1	W	I	F	2015
Sonso	Irene's	1	W	I	M	2016
Sonso	Mukwana's	1	W	I	?	2016
Sonso	Deli's	1	W	I	F	2017
Sonso	Upesi's	1	W	I	F	2017
Sonso	Ramula's	1	W	I	?	2017
Sonso	Unidentified	2	W	I	?	2018
Sonso	Unidentified	2	W	I	?	2018

(*continued*)

Table 4. Continued

Chapter number	Name of victim	Certainty of killing	Within/outside group	Age of victim	Sex of victim	Year
Sonso	Unidentified	4	W?	I	M	1999
Sonso	Kalema's	4	W	I	F	2013
Sonso	Kutu's	4	W	I	F	2013
Sonso	Kewaya's	4	W	I	F	2013
Sonso	Melissa's	4	W	I	F	2014
Sonso	Mukwano's	4	W	I	?	2017
Sonso	MON's	4	W	I	?	2017
Sonso	Rose's	5	W	I	F	2011
Sonso	Janie's	5	W	I	F	2014
Goualougo	Nameless	5	W	I	?	2006
Lomako	Nameless	4	W	I	F	n.d.

Key

Column 1: Research community

Column 2: Name of victim

Column 3: Status of killing
   1 A certain killing
   2 A killing beyond reasonable doubt
   3 A very likely killing
      1, 2, and 3 unshaded. 1, 2, and 3 referred to in text as "likely killings"
   4 A possible killing
      Light shading. 1-4 referred to in text as "certain to possible killings"
   5 A hypothetical killing
      Dark shading

Column 4: Group of victim
   O Victim from outside the group
   W Victim from within the group
   ? Victim group unknown

Column 5: Age of victim
   A Adult
   As Adolescent
   Juv Juvenile
   I Infant
   ? Unknown

Column 6: Sex of victim
   F Female
   M Male
   ? Unknown

Column 7: Date of killing

Table 5. Unknown Group Adult Killings

Location	Victim	Certainty of killing	Within/outside group	Age of victim	Sex of victim	Year
Gombe	Figan	5	?	A	M	1982
Gombe	Evered	5	?	A	M	1993
Loango		2	?	Juv	M	2018
Loango		4	?	A	M	2006
Loango		4	?	A	M	2008

Key

Column 1: Research community

Column 2: Name of victim

Column 3: Status of killing
  1 A certain killing
  2 A killing beyond reasonable doubt
  3 A very likely killing
    1, 2, and 3 unshaded. 1, 2, and 3 referred to in text as "likely killings"
  4 A possible killing
    Light shading. 1-4 referred to in text as "certain to possible killings"
  5 A hypothetical killing
    Dark shading

Column 4: Group of victim
  O Victim from outside the group
  W Victim from within the group
  ? Victim group unknown

Column 5: Age of victim
  A Adult
  As Adolescent
  Juv Juvenile
  I Infant
  ? Unknown

Column 6: Sex of victim
  F Female
  M Male
  ? Unknown

Column 7: Date of killing

Table 6. Unknown Group Infant Killings

Location	Victim	Certainty of killing	Within/outside group	Age of victim	Sex of victim	Year
Busingiro	Nameless	4	?	I	?	1967
Sonso	Nameless	2	?	I	?	1995
Sonso	Nameless	1	?	I	M	1995
Sonso	Nameless	2	?	I	?	1993
Sonso	Nameless	4	?	I	?	1991
Sonso	Nameless	5	?	I	?	1997
Loango	Nameless	2	?	I	?	2007
Loango		2	?	I	?	2018
Loango		2	?	I	?	2019
Loango		2	?	I	F	2019
Loango		4	?	I	?	2017

Key

Column 1: Research community

Column 2: Name of victim

Column 3: Status of killing
   1 A certain killing
   2 A killing beyond reasonable doubt
   3 A very likely killing
      1, 2, and 3 unshaded. 1, 2, and 3 referred to in text as "likely killings"
   4 A possible killing
      Light shading. 1-4 referred to in text as "certain to possible killings"
   5 A hypothetical killing
      Dark shading

Column 4: Group of victim
   O Victim from outside the group
   W Victim from within the group
   ? Victim group unknown

Column 5: Age of victim
   A Adult
   As Adolescent
   Juv Juvenile
   I Infant
   ? Unknown

Column 6: Sex of victim
   F Female
   M Male
   ? Unknown

Column 7: Date of killing

References

ABC/Discovery News. (1999). Deborah Amos reporting, Broadcast June 12, 1999. Tape in author's possession.

Abler, T. (1992). Beavers and muskets: Iroquois military fortunes in the face of European colonization. In Ferguson, R.B., & Whitehead, N.L. (Eds.), *War in the tribal zone: Expanding states and indigenous warfare* (pp. 151–174). Schools of American Research Press.

Abouheif, E., Fave, M.-J., Ibarraran Viniegra, A.S., Lesoway, M.P., Rafiqi, A.M., & Rajakumar, R. (2014). Eco-evo-devo: The time has come. In Landry, C.R., & Aubin-Horth, N. (Eds.), *Ecological genomics: Ecology and the evolution of genes and genomes* (pp. 107–125). Advances in Experimental Medicine and Biology 781. Springer.

Adams, H.R., Sleeman, J.M., Rwego, I., & New, J.C. (2001). Self-reported medical history survey of humans as a measure of health risk to the chimpanzees (*Pan troglodytes schweinfurthii*) of Kibale National Park, Uganda. *Oryx, 35*, 308–312.

Afghanistan Research Reachback Center White Paper. (2009). *My cousin's enemy is my friend: A study of Pashtun "tribes" in Afghanistan*. US Army: TRADOC G2 Human Terrain System. https://smallwarsjournal.com/documents/cousinsenemy.pdf. Accessed March 25, 2020.

African Wildlife Foundation. (2008). *A big win for conservation in DRC—Lomako Yokokala Faunal Reserve officially gazetted*. https://www.awf.org/news/big-win-conservation-drc-lomako-yokokale-faunal-reserve-officially-gazetted. Accessed March 2020.

Agapow, P.M., Bininda Emonds, O.R., Crandall, K.A., Gittleman, J.L., Mace, G.M., Marshall, J.C., & Purvis, A. (2004). The impact of species concept on biodiversity studies. *Quarterly Review of Biology, 79*(2), 161–179.

Albrecht, H., & Coghill Dunnett, S. (1971). *Chimpanzees in western Africa*. R. Piper and Company Verlag.

Amati, S., Babweteera, F., & Wittig, R.M. (2008). *Snare removal by a chimpanzee of the Sonso community*. Budongo Conservation Field Station (BCFS). http://mahale.web.infoseek.co.jp/PAN/15_1/15(1)_03.html. Accessed May 21, 2014.

Amsler, S.J. (2009). *Ranging behavior and territoriality in chimpanzees at Ngogo, Kibale National Park, Uganda*. PhD dissertation, University of Michigan, Ann Arbor.

Amsler, S.J. (2010). Energetic costs of territorial boundary patrols by wild chimpanzees. *American Journal of Primatology, 72*, 93–103.

Anderson, D.P., Nordheim, E.K., Boesch, C., & Mormond, T.C. (2002). Factors influencing fission-fusion groping in chimpanzees in the Tai National Park, Cote d'Ivoire. In Boesch, C., Hohmann, G., & Marchant, L.F. (Eds.), *Behavioural diversity in chimpanzees and bonobos* (pp. 90–101). Cambridge University Press.

Anderson, J.A., Johnston, R.A., Lea, A.J., Campos, F.A., Voyles, T.N., Akinyi, M.Y., Alberts, S.C., Archie, E.A., & Tung, J. (2021). High social status males experience accelerated epigenetic aging in wild baboons. *eLife, 10*, e66128.

Anestis, S.F. (2004). Female genito-genital rubbing in a group of captive chimpanzees. *International Journal of Primatology, 25*, 477–488.

Animal Planet. (2017). *Rise of the warrior apes*. Discovery.

Anonymous. (1996). A human infant killed by a wild chimpanzee. *Pan Africa News, 3*(1), May. Unpaginated. http://mahale.main.jp/PAN/index.html. Accessed May 4, 2020.

Anonymous. (2019). Name withheld e-mail to author, September 9, 2019.

Arandjelovic, M., Head, J., Rabanal, L.I., Schuert, G., Mettke, E., Boesch, C., Robbins, M.M., & Vigilant, L. (2011). Non-invasive genetic monitoring of wild central chimpanzees. *PLoS One, 6(3)*, 1–11, e14761.

Arcadi, A.C. (2018). *Wild chimpanzees: Social behavior of an endangered species*. Cambridge University Press.

Arcadi, A.C., & Wrangham, R.W. (1999). Infanticide in chimpanzees: Review of cases and a new within group observation from the Kanywara Study Group in Kibale National Park. *Primates, 40*, 337–351.

Archer, J. (1991). The influence of testosterone on human aggression. *British Journal of Psychology, 82*(1), 1–28.

Ardrey, R. (1961). *African genesis*. Dell.

Ardrey, R. (1968). *The territorial imperative*. Atheneum.

Arkush, E.N., & Allen, M.W. (Eds.). (2006). *The archaeology of warfare: Prehistories of raiding and conquest*. University of Florida Press.

Asiimwe, C. (2019). Sonso and Waibira chimpanzees suffer a respiratory infection outbreak. *Budongo Conservation Field Station*, April 29. http://www.budongo.org/news/sonso-and-waibira-chimpanzees-suffer-a-respitatoy-infection-outbreak. Accessed April 8, 2020.

Aureli, F. (2010). Unsolicited e-mail to the author, October 23, 2010.

Aureli, F., & de Waal, F. (Eds.). (2000). *Natural conflict resolution*. University of California.

Aureli, F., Schaffner, C.M., Boesch, C., Bearder, S.K., Call, J., Chapman, C.A., Conner, R., Di Fiore, A., Dunbar, R.I.M., Henzie, S.P., Holekamp, K., Korstjens, A.H., Layton, A.H., Lee, R., Lehmann, J., Ramos-Fernandez, G., Strier, K.B., & van Schaik, C.P. (2008). Fission-fusion dynamics. *Current Anthropology, 49*, 627–654.

Babweteera, F., Plumptre, A., & Obua, J. (2000). Effect of gap size and age on climber abundance and diversity in Budongo Forest Reserve, Uganda. *African Journal of Ecology, 38*, 230–237.

Babweteera, F., Reynolds, V., & Zuberbühler, K. (2008). Conservation and research in the Budongo Forest Reserve, Masindi District, Western Uganda. In Wrangham, R., & Ross, E. (Eds.), *Science and conservation in African forests: The benefits of long-term research* (pp. 145–157). Cambridge University Press.

Babweteera, F., Sheil, D., Reynolds, V., Plumptre, K., Zuberbuhler, K., Hill, C.M., Webber, A., & Tweheyo, M. (2011). Environmental and anthropogenic changes in and around Budongo Forest Reserve. In Plumptre, A.J. (Ed.), *The ecological impact of long-term changes in Africa's Rift Valley* (pp. 31–53). Nova Science Publishing.

Badrian, A., & Badrian, N. (1977). Pygmy chimpanzees. *Oryx, 13*, 463–468.

Badrian, A., & Badrian, N. (1984). Social organization of *Pan paniscus* in the Lomako Forest, Zaire. In Sussman, R.L. (Ed.), *The pygmy chimpanzee* (pp. 325–346). Springer.

Badrian, N., & Malenky, R.K. (1984). Feeding ecology of *Pan paniscus* in the Lomako Forest, Zaire. In Sussman, R.L. (Ed.), *The pygmy chimpanzee* (pp. 275–299). Springer.

Bahram, R., Burke, J.E., & Lanzi, G.L. (2004). Head and neck injury from a leopard attack: Case report and review of the literature. *Journal of Oral and Maxillofacial Surgery*, 62, 247–249.

Bailey, T.N. (1993). *The African leopard: Ecology and behavior of a solitary felid*. Columbia University Press.

Baldwin, P.J., McGrew, W.C., & Tutin, C.F.G. (1982). Wide-ranging chimpanzees at Mt. Assirik, Senegal. *International Journal of Primatology*, 3, 367–385.

Balee, W. (1984). The ecology of ancient Tupi warfare. In Ferguson, R.B. (Ed.), *Warfare, culture and environment* (pp. 241–265). Academic Press.

Barnard, A. (1983). Contemporary hunter-gatherers: Current theoretical issues in ecology and social organization. *Annual Review of Anthropology*, 12, 193–214.

Bartlett, T.Q., Sussman, R.W., & Cheverud, J.M. (1993). Infant killing in primates: A review of observed cases with specific reference to the sexual selection hypothesis. *American Anthropologist*, 95(4), 958–990.

Basabose, A.K. (2004). Fruit availability and chimpanzee party size at Kahuzi montane forest, Democratic Republic of Congo. *Primates*, 45, 211–219.

Basabose, A.K. (2005). Ranging patterns of chimpanzees in a montane forest of Kahuzi, Democratic Republic of Congo. *International Journal of Primatology*, 26, 32–46.

Basabose, A.K., Inoue, E., Kamungu, S., Murhabale, B., Akomo-Okoue, E.F., & Yamagiwa, J. (2015). Estimation of chimpanzee community size and genetic diversity in Kahuzi Biega National Park, Democratic Republic of Congo. *American Journal of Primatology*, 9, 1015–1025.

Bates, L.A., & Byrnes, R.W. (2009). Sex differences in the movement patterns of free-ranging chimpanzees (*Pan troglodytes schweinfurthii*): Foraging and border checking. *Behavioral Ecology and Sociobiology*, 64, 247–255.

Bauer, H.R. (1980). Chimpanzee society and social dominance in evolutionary perspective. In Omark, D.R., Strayer, F.F., & Freedman, D.G. (Eds.), *Dominance relations: An ethological view of human conflict and social interaction* (pp. 97–119). Garland STPM Press.

Baumard, N. (2013). A mutualistic approach to morality: The evolution of fairness by partner choice. *Behavioral and Brain Sciences*, 36, 59–78.

BBC. (2004). The demonic ape. *Science and Nature* [TV and radio]. https://www.bbc.co.uk/science/horizon/2004/demonicapetrans.shtm. Accessed March 3, 2020.

Beck, J., & Chapman, H. (2008). A population estimate of the endangered chimpanzee *Pan troglodytes vellerosus* in a Nigerian montane forest: Implications for conservation. *Oryx*, 42, 448–451.

Beehner, J.C., & Bergman, T.J. (2017). The next step for stress research in primates: To identify relationships between glucocorticoid secretion and fitness. *Hormones and Behavior*, 91, 68–93.

Berkhoudt, K. (n.d.). Behind the rhetorics: "Community conservation" around Kibale National Park, Uganda. *AfrikaStudies.nl*. http://afrikastudies.nl/downloads-newsletters/nl1109/pdf/Karin_Berkhoudt.pdf. Accessed June 10, 2014.

Bila-Isia, I., Nzala, A.B., & Bokika, J.C. (2013). People and bonobos in the southern Lake Tumba Landscape, Democratic Republic of Congo. *American Journal of Human Ecology*, 2(2), 44–53.

Bishop, N., Bishop, N., Hrdy, S.B., Teas, J., & Moore, J. (1981). Measures of human influence in habitats of South Asian monkeys. *International Journal of Primatology, 2*(2), 153–167.

Bjork, A., Liu, W., Wertheim, J.O., Hahn, B.H., & Worobey, M. (2010). Evolutionary history of chimpanzees inferred from complete mitochondrial genomes. *Molecular Biology and Evolution, 28*, 615–623.

Blasse, A., Calvignac-Spencer, S., Merkel, K., Goffe, A.S., Boesch, C., Mundry, R., & Leendertz, F.H. (2013). Mother-offspring transmission and age-dependent accumulation of Simian Foamy Virus in wild chimpanzees. *Journal of Virology, 87*, 5193–5204.

Blount, B.G. (1990). Issues in bonobo (*Pan paniscus*) sexual behavior. *American Anthropologist, 93*, 702–714.

Bludau, A., Royer, M., Meister, G., Neumann, I.D., & Menon, R. (2019). Epigenetic regulation of the social brain. *Trends in Neurosciences, 42*, 471–484.

Blumberg, M.S. (2005). *Basic instinct: The genesis of behavior*. Thunder's Mouth Press.

Blundell, V. (1980). Hunter-gatherer territoriality: Ideology and behavior in Northwest Australia. *Ethnohistory, 27*, 103–117.

Boas, F. (1912). *An anthropologist's view of war*. Carnegie Endowment for International Peace, International Conciliation Pamphlet, no. 52.

Boehm, C. (1997). Egalitarian behavior and the evolution of political intelligence. In Byrne, D., & Whiten, A. (Eds.), *Machiavellian intelligence* (Vol. 2, pp. 341–364). Cambridge University Press.

Boehm, C. (1999). *Hierarchy in the forest: The evolution of egalitarian behavior*. Harvard University Press.

Boehm, C. (2000). Conflict and the evolution of social control. *Journal of Consciousness Studies, 7*, 79–101.

Boehm, C. (2012). *Moral origins: The evolution of virtue, altruism, and shame*. Basic Books.

Boehm, C. (2018a). Collective intentionality: A basic and early component of moral evolution. *Philosophical Pyschology, 31*, 680–702.

Boehm, C. (2018b). Ancestral precursors, social control, and social selection in the evolution of morals. In Boehm, C. (Ed.), *Chimpanzees and human evolution* (pp. 746–790). Harvard University Press.

Boesch, C. (1991a). The effects of leopard predation on grouping patterns in forest chimpanzees. *Behaviour, 117*, 220–241.

Boesch, C. (1991b). Symbolic communication in wild chimpanzees. *Human Evolution, 6*, 81–90.

Boesch, C. (1994). Chimpanzees-red colobus monkeys: A predator-prey system. *Animal Behavior, 47*, 1135–1148.

Boesch, C. (1996). Social groupings in Tai chimpanzees. In McGrew, W.C., Marchant, L.F., & Nishida, T. (Eds.), *Great ape societies* (pp. 101–113). Cambridge University Press.

Boesch, C. (2008). Why do chimpanzees die in the forest? The challenges of understanding and controlling for wild ape health. *American Journal of Primatology, 70*, 722–726.

Boesch, C. (2009). *The real chimpanzee: Sex strategies in the forest*. Cambridge University Press.

Boesch, C. (2010). Patterns of chimpanzee's intergroup violence. In Hogh-Olesen, H. (Ed.), *Human morality and sociality: Evolutionary and comparative perspectives* (pp. 132–159). Palgrave Macmillan.

Boesch, C. (2011). Our cousins in the forest—or bushmeat? In Robbins, M.M., & Boesch, C. (Eds.), *Among African apes: Stories and photos from the field* (pp. 77–87). University of California Press.
Boesch, C. (2012). *Wild cultures: A comparison between chimpanzee and human cultures.* Cambridge University Press.
Boesch, C. (2019). War and peace in the Tai chimpanzee forest: Running a long-term chimpanzee research project. In Boesch, C., Wittig, R., Crockford, C., Vigilant, L., Deschner, T., & Leendertz, F. (Eds.), *The chimpanzees of the Tai Forest: 40 years of research* (pp. 1–27). Cambridge University Press.
Boesch, C., & Boesch, H. (1989). Hunting behavior of wild chimpanzees in the Tai National Park. *American Journal of Physical Anthropology, 78*, 547–573.
Boesch, C., Boesch, H., Bi, Z.B.G., Normand, E., & Herbinger, I. (2008a). The contribution of long-term research by the Tai Chimpanzee Project to conservation. In Wrangham, R.W., & Ross, E. (Eds.), *Science and conservation in African forests: The benefits of long-term research* (pp. 184–200). Cambridge University Press.
Boesch, C., & Boesch-Achermann, H. (1995). Epidemics and wild chimpanzee study groups: Tai chimpanzees confronted with a fatal Ebola virus. *Pan Africa News, 2*(2), unpaginated. http://mahale.main.jp/PAN/index.html. Accessed May 4, 2020.
Boesch, C., & Boesch-Achermann, H. (2000). *The chimpanzees of the Tai Forest: Behavioural ecology and evolution.* Oxford University Press.
Boesch, C., Bole, C., Eckhardt, N., & Boesch, H. (2010). Altruism in forest chimpanzees: The case of adoption. *PLoS One*, 5. http://www.plosone.org/article/info%3Adoi%2F10.1371%2Fjournal.pone.0008901. Accessed June 23, 2014.
Boesch, C., Crockford, C., Herbinger, I., Wittig, R., Moebius, Y., & Normand, E. (2008b). Intergroup conflicts among chimpanzees in Tai National Park: Lethal violence and the female perspective. *American Journal of Primatology, 70*, 519–532.
Boesch, C., Gnakouri, C., Marques, L. Nohon, G., Herbinger, I., Lauginie, F., Boesch, H., Kouame, S., Traore, M., & Akindes, F. (2008c). Chimpanzee conservation and theater: A case study of an awareness project around the Tai National Park, Cote d'Ivoire. In Stoinski, T.S., Steklis, H., & Mehlman, P.T. (Eds.), *Conservation in the 21st century: Gorillas as a case study* (pp. 128–135). Springer.
Boesch, C., Head, J., Tagg, N., Arandjelovic, M., Vigilant, L., & Robbins, M.M. (2007). Fatal chimpanzee attack in Loango National Park, Gabon. *International Journal of Primatology, 28*, 1025–1034.
Boesch, C., Kohou, G., Nene, H., & Vigilant, L. (2006). Male competition and paternity in wild chimpanzees of the Tai Forest. *American Journal of Physical Anthropology, 130*, 103–115.
Boesch, C., & O'Connell, S. (2012). *Chimpanzee: The making of the film.* Disney Editions.
Boesch-Acherman, H., & Boesch, C. (1994). The Tai chimpanzee project in Cote d'Ivoire, West Africa. https://www.researchgate.net/publication/277037385_The_Tai_Chimpanzee_Project_in_Cote_d%27Ivoire_West_Africa. Accessed April 4, 2020.
Bogart, S.L., & Pruetz, J.D. (2010). Insectivory of savanna chimpanzees (*Pan troglodytes verus*) at Fongoli, Senegal. *American Journal of Physical Anthropology, 145*, 11–20.
Bonnell, T.R., Reyna-Hurtado, R., & Chapman, C.A. (2011). Post-logging recovery time is longer than expected in an East African tropical forest. *Forest Ecology and Management, 261*, 855–864.

Book, A.B., Starzyk, K.B., & Quinsey, V.L. (2001). The relationship between testosterone and aggression: A meta-analysis. *Aggression and Violent Behavior, 6*, 579–599.

Booker Tate. (n.d.). Kinyara Sugar Works Limited. http://www.booker-tate.co.uk/media/4306/uganda_-_kinyara_-_february_2013.pdf. Accessed May 8, 2014.

Bortolamiol, S., Cohen, M., Potts, K., Pennec, F., Rwaburindore, P., Kasenene, J., Seguya, A., Vignaud, Q., & Krief, S. (2014). Suitable habitats for endangered frugivorous mammals: Small-scale comparison, regeneration forest and chimpanzee density in Kibale National Park, Uganda. *PLoS One, 9*(7), 1–12.

Bortolamiol, S., Cohen, M., Jiguet, F., Pennec, F., Seguya, A., & Krief, S. (2016). Chimpanzee non-avoidance of hyper-proximity to humans. *Journal of Wildlife Management, 80*(5), 924–934.

Bower, B. (2010). Female chimps play with "dolls." *US News and World Reports Science News.* http://www.usnews.com/science/articles/2010/12/20/female-chimps-play-with-dolls. Accessed May 27, 2020.

Boyer Ontl, K.M. (2017). *Chimpanzees in the island of gold: Impacts of artisanial small-scale gold mining chimpanzees (Pan troblodytes verus) in Fongoli, Senegal.* Doctoral dissertation, Iowa State University, Department of Anthropology.

Bradshaw, G.A. (2009). *Elephants on the edge: What animals teach us about humanity.* Yale University Press.

Bradshaw, G.A., Capaldo, T., Lindner, L., & Grow, G. (2008). Building an inner sanctuary: Complex PTSD in chimpanzees. *Journal of Trauma and Dissociation, 9*, 9–34.

Bradshaw, G.A., Capaldo, T., Lindner, L., & Grow, G. (2009). Developmental context effects on bicultural posttrauma self repair in chimpanzees. *Developmental Psychology, 45*, 1376–1388.

Bradshaw, G.A., Schore, A.N., Brown, J.L., Poole, J.H., & Moss, C.J. (2005). Elephant breakdown. *Nature, 433*, 807.

Brain, C.K. (1981). *The hunters or the hunted? An introduction to African cave taphonomy.* University of Chicago Press.

Brand, C.M., White, F.J., Wakefield, M.L., Waller, M.T., Ruiz-López, M.J., & Ting, N. (2016). Initiation of genetic demographic monitoring of bonobos (*Pan paniscus*) at Iyema, Lomako Forest, DRC. *Primate Conservation, 30*, 103–111.

Bray, J., & Gilby, I.C. (2020). Social relationships among adult male chimpanzees (*Pan troglodytes schweinfurthii*): Variation in the strength and quality of social bonds. *Behavioral Ecology and Sociobiology ,74*, 1–19. https://doi.org/10.1007/s00265-020-02892-3.

Bray, J., Pusey, A.E., & Gilby, I.C. (2016). Incomplete control and concessions explain mating skew in male chimpanzees. *Proceedings of the Royal Society B, 283*(1842), 20162071.

Brewer, S. (1978). *The chimps of Mt. Asserik.* Alfred A. Knopf.

Brewer Marsden, S., & McGrew, W.C. (1990). Chimpanzee use of a tool-set to get honey. *Folia Primatologica, 54*, 100–104.

Brewer Marsden, S., Marsden, D., & Emery Thompson, M. (2006). Demographic and life history parameters of free-changing chimpanzees at the Chimpanzee Rehabilitation Project, River Gambia National Park. *International Journal of Primatology, 27*, 391–410.

Brody, J.E. (1996). Gombe chimps archived on video and CD-ROM. *New York Times*, February 20, C1, C8.

Brüne, M., Brüne-Cohrs, U., McGrew, W., & Preuschoft, S. (2006). Psychopathology in great apes: Concepts, treatment options and possible homologies to human psychiatric disorders. *Neuroscience and Biobehavioral Reviews, 30*, 1246–1259.

Budongo Conservation Field Station. (n.d.). Overview. http://www.budongo.org/conservation-research/overview/. Accessed April 8, 2020.

Budongo's weblogongo: Blogging in the jungle. http://budongo.wordpress.com. Accessed May 26, 2020.

Buirksi, B., & Plutchik, R. (1991). Measurement of deviant behavior in a Gombe chimpanzee: Relation to later behavior. *Primates, 32*, 207–211.

Bullinger, A., Burkart, J., Melis, A., & Tomasello, M. (2013). Bonobos, *Pan paniscus*, chimpanzees, *Pan troglodytes*, and marmosets, *Callithrix jacchus*, prefer to feed alone. *Animal Behaviour, 85*, 51–60.

Burggren, W.W. (2014). Epigenetics as a source of variation in comparative animal physiology–or–Lamarck is lookin' pretty good these days. *Journal of Experimental Biology, 217*(5), 682–689.

Burt, W.H. (1943). Territoriality and home range concepts as applied to mammals. *Journal of Mammalogy, 24*, 346–352.

Bush, E.R., Whytock, R.C., . . . Abernethy, K. (2020). Long-term collapse in fruit availability threatens Central African forest megafauna. *Science, 370*, 1219–1222.

Busse, C. (1978). Do chimpanzees hunt cooperatively? *American Naturalist, 112*, 767–770.

Busse, C. (1980). Leopard and lion predation upon chacma baboons living in the Moremi Wildlife Reserve. *Botswana Notes and Records, 12*, 15–20.

Butynski, T.M. (2003). The robust chimpanzee *Pan troglodytes*: Taxonomy, distribution, abundance, and conservation status. In Kormos, R., Boesch, C., Bakarr, M.I., & Butynski, T. (Eds.), *West African chimpanzees: Status survey and conservation action plan* (pp. 5–12). IUCN/SSC Primate Specialist Group, IUCN, Gland, Switzerland.

Bygott, J.D. (1974). *Agonistic behavior and dominance in wild chimpanzees*. PhD dissertation, Cambridge University.

Bygott, J.D. (1979). Agonistic behavior, dominance, and social structure in wild chimpanzees of the Gombe National Park. In Hamburg, D.A., & McCown, E. (Eds.), *The great apes* (pp. 405–427). Benjamin/Cummings Publishing.

Bygott, J.D. (1992). *Gombe Stream National Park*. Tanzania National Parks/African Wildlife Foundation.

Cain, C.E., Blekhman, R., Marioni, J.C., & Gilad, Y. (2011). Gene expression differences among primates are associated with changes in a histone epigenetic modification. *Genetics, 187*, 1225–1234.

Call, J. (2019). Bonobos, chimpanzees and tools: Integrating species-specific psychological biases and socio-ecology. In Boesch, C., Wittig, R., Crockford, C., Vigilant, L., Deschner, T., & Leendertz, F. (Eds.), *The chimpanzees of the Tai Forest: 40 years of research* (pp. 171–180). Cambridge University Press.

Campbell, C.J., Fuentes, A., MacKinnon, K.C., & Panger, M. (2007). Where we have been, where we are, and where we are going: The future of primatological research. In Campbell, C.J., Fuentes, A., MacKinnon, K.C., Panger, M., & Bearder, S.K. (Eds.), *Primates in perspective* (pp. 702–706). Oxford University Press.

Campbell, G., Kuehl, H., Kouame, P.N., & Boesch, C. (2008). Alarming decline of West African chimpanzees in Cote d'Ivoire. *Current Biology, 18*, PR903–PR904.

Carneiro, R. (1998). What happened at the flashpoint? Conjectures on chiefdom formation at the very moment of conception. In Redmond, E. (Ed.), *Chiefdoms and chieftaincy in the Americas* (pp. 18–42). University of Florida Press.

Carvalho, J.S., Graham, B., . . . Kuhl, H.S. (2021). Predicting range shifts of African apes under global change scenarios. *Diversity and Distributions, 27,* 1663–1679.

Casanova, C., Mondragon-Ceballos, R., & Lee, P.C. (2007). Innovative social behavior in chimpanzees (*Pan troglodytes*). *American Journal of Primatology, 70,* 54–61.

Cashdan, E. (1983). Territoriality among human foragers: Ecological models and an application to four Bushman groups. *Current Anthropology, 24,* 47–66.

Caspi, A., McClay, J., Moffitt, T.E., Mill J., Martin, J., Craig, I.W., Taylor, A., & Poulton, R. (2002). Role of genotype in the cycle of violence in maltreated children. *Science, 297,* 851–854.

Caswell, J.L., Malick, S., . . . Reich, D. (2008). Analysis of chimpanzee history based on genome sequence alignments. *PLoS Genetics, 4,* e1000057.

CBS. (2010). What drives a chimp to murder? *CBS News.* http://www.cbsnews.com/stories/2010/06/21/tech/main6605085.shtml. Accessed June 10, 2014.

Cech, T.R., & Steitz, J.A. (2014). The noncoding RNA revolution—Trashing old rules to forge new ones. *Cell, 157,* 77–94.

Chagnon, N. (1968). *Yanomamo: The fierce people.* Holt, Rinehart, Winston.

Chagnon, N. (1988). Life histories, blood revenge, and warfare in a tribal population. *Science, 239,* 985–992.

Chagnon, N., & Irons, W. (Eds.). (1979). *Evolutionary biology and human social behavior: An anthropological perspective.* Duxbury.

Chapais, B. (1991). Primate and the origins of aggression, power, and politics among humans. In Loy, J.D., & Peters, C.B. (Eds.), *Understanding behavior: What primate studies tell us about human behavior* (pp. 190–228). Oxford University Press.

Chapman, C.A., Chapman, L.J., Ghai, R., Hartter, J., Jacob, A.L., Lwanga, J.S., Omeja, P., Rothman, J.M., & Twinomugisha, D. (2011). Complex responses to climate and anthropogenic changes: An evaluation based on long-term data from Kibale National Park, Uganda. In Plumptre, A.J. (Ed.), *The ecological impact of long term changes in Africa's Rift Valley* (pp. 73–94). Nova Science.

Chapman, C.A., Chapman, L.J., Struhsaker, T.T., Zanne, A.E., Clark, C.J., & Poulsen, J.R. (2005). A long term evaluation of fruiting technology: Importance of climate change. *Journal of Tropical Ecology, 21,* 31–45.

Chapman, C.A., & Lambert, J.E. (2000). Habitat alteration and the conservation of African primates: Case study of Kibale National Park, Uganda. *American Journal of Primatology, 50,* 169–185.

Chapman, C.A., White, F.J., & Wrangham, R.W. (1994). Party size in chimpanzees and bonobos. In Wrangham, R.W., McGrew, W.C., de Waal, F.B.M., & Heltne, P. (Eds.), *Chimpanzee cultures* (pp. 41–58). Harvard University Press.

Chapman, C.A., & Wrangham, R.W. (1993). Range use of the forest chimpanzees of Kibale: Implications for the understanding of chimpanzee social organization. *American Journal of Primatology, 31,* 263–273.

Chen, F.-C., Vallener, E.J., Wang, H., Tzeng, C.-S., & Li, W.-H. (2001). Divergence between human and chimpanzee estimated from large-scale alignments of genomic sequences. *Journal of Heredity, 92,* 481–489.

Cheney, D.L. (1986). Interactions and relationships between groups. In Smuts, B.B., Cheney, D.L., Seyfarth, R.M., Wrangham, R.W., & Struhsaker, T.T. (Eds.), *Primate societies* (pp. 267–281). University of Chicago Press.

Chesterman, N.S., Angedakin, S., Mbabazi, G., Tibisimwa, J., & Sandel, A.A. (2019). Evidence and ecology of historic human settlements in Kibale National Park, Uganda. *Human Ecology, 47*, 765–775.

Chitayat, A.B., Wich, S.A., Lewise, M., Stewart, F.A., & Piel, A.K. (2021). Ecological correlates of chimpanzee (*Pan troglodytes schweinfurthii*) density in Mahale Mountains National Park, Tanzania. *PLoS One, 16*(2), e0246628.

Christie, T., Juhn, D., & Peal, A. (2007). Fragmentation and clearance of Liberia's forests during 1986–2000. *Oryx, 41*, 539–543.

Cibot, M., Bortolamiol, S., Seguya, A., & Krief, S. (2015). Chimpanzees facing a dangerous situation: A high traffic asphalted road in the Sebitoli area of Kibale National Park, Uganda. *American Journal of Primatology, 77*, 890–900.

Clay, Z., & de Waal, F.B. (2013a). Bonobos respond to distress in others: Consolation across the age spectrum. *PLoS One, 8*, p.e55206.

Clay, Z., & de Waal, F.B. (2013b). Development of socio-emotional competence in bonobos. *Proceedings of the National Academy of Sciences, 110*(45), 18121–18126.

Clay, Z., Furuichi, T., & de Waal, F.B. (2016). Obstacles and catalysts to peaceful coexistence in chimpanzees and bonobos. *Behavior, 153*, 1293–1239.

Clutton-Brock, T. (2009). Cooperation between non-kin in animal societies. *Nature, 462*, 51–57.

Collins, A. (2003). Health guidelines for visiting researcher in Gombe National Park to minimize risk of disease transmission among primates (Updated 9/01/03). *Pan Africa News, 10*(1), unpaginated. http://mahale.main.jp/PAN/index.html. Accessed May 4, 2020.

Collins, A., & Goodall, J. (2008). Long term research and conservation in Gombe National Park, Tanzania. In Wrangham, R., & Ross, E. (Eds.), *Science and conservation in African forests: The benefits of long-term research* (pp. 158–172). Cambridge University Press.

Colyn, M., Gautier-Hion, A., & Verheyen, W. (1991). A re-appraisal of palaeoenvironmental history in Central Africa: Evidence for a major fluvial refuge in the Zaire Basin. *Journal of Biogeography, 18*, 403–407.

Conklin-Brittain, N.L., Wrangham, R.W., & Hunt, K.D. (1998). Dietary response of chimpanzees and cercopithecines to seasonal variation in fruit abundance. II. Macronutrients. *International Journal of Primatology, 19*, 971–998.

Conniff, R. (2003). Rethinking primate aggression. *Smithsonian Magazine.* https://www.smithsonianmag.com/science-nature/rethinking-primate-aggression-86813532/. Accessed June 6, 2021.

Constable, J.L., Mary, V.A., Goodall, J., & Pusey, A.E. (2001). Noninvasive paternity assignment in Gombe chimpanzees. *Molecular Ecology, 10*, 1279–1300.

Coolidge, H.J. (1933). *Pan paniscus*: Pigmy chimpanzee from south of the Congo River. *American Journal of Physical Anthropology, 18*, 1–59.

Corredor-Ospoina, N., Kreyer, M., Rossi, G., Hohmann, G., & Fruth, B. (2021). First report of a leopard (*Panthera pardus*)–bonobo (*Pan paniscus*) encounter at the LuiKotale study site, Democratic Republic of the Congo. *Primates.* https://doi.org/10.1007/s10 329-021-00897-8

Coscolla, M., Lewin, A., Metzger, S., Maetz-Rennsing, K., Calvignac-Spencer, S., Nitsche, A., Dabrowski, P.W., Radonic, A., Niemann, S., Parkhill, J., Couacy-Hymann, E., Feldman, J., Comas, I., Boesch, C., Gagneux, S., & Leendertz, F.H. (2013). Novel mycobacterium tuberculosis complex isolate from a wild chimpanzee. *Emerging Infectious Diseases, 19*, 969–976.

Cox, D., Panta K., & Appell, P. (n.d.). Budongo ecotourism. *Budongo Ecotourism Project/ the Jane Goodall Institute*. http://www.janegoodall.org/programs/budongo-ecotourism-project-0. Accessed May 9, 2014.

Crevecoeur, I., Dias-Meirinho, M.-H., Zazzo, A., Antoine, D., & Bon, F. (2021). New insights on interpersonal violence in the Late Pleistocene based on the Nile valley cemetery of Jebel Sahaba. *Nature: Scientific Reports, 11*, 1–13. https://doi.org/10.1038/s41598-021-89386-y

Crews, D., Gillette, R., Miller-Crews, I., Gore, A.C., & Skinner, M.K. (2014). Nature, nurture and epigenetics. *Molecular and Cellular Endocrinology, 398*, 42–52.

Crockford, C., Herbinger, I., Vigilant, L., & Boesch, C. (2004). Wild chimpanzees produce group-specific calls: A case for vocal learning? *Ethology, 110*, 221–243.

Crofoot, M.C., & Wrangham, R.W. (2010). Intergroup aggression in primates and humans: The case for a unified theory. In Kappeler, P.M., & Silk, J.B. (Eds.), *Mind the gap* (pp. 171–195). Springer Press.

Cronin, K.A., De Groot, E., & Stevens, J.M. (2015). Bonobos show limited social tolerance in a group setting: A comparison with chimpanzees and a test of the relational model. *Folia Primatologica, 86*, 164–177.

Cronk, L., & Leech, B.L. (2013). *Meeting at Grand Central: Understanding the social and evolutionary roots of cooperation* (pp. 18–46). Princeton University Press.

Curtin, R., & Dolhinow, P. (1978). Primate social behavior in a changing world. *American Scientist, 66*, 468–475.

Dagg, A.I. (1999). Sexual selection is debatable. *Anthropology News*, December, 20.

Dahl, J.F. (1985). The external genitalia of female pygmy chimpanzees. *Anatomical Record, 211*, 24–28.

Dahl, J.F. (1986). Cyclic perineal swelling during the intermenstrual intervals of captive female pygmy chimpanzees (*Pan paniscus*). *Journal of Human Evolution, 15*, 369–385.

D'Amour, D.E., Hohmann, G., & Fruth, B. (2006). Evidence of leopard predation on bonobos (*Pan paniscus*). *Folia Primatologica, 77*, 212–217.

Danchin, E., Charmantier, A., Champagne, F.A., Mesoudi, A., Pujol, B., & Blanchet, S. (2011). Beyond DNA: Integrating inclusive inheritance into an extended theory of evolution. *Nature Reviews Genetics, 12*, 475–486.

Danchin, E., Pocheville, A., & Huneman, P. (2019). Early in life effects and heredity: Reconciling neo-Darwinism with neo-Lamarckism under the banner of the include evolutionary synthesis. *Philosophical Transaction of the Royal Society B, 374*, 20180113, 1–13.

Darmangeat, C. (2019). Vanished wars of Australia: the archaeological invisibility of aboriginal collective conflicts. *Journal of Archaeological Method and Theory, 26*, 1556–1590.

Dart, R. (1959). *Adventures with the missing link*. Harper and Brothers.

Darwin Initiative. (2016). *Alternative sustainable livelihood sources for forest-edge hunting communities*. LTS International Ltd. https://www.darwininitiative.org.uk/assets/uploads/2016/09/Uganda-MTR-Final-Report.pdf. Accessed March 9, 2020.

Dean, L.G., Vale, G.L., Laland, K.N., Flynn, E., & Kendal, R.L. (2014). Human cumulative culture: A comparative perspective. *Biological Review, 89*, 284–301.

de Manuel, M., Kuhlwim, M., Frandsen, P., Sousa, V.C., Desai, T. Prado-Martinez, J., Hernandez-Rodriguez, J., Dupanloup, I., Lao, O., Hallast, P., & Schimdt, J.M. (2016). Chimpanzee genomic diversity reveals ancient admixture with bonobos. *Science, 354*, 477–481.

de Pelham, A., & Burton, F.D. (1976). Reply to Teleki. *Current Anthropology, 18*, 108–109.

Desai, N.P., Fedurek, P., Slocumbe, K.E., & Wilson, M.L. (2021). Chimpanzee pant-hoots encode information about individual but not group differences. *bioRxiv.* https://www.biorxiv.org/content/10.1101/2021.03.09.434515v1.abstract. Accessed October 21, 2021.

de Waal, F. (1986). The brutal elimination of a rival among captive male chimpanzees. *Ethology and Sociobiology, 7*, 237–251.

de Waal, F. (1987). Tension regulation and nonreproductive functions of sex in captive bonobos (*Pan paniscus*). *National Geographic Research, 3*, 318–335.

de Waal, F. (1989a). Behavioral contrasts between bonobo and chimpanzee. In Heltne, P.G., & Marquardt, L.A. (Eds.), *Understanding chimpanzees* (pp. 154–175). Harvard University Press.

de Waal, F. (1989b). Dominance style and primate social organization. In Standen, V., & Foley, R.A. (Eds.), *Comparative socioecology* (pp. 243–263). Blackwell Scientific Publications.

de Waal, F. (1989c). *Chimpanzee politics: Power and sex among apes.* Johns Hopkins University Press.

de Waal, F.B. (1990). Sociosexual behavior used for tension regulation in all age and sex combinations among bonobos. In Feierman, J.R. (Ed.), *Pedophilia: Biosocial dimensions* (pp. 378–393). Springer.

de Waal, F.B. (1995). Bonobo sex and society. *Scientific American, 272*(3), 82–88.

de Waal, F.B. (1997). *Bonobo: The forgotten ape, with photographs by Frans Lanting.* Berkeley.

de Waal, F.B. (2001a). Apes from Venus: Bonobos and human social evolution. In de Waal, F.B.M. (Ed.), *Tree of origin: What primate behavior can tell us about human social evolution* (pp. 41–68). Harvard University Press.

de Waal, F.B. (2001b). *The ape and the sushi master: Cultural reflections by a primatologist.* Basic Books.

de Waal, F.B. (2005). *Our inner ape: A leading primatologist explains why we are who we are.* Riverhead Books.

de Waal, F.B. (2008). Foreword. In Furuichi, T., & Thompson, J. (Eds.), *The bonobos: Behavior, ecology and conservation* (pp. 11–18). Springer.

de Waal, F.B. (2013). *The bonobo and the atheist: In search of humanism among the primates.* WW Norton & Company.

de Waal, F. (2016). *Primates and philosophers: How morality evolved.* Princeton University Press.

de Waal, F.B., & Harcourt, A.H. (1992). Coalitions and alliances: A history of ethological research. In Harcourt, A.H., & de Waal, F.B. (Eds.), *Coalitions and alliances in humans and other animals* (pp. 1–21). Oxford University Press.

de Waal, F.B., & Luttrel, L.M. (1988). Mechanisms of social reciprocity in three primate species: Symmetrical relationship characteristics of cognition? *Ethology and Sociobiology, 9*, 101–118.

de Waal, F.B., Smith Churchland, P., & Parmigiani, S. (Eds.). (2014). *Evolved morality: The biology and philosophy of human conscience.* Brill.

de Wasseige, C., Devers, D., de Marcken, R., Eba'a, A., Nasi, R., & Mayaux, P. (Eds.). (2008). *The forests of the Congo Basin: State of the forest 2008.* Publications of the Office of the European Union.

Diamond, J. (2012). *The world until yesterday.* Penguin.

Dickins, T.E., & Rahman, Q. The extended evolutionary synthesis and the role of soft inheritance in evolution. *Proceedings of the Royal Society, B, 279,* 2913–2921.

Dirven, B.C.J., Homberg, J.R., Kozicz, T., & Henckens, M.J.A.G. (2017). Epigenetic programming of the neuroendocrine stress response by adult life stress. *Journal of Molecular Endocrinology, 59,* R11–R31.

Donne, J. (2001). One chimp, two chimps, three chimps: Four months of the chimpanzee population census of Budongo. *Budongo Forest Project.* http://culture.st-and.ac.uk/bcfs/documents/newsletter/newsletter1_2.html. Accessed May 8, 2014.

Doran, D.M., Jungers, W.L., Sugiyama, Y., Fleagle, J.G., & Heesy, C.P. (2002). Multivariate and phylogenetic approaches to understanding chimpanzee and bonobo behavioral diversity. In Boesch, C., Hohmann, G., & Marchant, L.F. (Eds.), *Behavioural diversity in chimpanzees and bonobos* (pp. 14–34). Cambridge University Press.

Draulans, D., & Van Krunkelsven, E. (2002). The impact of war on forest areas in the Democratic Republic of Congo. *Oryx, 36,* 35–40.

Duffy, K.G., Wrangham, R.W., & Silk, J.B. (2007). Male chimpanzees exchange political support for mating opportunities. *Current Biology, 17,* 586.

Dulac, D., 2010. Brain function and chromatin plasticity. *Nature, 465,* 728–735.

Dunay, E., Apakupakul, K., Leard, S., Palmer, J.L., & Deem, S.L. (2018). Pathogen transmission from humans to great apes is a growing threat to primate conservation. *EcoHealth, 15,* 148–162.

Dupain, J., & Van Elsacker, L. (2001). Status of the proposed Lomako Forest Bonobo Reserve: A case study of the bushmeat trade. In Galdikas, B.F.M., Briggs, N.E., Sheeran, L.K., Shapiro, G.L., & Goodall, J. (Eds.), *All apes great and small: Volume I, African apes* (pp. 259–273). Springer.

Dupain, J., Van Krunkelsven, E., Van Elsacker, L., & Verheyen, R.F. (2000). Current status of the bonobo (*Pan paniscus*) in the proposed Lomako Reserve (Democratic Republic of Congo). *Biological Conservation, 94,* 265–272.

Dyson-Hudson, R., & Smith, E.A. (1978). Human territoriality: An ecological reassessment. *American Anthropologist, 80,* 21–41.

Eagly, A., & Wood, W. (2003). The origins of sex differences in human behavior: Evolved dispositions versus social roles. In Travis, C.B. (Ed.), *Evolution, gender, and rape* (pp. 265–304). MIT Press.

East African. (2004). "Drunk and disorderly" chimps attacking Ugandan children, February 9. https://www.theeastafrican.co.ke/magazine/434746-242460-c5tndh/index.html. Accessed April 11, 2020.

Edgerton, R.B. (2000). *Warrior women: The Amazons of Dahomey and the nature of war.* Westview Press.

Eggeling, W.J. (1947). Observations on the ecology of the Budongo Rain Forest, Uganda. *Journal of Ecology, 34,* 20–87.

Einstein, A. (1932). *Why war? A letter from Albert Einstein to Sigmund Freud.* https://en.unesco.org/courier/may-1985/why-war-letter-albert-einstein-sigmund-freud. Accessed November 16, 2022.

Emery Thompson, M., Kahlenberg, S.M., Gilby, I.C., & Wrangham, R.W. (2007). Core area quality is associated with variance in reproductive success among female chimpanzees at Kibale National Park. *Animal Behaviour, 73*, 501–512.

Emery Thompson, M., Machanda, Z.P., Scully, E.J., Enigk, D.K., Otali, E., Muller, M.N., Goldberg, T.L., Chapman, C.A., & Wrangham, R.W. (2018). Risk factors for respiratory illness in a community of wild chimpanzees (*Pan troglodytes schewinfurthii*). *Royal Society Open Science, 2018*, 1–17.

Emery Thompson, M., Muller, M.N., Wrangham, R.W., Lwanga, J.S., & Potts, K.B. (2009). Urinary C-peptide tracks seasonal and individual variation in energy balance in wild chimpanzees. *Hormones and Behavior, 55*, 299–305.

Emery Thompson, M., Newton-Fisher, N., & Reynolds V. (2006). Probable community transfer of parous adult female chimpanzees in the Budongo Forest, Uganda. *International Journal of Primatology, 27*, 1601–1617.

Estrada, A., Garber, P.A., . . . Li, B. (2017). Impending extinction crisis of the world's primates: Why primates matter. *Science Advances, 3*, e1600946.

Fadiman, J.A. (1982). *An oral history of tribal warfare: The Meru of Mt. Kenya.* Ohio University Press.

Fagiolini, M., Jensen, C.L., & Champagne, F.A. (2009). Epigenetic influences on brain development and plasticity. *Current Opinion in Neurobiology, 19*, 207–212.

Fahy, G.E., Richards, M., Riedel, J., Hublin, J.J., & Boesch, C., (2013). Stable isotope evidence of meat eating and hunting specialization in adult male chimpanzees. *Proceedings of the National Academy of Sciences, 110*(15), 5829–5833.

Fallow, A. (2003). Frodo: The alpha male. *National Geographic Online.* https://web.archive.org/web/20111227200328/http://ngm.nationalgeographic.com/ngm/0304/feature4/online_extra2.html. Accessed June 22, 2020.

Far Horizons. (2011). Journeys discovering Africa, East Africa update. https://myemail.constantcontact.com/East-Africa-Update-From-The-Far-Horizons--June-2011.html?soid=1102589984134&aid=A3AvTx-8vN8. Accessed May 2, 2020.

Farmer, K.H., Buchanan-Smith, H.M., & Jamart, A. (2006). Behavioral adaptation of *Pan troglodytes troglodytes. International Journal of Primatology, 27*, 747–765.

Fawcett, K., & Muhumza, G. (2000). Death of a wild chimpanzee community member: Possible outcome of intense sexual competition. *American Journal of Primatology, 51*, 243–247.

Fay, J.M., Carroll, R., Kerbis Peterhans, J.C., & Harris, D. (1995). Leopard attack on and consumption of gorillas in the Central African Republic. *Journal of Human Evolution, 29*, 93–99.

Fedurek, P., Tkaczynski, P., Asilimwe, C., Hobaiter, C., Samuni, L., Lowe, A.E., Dijirian, A.G., Zuberbuhler, K., Wittig, R.M., & Crockford, R.M. (2020). Maternal cannibalism in two populations of wild chimpanzees. *Primates, 61*, 181–187.

Feldblum, J.T., Manfredi, S., Gilby, I.C., & Pusey, A.E. (2018). The timing and causes of a unique chimpanzee community fission preceding Gombe's 'Four-Year War.' *American Journal of Physical Anthropology, 166*, 730–734.

Feldblum, J.T., Wroblewski, E.E., Rudicell, R.S., Hahn, B.H., Paiva, T., Cetinkaya-Rundel, M., Pusey, A.E., & Gilby, I.C. (2014). Sexually coercive male chimpanzees sire more offspring. *Current Biology, 24*, 2855–2860.

Ferdowsian, H.R., Durham, D.L., Kimwele, C., Kranendonk, G., Otali, E., Akugizibwe, T., Mulcahy, J.B., Ajarova, L., & Johnson, C.M. (2011). Signs of mood and anxiety disorder in chimpanzees. *PLoS One, 6*, 1–11.

Ferguson, R.B. (1984a). Introduction: Studying war. In Ferguson, R.B. (Ed.), *Warfare, culture, and environment* (pp. 1–81). Academic Press.

Ferguson, R.B. (1984b). A re-examination of the causes of Northwest Coast warfare. In Ferguson, R.B. (Ed.), *Warfare, culture, and environment* (pp. 267–328). Academic Press.

Ferguson, R.B. (1988). How can anthropologists promote peace? *Anthropology Today, 4*(3), 1–3.

Ferguson, R.B. (1989a). Game wars? Ecology and conflict in Amazonia. *Journal of Anthropological Research, 45*, 179–206.

Ferguson, R.B. (1989b). Anthropology and war: Theory, politics, ethics. In Turner, P.R., & Pitt, D. (Eds.), *The anthropology of war and peace: Perspectives on the nuclear age* (pp. 141–159). Bergin and Garvey.

Ferguson, R.B. (1990a). Explaining war. In Haas, J. (Ed.), *The anthropology of war* (pp. 26–55). Cambridge University Press.

Ferguson, R.B. (1990b). Blood of the Leviathan: Western contact and warfare in Amazonia. *American Ethnologist, 17*, 237–257.

Ferguson, R.B. (1992a). A savage encounter: Western contact and the Yanomami war complex. In Ferguson, R.B., & Whitehead, N.L. (Eds.), *War in the tribal zone: Expanding states and indigenous warfare* (pp. 199–227). School of America Research Press.

Ferguson, R.B. (1992b). Tribal warfare. *Scientific American, 266*(1), 108–113.

Ferguson, R.B. (1993). When worlds collide: The Columbian encounter in global perspective. *Human Peace, 10*(1), 9–10.

Ferguson, R.B. (1995a). *Yanomami warfare: A political history*. School of American Research.

Ferguson, R.B. (1995b). Infrastructural determinism. In Murphy, M., & Margolis, M. (Eds.), *Science, materialism, and the study of culture* (pp. 21–38). University Press of Florida.

Ferguson, R.B. (1997). Tribe, tribal organization. In Barfield, T. (Ed.), *The dictionary of anthropology* (pp. 475–476). Blackwell Publishers.

Ferguson, R.B. (1999). A paradigm for the study of war and society. In Raaflaub, K., & Rosenstein, N. (Eds.), *War and society in the ancient and medieval worlds* (pp. 409–458). Harvard University Press and Center for Hellenic Studies.

Ferguson, R.B. (2001). Materialist, cultural, and biological theories on why Yanomami make war. *Anthropological Theory, 1*, 99–116.

Ferguson, R.B. (2003). Introduction: Violent conflict and control of the state. In Ferguson, R.B. (Ed.), *The state, identity, and violence: Political disintegration in the post Cold War world* (pp. 1–58). Routledge.

Ferguson, R.B. (2006a). Archaeology, cultural anthropology, and the origins and intensification of war. In Arkush, E., & Allen, M. (Eds.), *The archaeology of war* (pp. 469–523). University of Florida Press.

Ferguson, R.B. (2006b). Tribal, "ethnic," and global wars. In Fitzduff, M., & Stout, C. (Eds.), *The psychology of resolving global conflicts: From war to peace* (pp. 41–69). Praeger.

Ferguson, R.B. (2008a). War before history. In de Souza, P. (Ed.), *The ancient world at war* (pp. 14–27). Thames and Hudson.

Ferguson, R.B. (2008b). Ten points on war. *Social Analysis, 52*(2), 32–49.

Ferguson, R.B. (2011a). Born to live: Challenging killer myths. In Cloninger, R., & Sussman, R. (Eds.), *Origins of cooperation and altruism* (pp. 249–270). New York.

Ferguson, R.B. (2011b). Plowing the human terrain: Toward global ethnographic surveillance. In McNamara, L.A., & Rubinstein, R.A. (Eds.), *Dangerous liaisons: Anthropologists and the national security state* (pp. 101–126). School of Advanced Research Press.

Ferguson, R.B. (2013a). Pinker's list: Exaggerating prehistoric war mortality. In Fry, D. (Ed.), *War, peace and human nature: The convergence of evolutionary and cultural views* (pp. 191–240). Oxford University Press.

Ferguson, R.B. (2013b). The prehistory of war and peace in Europe and the Near East. In Fry, D. (Ed.), *War, peace and human nature: The convergence of evolutionary and cultural views* (pp. 112–131). Oxford University Press.

Ferguson, R.B. (2013c). Full spectrum: The military invasion of anthropology. In Whitehead, N.L., & Finnstrom, S. (Eds.), *Virtual war and magical death: Technologies and imaginaries for terror and killing* (pp. 85–110). Duke University Press.

Ferguson, R.B. (2014a). Anthropologist finds flaw in claim that chimp raids are "adaptive." John Horgan *Scientific American* blog Cross-Check, November 25. https://blogs.scientificamerican.com/cross-check/anthropologist-finds-flaw-in-claim-that-chimp-raids-are-8220-adaptive-8221/. Accessed February 29, 2020.

Ferguson, R.B. (2014b). Ferguson challenges claim that chimp violence is adaptive. John Horgan *Scientific American* blog Cross-Check, September 18. https://blogs.scientificamerican.com/cross-check/anthropologist-brian-ferguson-challenges-claim-that-chimp-violence-is-adaptive/. Accessed February 29, 2020.

Ferguson, R.B. (2015). History, explanation, and war among the Yanomami: A response to Chagnon's *Noble Savages. Anthropological Theory, 15*, 377–406.

Ferguson, R.B. (2018). War may not be in our nature after all. *Scientific American, 319*(3), 76–81.

Ferguson, R.B. (2019). Comment to P. Wiessner, Collective action for war and for peace: Case study among the Enga of Papua New Guinea. *Current Anthropology, 60*(2), 236–237.

Ferguson, R.B. (2021). Masculinity and war. *Current Anthropology, 62*, Supplement 23, S112–S124.

Ferguson, R.B., & Whitehead, N.L. (Eds.). (1992a). *War in the tribal zone: Expanding states and indigenous warfare*. School of American Research Press.

Ferguson, R.B., & Whitehead, N.L. (1992b). The violent edge of empire. In Ferguson, R.B., & Whitehead, N.L. (Eds.), *War in the tribal zone: Expanding states and indigenous warfare* (pp. 1–30). School of American Research Press.

Ferguson, R.B., & Whitehead, N.L. (1992c). Provisional diagrams from the Advanced Seminar. In Ferguson, R.B., & Whitehead, N.L. (Eds.), *War in the tribal zone: Expanding states and indigenous warfare* (pp. 251–253). School of American Research Press.

Ferguson, R.B., & Whitehead, N.L. (2000). Preface to the Second Printing. In Ferguson, R.B., & Whitehead, N.L. (Eds.), *War in the tribal zone: Expanding states and indigenous warfare* (pp. xi–xl). School of American Research Press.

Filkins, D. (2010). Afghan tribe, vowing to fight Taliban, to get U.S. aid in return. *New York Times*, January 28. https://www.nytimes.com/2010/01/28/world/asia/28tribe.html. Accessed March 25, 2020.

Fischer, A., Pollack, J., Thalmann, O., Nickel, B., & Paabo, S. (2006). Demographic history and genetic differentiation. *Current Biology, 16*, 1133–1138.

Flack, J.C., Girvan, M., de Waal, F.B., & Krakauer, D.C. (2006). Policing stabilizes construction of social niches in primates. *Nature, 439*, 426–429.

Flack, J.C., Krakauer, D.C., & de Waal, F.B. (2005). Robustness mechanisms in primate societies: A perturbation study. *Proceedings of the Royal Society of London B: Biological Sciences, 272*, 1091–1099.

Fleury-Brugiere, M.-C., & Brugiere, D. (2002). A population density estimate of the chimpanzee in the Haut-Niger National Park, Republic of Guinea. *Pan Africa News, 9*(1), unpaginated. http://mahale.main.jp/PAN/index.html. Accessed May 4, 2020.

Foer, J. (2010). The truth about chimps. *National Geographic Magazine* [online]. http://ngm.nationalgeographic.com/print/2010/02/congo-chimps/foer-text. Accessed May 22, 2014.

Foerster, S., McLellan, K., Schroepfer-Walker, K., Murray, C.M., Krupenye, C., Gilby, I.C., & Pusey, A.E. (2015). Social bonds in the dispersing sex: Partner preference among adult female chimpanzees. *Animal Behavior, 71*, 136–144.

Formenty, P., Boesch, C., Wyers, M., Steiner, C., Donati, F., Dind, F., Walker, F., & Le Guenno, B. (1999). Ebola virus outbreak among wild chimpanzees living in a rain forest of Côte d'Ivoire. *Journal of Infectious Diseases, 179*, Supplement 1, S120–S126.

Formenty, P., Karesh, W., Fromenty, J-M., & Wallis, J. (2003). Infectious diseases in west Africa: A common threat to chimpanzees and humans. In Kormos, R., Boesch, C., Bakarr, M.I., & Butynski, T.M. (Eds.), *West African chimpanzees* (pp. 169–174). IUCN The World Conservation Union.

Fossey, D. (1984). Infanticide in mountain gorillas (*Gorilla gorilla beringei*) with comparative notes on chimpanzees. In Hasfater, G., & Hrdy, S.B. (Eds.), *Infanticide: Comparative and evolutionary perspectives* (pp. 217–236). Routledge.

Foster, M.W., Gilby, I.C., Murray, C.M., Johnson, A., Wroblewsi, E.E., & Pusey, A.E. (2008). Alpha male chimpanzee grooming patterns: Implication for dominance "style." *American Journal of Primatology, 71*, 136–144.

Fourrier, M., Sussman, R.W., Kippen, R., & Childs, G. (2008). Demographic modeling of a predator-prey system and its implication for the Gombe population of *Procolobus rufomitratus tephrosceles*. *International Journal of Primatology, 29*(2), 497–508.

Fowler, A., & Summer, V. (2007). Subsistence technology of Nigerian chimpanzees. *International Journal of Primatology, 28*, 997–1023.

Fowler A., & Hohmann, G. (2010). Cannibalism in wild bonobos (*Pan paniscus*) at Lui Kotale. *American Journal of Primatology, 72*, 509–514.

Fowles, S.M. (2002). From social type to social process: Placing "tribe" in a historical framework. In Parkinson, W.A. (Ed.), *The archaeology of tribal societies* (pp. 13–33). Archaeological Series 15. International Monographs in Prehistory.

Freeman, H.D., & Gosling, S.D. (2010). Personality in nonhuman primates: A review and evaluation of past research. *American Journal of Primatology, 72*, 653–671.

Freud, S. (1932). *Why war? A letter from Freud to Einstein*. https://en.unesco.org/courier/marzo-1993/why-war-letter-freud-einstein. Accessed November 16, 2022.

Fried, M. (1967). *The evolution of political society: An essay in political anthropology*. Random House.
Fried, M. (1975). *The notion of tribe*. Cummings Publishing.
Fried, M., Harris, M., & Murphy, R. (1968). Foreword: Fink out or teach in. In Fried, M., Harris, M., & Murphy, R. (Eds.), *War: The anthropology of armed conflict and aggression* (pp. ix–xix). Natural History Press.
Fry, D. (2006). *The human potential for peace: An anthropological challenge to assumptions about war and violence*. Oxford University Press.
Fry, D. (Ed.). (2013). *War, peace, and human nature: The convergence of evolutionary and cultural views*. Oxford University Press.
Fry, D. (2018). The evolutionary logic of human peaceful behavior. In Verbeek, P., & Peter, B.A. (Eds.), *Peace Ethology: Behavioral processes and systems of peace* (pp. 249–265). John Wiley and Sons.
Fry, D.P., Keith, C., & Soderberg, P. (2020). Social complexity, inequality, and war before farming: Congruence of comparative forager and archaeological data. In Moreau, L. (Ed.), *Social inequality before farming? Multidisciplinary approaches to the investigation of egalitarian and non-egalitarian social relationships in prehistoric and extant hunter-gatherer societies* (pp. 303–320). University of Cambridge, McDonald Institute Monographs.
Fry, D., & Soderberg, P. (2013). Lethal aggression in mobile forager bands and implications for the origins of war. *Science, 341*, 270–273.
Fry, D.P., & Soderberg, P. (2014). Myths about hunter-gatherers redux: Nomadic forager war and peace. *Journal of Aggression, Conflict, and Peace Research, 6*, 256–266.
Fruth, B., & Hohmann, G. (2018). Food sharing across borders: First observations of inter-community meat sharing by bonobos at LuiKotale, DRC. *Human Nature, 29*, 91–103.
Fuentes, A. (2004). "It's not all sex and violence": Integrated anthropology and the role of cooperation and social complexity in human evolution. *American Anthropologist, 106*, 710–118.
Fuentes, A. (2012). Ethnoprimatology and the anthropology of the human–primate interface. *Annual Review of Anthropology, 41*, 101–117.
Fuentes, A. (2015). Integrative anthropology and the human niche: Toward a contemporary approach to human evolution. *American Anthropologist, 117*, 302–315.
Fuentes, A., & Hockings, K.J. (2010). The ethnoprimatological approach in primatology. *American Journal of Primatology, 72*, 841–847.
Fuentes, A., & Wolfe, L.D. (Eds.). (2002). *Primates face to face: Conservation of human-nonhuman primate interconnections*. Cambridge University Press.
Fukuyama, F. (1998). Women and the evolution of world politics. *Foreign Affairs, 77*, 24–40.
Furuichi, T. (2000). Possible case of predation on a chimpanzee by a leopard in the Petit Loango Reserve, Gabon. *Pan Africa News, 7*(2), unpaginated. http://mahale.main.jp/PAN/index.html. Accessed May 4, 2020.
Furuichi, T. (2009). Factors underlying party size differences between chimpanzees and bonobos: A review and hypotheses for future study. *Primates, 50*, 197–209.
Furuichi, T. (2011). Female contributions to the peaceful nature of bonobo society. *Evolutionary Anthropology: Issues, News, and Reviews, 20*, 131–142.

Furuichi, T. (2020). Variation in intergroup relationships among species and among and within local populations of African apes. *International Journal of Primatology, 41,* 203–223.

Furuichi, T., Harhisa I., & Angoue-Ovono, S. (1997). Population density of chimpanzees and gorillas in the Petit Loango Reserve, Gabon: Employing a new method to distinguish between nests of the two species. *International Journal of Primatology, 18,* 1029–1046.

Furuichi, T., Hashimoto, C., & Tashiro, Y. (2001). Fruit availability and habitat use by chimpanzees in the Kalinzu Forest, Uganda: Examination off fallback foods. *International Journal of Primatology, 22,* 929–945.

Furuichi, T., Idani, G.I., Ihobe, H., Hashimoto, C., Tashiro, Y., Sakamaki, T., Mulavwa, M.N., Yangozene, K., & Kuroda, S. (2012). Long-term studies on wild bonobos at Wamba, Luo Scientific Reserve, DR Congo: Towards the understanding of female life history in a male-philopatric species. In Kappeler, P.M., & Watts, D.P. (Eds.), *Long-term field studies of primates* (pp. 413–433). Springer.

Furuichi, T., Idani, G.I., Ihobe, H., Kuroda, S., Kitamura, K., Mori, A., Enomoto, T., Okayasu, N., Hashimoto, C., & Kano, T. (1998). Population dynamics of wild bonobos (*Pan paniscus*) at Wamba. *International Journal of Primatology, 19,* 1029–1043.

Furuichi, T., & Ihobe, H. (1994). Variation in male relationships in bonobos and chimpanzees. *Behaviour, 130,* 211–228.

Furiuichi, T., Mulavwa, M., Yangozene, K., Yama-Yamba, M., Motemo-Salo, B., Idani, G., Ihobe, H., Hashimoto, C., Tashiro, Y., & Mwanza, N. (2008). Relationships among fruit abundance, ranging, rate and party size and composition of bonobos at Wamba. In Furuichi, T., & Thompson, J. (Eds.), *The bonobos: Behavior, ecology and conservation* (pp. 135–149). Springer.

Furuichi, T., Sanz, C., Koops, K., Sakamaki, T., Ryu, H., Tokuyama, N., & Morgan, D. (2015). Why do wild bonobos not use tools like chimpanzees do? *Behaviour, 152,* 425–460.

Gagneux, P., Wills, C., Gerloff, U., Tautz, D., Morin, P.A., Boesch, C., Fruth, B., Hohmann, G., Ryder, O.A., & Woodruff, D. (1999). Mitochondrial sequences show diverse evolutionary histories of African hominoids. *Proceedings of the National Academy of Sciences, 96,* 5077–5082.

Gant, J. *One tribe at a time: A strategy for success in Afghanistan.* Nine Sisters Imports. http://www.operationspaix.net/DATA/DOCUMENT/5042~v~One_Tribe_at_a_Time_A_Strategy_for_Success_in_Afghanistan.pdf. Accessed March 25, 2020.

Gat, A. (2015). Proving communal warfare among hunter-gatherers: The quasi-Rousseauan error. *Evolutionary Anthropology, 24,* 111–126.

Gaulin, S.J.C., Kurland, J.A., & Strum, S.C. (1976). Primate predation and bioenergetics. *Science, 191,* 314–317.

Gavin, M. (2004). Chimps and humans in conflict. *BBC Science and Nature.* http://www.bbc.co.uk/print/nature/animals/features/325feature1.shtml. Accessed May 25, 2004.

Genin, E. (2020). Missing heritability of complex diseases: Case solved? *Human Genetics, 139,* 103–113.

Georgiev, A.V., Russell, A.F., Emery Thompson, M., Otali, E., Muller, M.N., & Wrangham, R.W. (2014). The foraging costs of mating effort in male chimpanzees (*Pan treoglogytes schweinfurthii*). *International Journal of Primatology, 35,* 725–745.

Gerloff, U., Hartung, B., Fruth, B., Hohmann, G., & Tautz, D. (1999). Intracommunity relationships, dispersal pattern and paternity success in a wild living community of Bonobos (*Pan paniscus*) determined from DNA analysis of faecal samples. *Proceedings of the Royal Society of London B: Biological Sciences, 266,* 1189–1195.

Ghiglieri, M.P. (1984). *The chimpanzees of Kibale Forest: A field study of ecology and social structure.* Columbia University Press.

Ghiglieri, M.P. (1987). War among the chimps. *Discover,* November 1987, 66–76.

Ghiglieri, M.P. (1988). *East of the Mountains of the Moon: Chimpanzee society in the African rain forest.* Collier Macmillan Publishers.

Ghiglieri, M.P. (1999). *The dark side of man: Tracing the origins of male violence.* Perseus Books.

Ghobrial, L., Lankester, F., Kiyang, J.A., Akih, A.E., de Vries, S., Fotso, R., Gadsby, E.L., Jenkins Jr, P.D., & Gonder, M.K. (2010). Tracing the origins of rescued chimpanzees reveals widespread chimpanzee hunting in Cameroon. *Biomed Central Ecology, 10.* http://www.biomedcentral.com/1472-6785/10/2. Accessed May 21, 2014.

Gibbons, A. (2004). Tracking the evolutionary history of a "warrior" gene. *Science, 304,* 818.

Gibbons, A. (2007). Spear-wielding chimps seen hunting bush babies. *Science, 315,* 1063.

Gilbert, S.F., Bosch, T.C.G., & Ledon-Rettig, C. (2015). Eco-evo-devo: Developmental symbiosis and developmental plasticity as evolutionary agents. *Nature Reviews/ Genetics, 16,* 611–622.

Gilby, I.C., Brent, L.J., Wroblewski, E.E., Rudicell, R.S., Hahn, B.H., Goodall, J., & Pusey, A.E. (2013a). Fitness benefits of coalitionary aggression in male chimpanzees. *Behavioral Ecology and Sociobiology, 67,* 373–381.

Gilby, I.C., & Connor, R.C. (2010). The role of intelligence in group hunting: Are chimpanzees different from other social predators? In Lonsdorf, E.V., Ross, S.R., & Matsuzawa, T. (Eds.) *The mind of the chimpanzee: Ecological and experimental perspectives* (pp. 220–223). University of Chicago Press.

Gilby, I.C., Eberly, L.E., & Wrangham, R.W. (2008). Economic profitability of social predation among wild chimpanzees: Individual variation promotes cooperation. *Animal Behaviour, 75,* 351–360.

Gilby, I.C., Machanda, Z.P., Mjungu, D.C., Rosen, J., Muller, M.N., Pusey, A.E., &Wrangham, R.W. (2015). Impact hunters catalyse cooperative hunting in two wild chimpanzee communities. *Philosophical Transactions of the Royal Society Series B, 370,* 20150005.

Gilby, I.C., Machanda, Z.P., O'Malley, R.C., Murray, C.M., Lonsdorf, E.V., Walker, K., Mjungu, D.C., Otali, E., Muller, M.N., Emery Thompson, M., Pusey, A.E., & Wrangham, R.W. (2017). Predation by female chimpanzees: Toward an understanding of sex difference in meat acquisition in the last common ancestor of *Pan* and *Homo. Journal of Human Evolution, 110,* 82–94.

Gilby, I.C., & Wawrzyniak, D. (2018). Meat eating by wild chimpanzees (*Pan troglodytes scheinfurthii*): Effects of prey age on carcass consumption sequence. *International Journal of Primatology, 39,* 127–140.

Gilby, I.C., Wilson, M.L., & Pusey, A.E. (2013). Ecology rather than psychology explains co-occurrence of predation and border patrols in male chimpanzees. *Animal Behavior, 86,* 61–74.

Gilby, I.C., & Wrangham, R.W. (2007). Risk-prone hunting by chimpanzees (*Pan troglodytes schweinfurthii*) increases during periods of high diet quality. *Behavioural Ecology and Sociobiology, 61*, 1771–1779.

Gilby, I.C., & Wrangham, R.W. (2008). Association patterns among wild chimpanzees (*Pan troglodytes schweinfurthii*) reflect sex differences in cooperation. *Behavioural Ecology and Sociobiology, 62*, 1831–1842.

Gillespie, T.R., Morgan, D., Deutsch, J.C., Kuhlenschmidt, M.S., Salzer, J.S., Cameron, K., Reed, T., & Sanz, C. (2009). A legacy of low-impact logging does not elevate prevalence of potentially pathogenic protozoa in free-ranging gorillas and chimpanzees in the Republic of Congo: Logging and parasitism in African apes. *EcoHealth, 6*, 557–564.

Glowacki, L. (2016). How the tribal warfare of our ancestors explains the Islamic State. *Washington Post*, March 24, 2016. https://www.washingtonpost.com/opinions/how-the-tribal-warfare-of-our-ancestors-explains-the-islamic-state/2016/03/24/d36baee6-e581-11e5-b0fd-073d5930a7b7_story.html. Accessed February 24, 2020.

Glowacki, L., & Wrangham, R. (2013). The role of rewards in motivating participation in simple warfare. *Human Nature, 24*, 444–460.

Glowacki, L., & Wrangham, R. (2015). Warfare and reproductive success in a tribal population. *Proceedings of the National Academy of Sciences, 112*, 348–353.

Glowacki, L., Wilson, M.L., & Wrangham, R.W. (2020). The evolutionary anthropology of war. *Journal of Economic Behavior and Organization, 178*, 963–982. http://dx.doi.org/10.1016/j.sebo.2017.09.014. Accessed February 22, 2020.

Gudsnuk, K., & Champagne, F.A. (2012). Epigenetic influence of stress and the social environment. *Institute for Laboratory Animal Research Journal, 53*, 279–288.

Goldberg, T.L. (1998). Biogeographic predictors of genetic diversity in populations of Eastern African Chimpanzees (*Pan troblodytes schweinfurthi*). *International Journal of Primatology, 19*, 237–254.

Goldberg, T.L., Gillespie, T.R., & Rwego, I.B. (2008). Health and disease in the people, primates, and domestic animals of Kibale National Park: Implications for conservation. In Wrangham, R.W., & Ross, E. (Eds.), *Science and conservation in African forests: The benefits of long-term research* (pp. 75–87). Cambridge University Press.

Goldberg, T.L., & Wrangham, R.L. (1997). Genetic correlates of social behaviour in wild chimpanzees: Evidence from mitochondrial DNA. *Animal Behavior, 54*, 559–570.

Goldman, A., Hartter, J., Southworth, J., & Binford, M. (2008). The human landscape around the Island Park: Impacts and responses to Kibale National Park. In Wrangham, R.W., & Ross, E. (Eds.), *Science and conservation in African forests: The benefits of long-term research* (pp. 129–144). Cambridge University Press.

Goldschmidt, W. (1998). Inducement to military participation in tribal societies. In Rubinstein, R.A., & Foster, M.L. (Eds.), *The social dynamics of peace and conflict: Culture in international security* (pp. 47–65). Westview Press.

Goldstein, J.S. (2001). *War and gender*. Cambridge University Press.

Gonder, M.K., Disotell, T.R., & Oates, J.F. (2006). New genetic evidence on the evolution of chimpanzee populations and implications for taxonomy. *International Journal of Primatology, 27*, 1103–1127.

Gonder, M.K., Locatelli, S., Ghobrial, L., Mitchell, M.W., Kujawski, J.T., Lankester, F.J., Stewart, C.-B., & Tishkoff, S.A. (2011). Evidence from Cameroon reveals differences in the genetic structure and histories of chimpanzee populations. *PNAS, 108*, 4766–4771.

Goodall, J. (1963). My life among wild chimpanzees. *National Geographic*, August, 272–308.

Goodall, J. (1965). Chimpanzees of the Gombe Stream Reserve. In DeVore, I. (Ed.), *Primate behavior: Field studies of monkeys and apes* (pp. 425–458). Holt, Rinehart and Winston Press.

Goodall, J. (1971). *In the Shadow of Man*. Houghton Mifflin Harcourt.

Goodall, J. (1977a). Infant-killing and cannibalism in free-living chimpanzees. *Folia Primatologica, 28*, 259–282.

Goodall, J. (1977b). Watching, watching, watching. *New York Times*, September 15, 24.

Goodall, J. (1979). Life and death at Gombe. *National Geographic, 155*, 592–620.

Goodall, J. (1983). Population dynamics during a 15 year period in one community of free-living chimpanzees in the Gombe National Park, Tanzania. *Zeitschrift für Tierpsychologie, 61*, 1–60.

Goodall, J. (1986). *The chimpanzees of Gombe: Patterns of behavior*. Belknap Press of Harvard University.

Goodall, J. (1988). *In the shadow of man*. San Diego State University.

Goodall, J. (1989). Area status report: Tanzania. In Heltne, P.G., & Marquardt, L.A. (Eds.), *Understanding chimpanzees* (pp. 360–361). Harvard University Press.

Goodall, J. (1990). *Through a window: My thirty years with the chimpanzees of Gombe*. Houghton Mifflin Company.

Goodall, J. (1992). Unusual violence in the overthrow of an alpha male chimpanzee at Gombe. In Nishida, T., McGrew, W.C., Marker, P., Pickford, M., & de Waal, F.B.M. (Eds.), *Topics in primatology Vol. 1: Human origins* (pp. 131–142). University of Tokyo Press.

Goodall, J. (1999). *Reason for hope: A spiritual journey*. Warner Books.

Goodall, J. (2000). *Africa in my blood: The early years*. Houghton Mifflin Company.

Goodall, J. (2001). *Beyond innocence: An autobiography in letters: The later years*. Houghton Mifflin Company.

Goodall, J. (2003). *Bridging the chasm: Helping people and the environment across Africa*. Environmental Change and Security Program. https://www.wilsoncenter.org/publication/bridging-the-chasm-helping-people-and-the-environment-across-africa. Accessed April 14, 2020.

Goodall, J., & Abrams, D., with Hudson, G. (2021). *The Book of hope: A survival guide for trying times*. Celadon Books.

Goodall, J., with Berman, P. (1999). *Reason for hope: A spiritual journey*. Warner Books.

Goodall, J., Bandora, A., Bergmann, E., Busse, C., Matama, H., Mpongo, E., Pierce, A., & Riss, D. (1979). Intercommunity interactions in the chimpanzee population of the Gombe National Park. In Hamburg, D.A., & McGown, E.R. (Eds.), *The great apes* (pp. 13–53). Benjamin/Cummings.

Goosens, B., Setchell, J.M., Tchidongo, E., Dilambaka, E., Vidal, C., Ancrenaz, M., & Jamart, A. (2005). Survival, interactions with conspecifics and reproduction in 37 chimpanzees released into the wild. *Biological Conservation, 123*, 461–475.

Gould, S.J. (1977). *Ontogeny and phylogeny*. Belknap Press of Harvard University.

Gould, S.J. (2002). *The structure of evolutionary theory*. Harvard University Press.

Granier, N., & Martinez, L. (2011). Conservation issues in the Nimba Mountains. In Marsuzawa, T., Humle, T., & Sugiyama, Y. (Eds.), *The chimpanzees of Bossou and Nimba* (pp. 381–192). Springer.

Grant, J.W.A., Chapman, C.A., & Richardson, K.S. (1992). Defended versus undefended home range size of carnivores, ungulates, and primates. *Behavioral Ecology and Sociobiology, 31*, 149–161.

Great Lakes Safaris. (n.d.). Kibale National Park map. http://safari-uganda.com/safariu/uganda/kibalemap.php. Accessed May 2, 2020.

Greene, M. (2005). *Jane Goodall: A biography*. Greenwood Press.

Greengrass, E. (2000a). The sudden decline of a community of chimpanzees at Gombe National Park. *Pan Africa News, 7*(1), unpaginated. http://mahale.main.jp/PAN/index.html. Accessed May 4, 2020.

Greengrass, E. (2000b). The sudden decline of a community of chimpanzees at Gombe National Park: A supplement. *Pan Africa News, 7*(2), unpaginated. http://mahale.main.jp/PAN/index.html. Accessed May 4, 2020.

Greengrass, E. (2009). Chimpanzees are close to extinction in southwest Nigeria. *Primate Conservation, 24*, 77–83.

Grieser Johns, B. (1996). Responses of chimpanzees to habituation and tourism in the Kibale Forest, Uganda. *Biological Conservation, 78*, 257–262.

Grieser Johns, B. (1997). *Population size and structure of the Ngogo chimpanzee community in the Kibale Forest, Uganda, and the impact of tourism*. Doctoral dissertation, University of London.

Gros-Louis, J., Perry, S., & Manson, J.H. (2003). Violent coalitionary attacks and intraspecific killing in wild white-faced capuchin monkeys (*Cebus capucinus*). *Primates, 44*, 341–346.

Grossmann, F., Hart, J.A., Vosper, A., & Ilambu, O. (2008). Range occupation and population estimates of bonobos in the Salonga National Park: Application to large-scale surveys of bonobos in the Democratic Republic of Congo. In Furuichi, T., & Thompson, J. (Eds.), *The bonobos: Behavior, ecology, and conservation* (pp. 189–216). Springer.

Gruber, T., & Clay, Z. (2016). A comparison between bonobos and chimpanzees: A review and update. *Evolutionary Anthropology: Issues, News, and Reviews, 25*, 239–252.

Gruber, T., Potts, K.B., Krupenye, C., Reynolds, V., Byrne, M.-R., Mackworth-Young, C., McGrew, W.C., & Zuberbühler, K. (2012). The influence of ecology on chimpanzee (*Pan troglodytes*) cultural behavior: A case study of five Ugandan chimpanzee communities. *Journal of Comparative Psychology, 126*, 446–457.

Gruber, T., Zuberbuhler, K., Clement, F., & van Schaik, C. (2015). Apes have culture but may not know that they do. *Frontiers in Psychology, 6*, 1–14.

Grutzmacher, K., Keil, V., Leinert, V., Leguillon, F., Henlin, A., Couacy-Hymann, E., Kondgen, S., Lang, A., Deschner, T., Witting, R.M., & Leendertz, F.H. (2016). Human quarantine: Toward reducing infectious pressure on chimpanzees at the Tai Chimpanzee Project, Cote d'Ivoire. *American Journal of Primatology, 80*, 1–6.

Haas, J. (1990). Warfare and the evolution of tribal polities in the prehistoric Southwest. In J. Haas (Ed.), *The anthropology of war* (pp. 171–189). Cambridge University Press.

Haas, J., & Piscitelli, M. (2013). The prehistory of warfare: Misled by ethnography. In Fry, D. (Ed.), *War, peace, and human nature: The convergence of evolutionary of cultural views* (pp. 168–190). Oxford University Press.

Hall, K., & Brosnan, S.F. (2016). A comparative perspective on the evolution of moral behavior. In Shackelford, T.K., & Hansen, R.D. (Eds.), *The evolution of morality* (pp. 157–176). Springer International.

Halloran, A.R., Cloutier, C.T., & Sesay, P.B., 2013. A previously undiscovered group of chimpanzees (*Pan troglodytes verus*) is observed living in the Tonkolili District of Sierra Leone. *American Journal of Primatology, 75*, 519–523.

Hamai, M., Nishida, T., Takasaki, H., & Turner, L.A. (1992). New records of within-group infanticide and cannibalism in wild chimpanzees. *Primates, 33*, 151–162.

Hamilton, C.A. (1984). *Deforestation in Uganda*. Oxford University Press.

Hanamura, S., Kiyono, M., Nakamura, M., Sakamaki, T., Itoh, N., Zamma, K., Kitopeni, R., Matumula, M., & Nishida, T. (2006). A new code of observation employed at Mahale: Prevention against a flu-like disease. *Pan Africa News, 13*(2), unpaginated. http://mahale.main.jp/PAN/index.html. Accessed May 4, 2020.

Hanamura, S., Kiyono, M., Lukasik-Braum, M., Mlengeya, T., Fujimoto, M., Nakamura, M., & Nishida, T. (2008). Chimpanzee deaths at Mahale caused by a flu-like disease. *Primates, 49*, 77–80.

Hanamura, S., Kooniyama, T., & Hosaka, K. (2015). In Nakamura, M., Hosaka, K., Itoh, N., & Zamma, K. (Eds.), *Mahale chimpanzees: 50 years of research* (pp. 354–371). Cambridge University Press.

Hance, J. (2010). Forest loss occurring around Kibale National Park in Uganda. *Mongabay.com*. http://print.news.mongabay.com/2010/0628-hance_landscape_effects.html. Accessed June 10, 2014.

Handwerk, B. (2010). Chimp "girls" play with "dolls" too: First wild evidence. *National Geographic Daily News*. http://news.nationalgeographic.com/news/2010/09/101220-chimpanzees-play-nature-nurture-science-animals-evolution/. Accessed June 10, 2014.

Haraway, D.J. (1989). *Primate visions: Gender, race, and nature in the world of modern science*. Psychology Press.

Hare, B., & Kwetuende, S. (2010). Bonbos voluntarily share their own food with others. *Current Biology, 20*, R230–R231.

Hare, B., & Woods, V. (2019). Cognitive comparisons of genus *Pan* support bonobo self-domestication. In Boesch, C., Wittig, R., Crockford, C., Vigilant, L., Deschner, T., & Leendertz, F. (Eds.), *The chimpanzees of the Tai forest: 40 years of research* (pp. 214–232). Cambridge University Press.

Hare, B., Melis, A.P., Woods, V., Hastings, S., & Wrangham, R. (2007). Tolerance allows bonobos to outperform chimpanzees on a cooperative task. *Current Biology, 17*, 619–623.

Hare, B., Wobber, V., & Wrangham, R. (2012). The self-domestication hypothesis: Evolution of bonobo psychology is due to selection against aggression. *Animal Behaviour, 83*, 573–585.

Harris, M. (1968). *The rise of anthropological theory: A history of theories of culture*. Thomas Crowell.

Harris, M. (1979). *Cultural Materialism: The struggle for a science of culture*. Random House.

Hart, J.A., Grossmann, F., Vosper, A., & Ilanga, J. (2008). Human hunting and its impact on bonobos in the Salonga National Park, Democratic Republic of Congo. In Furuichi, T., & Thompson, J. (Eds.), *The bonobos: Behavior, ecology, and conservation* (pp. 245–271). Springer.

Hartter, J., & Goldman, A. (2010). Local responses to a forest park in western Uganda: Alternative narratives on fortress conservation. *Oryx, 45*, 60–68.

Hartter, J., Ryan, S.J., MacKenzie, C.A., Goldman, A., Dowhaniu, N., Palace, M., Diem, J.E., & Chapman, C.A. (2015). Now there is no land: A story of ethnic migration in a protected area landscape in western Uganda. *Population and Environment, 36*, 452–479.

Hartter, J., & Southworth, J. (2009). Dwindling resources and fragmentation of landscapes around parks: Wetlands and forest patches around Kibale National Park, Uganda. *Landscape Ecology, 24*, 643–656.

Hasegawa, T., Hiraiwa, M., Nishida, T., & Takasaki, H. (1983). New evidence on scavenging behavior in wild chimpanzees. *Current Anthropology, 24*, 231–232.

Hasegawa, T. (1989). Sexual behavior of immigrant and resident female chimpanzees at Mahale. In Heltne, P.G., & Marquardt (Eds.), *Understanding chimpanzees* (pp. 90–103). Harvard University Press.

Hashimoto, C. (1998). Chimpanzees of the Kalinzu Forest, Uganda. *Pan Africa News, 5*(1), unpaginated. http://mahale.main.jp/PAN/index.html. Accessed May 4, 2020.

Hashimoto, C. (1999). Snare injuries of chimpanzees in the Kalinzu Forest, Uganda. *Pan Africa News, 6*(2), unpaginated. http://mahale.main.jp/PAN/index.html. Accessed May 4, 2020.

Hashimoto, C., Cox, D., & Furuichi, T. (2007). Snare removal for conservation of chimpanzees in the Kalinzu Forest Reserve, Uganda. *Pan Africa News, 14*(1), unpaginated. http://mahale.main.jp/PAN/index.html. Accessed May 4, 2020.

Hashimoto, C., & Furuichi, T. (2005). Possible intergroup killing in the Kalinzu Forest, Uganda. *Pan Africa News, 12*(1), unpaginated. http://mahale.main.jp/PAN/index.html. Accessed May 4, 2020.

Hashimoto, C., & Furuichi, T. (2006). Frequent copulations by females and high promiscuity in chimpanzees in the Kalinzu Forest, Uganda. In Newton-Fisher, N.E., Notman, H., Paterson, J.D., & Reynolds, V. (Eds.), *Primates of western Uganda* (pp. 247–257). Springer.

Hashimoto, C., & Furuichi, T. (2015). Sex differences in ranging and association patterns in chimpanzees in comparison with bonobos. In Furuichi, T. Yamigiwa, J., & Aurelli, F. (Eds.), *Dispersing primate females: Life histories and social strategies in male-philopatric species* (pp. 105–126). Springer.

Hashimoto, C., Isaji, M., Mouri, K., & Takemoto, H. (2020). Intergroup encounters of chimpanzees (*Pan troglodytes*) from the female perspectives. *International Journal of Primatology, 41*, 171–180.

Hashimoto, C., Tashiro, Y., Kimura, D., Enomoto, T., Ingmanson, E.J., Idani, G.I., & Furuichi, T. (1998). Habitat use and ranging of wild bonobos (*Pan paniscus*) at Wamba. *International Journal of Primatology, 19*, 1045–1060.

Hashimoto, C., Tashiro, Y., Hibino, E., Mulavwa, M., Yangozene, K., Furuichi, T., Idani, G.I., & Takenaka, O. (2008). Longitudinal structure of a unit-group of bonobos: Male philopatry and possible fusion of unit-groups. In Furuichi, T., & Thompson, J. (Eds.), *The bonobos: Behavior, ecology, and conservation* (pp. 107–119). Springer.

Haslam, M. (2014). On the tool use behavior of the bonobo chimpanzee last common ancestor, and the origins of hominine stone tool use. *American Journal of Primatology, 76*, 910–918.

Hauser, M.D. (1998). *Project description: Intergroup aggression in wild chimpanzees*. National Science Foundation proposal #9812781.

Hauser, M.D. (2005). *Moral minds: How nature designed our universal sense of right and wrong*. Ecco Press.

Hawks, J. (2007). Fongoli savanna cave chimps. John Hawks blog. http://johnhawks.net/weblog/reviews/chimpanzees/comparison/fongoli_caves_open_country_2007.html. Accessed May 3, 2020.

Hayakawa, T., Nakashima, M., & Nakamura, M. (2010). Immigration of a large number of adolescent female chimpanzees into the Mahale M Group. *Pan Africa News, 18*(1). http://mahale.main.jp/PAN/index.html. Accessed May 4, 2020.

Head, J. (2011). Keeping it in the family: Tribal warfare between chimpanzee communities. In Robbins, M.M., & Boesch, C. (Eds.), *Among African apes: Stories and photos from the field* (pp. 101–115). University of California Press.

Head, J.S., Boesch, C., Makaga, L., & Robbins, M.M. (2011). *International Journal of Primatology, 32*, 755–775.

Head, J.S., Boesch, C., Robbins, M.M., Rabanal, L.I., Makaga, L., & Kuhl, H.S. (2013). Effective sociodemographic population assessment of elusive species in ecology and conservation management. *Ecology and Evolution* [online]. http://www.eva.mpg.de/primat/staff/boesch/pdf/Head_et_al_Ecology_and_Evolution_2013.pdf. Accessed June 4, 2014.

Head, J.S., Robbins, M.M., Mundry, R., Makaga, L., & Boesch, C. (2012). Remote video-camera traps measure habitat use and competitive exclusions among sympatric chimpanzee, gorilla and elephant in Loango National Park, Gabon. *Journal of Tropical Ecology, 28*, 571–583.

Heard, E., & Martienssen, R.A. (2014). Transgenerational epigenetic inheritance: Myths and mechanisms. *Cell, 157*, 95–109.

Heinsohn, R. (1997). Group territoriality in two populations of African lions. *Animal Behaviour, 53*, 1143–1147.

Henschel, P., Abernethy, K.A., & White, L.J.T. (2005). Leopard food habits in the Lope National Park, Gabon, Central Africa. *African Journal of Ecology, 43*, 21–28.

Herbinger, I., Boesch, C., & Rothe, H. (2001). Territory characteristics among three neighboring chimpanzee communities in the Tai National Park, Cote d'Ivoire. *International Journal of Primatology, 22*, 143–167.

Herbinger, I., Papworth, S., Boesch, C., & Zuberbühler, K. (2009). Vocal, gestural and locomotor responses of wild chimpanzees to familiar and unfamiliar intruders: A playback study. *Animal Behaviour, 78*, 1389–1396.

Herman, J.J., Spencer, H.G., Donohue, K., & Sultan, S.E. (2014). How stable "should" epigenetic modifications be? Insights from adaptive plasticity and bet hedging. *Evolution, 68*, 632–643.

Hernando-Herraez, I., Prado-Martinez, J., Garg, P., Fernandez-Callejo, M., Heyn, H., Hvilsom, C., Navarro, A., Esteller, M., Sharp, A.J., & Marques-Bonet, T. (2013). Dynamics of DNA methylation in recent human and great ape evolution. *PLoS Genetics, 9*, p.e1003763.

Herrman, E., & Tomasello, M. (2012). Human cultural cognition. In Mitani, J.C., Call, J., Kappeler, P.M., Palombit, R.A., & Silk, J. (Eds.), *The evolution of primate societies* (pp. 701–714). University of Chicago Press.

Hey, J. (2006). On the failure of modern species concepts. *Trends in Ecology and Evolution, 21*, 447–450.

Hicks, T.C., Kuhl, H.S., Boesch, C., Dieguez, P., Ayimisin, A.E., Fernandez, R.M., Zungawa, D.B., Kambere, M., Swinkels, J., Menken, S.B.J., Hart, J., Mundry, R., & Roessingh, P. (2019). Bili-Uere: A chimpanzee behavioural realm in northern Democratic Republic of Congo. *Folia Primatologica, 90,* 3–64.

Hicks, T.C., Menken, S.B.J., Laudisoit, A., & Hart, J. (2019). Handling and consumption of vertebrate prey by chimpanzees (*Pan troglodytes schweinfurthii*) in the Northern Democratic Republic of the Congo. In Jensvold, M.L.A. (Ed.), *Chimpanzee behaviour* (pp. 1–34). Nova Science Publishers. https://www.novapublishers.com/wp-content/uploads/2020/03/978-1-53615-906-6_ch1.pdf. Accessed September 28, 2021.

Hill, K. (2009). Animal "culture." In Laland, K.N., & Galef, B.G. (Eds.), *The question of animal culture* (pp. 269–287). Harvard University Press.

Hill, K., Boesch, C., Goodall, J., Pusey A., Williams, J., & Wrangham, R. (2001). Mortality rates among wild chimpanzees. *Journal of Human Evolution, 40,* 437–450.

Hiraiwa-Hasegawa, M., Hasegawa, T., & Nishida, T. (1984). Demographic study of a large-sized unit-group of chimpanzees in the Mahale Mountains, Tanzania: A preliminary report. *Primates, 25,* 401–413.

Hirata, S., Shinya, Y. Takemoto, H., & Matsuzawa, T. (2010). A case report of meat and fruit sharing in a pair of wild bonobos. *Pan Africa News, 17*(2), unpaginated. http://mahale.main.jp/PAN/index.html. Accessed May 4, 2020.

Hitonaru, N. (2004). Increased hunting of yellow baboons (*Papio cynocephalus*) by M group chimpanzees at Mahale. *Pan Africa News, 11*(2), unpaginated. http://mahale.main.jp/PAN/index.html. Accessed May 4, 2020.

Hladik, C.M. (1977). Chimpanzees of Gabon and chimpanzees of Gombe: Some comparative data on the diet. In Clutton-Brock, T.H. (Ed.), *Primate ecology: Studies of feeding and ranging behavior in lemurs, monkeys and apes* (pp. 481–501). Academic Press.

Hobaiter, C., Samuni, L., Mullins, C., Akankwasa, W.J., & Zuberbühler, K. (2017). Variation in hunting behaviour in neighbouring chimpanzee communities in the Budongo forest, Uganda. *PLoS One, 12,* p.e0178065.

Hoberg, E.P., & Brooks, D.R. (2015). Evolution in action: Climate change, biodiversity dynamics and emerging infectious disease. *Philosophical Transactions of the Royal Society B, 370,* 20130553, 1–7.

Hockings, K.J. (2009a). Use of wild and cultivated foods by chimpanzees at Bossou, Republic of Guinea: Feeding dynamics in a human-influenced environment. *American Journal of Primatology, 71,* 636–646.

Hockings, K.J. (2009b). Living at the interface: Human-chimpanzee competition, coexistence and contact in Africa. *Interaction Studies, 10,* 183–205.

Hockings, K.J. (2010). Human-chimpanzee competition and conflict in Africa: A case study of coexistence in Bossou, Republic of Guinea. In Lonsdorf, E.V., Ross, S.R., & Matsuzawa, T. (Eds.), *The mind of the chimpanzee: Ecological and experimental perspectives* (pp. 347–360). Chicago University Press.

Hockings, K.J. (2011). The crop-raiders of the sacred hill. In Matsuzawa, T., Humle, T., & Sugiyama, Y. (Eds.), *The chimpanzees of Bossou and Nimba* (pp. 211–220). Springer Press.

Hockings, K.J., Anderson, J.R., & Matsuzawa, T. (2009). Use of wild and cultivated foods by chimpanzees at Bossou, Republic of Guinea: Feeding dynamics in a human-influenced environment. *American Journal of Anthropology, 71,* 636–646.

Hockings, K.J., Anderson, J.R., & Matsuzawa, T. (2012). Socioecological adaptations by chimpanzees, *Pan troglodytes verus*, inhabiting an anthropogenically impacted habitat. *Animal Behaviour, 83*, 801–810.

Hockings, K.J., & McLennan, M.R. (2012). From forest to farm: Systematic review of cultivar feeding by chimpanzees: Management implications for wildlife in anthropogenic landscapes. *PloS ONE, 7*, e33391, 1–11.

Hockings, K.J., McLennan, M.R., ... Hill, C.M. (2015). Apes in the anthropocene: Flexibility and survival. *Trends in Ecology and Evolution, 30*, 215–222.

Hockings, K.J., Yamakoshi, G., Kabasawa, A., & Matsuzawa, T. (2010). Attacks on local persons by chimpanzees in Bossou, Republic of Guinea: Long-term perspectives. *American Journal of Primatology, 71*, 1–10.

Hoffmann, C., Zimmermann, F., Biek, R., Kuehl, H., Nowak, K., Mundry, R., Agbor, A., Angedakin, S., Arandjelovic, M., Blankenburg, A., & Brazolla, G. (2017). Persistent anthrax as a major driver of wildlife mortality in a tropical rainforest. *Nature, 548*, 82–86.

Hohmann, G. (2001). Association and social interactions between strangers and residents in Bonobos (*Pan paniscus*). *Primates, 42*, 91–99.

Hohmann, G., Fowler, A., & Ortmann, S. (2006). Frugovory and gregariousness of Salonga bonobos and Gashaka chimpanzees: The influence of abundance and nutritional quality of fruit. In Hohman, G., Robbins, M.M., & Boesch, C. (Eds.), *Feeding ecology in apes and other primates* (pp. 123–159). Cambridge University Press.

Hohmann, G., & Fruth, B. (1993). Field observations on meat sharing among bonobos (*Pan-paniscus*). *Folia Primatologica, 60*, 225–229.

Hohmann, G., & Fruth, B. (2000). Use and function of genital contacts among female bonobos. *Animal Behaviour, 60*, 107–120.

Hohmann, G., & Fruth, B. (2002). Dynamics in social organization of bonobos (*Pan paniscus*). In Boesch, C., Hohmann, G., & Marchant, L. (Eds.), *Behavioural Diversity in Chimpanzees and Bonobos* (pp. 138–150). Cambridge University Press.

Hohmann, G., & Fruth, B. (2003a). Culture in bonobos? Between species and within species variation in behavior. *Current Anthropology, 44*, 563–571.

Hohmann, G., & Fruth, B. (2003b). Intra-and inter-sexual aggression by bonobos in the context of mating. *Behaviour, 140*, 1389–1413.

Hohmann, G., & Fruth, B. (2003c). Lui Kotal: A new site for field research on bonobos in the Salonga National Park. *Pan Africa News, 10*(2), unpaginated. http://mahale.main.jp/PAN/index.html. Accessed May 4, 2020.

Hohmann, G., & Fruth, B. (2007). New records on prey capture and meat eating by bonobos at Lui Kotale, Salonga National Park, Democratic Republic of Congo. *Folia Primatologica, 79*, 103–110.

Hohmann, G., & Fruth, B. (2011). Is blood thicker than water? In Robbins, M.M., & Boesch, C. (Eds.), *Among African apes: Stories and photos from the field* (pp. 61–76). University of California Press.

Hohmann, G., Vigilant, L., Mundry, R., & Behringer, V. (2017). Aggression by male bonobos against immature individuals does not fit with predictions of infanticide. *Aggressive Behavior, 45*, 300–309.

Holloway, R. (1992). Culture: A human domain. *Current Anthropology, 33*, 47–64.

Home Box Office. (1990). *Chimps, so like us.* Direct Cinema Ltd.

Hooper, R. (2011). Going ape: Ultraviolence and our primate cousins. *CultureLab*. http://www.newscientist.com/blogs/culturelab/2011/06/going-ape-ultraviolence-and-our-primate-cousins.html. Accessed June 4, 2014.

Hopkins, W.D., Stimpson, C.D., & Sherwood, C.C. (2019). Social cognition and brain organization in chimpanzees (*Pan troglodytes*) and bonobos (*Pan paniscus*). In Boesch, C., Wittig, R., Crockford, C., Vigilant, L., Deschner, T., & Leendertz, F. (Eds.), *The chimpanzees of the Tai Forest: 40 years of research* (pp. 200–213). Cambridge University Press.

Horiuchi, S. (2004). A competition model within and across groups explaining the contrast between the societies of chimpanzees and bonobos. *Population Ecology*, 46, 65–70.

Horn, A.D. (1980). Some observations on the ecology of the bonobo chimpanzee (*Pan paniscus*, Schwarz 1929) near Lake Tumba, Zaire. *Folia Primatologica*, 34, 145–169.

Hosaka, K. (1995a). Epidemics and wild chimpanzee study groups. *Pan Africa News*, 2(1), unpaginated. http://mahale.main.jp/PAN/index.html. Accessed May 4, 2020.

Hosaka, K. (1995b). Mahale: A single flu epidemic killed at least 11 chimps. *Pan Africa News*, 2(2), unpaginated. http://mahale.main.jp/PAN/index.html. Accessed May 4, 2020.

Hosaka, K. (2015a). Who's who. In Nakamura, M., Hosaka, K., Itoh, N., & Zamma, K. (Eds.), *Mahale chimpanzees: 50 years of research* (pp. 48–67). Cambridge University Press.

Hosaka, K. (2015b). Intimidation display. In Nakamura, M., Hosaka, K., Itoh, N., & Zamma, K. (Eds.), *Mahale chimpanzees: 50 years of research* (pp. 435–447). Cambridge University Press.

Hosaka, K. (2015c). Hunting and food sharing. In Nakamura, M., Hosaka, K., Itoh, N., & Zamma, K. (Eds.), *Mahale chimpanzees: 50 years of research* (pp. 274–290). Cambridge University Press.

Hosaka, K., Matsumoto-Oda, A., Huffman, M.A., & Kawanaka, K. (2000). Reactions to dead bodies of conspecifics by wild chimpanzees in the Mahale Mountains, Tanzania. *Primate Research*, 16, 1–15.

Hosaka, K., & Nakamura, M. (2015a). Male-male relationships. In Nakamura, M., Hosaka, K., Itoh, N., & Zamma, K. (Eds.), *Mahale chimpanzees: 50 years of research* (pp. 387–398). Cambridge University Press.

Hosaka, K., & Nakamura, M. (2015b). Conservation and the future. In Nakamura, M., Hosaka, K., Itoh, N., & Zamma, K. (Eds.), *Mahale chimpanzees: 50 years of research* (pp. 679–690). Cambridge University Press.

Hosaka, K., Nishida, T., Hamai, M., Matsumoto-Oda, A., & Uehara, S. (2001). Predation of mammals by the chimpanzees of the Mahale Mountains, Tanzania. In Galdikas, B.M.F., Briggs, N.E., Sheehan, L.K., Shapiro, G.L., & Goodall, J. (Eds.), *All apes great and small. Volume 1: African apes* (pp. 107–130). Kluwer Academic.

Hosey, G., Melfi, V., Formella, I., Ward, S.J., Tokarski, M., Brunger, D., Brice, S., & Hill, S.P. (2016). Is wounding aggression in zoo-housed chimpanzees and ring-tailed lemurs related to zoo visitor numbers? *Zoo Biology*, 35, 205–209.

Hrdy, S.B. (1974). Male–male competition and infanticide among the langurs (*Presbythe entellus*) of Abu, Rajasthan. *Folia Primatologica*, 22, 19–58.

Hrdy, S.B. (1999). *Mother Nature: A history of mothers, infants, and natural selection*. Pantheon.

Hrdy, S.B., & Hausfater, G. (1984a). Comparative and evolutionary perspectives on infanticide: Introduction and overview. In Hausfater, G., & Hrdy, S.B. (Eds.), *Infanticide: Comparative and evolutionary perspectives* (pp. xiii–xxvi). Aldine.

Hrdy, S.B., & Hausfater, G. (1984b). Preface. In Hausfater, G., & Hrdy, S.B. (Eds.), *Infanticide: Comparative and evolutionary perspectives* (pp. xi–xii). Aldine.

Hughes, N., Rosen, N., Gretsky, N., & Sommer, V. (2011). Will the Nigeria-Cameroon chimpanzee go extinct? Models derived from intake rates of ape sanctuaries. In Sommer, V., & Ross, C. (Eds.), *Primates of Gashaka: Socioecology and conservation in Nigeria's biodiversity hotspot* (pp. 493–523). Springer.

Humle, T. (2003). Chimpanzees and crop raiding in West Africa. In Kormos, R., Boesch, C., Bakarr, M.I., & Butynski, T.M. (Eds.), *West African chimpanzees: Status survey and conservation action plan* (pp. 147–150). IUCN/The World Conservation Union.

Humle, T. (2011). The 2003 epidemic of a flu-like respiratory disease at Bossou. In Matsuzawa, T., Humle, T., & Sugiyama, Y. (Eds.), *The chimpanzees of Bossou and Nimba* (pp. 211–220). Springer.

Humle, T., & Kormos, R. (2011). The Chimpanzees of Yeale, Nimba. In Matsuzawa, T., Humle, T., & Sugiyama, Y. (Eds.), *The chimpanzees of Bossou and Nimba* (pp. 267–275). Springer.

Humle, T., & Matsuzawa, T. (2000). Behavioural diversity among the wild chimpanzee populations of Bossou and neighbouring areas, Guinea and Cote d'Ivoire, West Africa. *Folia Primatologica, 72,* 7–68.

Huneman, P. (2021). *Inclusive fitness teleology and Darwinian explanatory pluralism: A theoretical sketch and an application to current controversies.* HAL archives-ouvertes, ID 031033162. https://hal.archives-ouvertes.fr/hal-03103162/document. Accessed June 1, 2021.

Hunt, K.D. (2000). Initiation of a new chimpanzee study site at Semliki-Toro Wildlife Reserve, Uganda. *Pan Africa News, 7*(2), unpaginated. http://mahale.main.jp/PAN/index.html. Accessed May 4, 2020.

Hunt, K.D. (2011). Is lethal violence an integral part of chimpanzee society? Like it or not, yes. *Psychology Today* [online], April 2011. http://www.psychologytoday.com/blog/the-naked-ape/201104/is-lethal-violence-integral-part-chimpanzee-society. Accessed May 21, 2014.

Hunt, K.D., & McGrew, W.C. (2002). Chimpanzees in the dry habitats of Assirik, Senegal and Semliki Wildlife Reserve, Uganda. In Boesch, C., Hohmann, G., & Marchant, L.F. (Eds.), *Behavioural diversity in chimpanzees and bonobos* (pp. 35–51). Cambridge University Press.

Hunter, R.G. (2012). Epigenetic effects of stress and corticosteroids in the brain. *Frontiers in Cellular Neuroscience, 6,* 18.

Hyeroba, D., Apell, P., & Otali, E. (2011). Managing a speared alpha male chimpanzee (*Pan troglodytes*) in Kibale National Park, Uganda. *Veterinary Record, 169,* 658.

Idani, G. (1990). Relations between unit-groups of bonobos at Wamba, Zaire: Encounters and temporary fusions. *African Study Monographs, 11,* 153–186.

Idani, G.I. (1991). Cases of inter-unit group encounters in pygmy chimpanzees at Wamba, Zaire. In *Primatology today: Proceedings of the XIIIth Congress of the International Primatological Society,* 235–238.

Idani, G.I., Mwanza, N., Ihobe, H., Hashimoto, C., Tashiro, Y., & Furuichi, T. (2008). Changes in the status of bonobos, their habitat, and the situation of humans at Wamba in the Luo Scientific Reserve, Democratic Republic of Congo. In Furuichi, T., & Thompson, J. (Eds.), *The bonobos: Behavior, ecology, and conservation* (pp. 291–302). Springer.

Igmanson, E. (1998). Comment in Stanford, C. The social behavior of chimpanzees and bonobos: Empirical evidence and shifting assumptions. *Current Anthropology, 39*(4), 409–410.

Ihobe, H. (1992). Male–male relationships among wild bonobos (*Pan paniscus*) at Wamba, Republic of Zaire. *Primates, 33*, 163–179.

Inaba, A. (2009). Power takeover occurred in M group of the Mahale Mountains, Tanzania, in 2007. *Pan Africa News, 16*(2), unpaginated. http://mahale.main.jp/PAN/index.html. Accessed May 4, 2020.

Ingold, T. (1987). *The appropriation of nature: Essays on human ecology and social relations.* University of Iowa Press.

Inoue, E., Inoue-Murayama, M., Vigilant, L., Takenaka, O., & Nishida, T. (2008). Relatedness in wild chimpanzees: Influence of paternity, male philopatry, and demographic factors. *American Journal of Physical Anthropology, 137*, 256–262.

Inogwabini, B.I., Bewa, M., Longwango, M., Abokome, M., & Vuvu, M. (2008). The bonobos of the Lake Tumba–Lake Maindombe hinterland: Threats and opportunities for population conservation. In Furuichi, T., & Thompson, J. (Eds.), *The bonobos: Behavior, ecology, and conservation* (pp. 273–290). Springer.

Inogwabini, B.I., Hall, J.S., Vedder, A., Curran, B., Yamagiwa, J., & Basabose, K. (2000). Status of large mammals in the mountain sector of Kahuzi-Biega National Park, Democratic Republic of Congo, in 1996. *African Journal of Ecology, 38*, 269–276.

Isabirye-Basuta, G. (1988). Food competition among individuals in a free-ranging chimpanzee community in Kibale Forest, Uganda. *Behaviour, 105*, 135–147.

Isabirye-Basuta, G., & Lwanga, J.S. (2008). Primate populations and their interactions with changing habitats. *International Journal of Primatology, 29*, 35–48.

Ishizuka, S., Takemoto, H., Sakamaki, T., Tokuyama, N., Toda, K. Hashimoto, C., & Furuichi, T. (2020). Comparisons of between-group differentiation in male kinship between bonobos and chimpanzees. *Scientific Reports, 10*. https://doi.org/10.1038/s41598-019-57133-z

Ishizuka, S., Toda, K., & Furuichi, T. (2020). Genetic analysis of migration pattern of female bonobos (*Pan paniscus*) among three neighboring groups. *International Journal of Primatology, 41*, 401–414.

Itani, J. (1980). Social structure of African great apes. *Journal of Reproduction and Fertility, 28*, 33–41.

Itani, J. (1982). Intraspecific killing among non-human primates. *Journal of Social and Biological Structures, 5*, 361–368.

Itani, J. (1980). Social structures of African great apes. *Journal of Reproductive Fertility, Supplement, 28*, 33–41.

Itani, J. (1996). Afterword: A new milestone in great ape research. In McGrew, W.C., Marchant, L.F., & Nishida, T. (Eds.), *Great ape societies* (pp. 305–308). Cambridge University Press.

Itani, J., & Suzuki, A. (1967). The social unit of chimpanzees. *Primates, 8*, 355–381.

Itoh, N., Sakamaki, T., Hamisi, M., Kitopeni, R., Bunengwa, M., Matumula, M., Athumani, K., Mwami, M., & Bunengwa, H. (1999). A new record of invasion by an unknown unit group into the center of M Group territory. *Pan Africa News, 6*(1), unpaginated. http://mahale.main.jp/PAN/index.html. Accessed May 4, 2020.

Itoh, N., Nakamura, M., Ihobe, H., Uehara, S., Zamma, K., Pintea, L., Seimon, A., & Nishida, T. (2011). Long-term changes in the social and natural environments surrounding the chimpanzees of the Mahale Mountains National Park. In Plumptre, A.J. (Ed.), *The ecological impact of long-term changes in Africa's Rift Valley* (pp. 249–277). Nova Science Publishers.

Izawa, K., & Itani, J. (1966). Chimpanzees in Kasakati Basin, Tanganyika. (I) Ecological study in the rainy season 1963–1964. *Kyoto University African Studies, 1*, 73–156.

Jablonka, E., & Lamb, M.J. (2008). Soft inheritance: Challenging the modern synthesis. *Genetics and Molecular Biology, 31*, 389–395.

Jablonka, E., & Noble, D. (2019). Systemic integration of different inheritance systems. *Current Opinion in Systems Biology, 13*, 52–58.

Jaeggi, A.V., Stevens, J.M., & Van Schaik, C.P. (2010a). Tolerant food sharing and reciprocity is precluded by despotism among bonobos but not chimpanzees. *American Journal of Physical Anthropology, 143*, 41–51.

Jaeggi, A.V., Burkart, J.M., & Van Schaik, C.P. (2010b). On the psychology of cooperation in humans and other primates: Combining the natural history and experimental evidence of prosociality. *Philosophical Transactions of the Royal Society of London B: Biological Sciences, 365*, 2723–2735.

Jenny, D., & Zuberbühler, K. (2005). Hunting behavior in West African forest leopards. *African Journal of Ecology, 43*, 197–200.

Jensen, K., Call, J., & Tomasello, M. (2007). Chimpanzees are vengeful but not spiteful. *Proceedings of the National Academy of Sciences, 104*, 13046–13050.

Johns, B.G. (1996). Responses of chimpanzees to habituation and tourism in the Kibale Forest, Uganda. *Biological Conservation, 78*, 257–262.

Jones, R. (1984). Hunters and history: A case study from Western Tasmania. In Schrire, C. (Ed.), *Past and present in hunter gatherer studies* (pp. 27–65). Academic Press.

Jones, T. (1998). Unification, deduction, and history: A reply to Steel. *Philosophy of Science, 65*, 672–681.

Kaburu, S.S.K., Inoue, S., & Newton-Fisher, N.E. (2013). Death of the alpha: Within-community lethal violence among chimpanzees of the Mahale Mountains National Park. *American Journal of Primatology, 75*, 789–797.

Kahlenberg, S.M., Emery Thompson, M., Muller, M.N., & Wrangham, R.W. (2008). Immigration costs for female chimpanzees and male protection as an immigrant counterstrategy to intrasexual aggression. *Animal Behaviour, 76*, 1497–1509.

Kahlenberg, S.M., & Wrangham, R.W. (2010). Sex differences in chimpanzees' use of sticks as play objects resemble those of children. *Current Biology, 20*, 1067–1068.

Kalan, A.K., et al. (2020). Environmental variability supports chimpanzee behavioral diversity. *Nature Communications, 11*, 1–9.

Kamenya, S. (2002). Human baby killed by Gombe Chimpanzee. *Pan Africa News, 9*(2), unpaginated. http://mahale.main.jp/PAN/index.html. Accessed May 4, 2020.

Kano, T. (1971). The chimpanzees of Filabanga, western Tanzania. *Primates, 12*, 229–246.

Kano, T. (1972). Distribution and adaptation of the chimpanzee on the eastern shore of Lake Tanganyika. *Kyoto University African studies, 7*, 37–129.

Kano, T. (1979). A pilot study on the ecology of pygmy chimpanzees, Pan paniscus. In Hamburg, D.A., & McGown, E.R. (Eds.), *The great apes* (pp. 123–135). Benjamin/Cummings.

Kano, T. (1984a). Distribution of pygmy chimpanzees (*Pan paniscus*) in the central Zaire basin. *Folia primatologica, 43*, 36–52.

Kano, T. (1984b). Observations of physical abnormalities among the wild bonobos (*Pan paniscus*) of Wamba, Zaire. *American Journal of Physical Anthropology, 63*, 1–11.

Kano, T. (1992). *The last ape: Pygmy chimpanzee behavior and ecology*. Stanford University Press.

Kano, T. (1996). Male rank order and copulation rate in a unit-group of bonobos at Wamba, Zaïre. In McGrew, W.C., Marchant, L.F., & Nishida, T. (Eds.), *Great ape societies* (pp. 135–145). Cambridge University Press.

Kano, T. (1998). Comment in Stanford, C. The social behavior of chimpanzees and bonobos: Empirical evidence and shifting assumptions. *Current Anthropology, 39*, 410–411.

Kano, T., & Mulavwa, M. (1984). Feeding ecology of the pygmy chimpanzees (*Pan paniscus*) of Wamba. In Susman, R.L. (Ed.), *The pygmy chimpanzee: Evolutionary biology and behavior* (pp. 233–274). Springer.

Kappeler, P.M., & Fichtel, C. (2015). Eco-evo-devo of the lemur syndrome: Did adaptive behavioral plasticity get canalized in a large primate radiation? *Zoology, 12(supplement), 12*, 1–16.

Kasenene, J.M., & Ross, E.A. (2008). Community benefits from long-term research programs: A case study from Kibale National Park, Uganda. In Wrangham, R.W., & Ross, E. (Eds.), *Science and conservation in African forests: The benefits of long-term research* (pp. 99–114). Cambridge University Press.

Kasozi, A.B.K. (1994). *The social origins of violence in Uganda, 1964–1985*. McGill-Queen's University Press.

Kaur, T., Singh, J., Tong, S., Humphrey, C., Clevenger, D., Tan, W., Szekely, B., Wang, Y. Li, Y., Muse, E.A., Kiyono, M., Hanamura, S., Inoue, E., Nakamura, M., Huffman, M.A., Jiang, B., & Nishida T. (2008). Descriptive epidemiology of fatal respiratory outbreaks and detection of a human-related metapneumovirus in wild chimpanzees (*Pan troglodytes*) at Mahale Mountains National Park, Western Tanzania. *American Journal of Primatology, 70*, 755–765.

Kawanaka, K. (1981). Infanticide and cannibalism in chimpanzees: With special reference to the newly observed case in the Mahale Mountains. *African Study Monographs, 1*, 69–99.

Kawanaka, K., & Nishida, T. (1974). Recent advances in the study of inter-unit-group relationships and social structure of wild chimpanzees of the Mahali Mountains. In *Proceedings from the Symposia of the Fifth Congress of the International Primatological Society* (pp. 173–186). International Primatological Society.

Keele, B., Jones, J.H., . . . Hahn, B.H. (2009). Increased mortality and AIDS-like immunopathology in wild chimpanzees infected with SIVcpz. *Nature, 460*, 515–519.

Keeley, L. (1996). *War before civilization: The myth of the peaceful savage*. Oxford University Press.

Keim, B. (2010). Girl chimpanzees may use sticks as dolls. *Wired Science*. http://www.wired.com/2010/12/chimp-dolls/. Accessed June 9, 2014.
Kelley, E.A., & Sussman, R.W. (2007). An academic genealogy on the history of American field primatologists. *American Journal of Physical Anthropology, 132*, 406–407.
Kelly, R. (Raymond). (1985). *The Nuer conquest: The structure and development of an expansionist system*. University of Michigan Press.
Kelly, R. (Raymond). (2000). *Warless societies and the origin of war*. University of Michigan Press.
Kelly R. (Raymond). (2005). The evolution of intergroup violence. *Proceedings of the National Academy of Sciences, 102*, 15294–15298.
Kelly, R. (Robert). (2013a). From the peaceful to the warlike: Ethnographic and archaeological insights into hunter-gatherers. In Fry, D. (Ed.), *War, peace, and human nature: The convergence of evolutionary of cultural views* (pp. 151–167). Oxford University Press.
Kelly, R. (Robert). (2013b). *The lifeways of hunter-gatherers: The foraging spectrum* (2nd ed.). Cambridge University Press.
Kemper, T.D. (1990). *Social structure and testosterone: Explorations of the socio-bio-social chain*. Rutgers University Press.
Kennedy, J., & Pavlicev, M. (2017). Female orgasm and the emergence of prosocial empathy: An evo-devo perspective. *Journal of Experimental Zoology: Molecular and Developmental Evolution, 330*, 66–75.
Kerbis Peterhans, J.C., Wrangham, R.W., Carter, M.L., & Hauser, M.D. (1993). A contribution to tropical rain forest taphonomy: Retrieval and documentation of chimpanzee remains from Kibale Forest, Uganda. *Journal of Human Evolution, 25*, 485–514.
Keverne, E.B. (2014). Significance of epigenetics for understanding brain development, brain evolution and behaviour. *Neuroscience, 264*, 207–217.
Kevles, B. (1976). *The wild apes: The primate studies of Goodall, Fossey, and Galdikas*. E.P. Dutton and Company.
Kingdon, J. (1989). *Island Africa*. Princeton University Press.
Kirchoff, C.A., Wilson, M.L., Mjungu, D.C., Raphael, J., Kamenya, S., & Collins, D.A. (2018). Infanticide in chimpanzees: Taphonomic case studies from Gombe. *American Journal of Physical Anthropology, 165*, 108–122.
Kitopeni, R., & Kasagula, M.B. (1995). Ntologi Falls??! *Pan Africa News, 2*(2), unpaginated. http://mahale.main.jp/PAN/index.html. Accessed May 4, 2020.
Klailova, M., Casanova, C., Jenschel, P., Lee, P., Rovero, F., & Todd, A. (2013). Non-human predator interactions with wild great apes in Africa and the use of camera traps to study their dynamics. *Folia Primatologica, 83*, 312–328.
Klein, H., Bockserger, G., Baas, P., Bunel, S., Theleste, E., Pika, S., & Deschner, T. (2021). Hunting of mammals by central chimpanzees (*Pan troglodytes troglodytes*) in the Loango National Park, Gabon. *Primates, 62*, 267–278.
Klopfer, P.H., & Gilbert, B.K. (1966). A note on retrieval and recognition of young in the elephant seal, *Mirounga angustirostris*. *Sonderdruck aus Zeitschrift fur Tierpsychologie, 6*, 575–760.
Kondgen, S., Calvignac-Spencer, S., Grutzmacher, K., Keil, V., Matz-Rensing, K., Nowak, K., Metzger, S., Kiyang, J., Lubke-Becker, A., Deschner, T., Wittig, R.M, Lankester, F., & Leendertz, F. (2017). Evidence for human Streptococcus pneumonia in wild and captive chimpanzees: A potential threat to wild chimpanzees. *Scientific Reports, 7*, 1–8.

Knauft, B. (1991). Reconsidering violence in simply human societies: Homicide among the Gebusi of New Guinea. *Current Anthropology, 28*, 457–500.

Kojima, S., Izumi, A., & Ceugniet, M. (2003). Identification of vocalizers by pant hoots, pant grunts and screams in a chimpanzee. *Primates, 44*, 225–230.

Kondgen, S., Kuhl, H., N'Goran, P.K., Walsh, P.D., Schenk, S., Emst, N., Biek, R., Formenty, P., Matz-Rensing, K., Schweiger, B., Junflen, S., Elierbrok, H., Nitsche, A., Briese, T., Lipkin, W.I., Pauli, G., Boesch, C., & Leendertz, F.H. (2008). Pandemic human viruses cause decline of endangered great apes. *Current Biology, 18*, 260–264.

Konner, M.J. (1993). Do we need enemies? The origins and consequences of rage. In Glick, R., & Roose, S. (Eds.), *Rage, power, and aggression* (pp. 173–193). Yale University.

Konner, M.J. (2006). Human nature, ethnic violence, and war. In Fitzduff, M., & Stout, C.E. (Eds.), *The psychology of resolving global conflicts: From war to peace. Volume 1: Nature vs nurture* (pp. 1–39). Praeger Security International.

Koops, K., Furuichi, T., & Hashimoto, C. (2015a). Chimpanzees and bonobos differ in intrinsic motivation for tool use. *Scientific Reports, 5*, 1–8.

Koops, K., McGrew, W.C., & Matsuzawa, T. Do chimpanzees (*Pan troglodytes*) use cleavers and anvils to fracture *Traculia africana* fruits? Preliminary data on a new form of percussive technology. *Primates, 51*, 175–178.

Koops, K., Schöning, C., Isaji, M., & Hashimoto, C. (2015b). Cultural differences in ant-dipping tool length between neighbouring chimpanzee communities at Kalinzu, Uganda. *Scientific Reports, 5*, 1–9.

Kormos, R., Humle, T., Brugiere, D., Fleury-Brugiere, M-C., Matsuzawa, T., Sugiyama, Y., Carter, J., Diallo, M.S., Sagno, C., & Tounkara, E.O. (2003). The Republic of Guinea. In Kormos, R., Boesch, C., Bakarr, M.I, & Butynski, T.M. (Eds.), *West African chimpanzees: Status survey and conservation action plan* (pp. 63–76). IUCN/The World Conservation Union.

Kouakou, C.Y., Boesch, C., Kuehl, H. (2009). Estimating chimpanzee population size with nest counts: Validating methods in Tai National Park. *American Journal of Primatology, 71*, 447–457.

Kouassi, J.A., Normand, E., Koné, I., & Boesch, C. (2017). Bushmeat consumption and environmental awareness in rural households: A case study around Taï National Park, Côte d'Ivoire. *Oryx, 53*, 293–299.

Kracke, W.H. (1978). *Force and persuasion*. University of Chicago Press.

Krebs, D.L. (2011). *The origins of morality: An evolutionary account*. Oxford University Press.

Krief, S., Berny, P., Gumisiriza, F., Gross, R., Demeneix, B., Fini, J.B., Chapman, C.A., Chapman, L.J., Seguya, A., & Wasswa, J. (2017). Agricultural expansion as risk to endangered wildlife: Pesticide exposure in wild chimpanzees and baboons displaying facial dysplasia. *Science of the Total Environment, 598*, 647–656.

Krief, S., Couturier, C., Bonnald, J., Okimat, J.P., Asalu, E., & Krief, J-M. (2020). COVID-19 and chimpanzees from a field perspective: Migration measures, ecological and economical situation after four months in Sebitoli, Kibale National, Park, Uganda. *Pan Africa News, 27(2)*, 16–20.

Krief, S., Huffman, M.A., Sevenet, T., Guillot, J., Bories, C., Hladik, C.M., & Wrangham, R.W. (2005). Noninvasive monitoring of the health of *Pan troglodytes schweinfurthii* in the Kibale National Park, Uganda. *International Journal of Primatology, 26*, 467–490.

Krief, S., Vermeulen, B., Lafosse, S., Kasenene, J.M., Nieguitsila, A., Berthelemy, M., Bain, O., & Guillot, J. (2010). Nodular worm infection in wild chimpanzees in Western Uganda: A risk for human health? *PloS Neglected Tropical Diseases, 4,* e630.

Kroeber, A. (1955). Nature of land-holding group. *Ethnohistory, 2,* 303–314.

Kroeber, C.B., & Fontana, B.L. (1986). *Massacre on the Gila: An account of the last major battle between American Indians, with reflections on the origin of war.* University of Arizona Press.

Kruuk, H., & Turner, M. 1967. Comparative notes on predation by lion, leopard, cheetah and wild dog in the Serengeti Area, East Africa. *Mammalia, 31,* 1–27.

Kuehl, H.S., Elzner, C., Moebius, Y., Boesch, C., & Walsh, P.D. (2008). The price of play: Self-organized infant mortality cycles in chimpanzees. *PloS One* 3, [online]. http://www.ncbi.nlm.nih.gov/pmc/articles/PMC2426927/. Accessed June 23, 2014.

Kuhl, H.S., Sop, T., Williamson, E.A., Mundry, R., Brugière, D., Campbell, G., Cohen, H., Danquah, E., Ginn, L., Herbinger, I., & Jones, S. (2017). The critically endangered Western chimpanzee declines by 80%. *American Journal of Primatology, 79,* 1–15.

Kuhl, H.S., Boesch, C., . . . Kalan, A.K. (2019). Human impact erodes chimpanzee behavioral diversity. *Science, 363,* 1453–1455.

Kuhar, C.W., Bettinger, T.L., Lehnhardt, K., Osuo, T., & Cox, T. (2010). Evaluating for long-term impact of an environmental education program at the Kalinzu Forest Reserve, Uganda. *American Journal of Primatology, 72,* 407–413.

Kuroda, S. (1979). Grouping of the pygmy chimpanzees. *Primates, 20,* 161–183.

Kuroda, S. (1980). Social behavior of the pygmy chimpanzees. *Primates, 21,* 181–197.

Kuroda, S. (1984). Interaction over food among pygmy chimpanzees. In Susman, R.L. (Ed.), *The pygmy chimpanzee: Evolutionary biology and behavior* (pp. 301–324). Springer.

Kutsukake, N., & Matsusaka, T. (2002). Incident of intense aggression by chimpanzees against an infant from another group in Mahale Mountain National Park, Tanzania. *American Journal of Primatology, 58,* 157–165.

Ladd, S. (2013). *Pimu's Murder- Steve Ladd, Greystoke Mahale.* [Online video]. http://vimeo.com/40444106. Accessed June 2, 2014.

Lahr, M.M., et al. (2016). Inter-group violence among early Holocene hunter-gatherers of West Turkana, Kenya. *Nature, 529,* 394–398.

Laland, K.N., & Janik, V.M. (2006). The animal cultures debate. *Trends in Ecology and Evolution, 21,* 542–547.

Laland, K.N., Sterelny, K., Odling-Smee, J., Hoppitt, W., & Uller, T. (2011). Cause and effect in biology revisited: Is Mayr's proximate-ultimate dichotomy still useful? *Science, 334,* 1512–1516.

Laland, K.N., Uller, T., Edelman, M., Sterelny, K., Muller, G.B., Moczek, A., Jablonka, E., & Odling-Smee, J. (2014). Does evolutionary theory need a rethink? Point, Yes, urgently. *Nature, 514,* 161–164.

Laland, K.N., Uller, T., Feldman, M.W., Sterelny, K., Muller, G.B., Moczek, A., Jablonka, E., & Odling-Smee, J. (2015). The extended evolutionary synthesis: Its structure, assumptions and predictions. *Proceedings of the Royal Society B, 282,* 20151019, 1–14.

Lambeth, S.P., Bloomsmith, M.A., & Alford, P.L. (1997). Effects of human activity on chimpanzee wounding. *Zoo Biology, 16,* 327–333.

Landecker, H., & Panofsky, A. (2013). From social structure to gene regulation, and back: A critical introduction to environmental epigenetics for sociology. *Annual Review of Sociology, 39*, 333–357.

Land Tenure Center. (1989). *Settlement in forest reserves, game reserves and national parks in Uganda*. Land Tenure Center, Nelson Institute for Environmental Studies.

Langat, A. (2019). For the famed chimps of Gombe, human encroachment takes a toll. Mongabay series: Global forests, global apes. https://news.mongabay.com/2019/02/for-the-famed-chimps-of-gombe-human-encroachment-takes-a-toll/. Accessed May 1, 2020.

Langergraber, K. (2012). Cooperation among kin. In Mitani, J., Call, J., Kappeler, P.M., Palombit, R.A., & Silk, J.B. (Eds.), *The evolution of primate societies* (pp. 491–513). University of Chicago Press.

Langergraber, K., Boesch, C., Inoue, E., Inoue-Murayama, M., Mitani, J.C., Nishida, T., Pusey, A., Reynolds, V., Schubert, G., Wrangham, R.W., Wroblewski, E., & Vigilant, L. (2011). Genetic and "cultural" similarity in wild chimpanzees. *Proceedings of the Royal Society B, 278*, 408–416.

Langergraber, K., Mitani, J., & Vigilant, L. (2007). The limited impact of kinship on cooperation in wild chimpanzees. *Proceedings of the National Academy of Sciences U.S.A., 104*, 7786–7790.

Langergraber, K., Mitani, J., & Vigilant, L. (2009). Kinship and social bonds in female chimpanzees (*Pan troglodytes*). *American Journal of Primatology, 71*, 840–851.

Langergraber, K., Mitani, J.C., Watts, D.P., & Vigilant, L. (2013). Male–female sociospatial relationships and reproduction in wild chimpanzees. *Behavioral Ecology and Sociobiology, 67*, 861–873.

Langergraber, K., Prüfer, K., Rowney, C., Boesch, C., Crockford, C., Fawcett, K., Inoue, E., Inoue-Muruyama, M., Mitani, J.C., Muller, M.N., Robbins, M.M., Schubert, G., Stoinski, T.S., Viola, B., Watts, D, Wittig, R.M., Wrangham, R.W., Zuberbühler, K., Paabo, S., & Vigilant, L. (2012). Generation times in wild chimpanzees and gorillas suggest earlier divergence times in great ape and human evolution. *PNAS, 109*, 15716–15721.

Langergraber, K., Rowney, C., Crockford, C., Wittig, R., Zuberbühler, K., & Vigilant, L. (2014). Genetic analyses suggest no immigration of adult females and their offspring into the Sonso community of chimpanzees in the Budongo Forest Reserve, Uganda. *American Journal of Primatology, 76*, 640–648.

Langergraber, K., & Vigilant, L. (2011). Genetic differences cannot be excluded from generating behavioural differences among chimpanzee groups. *Proceedings of the Royal Society B, 278*, 2094–2095.

Langoya, C.D., & Long, C. (1997). Local communities and ecotourism development in Budongo Forest Reserve, Uganda. *Budongo Forest Ecotourism Project* [online]. http://www.edi.org.uk/sites/edi.org.uk/files/edi-assets/publications-opinion-files/1172.pdf. Accessed May 9, 2014.

Laporte, N., Walker, W., Stabach, J., & Landsberg, F. (2008). Monitoring forest–savanna dynamics in Kibale National Park with satellite imagery (1989–2003): Implications for the management of wildlife habitat. In Wrangham, R.W., & Ross, R. (Eds.), *Science and conservation in African forests: The benefits of long-term research* (pp. 38–50). Cambridge University Press.

Latzman, R.D., Hopkings, W.D., Keebaugh, A.C., & Young, L.J. (2014). Personality in chimpanzees (*Pan troglodytes*): Exploring the hierarchical structure of associations with the vasopressin V1A receptor gene. *PloS ONE, 9*, e95741, 1–2.

Latzman, R.D., Hecht, L.K., Freeman, H.D., Schapiro, S.J., & Hopkings, W.D. (2015a). Neuroanatomical correlates of personality in chimpanzees (*Pan troglodytes*): Associations between personality and frontal cortex. *Neuroimage, 123*, 63–71.

Latzman, R.D., Freeman, H.D., Schapiro, S.J., & Hopkins, W.D. (2015b). The contribution of genetics and early rearing experiences to hierarchical personality dimensions in chimpanzees (*Pan troglodytes*). *Journal of Personality and Social Psychology, 109*, 889–900.

Lawler, R. (2011). Feeding competition, cooperation, and the causes of primate sociality: A commentary on the model proposed by Sussman et al. *American Journal of Primatology, 73*, 84–90.

Layton, R. (1986). Political and territorial structures among hunter-gatherers. *Man, 21*(1), 18–33.

Leakey, L., & Ardrey, R. (1971). Aggression and violence in man: A dialogue between Dr. Louis Leakey and Mr. Robert Ardrey. *Munger Africana Library Notes, 9*.

Lee, M.E., Alonso, A., Dallmeier, F., Campbell, P., & Pauwels, O.S.G. (2006). The Gamba complex of protected areas: An illustration of Gabon's biodiversity. *Bulletin of the Biological Society of Washington, 12*, 229–241.

Lee, R. (2018). Hunter-gatherers and human evolution: New light on old debates. *Annual Review of Anthropology, 47*, 513–531.

Leech, B.L., & Cronk, L. (2017). Coordinated policy action and flexible coalitional psychology: How evolution made humans so good at politics. *Cognitive Systems Research, 43*, 89–99.

Leendertz, F.H., Ellerbrok, H., Boesch, C., Couacy-Hymann, E., Matz-Rensing, K., Hakenbeck, R., Bergmann, C., Abaza, P., Junglen, S., Moebius, Y., Vigilant, L., Formenty, P., & Pauli, G. (2004). Anthrax kills wild chimpanzees in a tropical rainforest. *Nature, 430*, 451–452.

Leendertz, S.A.J., Locatelli, S., Boesch, C., Formenty, P., Liegeois, F., Ayouba, A., Peeters, M., & Leendertz, F.H. (2011). No evidence for transmission of SIVwrc from western red colobus monkeys (*Piliocolobus badius badius*) to wild west African chimpanzees (*Pan troglodytes verus*) despite high exposure through hunting. *BMC Microbiology, 11*, [online]. http://www.biomedcentral.com/content/pdf/1471-2180-11-24.pdf. Accessed June 23 2014.

Legrain, L., Stevens, J., Alegria Iscoa, J., & Destrebecqz, A. (2011). A case study of conflict management in bonobos: How does a bonobo (*Pan paniscus*) mother manage conflicts between her sons and her female coalition partner? *Folia primatologica, 82*, 236–243.

Le Hellaye, Y., Goosens, B, Jamart, A., & Curtis, D.J. (2010). Acquisition of fission-fusion social organization in a chimpanzee (*Pan troglodytes troglodytes*) community released into the wild. *Behavioral Ecology and Sociobiology, 64*, 349–360.

Lehman, J., & Boesch, C. (2005). Bisexually bonded ranging in chimpanzees (*Pan troglodytes verus*). *Behavioral Ecology and Sociobiology, 57*, 525–535.

Lehman Haupt, C. (1971). David and Goliath and Mike and Flo. *New York Times*, November 26, 35.

Lehmann, J., & Boesch, C. (2008). Sexual differences in chimpanzee sociality. *International Journal of Primatology, 29*, 65–81.

Lema, S.C. (2020). Hormones, developmental plasticity, and adaptive evolution: Endocrine flexibility as a catalyst for "plasticity-first" phenotypic divergence. *Molecular and Cellular Endocrinology, 502*, 110678, 1–14.

Lemoine, S., Boesch, C., Preis, A., Samuni, L., Crockford, C., & Wittig, R.M. (2020). Group dominance increases territory size and reduces neighbor pressure in wild chimpanzees. *Royal Society Open Science, 7*, 200577, 1–15.

Lepp, A. (2008). Tourism and dependency: An analysis of Bigodi village, Uganda. *Tourism Management, 29*, 1206–1214.

Leroux, M., Monday, G., Chandia, B., Akankwasa, J.W., Zuberbuhler, K., Hobaiter, C., Crockford, C., Townsend, S.W., Asiimwe, C., & Fedurek, P. (2021). First observation of a chimpanzee with albinism in the wild: Social interactions and subsequent infanticide. *American Journal of Primatology*, 1–7. https://doi.org/10.1002/ajp.23305

Lewis, R.J. (2002). Beyond dominance: The importance of leverage. *Quarterly Review of Biology, 77*, 149–164.

Linden, E. (2002). The wife beaters of Kibale. *Time Magazine*, August 19, 56–57.

Linder, J.M., & Palkovitz, R.E. (2016). The threat of industrial oil palm expansion to primates and their habitats. In Waller, M. (Ed.), *Ethnoprimatology: Primate conservation in the 21st century* (pp. 21–45). Springer.

Lindshield, S., Danielson, B.J., Rothman, J.M., & Pruetz, J.D. (2017). Feeding in fear? How adult male western chimpanzees (*Pan troglodytes verus*) adjust to predation and savanna habitat pressures. *American Journal of Physical Anthropology, 163*, 480–496.

Lingomo, B., & Kimura, D. (2009). Taboo of eating bonobo among the Bongando people in the Wamba Region, Democratic Republic of Congo. *African Study Monographs, 30*(4), 209–225.

Lobon, I., Tucci, S., De Manuel, M., Ghirotto, S., Benazzo, A., Prado-Martinez, J., Lorente-Galdos, B., Nam, K., Dabad, M., Hernandez-Rodriguez, J., & Comas, D. (2016). Demographic history of the genus *Pan* inferred from whole mitochondrial genome reconstructions. *Genome Biology and Evolution, 8*, 2020–2030.

Lonsdorf, E.V., Travos, D., Puseyu, A.E., Goodall, J., Mcgrew, W.C. (2006). Using retrospective health data from the Gombe chimpanzee study to inform future monitoring efforts. *American Journal of Primatology, 68*, 897–908.

Lonsdorf, E.V., Murray, C.M., Lonsdorf, E.V., Travis, D.A., Gilby, I.C., Chosy, J., Goodall, J., & Pusey, A. (2011). A retrospective analysis of factors correlated to chimpanzee (*Pan troglodytes schweifurthii*) respiratory health at Gombe National Park, Tanzania. *EcoHealth, 8*, 26–35.

Lonsdorf, E.V., Gillespie, T.R., ... Travis, D.A. (2016). Socioecological correlates of clinical signs in two communities of wild chimpanzees (*Pan troglodytes*) at Gombe National Park, Tanzania. *American Journal of Primatology, 80*, e22562, 1–20.

Lopresti-Goodman, S.M., Kameka, M., & Dube, A. (2013). Stereotypical behaviors in chimpanzees rescued from the African bushmeat and pet trade. *Behavioral Sciences, 3*, 1–20.

Lorenz, K. (1966). *On Aggression*. Harcourt, Brace and World.

Lowe, A.E., Hobaiter, C., Aslimwe, C., & Zuberbuhler, K. (2019). Intra-community infanticide in wild, eastern chimpanzees: A 24-year review. *Primates, 61*, 69–83.

Lucchesi, S. (2021). Better together? How intergroup associations affect energy balance and feeding behavior in wild bonobos. *Behavioral Ecology and Sociobiology, 75*, 1–14.

Lukas, D., Reynolds, V., Boesch, C., & Vigilant, L. (2005). To what extent does living in a group mean living with kin? *Molecular Ecology, 14*, 2181–2196.

Lukasik-Braum, M., & Spelman, L. (2008). Chimpanzee respiratory disease and visitation rules at Mahale and Gombe National Parks in Tanzania. *American Journal of Primatology, 70*, 734–737.

Luncz, L., & Boesch C. (2015). The extent of cultural variation between adjacent chimpanzee (*Pan troglodytes verus*) communities: A microecological approach. *American Journal of Physical Anthropology, 156*, 67–75.

Luncz, L., Mundry, R., & Boesch, C. (2012). Evidence for cultural differences between neighboring chimpanzee communities. *Current Biology, 22*, 922–926.

Lwanga, J.S., Butynski, T.M., & Struhsaker, T.T. (2000). Tree population dynamics in Kibale National Park, Uganda 1975–1998. *African Journal of Ecology, 38*, 238–247.

Lwanga, J.S. (2003). Localized tree mortality following the drought of 1999 at Ngogo, Kibale National Park, Uganda. *African Journal of Ecology, 41*, 194–196.

Lwanga, J.S. (2006). Spatial distribution of primates in a mosaic of colonizing and old growth forest at Ngogo, Kibale National Park, Uganda. *Primates, 47*, 230–238.

Lwanga, J.S., & Isabirye-Basuta, G. (2008). Long-term perspectives on forest conservation: Lessons from research in Kibale National Park. In Wrangham, R., & Ross, E. (Eds.), *Science and conservation in African forests: The benefits of longterm research* (pp. 63–74). Cambridge University Press.

Lwanga, J.S., Struhsaker, T.T., Struhsaker, P.J., Butynski, T.M., & Mitani, J.C. (2011). Primate population dynamics over 32.9 years at Ngogo, Kibale National Park, Uganda. *American Journal of Primatology, 73*, 997–1011.

Lycett, S.J., Collard, M., & McGrew, W.C. (2007). Phylogenetic analyses of behavior support existence of culture among wild chimpanzees. *Proceedings of the National Academy of Sciences, 104*, 17588–17592.

Lycett, S.J., Collard, M., & McGrew, W.C. (2009). Cladistic analyses of behavioural variation in wild *Pan troglodytes*: Exploring the chimpanzee culture hypothesis. *Journal of Human Evolution, 57*, 337–349.

Lycett, S.J., Collard, M., & McGrew, W.C. (2010). Are behavioral differences among wild chimpanzee communities genetic or cultural? An assessment using tool use data and phylogenetic methods. *American Journal of Physical Anthropology, 142*, 461–467.

Lycett, S.J., Collard, M., & McGrew, W.C. (2011). Correlations between genetic and behavioural dissimilarities in wild chimpanzees (*Pan troglodytes*) do not undermine the case for culture. *Proceedings of the Royal Society of London B: Biological Sciences, 278*, 2091–2093.

Mackenzie, C.A., Chapman, C.A., & Sengupta, R. (2011). Spatial patterns of illegal resource extraction in Kibale National Park, Uganda. *Environmental Conservation, 39*, 38–50.

MacKinnon, K.C., & Fuentes, A. (2011). Primates, niche construction, and social complexity: The roles of social cooperation and altruism. In Cloninger, R., & Sussman, R. (Eds.), *Origins of cooperation and altruism* (pp. 121–143). Springer.

Macfie, E.J., & Williamson, E.A. (2010). *Best practice guidelines for great ape tourism.* International Union for Conservation of Nature.

Madden, R. (2002). You looking at me? *Sunday Telegraph*, January13. http:www.discovery initiatives.com/articleschimp.asp. Accessed May 23, 2004.

Maher, B. (2008). The case of the missing heritability. *Nature, 456*, 18–21.

Maki, S., Alford, P.L., & Bramblett, C. (1987). The effects of unfamiliar humans on aggression in captive chimpanzee groups. (Abstract). *American Journal of Primatology, 12*, 358.

Malenky, R.K., Kuroda, S., Vineberg, E.O., & Wrangham, R.W. (1994). The significance of terrestrial herbaceous foods for bonobos, chimpanzees and gorillas. In Wrangham, R.W., McGrew, W.C., de Waal, F.B.M., & Heltne, P. (Eds.), *Chimpanzee cultures* (pp. 59–75). Harvard University Press.

Maley, J. (1996). The African rain forest: Main characteristics of changes in vegetation and climate from the Upper Cretaceous to the Quaternary. *Proceedings of the Royal Society of Edinburgh. Section B. Biological Sciences, 104*, 31–73.

Malinowski, B. (1941). An anthropological analysis of war. *American Journal of Sociology, 46*, 521–550.

Malone, N.M., Fuentes, A., & White, F.J. (2010). Ethics commentary: Subjects of knowledge and control in field primatology. *American Journal of Primatology, 72*, 779–784.

Manson, J.H., & Wrangham, R.W. (1991). Intergroup aggression in chimpanzees and humans. *Current Anthropology, 32*, 369–390.

Marchant, L.F., & McGrew, W.C. (1991). Comment in Manson, J.H., & Wrangham, R.W. Intergroup aggression in chimpanzees and humans. *Current Anthropology, 32*, 369–390.

Markham, A.C., Lonsdorf, E.V., Pusey, A.E., & Murray, C.M. (2015). Maternal rank influences the outcome of aggressive interactions between immature chimpanzees. *Animal Behaviour, 100*, 192–198.

Marshall, M. (2015). Chimpanzees over-hunt prey almost to extinction. BBC Earth, http://www.bbc.com/earth/story/20150728-chimps-nearly-wiped-out-monkeys. Accessed May 3, 2020.

Martinez-Inigo, L., Bass, P., Klein, H., Pika, S., & Deschner, T. (2021a). Intercommunity interactions and killings in central chimpanzees (*Pan troglodytes troglodytes*) from Loango National Park, Gabon. *Primates*. https://doi.org/10/1007/s10329-021-00921-x

Martinez-Inigo, L., Bass, P., Klein, H., Pika, S., & Deschner, T. (2021b). Home range size in central chimpanzees (*Pan troglodytes troglodytes*) from Loango National Park, Gabon. *Primates*, 1–12. https://doi.org/10.1007/s10329-021-00927-5

Massaro, A.P., Wroblewski, E.E., Mjungu, D.C., Foerster, S., Walker, K., Desai, N., Kamenya, S., Simmons, N.M., Rudicell, R.S., Hahn, B.H., Pusey, A.E., & Wilson, M.L. (2020). Demographic factors influence the relative costs and benefits of intragroup killing. https://www.google.com/search?client=firefox-b-1-d&q=%22demographic+factors+influence+the+relative+costs+and+benefits+of+chimpanzee+intergroup+killing%22&spell=1&sa=X&ved=2ahUKEwj-uebil-fsAhXclXIEHf0XAcEQBSgAegQIAxAq&biw=1280&bih=537. Accessed November 3, 2020.

Massaro, A.P., Wroblewski, E., Mjungu, D., Boehm, E., Desai, N., Foerster, S., Rudicell, R., Hahn, B., Pusey, A., & Wilson, M.L. (n.d.). Female monopolizability promotes within-community killing in chimpanzees. *Research Square*. https://doi.org/10.21203/rs.3.rs-163673/v1

Massen, J., Antonides, A., Arnold, A-M., Bionda, T., & Koski, S.E. (2013). A behavioral view on chimpanzee personality: Exploration tendency, persistence, boldness, and tool-orientation measured with group experiments. *American Journal of Primatology, 75*, 947–958.

Masters, R. (2004). Survival of the fittest, review of *Darwin and International Relations*. *International Review, 26*, 82–83.

Matsumoto-Oda, A., Hosaka, K., Huffman, M.A., & Kawanaka, K. (1998). Factors affecting party size in chimpanzees of the Mahale Mountains. *International Journal of Primatology, 19*, 999–1011.

Matsumoto-Oda, A., & Kasagula, M.B. (2000). Preliminary study of feeding competition between baboons and chimpanzees in the Mahale Mountains National Park, Tanzania. *African Study Monographs, 21*, 147–157.

Matsuzawa, T. (1997). The death of an infant chimpanzee at Bossou, Guinea. *Pan Africa News, 4*(1), unpaginated. http://mahale.main.jp/PAN/index.html. Accessed May 4, 2020.

Matsuzawa, T., & Humle, T. (2011). Bossua: 33 Years. In Matsuzawa, T., Humle, T., & Sugiyama, Y. (Eds.), *The chimpanzees of Bossou and Nimba* (pp. 3–10). Springer.

Matsuzawa, T., & Kourouma, M. (2008). The Green Corridor Project: Long term research and conservation in Bossou, Guinea. In Wrangham, R., & Ross, E. (Eds.), *Science and conservation in African forests: The benefits of long-term research* (pp. 201–212). Cambridge University Press.

Matsuzawa, T., Ohashi, G., Humle, T., Granier, N., Kourouma, M., & Soumah, A.G. (2011). Green Corridor Project: Planting trees in the savanna between Bossou and Nimba. In Matsuzawa, T., Humle, T., & Sugiyama, Y. (Eds.), *The chimpanzees of Bossou and Nimba* (pp. 361–379). Springer.

Matsuzawa, T., Sakura, O., Kimura, T., Hamada, Y., & Sugiyama, Y. (1990). Case report on the death of a wild chimpanzee (*Pan troglodytes verus*). *Primates, 31*, 635–641.

Max Planck Institute. (2017). *Chimpanzee groups*. Max-Planck-Institut fur evolutionare Anthropologie. https://www.eva.mpg.de/primat/research-groups/chimpanzee/field-sites/tai-chimpanzee-project/chimpanzee-groups/html. Accessed May 11, 2018.

Maybury-Lewis, D. (1974). *Akwe-Shavante society*. Oxford University Press.

McCarthy, M. (2010). Chimpanzees "launch murderous sprees to expand their territories." *The Independent* [online]. http://www.independent.co.uk/environment/nature/chimpanzees-launch-murderous-sprees-to-expand-their-territories-2006829.html. Accessed June 10, 2014.

McComb, K., Packer, C., & Pusey, A. (1994). Roaring and numerical assessment in contests between groups of female lions, *Panthera leo*. *Animal Behavior, 47*, 379–387.

McEwen, B.S. (2018). Redefining neuroendocrinology: Epigenetics of brain-body communication over the life course. *Frontiers in Neuroendocrinology, 49*, 8–30.

McGrew, W.C. (1992). *Chimpanzee material culture: Implications for human evolution*. Cambridge University Press.

McGrew, W. (2010). (Review of) Christophe Boesch: *The real chimpanzees: Sex strategies in the forest*. *Primates, 51*, 189–190.

McGrew, W. (2017). Field studies of *Pan troglodytes* reviewed and comprehensively mapped, focussing on Japan's contribution to cultural primatology. *Primates, 58*, 237–258.

McGrew, W.C., Baldwin, P.J., & Tutin, C.E.G. (1981). Chimpanzees in a hot, dry and open habitat: Mt. Assirik, Senegal, West Africa. *Journal of Human Evolution, 10*, 227–244.

McGrew/Pierce. (2009). (McGrew, W. Foreword to Pierce, A.H. 1974). An encounter between a leopard and a group of chimpanzees at Gombe National Park. *Pan Africa News*, *16*(4), unpaginated http://mahale.main.jp/PAN/index.html. Accessed May 17, 2020.

McLennan, M.R., & Hill, C.M. (2010). Chimpanzee responses to researchers in a disturbed forest-farm mosaic at Bulindi, Western Uganda. *American Journal of Primatology*, *72*, 907–918.

McLennan, M.R., & Hill, C.M. (2012). Troublesome neighbours: Changing attitudes towards chimpanzees (*Pan troglodytes*) in a human-dominated landscape in Uganda. *Journal for Nature Conservation*, *20*, 219–227.

McLennan, M.R., & Hockings, K.J. (2016). The aggressive apes? Causes and contexts of great ape attacks on local persons. In Angelici, F. (Ed.), *Problematic wildlife: A cross-disciplinary approach* (pp. 373–394). Springer International.

McLennan, M.R., Hyeroba, D., Asiimwe, C., Reynolds, V., & Wallis, J. (2012). Chimpanzees in mantraps: Lethal crop protection and conservation in Uganda. *Oryx*, *46*, 598–603.

Meilinger, P.S. (1997). Review of *Demonic males: Apes and the origins of human violence*; *War before civilization: The myth of the peaceful savage*; *A history of warfare*. *Journal of Military History*, *61*, 598–601.

Meggitt, M. (1968). *Desert people: A study of Walbiri aborgines of Central Australia*. University of Chicago Press.

Mesoudi, A., Blanchet, S., Charmantier, A., Danchin, E., Fogarty, L., Jablonka, E., Laland, K.N., Morgan, T.J.H., Muller, G.B., Odling-Smee, F.J., & Pujol, B. (2013). Is non-genetic inheritance just a proximate mechanism? A corroboration of the extended evolutionary synthesis. *Biological Theory*, *7*, 189–195.

Middleton, L., & Else, L. (2005). Close encounters. *New Scientist*, *186*(2502), 46–47.

Milam, E.L. (2019). *Creatures of Cain: The hunt for human nature in Cold War America*. Princeton University Press.

Miller, J.A., Pusey A.E., Gilby, I.C., Schroepfer-Walker, K., Markham, A.C., & Murray, C.M. (2014). Competing for space: Female chimpanzees are more aggressive inside than outside their core areas. *Animal Behaviour*, *10*, 147–152.

Mitani, J.C. (2006). Review of *The chimpanzees of the Budongo Forest*, by Vernon Reynolds, *International Journal of Primatology*, *27*, 1491–1493.

Mitani, J.C. (2008). Chimpanzee behavior: There's no place like home. *Current Biology*, *18*, 166–167.

Mitani, J.C. (2009). Male chimpanzees form enduring and equitable social bonds. *Animal Behaviour*, *77*, 633–640.

Mitani, J.C., & Amsler, S.J. (2003). Social and spatial aspects of male subgrouping in a community of wild chimpanzees. *Behaviour*, *140*, 869–884.

Mitani, J.C., Merriwether, D.A., & Zhang, C. (2000). Male affiliation, cooperation and kinship in wild chimpanzees. *Animal Behavior*, *59*, 885–893.

Mitani, J.C., & Rodman, P.S. (1979). Territoriality: The relation of ranging pattern and home range size to defendability, with an analysis of territoriality among primate species. *Behavioral Ecology and Sociobiology*, *5*, 241–251.

Mitani, J.C., Struhsaker, T.T., & Lwanga, J.S. (2000). Primate community dynamics in old growth forest over 23.5 years at Ngogo, Kibale National Park, Uganda: Implications for conservation and census methods. *International Journal of Primatology*, *21*, 269–285.

Mitani, J.C., & Watts, D.P. (1999). Demographic influences on the hunting behavior of chimpanzees. *N American Journal of Physical Anthropology, 109*, 439–454.

Mitani, J.C., & Watts, D.P. (2001). Why do chimpanzees hunt and share meat? *Animal Behaviour, 61*, 915–924.

Mitani, J.C., & Watts, D.P. (2003). Field research at Ngogo, Kibale National Park, Uganda. *Pan Africa News, 10*(1), unpaginated. http://mahale.main.jp/PAN/index.html. Accessed May 4, 2020.

Mitani, J.C., & Watts, D.P. (2005). Correlates of territorial boundary patrol behavior in wild chimpanzees. *Animal Behaviour, 70*, 1079–1086.

Mitani, J.C., Watts, D.P., & Amsler, S.J. (2010). Lethal intergroup aggression leads to territorial expansion in wild chimpanzees. *Current Biology, 20*, 507–508.

Mitani, J.C., Watts, D., & Lwanga, J. (2002a). Ecological and social correlates of party size and composition. In Boesch, C., Hohmann, G., & Marchant, L. (Eds.), *Behavioral diversity in chimpanzees and bonobos* (pp. 101–111). Cambridge University Press.

Mitani, J.C., Watts, D.P., & Muller, M.N. (2002a). Recent developments in the study of wild chimpanzee behavior. *Evolutionary Anthropology, 11*, 9–25.

Mitani, J.C., Watts, D., Pepper, J., & Merriwether, D.A. (2002b). Demographic and social constraints on male chimpanzee behavior. *Animal Behaviour, 63*, 727–737.

Mjungu, D.C. (2010). *Dynamics of intergroup competition in two neighboring chimpanzee communities*. Doctoral dissertation, University of Minnesota.

Mjungu, D., & Collins, A. (n.d.). *Gombe gets a new alpha: The fall of Ferdinand*. Jane Goodall Research Center. https://janegoodall.ca/our-stories/gombe-gets-new-alpha-fall-ferdinand-2/. Accessed May 1, 2020.

Mjungu, D.C., Lipende, I., Walker, K.S., Gilby, I.C., Murray, C., Wroblewski, E., Ramirez, M., Hahn, B., Pusey, A.E., & Wilson, M.L. (2014). Within-group infanticide and infanticidal attempts by the alpha male chimpanzee at Gombe National Park. *American Journal of Physical Anthropology, 153*, 187–188.

Mjungu, D., Wilson, M.L., Foerster, S., & Pusey, A.E. (2016). *Fighting back: Population recovery and expansion of the range size of the Mitumba chimpanzee community in Gombe National Park, Tanzania* (No. e1806v1). PeerJ Preprints. https://peerj.com/preprints/1806/. Accessed September 5, 2020.

Montagu, A. (Ed.). (1968). *Culture: Man's adaptive dimension*. Oxford University Press.

Moore, D.L., Langergraber, K.E., & Vigilant, L. (2015). Genetic analyses suggest male philopatry and territoriality in savanna-woodland chimpanzees (*Pan troglodytes schweinfurthii*) of Ugalla, Tanzania. *International Journal of Primatology, 36*, 377–397.

Moore, J. (1992). Review of *The egalitarians: Human and chimpanzee*. *American Journal of Physical Anthropology, 88*(2), 259–262.

Moore, J. (1998). Comment on Stanford, The social behavior of chimpanzees and bonobos. *Current Anthropology, 39*, 412–413.

Moore, J., & Collier, M. (1999). *African apes study sites*. http://weber/ucsd.edu/~jmoore/apesites/ApeSite.html. Accessed March 4, 2002.

Moore, L.D., Le, T., & Fan, G. (2013). DNA methylation and its basic function. *Neuropsychopharmacology, 38*, 23–38.

Moore, N.C. (2010). Chimpanzee gangs kill for land, new study shows. *US News*. [Online]. http://www.usnews.com/science/articles/2010/06/22/chimpanzee-gangs-kill-for-land-new-study-shows. Accessed June 10, 2014.

Moreno, J.D., & Schulkin, J. (2019). Epineuromics: Implications for development. *New Ideas in Psychology, 53*, 32–36.

Morgan, D., & Sanz, C. (2003). Naïve encounters with chimpanzees in the Goualougo Triangle Republic of Congo. *International Journal of Primatology, 24*, 369–381.

Morgan, D., Sanz, C., Onononga, J.R., & Strindberg, S. (2006). Ape abundance and habitat use in the Goualougo Triangle, Republic of Congo. *International Journal of Primatology, 27*, 147–179.

Morin, M. (2014). Monkey see, monkey kill: The evolutionary roots of lethal combat. *Los Angeles Times*. http://latimes.com/science/sciencenow/la-sci-sn-chimpanee-violence-20140916-story.html. Accessed July 11, 2015.

Morin, P.A., Moore, J.J., Chakraborty, R., Jin, L., Goodall, J., & Woodruff, D.S. (1994). Kin selection, social structure, gene flow, and the evolution of chimpanzees. *Science, 265*, 1193–1201.

Morris, I. (2014). *War! What is it good for?* Farrar, Straus and Giroux.

Morris, R., & Morris, D. (1966). *Men and apes*. McGraw Hill.

Moskowitz, C. (2010). Chimps kill chimps for land. *NBC News* Science. http://www.nbcnews.com/id/37830165/ns/technology_and_science-science/t/chimps-kill-chimps-land/#.Xq8XzTfsa3A. Accessed May 3, 2020.

MSI. (1994). *Evaluation of the Kibale Forest Conservation and management project under the Action Program for the Environment*. United States Agency for International Development. http://pdf.usaid.gov/pdf_docs/PDABN426.pdf. Accessed June 29, 2011.

MUBFS. (n.d.). Makerere University Biological Field Station: The environment. *Chapman Research* [Online]. http://chapmanresearch.mcgill.ca/Kibale/Environment.html. Accessed June 9, 2014.

Muehlenbein, M.P. (2005). Parasitological analyses of the male chimpanzees (*Pan troglodytes schweinfurthii*) at Ngogo, Kibale National Park, Uganda. *American Journal of Primatology, 65*, 167–179.

Muehlenbein, M.P., Watts, D.P., & Wittens, P.L. (2004). Dominance rank and fecal testosterone levels in adult male chimpanzees (*Pan troglodytes schweinfurthii*) at Ngogo, Kibale National Park, Uganda. *American Journal of Primatology, 64*, 71–82.

Mugisha, A. (2008). Potential interactions of research with the development and management of ecotourism. In Wrangham, R.W., & Ross, E. (Eds.), *Science and conservation in African forests: The benefits of long-term research* (pp. 115–128). Cambridge University Press.

Muhabwe, R.R. (2008). *Kibale Conservation Area monitoring and research plan implemented: Status report*. Kibale Conservation Area.

Muhumuza, F., Kutegeka, S., & Wolimbwa, A. (2007). Wealth distribution, poverty and timber governance in Uganda: A case study of Budongo Forest Reserve. *USAID ACODE Policy Research Series No. 26*.

Muller, M.N. (2000). The knuckle-walking wounded. *Natural History, 109*, 44–46.

Muller, M.N. (2002). Agonistic relations among Kanyawara chimpanzees. In Boesch, C., Hohmann, G., & Marchant, L. (Eds.), *Behavioral diversity in chimpanzees and bonobos* (pp. 112–124). Cambridge University Press.

Muller, M.N. (2007). Chimpanzee violence: Femmes fatales. *Current Biology, 17*, 365–366.

Muller, M.N. (2011). Review of Christophe Boesch: *The real chimpanzees: Sex strategies in the forest*. *International Journal of Primatology, 32*, 524–529.

Muller, M.N., Emery Thompson, M., & Wrangham, R.W. (2006). Male chimpanzees prefer mating with old females. *Current Biology, 16*, 2234–2238.

Muller, M.N., Enigk, D.K., Fox, S.A., Lucore, J., Machanda, Z.P., Wrangham, R.W., & Emery Thompson, M. (2021). Aggression, glucocorticoids, and the chronic costs of status competition for wild male chimpanzees. *Hormones and Behavior, 130*, 104965, 1–12.

Muller, M.N., Kahlenberg, S.M., Emery Thompson, M., & Wrangham, R.W. (2007). Male coercion and the costs of promiscuous mating for female chimpanzees. *Proceedings of the Royal Society B, 274*, 1009–1014.

Muller, M.N., Kahlenberg, S.M., Emery Thompson, M., & Wrangham, R.W. (2011). Sexual coercion by male chimpanzees shows that female choice may be more apparent than real. *Behavioural Ecology and Sociobiology, 65*, 921–933.

Muller, M.N., Kahlenberg, S.M., & Wrangham, R.W. (2009). Male aggression against females and sexual coercion in chimpanzees. In Muller, M.N., & Wrangham, R.W. (Eds.), *Sexual coercion in primates and humans: An evolutionary perspective on male aggression against females* (pp. 184–217). Harvard University Press.

Muller, M.N., Machanda, Z.P., Enigk, D.E., & Wrangham, R.W. (2013). *Intergroup aggression and within-group cohesion in wild chimpanzees.* Paper presented at the 82nd Annual Meeting of the American Association of Physical Anthropologists, Knoxville, Tennessee, April 9–13.

Muller, M.N., & Mitani, J.C. (2005). Conflict and cooperation in wild chimpanzees. *Advances in the Study of Behavior, 35*, 275–331.

Muller, M.N., Mpongo, E., Stanford, C.B., & Boehm, C. (1995). A note on scavenging by wild chimpanzees. *Folia Primatologica, 65*, 43–47.

Muller, M.N., & Wrangham, R.W. (2004). Dominance, cortisol and stress in wild chimpanzees *(Pan troglodytes schweinfurthii)*. *Behavioral Ecology and Sociobiology, 55*, 332–340.

Muller, M.N., & Wrangham, R.W. (2013). Mortality rates among Kanyawara chimpanzees. *Journal of Human Evolution, 66*, 107–114.

Murray, C.M., Stanton, M.A., Lonsdorf, E.V., Wroblewski, E.E., & Pusey, A.E. (2016). Chimpanzee fathers bias their behaviour towards their offspring. *Royal Society Open Science, 3*(11), 1–10.

Murray, C.M., Gilby, I.C., Mane, S.V., & Pusey, A.E. (2008). Adult male chimpanzees inherit maternal ranging patterns. *Current Biology, 18*, 20–24.

Murray, C.M., Wroblewski, E., & Pusey, A.E. (2007). New case of intragroup infanticide in the chimpanzees of Gombe National Park. *International Journal of Primatology, 28*, 23–37.

Murphy, R. (1957). Intergroup hostility and social cohesion. *American Anthropologist, 59*, 1018–1035.

Mutai, W. (2011). Face the future: Payment for ecosystem services training, Uganda. *Forest Trends* [online]. http://forest-trends.org/~foresttr/documents/files/doc_2741.pdf. Accessed July 5, 2011.

Mwendya, A. (2010). An experience with contract farming in Uganda's sugar industry. In Cotula, L., & Leonard, R. (Eds.), *Alternatives to land acquisitions: Agricultural investment and collaborative business models* (pp. 33–40). International Institute for Environment and Development.

Myers, N. (1976). *The leopard* Panthera pardus *in Africa*. International Union for Conservation of Nature and Natural Resources.

Nackoney, J., Molinario, G., Potapov, P., Turubanova, S., Hansen, M.C., & Furuichi, T. (2014). Impacts of civil conflict on primary forest habitat in northern Democratic Republic of the Congo, 1990–2010. *Biological Conservation, 170*, 321–328.

Nakamura, M. (1997). First observed case of chimpanzee predation on yellow baboons (*Papio cynocephalus*) at the Mahale Mts. National Park. *Pan Africa News, 4*(2), unpaginated. http://mahale.main.jp/PAN/index.html. Accessed May 4, 2020.

Nakamura, M., Corp, N., Fujimoto, M., Fujita, S., Hanamura, S., Hayaki, H., Hosaka, K., Huffman, M.A., Inaba, A., Inoue, E., Itoh, N., Kutsukake, N., Kiyono-Fuse, M., Kooriyama, T., Marchant, L.F., Matsumoto-Oda, A., Matsusaka, T., McGrew, W.C., Mitani, J.C., ... Zamma, K. (2013). Ranging behavior of Mahale chimpanzees: A 16 year study. *Primates, 54*, 171–182.

Nakamura, M., & Fukuda, F. (1999). Chimpanzees to the east of the Mahale Mountains. *Pan Africa News, 6*(1), unpaginated. http://mahale.main.jp/PAN/index.html. Accessed May 4, 2020.

Nakamura, M., Hosaka, K., & Takahata, Y. (2015). Research history. In Nakamura, M., Hosaka, K., Itoh, N., & Zamma, K. (Eds.), *Mahale chimpanzees: 50 years of research* (pp. 21–32). Cambridge University Press.

Nakamura, M., & Itoh, N. (2015). Conspecific killings. In Nakamura, M., Hosaka, K., Itoh, N., & Zamma, K. (Eds.), *Mahale chimpanzees: 50 years of research* (pp. 372–383). Cambridge University Press.

Nakamura, M., & Nishida, T. (2009). Chimpanzee tourism in relation to the viewing regulations at the Mahale Mountains National Park, Tanzania. *Primate Conservation, 24*, 85–90.

Nakazawa, N., Hanamura, S., Inoue, E., Nakatsukasa, M., & Nakamura, M. (2013). A leopard ate a chimpanzee: First evidence from East Africa. *Journal of Human Evolution*. http://dx.doi.org/10.1016/j.jhevol.2013.04.003. Accessed June 2, 2014.

National Geographic. (1967). *Miss Goodall and the wild chimpanzees* (videorecording). National Geographic Society.

Naturinda, S. (2011). Government sells stake in Kinyara Sugar Works. *Daily Monitor*. http://www.monitor.co.ug/News/National/-/688334/1244762/-/view/printVersion/-/x74g7lz/-/index.html. Accessed May 11, 2014.

Naughton Treves, L. (1996). *Uneasy neighbors: Wildlife and farmers around Kibale National Park, Uganda*. PhD dissertation, University of Florida, Gainesville.

Negrey, J.D., Reddy, R.B., Scully, E.J., Phillips-Garcia, S., Owens, L.A., Langergraber, K.E., Mitani, J.C., Emery Thompson, M., Wrangham, R.W., Muller, M.N., Otali, E., Machanda, Z., Hyeroba, D., Grindle, K.A., Pappas, T.E., Palmenberg, A.C., Gern, J.E., & Goldberg, T.L. (2019). Simultaneous outbreads of respiratory disease in wild chimpanzees caused by distinct viruses of human origin. *Emerging Microbes and Infections, 8*, 139–149.

Newton-Fisher, N. (1997). *Tactical behaviour and decision making in wild chimpanzees*. PhD dissertation, University of Cambridge, Cambridge.

Newton-Fisher, N. (1998). The socio-ecology of Budongo's chimps. *Budongo Forest Project Newsletter*, 1. http://culture.st-and.ac.uk/bcfs/documents/newsletter/newsletter1_2.html. Accessed May 8, 2014.

Newton-Fisher, N. (1999a). The diet of chimpanzees in the Budongo Forest Reserve, Uganda. *African Journal of Ecology, 37*, 344–354.

Newton-Fisher, N. (1999b). Infant killers of Budongo. *Folia Primatologica, 70,* 167–169.

Newton-Fisher, N. (2000). Male core areas: Ranging by Budongo Forest chimpanzees. *Pan Africa News, 7*(1), unpaginated. http://mahale.main.jp/PAN/index.html. Accessed May 4, 2020.

Newton-Fisher, N. (2002). Ranging patterns of male chimpanzees in the Budongo Forest, Uganda. In Harcourt, C.S., & Sherwood, B.R. (Eds.), *New perspectives in primate evolution and behaviour* (pp. 287–308). Westbury Academic and Scientific Publishing.

Newton-Fisher, N. (2003). The home range of the Sonso community of chimpanzees from the Budongo Forest, Uganda. *African Journal of Ecology, 41,* 151–156.

Newton-Fisher, N. (2004). Hierarchy and social status in Budongo chimpanzees. *Primates, 45,* 81–87.

Newton-Fisher, N. (2006). Female coalitions against male aggression in wild chimpanzees of the Budongo Forest. *International Journal of Primatology, 27,* 1589–1599.

Newton-Fisher, N., & Davis, C.L. (2004/2018). Sonso community chimpanzees [online]. http://www.budongo.org/media/1279/2018-02-official-list-sonso-chimpanzees.pdf. Accessed February 23, 2020.

Newton-Fisher, N., & Emery Thompson, M. (2012). Comparative evolutionary perspectives on violence. In Shackleford T.K., & Weekes-Shackleford, V.A. (Eds.), *The Oxford handbook of evolutionary perspectives on violence, homicide, and war*. Oxford University Press.

Newton-Fisher, N., Emery Thompson, M., Reynolds, V., Boesch, C., & Vigilant, L. (2010). Paternity and social rank in wild chimpanzees (*Pan troglodytes*) from the Budongo Forest, Uganda. *American Journal of Primatology, 142,* 417–428.

New Vision. (2006). Chimpanzees on the run. *Africa News*. http://allafrica.com/stories/200606190434.html. Accessed August 15, 2014.

New York Times. (1975). Raiders kidnap 3 U.S. students at Tanzanian wildlife station. *New York Times*, May 22, 2.

Nicoglou, A. (2015). Phenotypic plasticity: From microevolution to macroevolution. In Heams, T., Huneman, P., Lecointre, G., & Silberstein, M. (Eds.), *Handbook of evolutionary thinking in the sciences* (pp. 285–317). Springer.

Ngogo Chimpanzee Project. (2014). Untitled. https://www.facebook.com/NgogoChimps/photos/have-you-ever-wondered-what-a-day-in-the-field-studying-wild-chimpanzees-is-like/833959323314774/. Accessed May 16, 2020.

N'Goran, P.K., Kouakou, C.Y., N'goran, E.K., Konaté, S., Herbinger, I., Yapi, F.A., Kuehl, H., & Boesch, C. (2013). Chimpanzee conservation status in the World Heritage Site Taï National Park, Côte d'Ivoire. *International Journal of Innovation and Applied Studies, 3,* 326–336.

Nishida, T. (1968). The social group of wild chimpanzees in the Mahali Mountains. *Primates, 9,* 167–224.

Nishida, T. (1970). Social behavior and relationship among wild chimpanzees of the Mahali mountains. *Primates, 11,* 47–87.

Nishida, T. (1979). The social structure of chimpanzees of the Mahale Mountains. In Hamburg, D.A., & McGown, E.R. (Eds.), *The great apes* (pp. 73–121). Benjamin/Cummings.

Nishida, T. (1980). On inter-unit-group aggression and intra-group cannibalism among wild chimpanzees. *Human Ethology Newsletter, 31,* 21–24.

Nishida, T. (1983). Alpha status and agonistic alliance in wild chimpanzees (*Pan troglodytes schweinfurthii*). *Primates, 24*, 318–336.

Nishida, T. (1989). Social interactions between resident and immigrant female chimpanzees. In Heltne, P.G., & Marquardt, L.A. (Eds.), *Understanding chimpanzees* (pp. 68–89). Harvard University Press.

Nishida, T. (1990). A quarter century of research in the Mahale Mountains: An overview. In Nishida, T. (Ed.), *The chimpanzees of the Mahale Mountains: Sexual and life history strategies* (pp. 3–36). University of Tokyo Press.

Nishida, T. (1994). Afterword: Review of recent findings on Mahale Chimpanzees: Implications and future research directions. In Wrangham, R.W., McGrew, W.C., de Waal, F.B.M., & Heltne, P.G. (Eds.), *Chimpanzee cultures* (pp. 373–396). Harvard University Press.

Nishida, T. (1996a). The death of Ntologi, the unparalleled leader of M Group. *Pan Africa News, 3*(1), unpaginated. http://mahale.main.jp/PAN/index.html. Accessed May 4, 2020.

Nishida, T. (1996b). Eradication of the invasive, exotic tree *Senna spectabilis* in the Mahale Mountains. *Pan Africa News, 3*(2), http://mahale.main.jp/PAN/index.html. Accessed May 4, 2020.

Nishida, T. (1997). Baboon invasion into chimpanzee habitat. *Pan Africa News, 4*(2), unpaginated. http://mahale.main.jp/PAN/index.html. Accessed May 4, 2020.

Nishida, T. (1998). Deceptive tactic by an adult male chimpanzee to snatch a dead infant from its mother. *Pan Africa News, 5*(2), unpaginated. http://mahale.main.jp/PAN/index.html. Accessed May 4, 2020.

Nishida, T. (2002). Competition between baboons and chimpanzees at Mahale. *Pan Africa News, 9*(2), unpaginated. http://mahale.main.jp/PAN/index.html. Accessed May 5, 2020.

Nishida, T. (2008). Why were guava trees cut down in Mahale Park? The question of exterminating all introduced plants. *Pan Africa News, 15*(1), unpaginated. http://mahale.main.jp/PAN/index.html. Accessed May 4, 2020.

Nishida, T. (2012). *Chimpanzees of the lakeshore: Natural history and culture at Mahale*. Cambridge University Press.

Nishida, T., Corp, N., Hamai, M., Hasegawa, T., Hiraiwa-Hasegawa, M., Hosaka, K., Hunt, K.D., Itoh, N., Kawanaka, K., Matsumoto-Oda, A., Mitani, J.C., Nakamura, M., Norikoshi, K., Sakamaki, T., Turner, L., Uehara, S., & Zamma, K. (2003). Demography, female life history, and reproductive profiles among the chimpanzees of Mahale. *American Journal of Primatology, 59*, 99–121.

Nishida, T., Hasegawa, T., Hayaki, H., Takahata, Y., & Uehara, S. (1992). Meat-sharing as a coalition strategy by an alphas male chimpanzee. *Topics in Primatology, 1*, 159–174.

Nishida, T., & Hiraiwa-Hasegawa, M. (1985). Responses to a stranger mother-son pair in the wild chimpanzee: A case report. *Primates, 26*, 1–13.

Nishida, T., & Hiraiwa-Hasegawa, M. (1986). Chimpanzees and bonobos: Cooperative relationships among males. In Smuts, B.B. Cheney, D.L., Seyfarth, R.M., Wrangham, R.W., & Struhsaker, T.T. (Eds.), *Primate societies* (pp. 165–177). University of Chicago Press.

Nishida, T., Hiraiwa-Hasegawa, M., Hasegawa, T., & Takahata, Y. (1985). Group extinction and female transfer in wild chimpanzees in the Mahale National Park, Tanzania. *Zeitschrift für Tierpsychologie, 67*, 284–301.

Nishida, T., Hosaka, K., Nakamura, M., & Hamai, M. (1995). A within-group gang attack on a young adult male chimpanzee: Ostracism of an ill-mannered member? *Primates, 36*, 207–211.

Nishida, T., & Kawanaka, K. (1972). Inter-unit-group relationships among wild chimpanzees of the Mahale Mountains. In Umesao, T. (Ed.), *Kyoto University African Studies, Vol. VII* (pp. 131–167). Committee of the Kyoto University Africa Primatological Expedition.

Nishida, T., & Kawanaka, K. (1985). Within-group cannibalism by adult male chimpanzees. *Primates, 26*, 274–284.

Nisihida, T., & Mwinuka, C. (2005). Introduction of seasonal park fee system to Mahale Mountains National Park: A proposal. *Pan Africa News, 12*(2), unpaginated. http://mahale.main.jp/PAN/index.html. Accessed May 4, 2020.

Nishida, T., & Nakamura, M. (2008). Long-term research and conservation in the Mahale Mountains, Tanzania. In Wrangham, R.W., & Ross, E. (Eds.), *Science and conservation in African forests: The benefits of long-term research* (pp. 173–183). Cambridge University Press.

Nishida, T., Uehara, S., & Nyundo, R. (1979). Predatory behavior among wild chimpanzees of the Mahale Mountains. *Primates, 20*, 1–20.

Nishida, T., Wrangham, R.W., Jones, J.H., Marshall, A., & Wakibara, J. (2001). Do chimpanzees survive the 21st century? In Brookfield Zoo (Ed.), *The apes: Challenges for the 21st Century conference proceedings* (pp. 43–51). Brookfield Zoo.

Nishida, T., Zamma, K., Matsusaka, T., Inaba, A., & McGrew, W.C. (2010). *Chimpanzee behavior in the wild: An audio-visual encyclopedia*. Springer.

Nishie, H., & Nakamura, M. (2018). A newborn infant snatched and cannibalized immediately after birth: Implications for "maternity leave" in chimpanzees. *American Journal of Physical Anthropology, 165*, 194–199.

Norikoshi, K. (1982). One observed case of cannibalism among wild chimpanzees of the Mahale Mountains. *Primates, 23*, 66–74.

Novak, S., & Hatch, M. (2009). Intimate wounds: Craniofacial trauma in women and female chimpanzees. In Wrangham, R.W., & Muller, M.N. (Eds.), *Sexual coercion in primates and humans: An evolutionary perspective on male aggression against females* (pp. 322–345). Harvard University Press.

Nunn, C., & Alitzer, S. (Eds.). (2006). *Infectious diseases in primates: Behavior, ecology and evolution*. Oxford University Press.

Nutter, F.B. (1996). Reports from the field: Gombe, Tanzania: Respiratory disease claims the lives of at least seven Gombe chimps. *Pan Africa News, 3*(1), unpaginated. http://mahale.main.jp/PAN/index.html. Accessed May 4, 2020.

Oates, J.F. (2006). Is the chimpanzee, *Pan troglodytes*, an endangered species? It depends on what "endangered" means. *Primates, 47*, 102–112.

O'Connell, S. (2004). Chimps behaving badly. *BBC Science and Nature*. http://www.bbc.co.uk/nature/animals/features/325chimp1.shtml. Accessed May 25, 2004.

O'Connor, R.M., Shaffie, R., Kang, G., & Ward, H.D. (2011). Cryptosporidiosis in patients with HIV/AIDS. *AIDS, 25*, 549–560.

O'Connor, S., Balme, J., Fyfe, J., & Oscar, J. (2013). Marking resistance? Change and continuity in the recent rock art of the south Kimberly. *Antiquity, 87*, 539–554.

Odling-Smee, F.J., Laland, K.N., & Feldman, M.W. (2003). *Niche construction: The neglected process in evolution*. Monographs in Population Biology, No. 37. Princeton University Press.

Oelse, V.M., Head, J.S., Robbins, M.M., Richards, M., & Richards, M. (2013). Niche differentiation and dietary seasonality among sympatric gorillas and chimpanzees in Loango National Park (Gabon) revealed by stable isotope analysis. *Journal of Human Evolution, 66*, 95–106.

O'Hara, S. (2003). Kwa heri, Jambo. *Budongo Forest Project, 5*(1), 2–3. http://culture.st-and.ac.uk/bcfs/documents/newsletter/newsletter1_2.html. Accessed May 8, 2014.

Ohashi, G. (2011). From Bossou to the forests of Liberia. In Matsuzawa, T., Humle, T., & Sugiyama, Y. (Eds.), *The chimpanzees of Bossou and Nimba* (pp. 313–315). Springer.

Ohashi, G., & Matsuzawa, T. (2011). Deactivation of snares by wild chimpanzees. *Primates, 52*, 1–5.

Olupot, W., & Plumptre, A.J. (2010). *Conservation research in Uganda's forests: A review of site history, research, and use of research in Uganda's forest parks and Budongo Forest Reserve*. Nova Science Publishers.

O'Malley, R.C., & Power, M.L. (2012). Nutritional composition of actual and potential insect prey for the Kasekela chimpanzees of Gombe National Park, Tanzania. *American Journal of Physical Anthropology, 149*, 493–503.

O'Malley, R.C., Stanton, M.A., Gilby, I.C., Lonsdorf, E.V., Pusey, A., Markham, A.C., & Murray, C.M. (2016). Reproductive state and rank influence patterns of meat consumption in wild female chimpanzees (*Pan troglodytes schewinfurtii*). *Journal of Human Evolution, 90*, 16–28.

Omeja, P.A., Chapman, C.A., Obua, J., Lwanga, J.S., Jacob, A.L., Wanyama, F., & Mugenyi, R. (2011). Intensive tree planting facilitates tropical forest biodiversity and biomass accumulation in Kibale National Park, Uganda. *Forest Ecology and Management, 261*, 703–709.

Onderdonk, D.A., & Chapman, C.A. (2000). Coping with forest fragmentation: The primates of Kibale National Park, Uganda. *International Journal of Primatology, 21*, 587–611.

O'Neill, M. (2018). Why chimpanzees go to "war": New study on infamous four-year feud documented by Jane Goodall in the 1970s reveals primates fight for the same reasons as humans. *Daily Mail*, March 26. http://www.dailymail.co.uk/sciencetech/article-5546617/Researchers-determined-cause-civil-war-chimpanzees-documented-1970s.html. Accessed March 27, 2018.

Onishi, E., Brooks, J., Leti, I., Monghiemo, C., Bokika, J.-C., Shintaku, Y., Idani, G., & Yamamoto, S. (2020). Nkala Forest: Introduction of a forest-savanna mosaic field site of wild bonobos and its future prospects. *Pan Africa News, 27*(1), 2–5.

Ortmann, S., Bradley, B.J., Stoller, C., & Ganzhorn, A.R. (2006). Estimating the quality and composition of wild animal diets. In Hohmann, G., Robbins, M.M., & Boesch, C. (Eds.), *Feeding ecology in apes and other primates: Ecological, physical, and behavioral aspects* (pp. 395–219). Cambridge University Press.

Otsuka, R., & Yamakoshi, G. (2020). Analyzing the popularity of YouTube videos that violate mountain gorilla tourism regulations. *PloS One, 15*(5), 1–20, e0232085.

Otterbein, K. (1987). Comment in Knauft, Reconsidering violence in simple human societies: Homicide among the Gebusi of New Guinea. *Current Anthropology, 28*, 485–486.

Otterbein, K. (1968). Internal war: A cross-cultural study. *American Anthropologist, 70,* 277–289.

Ortner, S. (1972). Is female to male as nature is to culture? *Feminist Studies, 1*(2), 5–31.

Packer, C. (1999). Infanticide is no fallacy. *American Anthropologist, 102,* 829–831.

Palagi, E., & Norscia, I. (2013). Bonobos protect and console friends and kin. *PLoS One, 8*(11), p.e79290.

Palombit, R.A. (2012). Infanticide: Male strategies and female counterstrategies. In Mitani, J.C., Call, J., Kappeler, P.M., Palombit, R.A., & Silk, J.B. (Eds.), *The evolution of primate societies* (pp. 432–468). University of Chicago Press.

Palombit, R.A. (2014). Infanticide as sexual conflict: Coevolution of male strategies and female counterstrategies. *Cold Spring Harbor Perspectives in Biology, 7,* a017640.

Palumbo, S., Mariotti, V., Iofrida, C., & Pellegrini, S. (2018). Genes and aggressive behavior: Epigenetic mechanisms underlying individual susceptibility to aversive enviornments. *Frontiers in Behavioral Neuroscience, 12,* 1–9.

Paoli, T. (2009). The absence of sexual coercion in bonobos. In Wrangham, R.W., & Muller, M.N. (Eds.), *Sexual coercion in primates and humans: An evolutionary perspective on male aggression against females* (pp. 410–423). Harvard University Press.

Paoli, T., & Palagi, E. (2008). What does agonistic dominance imply in bonobos? In Furuichi, T., & Thompson, J. (Eds.), *The bonobos: Behavior, ecology, and conservation* (pp. 39–54). Springer.

Paoli, T., Palagi, E., & Tarli, S.M. (2006). Reevaluation of dominance hierarchy in bonobos (Pan paniscus). *American Journal of Physical Anthropology, 130,* 116–122.

Parish, A.R. (1996). Female relationships in bonobos (*Pan paniscus*). *Human Nature, 7,* 61–96.

Parish, A.R. (1994). Sex and food control in the "uncommon chimpanzee": How bonobo females overcame a phylogenetic legacy of male dominance. *Ethology and Sociobiology, 15,* 157–179.

Parish, A.R., & De Waal, F.B. (2000). The other "closest living relative." How bonobos (*Pan paniscus*) challenge traditional assumptions about females, dominance, intra-and intersexual interactions, and hominid evolution. *Annals of the New York Academy of Sciences, 907,* 97–113.

Parker, I. (2007). Swingers: Bonobos are celebrated as peace-loving, matriarchal, and sexually liberated. Are they? *New Yorker,* July 30, 48–61.

Parkinson, W.A. (2002). Introduction: Archaeology and tribal societies. In Parkinson, W.A. (Ed.), *The archaeology of tribal societies* (pp. 1–12). International Monographs in Prehistory.

Parsons, M.B., Travis, D., Lonsdorf, E.V., Lipende, I., Roellig, D.M.A., Kamenya, S., Zhang, H., Xiao, L., & Gillespie, T.R. (2015). Epidemiology and molecular characterization of Cryptosporidium spp. in humans, wild primates, and domesticated animals in the Greater Gombe ecosystem, Tanzania. *PLoS Neglected Tropical Diseases.* https://journals.plos.org/plosntds/article?id=10.1371/journal.pntd.0003529. Accessed September 9, 2020.

Paterson, J.D. (2005). In *Abstracts of the XIXth Congress The International Primatological Society.*

Patrick, R., Patrick, D., & Hunt, K.D. (2011). Long term changes at Toro-Semliki Wildlife Reserve. In Plumptre, A.J. (Ed.), *Long term changes in Africa's Rift Valley: Impacts on biodiversity and ecosystem* (pp. 56–69). Nova Science Publishers.

Patrono, L.V., & Leendertz, F. (2019). Acute infectious diseases occurring in the Tai chimpanzee population: A review. In Boesch, C., Wittig, R., Crockford, C., Vigilant, L., Deschner, T., & Leendertz, F. (Eds.), *The chimpanzees of the Tai Forest: 40 years of research* (pp. 385–393). Cambridge University Press.

Patterson, N., Richter, D.J., Gnerre, S., Lander, E.S., & Reich, D. (2006). Reply to: Complex speciation of humans and chimpanzees. *Nature, 452,* 3–4.

Peterson, D. (2006). *Jane Goodall: The woman who redefined man.* Houghton Mifflin Company.

Peterson, N. (1974). Hunter-gatherer territoriality: The perspectives from Australia. *American Anthropologist, 78,* 53–68.

Peterson, N. (1976). A reply to Thomas P. Myers. *American Anthropologist, 78,* 355–356.

Peterson, N. (1993). Demand sharing: Reciprocity and the pressure for generosity. *American Anthropologist, 95,* 860–874.

Pickering, T.R., & Dominguez-Rodrigo, M. (2010). *Open Anthropology Journal, 3,* 107–113.

Pika, S., Klein, H. Bunel, S., Baas, P., Theleste, E., & Deschner, T. (2019). Wild chimpanzees (*Pan troglodytes troglodytes*) exploit tortoises (*Kinixys erosa*) via percussive technology. *Scientific Reports, 9,* 1–7. https://doi.org/10.1038/s41598-019-43301-8

Pilbrow, V., & Groves, C. (2013). Evidence for divergence in populations of bonobos (*Pan paniscus*) in the Lomami-Lualaba and Kasai-Sankuru regions based on preliminary analysis of craniodental variation. *International Journal of Primatology, 34,* 1244–1260.

Pintea, L. (2012). Modeling potential conflict between agricultural expansion and biodiversity in the greater Mahale ecosystem, Tanzania. *African Biodiversity Collaborative Group.* http://frameweb.org/adl/en-US/9867/file/1410/H.1%20JGI%20AGR-Bodiversity%20Conflict%20Final%201.pdf. Accessed on June 2, 2014.

Pintea, L., Pusey, A., Wilson, M., Gilby, I., Collins, A., Kamenya, S., & Goodall, J. (2011). Long-term ecological changes affecting the chimpanzees of gombe national park, Tanzania Long-term ecological changes affecting the chimpanzees of gombe national park, Tanzania. In Plumptre, A.J. (Ed.), *The ecological impact of long-term changes in Africa's Rift Valley* (pp. 227–247). Nova Science Publishers.

Plomin, R. (2011). Commentary: Whey are children in the same family so different? Non-shared environment three decades later. *International Journal of Epidemiology, 40,* 582–592.

Plumptre, A.J. (1996). Changes following 60 years of selective timber harvesting in the Budongo Forest Reserve, Uganda. *Forest Ecology and Management, 89,* 101–113.

Plumptre, A.J., Cox, D., & Mugume, S. (2003). *The status of chimpanzees in Uganda.* Albertine Rift Technical Reports, 2. World Conservation Society.

Plumptre, A.J., & Reynolds, V. (1994). The effect of selective logging on the primate populations in the Budongo Forest Reserve, Uganda. *Journal of Applied Ecology, 31,* 631–641.

Plumptre, A.J., & Reynolds, V. (1996). Censusing chimpanzees in the Budongo Forest, Uganda. *International Journal of Primatology, 17,* 85–99.

Potts, K.B. (2011). The long-term impact of timber harvesting on the resource base of chimpanzees in Kibale National Park, Uganda. *Biotropica, 43,* 256–264.

Potts, K.B., Watts, D.P., Wrangham, R.W. (2011). Comparative feeding ecology of two communities of chimpanzees (*Pan troglodytes*) in Kibale National Park, Uganda. *International Journal of Primatology, 32,* 669–690.

Potts, K.B., Baken, E., Ortmann, S., Watts, D.P., & Wrangham, R.W. (2015). Variability in population density is paralleled by large differences in foraging efficiency in chimpanzees (*Pan troglodytes*). *International Journal of Primatology, 36,* 1101–1119.

Potts, R. (2013). Hominin evolution in settings of strong environmental variability. *Quaternary Science Reviews, 73,* 1–13.

Povinelli, D.J., & Vonk, J. (2003). Chimpanzee minds: Suspiciously human? *Trends in Cognitive Sciences, 7,* 157–160.

Power, M.G. (1991). *The egalitarians—human and chimpanzee: An anthropological view of social organization.* Cambridge University Press.

Power, M.G. (1995). Gombe revisited: Are chimpanzees violent and hierarchical in the "free" state? *General Anthropology, 2,* 5–9.

Powledge, T.M. (2011). Behavioral epigenetics: How nurture shapes nature. *BioScience, 61,* 588–592.

Pradhan, G.R., Pandit, S.A., & Van Schaik, C.P. (2014). Why do chimpanzee males attack the females of neighboring communities? *American Journal of Physical Anthropology, 155,* 430–4345.

Prado-Martinez, J., Sudmatt, P.H., ... Marques-Bonet, T. (2013). Great ape genetic diversity and population history. *Nature, 499,* 471–475.

Pruetz, J.D. (2006). Feeding ecology of savanna chimpanzees (*Pan troglodytes verus*) at Fongoli, Senegal. In Hohmann, G., Robbins, M.M., & Boesch, C. (Eds.), *Feeding ecology in apes and other primates: Ecological, physical and behavioral aspects* (pp. 161–183). Cambridge University Press.

Pruetz, J.D. (2007). Evidence of cave use by savanna chimpanzees (*Pan troglodytes verus*) at Fongoli, Senegal: Implications for thermoregulatory behavior. *Primates, 48*(2), 316–319.

Pruetz, J.D., Ballahira, R., Camara, W., Lindshield, S., Marshack, J.L., Olson, A., Sahdiako, M., & Villalobos-Flores, U. (2012). Update on the Assirik chimpanzee (*Pan troglodytes verus*) population in Niokolo Koba National Park, Senegal. *Pan Africa News, 19*(1), unpaginated. http://mahale.main.jp/PAN/index.html. Accessed May 4, 2020.

Pruetz, J.D., & Bertolani, P. (2007). Savanna chimpanzees, *Pan troglodytes verus*, hunt with tools. *Current Biology, 17,* 1–6.

Pruetz, J.D., Bertolani, P., Ontl, K.B., Lindshield, S., Shelley, M., & Wessling, E.G. (2015). New evidence on the tool-assisted hunting exhibited by chimpanzees (*Pan troglodytes verus*) in a savannah habitat at Fongoli, Sénégal. *Royal Society Open Source Publishing, 2*(4), 1–11.

Pruetz, J.D., & Herzog, N.M. (2017). Savanna chimpanzees at Fongoli, Senegal, navigate a fire landscape. *Current Anthropology, 58*(S16), 5337–5350.

Pruetz, J.D., & Kante, D. (2010). Successful return of a wild infant chimpanzee (*Pan troglodytes verus*) to its natal group after capture by poachers. *African Primates, 7,* 35–41.

Pruetz, J.D., & Lindshield, S. (2012). Plant-food and tool transfer among savanna chimpanzees at Fongoli, Senegal. *Primates, 53,* 133–145.

Pruetz, J.D., Marchant, L.F., Arno, J., & McGrew, W.C. (2002). Survey of savanna chimpanzees (*Pan troglodytes verus*) in southeastern Senegal. *American Journal of Primatology*, 58, 35–43.

Pruetz, J.D., & Marschack, J.L. (2009). Savanna chimpanzees (*Pan troglodytes verus*) prey on patas monkeys (*Erythrocebus patas*) at Fongoli, Senegal. *Pan Africa News*, 16(2), unpaginated. http://mahale.main.jp/PAN/index.html. Accessed May 4, 2020.

Pruetz, J.D., Ontl, K.B., Cleaveland [OK], E., Lindshield, S., Marshack, J., & Wessling, E.G. (2017). Intragroup lethal aggression in West African Chimpanzees (*Pan troglodytes verus*): Inferred killing of a former alpha male at Fongoli, Senegal. *International Journal of Primatology*, 38, 31–57.

Purcell, Z. (2002). Chimpanzee viewing and regulation: Mahale Mountains National Park. *Pan Africa News*, 9(2), unpaginated. http://mahale.main.jp/PAN/index.html. Accessed May 4, 2020.

Pusey, A.E. (1979). Intercommunity transfer of chimpanzees in Gombe National Park. In Hamburg, D.A., & McCown, E.R (Eds.), *The great apes* (pp. 465–479). Benjamin/Cummings.

Pusey, A.E. (1980). Inbreeding avoidance in chimpanzees. *Animal Behaviour*, 28, 543–552.

Pusey, A.E. (2010). Review of *The real chimpanzee: Sex strategies in the forest*, by C. Boesch. *Quarterly Review of Biology*, 85, 380.

Pusey, A.E., Murray, C., Wallauer, W., Wilson, M., Wroblewski, E.E., & Goodall, J. (2008). Severe aggression among female *Pan troglodytes schweinfurthii*. *International Journal of Primatology*, 29, 949–973.

Pusey, A.E., Oehlert, G.W., Williams, J.M., & Goodall, J. (2005). Influence of ecological and social factors on body mass of wild chimpanzees. *International Journal of Primatology*, 26, 3–31.

Pusey, A.E., Pintea., L., Wilson, M.L., Kamenya, S., & Goodall, J. (2007). The contribution of long-term research at Gombe National Park to chimpanzee conservation. *Conservation Biology*, 21, 623–634.

Pusey, A.E., & Schropefer-Walker, K. (2013). Female competition in chimpanzees. *Philosophical Transactions of the Royal Society B*, 368, 1631.

Pusey, A.E., Williams, J., & Goodall, J. (1997). The influence of dominance rank on the reproductive success of female chimpanzees. *Science*, 277, 828–831.

Quammen, D. (2003). Jane in the forest again. *National Geographic Magazine*. http://ngm.nationalgeographic.com/2003/04/jane-goodall/goodall-text. Accessed 22 May 22, 2014.

Raubenheimer, D., Simpson, S.J., & Mayntz, D. (2009). Nutrition, ecology and nutritional ecology: Toward an integrated framework. *Nutritional Ecology*, 23, 4–16.

Redmond, E.M. (1998). *Chiefdoms and chieftaincy in the Americas*. University of Florida Press.

Rees, A. (2009). *The infanticide controversy*. University of Chicago Press.

Riedel, J., Franz, M., & Boesch, C. (2011). How feeding competition determines female chimpanzee gregariousness and ranging in the Tai National Park, Cote d'Ivoire. *American Journal of Primatology*, 73, 305–313.

Reinartz, G.E., Isia, I.B., Ngamankosi, M., & Wema, L.W. (2006). Effects of forest type and human presence on bonobo (*Pan paniscus*) density in the Salonga National Park1. *International Journal of Primatology*, 27, 603–634.

Renaud, A., Jamart, A., Goosens, B., & Ross, C. (2013). A longitudinal study on feeding behaviour and activity patterns of released chimpanzees in Conkouati-Douli National Park, Republic of Congo. *Animals, 3*, 532–550.

Reynolds, H. (1978). Aboriginal-European contact history. *Journal of Australian Studies, 3*, 52–64.

Reynolds, V. (1965). *Budongo: An African forest and its chimpanzees*. Natural History Press.

Reynolds, V. (1966). Open groups in Hominid evolution. *Man, 1*, 441–452.

Reynolds, V. (1975). How wild are the Gombe chimpanzees? *Man, 10*, 123–125.

Reynolds, V. (1980). Sociobiology and the idea of primordial discrimination. *Ethnic and Racial Studies, 3*, 303–315.

Reynolds, V. (1994). Research at Budongo Forest, Uganda. *Pan African News, 1*(1), unpaginated.

Reynolds, V. (2000). Learning from the past, looking towards the future. *Budongo Forest Project Newsletter, 3*(1). http://culture.st-and.ac.uk/bcfs/documents/newsletter/newsletter3_1.html-2002. Accessed May 8, 2014.

Reynolds, V. (2005). *The chimpanzees of Budongo Forest: Ecology behaviour and conservation*. Oxford University Press.

Reynolds, V. (2006a). Budongo's chimpanzees and the Kinyara Sugar Works. *Budongo Forest Project, 7*(1), 4–6. http://culture.st-and.ac.uk/bcfs/documents/newsletter/newsletter1_2.html. Accessed May 8, 2014.

Reynolds, V. (2006b). Threats to, and protection of, the chimpanzees of the Budongo Forest Reserve. In Newton-Fisher, N.E., Notman, H., Paterson, J.D., & Reynolds, V. (Eds.), *Primates of Western Uganda* (pp. 391–403). Springer.

Reynolds, V. (2010). *Back to Budongo*. Intype Libra Ltd.

Reynolds, V. (n.d.). Project history, research and conservation: Overview, and publications. *Budongo Conservation Field Station*. http://culture.st-and.ac.uk/bcfs/documents/history.html. Accessed, May 14, 2014.

Reynolds, V., & Reynolds, F. (1965). Chimpanzees of the Budongo Forest. In De Vore, I. (Ed.), *Primate behavior: Field studies of monkeys and apes* (pp. 368–424). Holt, Rinehart and Winston.

Reynolds, C., Wallis, J., & Kyamanywa, R. (2003). Fragments, sugar and chimpanzees in Masindi District, Western Uganda. In Marsh, L.K. (Ed.), *Primates in fragments: Ecology in conservation* (pp. 309–320). Kluwer Academic/Plenum Publishers.

Reynolds, V., Lloyd, A.W., English, C.J., Lyons, P., Dodd, H., Hobaiter, C., Newton-Fisher, N., Mullins, C., Lamon, N., Schel, A.M., & Fallon, B. (2015). Mineral acquisition from clay by Budongo Forest chimpanzees. *PLoS One, 10*, e.0134075.

Reynolds, V., Lloyd, A.W., Babweteera, F., & English, C.J. (2009). Decaying *Raphia farinifera* palm trees provide a source of sodium for wild chimpanzees in the Budongo Forest, Uganda. *PloS One, 4*, e6194.

Riches, D. The phenomenon of violence. In Riches, D. (Ed.), *The anthropology of violence* (pp. 1–27). Basil Blackwell.

Riley, E.P. (2006). *Ethnoprimatology: Toward reconciliation of biological and cultural anthropology*. University of Nebraska–Lincoln, Digital Commons@University of Nebraska-Lincoln. https://digitalcommons.unl.edu/cgi/viewcontent.cgi?article=1007&context=icwdmeea. Accessed April 4, 2020.

Riley, E.P., & Ellwanger, A.L. (2013). Methods in ethnoprimatology: Exploring the human-non-human primate interface. In Sterling, E.J., Bynum, N., & Blair, M.E. (Eds.), *Primate ecology and conservation: A handbook of techniques* (pp. 128–150). Oxford University Press.

Riss, D.C., & Busse, C.D. (1977). Fifty-day observation of a free-ranging adult male chimpanzee. *Folia Primatologica, 28*, 283–297.

Roberts, T. (2005). *Frontier justice: A history of the Gulf country to 1900*. University of Queensland Press.

Rodseth, L., & Wrangham, R. (2004). Human kinship: A continuation of politics by other means? In Chapais, B., & Berman, C. (Eds.), *Kinship and behavior in primates* (pp. 389–419). Oxford University Press.

Rodseth, L. Wrangham, R.W., Harrigan, A.M., & Smuts, B.B. (1991). The human community as a primate society. *Current Anthropology, 32*, 221–254.

Romero, T., Castellanos, M.A., & de Waal, F.B. (2010). Consolation as possible expression of sympathetic concern among chimpanzees. *Proceedings of the National Academy of Sciences, 107*, 12110–12115.

Roscoe, P. (2007). Intelligence, coalitional killings, and the antecedents of war. *American Anthropologist, 109*, 485–495.

Roscoe, P. (2011). "Dead Birds:" The "theater" of war among the Dugum Dani. *American Anthropologist, 113*, 56–70.

Roscoe, P. (2014). The end of war in Papua New Guinea: "Crime" and "tribal warfare" in post-colonial states. *Anthropologica, 56*, 327–339.

Rubenstein, D.I., & Wrangham, R.W. (Eds.). (1986). *Ecological aspects of social evolution: Birds and mammals*. Princeton University Press.

Rubin, A.J. 2010. Afghan tribal rivalries bedevil a U.S. plan. *New York Times*, March 11, https://www.nytimes.com/2010/03/12/world/asia/12afghan.html. Accessed March 25, 2020.

Rudicell, R.S., Jones, J.H., . . . Wilson, M.L. (2010). Impact of simian immunodeficient virus infection on chimpanzee population dynamics. *PloS Pathogens, 6*(9), 1–17.

Ryu, H., Hill, D.A., Sakamaki, T., Garai, C., Tokuyama, N., & Furuichi, T. (2020). Occurrence and transmission of flu-like illness among neighboring bonobo groups at Wamba. *Primates, 61*, 775–784.

Sahlins, M. (1961). The segmentary lineage: An organization of predatory expansion. *American Anthropologist, 63*, 322–345.

Sahlins, M. (1987). *Islands of history*. University of Chicago Press.

Sabbi, K., & Enigk, D. (2015). Kanyawara has a new alpha male. Kibale Chimpanzee Project. https://kibalechimpanzees.wordpress.com/2015/02/21/kanyawara-has-a-new-alpha-male/. Accessed May 17, 2020.

Sakamaki, T. (2013). Social grooming among wild bonobos (*Pan paniscus*) at Wamba in the Luo Scientific Reserve, DR Congo, with special reference to the formation of grooming gatherings. *Primates, 54*, 349–359.

Sakamaki, T., Itoh, N., & Nishida, T. (2001). An attempted within-group infanticide in wild chimpanzees. *Primates, 42*, 359–366.

Sakamaki, T., Maloueki, U., Bakaa, B., Bongoli, L., Kasalevo, P., Terada, S., & Furuichi, T. (2016). Mammals consumed by bonobos (*Pan paniscus*): New data from the Iyondji forest, Tshuapa, Democratic Republic of the Congo. *Primates, 57*, 295–301.

Sakamaki, T., & Nakamura, M. (2015). Intergroup relationships. In Nakamura, M., Hosaka, K., Itoh, N., & Zamma, K. (Eds.), *Mahale chimpanzees: 50 years of research* (pp. 128-139). Cambridge University Press.

Sakamaki, T., Nakamura, M., & Nishida, T. (2007). Evidence of cultural differences in diet between two neighboring unit groups of chimpanzees in Mahale Mountains National Park, Tanzania. *Pan Africa News, 14*(1), unpaginated. http://mahale.main.jp/PAN/index.html. Accessed May 4, 2020.

Sakamaki, T., Ryu, H., Toda, K., Tokuyama, N., & Furuichi, T. (2018). Increased frequency of intergroup encounters in wild bonobos (*Pan paniscus*) around the yearly peak in fruit abundance at Wamba. *International Journal of Primatology, 39,* 685-704.

Samson, D.R. (2012). The chimpanzee nest quantified: Morphology and ecology of arboreal sleeping platforms within the dry habitat site of Toro-Semliki Wildlife Reserve, Uganda. *Primates, 53,* 357-364.

Samson, D.R., & Hunt, K.D. (2014). Is chimpanzee (*Pan troglodytes schweinfurthii*) low population density linked with low levels of aggression? *Pan Africa News, 21*(2), unpaginated. http://mahale.main.jp/PAN/index.html. Accessed May 4, 2020.

Samuni, L., Mielke, A., Preis, A., Crockford, C., & Wittig, R.M. (2020). Intergroup competition enhances chimpanzee (*Pan troglodytes verus*) in-group cohesion. *International Journal of Primatology, 20,* 342-362.

Samuni, L., Preis, A., Deschner, T., Crockford, C., & Wittig, R.M. (2018). Reward of labor coordination and hunting success in wild chimpanzees. *Communications Biology, 1,* Article # 138, 1-9.

Samuni, L., Preis, A., Mundry, R., Deschner, T., Crockford, C., & Wittig, R.M. (2017). Oxytocin reactivity during intergroup conflict in wild chimpanzees. *Proceedings of the National Academy of Sciences, 114,* 268-273.

Sandel, A.A., & Watts, D.P. (2021). Lethal coalitionary aggression associated with a community fission in chimpanzees (*Pan troglodytes*) at Ngogo, Kibale National Park, Uganda. *International Journal of Primatology, 42,* 26-48.

Sannen, A., Heistermann, M., Van Elsacker, L., Möhle, U., & Eens, M. (2003). Urinary testosterone metabolite levels in bonobos: A comparison with chimpanzees in relation to social system. *Behaviour, 140,* 683-696.

Sanz, C.M. (2004). *Behavioral ecology of chimpanzees in a central African forest:* Pan troglodytes troglodytes *in the Goualougo Triangle, Republic of Congo*. PhD dissertation, Washington University.

Sanz, C.M.M., & Morgan, D.B. (2007). Chimpanzee tool technology in the Goualougo Triangle, Republic of Congo. *Journal of Human Evolution, 52,* 420-433.

Sanz, C.M.M., & Morgan, D.B. (2013). Ecological and social correlates of chimpanzee tool use. *Philosophical Transactions of the Royal Society B, 368*(1630), 1-14. http://dx.doi.org/10.1098/rstb.2012.0416. Accessed May 22, 2014.

Sanz, C.M.M., Morgan, D.B., & Gulick, S. (2004). New insights into chimpanzees, tools, and termites from the Congo Basin. *American Naturalist, 164,* 567-581.

Sanya, S. (2012). Kaliro Sugar Factory to ease sugar deficit. *New Vision*, http://www.newvision.co.ug/mobile/Detail.aspx?NewsID=639237&CatID=3. Accessed May 14, 2014.

Sapolsky, R.M. (1982). The endocrine stress-response and social status in the wild baboon. *Hormones and Behavior, 16*(3), 279-292.

Sapolsky, R.M. (1998). *The trouble with testosterone: And other essays on the biology of the human predicament.* Simon and Schuster.

Sapolsky, R.M. (2005). The influence of social hierarchy on primate health. *Science, 308,* 648–652.

Sapolsky, R.M. (2013). Rousseau with a tail: Maintaining a tradition of peace among baboons. In Fry, D. (Ed.), *War, peace and human nature: The convergence of evolutionary and cultural views* (pp. 421–438). Oxford University Press.

Sapolsky, R.M. (2019). This is your brain on nationalism. *Foreign Affairs, 98*(2), September/October, 42–47. htps://www.foreignaffairs.com/articles/2019-02-12/your-brain-nationalism. Accessed September 12, 2020.

Sapolsky, R.M. (2021). Glucocorticoids, the evolution of the stress-response, and the primate predicament. *Neurobiology of Stress, 14,* 100320, 1–14.

Sapolsky, R.M., & Share, L.J. (2004). A pacific culture among wild baboons: Its emergence and transmission. *PLoS Biology, 2*(4), 1–8.

Savage-Rumbaugh, E.S., & Wilkerson, B.J. (1978). Socio-sexual behavior in *Pan paniscus* and *Pan troglodytes*: A comparative study. *Journal of Human Evolution, 7,* 327–344.

Scarf, M. (1973). Goodall and chimpanzees at Yale. *New York Times,* February 18, 14.

Schaller, G.B. (1972). *The Serengeti lion: A study of predator-prey relations.* University of Chicago Press.

Schaller, G.B. (1976). *The mountain gorilla: Ecology and behavior.* University of Chicago Press.

Schubert, G., Stoneking, C.J., Arandjelovic, M., Boesch, C., Eckhardt, N., Hohmann, G., Langergraber, K., Lukas, D., & Vigilant, L. (2011). Male-mediated gene flow in patrilocal primates. *PLoS One, 6*(7), 1–10. http://www.plosone.org/article/info%3Adoi%2F10.1371%2Fjournal.pone.0021514. Accessed June 23, 2014.

Schubert, G., Vigilant, L., Boesch, C., Klenke, R., Langergraber, K., Mundry, R., Surbeck, M., & Hohmann, G. (2013). Co-residence between males and their mothers and grandmothers is more frequent in bonobos than chimpanzees. *PLoS One, 8*(12), 1–11.

Sekercoglu, C.H. (2002). Effects of forestry practices on vegetation structure and bird community of Kibale National Park, Uganda. *Biological Conservation, 107,* 229–240.

Semliki Chimpanzee Project. (n.d.a). *History of the Reserve.* Semliki Chimpanzee Project. http://www.indiana.edu/~semliki/reserveHistory.shtml. Accessed May 21, 2014.

Semliki Chimpanzee Project. (n.d.b). *Mugiri community.* Semliki Chimpanzee Project. http://www.indiana.edu/~semliki/reserveHistory.shtml. Accessed May 21, 2014.

Service, E.L. (1971). *Primitive social organization: An evolutionary perspective* (2nd ed.). Random House.

Sharma, A. (2015). Systems genomics analysis centered inheritance supports development of a unified theory of biology. *Journal of Experimental Biology, 218,* 3368–3373.

Shea, B.T. (1983). Paedomorphosis and neoteny in the pygmy chimpanzee. *Science, 222,* 521–522.

Sherrow, H.M. (2009). Book review: *The Bonobos: Behavior, ecology, and conservation. American Journal of Physical Anthropology, 139,* 276–277.

Sherrow, H. (2012). Adolescent male chimpanzees at Ngogo, Kibale National Park, Uganda have decided dominance relationships. *Folia Primatologica, 83,* 67–75.

Sherrow, H.M., & Amsler, S.J. (2007). New intercommunity infanticides by the chimpanzees of Ngogo, Kibale National Park, Uganda. *International Journal of Primatology, 28*, 9–22.

Sherry, D.S., & Ellison, P.T. (2007). Potential applications of urinary C peptide of insulin for comparative energetics research. *American Journal of Physical Anthropology, 133*, 771–778.

Shilton, D., Breski, M., Dor, D., & Jablonka, E. (2020). Human social evolution: Self-domestication or self-control. *Frontiers in Psychology, 11*, 1–21.

Shimada, M. (2003). A note on the southern neighboring groups of M group in the Mahale Mountains National Park. *Pan Africa News, 10*(1), unpaginated. http://mahale.main.jp/PAN/index.html. Accessed May 4, 2020.

Siebert, C. (2006). An elephant crackup? *New York Times Magazine*, October 8. https://www.nytimes.com/2006/10/08/magazine/08elephant.html. Accessed June 21, 2019.

Silk, J.B. (2002). The form and function of reconciliation in primates. *Annual Review of Anthropology, 31*, 21–44.

Silk, J.B. (2014). The evolutionary roots of lethal conflict. *Nature, 513*, 321–322.

Silk, J.B., & Stanford, C. (1999). Infanticide article disputed. *Anthropology News*, September, 27–29.

Sillitoe, P. (1978). Big men and war in New Guinea. *Man, 13*, 252–271.

Skinner, M.K. (2015). Environmental epigenetics and a unified theory of the molecular aspects of evolution: A Neo-Lamarckian concept that facilitates Neo-Darwinian evolution. *Genome Biology and Evolution, 7*, 1296–1302.

Skorupa, J.P. (1986). Responses of rainforest primates to selective logging in Kibale Forest, Uganda: A summary report. In Benirschke, K. (Ed.), *Primates: The road to self-sustaining populations* (pp. 57–70). Springer.

Slocombe, K.E., Townsend, S.W., & Zuberbühler, K. (2009). Wild chimpanzees (*Pan troglodytes schweinfurthii*) distinguish between different scream types: Evidence from a playback study. *Animal Cognition, 12*, 441–449.

Smells Like Science. (2010). Q&A with primatologist John Mitani. *Smells Like Science.* http://smellslikescience.com/qa-with-primatologist-john-mitani/. Accessed June 10, 2014.

Smith, L., & Marsh, S. (2003). Chimps eat children in war of survival. *Times Online World News.* http://www.timesonline.co.uk/article/0,,3-947568,00.html. Accessed May 14, 2014.

Smith, R.M. (1977). Movement patterns and feeding behaviour of leopard in the Rhodes Matopos National Park, Rhodesia. *Arnoldia, 8*(13), 1–16.

Smuts, B.B., & Smuts, R.W. (1993). Chimps eat children in war of survival. *Advances in the Study of Behavior, 22*, 1–63.

Sober, E., & Wilson, D.S. (1988). *Unto others: The evolution and psychology of unselfish behavior.* Harvard University Press.

Solomon, J., Jacobson, S.K., Wald, K.D., & Gavin, M. (2007). Estimating illegal resource use at a Ugandan park with the randomized response technique. *Human Dimensions of Wildlife, 12*, 75–88.

Sommer, R.J. (2020). Phenotypic plasticity: From theory and genetics to current and future challenges. *Genetics, 215*, 1–13.

Sommer, V. (2000). The holy wars about infanticide: Which side are you on? And why? In Van Schaik, C.P., & Janson, C.H. (Eds.), *Infanticide by males and its implications* (pp. 9–26). Cambridge University Press.

Sommer, V., Bauer, J., Fowler, A., & Ortmann, S. (2011). Patriarchal chimpanzees, matriarchal bonobos: Potential ecological causes of a *Pan* dichotomy. In Sommer, V., & Ross, C. (Eds.), *Primates of Gashaka. Developments in primatology: Progress and prospects* (pp. 460–501). Springer.

Sousa, J., Barata, A.V., Sousa, C., Casanova, C.C.N., & Vicente, L. (2011). Chimpanzee oil-palm use in southern Cantanhez National Park, Guinea-Bissau. *American Journal of Primatology, 73*, 485–497.

Southall, A. (1980). Social disorganisation in Uganda: Before, during, and after Amin. *Journal of Modern African Studies, 18*, 627–656.

Southern, L.M., Deschner, T., & Pika, S. (2021). Lethal coalitionary attacks of chimpanzees (*Pan troglodytes troglodytes*) on gorillas (*Gorilla gorilla gorilla*) in the wild. *Scientific Reports, 11*. https://doi.org/10.1038/s41598-021-983829-x

Southworth, J., Hartter, J., Binford, M.W., Goldman, A., Chapman, C.A., Chapman, L.J., Omeja, P., & Binford, E. (2010). *Tropical Conservation Science, 3*, 122–142.

Sowter, A. (2007). Conservation in Budongo and the role of environmental education. *Budongo Forest Project, 8*, 8–9. http://culture.st-and.ac.uk/bcfs/documents/newsletter/newsletter1_2.html. Accessed May 8, 2014.

Spencer, B., & Gillen, F.J. (1969a). *Northern tribes of central Australia*. Humanities Press.

Spencer, B., & Gillen, F.J. (1969b). *The native tribes of central Australia*. Humanities Press.

Spira, C., Kirkby, A., Kujirakwinja, & Plumptre, A.J. (2019). The socio-economics of artisanal mining and bushmeat hunting around protected areas: Kahuzi-Biega National Park and Itombwe Nature Reserve, eastern Democratic Republic of Congo. *Oryx, 53*, 136–144.

Sponsel, L.E. (1997). The human niche in Amazonia: Explorations in ethnoprimatology. In Kinzey, W.G. (Ed.), *New world primates: Ecology, evolution and behavior* (pp. 143–165). Aldine de Gruyter.

Stade, G. (1972). (Review of) The Serengeti lion. *New York Times*, December 3, BR6–7.

Stanford, C.B. (1995). The influence of chimpanzee predation on group size and antipredator behaviour in red colobus monkeys. *Animal Behaviour, 49*, 577–587.

Stanford, C.B. (1998a). *Chimpanzee and red colobus: The ecology of predator and prey*. Harvard University Press.

Stanford, C.B. (1998b). The social behavior of chimpanzees and bonobos. *Current Anthropology, 39*, 399–420.

Stanford, C.B. (2001). The ape's gift: Meat-eating, meat-sharing, and human evolution. In Frans de Waal (Ed.), *Tree of origin: What primate behavior can tell us about human social evolution* (pp. 96–117). Harvard University Press.

Stanford, C.B. (2012). *Planets without apes*. Harvard University Press.

Stanford, C.B., Wallis, J., Matama, H., & Goodall, J. (1994). Patterns of predation by chimpanzees on red colobus monkeys in Gombe National Park, 1982–1991. *American Journal of Physical Anthropology, 94*, 213–228.

Steel, D. (1998). Warfare and western manufactures: A case study of explanation in anthropology. *Philosophy of Science, 65*, 649–671.

Stevens, J.M., Vervaecke, H., De Vries, H., & Van Elsacker, L. (2006). Social structures in *Pan paniscus*: Testing the female bonding hypothesis. *Primates, 47*, 210–217.

Stevens, J.M., Vervaecke, H., De Vries, H., & van Elsacker, L. (2007). Sex differences in the steepness of dominance hierarchies in captive bonobo groups. *International Journal of Primatology, 28*, 1417–1430.

Stevens, J.M.G., Vervaecke, H., & van Elsacker, L. (2008). The bonobo's adaptive potential: Social relations under captive conditions. In Furuichi, T., & Thompson, J. (Eds.), *The bonobos: Behavior, ecology, and conservation* (pp. 19–38). Springer-Verlag.

Stevens, W.K. (1997). Logging sets off an apparent chimp war. *New York Times*, May 13, 3.

Steward, J. (1955). Theory and application in a social science. *Ethnohistory, 2*, 292–302.

Stocking, G.W. (1966). Franz Boas and the culture concept in historical perspective. *American Anthropologist, 68*, 867–882.

Stringberg, S., et al. (2018). Guns, germs, and trees determine density and distribution of gorillas and chimpanzees in Western Equatorial Africa. *Science Advances, 4*, 1–14.

Stumpf, R.M. (2011). Chimpanzees and bonobos: Inter- and intraspecies diversity. In Campbell, C., Fuentes, A., MacKinnon, K., Bearder, S., & Stumpf, R. (Eds.), *Primates in perspective* (pp. 340–356). Oxford University Press.

Struhsaker, T. (1975). *The red colobus monkey*. University of Chicago Press.

Struhsaker, T. (1997). *Ecology of an African rain forest*. University Press of Florida.

Struhsaker, T. (2008). Long-term research and conservation in Kibale National Park. In Wrangham, R.W., & Ross, E. (Eds.), *Science and conservation in African forests: The benefits of long-term research* (pp. 27–37). Cambridge University Press.

Struhsaker, T.T., Lwanga, J.S., & Kasenene, J.M. (1996). Elephants, selective logging and forest regeneration in the Kibale Forest, Uganda. *Journal of Tropical Ecology, 12*, 45–64.

Stumpf, R. (2007). Chimpanzees and bonobos: Diversity within and between species. In Campbell, C., Fuentes, A., MacKinnon, K., Bearder, S., & Stumpf, R. (Eds.), *Primates in Perspective* (pp. 321–344). Oxford University Press.

Stumpf, R.M., & Boesch, C. (2006). The efficacy of female choice in chimpanzees of the Tai Forest, Cote d'Ivoire. *Behavioral Ecology and Sociobiology, 60*, 749–765.

Stumpf, R.M., & Boesch, C. (2010). Male aggression and sexual coercion in wild West African chimpanzees, *Pan troglodytes verus*. *Animal Behaviour, 79*, 333–342.

Sugiyama, Y. (1968). Social organization of chimpanzees in the Budongo Forest, Uganda. *Primates, 9*, 225–258.

Sugiyama, Y. (1984). Population dynamics of wild chimpanzees at Bossou, Guinea, between 1976 and 1983. *Primates, 25*, 391–400.

Sugiyama, Y. (1994). Research at Bossou, Guinea. *Pan Africa News, 1*(1), 61–68. http://mahale.main.jp/PAN/index.html. Accessed May 4, 2020.

Sugiyama, Y. (1999). Socioecological factors of male chimpanzee migration at Bossou, Guinea. *Primates, 40*, 61–68.

Sugiyama, Y. (2004). Demographic parameters and life history of chimpanzees at Bossou, Guinea. *American Journal of Physical Anthropology, 124*, 154–165.

Sugiyama, Y., & Fujita, S. (2011). The demography and reproductive parameters of Bossou Chimpanzees. In Matsuzawa, T., Humle, T., & Sugiyama, Y. (Eds.), *The chimpanzees of Bossou and Nimba* (pp. 23–34). Springer.

Sugiyama, Y., Kawamoto, S., Takenaka, O., Kumazaki, K., & Miwa, N. (1993). Paternity discrimination and inter-group relationships of chimpanzees at Bossou. *Primates, 34*, 545–552.

Sugiyama, Y., & Koman, J. (1979). Social structure and dynamics of wild chimpanzees at Bossou, Guinea. *Primates, 20*, 323–339.

Surbeck, M., Boesch, C., Girard-Buttoz, C., Crockford, C., Hohmann, G., & Wittig, R.M. (2017a). Comparison of male conflict behavior in chimpanzees (*Pan troglodytes*) and bonobos (*Pan paniscus*), with specific regard to coalition and post-conflict behavior. *American Journal of Primatology, 79*(6), 1–11.

Surbeck, M., Deschner, T., Schubert, G., Weltring, A., & Hohmann, G. (2012a). Mate competition, testosterone and intersexual relationships in bonobos, *Pan paniscus*. *Animal Behaviour, 83*, 659–669.

Surbeck, M., Deschner, T., Weltring, A., & Hohmann, G. (2012b). Social correlates of variation in urinary cortisol in wild male bonobos (*Pan paniscus*). *Hormones and Behavior, 62*, 27–35.

Surbeck, M., Girard-Buttoz, C., Boesch, C., Crockford, C., Fruth, B., Hohmann, G., Langergraber, K.E., Zuberbuhler, K., Wittig, R.M., & Mundry, R. (2017b). Sex specific association patterns in bonobos and chimpanzees reflect species differences in cooperation. *Royal Society Open Science, 4*, 161081.

Surbeck, M., & Hohmann, G. (2008). Primate hunting by bonobos at LuiKotale, Salonga National Park. *Current Biology, 18*, R906–R907.

Surbeck, M., & Hohmann, G. (2013). Intersexual dominance relationships and the influence of leverage on the outcome of conflicts in wild bonobos (*Pan paniscus*). *Behavioral Ecology and Sociobiology, 67*, 1767–1780.

Surbeck, M., Langergraber, K.E., Fruth, B., Vigilant, L., & Hohmann, G. (2017c). Male reproductive skew is higher in bonobos than chimpanzees. *Current Biology, 27*, R623–R641.

Surbeck, M., Mundry, R., & Hohmann, G. (2011). Mothers matter! Maternal support, dominance status and mating success in male bonobos (*Pan paniscus*). *Proceedings of the Royal Society of London B: Biological Sciences, 278*, 590–598.

Surbeck, M., et al. (2019). Males with a mother living in their group have higher paternity success in bonobos but not chimpanzees. *Current Biology, 29*, R354–R355.

Susman, R.L. (1984). The locomotor behavior of *Pan paniscus* in the Lomako forest. In Susman, R. (Ed.), *The pygmy chimpanzee* (pp. 369–393). Springer.

Sussman, R.W. (1999). The myth of man the hunter/man the killer and the evolution of human morality. In Sussman, R.W. (Ed.), *The biological basis of human behavior* (2nd ed., pp. 121–128). Upper Saddle River, NJ: Prentice Hall.

Sussman, R.W., & Chapman, A. (Eds.). (2004). *The origin and nature of sociality*. Aldine de Gruyter.

Sussman, R.W., Cheverud, J.M., & Bartlett, T.Q. (1995). Infant killing as an evolutionary strategy: Reality or myth. *Evolutionary Anthropology, 3*, 149–151.

Sussman, R.W., & Cloninger, C.R. (Eds.). (2011). *Origins of altruism and cooperation*. Springer.

Sussman, R.W., & Garber, P. (2004). Rethinking sociality: Cooperation collective action, and competition in primate social interactions. In Sussman, R., & Chapman, A. (Eds.), *The origin and nature of sociality* (pp. 161–190). Aldine de Gruyter.

Sussman, R.W., Garber, P.A., & Cheverud, J.M. (2005). Importance of cooperation and affiliation in the evolution of primate sociality. *American Journal of Physical Anthropology*, 128, 84–97.
Sussman, R.W., & Hart, D. (2010). Gentle savage or bloodthirsty brute. In Evans Pim, J. (Ed.), *Nonkilling societies* (pp. 55–80). Center for Global Nonkilling.
Sussman, R.W., & Marshack, J. (2010). Are humans inherently killers? *Global Nonkilling Working Papers*, 1, 7–28. Center for Global Nonkilling.
Suzuki, A. (1971). Carnivority and cannibalism observed among forest-living chimpanzees. *Journal of the Anthropological Society of Nippon*, 79, 30–48.
Takahata, Y. (1985). Adult male chimpanzees kill and eat a male newborn infant: Newly observed intragroup infanticide and cannibalism in Mahale National Park, Tanzania. *Folia Primatologica*, 44, 161–170.
Takahata, Y. (2015). Disappearance of K-group male chimpanzees: Re-examination of group extinction. In Nakamura, M., Hosaka, K., Itoh, N., & Zamma, K. (Eds.), *Mahale chimpanzees: 50 years of research* (pp. 119–127). Cambridge University Press.
Takahata, H., & Takahata, Y. (1989). Inter-unit-group transfer of an immature male common chimpanzee and his social interactions in the non-natal group. *African Study Monographs*, 9, 209–220.
Takahata, Y., Ihobe, H., & Idani, G.I. (1996). Comparing copulations of chimpanzees and bonobos: Do females exhibit proceptivity or receptivity? In McGrew, W.C., Marchant, L.F., & Nishida, T. (Eds.), *Great ape societies* (pp. 146–157). Cambridge University Press.
Takasaki, H. (2000). Traditions of the Kyoto School of field primatology in Japan. In Strum, S.C., & Fedigan, L.M. (Eds.), *Primate encounters: Models of science, gender, and society* (pp. 151–164). University of Chicago Press.
Takemoto, H., Kawamoto, Y., & Furuichi, T. (2015). How did bonobos come to range south of the Congo River? Reconsideration of the divergence of *Pan paniscus* from other Pan populations. *Evolutionary Anthropology: Issues, News, and Reviews*, 24, 170–184.
Takemoto, H., Kawamoto, Y., & Furuichi, T. (2019). The formation of Congo River and the origin of bonobos: A new hypothesis. In Boesch, C., Wittig, R., Crockford, C., Vigilant, L., Deschner, T., & Leendertz, F. (Eds.), *The chimpanzees of the Tai Forest: 40 years of research* (pp. 235–248). Cambridge University Press.
Tammen, S.A., Friso, S., & Choi, S.W. (2013). Epigenetics: The link between nature and nurture. *Molecular Aspects of Medicine*, 34, 753–764.
Tan, J., & Hare, B. (2013). Bonobos share with strangers. *PLoS One*, 8(2), 1–11.
Tan, J., & Hare, B. (2019). Prosociality among non-kin in bonobos and chimpanzees compared. In Boesch, C., Wittig, R., Crockford, C., Vigilant, L., Deschner, T., & Leendertz, F. (Eds.), *The chimpanzees of the Tai Forest: 40 years of research* (pp. 140–154). Cambridge University Press.
Tang, S. (2015). The onset of ethnic war: A general theory. *Sociological Theory*, 33, 256–279.
TAWIRI. (2018). *Tanzania Chimpanzee Conservation Action Plan 2018–2023*. Tanzania Wildlife Research Institute. https://www.researchgate.net/publication/332865978_T anzania-Chimpanzee-Conservation-Action-Plan-2018#fullTextFileContent. Accessed May 1, 2020.
Taylor, D., Robertshaw, P., & Marchant, R.A. (2000). Environmental change and political-economic upheaval in precolonial western Uganda. *The Holocene*, 10, 527–536.

Teelen, S. (2007). Primate abundance along five transect lines at Ngogo, Kibale National Park, Uganda. *American Journal of Primatology, 69,* 1030–1044.

Teelen, S. (2008). Influence of chimpanzee predation on the red colobus population at Ngogo, Kibale National Park, Uganda. *Primates, 49,* 41–49.

Teleki, G. (1973). *The predatory behavior of wild chimpanzees.* Associated University Presses.

Teleki, G. (1974). Chimpanzee subsistence and technology: Materials and skills. *Journal of Human Evolution, 3,* 575–584.

Teleki, G. (1977). *Spatial and temporal dimensions of routine activities performed by chimpanzees in Gombe National Park, Tanzania: An ethological study of adaptive strategy.* Doctoral dissertation, Pennsylvania State University.

Teleki, G. (1981). The omnivorous diet and eclectic feeding habits of chimpanzees in Gombe National Park, Tanzania. In Harding, R.S.O., & Teleki, G. (Eds.), *Omnivorous primates: Gathering and hunting in human evolution* (pp. 303–343). Columbia University Press.

Teleki, G., Hunt, E.E., & Pfifferling, J.H. (1976). Demographic observations (1963–1973) on the chimpanzees of Gombe National Park, Tanzania. *Journal of Human Evolution, 5,* 559–598.

Tennie, C., Gilby, I.C., & Mundry, R. (2009). The meat-scrap hypothesis: Small quantities of meat may promote cooperative hunting in wild chimpanzees (*Pan troglodytes*). *Behavioral Ecology and Sociobiology, 63,* 421–431.

Terio, K.A., Lonsdorf, E.V., Kinsel, M.J., Raphael, J., Lipende, I., Collins, A., Li, Y., Hahn, B.H., & Travis, D.A. (2018). Oesophagostomiasis in non-human primates of Gombe National Park, Tanzania. *American Journal of Primatology, 80,* 1–9 e22572.

The Economist. (2010). Killer instincts. Economist.com. http://www.economist.com/node/16422404/print. Accessed June 10, 2014.

Thaxton, M. (2006a). *What can be done to protect the chimpanzees and other great apes of Africa.* Population Reference Bureau. http://www.prb.org/Publications.Articles/2006/WhatCanBeDonetoProtecttheChimpanzeesandOtherGreatApesofAfrica.aspx. Accessed July 26, 2015.

Thaxton, M. (2006b). *Why the chimpanzees of Gombe National Part are in jeopardy.* Gombe. Population Reference Bureau. http://www.prb.org/Publications/Articles/2006/WhytheChimpanzeesofGombeNationalParkAreinJeopardy.aspx. Accessed July 25, 2015).

Thayer, B.A. (2004). *Darwin and international relations: On the evolutionary origins of war and ethnic conflict.* University of Kentucky Press.

Theofanopoulou, C., Gastaldon, S., O'Rourke, T.O., Samuels, B.D., Messner, A., Martins, P.T., Delogu, F., Alamri, S., & Boeckx. (2017). Self-domestication in *Homo sapiens*: Insights from comparative genomics. *PLoS One, 12*(10), 1–23. https://doi.org/10.1371/journal.pone.0185306

Thomas, D.K. (1961). The Gombe Stream Game Reserve. *Tanganyika Notes and Records, 56,* 34–39.

Thompson, J.A.M. (2002). Bonobos of the Lukuru Wildlife Research Project. In Boesch, C., Hohmann, G., & Marchant, L.F. (Eds.), *Behavioural diversity in chimpanzees and bonobos* (pp. 61–70). Cambridge University Press.

Thompson, J.A.M. (2003). A model of the biogeographical journey from proto-pan to Pan paniscus. *Primates, 44,* 191–197.

Thompson, M.E. (2017). Energetics of feeding, social behavior, and life history in nonhuman primates. *Hormones and Behavior, 91*, 84–96.
Thompson, M.E., Muller, M.N., Wrangham, R.W., Lwanga, J.S., & Potts, K.B. (2009). Urinary C-peptide tracks seasonal and individual variation in energy balance in wild chimpanzees. *Hormones and Behavior, 55*, 299–305.
Thompson, M.E., Newton-Fisher, N.E., & Reynolds, V. (2006). Probable community transfer of parous adult female chimpanzees in the Budongo Forest, Uganda. *International Journal of Primatology, 27*, 1601–1617.
Thompson-Handler, N. (1990). *The Pygmy chimpanzee: Sociosexual behavior, reproductive biology and life history.* PhD dissertation, Yale University.
Thompson-Handler, N., Malenky, R.K., & Badrian, N. (1984). Sexual behavior of *Pan paniscus* under natural conditions in the Lomako Forest, Equateur, Zaire. In Sussman, R.L. (Ed.), *The pygmy chimpanzee* (pp. 347–368). Springer.
Toda, K., & Furuichi, T. (2020). Low resistance of senior resident females toward female immigration in Bonobos (*Pan paniscus*) at Wamba, Democratic Republic of Congo. *International Journal of Primatology, 41*, 415–427.
Tokuyama, N., Sakamaki, T., & Furuichi, T. (2019). Inter-group aggressive interaction patterns indicate male mate defense and female cooperation across bonobo groups at Wamba, Democratic Republic of Congo. *American Journal of Physical Anthropology, 170*, 535–550.
Tokuyama, N., Toda, K., Poiret, M-L., Iyokango, B., Bakas, B., & Ishzuka, S. (2021). Two wild female bonobos adopted infants from a different social group at Wamba. *Scientific Reports, 11*, 1–11. http://doi.org/10.1038/s41598-021-83667-2
Tomasello, M. (1990). Cultural transmission in the tool use and communicatory signaling of chimpanzees. In Parker, S.T., & Gibson, K.R. (Eds.), *"Language" and intelligence in monkeys and apes: Comparative developmental perspectives* (pp. 274–311). Cambridge University Press.
Tomasello, M. (1999). The human adaptation for culture. *Annual Review of Anthropology, 28*, 509–529.
Tomasello, M. (2009). The question of chimpanzee culture, plus postscript. In Laland, K.N., & Galef, B.G. (Eds.), *The question of animal culture* (pp. 198–220). Harvard University Press.
Tomasello, M. (2016). The ontogeny of cultural learning. *Current Opinion in Psychology, 8*, 1–4.
Tokuyama, N., Moore, D.L., Graham, K.E., Lokasola, A., & Furuichi, T. (2017). Cases of maternal cannibalism in wild bonobos (*Pan paniscus*) from two different field sites, Wamba and Kokolopori, Democratic Republic of the Congo. *Primates, 58*, 7–12.
Townsend, S.W., Slocombe, K.E., Emery-Thompson, M., & Zuberbühler, K. (2007). Female-led infanticide in wild chimpanzees. *Current Biology, 17*, 355–356.
Tretola, M., Relli, V., Simeone, P., & Alberti, S. (2015). Epigenetic inheritance and the missing heritability. *Human Genomics, 9*, 1–12.
Trudeau, M.B., Bergmann-Riis, E., & Hamburg, D.A. (1981). Towards an evolutionary perspective on aggressive behavior: The chimpanzee evidence. In Hamburg, D.A., & B. Trudeau, M.B. (Eds.), *Biobehavioral aspects of aggression* (pp. 27–40). Alan R. Liss.
Tsukahura, T. (1993). Lions eat chimpanzees: The first evidence of predation by lions on wild chimpanzees. *American Journal of Primatology, 29*, 1–11.

Tumusiime, D.M., Eilu, G., Tweheyo, M., & Babweteera, F. (2010). Wildlife snaring in Budongo Forest Reserve, Uganda. *Human Dimensions of Wildlife, 15*, 129–144.

Tung, J., & Gilad, Y. (2013). Social environmental effects on gene regulation. *Cellular and Molecular Life Sciences, 70*, 4323–4339.

Turnbull-Kemp, P. (1967). *The leopard.* Howard Timmins.

Turner, L., & Nishida, T. (1994). Tanzania. *Pan Africa News, 1*(2), unpaginated. Accessed October 9, 2020.

Turney-High, H. (1971). *Primitive war: Its practice and concepts.* University of South Carolina Press.

Tutin, C.E.G., Ancrenaz, M., Paredes, J., Vacher-Vallas, M., Vidal, C., Goossens, B., Bruford, M.W., & Jamart, A. (2001). Conservation biology framework for the release of wild-born orphaned chimpanzees into the Conkouati Reserve, Congo. *Conservation Biology, 15*, 1247–1257.

Tutin, C.E.G., & Fernandez, M. (1991). Responses of wild chimpanzees and gorillas to the arrival of primatologists: Behaviour observed during habituation. In Box, H.O. (Ed.), *Primate responses to environmental change* (pp. 187–197). Chapman and Hall.

Tutin, C.E.G., & Fernandez, M. (1993a). Composition of the diet of chimpanzees and comparisons with that of sympatric lowland gorillas in the Lope Reserve, Gabon. *American Journal of Primatology, 30*, 195–211.

Tutin, C.E.G., & Fernandez, M. (1993b). Relationship between minimum temperature and fruit production in some tropic forest trees in Gabon. *Journal of Tropical Biology, 9*, 241–248.

Tutin, C.E.G., Fernandez, M., Rogers, M.E., Williamson, E.A., & McGrew, W. 1991. Foraging profiles of sympatric lowland gorillas and chimpanzees in the Lope Reserve, Gabon. *Philosophical Transactions of the Royal Society B, 334*, 179–186.

Tutin, C.E.G., McGrew, W.C., & Baldwin, P.J. (1983). Social organization of savanna-dwelling chimpanzees, *Pan troglodytes verus*, at Mt. Assirik, Senegal. *Primates, 24*, 154–173.

Tutin, C.E.G., & Oslisy, R. (1995). *Homo, Pan* and *Gorilla*: Co-existence over 60,000 years at Lope in Central Gabon. *Journal of Human Evolution, 28*, 597–602.

Tuttle, R.H. (1986). *Apes of the world: Their social behavior, communication, mentality, and ecology.* Noyes Publications.

Tuttle, R.H. (2014). *Apes and human evolution.* Harvard University Press.

Tweh, C.G., Lormie, M.M., Kouakou, C.Y., Hillers, A., Kühl, H.S., & Junker, J. (2015). Conservation status of chimpanzees *Pan troglodytes verus* and other large mammals in Liberia: A nationwide survey. *Oryx, 49*, 710–718.

Tweheyo, M., & Babweteera, F. (2007). Production, seasonality and management of chimpanzee food trees in Budongo Forest, Uganda. *African Journal of Ecology, 45*, 535–544.

Tweheyo, M., & Lye, K.A. (2005). Patterns of frugivory of the Budongo Forest Chimpanzees, Uganda. *African Journal of Ecology, 43*, 282–290.

Tylor, E.B. 1970 (orig. 1881). *Anthropology.* University of Michigan.

Uehara, S. (1997). Predation on mammals by the chimpanzee (*Pan troglodytes*). *Primates, 38*, 193–214.

Uehara, S., Haraiwa-Hasegawa, M., Hosaka, K., & Hamai, M. (1994b). The fate of defeated alpha male chimpanzees in relation to their social networks. *Primates, 35*, 49–55.

Uehara, S., Nishida, T., Takasaki, H., Norikoshi, K., Tsukahara, T., Nyundo, R., & Hamai, M. (1994a). A lone male chimpanzee in the wild: The survivor of a disintegrated unit-group. *Primates, 35,* 275–281.

Uller, T., Feiner, N., Radersma, R., Jackson I.S., & Rago, A. (2019). Developmental plasticity and evolutionary explanations. *Evolution and Development, 22,* 47–55.

University of St. Andrews. (2007). Female of the species as deadly as the male. https://news.st-andrews.ac.uk/archive/female-of-the-species-as-deadly-as-the-male/. Accessed February 16, 2020.

Vaesen, K. (2014). Chimpocentrism and reconstructions of human evolution (a timely reminder). *Studies in History and Philosophy of Science Part C: Studies in History and Philosophy of Biomedical Sciences, 45,* 12–21.

Van Lawick-Goodall, J., & van Lawick, H. (1967). *My friends, the wild chimpanzees.* National Geographic Society.

van Lawick-Goodall, J. (1968). The behaviour of free-living chimpanzees in the Gombe Stream Reserve. *Animal Behaviour Monographs, 1,* 163–311.

van Lawick-Goodall, J. (1973a). The behavior of chimpanzees in their natural habitat. *American Journal of Psychiatry, 130*(1), 1–12.

van Lawick-Goodal, J. (1973b). Cultural elements in a chimpanzee community. *IVth International Congress of Primatology, Vol. I: Precultural Primate Behavior,* 144–184.

van Leeuwen, K.L., Hill, R.A., & Korstjens, A.H. (2020). Classifying chimpanzee (*Pan troglodytes*) landscapes across large-scale environmental gradients in Africa. *International Journal of Primatology, 41,* 800–821. https://doi.org/10.1007/s10764-020-00164-5

van Orsdol, K.G. (1986). Agricultural encroachment in Uganda's Kibale Forest. *Oryx, 20,* 115–117.

van Schaik, C.P. (2000). Social counterstrategies against infanticide by males in primates and other mammals. In Kappeler, P.M. (Ed.), *Primate males: Causes and consequences of variation in group composition* (pp. 34–52). Cambridge University Press.

van Schaik, C.P. (2016). *The primate origins of human nature.* John Wiley and Sons.

van Schaik, C.P., & Janson, C.H. (Eds.). (2000a). *Infanticide by males and its implications.* Cambridge University Press.

van Schaik, C.P., & Janson, C.H. (2000b). Infanticide by males: Prospectus. In van Schaik, C.P., & Janson, C.P. (Eds.), *Infanticide by males and its implications* (pp. 1–6). Cambridge University Press.

Vencl, S. (1984). War and warfare in archaeology. *Journal of Anthropological Archaeology, 3,* 116–132.

Vergano, D. (2010). Female chimps play with stick "dolls." *USA Today.* http://content.usatoday.com/communities/sciencefair/post/2010/12/female-chimps-play-with-stick-dolls/1#.U5ZWKXJdWSo. Accessed June 9, 2014.

Vervaecke, H., Stevens, J., & van Elsacker, L. (2004). Pan continuity: Bonobo-chimpanzee hybrids. *Folia Primatolica, 75,* 59.

Vigil, J.D. (2003). Urban violence and street gangs. *Annual Review of Anthropology, 32,* 225–242.

Vigilant, L. (2019). Insights from genetic analysis of the Tai chimpanzees. In Boesch, C., Wittig, R., Crockford, C., Vigilant, L., Deschner, T., & Leendertz, F. (Eds.), *The chimpanzees of the Tai Forest: 40 years of research* (pp. 70–77). Cambridge University Press.

Vigilant, L., Hofreiter, M., Siedel, H., & Boesch, C. (2001). Paternity and relatedness in wild chimpanzee communities. *Proceedings of the National Academy of Sciences of the United States, 98,* 12890–12895.

Virgens, M.Y.F. (2013). Aggressive behavior of chimpanzees at the Oakland Zoo. http://academia.edu/3227659/Aggressive_Behavior_of_chimpanzees_in_the_Oakland_zoo. Accessed July 13, 2013.

Wade, N. (2003). A course in behavior and evolution, taught by chimps. *International Herald Tribune,* November 27, 10.

Wade, N. (2006). The twists and turns of history, and DNA. *New York Times,* March 12, https://www.nytimes.com/2006/03/12/weekinreview/the-twists-and-turns-of-history-and-of-dna.html. Accessed February 16, 2020.

Wade, N. (2010). Chimps that wage war and annex rival territory. *New York Times Science Supplement,* June 22, D1.

Wainschetein, P., Jain, D.P., Yengo, L., Zheng, Z., & TOPMed Anthropometry Working Group, Trans-Omics for Precision Medicine Consortium. (2019). Recovery of trait heritability from whole genome sequence data. bioRxvi preprint. https://www.biorxiv.org/content/biorxiv/early/2019/03/25/588020.full.pdf. Accessed June 9, 2021.

Wakefield, M.L. (2008). Grouping patterns and competition among female *Pan troglodytes schweinfurthii* at Ngogo, Kibale National Park, Uganda. *International Journal of Primatology, 29,* 907–929.

Wakibara, J. (1998). Observations on the pilot control of *Senna spectabilis,* an invasive exotic tree in the Mahale Mountains National Park, Western Tanzania. *Pan Africa News, 5,* unpaginated. http://mahale.main.jp/PAN/index.html. Accessed May 4, 2020.

Walker, J. (1935). A case of leopard bite, with a note on claw marks. *Lancet, 226,* 133.

Walker, K.K., & Hare, B. (2017). Bonobo baby dominance: Did female defense of offspring lead to reduced male aggression? In Hare, B., & Yamamoto, S. (Eds.), *Bonobo cognition and behavior* (pp. 49–64). Brill.

Walker, K.K., & Pusey, A.E. (2020). Inbreeding risk and maternal support have opposite effects on female chimpanzee dispersal. *Current Biology, 30,* R62–R63.

Walker, K.K., Rudicell, R.S., Li, Y., Hahn, B.H., Wroblewski, E., & Pusey, A.E. (2018). Chimpanzees breed with genetically dissimilar mates. *Royal Society Open Science, 4,* 1–13.

Waller, J.C., & Reynolds, V. (2001). Limb injuries resulting from snares and traps in chimpanzees (*Pan troglodytes schweinfurthii*) of the Budongo Forest, Uganda. *Primates, 42,* 135–139.

Waller, M.T., & Pruetz, J. (2016). Competition between chimpanzees and humans: The effects of harvesting non-timber forest products. In Waller, M.T. (Ed.), *Ethnoprimatology, developments in primatology: Progress and prospects* (pp. 157–177). Springer International.

Waller, M.T., & White, F.J. (2016). The effects of war on bonobos and other non-human primates in the Democratic Republic of the Congo. In Waller, M. (Ed.), *Ethnoprimatology: Primate conservation in the 21st century* (pp. 179–192). Springer International.

Wallis, J., & Lee, D.R. (1999). Primate conservation: The prevention of disease transmission. *International Journal of Primatology, 20,* 803–826.

Walsh, P.D. (2008). A rant on infectious disease and ape research priorities. *American Journal of Primatology, 70,* 719–721.

Walsh, P.D., Abernethy, K.A., Bermejo, M., Beyers, R., De Wachter, P., Akou, M.E., Huijbregts, B., Mambounga, D.I., Toham, A.K., Kilbourn, A.M., Lahm, S.A., Latour, S., Maisels, F., Mbina, C., Mihindou, Y., Obiang, S.N., Effa, E.N., Starkey, M.P., Telfer, P., Thibault, M., Tutin, C.E.G., White, L.J.T., & Wilkie, D.S. (2003). Catastrophic ape decline in western equatorial Africa. *Nature, 422*, 611–614.

Wanyama, F., Muhabwe, R., PLumptre, A.J., Chapman, C.A., & Rothman, J.M. (2009). Censusing large mammals in Kibale National Park: Evaluation of the intensity of sampling required to determine change. *African Journal of Ecology, 48*, 953–961.

Warner, W.L. (1958). *A black civilization: A study of an Australian tribe*. Harper and Row.

Washington University. (2003). *Chimps with little or no human contact discovered in remote African rain forest*. https://source.wustl.edu/2003/05/chimps-with-little-or-no-human-contact-discovered-in-remote-african-rain-forest/. Accessed April 24, 2020.

Wasserstrom, R. (2016). Waorani warfare on the Ecuadorian frontier, 1885–2013. *Journal of Latin American and Caribbean Anthropology, 21*, 497–516.

Watts, D.P. (2002). Reciprocity and interchange in the social relationships of wild male chimpanzees. *Behaviour, 139*, 343–370.

Watts, D.P. (2003). Intracommunity coalitionary killing of an adult male chimpanzee at Ngogo, Kibale National Park, Uganda. *International Journal of Primatology, 25*, 507–521.

Watts, D.P. (2007). Effects of male group size, parity, and cycle stage on female chimpanzee copulation rates at Ngogo, Kibale National Park, Uganda. *Primates, 48*, 222–231.

Watts, D.P. (2008a). Tool use by chimpanzees at Ngogo, Kibale National Park, Uganda. *International Journal of Primatology, 29*, 83–94.

Watts, D.P. (2008b). Scavenging by chimpanzees at Ngogo and the relevance of chimpanzee scavenging to early hominin behavioral ecology. *Journal of Human Evolution, 54*, 125–133.

Watts, D.P. (2010). Dominance, power, and politics in nonhuman and human primates. In Kappeler, P.M., & Silk, J.B. (Eds.), *Mind the gap* (pp. 109–133). Springer.

Watts, D.P. (2012). Long-term research on chimpanzee behavioral ecology in Kibale National Park, Uganda. In Kappeler, P.M., & Watts, D.P. (Eds.), *Long-term field studies of primates* (pp. 313–338). Springer.

Watts, D.P. (2020). Meat eating by nonhuman primates: A review and synthesis. *Journal of Human Evolution, 149*, 1–25. https://doi.org/101016/j.jhevol.2020.102882

Watts, D.P., & Amsler, S.J. (2013). Chimpanzee red colobus encounter rates show a red colobus population decline associated with predation by chimpanzees at Ngogo. *American Journal of Primatology, 75*, 927–937.

Watts, D.P., & Mitani, J.C. (2000). Infanticide and cannibalism by male chimpanzees at Ngogo, Kibale National Park, Uganda. *Primates, 41*, 357–365.

Watts, D.P., & Mitani, J.C. (2001). Boundary patrols and intergroup encounters in wild chimpanzees. *Behaviour, 138*, 299–327.

Watts, D.P., & Mitani, J.C. (2002a). Hunting behavior of chimpanzees at Ngogo, Kibale National Park, Uganda. *International Journal of Primatology, 23*, 1–27.

Watts, D.P., & Mitani, J.C. (2002b). Hunting and meat sharing by chimpanzees at Ngogo, Kibale National Park, Uganda. In Boesch, C., Hohmann, G., & Marchant, L. (Eds.), *Behavioural diversity in chimpanzees and bonobos* (pp. 244–255). Cambridge University Press.

Watts, D.P., Mitani, J.C., Amsler, S.J., & Lwanga, J. (2011). Decrease in hunting by chimpanzees in response to over-harvesting of red colobus monkeys at Ngogo, Kibale National Park, Uganda. *American Journal of Physical Anthropology, 144*, 306–307.

Watts, D.P., Mitani, J.C., & Sherrow, H.M. (2002). New cases of inter-community infanticide by male chimpanzees at Ngogo, Kibale National Park, Uganda. *Primates, 43*, 263–270.

Watts, D.P., Muller, M., Amsler, S.J., Mbabazi, G., & Mitani, J.C. (2006). Lethal intergroup aggression by chimpanzees in Kibale National Park, Uganda. *American Journal of Primatology, 68*, 161–180.

Watts, D.P., Potts, K.B., Lwanga, J.S., & Mitani, J.C. (2012a). Diet of chimpanzees (*Pan troglodytes schweinfurthii*) at Ngogo, Kibale National Park, Uganda, 1. Diet composition and diversity. *American Journal of Primatology, 74*, 114–129.

Watts, D.P., Potts, K.B., Lwanga, J.S., & Mitani, J.C. (2012b). Diet of chimpanzees (*Pan troglodytes schweinfurthii*) at Ngogo, Kibale National Park, Uganda, 2: Temporal variation and fallback foods. *American Journal of Primatology, 74*, 130–144.

Webber, A.D., Hill, C.M., & Reynolds, V. (2007). Assessing the failure of a community-based human-wildlife conflict mitigation project in Budongo Forest Reserve, Uganda. *Oryx, 41*, 177–184.

Weisner, P. (2019). Collective action for war and for peace: A case study among the Enga of Papua New Guinea. *Current Anthropology, 60*, 224–244.

Weiss, R.A., & McMichael, A.J. (2004). Social and environmental risk factors in the emergence of infectious diseases. *Nature Medicine, 10*, S 70–76.

Weiss, A., Staes, N., Pereboom, J.J., Inoue-Murayama, M., Stevens, J.M., & Eens, M. (2015). Personality in bonobos. *Psychological Science, 26*, 1430–1439.

Weiss, A., Wilson, M.L., Collins, D.A., Mjungu, D., Kamenya, S., Foerster, S., & Pusey, A.E. (2017). Personality in the chimpanzees of Gombe National Park. *Scientific Data, 4*, 170146.

Wendorf, F. (Ed.). (1968). *The prehistory of Nubia*. Southern Methodist University Press.

Wessling, E.G., Deschner, T., Mundry, R., Pruetz, J.D., Wittig, R.M., & Kuhl, H.S. (2018). Seasonal variation in physiology challenges the notion of chimpanzees (*Pan troglodytes verus*) as a forest-adapted species. *Frontiers in Ecology and Evolution, 6*, 1–21.

West-Eberhard, M.J. (2003). *Developmental plasticity and evolution*. Oxford University Press.

Whitehead, H., Laland, K.N., Rendell, L., Thorogood, R., & Whiten, A. (2019). The reach of gene-culture coevolution in animals. *Nature Communications, 10*, 2405, 1–10. https://doi.org/10.1038/s41467-019-10293-y.

Whitten, A. (2021). The burgeoning reach of animal culture. *Science, 372*, 6537, 46–53.

Wich, S.A., Garcia-Ulloa, J., Kühl, H.S., Humle, T., Lee, J.S., & Koh, L.P. (2014). Will oil palm's homecoming spell doom for Africa's great apes? *Current Biology, 24*, 1659–1663.

White, F.J. (1988). Party composition and dynamics in *Pan paniscus*. *International Journal of Primatology, 9*(3), 179–193.

White, F.J. (1992). Pygmy chimpanzee social organization: Variation with party size and between study sites. *American Journal of Primatology, 26*, 203–214.

White, F.J. (1996a). Pan paniscus 1973 to 1996: Twenty-three years of field research. *Evolutionary Anthropology Issues News and Reviews, 5*, 11–17.

White, F.J. (1996b). Comparative socio-ecology of *Pan paniscus*. In McGrew, W.C., Marchant, L.F., & Nishida, T. (Eds.), *Great ape societies* (pp. 29–44). Cambridge University Press.

White, F.J., & Burgman, M.A. (1990). Social organization of the pygmy chimpanzee (*Pan paniscus*): Multivariate analysis of intracommunity associations. *American Journal of Physical Anthropology, 83*, 193–201.

White, F.J., & Chapman, C.A. (1994). Contrasting chimpanzees and pygmy chimpanzees: Nearest neighbor distances and choices. *Folia Primatolgica, 63*, 181–191.

White, F.J., Waller, M., Boose, K., Merrill, M.Y., & Wood, K.D. (2015). Function of loud calls in wild bonobos. *Journal of Anthropological Sciences, 93*, 1–13.

White, F.J., Waller, M.T., Cobden, A.K., & Malone, N.M. (2008). Lomako bonobo population dynamics, habitat productivity, and the question of tool use. *American Journal of Physical Anthropology, Supplement, 466*, 222.

White, F.J., & Wood, K.D. (2007). Female feeding priority in bonobos, *Pan paniscus*, and the question of female dominance. *American Journal of Primatology, 69*, 837–850.

White, L., & Tutin, C. (2001). Why chimpanzees and gorillas respond differently to logging: A cautionary tale from Gabon. In Weber, W., White, L.J.T., Vedder, A., & Naughton-Treves, L. (Eds.), *African rain forest ecology and conservation: An interdisciplinary perspective* (pp. 449–462). Yale University Press.

Whitesell, S.E., Kyampaire, O., & Lilleholm, R.J. (1997). Human dimensions research needs in Uganda's Kibale National Park. *The George Wright Forum, 14*, 65–71.

Whitty, J. (2010). Girl chimps make dolls. *Mother Jones*. http://www.motherjones.com/blue-marble/2010/12/girl-chimps-make-dolls. Accessed June 9, 2014.

Wilkins, A.S., Wrangham, R.W., & Fitch, T. (2014). The "domestication syndrome" in mammals: A unified explanation based on neural crest cell behavior and genetics. *Genetics, 197*, 795–808.

Williams, J.M. (1999). *Female strategies and the reasons for territoriality in chimpanzees: Lessons from three decades of research at Gombe*. Doctoral dissertation, University of Minnesota.

Williams, J.M., Londsdorf, E.V., Wilson, M.L., Schumacher-Stankey, J., Goodall, J., & Pusey, A.E. (2008). Causes of death in the Kasekela chimpanzees of Gombe National Park, Tanzania. *American Journal of Primatology, 70*, 766–777.

Williams, J.M., Oehlert, G.W., Carlis, J.V., & Pusey, A.E. (2004). Why do male chimpanzees defend a group range? *Animal Behaviour, 68*, 523–532.

Williams, J.M., Pusey, A.E., Carlis, J.V., Farm, B.P., & Goodall, J. (2002). Female competition and male territorial behaviour influence female chimpanzees patterns. *Animal Behavior, 63*, 347–360.

Williams, N.M. (1983). Yolngu concepts of land ownership. In Peterson, N., & Langston, M. (Eds.), *Aborigines, land and land rights*. Australian Institute of Aboriginal Studies.

Williams, R.C., Nash, L.T., Scarry, C.J., Videan, E.N., & Fritz, J. (2010). Factors affecting wounding aggression in a colony of captive chimpanzees (*Pan troglodytes*). *Zoo Biology, 29*, 351–354.

Wilson, E.O. (1980). *Sociobiology: The abridged edition*. Harvard University Press.

Wilson, E.O. (2012). *The social conquest of Earth*. Liveright Publishers.

Wilson, M.L. (2001). *Imbalances of power: How chimpanzees respond to the threat of intergroup aggression*. PhD dissertation, Harvard University.

Wilson, M.L. (2012). Long-term studies of the chimpanzees of Gombe National Park, Tanzania. In Kappeler, P.M., & Watts, D.P. (Eds.), *Long-term field studies of primates* (pp. 339–385). Springer.

Wilson, M.L. (2013). Chimpanzees, warfare, and the invention of peace. In Fry, D. (Ed.), *War, peace, and human nature: The convergence of evolutionary of cultural views* (pp. 361–388). Oxford University Press.

Wilson, M.L., Boesch, C., et al. (2014a). Lethal aggression in *Pan* is better explained by adaptive strategies than human impacts. *Nature, 513*, 414–417.

Wilson, M.L., et al. (2014b). Chimp violence researchers respond to criticism on cross-check. John Horgan's blog Cross-Check. *Scientific American*. https://blogs.scientificamerican.com/cross-check/chimp-violence-researchers-respond-to-criticism-on-cross-check/. Accessed February 29, 2020.

Wilson, M.L., Britton, N.F., & Franks, N.R. (2002). Chimpanzees and the mathematics of battle. *Proceedings of the Royal Society B: Biological Sciences, 269*, 1107–1112.

Wilson, M.L., Collins, A., Wallauer, W.R., & Kamenya, S. (2005). *Gombe Stream Research Centre 2005 Annual Report*. Gombe Stream Research Centre. The Jane Goodal Institute.

Wilson, M.L., Glowacki, L. (2017). Violent cousins: Chimpanzees, humans, and the roots of war. In Muller, M.N. Wrangham, R.W., & Pilbeam, D.R. (Eds.), *Chimpanzees and human evolution* (pp. 464–508). Belknap Press of Harvard University Press.

Wilson, M.L., Hauser, M.D., & Wrangham, R.W. (2001). Does participation in intergroup conflict depend on numerical assessment, range location, or rank for wild chimpanzees? *Animal Behaviour, 61*, 1203–1216.

Wilson, M.L, Hauser, M.D., & Wrangham, R.W. (2007). Chimpanzees (*Pan troglodytes*) modify grouping and vocal behaviour in response to location-specific risk. *Behaviour, 144*, 1621–1653.

Wilson, M.L., Lonsdorf, E.V., Mjungu, D.C., Kamenya, S., ... Goodall, J. (2020). Research and conservation in the greater Gombe ecosystem: Challenges and opportunities. *Biological Conservation, 252*, 1–11.

Wilson, M.L., Kahlenberg, S.M., Wells, M., & Wrangham, R.W. (2011). Ecological and social factors affect the occurrence and outcomes of intergroup encounters in chimpanzees. *Animal Behaviour, 83*(1), 277–291.

Wilson, M.L., Wallauer, W.R., & Pusey, A.E. (2004). New cases of intergroup violence among chimpanzees in Gombe National Park, Tanzania. *International Journal of Primatology, 25*, 523–549.

Wilson, M.L., & Wrangham, R.W. (2003). Intergroup relations in chimpanzees. *Annual Review of Anthropology, 32*, 363–392.

Wittig, R., & Boesch, C. (2019). Demography and life history of five chimpanzee communities in Tai National Park. In Boesch, C., Wittig, R., Crockford, C., Vigilant, L., Deschner, T., & Leendertz, F. (Eds.), *The chimpanzees of the Tai Forest: 40 years of research* (pp. 127–140). Cambridge University Press.

Wittig, R.M., & Boesch, C. (2003). Food competition and linear dominance hierarchy among female chimpanzees of the Tai National Park. *International Journal of Primatology, 24*, 847–867.

Wittiger, L., & Boesch, C. (2013). Female gregariousness in Western Chimpanzees (*Pan troglodytes verus*) is influenced by resource aggregation and the number of females in estrus. *Behavioral Ecology and Sociobiology, 67*, 1097–1111.

Wobber, V., Hare, B., Maboto, J., Lipson, S., Wrangham, R., & Ellison, P.T. (2010a). Differential changes in steroid hormones before competition in bonobos and chimpanzees. *Proceedings of the National Academy of Sciences, 107*, 12457–12462.

Wobber, V., Wrangham, R., & Hare, B. (2010b). Bonobos exhibit delayed development of social behavior and cognition relative to chimpanzees. *Current Biology, 20*, 226–230.

Wolf, E. (1987). *Europe and the people without history*. University of California Press.

Wood, B.M., Watts, D.P., Mitani, J.C., & Langergraber, K.E. (2017). Favorable ecological circumstances promote life expectancy in chimpanzees similar to that of human hunter-gatherers. *Journal of Human Evolution, 105*, 41–56.

Won, Y.-J., & Hey, J. (2005). Divergence population genetics of chimpanzees. *Molecular Biology and Evolution, 22*, 297–307.

Wood, W. (1998). Interactions among environmental enrichment, viewing crowds and zoo chimpanzees (*Pan troglodytes*). *Zoo Biology, 17*, 211–230.

World Science. (2010). *Chimps kill each other for territory, study finds*. http://www.freerepublic.com/focus/chat/2539103/posts. Accessed April 24, 2020.

World Heritage Center. (n.d.). *Tai National Park*. https://whc.unesco.org/document/152954. Accessed September 30, 2018.

World Wildlife Fund. (n.d.). *Chimpanzees*. https://wwf.panda.org/knowledge_hub/endangered_species/great_apes/chimpanzees/. Accessed April 24, 2020.

Wrangham, R.W. (1974). Artificial feeding of chimpanzees and baboons in their natural habitat. *Animal Behavior, 22*, 83–93.

Wrangham, R.W. (1975). *Behavioral ecology of chimpanzees in Gombe National Park, Tanzania*. Doctoral dissertation, University of Cambridge.

Wrangham, R.W. (1977). Feeding behavior of chimpanzees in Gombe National Park, Tanzania. In Clutton-Brock, T.H. (Ed.), *Primate ecology: Studies of feeding and ranging behavior in lemurs, monkey and apes* (pp. 503–538). Academic Press.

Wrangham, R.W. (1979a). On the evolution of ape social systems. *Social Science Information, 18*, 335–368.

Wrangham, R.W. (1979b). Sex differences in chimpanzee dispersion. In Hamburg, D.A., & McCown, E. (Eds.), *The great apes* (pp. 481–489). Benjamin Cummings.

Wrangham, R.W. (1982a). Natural selection in sociobiology. In King's College Sociobiology Group, Cambridge (Eds.), *Current problems in sociobiology* (pp. 5–7). Cambridge University Press.

Wrangham, R.W. (1982b). Mutualism, kinship, and social evolution. In Kings College Sociobiology Group (Eds.), *Current problems in sociobiology* (pp. 269–290). Cambridge University Press.

Wrangham, R.W. (1987). The significance of African apes for reconstructing human social evolution. In Kinzey, W.G. (Ed.), *The evolution of human behavior: Primate models* (pp. 67–71). State University of New York Press.

Wrangham, R.W. (1988). War in evolutionary perspective. In Pines, D. (Ed.), *Emerging syntheses in science: Proceeding of the founding workshop of the Santa Fe Institute, Santa Fe, New Mexico* (Vol. 1, pp. 77–82). Addison-Wesley.

Wrangham, R.W. (1993). The evolution of sexuality in chimpanzees and bonobos. *Human Nature, 4*, 47–79.

Wrangham, R.W. (1995). Ape cultures and missing links. *Symbols*, Spring, 2–9, 30.

Wrangham, R.W. (1998). Is military incompetence adaptive? *Evolution and Human Behavior, 20,* 3–17.
Wrangham, R.W. (1999). Evolution of coalitionary killing. *Yearbook of Physical Anthropology, 4,* 1–30.
Wrangham, R.W. (2000). The snare patrol. *Natural History, 109,* 46.
Wrangham, R.W. (2001). Moral decisions about wild chimpanzees. In Beck, B.B., Stoinski, T.S., Hutchins, M., Maple, T.L., & Norton, B. (Eds.), *Great apes and humans: The ethics of coexistence* (pp. 230–243). Smithsonian Institution Press.
Wrangham, R.W. (2004). Killer species. *Daedalus, 133,* 25–35.
Wrangham, R.W. (2005). Planet of the apes. *Harper's Magazine, 310,* 15–19.
Wrangham, R.W. (2006). Introduction. In Hohmann, G., Robbins, M.M., & Boesch, C. (Eds.), *Feeding ecology in apes and other primates: Ecological, physical and behavioral aspects* (pp. 237–241). Cambridge University Press.
Wrangham, R. (2006). Why apes and humans kill. In Jones, M., & Fabian, A.C. (Eds.), *Conflict* (pp. 43–62). Darwin College Lecture Series, 18. Cambridge University Press.
Wrangham, R.W. (2010). Chimpanzee violence is a serious topic: A response to Sussman and Marshack's critique of *Demonic males: Apes and the origins of human violence. Global Nonkilling Working Papers, 1,* 29–47.
Wrangham, R.W. (2018). Two types of aggression in human evolution. *Proceedings of the National Academy of Sciences, 115*(2), 245–253.
Wrangham, R.W. (2019). *The goodness paradox: The strange relationship between virtue and violence in human evolution.* Pantheon Books.
Wrangham, R.W. (2021). Targeted conspiratorial killing, human self-domestication and the evolution of groupishness. *Evolutionary Human Sciences, 3,* e26, 1–21.
Wrangham, R.W., & Bergman-Riss, E.V.Z.B. (1990). Rates of predation on mammals by Gombe chimpanzees, 1972–1975. *Primates, 31,* 157–170.
Wrangham, R.W., Chapman, C.A., Clark-Arcadi, A.P., & Isabirye-Basuta, G. (1996). Social ecology of Kanyawara chimpanzees: Implications for understanding the costs of great ape groups. In McGrew, W.C., Marchant, L.F., & Nishida, T. (Eds.), *Great ape societies* (pp. 45–57). Cambridge University Press.
Wrangham, R.W., Crofoot, M., Lundy, R., & Gilby, I. (2007). Use of overlap zones among group-living primates: A test of the risk hypothesis. *Behaviour, 144,* 1599–1619.
Wrangham, R.W., & Glowacki, L. (2012). Intergroup aggression in chimpanzees and war in nomadic hunter-gatherers: Evaluating the chimpanzee model. *Human Nature, 23,* 5–29.
Wrangham, R.W., & Mugume, S. (2000). Snare removal program in Kibale National Park: A preliminary report. *Pan Africa News, 7*(2), unpaginated. http://mahale.main.jp/PAN/index.html. Accessed May 4, 2020.
Wrangham, R.W., & Otoli, E. (2011). Teddy's death and the aftermath. *Kibale Chimpanzee Project* [online]. http://kibalechimpanzees.wordpress.com/2011/06/23/teddys-death-and-the-aftermath/. Accessed June 9, 2014.
Wrangham, R.W., & Peterson, D. (1996). *Demonic males: Apes and the origins of human violence.* Houghton Mifflin.
Wrangham, R.W., & Pilbeam, D. (2001). African apes as time machines. In Galdikas, B.M.F., Briggs, N.E., Sheeran, L.K., Shapiro, G.L., & Goodall, J. (Eds.), *All apes great and small: Volume 1: African apes* (pp. 5–17). Kluwer Academic/Plenum Publishers.

Wrangham, R.W., & Smuts, B.B. (1980). Sex differences in the behavioural ecology of chimpanzees in the Gombe National Park, Tanzania. *Journal of Reproduction and Fertility. Supplement, 28*, 13–31.

Wrangham, R.W., & Wilson, M.L. (2004). Collective violence: Comparisons between youths and Chimpanzees. *Annals of the New York Academy of Sciences, 1036*, 233–256.

Wrangham, R.W., Wilson, M.L., & Muller, M.N. (2006). Comparative rates of violence in chimpanzees and humans. *Primates, 47*, 14–26.

Wray, G.A., Hoekstra, H.E., Futuyama, D.J., Lenski, R.E., Macay, T.F.C., Schluter, D., & Strassmann, J.E. (2014). Does evolutionary theory need a rethink? No, all is well. *Nature, 514*, 161–164.

Wright, C. (2002). Going ape. *Boston Phoenix.* http://www.bostonphoenix.com/boston/news_features/top/features/documents/02537776.htm. Accessed June 9, 2014.

Wroblewski, E.E., Murray, C.M., Keele, B.F., Schumacher-Stankey, J.C., Hahn, B.H., & Pusey, A.E. (2009). Male dominance rank and reproductive success in chimpanzees, *Pan troglodytes schweinfurthii. Animal Behaviour, 77*, 873–885.

Yale, G., Bhanurekha, V., & Ganesan, P.I. (2013). Anthropogenic factors responsible for emerging and re-emerging infectious diseases. *Current Science, 105*, 940–946.

Yamagiwa, J., & Basabose, A.K. (2006). Diet and seasonal changes in sympatric gorillas and chimpanzees at Kahuzi-Biega National Park. *Primates, 47*, 74–90.

Yamagiwa, J., Basabose, A.K., Kahekwa, J., Bikaba, D., Matsubara, M., Ando, C., Iwasaki, N., & Sprague, D.S. (2011). Long-term changes in habitats and ecology of African apes in Kahuzi-Biega National Park, Democratic Republic of Congo. In Plumptre, A.J. (Ed.), *The ecological impact of long-term changes in Africa's Rift Valley* (pp. 203–225). Nova Science.

Yamakoshi, G. (2011). The "prehistory" before 1976: Looking back on three decades of research on Bossou Chimpanzees. In Matsuzawa, T., Humle, T., & Sugiyama, Y. (Eds.), *The chimpanzees of Bossou and Nimba* (p. 35–44). Springer.

Yamakoshi, G. (2004). Food seasonality and socioecology in *Pan*: Are west African chimpanzees another bonobo? *African Study Monographs, 25*, 45–60.

Yao, TB., Oszwald, J., Bigot, S., & Servat, E. (2005). Risques de deforestation dans le domain permanent de l'etat en Cote d'Ivoire: Quel avenir pour ces dernier massifs forestiers? *Teledetection, 5*, 105–121.

Yong, E. (2019). A scientist witnessed poachers killing a chimp. *The Atlantic.* https://www.theatlantic.com/science/archive/2019/08/death-chimpanzee/595303/. Accessed May 16, 2020.

Zamma, K., & Fujita, S. (2004). Genito-genital rubbing among the chimpanzees of Mahale and Bossou. *Pan Africa News, 11*(2), unpaginated. http://mahale.main.jp/PAN/index.html. Accessed May 4, 2020.

Zamma, K., Hanamura, S., & Sakamaki, T. (2015). Chimpanzee distribution: Accumulation of survey reports. In Nakamura, M., Hosaka, K., Itoh, N., & Zamma, K. (Eds.), *Mahale chimpanzees: 50 years of research* (pp. 33–47). Cambridge University Press.

Zefferman, M.R., Baldini, R., & Mathew, S. (2015). Solving the puzzle of human warfare requires an explanation of battle raids and cultural institutions. *Proceedings of the National Academy of Science, 122*, E2557.

Zeppel, H.D. (2006). *Indigenous ecotourism: Sustainable development and management.* CABI North America.

Zhang, X., & Ho, S.M. (2011). Epigenetics meets endocrinology. *Journal of Molecular endocrinology, 46*, R11–R32.

Zihlman, A., & Bolter, D.R. (2004). Mammalian and primate roots of human sociality. In Sussman, R.W., & Chapman, A.R. (Eds.), *The origins and nature of sociality* (pp. 23–52). Aldine de Gruyter.

Zuberbühler, K. (2007). Editorial. *Budongo Conservation Field Station News, 8*(1), http://culture.st-and.ac.uk/bcfs/documents/newsletter/newsletter1_2.html. Accessed May 8, 2014.

Zuberbühler, K., & Jenny, D. (2002). Leopard predation and primate evolution. *Journal of Human Evolution, 43*, 873–886.

Index

For the benefit of digital users, indexed terms that span two pages (e.g., 52–53) may, on occasion, appear on only one of those pages.
Note: Figures are indicated by an *f* following the page number.

Abrams, Douglas, 8
adaptationism. *See also* human demonic/
    adaptationist warfare
  explanations of killing, 89–93
  food abundance and, 402–3
  Four Year War, 87, 89–93
  gene-sharing males, 13
  human impact and, 406, 416
  human war and, 419–22, 437, 438–39,
    443, 449
  infanticide paradigm, 377–78
  intergroup killing/violence, 391–92, 393,
    403–5, 404*f*
  maximizing reproductive success, 9–10
  plasticity led adaptation, 364, 368
  sociocognitive adaptations, 437
  Sonso chimpanzees, 246–47
aggressive territorial defense, 205–8
al Qaeda, 451
alpha males
  deposed alphas among Mahale
    chimpanzees, 118–19
  Fongoli chimpanzees, 280
  Kasakela group, 37, 67
  killing of, 130–31, 138–39, 280
  Ngogo chimpanzees, 188–89
American Anthropological Association, 207
Animal Planet, 175
anthrax, 290
anthropogenic changes, 25, 31, 75, 94–95,
    133. *See also* human impact
anthropogenic disease, 73, 131, 298. *See also*
    disease
Ardrey, Robert, 3
artificial provisioning, 25, 58, 70, 122, 139,
    163, 189. *See also* banana feeding
assaults on females, 57–58, 193–94, 206,
    209–11, 245
The Atlantic, 156

baboon-chimpanzee aggression, 3, 50–53,
    132–33, 133*f*
Badrian, Alison, 326–27
Badrian, Noel, 326–27
Baldwin Effect, 364
banana competition, 5–6, 54, 68
banana feeding, 3, 47–53, 49*f*, 55, 58, 59,
    60, 70, 171, 410. *See also* artificial
    provisioning
band-and-village societies, 422–25
Batoro people, 147
battered females, 209–10
biological determinism, 21
bipedal swaggering, 321
Blumberg, Mark, 367
Boas, Franz, 436–37
body mass, 90
Boehm, Christopher, 63
Boesch, Christophe, 265
bonobos. *See also* evolutionary development
    in bonobos *vs.* chimpanzees;
    LuiKotale bonobos; Wamba bonobos
  absence of panicide, 350–52
  associating behaviors, 338–39
  coalitional relationships, 349–50
  contrasting types, 317–18
  demonic perspective, 357–60
  display violence, 348–49
  ecological conditions, 335–36
  female cohesiveness, 354–55
  female dominance, 345, 353–54
  female fighting, 339–41, 340*f*, 341*f*
  food abundance and, 335–36, 337*f*, 358–59
  gender differences, 337–38
  GG rubbing, 339–42, 340*f*, 341*f*, 367
  Gombe paradigm and, 323–24
  human impact on, 324–25, 415
  intergroup killing/violence, 322–23, 330
  intersexual dominance, 342–45

bonobos. (*cont.*)
   interspecies differences and, 337–38
   introduction to, 315
   learned traditions, 355–57
   lone males, 359–60
   male status competition, 345–50
   mother-son relationships, 346–48, 350
   nature/nurture divide, 366–70
   provisioning of, 321, 322–23, 324
   research studies on, 317, 325–26
   sex differences, 338–39
   sexual behavior, 318–19
   social evolution, 353–54
   social organization, 335, 338–42
   species overview, 316–19
   territorial organization, 252, 253*f*
   tool use, 338–39
The Book of Hope (Goodall, Abrams), 8
border/boundary patrolling, 110–11, 121, 135, 157–58, 159*f*, 160*f*, 168, 185, 187, 200–1, 207–8, 229–31, 279, 296
Bossou chimpanzees, 280–84
Budongo chimpanzees. *See also* Sonso chimpanzees
   adaptationism and, 246–47
   conservation impact, 226
   food scarcity, 218
   hardwood logging and, 218, 223–24
   human impact, 217–18, 223–27, 241–47, 413–14
   infant-killing, 223
   intergroup killing/violence, 219–23, 240–46
   introduction to, 217
   islandization, 218
   open groups, 3
   sugar production and, 224–25
   territorial organization, 219–20, 222*f*
   tourism impact, 226
   wire snares and, 225
Bush, George, 451
Bygott, David, 5

cannibalism
   of baboon competitors, 58
   by bonobos, 331
   of infants, 44, 57, 97–98, 304–5, 331, 385, 386–87, 410
captive chimpanzees, 45, 356

Central African chimpanzees
   Conkouati-Douli chimpanzees, 262–63
   Goualougo Triangle chimpanzees, 259–62, 261*f*
   introduction to, 259
   Loango National Park chimpanzees, 264–74
   Lope National Park chimpanzees, 263–64
   Moto chimpanzees, 260–62
certain killings, 42, 86, 375, 387
chimpanzee reunions, 33–35
chimpanzee violence. *See also* evolutionary development in bonobos *vs.* chimpanzees; specific chimpanzee groups
   disappeared chimpanzees, 116–19
   gorillas and, 272
   human influence on, 5–6
   image of peace, 3–4
   revisionary thinking about, 4
   sociobiology/selfish-gene/inclusive fitness theory, 361–66
   trauma in captivity, 152
   unhabituated chimpanzees, 37, 151, 177, 229, 268
The Chimpanzees of Gombe (Goodall), 7, 8, 32–33
Chrysophyllum albidum food source, 194–96
city gangs, 421–22
civil wars, 420–21
close kin shared genes, 9, 295, 316, 354. *See also* epigenetics
coalitional aggression/killing, 12, 138, 163, 179, 185, 238, 372, 403–4, 435
collective killing, 427, 439–40
collective violence, 15, 16, 20, 420–21, 428, 446
competition-for-scarce-resources (CSR), 22–23
Conkouati-Douli chimpanzees, 262–63
contemporary human war, 450–51
crop raiding, 31, 73, 172, 193, 225–26, 281, 407
Cryptosporidium, 74–75
cultural materialism, 441–42, 449, 454
culture and human war, 436–37, 440–42

The Dark Side of Man: Tracing the Origins of Male Violence (Ghiglieri), 14, 19, 109, 146–47

Dawkins, Richard, 9, 10
dechimpized, 7
deforestation, 71, 94, 117, 149, 255, 259, 288, 290, 412
demonic females, 238–39
demonic males
   bonobos vs. chimpanzees, 357–60
   Four Year War, 89, 95–98
   human war and, 419–22, 454–55
   imbalance of power hypothesis, 13–21
   inclusive fitness theory and, 9, 10, 11
   interference mutualism, 11–12
   Niokolo Koba chimpanzees, 277–78
   philopatry and, 396
   scientific methods and, 10–11
   social organization and, 335
   sociobiology and, 9–13, 18, 19, 361, 384, 395
   sociobiology/selfish-gene/inclusive fitness theory, 361–66
   tendencies to war, 9–10
Demonic Males: Apes and the Origins of Human Violence (Peterson), 14, 19, 399, 443–44
developmental psychology, 363
disappeared chimpanzees, 116–19
disease
   anthropogenic disease, 73, 131, 298
   Cryptosporidium, 74–75
   Four Year War, 73–77
   Kibale chimpanzees, 154–56
   Mahale chimpanzees, 131–32
   Mitumba and, 75–76
   Oesophagostomiasis, 74
   skinny male syndrome, 74, 84, 100
   Sonso chimpanzees, 247
   Tai chimpanzees, 289–91
display killing/violence. *See also* status-linked violence
   bonobos, 348–49
   infanticide and, 382
   male status competition, 26–28, 63, 345, 350, 354, 410
   Ngogo chimpanzees, 186–89
   Tai chimpanzees, 309–10
display violence hypothesis (DVH), 63–64
domestication syndrome (DS), 361
dominance drive, 16, 17, 22, 27, 305, 335, 345, 419, 421

Eastern African chimpanzees
   bonobos and, 252, 253*f*
   Filabanga chimpanzees, 257–58
   intergroup killing/violence, 254–55
   Kahuzi-Biega chimpanzees, 257
   subspecies and geography, 251–52
   Toro-Semiliki chimpanzees, 255–56
   Ugalla chimpanzees, 257–58
ebola, 289–90
eco-evo-devo, 366–68
egalitarianism, 26, 422, 427–28, 440, 442, 447–49
The Egalitarians-Human and Chimpanzee (Power), 24–25
epigenetics
   biology and, 362–63
   of bonobos, 366–68
   close kin shared genes, 9
   demonic perspective, 361–62
   gene-sharing males, 13, 396
   Modern Synthesis and, 365–66
   nature- nurture interaction, 363–64, 368–72
   niche selection, 365
   plasticity, 364
   regulation of gene expression, 363–64, 367
   social behavior, 365
ethnic violence, 421, 452
ethnoprimatology, 24–25, 281
evolutionary development in bonobos vs. chimpanzees
   demonic perspective, 357–60
   developmental biology, 362–63
   eco-evo-devo, 366–68
   endocrinology and, 369–70
   epigenetics, 363–64, 367
   evolutionism, 357
   extended evolutionary synthesis, 365, 366
   food abundance and, 358–59
   learned traditions, 355–57
   lone males, 359–60
   missing heritabilities, 362
   Modern Synthesis, 365–66
   nature/nurture divide, 366–70
   neurobiology and, 369–70
   niche selection, 365, 368
   plasticity, 364, 368
   power imbalances, 359
   self-domestication hypothesis, 324

evolutionary development in bonobos vs.
    chimpanzees (cont.)
  self-sustaining organization, 354–55
  social behavior inheritance, 365
  social evolution, 353–54, 368
  sociobiology/selfish-gene/inclusive fitness
    theory, 361–66
  summary of, 370–72
extended evolutionary synthesis (EES),
  365, 366
external killings/violence, 79–83, 94–98
Eyengo (Ranger) community, 328–30

female fighting, 339–41
female immigration, 170, 229, 243, 400
Ficus mucuso food source, 169–70, 194–96
Filabanga chimpanzees, 257–58
First Congo War, 324–25
fission/fusion pattern
  in bonobos, 322, 359
  define limits of, 4
  defined, 13
  Ngogo chimpanzees, 190–91
Fongoli chimpanzees, 278–80
food abundance
  adaptationist theory and, 402–3
  aggregation and association of females,
    352, 354
  bonobos and, 335–36, 337f, 358–
    59, 366–67
  cohesive groupings and, 354
  population density and, 229, 238, 247
  reduction of rivals and, 404–5
  seasonal periods of, 179, 196
food scarcity
  Budongo chimpanzees, 218
  competition for resources, 301
  Gombe chimpanzees, 72, 74
  gorillas and, 272–73
  group conflict and, 88
  Kalande chimpanzees, 73
  Loango National Park chimpanzees,
    273f, 273–74
  Ngogo chimpanzees, 179–81, 194
  Sonso chimpanzees, 218
  Tai chimpanzees, 301–2
forager exclusivity, 433
Foreign Affairs, 389, 451
Four Year War. *See also* Gombe chimpanzees

  brief overview, 38–42
  context of, 33, 56–57, 58, 62, 228
  demonic vision of chimpanzees, 65–
    68, 105
  exiting conflict, 41–42
  Gombe paradigm and, 107–8
  human impact and, 44–50, 101
  hunting by chimpanzees, 49f, 50–
    55, 92–93
  intergroup killing/violence, 84–86, 87, 99–
    100, 399–401
  introduction to, 4, 5–6, 7, 31, 32–33
  Kalande community invasion, 59–68
  leaders of, 95–98
  number of killings, 40–43
  observation by researchers, 45–50, 46f
  porous intergroup boundaries, 36–38
  reasons for, 59–61, 64–65
  red colobus monkeys and, 53–55
  start of, 56, 98
  status competition and, 63–64
  territorial organization, 33–38, 90–91, 91f
  varieties of violence, 33
Furuichi, Takeshi, 319

gang warfare by humans, 421–22
gene-sharing males, 13, 396. *See also*
  epigenetics
genocide, 9, 284, 385, 420–21, 423, 426, 432
Genome Wide Association Studies
  (GWAS), 362
GG rubbing, 340f, 341f, 339–42, 367
Ghiglieri, Michael, 12–13, 14, 109, 146–
  47, 167–69
Gombe chimpanzees. *See also* Four Year War
  adaptationist explanations of killing,
    87, 89–93
  ambiguous observations, 34f, 35–36
  assaults by humans, 72–73
  assaults on mothers, 57–58, 83
  baboon-chimpanzee aggression, 3, 50–53
  banana feeding, 47–53, 49f, 55, 58,
    59, 60, 70
  body mass and, 90
  chimpanzee reunions, 33–35
  competition for food, 59–61
  conservation and, 71–72
  demographic collapse, 76–77
  demonic males perspective, 89, 95–98

disease impact on, 73–77
display violence hypothesis, 63–65
external killings/violence, 79–83, 94–98
field operations, 32–33
frustration and favoritism in, 59
Gombe National Park overview, 31–32
Goodall, Jane and, 32–33, 69–70
habitat destruction, 71
human impact hypothesis (HIH), 68, 94–95
human impact on, 44–50, 46f, 70–73, 410–11
hunting by, 49f, 50–55, 92–93
imbalance of power hypothesis, 87–88
infant-eating, 56–57
infant-killing, 83
infectious diseases, 74–75
internal killing/violence, 84–86, 87, 99–100, 399–401
interpretation of, 87
introduction to, 4, 5–6, 69
Ngogo chimpanzees and, 89–93
number of killings, 40–43
observation by researchers, 45–50, 46f
payback violence, 27, 67, 87, 98, 100–1, 375
politics and, 63, 77–79
porous intergroup boundaries, 36–38
post-invasion stability, 77
psychology and, 61–62
red colobus monkeys and, 53–55
research impact on, 70–71
rival coalition reduction hypothesis and, 68, 78, 88–89
sex/sexual competition and, 62, 93
status-linked violence, 63–65, 98–101
territorial organization, 33–38, 90–91, 91f
tourism impact on, 70–71
varieties of violence, 33
victim coding, 43
Gombe paradigm, 19, 22, 25, 87, 101, 107–10, 120, 121, 139, 219, 230, 232, 256, 323–24, 419, 441. *See also* theoretical alternatives to Gombe paradigm
Gombe Stream Research Center, 6
Goodall, Jane
  on banana feeding, 3, 50–51, 60
  on beatings, 304, 310
  chimpanzee subgroups, 3–4
  chimpanzees playing with objects, 212–13

on culture, 436–37, 440–42
Four Year War and, 32–33
as hero and scientist, 8
human-chimpanzee comparisons, 4
human influence on chimpanzee violence, 5–6
on language, 437, 438
on Mahale chimpanzees, 125
natural history approach, 10–11
start of research, 3–4
on tendencies to war, 9
view of human nature, 6–8
The Goodness Paradox (Wrangham), 18, 20, 431–32, 453
gorillas, chimpanzee attacks on, 272
Goualougo Triangle chimpanzees, 259–62, 261f
Great Disappearance, 117, 118, 134–35
Great Revision, 4, 35
Grieser-Johns, Bettina, 147

habitat destruction/loss
  Four Year War, 71
  human impact, 407
  immigration and, 71
  Kanyawara chimpanzees, 192–93, 195f
  Kibale chimpanzees, 145, 148–50, 155f, 166, 170–71
  Lomako bonobos, 330–31
  Mahale chimpanzees, 135, 136–37
hardwood logging, 148–49, 193, 218, 223–24
Harris, Marvin, 441–42
HELP (Habitat Ecologique et Liberte des Primates), 262
high-status males, 63, 117, 130, 138, 387, 411. *See also* alpha males
Hinde, Robert, 32–33
Hohmann, Gottfried, 326–27
Hrdy, Sarah, 376, 383
human demonic/adaptationist warfare
  band-and-village societies, 422–25
  city gangs, 421–22
  civil wars, 420–21
  continual hostility, 426–28
  evolution and, 425
  forager exclusivity, 433
  genocide, 420–21, 423
  hunter-gatherer territoriality, 434–35
  introduction to, 419

552 INDEX

human demonic/adaptationist warfare (cont.)
    military horizon and, 419–20
    outgroup members, 428–31
    overview of, 419–22
    raids, 428–31
    social units and, 422–23
    territorial foundation, 432–35
    theoretical application, 425–28
    tribe concept, 423–25
    war-risk hypothesis, 429–32
human impact
    adaptationism and, 406, 416
    anthropogenic changes, 25, 31, 75, 94–95, 133
    bonobos, 324–25, 415
    Bossou chimpanzees, 281–82
    Budongo chimpanzees, 217–18, 223–27, 241–47, 413–14
    on chimpanzee violence, 5–6
    disturbance factor, 407–8
    Fongoli chimpanzees, 279
    Four Year War, 44–50, 46f, 70–73, 410–11
    Kibale chimpanzees, 145, 147–48, 156, 171, 412–13
    Mahale chimpanzees, 125–26, 130, 411–12
    narrative summary, 410–15
    Ngogo chimpanzees, 412–13
    overview of, 23–25
    provisioned bonobos, 321, 322–23, 324
    provisioned chimpanzees, 25, 72, 122–23, 145, 408
    refutation of, 406–10
    on sexually selected infanticide, 386–87
    size of protected areas, 408–9
    smaller cases, 414
    Sonso chimpanzees, 245–46, 247
    summary of, 415–16
    Tai chimpanzees, 303, 414–15
human impact hypothesis (HIH)
    Four Year War, 68, 94–95
    human disruption variable, 407–8
    infanticide and, 375
    Mahale chimpanzees, 140
    Ngogo chimpanzees, 189–90
    overview of, 23–25
human war
    adaptationism and, 437, 438–39, 443, 449
    ancient states and, 449–50
    anthropology of, 443
    collective killing, 427, 439–40
    comparative politics of, 448–50
    contemporary human war, 450–51
    cultural materialism, 441–42
    culture and, 436–37, 440–42
    demonic males and, 419–22, 454–55
    First Congo War, 324–25
    as human nature, 454–55
    identerism and, 451–53
    introduction to, 436
    language of, 437–40
    moral conversion and, 440
    origins of, 439–40
    politics and, 440–42
    primordialism, 451–52
    sociocognitive adaptations, 437
    Superstructural ideology, 441–42, 444–47, 452–53
    symbolic construction of, 437–40
    in tribal zones, 445–48
    Western contact and, 437–40
    Yanomami people, 443–45
hunt-and-kill propensity, 14
hunting by bonobos, 331–33
hunting by chimpanzees
    Four Year War, 49f, 50–55, 92–93
    Kanyawara chimpanzees, 196–97
    monkey hunting, 358
    Ngogo chimpanzees, 181–86, 184f
    Sonso chimpanzees, 239–40
    Tai chimpanzees, 295–96
hunting by humans, 288–89
Hussein, Saddam, 451
hypothetical killings, 42, 408

identerism and human war, 451–53
imbalance of power hypothesis (IoPH)
    access to resources, 22–23
    advantage in numbers, 16–17
    applied to humans, 17–19
    demonic males perspective, 13–21
    dominance drive, 16, 17
    Four Year War, 87–88
    Kalande expansion, 66
    Kanyawara chimpanzees, 201
    key concepts, 13–14
    natural selection and, 10, 12, 15, 16–17, 18, 315
    sufficient to kill, 15, 121

urge to kill and, 14–19
immigration and habitat destruction, 71
inclusive fitness theory, 9–10, 11, 13, 101, 361, 366, 371, 396, 405, 430, 436
infanticide (infant-killing). *See also* sexually selected infanticide
  Budongo chimpanzees, 223, 231–33, 237–39
  cannibalism and, 44, 57, 97–98, 304–5, 331, 385, 386–87, 410
  Four Year War, 83
  Kibale chimpanzees, 158–62, 159*f*
  Loango National Park chimpanzees, 269, 271
  Mahale chimpanzees, 113, 126–35, 139
  Ngogo chimpanzees, 185–86
  Sonso chimpanzees, 231–33, 237–39, 242–45, 243*f*
infectious diseases, 74–75
intent to kill, 7, 19, 296–97, 300, 394–95
inter-unit-group interactions, 4, 110, 111, 124*f*
intercommunity aggression, 15, 185, 207, 333, 388–89, 399
interference mutualism (IM), 11–12
intergroup killing/violence. *See also* infanticide; panicide
  adaptive benefits, 391–92, 393
  adaptive variables, 403–5, 404*f*
  assaults on females, 57–58, 193–94, 206, 209–11, 245
  attackers, 393
  Budongo chimpanzees, 219–23
  chimpanzee *vs.* human, 12, 14–15
  clade ancestry, 401–2
  differing perspectives on, 388–90
  East African chimpanzees, 254–55
  Four Year War, 84–86, 87, 99–100, 399–401
  inside *vs.* outside, 397–98
  instances of, 390
  introduction to, 388
  Kanyawara chimpanzees, 197–208, 200*f*
  Kibale chimpanzees, 158–62
  Loango National Park chimpanzees, 264–74
  Lomako bonobos, 330
  LuiKotale bonobos, 333–34
  Mahale chimpanzees and, 107–10, 111–15, 123–25

male aggression sex bias, 392–96
male numbers and density, 402–3
mating and, 398–99
models of, 401–5
Ngogo chimpanzees, 175–78, 185–86
observations of, 391
outside females, 398–401
outside males, 393–95
philopatric males, 396
rarity of, 390–92
resource competition hypothesis and, 395, 401
rival coalition reduction hypothesis and, 397
rival males, 395–98
Sonso chimpanzees, 240–46
summary of, 405
Tai chimpanzees, 296–301, 304–11
victims, 393
internal killing/violence. *See also* infanticide
  Four Year War, 84–86, 87, 99–100, 399–401
  Kasakela group, 84
  sexually selected infanticide, 380–82
  Sonso chimpanzees, 233–34
intersexual dominance in bonobos, 342–45
intimidation displays, 128–29
intracommunity aggression, 7, 78, 85–86
Isabirye-Basuta, Gilbert, 147, 193
islandization, 150–51, 218, 287–91, 293

Jane Goodall Institute (JGI), 6, 8, 71–72

Kahama group
  attacks on, 4, 5–6, 7
  brief overview of Four Year War, 38–42
  competition for food, 59–61
  Kalande community invasion, 59–68
  territorial organization, 36–37
Kahuzi-Biega chimpanzees, 257
Kakombe chimpanzees, 4, 36, 38–42
Kalande chimpanzees
  community invasion, 59–68
  crop raiding by, 73
  demographic collapse, 76–77
  external violence, 79–83
Kalinzu chimpanzees, 252–54, 254*f*
Kano, Takayoshi, 319–20
Kanyanchu chimpanzees, 179–81

Kanyawara chimpanzees
  aggressive territorial defense, 205–8
  battered females, 209–10
  boundary patrolling, 200–1, 207–8
  coercion by males, 210–11
  demographics of, 193–94
  geopolitics, 197–98, 208
  habitat destruction/loss, 192–93, 195*f*
  hunting by chimpanzees, 196–97
  intergroup killing/violence, 197–208, 200*f*
  introduction to, 192
  NSF research method, 205–8
  panicide, 192, 203, 208
  principle foods, 194–96
  sex-specific predispositions, 211–13
  unsavory behaviors, 209–13
  Wantabu community, 198–99
Kasakela chimpanzees
  attacks by, 4, 5–6, 7
  brief overview of Four Year War, 38–42
  competition for food, 59–61
  infant-eating and, 56–57
  internal violence, 84, 85
  territorial organization, 36–38
Kibale chimpanzees. *See also* Kanyawara chimpanzees; Ngogo chimpanzees
  boundary patrolling, 157–58, 159*f*, 160*f*, 164, 168
  demonic males perspective, 164
  disease impact, 154–56
  food scarcity, 179–81, 194, 218, 272–73, 301
  habitat destruction/loss, 145, 148–50, 155*f*, 166, 170–71
  human impact, 145, 147–48, 156, 171, 412–13
  infant-killing, 158–62, 159*f*
  intergroup killing/violence, 158–62
  introduction to, 145
  islandization of, 150–51
  Ngogo territorial conflict, 157–65, 166–78
  overview of Kibale National Park, 146
  research on, 146–47, 163–65
  territorial organization, 150–51, 162–63, 171–75
  tourism impact, 152–54
  wire snares and, 151–52
killing beyond reasonable doubt, 42, 375
kin selection, 9, 13, 18, 392, 396

Kortlandt, Adriaan, 280
Kyoto School, 105–6

Lake Tanganyika Catchment Reforestation and Education Project (TACARE), 71–72
language of human war, 437–40
Leakey, Louis, 3, 32
learned traditions of bonobos, 355–57
leopard attacks, 81–83, 265–68, 288
lethal raiding, 14, 357, 420–21
linear dominance hierarchy, 346
Loango National Park chimpanzees
  attacks on gorillas, 272
  food scarcity and, 273*f*, 273–74
  global warming and, 273–74
  infant-killing, 269, 271
  intergroup killing/violence, 264–74
  leopard attacks, 265–68
  territoriality, 270–71
Lomako bonobos
  blobs grouping, 327–28
  Eyengo (Ranger) community, 328–30
  habitat destruction/loss, 330–31
  intergroup violence, 330
  intersexual dominance, 343–44
  introduction to, 326–28
  male status competition, 346
  research complications, 326–27
  social groups, 327
lone males, 359–60
Lope National Park chimpanzees, 263–64
LuiKotale bonobos
  hunting by bonobos, 331–33
  intergroup killing/violence, 333–34
  intersexual dominance, 344–45
  introduction to, 331–33
  male status competition, 346

Mahale chimpanzees
  age-sex pyramid and, 120–21
  baboon-chimpanzee aggression, 132–33, 133*f*
  boundary patrols and incursions, 110–11
  deposed alphas, 118–19
  disappeared chimpanzees, 116–19
  disease impact on, 131–32
  Gombe paradigm and, 107–10, 120, 121
  habitat loss, 135, 136–37

human impact on, 125–26, 130, 411–12
human settlement and, 106–7
hunting by chimpanzees, 134
infant-killing, 113, 126–35
initial observations, 122–23
intergroup killing/violence and, 107–10, 111–15, 139–41
introduction to, 105
investigators of, 105–7
Kyoto School and, 105–6
landscape transformation, 133
mystery groups and, 135–36
paradigmatics and, 140–41
politics and, 140
provisioning of, 25, 72, 122–23, 125–26
range changes, 134–35
revising disappearance thoughts, 119–21
severe fighting, 123–25
sexual coercion hypothesis, 380
status-linked violence, 129–30
tourism impact on, 131–32, 137
transfers of females and sons, 114
war among, 110–11
male emigration of Bossou chimpanzees, 283–84
male philopatry, 13, 295, 396, 435
male status competition, 26–28, 63, 345–50, 354, 410
Max Planck Institute, 326–27
meat eating, 53–54
Mimusops bagshawei food source, 196
Mitani, John, 207
Mitumba chimpanzees, 84–86
modern synthesis (MS), 362, 365–66
Montagu, Ashley, 3
Morgan, David, 259–60
Moto chimpanzees, 260–62
Mt. Assirik chimpanzees. *See* Niokolo Koba chimpanzees
Muller, Mark, 207

National Geographic, 4, 33, 261–62
National Science Foundation, 205
natural history approach, 10–11
natural selection, 10, 12, 15, 16–17, 18, 315, 362, 363–64, 397
nature/nurture divide, 366–70
New York Times, 63
New Yorker, 326–27

Ngogo chimpanzees
conquest and, 162–63, 176–78
display killing, 186–89
drought impact, 180
evidence of population growth, 167–69, 168*f*
Ficus mucuso food source, 169–70
fissioning of, 190–91
food scarcity, 179–81
Four Year War and, 89–93
geopolitics, 171–75
historic contextualization, 189–90
human impact, 412–13
hunting by chimpanzees, 181–86, 184*f*
infant-killing, 185–86
intergroup killing/violence, 175–78, 185–86
overview of, 166–67
population growth, 183
status-linked violence, 186–89
territorial conflict, 157–65, 166–78
niche selection, 365, 368
Niokolo Koba chimpanzees, 275–78
Nishida, Toshisada, 4, 105–6
non-fig fruits (NFF), 180
non-interference mutualism (NIM), 11–12
nonkilling, 294, 302–3, 415
Nouabale-Ndoki National Park (NNNP), 259
nutritional needs of chimpanzees, 53–54

observation by researchers, 45–50
Oesophagostomiasis, 74
oil palm *(Elaeis guineensis)*, 44
open groups, 3

Pan paniscus. See bonobos
Pan troglodytes schweinfurthii. See Eastern African chimpanzees
Pan troglodytes troglodytes. See Central African chimpanzees
Pan troglodytes verus. See West African chimpanzees
panicide. *See also* intergroup killing/violence; sexually selected infanticide
absence in bonobos, 350–52
Central African chimpanzees, 267, 268, 269
Four Year War, 82, 94
Gombe chimpanzees, 40, 41, 43, 52, 57

panicide (*cont.*)
  human impact and, 409–10, 414, 415
  infant killing and, 375–76
  Kanyawara chimpanzees, 192, 203, 208
  Kibale chimpanzees, 162, 163
  Mahale chimpanzees, 109, 113, 116, 118
  sexually selected infanticide and, 375–76
  Sonso chimpanzees, 240, 246
  Tai chimpanzees, 311
*pan*ology/panologists, 19, 22, 23, 25, 94, 101, 114, 201, 258, 284, 388, 390, 409–10, 416, 431, 436, 448
Paradise Lost period, 6
payback violence, 27, 67, 87, 98, 100–1, 375
philopatry, 13–14, 108, 257, 258, 283, 295, 317–18, 356, 396, 435
pitsawing, 232, 234
plant *vs.* animal foods, 53–54
plasticity led adaptation, 364, 368
politics
  Four Year War, 63, 77–79
  of human war, 448–50
  Kanyawara chimpanzees, 197–98, 208
  Mahale chimpanzees, 140
  Ngogo chimpanzees, 171–75
  Tai chimpanzees, 306–10
porous intergroup boundaries, 36–38
possible killing, 42, 43, 268, 375, 393, 397, 411
postgenomic evolutionary theory, 362
Power, Margaret, 5, 24–25, 164, 165
primordialism, 451–52
provisioned bonobos, 321, 322–23, 324
provisioned chimpanzees, 25, 72, 122–23, 145, 408

raids/raiding, 428–31
Reason for Hope (Goodall), 19
red colobus monkeys, 53–55, 134, 295–96
reproductive competition, 94–95, 138, 234, 306
resource competition hypothesis (RCH)
  intergroup killing/violence and, 395, 401
  Kibale chimpanzees, 145
  Mahale chimpanzees, 140
  Ngogo chimpanzees, 189–90
  theory of, 22–23
Reynolds, Frances, 219–20
Reynolds, Vernon, 3, 219–20
rival coalition reduction hypothesis (RCRH)
  Conkouati-Douli chimpanzees, 262–63
  demonic males and, 88–89
  intergroup killing/violence and, 397
  Kalande chimpanzees, 68
  Kanyawara chimpanzees, 192
  Kasakela chimpanzees, 78
  Kibale chimpanzees, 145
  Mahale chimpanzees, 127–28, 136, 140
  sexually selected infanticide and, 378, 384–86
  Sonso chimpanzees, 230–31, 233, 247
  theory of, 22–23
rival males, 395–98

Sanz, Crickette, 259–60
savanna baboons, 356–57
Second Congo War, 324–25
self-domestication hypothesis, 324
The Selfish Gene (Dawkins), 9, 10
sex/sexual competition in Four Year War, 62, 93
sex-specific behavioral predispositions, 211–13
sexual coercion hypothesis, 379–80
sexually selected infanticide hypothesis (SSIH), 243–45
sexually selected infanticide (SSI)
  adaptive infanticide paradigm, 377–78
  by chimpanzees, 378
  external killings, 384–87
  by females, 382–84
  human impact on, 386–87
  internal killings, 380–82
  introduction to, 375
  overview of, 376–78
  as reproductive strategy, 382–84
  resource competition, 382–83
  rival coalition reduction hypothesis and, 378, 384–86
  sexual coercion hypothesis, 379–80
  steep hierarchy, 381
  tallies on, 375–76
  within-group, 379–82
shared genes, 9
skinny male syndrome, 74, 84, 100
small farms/farmers, 149–50
snaring. *See* wire snares
social isolation, 282, 422
social organization, 46, 335, 338–42

sociobiology
    adaptive infanticide paradigm, 377
    anthropological theory, 443, 454
    demonic males perspective and, 9–13, 18, 19, 361, 384, 395
    food abundance and, 383
    Gombe paradigm, 101
    human impact and, 24
    Kasakela chimpanzees, 62
    Mahale chimpanzees, 106, 107–8, 114, 119, 126
    sexually selected infanticide and, 376, 380, 381
    Sonso chimpanzees, 243
Sociobiology: The New Synthesis (Wilson), 9
sociobiology/selfish-gene/inclusive fitness theory, 361–66
Sonso chimpanzees
    adaptationism and, 246–47
    boundary patrolling, 229–31
    demonic females, 238–39
    disease impact, 247
    early observations, 228–29
    father genotypes, 236
    Gombe paradigm and, 232
    human impact, 245–46, 247
    hunting by chimpanzees, 239–40
    infant-killing, 231–33, 237–39, 242–45, 243f
    intergroup killing/violence, 240–46
    internal killing, 233–34
    introduction to, 228
    newcomers to, 234–37
    overview of, 229–31
    pitsawing, 232, 234
    population pressure, 238
    rival coalition reduction hypothesis, 230–31, 233, 247
    Y chromosome haplotypes, 235–36
Speck, Frank, 433
Sponsel, Leslie, 24
status-linked violence. *See also* display killing/violence
    Four Year War, 63–65, 98–101
    human impact and, 415–16
    Mahale chimpanzees, 129–30
    male status competition, 26–28, 63, 345–50, 354, 410
    Ngogo chimpanzees, 186–89

rival males, 395–98
sugar production impact, 224–25
sugarcane raids, 106
Sugiyama, Yukimaru, 221–23, 280, 283–84
Superstructural ideology, 441–42, 444–47, 452–53
Susman, Randall, 326–27
Suzuki, Akira, 221
symbolic construction of human war, 437–40

Tai chimpanzees
    brutality among, 304–5
    demographic decline, 291–93, 292f
    devastation of, 287–91
    disease impact, 289–91
    display violence, 309–10
    exceptionalism and, 305
    external killings and, 309
    field observations on, 310–11
    food scarcity, 301–2
    gender differences in behavior, 294–95, 298–99
    Gombe paradigm and, 293
    human impact, 303, 414–15
    hunting by chimpanzees, 295–96
    hunting by humans, 288–89
    intergroup killing/violence, 296–301, 304–11
    introduction to, 287
    islandization of, 287–91, 293
    leopard attacks, 288
    politics of, 306–10
    reproductive competition, 306
    sophistication in confrontations, 300
    strategic planning by, 299
    territoriality, 302, 303
    tourism impact, 291
Tanzania National Parks Authority, 72
Teleki, Geza, 35–36
territorial acquisition, 88, 101, 162–63
territoriality
    Budongo chimpanzees, 219–20, 222f
    Four Year War, 33–38, 90–91, 91f
    Loango National Park chimpanzees, 270–71
    Mahale chimpanzees, 123, 124f
    Niokolo Koba chimpanzees, 276–77
    nonkilling, 294, 302–3
    Tai chimpanzees, 302, 303

theoretical alternatives to Gombe paradigm
  competition for scarce resources, 22–23
  ethnoprimatology, 24
  human impact hypothesis, 23–26
  resource competition hypothesis, 22–23
  rival coalition reduction
    hypothesis, 22–23
  status-linked violence, 26–28
Time Magazine, 209
Toro-Semiliki chimpanzees, 255–56
tourism impact
  Budongo chimpanzees, 226
  Four Year War, 70–71
  Kibale chimpanzees, 152–54
  Mahale chimpanzees, 131–32, 137
  Tai chimpanzees, 291
tribal zones, 445–48
tribe concept, 423–25
Tylor, Edward, 436

Ugalla chimpanzees, 257–58
unhabituated chimpanzees, 37, 151, 177, 229, 268
urge to kill, 14–19, 115, 204
Uvariopsis congensis food source, 180–81, 196, 199, 412–13

very likely killing, 42, 43, 78, 192, 375
victim coding, 43
Village Land Forest Reserves, 72

Wamba bonobos. *See also* Lomako bonobos
  aggression of, 321–25

  groupings, 320–21
  intersexual dominance, 343
  introduction to, 319–21
  male status competition, 346
  overview of, 319–26
  research studies on, 317, 325–26
Wantabu community, 198–99
war, chimpanzees, 110–11. *See also* Four Year War
war, human. *See* human war
war-risk hypothesis, 429–32
"war" vs. war, xi–xiv
Washington Post, 432
West African chimpanzees
  Bossou chimpanzees, 280–84
  Fongoli chimpanzees, 278–80
  introduction to, 251–52, 275
  Niokolo Koba chimpanzees, 275–78
White, Frances, 326–27
Wildlife Conservation Society, 262
Wilkie, Leighton, 32
Wilson, E. O., 9
Wilson, Michael, 192
wire snares, 25–26, 72–73, 147, 151–52, 225, 252–53, 254f, 281–82
Wolf, Eric, 450
World Heritage Site, 287–88
World Wildlife Foundation (WWF), 291
Wrangham, Richard, 152

xenophobia, 7, 13, 19, 305, 451–52

Yanomami people, 443–45